Contemporary Employment Relations

Contemporary Employment Relations

A Critical Introduction

SECOND EDITION

STEVE WILLIAMS

AND DEREK ADAM-SMITH

OXFORD
UNIVERSITY PRESS

OXFORD
UNIVERSITY PRESS

Great Clarendon Street, Oxford OX2 6DP

Oxford University Press is a department of the University of Oxford.
It furthers the University's objective of excellence in research, scholarship,
and education by publishing worldwide in

Oxford New York

Auckland Cape Town Dar es Salaam Hong Kong Karachi
Kuala Lumpur Madrid Melbourne Mexico City Nairobi
New Delhi Shanghai Taipei Toronto

With offices in

Argentina Austria Brazil Chile Czech Republic France Greece
Guatemala Hungary Italy Japan Poland Portugal Singapore
South Korea Switzerland Thailand Turkey Ukraine Vietnam

Oxford is a registered trade mark of Oxford University Press
in the UK and in certain other countries

Published in the United States
by Oxford University Press Inc., New York

First published 2005
Second edition 2010

British Library Cataloguing in Publication Data

Data available

Library of Congress Cataloging in Publication Data

Williams, Steve, 1968-
   Contemporary employment relations: a critical introduction / Steve Williams and
Derek Adam-Smith. --2nd
      p. cm.
   ISBN 978-0-19-954543-8
1. Industrial relations. 2. Labor unions. 3. Labor contract. 4. Industrial relations--Great
Britain. 5. Labor unions--Great Britain. 6. Labor contract--Great Britain. I. Adam-Smith,
Derek. II. Title.
   HD6971.W63 2009
   658.3'153--dc22

                                                                                  2009039596

Typeset by Macmillan Publishing Solutions
Printed in Italy
on acid-free paper by
Lego S.p.A

ISBN 978-0-19-954543-8

1 3 5 7 9 10 8 6 4 2

ACKNOWLEDGEMENTS

Much of this second edition was prepared by Steve Williams during a semester's study leave. Steve thanks his colleagues in the Department of Human Resource and Marketing Management at the University of Portsmouth Business School for their support. Thanks also to Rebecca Harris for her help with some of the diagrams. The Ethical Trading Initiative kindly gave us permission to reproduce elements of its Base Code. Sarah Pass and *People Management* magazine kindly gave us permission to use Sarah's article on high performance management. We continued to benefit from the exceptional support of Oxford University Press while working on the second edition of this book, particularly Angela Adams, Fran Griffin, Kirsty Reade, and Hannah Brannon. We received very helpful feedback on draft chapters from the publisher's reviewers: Dr Vaughan Ellis, Edinburgh Napier University; Dr Enda Hannon, Kingston Business School; Brian Critchley, London Metropolitan University; David Banner, University of Westminster; Jerome Snook, Nottingham Trent University; Dr Frank Carr, University of Bedfordshire; Patrick Gunnigle, University of Limerick; James Richards, Heriot-Watt University; Dr Margaret May, London Metropolitan University; Alan Ryan, De Montfort University; Cecilie Bingham, University of Westminster; Dr Jean Jenkins, Cardiff University; Richard Warren, Manchester Metropolitan University; and Dr Amanda Pyman, University of Kent. Our thanks go to them. We also acknowledge the kind permission of the following organizations and publishers to use their copyright material:

The European Trade Union Institute for the end of Chapter 3 case study;
Routledge for Figure 5.3 and Table 5.1;
Wolters Kluwer (UK) Limited for the end of Chapter 4 case study;
Sage for Table 5.2 and the end of Chapter 7 case study;
Blackwell for Tables 6.1, 6.2, 6.3, and 9.1;
Crown copyright is reproduced under Class License Number C2006010631 with the permission of OPSI and the Queen's Printer for Scotland.

BRIEF CONTENTS

How to use this book   xiii
How to use the online resource centre   xv
List of tables   xvii
List of boxes   xix
List of figures   xxii
List of abbreviations   xxiii
Preface: About this book   xxvii

PART 1 Introducing Employment Relations

1   The nature of employment relations   3

PART 2 Contemporary Employment Relations in Context

2   Employment relations in the contemporary economy   41

3   The politics of employment relations   82

4   Social divisions and employment relations   121

PART 3 Key Issues in Contemporary Employment Relations

5   Managing employment relations   169

6   Representation at work   211

7   Contemporary developments in pay and working time   255

8   Experiencing employment relations: involvement,
    insecurity, intensification   298

9   Conflict and employment relations   328

PART 4 Conclusion

10 **Employment relations: regulating, experiencing, and contesting the employment relationship**   371

Glossary   381
Bibliography   385
Index   415

DETAILED CONTENTS

How to use this book   xiii
How to use the online resource centre   xv
List of tables   xvii
List of boxes   xix
List of figures   xxii
List of abbreviations   xxiii
Preface: About this book   xxvii

PART 1 Introducing Employment Relations

1   The nature of employment relations   3

1.1 Introduction   3
     Introductory case study: the relevance of employment relations   4

1.2 The employment relationship and employment relations   4

1.3 Employment relations as a 'field of study'   11

1.4 Employment relations: actors, processes, outcomes,
     and contexts   17

Conclusion   34

ASSIGNMENT AND DISCUSSION QUESTIONS   35
CHAPTER CASE STUDY: MANAGING WITH UNIONS IN THE ROYAL MAIL   36

PART 2 Contemporary Employment Relations in Context

2   Employment relations in the contemporary economy   41

2.1 Introduction   41
     Introductory case study: agency workers and employment flexibility   42

2.2 Employment relations in the 'new' economy   42

2.3 Employment relations in a global economy I: multinational
     companies and union responses   56

2.4 Employment relations in a global economy II: regulating
     international labour standards   66

Conclusion   79

ASSIGNMENT AND DISCUSSION QUESTIONS   79
CHAPTER CASE STUDY: UNION ORGANIZATION OF 'ATYPICAL' WORKERS   80

3   The politics of employment relations   82

3.1   **Introduction**   82
       Introductory case study: the European Union's Agency Workers' Directive   83

3.2   **State policy and employment relations in Britain**   83

3.3   **Labour and employment relations in Britain 1997–2009**   93

3.4   **Employment relations and the politics
       of European integration**   102

Conclusion   118

ASSIGNMENT AND DISCUSSION QUESTIONS   119
CHAPTER CASE STUDY: TRADE UNIONS AND THE EURO   120

4   Social divisions and employment relations   121

4.1   **Introduction**   121
       Introductory case study: pregnancy discrimination at work   122

4.2   **Workplace inequality and employment relations**   122

4.3   **Public policy, anti-discrimination legislation,
       and equality at work**   128

4.4   **Managing equality and diversity at work**   141

4.5   **Trade unions, collective bargaining, and the pursuit
       of workplace equality**   153

Conclusion   163

ASSIGNMENT AND DISCUSSION QUESTIONS   163
CHAPTER CASE STUDY: EMPLOYER ATTITUDES TO EMPLOYEES' WORK–LIFE BALANCE   164

PART 3 Key Issues in Contemporary Employment Relations

5   Managing employment relations   169

5.1   **Introduction**   169
       Introductory case study: engaging employees at McDonalds   170

5.2   **Managing with trade unions**   171

5.3   **Challenging unions**   175

5.4   **Human resource management and employment relations**   184

5.5   **Managing employment relations in non-union
       environments**   195

5.6   **Conceptualizing the management of employment
       relations**   202

Conclusion   208

ASSIGNMENT AND DISCUSSION QUESTIONS   209
CHAPTER CASE STUDY: HUMAN RESOURCE MANAGEMENT AND THE HOTEL INDUSTRY   210

6   Representation at work   **211**

6.1   Introduction   **211**
        Introductory case study: revitalizing trade unions: the case of Community   212

**6.2   Trade unions, worker representation, and the rise
        of a 'representation gap'**   **212**

6.3   Non-union forms of employee representation   **221**

6.4   Partnership agreements   **234**

6.5   Organizing unionism   **243**

Conclusion   **252**

ASSIGNMENT AND DISCUSSION QUESTIONS   253
CHAPTER CASE STUDY: E-UNIONS   253

7   Contemporary developments in pay and working time   **255**

7.1   Introduction   **255**
        Introductory case study: the 'fair tips' campaign   256

7.2   The changing pattern of pay determination in Britain   **256**

7.3   Pay inequality, low pay, and the National Minimum Wage   **273**

7.4   Developments in working time   **284**

Conclusion   **295**

ASSIGNMENT AND DISCUSSION QUESTIONS   295
CHAPTER CASE STUDY: THE NATIONAL MINIMUM WAGE AND THE HAIRDRESSING INDUSTRY   296

**8   Experiencing employment relations: involvement,
        insecurity, intensification**   **298**

8.1   Introduction   **298**
        Introductory case study: employment relations in a recession   299

8.2   Developments in employee involvement and participation   **299**

8.3   Redundancy and insecurity   **307**

8.4   The intensification of work   **318**

Conclusion   **326**

ASSIGNMENT AND DISCUSSION QUESTIONS   326
CHAPTER CASE STUDY: WORK INTENSIFICATION IN THE PUBLIC SECTOR   327

9   Conflict and employment relations   **328**

9.1   Introduction   **328**
        Introductory case study: the US writers' strike   329

9.2   Strikes and employment relations   **329**

9.3   Other forms of industrial conflict   **342**

9.4   Resolving disputes in employment relations   **352**

Conclusion   **365**

ASSIGNMENT AND DISCUSSION QUESTIONS   366
CHAPTER CASE STUDY: A BRITISH AIRWAYS CASE   367

PART 4 Conclusion

**10 Employment relations: regulating, experiencing,
     and contesting the employment relationship**   371

Regulating the employment relationship   **371**

Experiencing the employment relationship   **374**

Contesting the employment relationship   **375**

Future prospects for employment relations   **377**

Glossary   381
Bibliography   385
Index   415

HOW TO USE THIS BOOK

There are many key features included in the chapters of *Contemporary Employment Relations* that are designed to help you both to learn and organize information. Some of these features emphasize how theory is applied in real organizations. Others help you to gain a deeper understanding of how this links to practice, in order to ground your theoretical understanding of contemporary employment relations from a critical perspective.

Chapter objectives:

The main objectives of this chapter are to:

* demonstrate the important influence which the political context exercises over employment relations;

* examine the main public policy developments in employment relations;

* assess and interpret the main features of Labour government policy towards employment relations after it was elected to office in 1997;

Chapter objectives
Each chapter opens with a bulleted outline of the main concepts and ideas. These serve as helpful signposts to what you can expect to learn from each chapter.

Introductory case study

Pregnancy discrimination at work

Despite being unlawful, studies show that each year tens of thousands of women workers are discriminated against on the grounds of their pregnancy. Between 2003 and 2005 the Equal Opportunities Commission (EOC) mounted a major investigation of pregnancy-related discrimination at work, including research with employers and a survey of 1,000 women who had worked during a recent pregnancy (EOC 2005). The EOC found that nearly a half (45 per cent) of the women they surveyed reported being discriminated against, which included being sacked in some cases. Other discriminatory practices included: failing to be get appropriate pay rises, and missing out on training opportunities. Young women, black and ethnic minority women, women who are relatively new to their jobs, and women on low incomes

Case studies
The book is packed with opening and closing case studies, which link the topics to real-life organizations to help you gain an understanding of employment relations in action.

INSIGHT INTO PRACTICE 5.4

Resisting union recognition at Kettle Chips

Kettle Chips is owned by the private equity firm Lion Capital and makes upmarket snacks and crisps at its factory in Norwich. In 2007 the Transport and General Workers' Union (TGWU)—now part of the Unite trade union—submitted a claim under the statutory union recognition procedure. Following an acrimonious battle between the union and employer, in October 2007 the workforce voted 206: 93 against union recognition. The firm claimed that its staff were relatively well paid, and enjoyed good benefits, including 25 days' holiday and comprehensive sick pay. Controversially, though, Kettle Chips hired the subsidiary of a prominent US union-busting firm, the Burke Group, to dissuade workers in the factory from voting for union recognition. Unite also claimed that managers had put undue influ-

Insights into practice boxes
These mini case studies show how employment relations have been played out in a wide range of real-world situations.

Employment relations reflection 6.1   Union Learning Representatives

Employers who recognize a trade union are obliged to give union representatives—shop stewards—a reasonable amount of time away from their work in order to undertake their union duties. A recognized union is also entitled to appoint safety representatives whose activities include investigating health and safety issues and making representations to managers. The 2002 Employment Act provided for the establishment of union learning representatives. Their role is designed to promote learning, training, and development activities, by raising awareness of the opportunities that are available to workers for example, or by encouraging employers to improve their provision.

By 2005, one estimate put the number of union learning representatives at 6,500. An evaluative study found that union learning representatives make an effective contribu-

Employment relations reflection boxes
These boxes allow you to pause for thought and consider a particular viewpoint on an issue.

INTERNATIONAL PERSPECTIVE 2.6

Globalization and the growth of the Indian call centre industry

One of the most prominent, and controversial, aspects of the way in which economic globalization affects employment concerns the growth of the call centre sector in India. Improvements in communication and information technologies enable companies to move jobs involving things like customer relations, telemarketing, payment processing, insurance claims, and credit card and loan applications to locations where labour is considerably cheaper. In India, wages are between 10 and 15 per cent of those offered in Britain. Moreover, firms can benefit from a highly educated and well-motivated pool of English-speaking labour. By 2004, the Indian call centre industry already employed 180,000 people and was growing at 20 per cent per annum. Many major companies,

International perspective boxes
In today's increasingly connected world, these boxes place employment relations in a 21st century global context.

Historical perspective boxes

To understand where we are now, you need to know what's gone before: these boxes provide the context for contemporary employment relations.

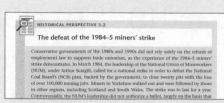

Legislation and policy boxes

These ensure you are up-to-date with the fast-changing and complex politico-legal framework of employment relations.

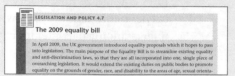

Section summaries and further reading

Section summaries act as signposts throughout the chapter, so you can ensure you are clear on each section before moving on. These will also be helpful for revision season, while the further reading suggestions are invaluable for exams and coursework.

Conclusions

Each chapter ends with a précis that summarizes the most important arguments developed within that chapter.

End-of-chapter assignment and discussion questions

Questions have been included at the end of every chapter to check you have grasped the key concepts and provide you with an opportunity for discussion.

Glossary

A list of key terms is included to provide you with a brief explanation of any technical terms introduced in the book.

HOW TO USE THE ONLINE RESOURCE CENTRE

To support this text, there is a wide range of web-based content for tutors and students. Students can go to the Online Resource Centre to find web links, annual updates and a comprehensive glossary. Tutors will be able to access a suite of customizable PowerPoint® slides, which can be used in lectures and seminars, alongside a guide to the case studies and end-of-chapter questions. Video resources are also provided to enliven seminars or supply to students via your VLE.

All these resources can be downloaded allowing them to be incorporated into your institution's existing virtual learning environment.

 http://www.oxfordtextbooks.co.uk/orc/williams_adamsmith2e/

FOR STUDENTS

Annotated web links

Links to websites relevant to each chapter direct students towards valuable sources of information and professional associations.

Glossary

Test yourself on the terms used in the book: click on a term and the 'card' will flip to reveal the definition or vice versa. You can even download these to your iPod or similar small screen device to use on the move.

Annual Updates

Regular updates to keep you informed of recent developments in contemporary employment relations.

FOR LECTURERS

PowerPoint® lecture slides

A suite of chapter-by-chapter PowerPoint® slides has been included for use in your lecture presentations. They are fully customizable so you can tailor them to match your own presentation style.

A guide to the case studies

Suggested points for students to include when answering the end-of-chapter case study questions.

A guide to the end-of-chapter questions

A suite of suggested answers to all end-of-chapter questions will provide you with a range of seminar resources.

A guide to web cases

Suggested answers to the web case studies to aid in your preparation for seminars and assignments.

Video clips

Two video clips featuring practitioners from the TUC and Molly Maid UK discussing employee relations in both a commercial and a not-for-profit organization.

Figures and tables from the text

All tables and figures from the text are provided for you to download for lecture presentations or to use with course materials or assignments.

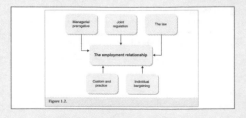

LIST OF TABLES

1.1	Major trade unions in the UK	22
1.2	UK unemployment, selected years 1979–2009	32
1.3	Female employees as a proportion of all employees in the UK, selected years 1984–2008	33
2.1	The proportion of UK jobs in manufacturing and service industries, selected years 1979–2008	43
2.2	Self-employment in the UK, 1984–2008	44
2.3	Occupational change in Britain during the 1990s	48
2.4	Occupational change in the UK in the 2000s	49
2.5	The proportion of temporary and part-time employees in the UK, selected years 1984–2008	52
2.6	The main approaches to promoting international labour standards	73
3.1	Positive and negative harmonization of labour standards	110
3.2	Accession dates of EU countries	113
4.1	Discrimination: key concepts	130
4.2	Parental leave: key concepts	135
4.3	The key characteristics of equal opportunities and diversity management approaches	147
4.4	The proportion of workplaces operating flexible working and leave arrangements for non-managerial employees, 1998 and 2004	150
5.1	Percentage of workplaces with a recognized union, 1980–98	176
5.2	New cases of union recognition and derecognition, 1995–2005	181
5.3	Trade union recognition, 1998 and 2004	182
6.1	Trade union membership and density in the UK, 1892–1979	213
6.2	Trade union membership and density, 1980–2008	218
6.3	Union density by sector and industry, UK 2008	220
7.1	Collective bargaining coverage by industry sector, 2004	259
7.2	Collective bargaining coverage by workplace size and organization size, 2004	260
7.3	Pay determination methods (employees), 2004	263
7.4	National Minimum Wage rates, 1999–2009	278
7.5	Number of hours usually worked each week by full-time employees in their main job, selected EU countries 2008	286
8.1	Percentage of workplaces with direct communications methods, 2004	300
8.2	The level and rate of redundancies in the UK, 1999–2008	310
8.3	The level and rate of redundancies in the UK, 2008	311
8.4	Work intensity, by selected job and workplace characteristics	320

8.5   The potential sources of work intensification   322
9.1   The level of strike activity in Britain, 1946–1989   332
9.2   The level of strike activity in Britain, 1990–2008   332
9.3   The main forms of 'organized' and 'unorganized' industrial conflict   343
9.4   Employment tribunal claims by jurisdiction, selected jurisdictions   361

LIST OF BOXES

Insight into practice

1.1	The effort bargain in action	6
1.2	Custom and practice in action	10
1.5	The role of the Trades Union Congress	23
2.1	Franchise arrangements—self-employment?	46
2.5	American multinationals in the UK and Ireland	60
2.7	The obstacles to effective labour internationalism	63
2.12	Flouting the code?	78
3.9	The outcomes of social dialogue	106
4.6	The individualized basis of responses to disability discrimination legislation	139
4.8	Racial disadvantage at work—the experiences of black and minority ethnic women trade unionists	144
4.9	Affinity groups as a diversity management tool	148
4.10	Family-friendly working—the experiences of professional women	152
4.11	Auditing union progress in the area of equality bargaining	157
4.12	Representing the interests of lesbian and gay members in British trade unions	159
5.4	Resisting union recognition at Kettle Chips	183
5.6	Managing employment relations in Ryanair	188
5.7	High commitment working—the view from below	193
5.8	Tipping as a source of management control?	205
6.4	The EWC agreement at Diageo	231
6.6	Partnership at Borg Warner	241
7.1	The survival of national bargaining in the electrical contracting industry	262
7.2	The erosion of national bargaining in the further education sector	269
7.8	The disruptive potential of overtime working	289
8.1	Communication practices in two aerospace firms	302
8.4	Voluntary redundancy—managerial control or employee choice?	312
8.5	Redundancy consultation	313
8.8	Work intensification in the airline industry	321
9.2	Sacking employees who are taking lawful strike action	338
9.3	'Living wage' campaigns in London	341
9.4	Employee sabotage in the contemporary service sector	347
9.5	Worker resistance and industrial conflict in a call centre	348

Employment relations reflection

1.3	The feminist critique of employment relations	15
1.4	New actors	17
1.7	Informal expectations and understandings—the case of workplace discipline	26

2.2   Homeworking in Britain   47
2.3   Flexibility and migrant labour   54
2.4   Globalization and migration   57
3.4   The outcome of political fund ballots   91
3.7   The trade unions and the Labour party—a growing rift?   101
4.1   The gender pay gap—an analysis   127
4.5   Accounting for the work—life balance movement   136
5.5   Towards a new public management?   187
5.9   Private equity and employment relations   207
6.1   Union Learning Representatives   217
6.3   Representing workers' interests beyond the workplace   223
6.8   Community unionism   250
7.3   Pay disputes in the public sector   271
7.4   Directors' pay and the growth of pay inequality   275
7.5   Campaigning for a 'living wage'   279
7.6   Unpaid work experience: opportunity or exploitation?   283
8.2   Varieties of team   305
8.3   Challenging redundancies   309
8.6   Migrant workers—a disposable workforce?   317
8.9   Job quality   325
9.6   Virtual industrial conflict   350
9.7   Negotiating power in action   353
9.9   The ACAS help-line service   359
9.10 The obstacles to effective workplace justice   364

International perspective

1.6   Union repression around the world   25
2.6   Globalization and the growth of the Indian call centre industry   62
2.8   Labour standards in export processing zones   69
2.10 The North American Free Trade Agreement and labour standards   75
3.3   Neo-liberalism and employment relations in New Zealand   90
3.8   The institutions of the European Union   103
3.12 The Irish Ferries dispute   116
4.4   Mainstreaming equality in the European Union   134
5.2   Anti-unionism in the United States   178
6.2   The system of works councils in Germany   222
6.7   'Justice for janitors' in Southern California   246
7.7   The 35-hour working week in France   288
8.7   European data on work pressures   319
9.1   Strikes and labour unrest in Dubai   335
9.8   The development of labour arbitration in China   355
10.1 The 'bossnapping' phenomenon   379

Historical perspective

1.8   Industrial democracy at work   29
3.1   The 'winter of discontent' 1978–9   87
3.2   The defeat of the 1984–5 miners' strike   89
5.1   Managing with the closed shop   174

Legislation and policy

2.9   The ILO's declaration of fundamental principles and rights at work   71
2.11 Elements of the Ethical Trading Initiative's 'base code'   76
3.5   The main elements of Labour's legislative programme   94
3.6   A ministerial view   97
3.10 Major European Union directives in the area
      of employment relations since 1993   107
4.2   The main equality and anti-discrimination legislation of the 1970s–90s   129
4.3   The development of equality and anti-discrimination legislation
      under Labour since 1997   132
4.7   The 2009 Equality Bill   140
5.3   The statutory recognition procedure in Britain   179
6.5   The Partnership Fund   237

LIST OF FIGURES

1.1	A simplified version of Dunlop's systems model	8
1.2	Sources of rules in employment relations	9
1.3	A framework for conceptualizing contemporary employment relations	35
4.1	Liberal and radical interventions used by trade unions to promote equality	160
5.1	A simplified model of the statutory union recognition procedure	180
5.2	The high commitment model	191
5.3	A framework for interpreting employment relations in small firms	199
5.4	Management approaches in non-union firms	203
9.1	Mobilization theory	340

LIST OF ABBREVIATIONS

ACAS	Advisory, Conciliation and Arbitration Service
APC&T	administrative, professional, clerical, and technical
ASLEF	Amalgamated Society of Locomotive Engineers and Firemen
ASTMS	Association of Supervisory, Technical, and Managerial Staff
BA	British Airways
BERR	(Department for) Business, Enterprise, and Regulatory Reform
BMA	British Medical Association
BME	black and minority ethnic
BUIRA	British Universities Industrial Relations Association
CAC	Central Arbitration Committee
CBI	Confederation of British Industry
CEEP	European Centre of Enterprises with Public Participation and of Enterprises of General Economic Interest
CEF	College Employers' Forum
CRE	Commission for Racial Equality
CSA	Child Support Agency
CSO	civil society organization
CWU	Communication Workers' Union
DRC	Disability Rights Commission
DTI	Department of Trade and Industry
EC	European Community
ECA	Electrical Contractors' Association
ECJ	European Court of Justice
EEC	European Economic Community
EEF	Engineering Employers' Federation
EES	European Employment Strategy
EHRC	Equality and Human Rights Commission
EI	employee involvement
EIF	European Industry Federation
EIRO	European Industrial Relations Observatory
EMU	Economic and Monetary Union
EO	equal opportunity
EOC	Equal Opportunities Commission
EPOS	electronic point of sale
EPZ	export processing zone
ERA	Employment Relations Act (1999)
ET	employment tribunal
ETI	Ethical Trading Initiative

ETUC	European Trade Union Confederation
EU	European Union
EWC	European Works Council
FBI	Federal Bureau of Investigation
FBU	Fire Brigades Union
FDI	foreign direct investment
FLA	Fair Labor Association
GCHQ	Government Communications Headquarters
GLA	Gangmasters Licensing Authority
GMB	General, Municipal and Boilermakers' Union
GSP	Generalized System of Preferences
GUF	Global Union Federation
HCA	healthcare assistant
HR	human resources
HRM	human resource management
HRMC	Her Majesty's Revenue and Customs
ICE	Information and Consultation with Employees (Regulations)
ICT	information and communications technology
IDS	Incomes Data Services
IFA	International Framework Agreement
ILO	International Labour Organization
ITF	International Transport Workers Federation
ITUC	International Trade Union Confederation
JCC	joint consultative committee
JIB	Joint Industry Board
JIC	Joint Industry Council
LGBT	lesbian, gay, bisexual, and transexual
LIFO	last in, first out
LPC	Low Pay Commission
MFGB	Miners' Federation of Great Britain
MNC	multinational company
MSF	Manufacturing Science and Finance Union
NAALC	North American Agreement on Labor Cooperation
NAFTA	North American Free Trade Agreement
NCB	National Coal Board
NEDC	National Economic Development Council
NGO	non-governmental organization
NHS	National Health Service
NIDL	New International Division of Labour
NMW	National Minimum Wage
NPM	New Public Management
NUM	National Union of Mineworkers
NUT	National Union of Teachers
OECD	Organization for Economic Cooperation and Development

OMC	Open Method of Coordination
PFI	Private Finance Initiative
PRB	Pay Review Body
PRP	performance-related pay
PSI	Public Services International
QMV	Qualified Majority Voting
RCN	Royal College of Nursing
RMT	Rail Maritime and Transport Union
RPA	Redundancy Payments Act (1965)
SEA	Single European Act
SEIU	Service Employees' International Union
SNB	Special Negotiating Body
SWU	Service Workers' Union
TELCO	The East London Communities' Organization
TGWU	Transport and General Workers' Union
TQM	Total Quality Management
TUC	Trades Union Congress
UCATT	Union of Construction and Allied Trades and Technicians
UCU	University and College Union
UDM	Union of Democratic Mineworkers
UEAPME	European Association of Craft, Small and Medium-Sized Enterprises
UNICE	Union of Industrial and Employers' Confederation of Europe
USDAW	Union of Shop Distributive and Allied Workers
WERS	Workplace Employment Relations Survey
WTO	World Trade Organization
WTR	Working Time Regulations

PREFACE: ABOUT THIS BOOK

The fundamental concern of employment relations as a field of study is with investigating the nature of the relationship that exists between an employer and his or her employees—or the employment relationship, as it is generally known (Edwards 2003). Given that employment is such an important aspect of people's lives in advanced industrialized societies like Britain, the need to understand the employment relationship is evidently a vital topic of enquiry in business studies and the wider social sciences.

Traditionally, studies of employment relations were often dominated by a concern with understanding the role of trade unions, membership bodies comprised of workers, and how their activities helped to regulate employment relationships. In other words, the emphasis was on how people's terms and conditions of employment—wages, hours, holidays, benefits, etc—were influenced by the actions of trade unions who, on behalf of the workforce as a whole, bargained collectively with employers. Such joint regulation, as it is known, remains an important element of contemporary employment relations.

Yet as will become evident, simply by focusing on how employment relationships are regulated is an inadequate foundation for understanding employment relations. We also need to consider the experiences of workers themselves, and how, often collectively in trade unions, they challenge and contest aspects of their employment relationships. Moreover, the decline of the trade unions means that we also have to fashion a broader, less restrictive approach to understanding contemporary employment relations, one that builds upon the traditional features of employment relations as a field of study, but which also takes into account the circumstances of the twenty-first-century environment in which it operates.

This book is distinguished by five main characteristics. First, it adopts an explicitly critical approach to employment relations. What do we mean by this? Rather than understanding employment relations just as concerning the regulation of employment relationships, we prefer to conceptualize it as the study of the way in which employment relationships are regulated, experienced, and contested. Clearly, we need to understand the ways in which the rules that govern the employment relationship are constituted, but how do workers experience the employment relationship, and how far, and in what ways, do they challenge, or contest, their employment situations? This is what distinguishes this study of employment relations from books about human resource management (HRM), which, by tending to adopt an explicitly managerial focus, largely neglect the implications of management decisions for employees, and their responses.

Second, the book treats employment relations in a more thematic way than is often the case in conventional accounts. These tend to be influenced by an assumption that trade unions and collective bargaining constitute its principal subject matter. Though still important, the diminishing significance of joint regulation means that such an approach is no longer tenable (Ackers and Wilkinson 2003). Rather than devote chapters to trade union organization and collective bargaining in their own right, we focus instead on the broader themes of employee representation (see Chapter 6), and developments in pay determination and working time (see Chapter 7). This more thematic approach better captures the broader conceptualization of employment relations advanced in this book.

Third, an important aim of this book is to establish the contemporary relevance of employment relations. The broader, critical approach—one that focuses on the way in which the employment relationship is regulated, experienced, and contested—allows us to consider a range of current employment relations issues. One purpose of the book is to demonstrate the continued importance of employment relations, based on the assumption that, as a field of study, its boundaries are wide-ranging, and cannot be restricted just to the study of trade unions and collective bargaining.

This is best illustrated with reference to a current area of interest. One of the most pressing matters in contemporary employment relations concerns efforts to ensure that the family responsibilities of working people are accommodated by employers. This is an issue—it concerns the way in which people's employment is regulated and experienced, and how they seek a more equitable balance between work and family commitments—which is by any measure something that concerns employment relations. Traditional approaches, those that focus on the institutions of trade unions and collective bargaining, would have paid little attention to the development of so-called family-friendly policies, not least because until relatively recently such topics rarely appeared on the male-dominated union bargaining agendas (see Chapter 4).

We are not suggesting that trade unions and collective bargaining are unimportant. On the contrary, they are important features of contemporary employment relations, as we demonstrate throughout the book. Where family-friendly policies are regulated jointly, they often function more effectively than if their existence depends upon the whim of managers, as we show in Chapter 4. But employment relations cannot be restricted just to the study of joint regulation; they encompass a much broader range of structures, processes, and activities.

Much of the book, but Chapters 2, 3, and 4 in particular, are informed by the need to consider employment relations in a broader context. Much of what happens at work is influenced by economic, political, and social changes. Thus there is the need to recognize that factors constituted mainly outside the workplace, such as gender for example, shape employment relations patterns and activities (Ackers 2002; Greene 2003). The contemporary focus is further informed by the inclusion of material taken from a wide range of recent and up-to-date research findings.

Fourth, our intention is to offer a relatively concise assessment of developments in employment relations. We do not aim to provide a comprehensive, encyclopaedic account of the subject, and important historical developments are not discussed in too great an amount of detail. We hope this book contributes to an understanding of contemporary employment relations and helps stimulate debate and provoke arguments over what is an endlessly fascinating, often controversial, and rarely consensual area of economic, social, and political life.

Fifth, while for reasons of space we concentrate largely on developments in Britain, it is important to recognize that employment relations is of international significance. European Union (EU) policies influence employment relations in important ways (see Chapter 3). At various points in the book we include examples taken from experiences in other countries. Moreover, in Chapter 2 we consider the implications of economic globalization for employment relations, and the policies and practices of multinational companies.

Before we set out the main features of this book, it is necessary to consider why it goes under the title of 'contemporary employment relations' rather than 'contemporary industrial relations'. As other writers have noted (Blyton and Turnbull 2004), the term 'industrial relations', although still widely used, is often associated with developments in traditional industries, like manufacturing, and with an emphasis on trade unions and joint regulation; 'employment relations', however, is more appropriate to understanding greater diversity in work and employment patterns. For this reason, it is better suited to the approach adopted here even though 'industrial' and 'employment' relations can be, and often are, used interchangeably.

The book is organized in four main sections. In Part 1, comprising Chapter 1, we provide an introduction to employment relations as a field of study, and present the main actors, processes, contexts, and outcomes of employment relations. In Part 2, we commence our thematic assessment of developments in contemporary employment relations by focusing on the important influence of contextual developments. In Chapter 2, for example, we consider the implications of labour market change, such as the growth of part-time work and other forms of flexible employment. The effects of economic globalization, and the policies and practices of multinational companies, are also considered in this chapter. Chapter 3 is about the political dimension of employment relations. We examine contemporary public policy developments and consider the implications of European integration for employment relations, respectively. In Chapter 4, we consider the implications of social divisions for employment relations. Inequality and disadvantage are durable features of jobs and the labour market, and we need to consider the interventions used to tackle them.

We continue with our thematic approach in Part 3 of the book, and examine five major issues in contemporary employment relations. Chapter 5 considers the management of employment relations, the implications of sophisticated HRM approaches, and the rise of non-unionism. Chapter 6 deals with the representation of employees' interests in contemporary employment relations. We critically assess the extent to which non-union arrangements, partnership agreements, and a more assertive form of union organizing can, respectively, provide workers with effective representation. In Chapter 7, we consider current developments in pay determination and the organization of working time. The distinctive feature of Chapter 8 is the way in which it highlights the experience of employees, and how the nature of that experience often puts them at odds with their employers. We consider three topics in particular: employee involvement and participation; redundancy and job insecurity; and work intensification. Following on from this, in Chapter 9 we assert the importance of conflict in contemporary employment relations. We discuss the various manifestations of industrial conflict, including the significance of strike activity, and explore methods of resolving disputes when they arise.

Part 4 of the book consists of a brief concluding chapter in which we draw together the main themes of the book in a way that demonstrates the relevance of employment relations to contemporary societies, and considers its future prospects.

Each chapter includes a number of supporting pedagogic features. Regular boxes devoted to employment relations reflections, insights into employment relations practice, international and historical perspectives, and legislation and policy interventions are used to illustrate the material in the main text. Each main section comes with a summary of the key points of the material covered in the preceding pages, and guidance on further reading suggestions, including appropriate website links. Each chapter commences with a brief introductory case study, which is designed to demonstrate the contemporary relevance of the subject matter, and a longer case study at the end, with questions attached. There are also assignment and discussion questions to reinforce learning activity. A glossary of key terms and concepts is found towards the end of the book. The companion website contains further relevant features, such as additional case studies and research updates.

PART 1

Introducing Employment Relations

1   The nature of employment relations   3

1

The Nature of Employment Relations

Chapter objectives:

The main objectives of this chapter are to:

* examine the characteristics of the employment relationship in capitalist market economies, and how it informs an understanding of the nature of employment relations;

* consider the perspectives applied to employment relations as a field of study;

* provide a critically informed assessment of approaches to employment relations; and

* introduce the main employment relations actors, processes, and outcomes, and the contexts in which they operate.

1.1 Introduction

Employment relations, which concerns how employment relationships are regulated, experienced, and contested, affects the majority of people who live in advanced, industrialized societies. In the UK, for example, close to 30 million people are in employment of some kind; many of those who are not depend upon the income generated from a parent's or partner's job for their subsistence. The purpose of this chapter is to consider the nature of employment relations, in three main sections. First, in Section 1.2 we investigate the nature of the employment relationship in market economies, and examine the main sources of rules that govern employment relationships. Second, in Section 1.3 we assess the main perspectives that have been applied to employment relations as a field of study. Third, in Section 1.4 we introduce the main actors and processes in employment relations, highlight the main outcomes of employment relations, and say something about the main contexts in which employment relations functions.

Introductory case study

The relevance of employment relations

One of the main objectives of this book is to demonstrate the relevance of employment relations in contemporary societies. An appreciation of how the relationship between workers and employers operates is essential if one is to develop a proper understanding of business and management today. The relevance of employment relations was clearly demonstrated in early 2009 when a number of companies around the UK suffered disruption after thousands of workers walked off their jobs to demonstrate their support for striking workers at the Lindsey oil refinery in Lincolnshire who were protesting about the use of foreign labour. Construction work on the expansion of the refinery, owned by the French oil company Total, was subcontracted to an Italian firm which had brought in its own workforce to do the job. Against a background of rising unemployment, many workers were angry that the work on the refinery was being undertaken by foreign workers, at lower rates of pay, instead of local workers. According to Stephen Briggs, one of the protesting workers, while they 'have got nothing against foreign workers, the fact is that there are a lot of people out of work and are looking for jobs' (BBC News website, 4 February 2009).

A good level of knowledge and understanding of employment relations is essential if we are to comprehend properly the causes, development, and implications of events like the refinery dispute. We need to understand how the relationship between employers and workers operates, and the factors that influence it, including the broader economic, political, and social factors. We need to be able to understand and explain why the relevant employment relations actors, especially managers, workers, and trade unions, behave in the ways that they do. We also need to understand why workers take action to protest against, or change, the terms of their employment relationships, and the methods they use to do so. A proper knowledge and understanding of contemporary employment relations makes important events like the refinery dispute of early 2009 comprehensible.

1.2 The employment relationship and employment relations

The basis of employment relations is the relationship that exists between an employer and an employee, or the 'employment relationship' as it is generally known. In essence, employment relations concerns the study of employment relationships (Edwards 2003). In this section we consider the nature of the employment relationship and examine how employment relationships are regulated, identifying the sources of the rules that govern employment relationships and that take the form of terms and conditions of employment, like pay, benefits, and working conditions.

1.2.1 The employment relationship as a 'wage-work bargain'

The notion of contract is ostensibly central to the employment relationship. Contractual relationships, and the capacity of the law to enforce contractual obligations and property rights, are defining features of capitalist market economies. With the development of capitalism in Britain, by the middle of the nineteenth century the system of wage labour, based on the notion of a contractual relationship between an employer and employee, had largely displaced traditional forms of work relations based on status, such as servitude (Burgess 1980). In theory, the employment contract captures the reciprocity evident in the agreement by an employer to provide workers with wages in exchange for their capacity to labour. Thus it is ostensibly characterized by the free and equal exchange of resources between the parties.

But is there such a thing, in reality, as an employment contract? The advantage of using a contractual framework to describe the employment relationship is that it captures the way in which the employment relationship is an economic transaction, something that concerns the willingness of workers to offer their capacity to labour in exchange for the promise of wages (Kahn-Freund 1977). But there are two fundamental problems with viewing the employment relationship in purely contractual terms.

First, the notion of a contract assumes that both parties to it come together in a free and equal way, without any obligation or pressure upon them to participate. However, the individual worker is in a much weaker position than the prospective employer. It is rare for workers to be in a position where they have as much freedom to choose between alternative offers of employment as employers have in selecting employees. Moreover, the consequences of refusing an offer of employment are potentially serious for the worker, since jobs, and the wages they attract, are most people's primary source of income. Employers can simply offer the job to someone else (Fox 1974).

Furthermore, by accepting an offer of employment, workers come under the authority of an employer. A purely contractual approach, then, fails to capture the way in which the employment relationship is a power relationship, characterized by the capacity of an employer to command and the obligation on the worker to obey (Kahn-Freund 1977). Thus the 'brute facts of power' (Fox 1974: 183) mean that it is inappropriate to consider the employment relationship as a contract, in the sense of a voluntary agreement between two equal parties. Indeed, British law has long recognized that the employment contract is not a purely economic relationship; it is infused by the assumption that the relationship between an employer and employee is akin to that which exists between masters and their servants. Thus the employment relationship cannot be equated with 'freedom of contract' (Wedderburn 1986).

The second reason why the employment relationship cannot be understood in pure contractual terms concerns the special nature of labour as a commodity. Employers do not buy employees in the way that a consumer purchases a tin of baked beans from a supermarket. Rather, they secure the capacity of employees to engage in productive work, their potential labour power; having hired an employee, the employer must then convert latent labour power into productive effort, through systems of control and supervision for example, or by eliciting employee commitment. Labour power, then, is an 'entirely fictitious commodity' (Polanyi 1957: 72); employers buy the capacity of workers to engage in productive effort. Therefore, 'labour differs from all other commodities in that it is enjoyed in use *and* is embodied in people' (Edwards 2003: 8).

The employment contract, then, is 'open-ended' or 'indeterminate' (Fox 1974; Marsden 1999). What this means is that when an employment contract is formed, it is impossible for the parties to specify all of the likely obligations. Neither the employer nor the employee can foresee all of the eventualities that may arise during the term of the contract.

In a commercial contract, a product or service is supplied for a price. In the labour contract, the worker sells an ability to work, which is translated into actual labour during the course of the working day. Expectations about standards of performance have to be built up during the process of production (Edwards 2003: 14).

The result is that the characteristics of the employment relationship are the outcome of both 'market' and 'managerial' relations (Flanders 1975). Market relations determine wages, or the price of a worker's employment, whereas managerial relations are concerned with establishing how much work is to be undertaken by the employee, of what kind, how quickly, and the sanctions for non-compliance (Edwards 2003).

Rather than viewing the employment relationship as a contract, then, it is generally more accurate to consider it as an ongoing series of contracts, which are continually being re-negotiated between employers and their employees as changes in their circumstances alter the expectations of the parties (Commons 1924), and thus their behaviour. The employment relationship is a process, one in which an employer, driven by a concern to produce goods or deliver services at minimum cost, seeks greater effort from employees whose main interest, obtained in the form of wages, is the maximum return possible for their labour. It can be conceptualized, then, as a 'wage-work' or 'effort bargain' (Behrend 1957), since both the employer and the employee seek to influence and adjust its terms in ways that are beneficial to their own interest (see Box 1.1 for an illustrative example).

INSIGHT INTO PRACTICE 1.1

The effort bargain in action

The way in which employers try to manipulate the effort bargain can be illustrated with reference to claims that postal workers are being expected to work faster to complete their delivery rounds within the allocated time. The postal operator Royal Mail faces greater competitive pressures; consequently, it is looking at making efficiency savings. One way of generating efficiencies is by working staff harder. In December 2008, the Communication Workers Union (CWU) claimed that the introduction of a new software system, known as Pegasus, which calculates the most efficient load that can be delivered in a round, was putting postal delivery workers under too much pressure. In particular, there was an assumption that delivery workers would maintain an average walking speed of four miles per hour while undertaking their rounds. The union alleged that such a speed was unachievable in practice, especially when you factor in the time postal workers spend waiting at doors to deliver packages that need signing for. Postal workers report that they frequently come under pressure to complete their rounds as quickly as possible. Bob Gibson, an official from the CWU, claimed that 'Royal Mail is using this system to meet financial savings without considering the physical realities of delivery needs. This is putting pressure on delivery workers and leading to bullying and harassment.' The Royal Mail denied it expected its delivery workers to walk so quickly, and stated that any bullying and harassment of staff would not be tolerated.

Sources
http://www.cwu.org; http://news.bbc.co.uk (11 December 2008)

An important implication of conceptualizing the employment relationship as an 'effort' or 'wage-work bargain' is that there is always the chance that the interests of employers and employees, or capital and labour, will come into conflict (Baldamus 1961). Thus underlying the employment relationship is a constant potential struggle over its terms, concerning what Goodrich called 'the frontier of control' (Hyman 1975). Some perspectives characterize the employment relationship as a 'stark conflict of interests' (Hyman 1975: 27), between an employer who is concerned to extract the maximum effort from employees at minimum cost, and an employee whose concern is to secure better wages, and limit the amount of work he or she is expected to undertake.

But it is overly simplistic to view the employment relationship just in terms of conflict between employers and employees; cooperation is also an essential feature (Edwards 1986, 2003). Employees share an interest with their employer in maintaining the competitiveness of their firm, for example, otherwise their jobs, and hence their livelihoods, are jeopardized (Kelly 1998). The employment relationship is, then, characterized both by cooperation and the potential for conflict. The power differential in favour of the employer renders it an essentially exploitative relationship; employers use their superior power to shift the terms of the wage-work bargain in a way that is favourable to their interest. Employees react to this, often by organizing themselves collectively in trade unions, to combat the imbalance of power. Although cooperation is an important characteristic of the employment relationship, there remains a basic antagonism between employers and employees that generates an inherent potential for conflict (Edwards 1986, 2003).

1.2.2 Regulating the employment relationship

A concern with how the terms of the employment relationship are established has long been a major concern of employment relations as a field of study. Thus its subject matter is concerned with the rules that govern the employment relationship, or the way in which it is regulated. By this we mean understanding how the terms of the employment relationship, such as pay, working hours, holiday entitlement, and the extent to which employees are able to influence decisions that affect them at work, are generated.

The systems-based approach to understanding employment relations, for example, is concerned with how the rules which govern employment relationships are established (Dunlop 1958). An employment relations system comprises four key elements (see Figure 1.1). First, there are three main groups of actors: managers, workers and trade unions, and governmental agencies. Second, these actors interact within specific contexts, the nature of the economic environment for example. Third, their interaction results in the production of a body of rules ('rule-making') which govern how employment relations operates (e.g. pay, working conditions). Negotiation between managers and unions is an example of a rule-making process. Fourth, an employment relations system is held together by an ideology: a 'set of ideas and beliefs commonly held by the actors that helps to bind or to integrate the system together as an entity' (Dunlop 1958: 16). An example of an ideology would be the preference for non-state intervention, or 'voluntarism' which long dominated employment relations in Britain (see Chapter 3).

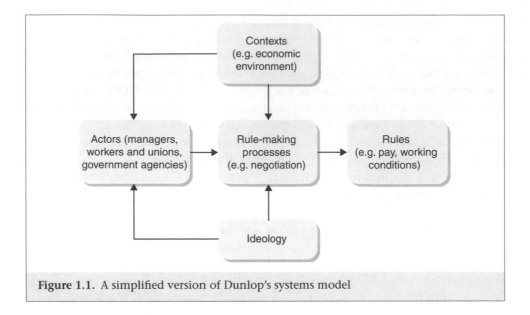

Figure 1.1. A simplified version of Dunlop's systems model

The rules-based approach, focusing on the regulation of the employment relationship, had a major influence on the development of employment relations as a field of study. It became defined as 'the study of the rules governing employment, together with the ways in which the rules are made and changed, interpreted, and administered. Put more briefly, it is the study of job regulation' (Clegg 1979: 1). If the regulation of the employment relationship is so important to developing an understanding of employment relations, how, then, do the rules originate?

Five main sources of rules can be identified which govern employment relationships (see Figure 1.2), although it is important to recognize that the influence of each will vary according to the situation. First, managers attempt to determine the terms of the employment relationship unilaterally, through the use of their prerogative. Exercising control over employees—the terms and conditions of their employment, and their behaviour—is an essential feature of management activity. The concept of managerial prerogative, or the 'right' to manage, is integral to understanding the management of employment relations. It should be understood primarily in ideological terms since it 'reflects an area of decision-making over which management believes it has (and acts as if it does have) sole and exclusive rights of determination and upon which it strenuously resists any interference ...' (Storey 1983: 102).

What factors influence this belief in the right of managers to exercise control over employment relations? Most obviously, managerial prerogative rests upon the role of management as the legitimate agent of the employer—the organization, and its shareholder owners. This is supported by statutory obligations that compel managers to undertake their function and operate in the interests of the shareholders. Managerial prerogative is also founded upon the belief that managers have the right to exercise control over employment relations by virtue of their abilities, expertise, and leadership skills (Storey 1983: 103–4). The right to manage, then, is important as an ideology, or set of ideas, to which many managers, especially senior ones, subscribe.

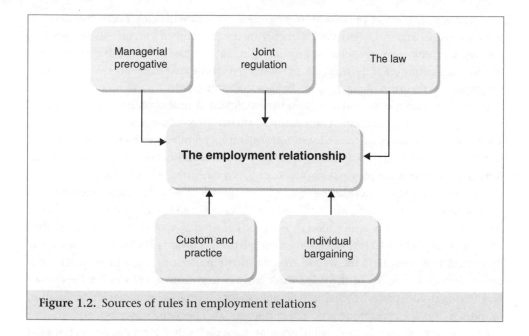

Figure 1.2. Sources of rules in employment relations

In practice, though, managerial prerogative is constrained in two important ways. First, it is necessarily influenced by the characteristics of the organizational environment, such as the state of product and labour markets. Low unemployment may oblige managers to improve pay and conditions in order to attract and retain employees. Second, the efforts of workers themselves, who, to a varying degree, challenge and contest managerial imperatives, limit the extent to which managers can exercise control in practice. Thus the nature of the employment relationship itself, as a wage-work bargain, implies that managerial prerogative, though important as an ideology that informs managers' behaviour, is never absolute.

The second source of rules concerns the ability of some workers to influence aspects of their own terms and conditions of employment by engaging in individual bargaining with employers. Given the power differential that exists in the employment relationship, few have the ability to exercise significant influence in this way, though individuals may obtain employer consent to relatively minor changes in work arrangements, such as starting and finishing times. Workers who possess particular skills for which there is high demand, in certain types of professional information technology work, for example, enjoy greater power to extract more favourable terms from employers. Perhaps the most obvious example of individual bargaining in practice concerns the activities of top professional sportspeople, footballers and the like, who, because of their exceptional individual talent, can negotiate with prospective employers (i.e. clubs) from a genuine position of strength.

Third, more commonly, though less so than used to be the case, the rules that govern the employment relationship are determined by collective bargaining between employers and trade unions, or 'joint regulation'. The unequal balance of power between the individual employee and employer in the employment relationship impels employees to combine in, and organize, trade unions, collective organizations of employees one of whose main purposes is to influence, principally through negotiations with employers, the terms of the wage-work bargain. Collective agreements are the outcome of the collective bargaining process. They may be procedural, setting out rules that govern the bargaining relationship between the employer and the union, or substantive, those that deliver concrete results to employees, in the form of pay rises or changes to working time, for example.

The fourth source of rules that govern the employment relationship emanate from the state, legislation in particular. Whereas the emphasis in Britain used to be on the desirability of joint regulation as a source of rules in employment relations (Flanders 1974), in recent years legislation has come to exercise an ever greater influence, in order to challenge discrimination for example (see Chapter 4), or to alleviate low pay (see Chapter 7).

Fifth, rules are also generated informally, through the day-to-day experiences of, and relationships between, managers and workers. Often referred to as 'custom and practice', informal rules are tacitly understood expectations of what is, and what is not, acceptable, and are an important feature of employment relations (Edwards 2003). Numerous workplace studies demonstrate the way in which unwritten, informal, and tacit understandings influence the terms of the wage-work bargain (e.g. Brown 1973; Scott 1994)—see Box 1.2 for an illustration. Workplace discipline, for example, and managerial toleration of indiscipline, are conditioned by tacit and informal expectations (see below).

These sources of rules do not exist in isolation from each other. Plenty of research studies demonstrate, for example, that the presence of robust joint regulation enhances the effectiveness of legislation designed to protect workers. Workplace health and safety legislation, for example, tends to be more rigorously enforced where trade unions are present.

Although it highlights the important role that trade unions often have in influencing managerial decision-making through joint regulation, the rules-based approach to understanding employment relations has a number of related weaknesses (Hyman 1975). First, it tends to concentrate on the formal institutions of job regulation, trade unions, and collective bargaining in particular, to a perhaps unwarranted degree.

Second, following on from this, the rules-based approach implies an emphasis on stability and order in the employment relationship; the processes by which workplace rules are challenged and changed, and the dynamic nature of the wage-work bargain,

---

◉) INSIGHT INTO PRACTICE 1.2

Custom and practice in action

In December 2004, a dispute arose between management and staff working in Post Office Counters, the retail arm of the Post Office, over Christmas opening hours. It was customary practice for staff to cease work at lunchtime on Christmas Eve, even though this had never been put in writing. Managers, however, wanted post offices to remain open until 5.30pm on 24 December, just like any other normal working day. They were concerned that the business would suffer if customers went elsewhere to do their last-minute Christmas shopping for stationery products and the like. This example demonstrates the importance of custom and practice rules in employment relations.

influenced, as it often is, by informal expectations and understandings based on custom and practice, tend to be neglected.

Third, it overlooks the way in which the employment relationship, understood as a wage-work bargain, is concerned with struggle as employees attempt to exercise control over their working lives. A proper understanding of employment relations, then, not only demands an analysis of how the employment relationship is regulated, but also how employees experience, challenge, and contest the rules.

SECTION SUMMARY AND FURTHER READING

- The employment relationship should be conceptualized not as a contract, but as a wage-work or effort bargain. This refers to the ongoing process of struggle over the terms of the employment relationship between an employer, who wishes to convert latent labour power into productive effort, and an employee, who is concerned with increasing the return, in the form of wages and better working conditions, from his or her labour.

- Conceptualizing it as a bargain implies that the potential for conflict is an inevitable feature of the employment relationship. Not only is there a basic antagonism between employer and employee, but the employment relationship is also exploitative, characterized by an imbalance of power, between a powerful employer and a relatively powerless individual employee.

- There are five sources of rules that govern employment relationships: managerial regulation; joint regulation; individual bargaining; the law; and custom and practice expectations. While the regulation of employment relations is a key feature of employment relations as a field of study, we also need to understand how people experience and challenge the rules.

Edwards (2003) is an excellent guide to the nature of both the employment relationship and employment relations. Flanders (1975) examines the nature of 'market' and 'managerial' relations in the employment relationship. See Storey (1983) for a detailed study of managerial prerogative.

 Visit our Online Resource Centre for web links to sites connected to this section. www.oxfordtextbooks.co.uk/williams_adamsmith2e

---

1.3 **Employment relations as a 'field of study'**

Employment relations is not an academic discipline in its own right; rather it is better conceptualized as a 'field of study' (Edwards 2003; Heery et al. 2008). Thus it does not have its 'own conceptual and theoretical analysis', but is an area in 'which a variety of disciplinary perspectives can be applied and tested' (Hyman 1994a: 3). The origins of employment relations as a field of study can be traced to the nineteenth century. This period saw the first major studies of the trade unions and collective bargaining (for example, Webb and Webb 1920a). It was also characterized by significant instances of worker unrest, the causes of which governments and official agencies were anxious to understand (Hyman 1989). A concern with investigating what became known as the 'labour problem' thus stimulated early studies of employment relations (Budd 2004; Heery et al. 2008).

These studies were largely influenced by theoretical perspectives drawn from the discipline of economics. Writers were concerned about the way in which the demand for, and the supply of, labour determined wage rates, for example. Studies of employment relationships in specific contexts discovered that the characteristics of the external labour market could not adequately explain differences in wage levels (Brown and Nolan 1988). Hence, there was an increasing emphasis on the way in which the institutions of job regulation, the bargaining role of trade unions in particular, shaped employment relationships (Ackers and Wilkinson 2003). Perspectives in this tradition were heavily influenced by the need for a proper historical understanding of the institutions they described. They were characterized by intricately detailed historical accounts of the development of trade unions and collective bargaining arrangements in particular (see Flanders and Clegg 1964).

1.3.1 Unitary and pluralist perspectives on employment relations

One of the leading writers on employment relations in Britain during the 1960s and 1970s, along with Flanders and Clegg, was Alan Fox. In 1966, he established a distinction between unitary and pluralist 'frames of reference' in employment relations. These frames of reference are perspectives that can be applied to employment relations; they are not theories of employment relations (Blyton and Turnbull 2004). Fox articulated them as 'ideologies of management' (Fox 1966: 10), beliefs held by managers that influence their approach to employment relations. They can be likened to lenses, tools which people use to 'perceive and define social phenomena', in this case the nature of the employment relationship, which thus influence and shape their actions (Fox 1974: 271).

The unitary perspective is characterized by an emphasis on cooperative relations at work. It rejects the assumption that a basic antagonism exists between employers and employees; conflict is largely caused by external agitators, trade unions, whose interference disrupts the harmonious state of relations that would otherwise exist. Holders of unitary beliefs rely on the 'liberal use of team or family metaphors' (Fox 1974: 249) when conceptualizing the nature of the employment relationship.

Managers, in particular, often use the team analogy to describe relations in their organizations, based on the assumption that employers and their employees share the same goals, something that renders managerial prerogative legitimate, and trade union representation unnecessary. In his evidence to the 1994 House of Commons Employment Committee investigation into the future of trade unions, for example, the then chief executive of Zurich Insurance contended that it 'is the job of the company to create an environment in which a trade union becomes irrelevant . . . the very nature of the unions, sitting in there in a divisive capacity, stops the employees and managers of an organization getting together as one team' (House of Commons Employment Committee 1994: 342).

The unitary perspective on employment relations is often criticized for advancing an unrealistic view of workplace life, in particular for denying the basic antagonism that characterizes the employment relationship. Yet, as a perspective on the nature of employment relations, and, moreover, one which is subscribed to by a great number of managers (Poole and Mansfield 1993), it must be taken seriously (Edwards 2003).

Most senior managers, if asked their views about the nature of the employment relationship, would articulate a unitary perspective, stressing the importance of common goals, shared objectives, and the absence of any conflict of interest between the employer and employee. These beliefs influence their behaviour, most notably the importance of upholding managerial prerogative, and of resisting what they see as trade union interference in the operation of their organizations.

There is evidence that the unitary perspective influences developments in contemporary employment relations. In a study of hotels, for example, Head and Lucas (2004) found that managers expressed hostility towards trade unions, rejected the notion that there was antagonism in the employment relationship, and emphasized the extent to which their organization was a 'happy team'. The food company studied by Wray (1996) attempted to secure the loyalty and cooperation of its employees, and thus render trade unions unnecessary, by offering relatively good benefits.

By contrast, the pluralist frame of reference is a perspective which recognizes the existence of a basic antagonism in the employment relationship, and hence the inevitable potential for conflict. The concept of pluralism is derived from political theory, where it is used to capture the way in which states and governments have to mediate between a potentially highly diverse range of competing interest groups when formulating their policies. Having to accommodate the views of a diversity—or plurality—of interests means that political power is not exercised in a straightforwardly top–down manner, but is more diffuse, linked to the respective influence of different interest groups over policy outcomes.

With regard to employment relations, pluralism recognizes that employers and employees may have different interests, which will need to be reconciled if the organization is to function effectively. The principal concern of pluralists is with ensuring that any conflict that arises from these differences of interest is managed appropriately, and contained in a way that prevents it from causing too much disruption. Thus there is an emphasis on developing procedures that are designed to resolve conflict, in particular the establishment of bargaining relationships with trade unions, given the array, or plurality, of interests that potentially exist within the organization.

Therefore, 'management has to face the fact that there are other sources of leadership, other focuses of loyalty, within the social system it governs, and that it is with these that management must share its decision-making' (Fox 1966: 8). In other words, managers cannot assume that the organization is characterized by shared interests and common goals; in particular employees will have divergent interests, and may want to express them through their own independent institutions, trade unions. 'At the heart of the pluralist position is a conviction that the employment relationship embraces two equally legitimate sets of interests, those of employers and those of employees' (Heery et al. 2008: 14–15). Unions, then, are not external agitators to be resisted if harmonious relations are to be upheld, but are the legitimate representatives of employees' interests.

The pluralist frame of reference was enormously influential in the development of employment relations as an academic field of study (Ackers and Wilkinson 2003; Hyman 1989). The emphasis on employment relations as the 'study of the institutions of job regulation' (Flanders 1975), noted above, was informed by a belief in the legitimacy of trade unions, and accorded a special role to collective bargaining as the means by which they secured their goals, something that became the 'dominant paradigm' (Ackers and Wilkinson 2003: 7).

During the 1960s and 1970s, the pluralist orthodoxy developed in the context of the emergence of employment relations as an important public policy issue (Ackers and Wilkinson 2003; Hyman 1989). Governments were concerned that particular characteristics of Britain's system of employment relations, most notably the growth of workplace bargaining between union representatives and managers, generated unnecessary levels of disruptive industrial conflict and inflationary wage increases.

From a pluralist perspective, the solution was not, as the holders of unitary views would argue, to resist the encroachment of the unions as a means of reasserting managerial authority; rather, stronger bargaining relationships between employers and unions should be encouraged, given the advantages of developing robust and effective procedures for containing, or institutionalizing, conflict through the joint regulation of the workplace. According to one leading pluralist, the 'paradox, whose truth managements have found it so difficult to accept, is that they can only regain control by sharing it' (Flanders 1975: 172). Until the 1980s, then, the pluralist perspective exercised an important influence over both public policy and management attitudes towards employment relations, though not at the expense of the latter's fundamentally unitary beliefs.

1.3.2 Challenges to pluralist orthodoxy

The main challenge to the pluralist employment relations orthodoxy of the 1960s and 1970s initially came from the development of radical perspectives on employment relations. These share with pluralism a belief in the essentially antagonistic nature of the employment relationship. However, they do not accept its assumption that conflict can be resolved by the development of procedures, or even the desirability of attempting to do so.

We do not deal with Marxist approaches to employment relations separately from the umbrella of radicalism (Edwards 1986). Generally, Marxism differs from other radical approaches in its emphasis on the way in which the exploitation of workers in the employment relationship generates class conflict between the working class, who produce goods and services, and the owners of capital, something that results in deepening class consciousness, and the development of a socialist political project (see Gall 2003b).

What criticisms, then, do radical approaches make of the pluralist perspective? First, it is argued that pluralism fails to address the issue of power seriously enough, assuming that, in an environment where bargaining relationships have been established, a balance of power exists between employers and unions (Fox 1974), although this has been rebutted by pluralist writers (Clegg 1975). Employers, by virtue of their ownership of, and control over, the production of goods or delivery of services, enjoy far greater power than even the most well-organized union (Fox 1974).

Second, radical writers contend that pluralism is an essentially conservative ideology, concerned with upholding the existing order in society rather than challenging it (Fox 1974; Goldthorpe 1977). Thus, while pluralism ostensibly appears to advance the interests of employees, by recognizing the desirability of union organization and collective bargaining, in fact the development of procedures ensures they are kept within narrow limits, and do not challenge the economic power of employers. Joint regulation contains conflict, resolves it, and thus ameliorates its potential for disruption in a way that helps the interests of capital rather than those of labour.

Following on from this, the third main criticism of the pluralist approach is that by focusing on procedural reform, it neglects the important substantive outcomes for employees (Hyman 1989). In other words, pluralism is more concerned with the system of joint regulation than whether or not it produces anything worthwhile for employees. However, it is suggested that the radical approach places an unwarranted emphasis on conflict and disorder in employment relations (Ackers and Wilkinson 2003).

During the late 1960s and the 1970s, a number of important sociological studies of workplace employment relations were strongly influenced by a radical perspective. Huw Beynon's study of Ford's Halewood car manufacturing plant is a particularly notable example of the genre (Beynon 1973). Since the 1980s, though, the influence of radical perspectives has waned (Ackers and Wilkinson 2005), largely because of the marked decline in the level of trade union membership and organization, decreasing strike levels, and the dwindling extent of collective bargaining activity. The main challenges to pluralist orthodoxy in employment relations now come from elsewhere, from feminist perspectives for example (see Box 1.3), and in particular from the resurgence of unitary thinking associated with the rise of human resource management techniques.

As we show in Chapter 5, there is growing interest in how organizations can develop sophisticated human resource management (HRM) approaches to engage and enhance the commitment of their staff as a means of realizing improvements in business performance. Contemporary 'human resource management follows the unitarist belief that effective management policies can align the interests of employees and employers and thereby remove conflicts of interest' (Budd 2004: 6). Growing interest in the 'neo-unitary' (Farnham and Pimlott 1995) character of HRM, demonstrates the extent to which perspectives drawn from the discipline of psychology, those concerning human relations at work in particular (Edwards 2003), such as the relationship between work, commitment, and performance, influence the study of employment relations.

The development of sophisticated HRM, and the associated ascendency of the unitary perspective, has challenged the position of employment relations as a field of study, given the extent to which, notwithstanding the increasing importance of radical perspectives, it was

---

Employment relations reflection 1.3   The feminist critique of employment relations

During the 2000s there has been a growth of interest in feminist perspectives on employment relations. Traditionally, matters such as trade unions and collective bargaining were studied without paying much attention to gender—defined as relations between men and women—and how it affects employment relations (Wacjman 2000); though there were some notable exceptions (e.g. Pollert 1981). The feminist critique of orthodox employment relations means that there is now a better appreciation of the influence on employment relations of factors that are constituted outside of workplaces, particularly gender, for example (Greene 2003). The development of feminist perspectives has contributed to a welcome broadening of the employment relations field (Heery et al. 2008); the challenges of reconciling paid work with family responsibilities, such as child care for example, have received more attention as a result.

concerned with the joint regulation of the workplace. The study of employment relations was founded upon the importance of trade unionism and collective bargaining, and under-pinned by a dominant pluralist perspective (Ackers and Wilkinson 2005; Heery et al. 2008).

By the 2000s, though, a field of study which 'focused on trade unions and collective bargaining had found it increasingly difficult to conceptualize a society in which both were increasingly marginal to the world of work' (Ackers and Wilkinson 2003: 12–13). While perspectives drawn from academic disciplines such as law (e.g. Davies and Freed-land 2007), geography (e.g. Herod, Peck, and Wills 2003), and politics (e.g. Ludlum and Taylor 2003) have increasingly enhanced our understanding of employment relations, its importance as an academic field of study dwindled during the 1980s and 1990s.

The purpose of this book, though, is to demonstrate that employment relations is about more than just trade unions and collective bargaining. Key elements of what makes employment relations distinctive as a field of study—the focus on the employment relationship and how it is regulated for example, and a concern with recognizing and promoting the interests of working people—mean that it remains a vital topic of contemporary enquiry (Ackers and Wilkinson 2005). Studying employment relations means that one has to recognize the importance of topics such as power and justice, and that employers and employees may have competing interests, things that are largely absent from HRM texts (BUIRA 2008). Thus an understanding of employment relations is essential in order to be able to comprehend, and critically evaluate, some of the key issues that affect business and management in twenty-first-century societies.

SECTION SUMMARY AND FURTHER READING

- The unitary perspective, which denies this basic antagonism in the employment relationship, can be criticized for being unrealistic, though its tenets influence the attitudes and behaviour of managers.

- Pluralism recognizes the potential for conflict, but tends to focus on how it can be contained by the development of procedures, collective bargaining arrangements in particular.

- Radical approaches, which developed out of a critique of pluralism, perhaps over-emphasize the degree of conflict and disorder in employment relations.

- As a field of study, employment relations was traditionally concerned with understanding the rules that govern employment relationships, in particular joint regulation, collective bargaining between trade unions and employers. This is too narrow an approach; it has been rendered untenable, moreover, by declining unionization and falling levels of collective bargaining. However, key elements of what makes employment relations distinctive as a field of study, notably a concern with the interests of workers, makes it a valuable topic of contemporary enquiry.

See Heery et al. (2008) for an assessment of pluralist orthodoxy in employment relations and the principal challenges to it. Hyman (1975) is the standard Marxist introduction to employment relations. For the nature of employment relations as a field of study, see Ackers and Wilkinson (2003).

 Visit our Online Resource Centre for web links to sites connected to this section. www.oxfordtextbooks.co.uk/williams_adamsmith2e

1.4 Employment relations: actors, processes, outcomes, and contexts

Having outlined the nature of the employment relationship and considered the main perspectives on employment relations as a field of study, the purpose of this section is to introduce the main actors, processes, and outcomes of employment relations, and illustrate the context which affects how it operates.

1.4.1 Employment relations actors

Clearly there are two fundamental actors in employment relations—workers and employers—without whom there could be no employment relationships. For the most part, though, employers vest day-to-day control of employment relations matters in the hands of appointed managers. Moreover, employers may combine in associations to handle employment relations matters. While the experiences of workers are integral to the approach taken in this book to employment relations as a field of study, they frequently organize in trade unions—collective bodies of workers that act to support and protect their interests. We have already established that legislation plays an ever increasing role in regulating employment relationships. Thus as well as examining the role of employers, managers, employers' associations, and unions in employment relations, the nature of state intervention is also worthy of scrutiny. In this section, then, we offer an overview of the three main employment relations actors—employers and management, trade unions, and the state. Bear in mind, though, that there are a range of other actors that play a role in contemporary employment relations (see Box 1.4).

Employers and management

Except in very small firms, the employing organization entrusts day-to-day control to salaried managers who are responsible, among other things, for managing employment

---

Employment relations reflection 1.4   New actors

Most studies of employment relations understandably focus on the activities of key actors like employers, workers, and trade unions. However, there is a growing interest in the role of other actors who come into contact with employment relations matters in some way, such as community-based organizations and non-governmental organizations (NGOs). The campaigning organization, Stonewall, for example, which lobbies on behalf of lesbian, gay, and bisexual people, works with employers to improve the way in which they manage sexual orientation issues. Vulnerable workers, particularly those who are based in parts of the economy where trade unions are weak, often rely on agencies like the network of Citizens' Advice Bureaux for help and support with employment-related matters (Abbott 2004). The increasing attention being given to these new and emerging employment relations actors illustrates how the boundaries of employment relations as a field of study are being widened. This is consistent with a shift towards the articulation of a broader understanding of employment relations in contemporary societies, one that expands its 'terrain to explore the links between employment and other spheres of social and economic life, and research new and previously neglected actors' (Heery and Frege 2006: 603).

relations. During the nineteenth and twentieth centuries, the development of the management function was particularly associated with the growth of large-scale enterprises and the increasing separation of ownership of the organization, shareholders in the private sector, from the control of activities within it, increasingly the province of expert managers. In a market economy their principal aim, in theory, is to manage the employment relationship efficiently in order to realize profitability, and thus maximize returns to shareholders. As we have already seen (see Section 1.2.2), a belief in managerial prerogative, or the 'right' to manage employment relationships unilaterally, without interference from third parties like trade unions, underpins managers' behaviour in employment relations.

Yet managerial efforts to secure employee compliance will always be frustrated and thus incomplete. The nature of the employment relationship as a wage-work bargain invariably limits the scope of managerial prerogative, and also provides workers with opportunities to challenge managerial control. Even in service industries, where workers' conduct is often highly prescribed, there is generally sufficient space for workers to behave in ways that do not accord with management expectations (Korczynski 2002).

Therefore in understanding how the employment relationship is managed, it is important not to oversimplify by concentrating solely on managerial attempts to secure control (Hyman 1987; Storey 1985). In order to realize the efficient production or delivery of goods and services, managers must secure a degree of legitimacy, or consent, among those they manage (Legge 2005).

A further challenge for managers concerns the dual function of labour. Employers are dependent upon their employees, but must also treat them as if they are disposable. On the one hand, employees, as the firm's human resources, are central to the realization of corporate objectives, and thus improvements in their loyalty, motivation, and commitment are essential if the organization is to be financially successful. Managers, then, may want to design and implement sophisticated and potentially costly personnel and HR techniques in order to secure the dedication of their employees; in other words, to foster a sense of dependency.

On the other hand, however, since labour costs often comprise a large proportion of an organization's budget, the workforce often bears the brunt of efforts to reduce expenditure. Moreover, the nature of the capitalist market economy means that firms constantly search out cheaper ways of producing goods and delivering services (Hyman 1975), something that makes employees inherently disposable.

Historically, employers sought to uphold managerial prerogative in the workplace by externalizing collective bargaining with trade unions through employers' associations. The origins of employers' associations in Britain can be traced to the late eighteenth and early nineteenth centuries; although these early organizations were local and transient in character, employers often combined to challenge the efforts of the nascent trade unions to organize workers (Clegg 1979; McIvor 1996).

The 1890s and 1900s saw the emergence of permanent national federations of employers, such as the Engineering Employers' Federation (EEF) (Wigham 1973); during the first half of the twentieth century they became a major employment relations actor in industries like building, engineering, and printing. The most important reason why employers organized in associations during this period was to negate the growing power of workplace trade unionism (Sisson 1983). By bargaining with unions away from the workplace, on a multi-employer basis, employers aimed to 'neutralize' union power in the workplace. In matters that went unregulated by collective agreements, particularly those pertaining to the organization and pace of work, the assumption was that management prerogative would predominate (Sisson 1987).

Although employers' associations sometimes engaged in crude anti-union activities, such as undermining strikes, their role in the joint regulation of employment relations, particularly through multi-employer collective bargaining and procedures for resolving disputes, became an important means of maintaining managerial control, and thus upholding employers' interests (McIvor 1996).

From the 1960s onwards, though, the role of employers' associations declined in significance, linked to the erosion of multi-employer bargaining. Increasing numbers of firms, especially larger ones, chose to develop organization-specific procedures for handling employment relations matters (Gospel 1992). The 1980s and 1990s saw the termination of multi-employer bargaining arrangements in industries such as retail banking, supermarkets, and engineering. Fewer than one in twenty private sector employees now have their pay determined by multi-employer bargaining (Kersley et al. 2006).

Unsurprisingly, given these developments, the membership of employers' associations fell. They have responded by focusing their activities on commercial matters, and the provision of employment relations advice (IRS 1998). Yet, employers' associations continue to be an integral feature of public sector employment relations, where multi-employer bargaining remains important.

One of the most notable features of employment relations since at least the 1960s has been the growing extent to which employers have sought to regain control over their own arrangements, and manage employment relations directly. At first, this took the form of a pluralist concern with responding to, and managing the consequences of, trade unionism. Since the 1980s, though, the managerial employment relations agenda has taken on a more unitary ethos, linked to the decline of both trade unionism and the joint regulation of employment relationships.

The rise of a sophisticated HRM approach to managing people at work, based on the use of techniques designed to raise organizational commitment and boost business performance, is emblematic of a more assertive managerial agenda in employment relations. We consider this in more detail in Chapter 5.

One indication that employers are taking the management of employment relations more seriously concerns the growing proportion of workplaces with access to specialist employment relations managers, those who have specific responsibility for managing human resources in organizations. In 2004, for example, nearly three-fifths (58 per cent) of workplaces were covered by a specialist employment relations manager, either in the workplace or at a higher level in the organization, up from 53 per cent in 1998 (Kersley et al. 2006). Moreover, the influence in contemporary employment relations enjoyed by non-HR specialists in organizations, like line managers, has increasingly been recognized (e.g. Purcell et al. 2003).

Trade unions

As we have already established, there is an imbalance of power in the employment relationship in favour of the employer. The main way in which workers attempt to challenge this power differential is to combine in collective organizations, trade unions, so that they can influence the terms of their employment relationships from a position of greater strength. One of the earliest and most well-known definitions of a trade union, dating from the end of the nineteenth century, refers to it as 'a continuous association of wage earners for the purpose of maintaining or improving the conditions of their working lives' (Webb and Webb 1920b: 1).

A proper definition should, however, be more specific about the means by which unions seek to improve the conditions of people's working lives. For our purposes, then, a trade union can be defined as a body comprised mainly of workers that, by means of collective organization and mobilization, represents and advances their interests both in the workplace and in society at large. It does so by providing workers with protection from the arbitrary exercise of managerial prerogative, bargaining with management over the terms and conditions of their employment, giving them influence over decisions that affect them at work, and by providing them with a means of effecting political changes that are favourable to their interests.

While one can trace their ancestry further back in time to the trade clubs and friendly societies of the eighteenth century, in Britain the trade unions originated in the nineteenth century during a period of sustained and rapid industrialization. Although there were attempts to form workers into unions during the early nineteenth century, these were generally transient bodies that either lacked formal organizational arrangements or were local affairs. The first stable and permanent national bodies date from around the middle of the nineteenth century and were mainly combinations of local organizations in industries such as engineering, construction, and printing (Hyman 2001b: 72).

Early union organization developed as a means by which skilled workers could maintain control of their craft, and of regulating the terms and conditions of their trades (Clegg, Fox, and Thompson 1964). A major function of the early trade unions was to provide their skilled craft-worker members with 'friendly benefits' such as unemployment and sick pay. In 'many industries it was the oldest form of trade union activity' (Webb and Webb 1920a: 153). Workers formed unions to defend and maintain their customary working practices and pay rates, and thus control their conditions of employment (Hyman 1975: 44).

During the second half of the nineteenth century, trade unionism began to take root in industries such as coal mining, the railways, and steel making, where craft practices, while evident, were much less deep-rooted (Hyman 2003), something that placed a greater onus on collective bargaining as a means of regulating pay and employment conditions. The main functions of the developing trade unions were thus to provide their members with benefits, to regulate the terms and conditions of employment, first through craft control but, as time progressed, more commonly through collective bargaining, and also through political activity. At the end of the nineteenth century the leading British trade unions of the time joined up with prominent socialist campaigners to establish an independent political party that would support the interests of workers and unions in parliament—the Labour party.

The main functions of the trade unions today continue to include regulating employment relationships through collective bargaining and political activity aimed at supporting the interests of working people; while most trade unions are independent of any political party, some of the major UK unions are affiliated to the Labour party, and all of them view political campaigning as a legitimate method of achieving their objectives. The rise of the welfare state during the twentieth century meant that providing membership benefits became a less important union function. Nevertheless, trade unions now play an important role in supporting and protecting workers, by representing them in grievance and disciplinary cases, for example (see Chapter 6).

Trade unions are ostensibly democratic bodies; organizations which comprise, and work on behalf of, their members. Trade union members pay a subscription—usually between £10 and £15 per month—to benefit from the services of their union, including the right to influence its policies. There is a large literature devoted to understanding the workings of union democracy (e.g. Edelstein and Warner 1975; Martin 1985)—defined as 'the extent to which the actions of union leaders are constrained by the needs and wishes of their members' (Heery and Fosh 1990: 15). One perspective holds that members' interests are best served by ensuring that unions are run by a cadre of expert officials who use their skills and know-how to represent them effectively (Allen 1954). An alternative approach holds that a more participatory approach is desirable, one that enables members to be directly involved in trade union decision-making themselves, rather than leaving it to expert officials (Fairbrother 1984).

In contemporary employment relations, though, the dominant approach to making sure that union policies reflect members' wishes is the representative democracy model. Union leaders are periodically elected and re-elected in a ballot of members, supposedly ensuring that the policies they pursue meet with the approval of their membership. However one understands trade union democracy, though, the unions are complex organizations whose activities are often marked by conflict over what their goals should be, and the most effective means of achieving them.

There are three broad types of trade union. Occupational unions organize and represent people working in specific occupations. ASLEF (the Amalgamated Society of Locomotive Engineers and Firemen), for example, recruits its members predominantly from the occupation of train driver. The second type is the industrial union. Industrial unions cover an entire industry sector, recruiting members from all levels and occupations within that industry. A good example of an industrial union is UCATT (Union of Construction and Allied Trades and Technicians), which operates in the construction industry. The third type of trade union is the general union. These are often large trade unions, which cover more than one industry, like Unison in the public sector for example, which has members in, among other places, health, education, and local government.

See Table 1.1 for a list of the major trade unions (those with more than 100,000 members) in Britain. The largest unions tend to be general unions, like the Transport and General Workers Union (TGWU) and Amicus, which in 2007 merged to form Unite the Union, the largest trade union in Britain. The list of unions in Table 1.1 also includes some notable industrial unions, such as the Union of Shop, Distributive, and Allied Workers (USDAW), which operates in the retail sector. Because occupational unions tend to be rather small, they are largely absent from the list in the table. However, both the Royal College of Nursing (RCN), a union of nurses, and the British Medical Association (BMA), which represents doctors, possess a strong occupational identity.

Table 1.1 Major trade unions in the UK

Trade union	Membership
Unison	1,343,000
Amicus*	1,176,594
Transport and General Workers Union (TGWU)*	761,336
General Municipal and Boilermakers union (GMB)	575,892
Royal College of Nursing (RCN)	394,196
National Union of Teachers (NUT)	368,066
Union of Shop Distributive and Allied Workers (USDAW)	341,291
Public and Commercial Services Union (PCS)	311,998
National Association of Schoolmasters Union of Women Teachers (NASUWT)	298,884
Communication Workers Union (CWU)	238,817
Association of Teachers and Lecturers (ATL)	207,075
British Medical Association (BMA)	138,909
Union of Construction Allied Trades and Technicians (UCATT)	128,914
University and College Union (UCU)	116,977
Prospect	101,532

* Amicus and the TGWU merged in 2007 to form Unite the Union.
Source: Certification Office (2008)

Another feature of Table 1.1 which is worth noting concerns the relatively large number of major trade unions which operate in the public sector; education unions like the National Union of Teachers (NUT) and the University and College Union (UCU), for example. During the nineteenth and twentieth centuries, the development of trade unions was concentrated among primary and manufacturing industries. However, since the 1970s employment in these areas has fallen substantially. At the same time, workers in the public sector have become increasingly unionized. The growing proportion of trade union members who work in the public sector, many of whom are employed in professional occupations like teaching, has had a marked effect on the character of trade unionism in Britain.

Finally, in this introduction to the role of the trade unions, it is important to mention the role and activities of the Trades Union Congress (TUC) – see Box 1.5. The TUC is a confederation of unions, and acts as the voice of the trade union movement in Britain. Very few major unions are not affiliated to the TUC; of those that appear in Table 1.1, only the RCN and BMA are outside it.

The state
Although management and unions are the principal parties in employment relations, it is also important to emphasize the strong, or 'pervasive' (Kelly 1998), influence of the state and its bodies. It is conventional to understand the effects of state activity on employment relations in four ways.

INSIGHT INTO PRACTICE 1.5

The role of the Trades Union Congress

Traditionally, the Trades Union Congress (TUC), which was founded in 1868, fulfils three broad roles in employment relations. First, it is involved in adjudicating disputes between unions concerning which of them should represent particular groups of workers, though this activity is now only of relatively minor importance (McIlroy and Daniels 2009). Second, it provides its union affiliates with services, such as education and training provision. Third, the TUC represents, and acts on behalf of, the trade union movement in general, in relations with government, for example. During the 1990s and 2000s the TUC's role changed in two key respects. One of the changes concerns the development of a more explicit campaigning role, on matters such as better rights for part-time workers, for example, and the need for vulnerable workers, like migrant workers, to have more protection. Linked to this, moreover, the TUC is trying to develop a role as the organization which speaks on behalf of working people as a whole, rather than just as the voice of the trade union interest. However, union mergers and amalgamations threaten the TUC's role. The trend towards so-called 'super-unions' like Unite, for example, which was formed from the merger of the Transport and General Workers Union and Amicus, potentially erodes the authority of the TUC (McIlroy and Daniels 2009).

First, employment in the state, or public, sector is a major element of contemporary employment relations and at various points in this book we consider some of its distinctive features, such as pay determination (see Chapter 7).

Second, states enact legislation in the area of employment relations, such as that designed to regulate trade union behaviour (see Chapter 3), or establish minimum wages (see Chapter 7). The European Union is also a source of employment legislation (see Chapter 3).

Third, states operate arrangements to assist employers and unions to resolve disputes, notably arbitration and conciliation machinery (see Chapter 9).

Fourth, the economic and political programmes followed by the governments of national states also have important implications for employment relations (see below and Chapter 3). In order to understand contemporary employment relations properly, then, it is essential to consider the important influence of the state.

One of the most popular approaches to conceptualizing the state is that of the German sociologist Max Weber, who understood the state in terms of the monopoly it enjoys over the legitimate use of physical force within certain defined territorial limits (see Pierson 1996). According to one prominent contemporary political scientist, the state is 'a system of relationships which defines the territory and membership of a community, regulates its internal affairs, conducts relations with other states (by peaceful and by warlike means) and provides it with identity and cohesion' (Jordan 1985: 1).

Liberal-pluralist approaches have long dominated attempts to understand the way in which groups mobilize and accrue power, and thus come to have their interests represented by the state (Miliband 1973). As a result, 'the making of public policy by governments is the end-product of a process of negotiation and accommodation in which citizens organized in groups to represent their interests exert pressure to realize their ambitions' (Pierson 1996: 72).

While the liberal-pluralist perspective encompasses a variety of distinctive strands, in respect of employment relations the state's role is generally seen to involve maintaining a balance between the competing interests of capital and labour, and accommodating the demands of both. Where an imbalance of power arises, particularly in favour of employers, the state acts, by introducing legislation for example, to ameliorate it. There are two fundamental problems with liberal-pluralist perspectives. First, they fail to account for the marked tendency of state policy to favour the interests of employers. Second, they assume that state intervention produces an equivalence of power between capital and labour when in reality the odds remain stacked against the latter (Miliband 1973).

However, a rather different assumption underpins new right, or neo-liberal, perspectives, as exemplified by the work of writers such as Hayek that became more prominent during the 1970s and 1980s. From this viewpoint, state intervention is treated as a fundamental threat to liberties; it stifles market forces and is liable to undermine the free society.

Whereas liberal-pluralist approaches consider state intervention in the area of employment relations as a largely progressive development, helping to ameliorate the imbalance of power between capital and labour, from a neo-liberal perspective, laws that make it easier for unions to operate endanger the liberties of individual workers and their employers to conduct their affairs in a manner of their own choosing. State regulation is desirable only in so far as it helps to protect and support free markets (see Dunleavy and O' Leary 1987). As we show in Chapter 3, state policy in contemporary employment relations is largely informed by such a perspective.

For a critical, and more sophisticated, appreciation of the role of the state in employment relations it is appropriate to draw upon Marxist perspectives. Although Marx himself did not develop an explicit theory of the state under capitalism (Hyman 1975), two distinct approaches to understanding its role can be inferred from his work. In his early writings, the state is treated as an instrument of class rule by the dominant capitalist interest (see Jordan 1985; Pierson 1996). In this approach, the emphasis is on the coercive, repressive role of the state, and the way in which its offices and policies are designed to undermine trade unions and the interests of labour in general in order to further those of capital. Kelly (1998), for example, suggests that the repression of trade unions, in particular the way in which strike activity is restricted and undermined, demonstrates the importance of the coercive role of the state in employment relations (see Box 1.6).

Yet state policy is not just characterized by the repression of the labour interest. Thus the second broad approach to understanding the role of the state under capitalism that can be inferred from Marx's writings, and that is particularly associated with the Italian Marxist theorist Antonio Gramsci, suggests that in order to maintain the long-term viability of capitalism, states need to win the favour, or consent, of those they govern. This provides a stable and ordered environment within which the capitalist order can flourish (Pierson 1996).

From this perspective, then, policies and legislation ostensibly designed to favour the labour interest, such as the nineteenth-century laws restricting the working hours of women and children (see Hyman 1975), in fact benefit capital in the long term. By seemingly favouring the interests of labour, they give the capitalist system, and the exploitative nature of the employment relationship that underpins it, added legitimacy. Thus in order to maintain the long-term viability of capitalism, states adopt

INTERNATIONAL PERSPECTIVE 1.6

Union repression around the world

State repression of trade unions and workers' rights is a marked feature of contemporary employment relations in many countries. The International Trade Union Confederation (ITUC) publishes an annual survey of violations of trade union rights around the world. Whereas many countries restrict the ability of trade unions to organize workers in some way, or limit opportunities for collective bargaining, the ICTU's survey of developments in 2007 demonstrates the violence exhibited towards independent trade unionism in some places. In Zimbabwe, for example, the government constantly harasses and intimidates union activists. One leader of a teachers' union died a few weeks after having been arrested and tortured by Robert Mugabe's regime. By far the most dangerous place to be a trade unionist, however, is Colombia in South America. While the number of assassinations of union activists there declined during the 2000s, there were still 39 such murders during 2007. The Colombian government claims that the violence is a consequence of years of civil war and the activities of numerous powerful armed groups of guerillas who control much of its territory. But there is evidence that the Colombian state encourages the killings.

Source
ITUC (2008)

policies or enact legislation that runs counter to the short-term interests of business (Dunleavy and O'Leary 1987).

Although Marxism offers a rather sophisticated understanding of the influence of the state on employment relations, suggesting that its approach is characterized by a mixture of coercion and consent (Kelly 1998), the extent to which state policies necessarily support the interests of capital has been questioned. Edwards (1986) contends that it is over-simplistic to view the state as the servant of one class and that state managers, policy-makers, and government officials have to accommodate the interests of both capital and labour.

The state does not just respond to demands from capital; it must also react to the concerns of labour. Policy reflects an accommodation between the demands of capital and those of labour, and does not simply flow from the interests of the former. Nevertheless, the state must still operate within a capitalist order, something that shapes, but does not determine, the character of its policies. This is even more pronounced given the imperatives of globalization (see Chapter 2).

1.4.2 Employment relations processes: collective bargaining, participation, and involvement

Formal processes play an important role in employment relations, in the form of collective bargaining, for example, or arrangements to resolve employee grievances and disciplinary matters. Processes that enable staff to be involved in, or informed about, decisions that affect them at work are also important features of contemporary employment relations. In this section we assess the nature of collective bargaining, and introduce the main dimensions of employee involvement and participation arrangements. Nevertheless, it is important not to underplay importance of informal expectations and understandings as they affect the wage-work bargain (see Box 1.7).

Collective bargaining

Collective bargaining can be considered in both narrow and broad terms. In its narrow sense, collective bargaining is simply a means of determining pay and conditions of employment. Beatrice and Sidney Webb, its first serious students, suggested that it is largely an economic process, the collective equivalent of individual bargaining (Webb and Webb 1920a). By acting collectively through trade unions, workers could secure more for themselves from the employment relationship than was possible from their individual efforts.

Employment relations reflection 1.7 Informal expectations and understandings—the case of workplace discipline

While formal processes are integral to the conduct of much employment relations, this should not lead us to overlook the importance of informal expectations and understandings, and their implications for the wage-work bargain. Take the case of workplace discipline for example. Formal procedures for disciplining staff suspected of transgressing organizational rules, and the application of formal sanctions like warnings as a result, are commonplace features of workplace life. In practice, however, workplace rules, whether or not they are obeyed, and whether or not managers choose to enforce them, are contingent upon the relationship between managers and workers. Discipline, then, 'means more than the application of sanctions by management. It also refers to the ways in which day-to-day understandings are negotiated between workers and managers: some rules are treated more seriously than others, and there is a process of shopfloor negotiation which defines which rules are respected and which are not' (Edwards and Whitston 1994: 320). Workplace rules are not laid down by managers, and then obeyed by workers, in an overly clear-cut manner. Rather, they are interpreted, and then adjusted, by managers and workers as part of the continuing process of negotiation and re-negotiation that characterizes the employment relationship as a wage-work bargain.

Andrew Scott (1994) offers a good example of this in his account of employment relations in a non-union chocolate factory. On coming across evidence that workers were leaving to go home before the end of a shift, and without tidying the changing room, managers instituted a 'first and last hour' rule. Anyone leaving the production line during the first and last hours of their shift without their manager's approval would receive a written warning. During the first few weeks of the new rule's existence, a number of workers received warnings as a result of breaching it. Having to ask permission to go to the toilet, for example, was, for the workers, a distasteful experience, and most considered the rule to be 'silly' and 'unfair' (Scott 1994: 113). Nor did the rule find favour among all the managers. They 'found it inconvenient and tiresome to spend two hours of each day making sure their staff did not slip away without permission and, moreover, they sensed that shop floor relations were not as friendly as they had been before the rule was introduced' (Scott 1994: 113). Not all managers, then, enforced the rule, though its continued existence in the rule-book meant that it could always be reimposed should they wish to enforce their authority more rigorously at any time.

Collective bargaining, however, is more than just a means of determining employment terms. It also fulfils a broader, political function. Flanders (1975) stressed that collective bargaining is a rule-making process. Not only does it set the terms and conditions on which labour is hired, but it also gives workers, through their unions, rights to challenge and influence managerial decisions over such things as the organization of work. Thus collective bargaining, since it is a process of 'job regulation', is an important means of giving workers voice over matters that affect them in their working lives.

The American writers Chamberlain and Kuhn (1965) identified two strands of this political aspect of collective bargaining. It is a rule-making process, allowing workers collectively to influence the terms of their employment, and also a system of industrial governance, in that it establishes a procedure that enables managements to reach deci-sions jointly with trade unions. It is inappropriate, therefore, to view collective bargaining simply as a device for determining pay and conditions. Rather, it 'is generally more useful to use the term to cover a broader set of joint regulatory behaviour, embracing all activity whereby employers deliberately permit representatives of employee collectivities to be involved in the management of the employment relationship' (Brown 1993: 197).

For pluralist writers, collective bargaining is the most effective means of regulating the employment relationship. For one thing, it enables workers to exercise influence over decisions that affect them at work. This was a particularly strong theme of the 1960s Donovan Royal Commission which, heavily imbued by the dominant pluralist thinking of the time, stated that where it was properly undertaken 'collective bargaining is the most effective means of giving workers the right to representation in decisions affecting their working lives, a right which is or should be the prerogative of every worker in a democratic society' (Royal Commission 1968: 54).

For the pluralists, though, collective bargaining not only gives workers a voice over matters that affect them at work, but is also an important means by which the inherent conflict in the employment relationship can be accommodated or, as it is often put, institutionalized. In other words, the presence of collective bargaining enables managers to contain conflict, to keep it within acceptable limits, and is therefore an effective means of managing employment relations and extending managerial control (Flanders 1975). Since the 1980s, though, the influence of collective bargaining has diminished (see Chapter 7), linked to the decline of the trade unions and the more unitary preferences of managers.

The principal radical critique of collective bargaining is that it contains workers' militancy within boundaries that are acceptable to employers. By institutionalizing conflict, it runs counter to the real interests of workers. It is suggested, moreover, that by becoming enmeshed in the process of bargaining with management, unions come to adopt a fundamentally conservative ethos, concerned with the procedural details of negotiations and agreements, rather than with advancing the substantive interests of their members. Whereas workers want to improve their terms and conditions of employment, and to secure greater influence over workplace decisions, in the bargaining process union leaders may prefer to focus upon establishing and maintaining stable relationships with employers, thus sustaining the institutional security of the union, rather than challenging them (Hyman 1989).

In practice, however, one cannot readily distinguish between union leaders' concern with stable and secure bargaining relationships and the desire of their members for improved pay and conditions. Workers have a concern with the security and survival of their union because, without it, they have no means of winning better employment terms. Moreover, the position of union leaders becomes problematic if, in the bargaining process, they are not seen to be delivering benefits for their members (Smith 2001).

Involvement and participation

In so far as it allows workers to influence decisions that affect their employment conditions and working environment, collective bargaining may be viewed as a form of participation and involvement (Clegg 1976, 1979). Generally, though, we use the terms employee involvement or participation to refer to arrangements that enable managers to communicate with their staff or that give workers some influence over organizational or workplace decisions.

A major problem, however, concerns the diversity of practices that can be accommodated under these labels. There is little commonality between arrangements that enable worker representatives to serve on company boards, for example, and those that allow managers simply to inform their staff about current organizational developments. Thus, 'participation and involvement are somewhat elastic terms and are amenable to a range of definitions' (Marchington and Wilkinson 2000: 342).

There are five areas where the potential for differing interpretations and conceptual misunderstandings exist. First, what is the purpose of participation? Is it driven largely by managers, with the aim of eliciting improved worker commitment and thus more output? Or is participation driven from the bottom up, through the collective organization and mobilization of workers, and designed to restrict the exercise of managerial prerogative? Thus it is important to recognize that terms like 'participation' and 'involvement' are often used in an imprecise way that invites confusion over their real meaning.

In a general sense, moreover, participation is something that can be supported by managements, unions, and workers alike (Blyton and Turnbull 2004). Nevertheless, some scope for clarity does exist. The term 'participation', for example, may be used to refer to arrangements that give workers some degree of influence over organizational and workplace decisions, sometimes collectively through trade unions. The term 'employee involvement' (EI) is more usefully applied to managerial initiatives that are designed to further the flow of communication at work as a means of enhancing the organizational commitment of employees (Hyman and Mason 1995).

Second, it is important to recognize differences over the subject matter, or scope, covered by participation. Does the content of participation encompass such wide-ranging matters as company decision-making, investment policies, planning, and future priorities? Or, as is generally more likely, is it restricted to a narrower, perhaps more trivial, range of issues such as the state of the car park or the staff canteen (Marchington et al. 1992)?

Third, following on from this, it is evident that the level at which participation takes place may vary. It can occur at the level of the organization, the workplace, or particularly in respect of teamworking initiatives, the work group.

Fourth, participation may be undertaken directly between management and the workforce, or indirectly, by means of workers' representatives, who may, or may not, be trade unionists.

Fifth, perhaps the greatest potential for ambiguity concerns the depth, or degree, of participation and involvement. There is a distinction to be drawn between those arrangements that enable workers, or their representatives, to exercise influence over organizational or workplace decisions, and those that simply allow managers to communicate information with their staff. The most pronounced form of participation, and by far the rarest, is control over the business by workers themselves (see Box 1.8).

Having outlined the meanings of, and conceptual difficulties associated with, participation and involvement at work, we now focus on one important aspect, the development of joint consultation arrangements in Britain. Joint consultation has long been a feature, albeit not always a prominent one, of Britain's employment relations landscape. It is a form of participation that is particularly amenable to managers since it renders their prerogatives relatively untouched in as much as they can secure employees' views without being bound by them. Workers 'influence but in no way determine managerial policy and practice' (Poole 1986: 71).

In theory, joint consultation committees (JCCs) are seen to be appropriate forums for matters where there is a supposed greater propensity for cooperation and a commonality of interests between management and workers, such as health, safety, and welfare issues,

HISTORICAL PERSPECTIVE 1.8

Industrial democracy at work

During the 1960s and 1970s, there was a wave of interest in workers' control and industrial democracy (Poole 1986). Threats of plant closures and job cuts associated with industrial restructuring stimulated a number of 'work-ins' in which workers and their unions attempted to maintain the operation of plants themselves. The most famous instance occurred following the announcement of the closure of the Upper Clyde Shipbuilders yard near Glasgow. Workers and shop stewards occupied the yard for a period of time in order to prevent its closure (Foster and Woolfson 1986).

There was also much interest evinced in how workers' interests could be represented on company boards of directors (Brannen 1983). In the 1970s, a government committee of inquiry recommended that union representatives should have equal parity with shareholders on the boards of large companies, with an 'intermediary' group of ostensibly independent directors appointed by mutual consent maintaining a balance between the two sides. Employer opposition and the hostility of influential union leaders, who were concerned about the threat to the primacy of collective bargaining, ensured that the proposals came to nothing. Nevertheless, in 1978–79 union representation was established on the board of the Post Office. An evaluation of this experiment found that while union officials were able to challenge management proposals and take the initiative in the boardroom, they had little influence on corporate decision-making. Not only did the so-called 'independent' directors tend to side with management, but also the union representatives themselves were weakened by internal differences and by their acceptance of the expertise and authority demonstrated by managers (Batstone, Ferner, and Terry 1983).

as opposed to the more explicitly conflictual collective bargaining relationship (Clegg 1979; Marchington 1989). However, it is often difficult to maintain a rigid distinction between consultation and collective bargaining, not least because union representatives will attempt to use consultation machinery as bargaining forums.

It is important to emphasize the diversity of joint consultation arrangements; Marchington (1989, 1994) identifies four ideal types. First, they can be operated as an alternative to collective bargaining machinery, particularly in firms where there is no recognized trade union.

Second, joint consultation can operate in such a way that it is marginal to the process of collective bargaining, covering relatively trivial welfare issues such as the state of the car parking and canteen facilities.

Third, it can be used as a way of competing with, or undermining, the collective bargaining process. In these cases managers will seek to consult, rather than bargain, with a union over as many issues as they can given that, with consultation, as opposed to bargaining, they reserve the right to make the final decisions.

Fourth, joint consultation can be operated in conjunction with, or as an adjunct to, the collective bargaining process, encompassing matters on which common interests appear to be more readily apparent. Thus it is clear that the practice of joint consultation cannot be equated with the cooperative relationships between managers and workers in an overly straightforward manner. Indeed, the 'four ideal types . . . demonstrate that JCCs can take a variety of forms in different workplaces, and that to conceive of consultation as a unified concept is both misguided and simplistic' (Marchington 1994: 683).

What, though, explains the waxing and waning of employer interest in participation initiatives such as joint consultation? Ramsay (1977) proposes the existence of cycles of participation. At particular times, such as during the 1960s and 1970s, employers foster participation as a means of containing and moderating worker militancy. Participation is embraced as a means of defusing industrial conflict and accommodating workers' demands as part of a more cooperative ethos to managing the employment relationship. The main problem with this approach, however, is that it assumes that the incidence of worker participation has a single causal factor when, in practice, participation initiatives are more likely the outcome of a number of considerations, of which accommodating worker militancy is just one. Nor does the 'cycles' approach explain why since the 1980s employers have been concerned to improve how they communicate with their employees, albeit a weak form of involvement and participation, during a period of pronounced union weakness (Ackers et al. 1992; Marchington and Wilkinson 2000).

Thus the concept of 'waves of interest' in participation has been developed in order to provide a more nuanced explanation of trends in employee involvement and worker participation (Marchington et al. 1992). According to this approach, participation may take different forms and be driven by a variety of motives. Thus 'rather than viewing EI or participation as either absent or present, as some absolute or unidimensional concept, we can analyse a number of different forms or aspects of participation' (Marchington et al. 1992: 25–6).

A further advantage of the 'waves of interest' approach is that it does not assume that historical patterns of participation repeat themselves in an overly mechanical way. Rather, 'waves come in different shapes and sizes, and last for different lengths of time in different organizations' (Marchington et al. 1992: 26). The benefits of this approach to understanding employee participation will become evident in later chapters when we consider the increasing interest of employers in communicating with their staff (Chapter 5), developments in employee information and consultation arrangements (Chapter 6), and the experiences of workers themselves (Chapter 8).

1.4.3 The outcomes of employment relations

Clearly, the production of rules that govern employment relationships is the most obvious outcome of employment relations. Collective bargaining, for example, involving the joint regulation of employment relationships, produces rules in the form of negotiated collective agreements between employers and trade unions. There are two types of collective agreement. Procedural agreements set out the details of how collective bargaining operates; specifying the topics that come within the scope of bargaining activity, for example. Substantive agreements concern the actual outcomes of the bargaining process; any changes to pay, hours, holidays, etc.—the substance of employment relationships—that result from a bargaining exercise.

While the main outcomes of collective bargaining concern the regulation of employment relationships, there has always been a strong interest in the broader social and economic implications of collective bargaining arrangements, on matters such as wage inequality, for example, and inflation (Heery et al. 2008). While the most obvious employment relations outcomes take the form of rules that govern employment relationships (see Section 1.2.2), we also need to take into account the broader implications of employment relations activities, beyond the workplace. Governments, for example, sometimes try to influence bargaining activities in order to regulate the overall level of earnings, in order to achieve their economic goals.

Traditionally, the main objective of employers in employment relations was to maintain and enhance their control over the workforce, linked to an efficiency rationale. Since the 1980s, moreover, there has been growing interest in how employment relations can be managed to engage, and win the organizational commitment of staff, with the goal of improving business performance (see Chapter 5). This development is associated with the neo-unitary challenge to pluralist orthodoxy mentioned above. However, a key feature of employment relations as a field of study, and one that distinguishes it from human resource management, is a concern with the outcomes for employees: not just with regard to tangible benefits like wages and benefits, but also more intangible effects such as job satisfaction, justice, and dignity at work (Ackers and Wilkinson 2005; Heery et al. 2008).

John W. Budd (2004) demonstrates that an efficiency rationale is just one of three objectives of the employment relationship, the others being equity and voice. The equity objective refers to the desirability of ensuring fair employment standards that reflect human dignity are in place, like an appropriate level of wages for example, or protection from being dismissed without adequate justification.

The voice objective concerns the ability of employees to enjoy meaningful influence over decisions that affect them at work (Budd 2004: 7–8). Since the employment relationship is a social relationship, one that involves human beings, those responsible for managing it are duty bound to respect their interests. 'As work is a fully human activity, employment outcomes and processes must respect human dignity and therefore the societal objectives of the employment relationship are efficiency, equity, and voice' (Budd 2004: 28–9).

While these three objectives can sometimes complement one another—workers who are treated fairly (equity) and have an opportunity to influence managerial decision-making (voice) may perform better (efficiency)—they often come into conflict. Managerial demands for greater work effort, for example, may lead to employment standards being undermined, or result in employees' views being disregarded, in pursuit of efficiency savings.

1.4.4 The contexts of employment relations

Employment relations operates in particular contexts, being affected by a wide range of economic, political, legal, and social influences. Here we provide an overview of the main contextual factors, supported by some illustrative examples.

First of all, employment relations is influenced by the nature of the economic environment. The economic recession of the early 1980s, for example, which hit the strongly unionized manufacturing sector particularly hard, generated high levels of unemployment. Between 1979 and 1984, the number of recorded unemployed rose from under one and a half million (5.4 per cent of the workforce) to over three million (11.8 per cent). During the 2000s, unemployment fell markedly, to less than five per cent of the workforce (see Table 1.2).

The recession which began in 2008, following the collapse of the banking sector, has had some profound implications for employment relations. In particular, it has led to a sharp rise in unemployment. In early 2009 the number of unemployed rose above the two million mark for the first time in twelve years. One of the main effects of the rise in unemployment has been to generate a greater level of job insecurity. This has encouraged a sense of injustice among some workers about employers' use of cheap foreign labour, leading to disputes in parts of the country (see the introductory case study).

Table 1.2 UK unemployment, selected years 1979–2009

Year	Total unemployed	Unemployment rate (%)
1979	1,432,000	5.4
1984	3,241,000	11.8
1989	2,082,000	7.2
1994	2,675,000	9.5
1999	1,728,000	6.0
2004	1,465,000	4.8
2008	1,777,000	5.7
2009 (1st quarter)	2,215,000	7.1

Source: Labour Force Survey, http://www.statistics.gov.uk

As we see in Chapter 2, employment relations is also affected by changes in the labour market and the composition of employment, like the use of more flexible employment arrangements, such as part-time and temporary work in particular. In the same chapter we examine the profound impact of economic globalization on employment relations around the world. A further important feature of employment change concerns the growing proportion of female and part-time employees in the labour market. Table 1.3 shows that between 1984 and 2008 the proportion of female employees grew to nearly a half.

Employment relations also operates within a political and legal context. We have already seen that the law is an important source of the rules that govern employment relationships; and, of course, the nature of the political system determines the kinds of laws that are enacted. During the 1980s and 1990s, for example, one of the key political aims of the Conservative governments under Margaret Thatcher and John Major was to weaken the role of the trade unions. This resulted in a number of pieces of legislation that heavily restricted how trade unions operate (see Chapter 3).

Political change, in the form of the Labour governments of Tony Blair and Gordon Brown after 1997, produced a change in emphasis. While Labour has done little to reverse the anti-union measures of their Conservative predecessors in government, it has not added to them. Labour has also been more ready to enact legislation that protects the interests of workers, through interventions like the National Minimum Wage. It also fashioned a less hostile approach to the European Union, something which has resulted in more employment legislation coming from that source—over information and consultation rights for workers, for example.

Finally, employment relations operates within a social context; the underpinning values and beliefs that influence people's attitudes and behaviour affect employment relations in important ways. There is evidence that since the 1980s Britain has become a more tolerant society. For example, the annual British Social Attitudes Survey demonstrates that prejudice against homosexuals has declined markedly. People have also become less prejudiced against working women.

Changes in social attitudes of this kind influence employment relations, by encouraging greater awareness and acceptance of equality and diversity measures, for example.

Table 1.3 Female employees as a proportion of all employees in the UK, selected years 1984–2008

Year	Female employees (%)
1984	43.7
1989	46.4
1994	48.5
1999	48.2
2004	48.7
2008	48.4

Source: Labour Force Survey, http://www.statistics.gov.uk

However, while the level of racial prejudice fell substantially during the 1990s, since the early 2000s it has edged up again, perhaps because of the negative way in which the media report immigration issues. Nearly one in five employees (18 per cent) believes that workers of Asian origin experience prejudicial treatment in their own workplace (Creegan and Robinson 2008).

SECTION SUMMARY AND FURTHER READING

- The main employment relations actors are employers and managers, workers and trade unions, and the state. However, the role of 'new actors' like community-based organizations and other non-governmental organizations is receiving greater scrutiny.

- The key employment relations processes are collective bargaining and arrangements that facilitate employee participation and involvement, such as joint consultation. Informal expectations and understandings also play a major role in employment relations.

- In terms of outcomes, employment relations is not just concerned with improvements in organizational efficiency; it is also marked by a focus on the implications for workers, notably the extent to which they experience fair and equitable treatment at work and the degree to which they can influence decision-making in organizations.

- Employment relations operates within a number of contexts; economic, industrial, political, and social changes all influence how employment relations functions.

See Heery et al. (2008) for further insights about the main employment relations actors, processes, and outcomes. Budd (2004: Chapter 1) is a particularly relevant source of material concerning employment relations outcomes.

 Visit our Online Resource Centre for web links to sites connected to this section. www.oxfordtextbooks.co.uk/williams_adamsmith2e

---

Conclusion

The main purpose of this chapter has been to introduce the nature of the employment relationship, to consider employment relations as a field of study, and to introduce the main actors, processes, and outcomes of employment relations, set against the key contexts within which employment relations operates. In essence, employment relations concerns how employment relationships are regulated; establishing the sources of the rules that govern employment relationships, in the form of terms and conditions of employment. On its own, however, it is not enough just to consider the regulation of employment relationships; we also need to understand the ways in which workers experience their employment relationships, and the circumstances under which they come to challenge the rules that govern how they are supposed to behave at work.

See Figure 1.3 for a diagram illustrating our conceptualization of contemporary employment relations. At the heart of employment relations is the relationship between an employer and an employee (the 'employment relationship'). Key employment relations actors (e.g. managers, unions, government agencies) are involved in regulating employment relationships (e.g. joint regulation or legal regulation). The regulation of employment relationships

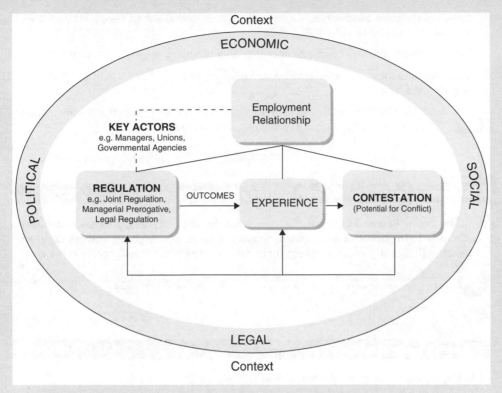

Figure 1.3. A framework for conceptualizing contemporary employment relations

in this way produces certain outcomes, not just narrow workplace rules, but also outcomes which take the form of broader, sometimes less tangible effects, like the implications for efficiency, equity, and voice (see Budd 2004). This latter point means that we have to be concerned with the way in which employees experience employment relations, and also with how the nature of this experience often puts them at odds with their employer. Thus the employment relationship is marked by an inherent potential for conflict, with the implication being that we need to understand the circumstances under which the terms of that relationship become contested, and also the form which that contestation takes. Finally, we have established that employment relations is influenced by aspects of the political, economic, legal, and social contexts within which it operates.

While employment relations, conceived narrowly as the study of trade unions and collective bargaining, may have become marginalized, the broader perspective, which we adopt here, views it as a field of study that continues to be highly relevant. It concerns the employment relationship, and all of the various features of, and influences over, that relationship, something that is of interest at an individual, organizational, and societal level.

Assignment and discussion questions

1   What are the main features of the employment relationship as a 'wage-work bargain'?

2   What is meant by the concept of managerial prerogative in employment relations? What are the main constraints on the exercise of managerial prerogative?

3 Which of the three perspectives—unitary, pluralist, or radical—most closely fits your own view of the world of work? Why?

4 Why is 'power' such an important concept in understanding employment relations?

5 With regard to the outcomes of employment relations, explain what is meant by 'efficiency', 'equity', and 'voice'?

 Visit our Online Resource Centre for web links to sites connected to this section. www.oxfordtextbooks.co.uk/williams_adamsmith2e

Take your learning further: online resource centre

Visit the Online Resource Centre that accompanies this book to enrich your understanding of Chapter 1: The nature of employment relations. Explore web links, test yourself using an interactive flashcard glossary, and keep up to date with the latest developments in the area.

 http://www.oxfordtextbooks.co.uk/orc/williams_adamsmith2e.

Chapter case study

Managing with unions in the Royal Mail

The Royal Mail is a highly unionized organization with postal workers, both those working in mail centres where post is sorted, and those delivering letters and parcels, represented by the Communication Workers' Union (CWU). Basic rates of pay are traditionally low, and workers often depend upon overtime payments and other allowances to bring their earnings up to a reasonable level. In some areas, employees' need to maximize earning opportunities led to them and the union controlling working arrangements, with managers unwilling or unable to deploy staff in a way consistent with operational efficiency.

Since the late 1980s, Royal Mail has faced increasing competition for its services. Other forms of communication such as e-mail and fax have not reduced the volume of mail, but have limited its potential increase. Private delivery operators have taken some business from the organization, however, and, as a result of an EU Directive, it is now required to compete on cost and service quality with private providers. In response to this increased competition, Royal Mail has sought to introduce, with union agreement, initiatives that would reduce overtime working, remove inefficient working practices, improve service quality, and implement a shorter working week. Managers and union representatives at each workplace were required to negotiate their own detailed agreements to implement the necessary changes.

The implementation, however, proved unpopular, even though a small majority of workers voted in favour of the national agreement. In many areas, staff who stood to lose the most voted against the principle of new working arrangements. Even where detailed workplace agreements had been reached by managers and union representatives, workers refused to accept their implementation. Between 1999 and 2001, there were frequent episodes of industrial action by postal workers opposed to the new arrangements. Of the several hundred stoppages of work, the overwhelming majority were unofficial; that is, taken without the support of the CWU leadership. These instances of industrial action were typically 'localized', based on just one workplace. However, on some occasions the action spread to other locations, generally where staff in one mail centre were required to sort mail diverted to it from another location where a strike was in progress.

An independent report published in 2001 which looked at employment relations in Royal Mail portrayed front-line managers as authoritarian; they closely directed and monitored the work of their staff: 'body watchers' as they often described themselves (Sawyer, Borkett, and Underhill 2001). Their permission was needed before an employee could go to the toilet, or get a drink of water. The application of misconduct rules and procedures for dealing with sickness absence were used as measures to punish employees in a mechanistic manner. A culture had emerged where managers intimidated employees, and union representatives antagonized managers who were unable to stand up to them.

The independent report recommended that Royal Mail management and the CWU should work more cooperatively to improve employment relations (Sawyer, Borkett, and Underhill 2001). Yet this has proved difficult to realize in practice. Faced with greater competition from private providers, Royal Mail managers claim that the postal service needs to be 'modernized' and made more efficient. While the CWU supports modernization in principle, it is concerned that some 40,000 of its members' jobs are at risk if Royal Mail puts all its proposals into effect. Employment relations remains highly conflictual. In 2007 the CWU organized national strike action over pay, pensions, and modernization issues.

In 2008 the government proposed selling off a stake in the Royal Mail to a private company such as TNT. This was presented as the only way in which the investment necessary to modernize the postal service could be obtained. The CWU vehemently opposes such a move, seeing it as likely to result in service cuts, major job losses, and the erosion of employment conditions. Employment relations in the Royal Mail look likely to be turbulent for some time to come.

1   What factors have contributed to the employment relations problems in the Royal Mail?

2   What interventions would improve management–union relations in the organization?

PART 2

Contemporary Employment Relations in Context

2 Employment relations in the contemporary economy   41

3 The politics of employment relations   82

4 Social divisions and employment relations   121

Employment Relations in the Contemporary Economy

Chapter objectives:

The main objectives of this chapter are to:

* examine the implications of developments associated with the rise of the so-called 'new' economy for employment relations;

* assess the impact of economic globalization and the activities of multi-national companies on employment relations;

* examine the responses of the international trade union movement to the challenges of globalization; and

* assess the nature of, and main approaches to, international labour standards.

2.1 Introduction

In this chapter, we examine the implications for employment relations of developments in the contemporary economy. In a capitalist market economy, employers buy the capacity of workers to engage in productive effort, or their latent labour power, in the labour market. Having hired someone, moreover, an employer must realize that worker's latent effort, by securing his or her compliance and gaining his or her consent, so that he or she is able to contribute appropriately to the production of goods and services. Changes in the economic context, by altering the power held by the parties, exercise a profound influence on the character and conduct of employment relations, particularly as organizations come under pressure to reduce labour costs, and increase the output of their staff, in order to maintain their competitiveness. To what extent do growing competitive pressures influence contemporary employment relations? We focus on two main developments in contemporary economic life: the implications of the so-called 'new' economy, and the effects of economic globalization.

Introductory case study

Agency workers and employment flexibility

One of the main themes of this chapter concerns the perceived desirability of flexible employment arrangements. One of the main ways in which employers try to secure flexibility is by hiring workers through temporary employment agencies. Not only does this enable them to make adjustments to workforce numbers in response to fluctuations in demand, but it can also be relatively cost-effective since agency workers can be paid less, and enjoy fewer rights, than directly employed staff. Faced with rapidly declining car sales as the result of the economic recession, in February 2009 BMW ended weekend working at its Cowley plant, near Oxford, which makes the Mini. Some 850 agency workers were sacked with one hour's notice. Because they were not employed directly by BMW, the agency staff enjoyed few employment rights, and were not entitled to any redundancy pay. They were simply paid one week's wages to cover the notice period. Yet many members of the supposedly 'temporary' workforce had worked in the plant for some years. One agency worker said he had been treated like a 'second class' employee: 'I've worked here for three-and-a-half years and now I've being sacked for no reason. I've been used'.

Angry workers reportedly booed and threw fruit at BMW managers on hearing that they were to lose their jobs. Union leaders, who were also targeted for criticism by some workers, expressed their disgust at the way in which the agency workers had been treated. Tony Woodley, joint leader of the Unite union, wrote to BMW accusing the company of treating workers with 'utter contempt'. He claimed that no one would 'treat a dog this way, never mind a loyal and committed workforce'. While the European Union has introduced legislation to give agency workers more rights (see Chapter 3), it is not expected to come into force until 2011 and would not have given the workers affected by BMW's shift closure much additional protection anyway. This case shows that the benefits of employment flexibility, which in this case amounted to the freedom enjoyed by BMW to dismiss workers as easily as possible, are often one-sided in favour of employers.

Sources: BBC News website 16 February 2009; BBC News website 19 February 2009; The *Guardian* 17 February 2009.

2.2 Employment relations in the 'new' economy

One of the most important influences on contemporary employment relations concerns developments in the economy, especially the changing composition of employment. During the latter part of the twentieth century, the UK underwent a process of de-industrialization, something that saw the decline of staple industries such as coal mining, iron and steel making, and shipbuilding, and also the erosion of the country's manufacturing capacity.

The importance of manufacturing industry as a source of economic dynamism should not be overlooked (Ackroyd and Proctor 1998). It makes up around a fifth of the UK's economy, and is responsible for some 60 per cent of its exports. Nevertheless, there has been a pronounced shift in employment in favour of the service sector—in banking, finance, retailing, leisure and hospitality, for example, and also in the public services (Beynon 1997). See Table 2.1 for details of how the proportion of manufacturing and services jobs in the economy has changed since the 1980s.

Table 2.1 The proportion of UK jobs in manufacturing and service industries, selected years 1979–2008

Year	Proportion of jobs in manufacturing (%)	Proportion of jobs in services (%)
1979	26.0	61.4
1984	20.5	67.5
1989	18.4	70.0
1994	15.8	74.2
1999	15.0	76.0
2004	11.6	80.0
2008	9.9	80.1

Source: Labour Force Survey, http://www.statistics.gov.uk

What have been the implications of these developments for employment relations? While it is important to recognize the diversity of its employment arrangements, the 'old industrial economy of Britain' was responsible for employing 'large numbers of highly unionized workers employed on full-time contracts' (Beynon 1997: 37), who were mainly men. The decline of employment levels in primary and manufacturing industries resulted in a large rise in economic inactivity and unemployment, particularly among men, since the increasing number of (frequently part-time) service sector jobs tend to be taken up by women (Bradley 1999).

High concentrations of male unemployment arose in the industrial regions of Britain, such as South Wales and North-East England (Nolan and Slater 2003). Moreover, de-industrialization eroded the membership and power of unions since many of the industries in decline were strongholds of trade unionism. Unions generally have a much weaker presence in the increasingly important private service sector.

What are the salient features of the 'new' economy, and what are their implications for employment relations? In the first place, the 'new' economy is supposedly characterized by a diminution in the significance of the employment relationship, given the increasing number of people who apparently work without one, as autonomous and independent self-employed, freelance contractors, for example.

Second, economic change is held to be transforming the nature of work itself, generating an increase in the proportion of people engaged in 'knowledge work'.

Third, the growth of flexible employment patterns, such as part-time and temporary work, is presented as advantageous both for employers, since it enables them to manage labour more efficiently, and workers, who are able to exercise more choice over their working arrangements. In the following sections we expose such claims to critical scrutiny, and demonstrate that the most prominent feature of employment relations in the contemporary economy is the growing power of capital relative to labour.

2.2.1 The end of the employment relationship?

One of the most prominent features of debates about the development of the 'new' economy concerns the supposedly greater significance of work undertaken by self-employed, freelance contractors who are not subject to the disciplines of an employment relationship. This is celebrated as a positive development since it signals that people are increasingly escaping the shackles of the employment relationship and looking to secure the independence that comes with working for oneself (Handy 1994; Leadbeater 1999).

People supposedly welcome the opportunity of working as 'free agents' (Barley and Kunda 2004), as self-employed temporary contractors who sell their expertise to a range of organizations, thus being liberated from the constraints associated with being in a relationship with, and thus under the control of, a single employer. If employment relationships are becoming less important, then clearly the relevance of employment relations as a field of study comes into question.

As can be seen from Table 2.2, between the mid 1980s and mid 1990s, the number of self-employed people in the UK grew by nearly a million. Self-employment was supported by successive Conservative governments who viewed its growth, and also that of small businesses in general, as the mark of a dynamic and competitive economy in which enterprise thrived (Goss 1991). While there is evidence that for some people, younger entrants to the labour market for example, the decision to become self-employed was a function of the absence of alternative job opportunities in a climate of high unemployment (MacDonald and Coffield 1991), in many cases it was a positive choice (Hakim 1988).

People often make a deliberate choice to become self-employed; the freedom and flexibility self-employment offers is viewed as highly desirable (Kirkpatrick and Hoque 2006), including the supposed ability to be able to turn down offers of work. In the media industry, for example, many freelance workers welcome the autonomy they gain from being self-employed (Platman 2004). Elsewhere, independence and autonomy are viewed as highly prized characteristics of freelance working arrangements.

More than three-quarters of the self-employed translators surveyed by Fraser and Gold (2001) expressed no wish to work for a company directly as an employee.

Table 2.2 Self-employment in the UK, 1984–2008

	No. of self-employed (000s)	Self-employed as a proportion of all those in employment (%)
1984	2,695	11.1
1988	3,216	12.3
1992	3,447	13.5
1996	3,506	13.5
2000	3,256	11.8
2004	3,618	12.7
2008	3,826	13.0

Source: Labour Force Survey, http://www.statistics.gov.uk

However, female translators were much more likely to have become freelance contractors because they had been obliged to do so by a 'change of circumstances', in particular the need to earn a living while raising a family. This demonstrates that people's choices in such situations are, given their domestic circumstances, frequently limited in practice.

Moreover, freelance translators tend to establish a wide client base. Over one-third worked for ten or more clients. With a growing demand for translation services, such workers enjoyed considerable autonomy since they were not dependent on a small number of companies for work. This can be contrasted with the experience of freelance editors and proofreaders. Stanworth and Stanworth (1995) found that they generally worked for just one or two publishing clients and were reliant, and therefore over-dependent, on them for commissions.

Thus the degree of control and autonomy enjoyed by freelance contractors varies according to such factors as their market situation (Fraser and Gold 2001). Moreover, it is important not to exaggerate the benefits of self-employment, since it can be associated with inferior employment conditions, like the absence of paid holidays, and may also be a source of considerable insecurity (Kirkpatrick and Hoque 2006).

The extent to which self-employment is stimulated by a desire for independence, autonomy, and control on the part of workers concerned should not be exaggerated. By far the most significant factor responsible for the growth of self-employment during the 1980s and 1990s was the changing pattern of labour use by employers, particularly their increased preference for sub-contracting arrangements as a way of reducing employment costs (Hakim 1988; Rees and Fielder 1992). Even the freelance translators studied by Fraser and Gold (2001) were able to work as self-employed contractors only because many large companies and European organizations had shut down their in-house translating arrangements, preferring to externalize such services.

Sub-contracting arrangements have a long history, especially in the construction industry. Often, sub-contract workers may undertake the same functions as a direct employee. In the construction industry, for example, 'people work as bricklayers or steel erectors or labourers on the large building sites of companies like Costain and Tarmac. They are paid by the company and to all intents and purposes are employees; but the companies do not recognise this relationship' (Beynon 1997: 33).

While this is done primarily for cost savings, it leaves the workforce, hired on short-term contacts, manifestly more exposed and vulnerable. Workers are obliged to bear more of the risks and costs of employment, given the unwillingness of companies to enter into a long-term and direct relationship with them. As contractors, workers do not benefit from the full range of employment rights. Moreover, although workers are often dependent upon client companies for work, these companies have no reciprocal obligations to them beyond the terms of the immediate contract.

One of the most popular forms of self-employment is the franchise arrangement. Under the 'business format' type of franchise, in exchange for a hefty fee, franchisees are provided by the franchiser company with a business format that they then operate as if it were their own business (Felstead 1991). Yet franchising cannot be equated with genuine self-employment, and can be used as a means of extending management control over workers (see Box 2.1).

INSIGHT INTO PRACTICE 2.1

Franchise arrangements—self-employment?

The case of the milk delivery company studied by O' Davison (1994) demonstrates that franchising cannot be equated with genuine self-employment, and that it can be used as a means of extending management control. In order to reduce costs, the company in question did away with direct employment on its milkrounds, obliging the delivery staff to operate as self-employed contractors. While the company made major cost savings as a result, it was no longer required to make National Insurance or pension contributions, for example; the 'very one-sided' franchise contract instituted 'some very specific controls over how franchisees must organize their work' (O' Davison 1994: 29, 30), including the wearing of an appropriate uniform. Thus the 'contract is seen as an effective substitute for what would once have been a job description and allows management to closely prescribe the day-to-day activities of the franchisee just as it would have controlled the activities of direct employees' (O' Davison 1994: 32).

Unlike Felstead (1991), who uses the term 'controlled self-employment' to describe the work situation of franchisees, based on her study of milk distribution, O' Davison (1994) prefers to conceptualize franchise arrangements as a type of employment relationship, albeit one that leaves the workers concerned more exposed and vulnerable.

Despite the claimed benefits of self-employment, and of freelance working arrangements, the total number of self-employed has scarcely grown since the early 1990s, fluctuating at a level close to the three-and-a-half million mark (see Table 2.2). Table 2.2 also shows that there has been no growth in the proportion of self-employed. Indeed, it actually fell during the late 1990s, to under 12 per cent of the workforce, before gradually rising again in the 2000s, to 13 per cent in 2008. This constancy is hardly a sign of the growth of a 'new' economy (Nolan and Slater 2003). There is little appetite on the part of most workers to go freelance and become self-employed contractors (McGovern et al. 2007).

While favourable market conditions may give self-employed workers some degree of control over their work, as in the case of the freelance translators, for example, most depend on clients for work and thus enjoy little real autonomy. This is particularly the case for homeworkers (see Box 2.2). Much so-called 'self-employment', moreover, is simply disguised employment, such as in the case of the milk delivery company (see Box 2.1). The employment relationship remains by far the most important means of organizing work in the contemporary economy.

2.2.2 Occupational change and the rise of the knowledge worker

A second feature of debates about the changing nature of work in the 'new economy' concerns the implications of occupational change, in particular the rise in the number of knowledge-based jobs undertaken by managers and professionals, for employment relations. The assumption is that the growth of knowledge work in the economy encourages a more cooperative employment relations environment.

Employment relations reflection 2.2   Homeworking in Britain

Advocates of the 'new' economy often emphasize that developments in information technology, the use of e-mail and internet facilities in particular, give people more opportunities to work from home, offering them greater autonomy and flexibility over their working lives, and liberating them from the rigid shackles of the traditional workplace (e.g. Leadbeater 1999). Studies of homeworkers suggest, however, that such a 'rosy picture' may be unjustified given that they are a highly differentiated group (Felstead and Jewson 2000). Those who 'sometimes' work from home, often male managers and professional employees, for example, people given the opportunity to do so largely as a benefit, should be distinguished from those who 'mainly' work at home, frequently low-paid women workers undertaking routine manual labour with minimal discretion.

Such work generally attracts low pay, often based on output, or 'piecework', and is characterized by poor and exploitative working conditions. Felstead and Jewson (2000: 91) cite the example of a woman who received £3.50 for every 100 bows she made from material provided by her employer, something that would take her at least six hours. A 2004 study by Oxfam, the Trades Union Congress and the National Group on Homeworking— *Made at Home*—found that workers often receive no maternity pay, sick pay, or paid holidays, and earn as little as 73 pence an hour for making Christmas crackers (Oxfam 2004a).

Since there are problems with its enforcement, many homeworkers did not benefit from the 1999 introduction of the National Minimum Wage. Employers, and other providers of work, have also been able to overestimate the pace at which homeworkers can assemble products, and thus publish theoretical hourly rates of pay that are unattainable in practice. However, in 2004 the UK government responded to concerns that many homeworkers were not receiving the minimum wage by tightening up the regulations governing piecework to ensure that 'fair piece rates' operate, based on the hourly minimum wage rate.

This is an area of longstanding interest. During the 1960s, the concept of 'post-industrialism' was developed by the American writer Daniel Bell as a means of analysing how technological change generated an increase in professional, managerial, and technical occupations, within which jobs were more highly skilled and inherently more satisfying for those who undertook them, relative to declining manual labour (Kumar 1986).

While evidence for such a change was decidedly lacking, during the 1980s there was a revival of post-industrial thinking, linked to the related concepts of 'post-Fordism' and 'flexible specialization' (Kumar 1995). At the heart of the former is the notion that the Fordist, mass-production-based economy was in terminal decline as a result of a transformation in the organization of capitalism, most notably technological change and the emergence of less predictable patterns of demand (Castells 1996). For Kumar (1995), flexible specialization is at the 'heart' of post-Fordism. New technology, the use of computer-controlled machinery in manufacturing in particular, enables firms to meet more unpredictable demand in a way that renders jobs more highly skilled, offering greater autonomy and control for those undertaking them (see Piore and Sabel 1984; Wood 1989).

While the flexible specialization thesis suggested that technological and economic change encouraged a new and more harmonious relationship between employers and workers in which conflict was rendered increasingly archaic, there are considerable doubts about its overall value. For one thing, it rested upon an over-simplistic view of the so-called mass-production economy; in many industrial sectors in Britain, such as food production for example, Fordist production techniques were never dominant (Pollert 1988a; Smith 1989).

Moreover, there was little evidence for the emergence of a cadre of highly skilled, functionally flexible workers who benefit from good employment conditions. The flexible specialization thesis fails to recognize that for many, including those in the expanding service sector, an area which it largely ignores, the introduction of new technology in banks, offices, and supermarkets, for example, often reduces autonomy and intensifies work (Hyman 1991; Poynter 2000).

During the 1990s and 2000s there has been a further revival of post-industrial thinking, based on the view that technological change and innovation increasingly generate jobs that demand higher levels of knowledge on the part of those who undertake them. The more widespread use of information technology and the rise of the internet as a business tool oblige companies increasingly to rely on workers' knowledge, not their labour, as a means of competitive advantage (Castells 2001). The development of the 'knowledge economy' is associated with changes in the occupational structure of advanced industrialized societies; in particular the growth in importance of professional and managerial jobs. In the UK the Labour government emphasized the importance of the emerging knowledge economy as a source of future growth and prosperity (Warhurst 2008).

One way in which we can assess the nature of changes in jobs is by classifying them into particular occupational categories. See Tables 2.3 and 2.4 for details of occupational change during the 1990s and 2000s. The way in which occupations are classified changed in 2000, so it is not possible to make direct comparisons between the 1990s and the 2000s. However, some broad trends are apparent. During the 1990s the proportion of managerial, professional, and associate professional jobs in the economy rose from 30.9 per cent in 1991 to 35.0 per cent in 1997 (see Table 2.3). This trend appears to have continued in the 2000s. Table 2.4 shows that between 2002 and 2008 the proportion of higher level and lower level managerial jobs in the economy rose from 40.8 per cent to 43.1 per cent.

There has been rather little change, however, in the proportion of routine, lower-level jobs. Between 1991 and 1997 the share of employment in personal and protective services (e.g. care assistants) rose (see Table 2.3). During the 2000s, the proportion

Table 2.3 Occupational change in Britain during the 1990s (% all in employment)

	Managerial	Professional	Associate professional & technicians	Clerical	Craft & related	Personal & protective services	Sales	Plants machine operatives
1991	12.7	9.4	8.8	17.8	12.8	9.9	8.3	10.7
1994	14.8	10.2	9.4	16.8	10.6	11.0	8.3	9.8
1997	15.0	10.0	10.0	16.6	10.1	11.6	8.7	9.6

Source: Labour Force Survey, http://www.statistics.gov.uk

Table 2.4 Occupational change in the UK in the 2000s (% all in employment)

	Higher managerial and professional	Lower managerial and professional	Intermediate	Small employers	Lower supervisory and technical	Semi-routine	Routine
2002	13.5	27.3	12.4	9.3	11.4	14.8	11.1
2005	14.3	28.2	12.2	9.9	10.8	14.4	10.2
2008	15.0	28.1	11.8	10.0	10.1	14.7	10.3

Note: Autumn 2002, 2005; 3rd quarter 2008.

Source: Labour Force Survey, http://www.statistics.gov.uk

of routine and semi-routine jobs in the economy has remained largely unchanged at about a quarter of the total (see Table 2.4). This suggests that we need to be careful not to exaggerate the shift to a knowledge economy; there are still a good many routine and low-skilled jobs in the labour market.

Nevertheless, it is sometimes assumed that the rise of the information-based, knowledge economy, in which jobs will increasingly be of a managerial, professional, and technical kind, reduces the need for traditional management approaches, and erodes the potential for conflict in the employment relationship. Not only is extensive management control redundant in the new knowledge economy, but also greater cooperation between employers and their employees is inevitable given the harmony of interests that arises between them. Thus 'the new economy is identified with a fresh pattern of work relations free from long-standing hierarchical and conflictual employment relations' (Nolan and Slater 2003: 77).

There are two major problems with this approach to assessing the nature of occupational change. First, the 'knowledge work' concept is a very crude and unsatisfactory tool for analysing the nature of occupational change (Thompson and Warhurst 1998). Can it be applied equally to a call centre operator, who relies upon information technology during the course of her work, and an information systems manager working for the same company?

Much so-called 'knowledge work' consists of rather basic, routine, and mundane data-processing activities that are founded upon the manual labour of workers, rather than what they contain in their heads. In financial services, for example, relatively few workers, those involved with developing information technology capabilities, or employed in the sales and marketing functions, enjoy a significant amount of autonomy in their jobs. The majority of workers, mainly women whose jobs involve routine data processing and handling customer enquiries, have experienced a decline in the conditions of their work such that they resembled the assembly-line process characteristic of traditional industrial society (Poynter 2000).

All jobs require workers to use knowledge; but the concept of 'knowledge work' implies the use of complex analytical and decision-making skills and a substantial amount of discretion and autonomy. Too often, though, 'simply using or applying knowledge in a job is enough for some to be regarded as a knowledge worker' (Warhurst and Thompson 2006: 792). Call centre workers and software developers both use sophisticated information and communications technologies as an integral feature of their jobs. Their employment relations arrangements, however, markedly differ. Software developers enjoy a far greater degree of discretion at work, and control over their own employment arrangements, than call centre workers (Baldry et al. 2007).

Even jobs in many so-called 'professional' occupations are marked by routine customer service work or information-processing activities, 'with low levels of discretion and analytical skill' (Fleming, Harley, and Sewell 2004: 735). When we examine the nature of occupations more closely, then, and in particular the content of the jobs that comprise them, we are presented with a rather different picture to that which has been advanced by advocates of the knowledge economy thesis.

The second problem with the proposition that there is a growing knowledge economy, which has encouraged a more cooperative employment relations climate, concerns the assumption that the labour market is increasingly being dominated by a rapidly growing proportion of people working in professional, managerial, and technical occupations. In reality, the nature of occupational change is rather more complex, involving the expansion of jobs at the top end of the labour market and those at the bottom, where low-skilled routine work, which contains little discretion or autonomy, is commonplace (Warhurst 2008). Thus 'while management, professional and technical jobs are expanding, so too are routine services jobs, particularly in personal services and retail and hospitality' (Thompson and Warhurst 2006: 793).

Moreover, much of the expansion of professional occupations has occurred as a result of restructuring in the public sector—changes to the delivery of education and health services, for example—not as part of a supposed shift to a knowledge economy (Nolan and Slater 2003). Assertions about the greater predominance of highly skilled, professional jobs in the economy should therefore be treated with a considerable degree of caution (Nolan and Wood 2003).

The concept of the 'new' economy, characterized by a greater degree of 'knowledge' work undertaken by highly skilled professionals, is highly misleading (Nolan and Wood 2003). Moreover, it serves to obscure the realities of wage labour in a capitalist market economy. There is evidence that, as private sector companies experience ever greater competitive pressures, and public sector organizations are increasingly constrained by budget limitations, employment relations in the contemporary economy is marked by the efforts of employers to secure more work for less reward from their employees.

This is amply demonstrated in Beynon et al.'s (2002) assessment of developments in seven public and private sector organizations. The behaviour of managers towards workers was strongly influenced by pressure to comply with exacting short-term financial targets in a way that was inimical to the development of long-term, stable, and secure employment relationships. Workers were increasingly treated as if they were 'commodities', to be used and disposed of as determined by organizational needs.

Based on this evidence, cooperative relations at work are scarce; the potential for conflict in the employment relationship seems to be growing rather than diminishing. This is particularly the case when we consider the likely implications of the economic recession which arose in 2008. Rising numbers of job losses, and the insecurity created by the economic downturn, not only put the potential for conflict in the employment relationship into clearer focus, but also seem likely to accentuate it (see Chapter 10).

2.2.3 A flexible labour market?

A third feature of debates about the development of a so-called 'new' economy concerns the more widespread use by companies of 'flexible' or 'non-standard' labour. In particular, the use of part-time and temporary staff is associated with the growing proportion of employment in service sector jobs, such as in retail, financial services, and hospitality (Felstead and Jewson 1999). By using part-time and temporary staff, rather than full-time and permanent employees, employers are able to align production or service delivery with anticipated demand and thus manage labour more efficiently.

The debate around flexible employment as a feature of the 'new economy' rests upon three main propositions. First, it is suggested that there has been a marked shift away from 'standard' jobs (i.e. full-time, permanent jobs) to non-standard forms of employment (part-time and temporary work). Flexible employment arrangements have become a commonplace feature of the management of labour in contemporary organizations. Part-time workers are present in four-fifths of workplaces; a similar proportion use at least one other type of flexible employment, workers on fixed-term contracts, for example, or agency workers (White et al. 2004).

Second, one of the most powerful arguments in favour of flexible employment arrangements is that, in addition to being convenient for employers, they allow people to exercise greater choice over their working lives. Women make up the overwhelming majority of workers holding part-time jobs, though there are some indications of a modest increase in the number of men working part-time (Robinson 1999). Nevertheless, some four-fifths (83 per cent) of part-time employees are women (Kersley et al. 2006). Part-time working arrangements are especially popular among women because they enable them to combine employment with family commitments (Hewitt 1993).

People often choose to take up temporary jobs since they are seen as a potential route into permanent employment (Robinson 1999). In some interpretations, temporary work assignments are unambiguously viewed as positive; they are a means by which workers can liberate themselves from the constraints of a full-time, permanent job and, by selling their services to a 'portfolio' of different clients, exercise greater choice over their working lives (Handy 1994; Leadbeater 1999).

The third proposition is that employers use flexible employment arrangements in a purposive manner, part of a more strategic approach to the management of labour, helping them to respond more effectively to fluctuations in demand for their products or services. The 'flexible firm' model (Atkinson 1984) posits that employers operate with 'core' and 'peripheral' groups of workers. It proposes that core employees will benefit from relative job security, receive good pay, conditions, and benefits, and be highly skilled, while being functionally flexible.

In other words, flexibility among valued core employees is achieved by enabling them to become multi-skilled, capable of undertaking a range of jobs. Around the core rests a peripheral group of non-standard workers, part-time, and temporary agency workers, people on fixed-term contracts and sub-contractors who are more disposable and whose numbers can be adjusted to meet variations in demand, in a way that insulates the privileged core employees.

However, there are a number of problems with the propositions that: first, the contemporary economy is characterized by a recent dramatic rise in the incidence of flexible employment; second, that part-time and temporary jobs are unambiguously beneficial for those who undertake them; and third, that flexible employment is managed by employers in a purposive, strategic way, consistent with the flexible firm model.

For one thing, the growth of flexible employment arrangements has been gradual and halting. Part-time employment, for example, has increased rather slowly. Table 2.5 shows that between 1984 and 2008 the proportion of employees in part-time employment rose from around a fifth of employees (21 per cent) to a quarter (25.3 per cent). Yet there is considerable variation by industry. Whereas over a half (53 per cent) of hotel and restaurant employees work part-time, just one in twenty (5 per cent) in manufacturing do so (Kersley et al. 2006: 78).

The share of temporary employment grew during the early 1990s; however, since the mid 1990s the proportion of employees in temporary employment has actually fallen, from 7.1 per cent in 1994 to 5.5 per cent in 2008 (see Table 2.5). European Union legislation, which compels employers to treat part-time and temporary staff no less favourably than their full-time, permanent equivalents when it comes to matters like pay, means that some of the cost benefits associated with using flexible employment have become less important (see Chapter Three and Chapter Four).

What about the second proposition—that flexible employment is positively chosen by the workers concerned, for whom it is beneficial? Many women are confined to relatively low-paid, poor quality part-time employment because of an absence of other alternatives. The emphasis on 'choice' pays insufficient heed to constraints such as childcare responsibilities (Beynon 1997; Felstead and Jewson 1999). There is plenty of evidence of women workers in particular being trapped in low-paid, part-time jobs which generally offer few opportunities for advancement compared to full-time ones (Bradley et al. 2000).

With regard to temporary work, it is important to recognize that people who undertake it cannot be treated as a homogeneous group. 'Short-term temporary workers', whose

Table 2.5 The proportion of temporary and part-time employees in the UK, selected years 1984–2008

Year	Temporary employees (%)	Part-time employees (%)
1984	5.5	21.0
1989	5.5	22.3
1994	7.1	24.5
1999	7.1	25.1
2004	6.1	25.9
2008	5.5	25.3

Source: Labour Force Survey, http://www.statistics.gov.uk

jobs are typically under a year in length, can be distinguished from 'fixed-term contract' workers, whose employment generally lasts for between one and three years (Gallie et al. 1998). Workers in the former category, often hired through employment agencies, have fewer opportunities to develop their careers and suffer from greater job insecurity than those in the latter, for example university researchers, whose pay and employment conditions are similar to their permanent counterparts. The use of fixed-term contracts is most common in the public services, especially health and education, where funding uncertainties and budgetary constraints often conspire to make it difficult for employers to offer staff a permanent contract (Beynon et al. 2002).

A notable feature of the labour market in the UK is the operation of private employment agencies that supply organizations with short-term staff. There are between 1.1 million and 1.5 million agency workers in the UK (BERR 2008). The agency employs the workers, or hires them as ostensibly self-employed contractors, thus sparing the organization from the costs, such as holiday pay, and duties that come with being an employer. In theory, workers can choose whether or not they want to take on an assignment, thus enabling them to work in a flexible manner of their own choice.

In reality, however, the mutuality embodied in this vision of the temporary assignment is rarely evident. In his study of temporary agency working in Leeds and Telford, Forde (2001) discovered that agencies reward those people whom they perceived to be good performers with regular assignments. Workers who refuse assignments, however, are less likely to be offered future ones.

Using agency-supplied staff transfers more of the costs and risks of employment from the organization to the worker (Forde 2001; Ward et al. 2001), since the former explicitly repudiates any of the obligations and responsibilities that would underpin an employment relationship, rendering the latter very much more vulnerable. See the introductory case study for how one company, in this case BMW, responded to economic difficulties by dismissing its agency workforce. They were, in the words of one of those who was sacked, treated as 'second-class' workers.

Studies of temporary workers highlight the irregularity of their earnings and, for those who are designated as self-employed, the absence of paid holidays and other benefits. Many undertake temporary assignments only because they have been unable to secure a permanent position (e.g. Grimshaw, Earnshaw, and Hebdon 2003). Many agency workers (between 20 and 30 per cent) choose such arrangements because of the flexibility they provide. Yet a much higher proportion—some 60 per cent—undertake temporary assignments not through choice, but because they cannot find permanent employment (BERR 2008). See Box 2.3 for details of the unscrupulous treatment frequently meted out to migrant workers hired through agencies.

The presence of short-term, financial pressures upon companies to reduce their headcount, that is the number of staff they directly employ, has encouraged the use of agency workers, who can thus be conveniently excluded from the official tally (Beynon et al. 2002). Companies also use agencies to 'screen' potential employees (Ward et al. 2001). For example, the pharmaceutical company studied by Bradley (1999), did not recruit any production workers itself. Rather, it took them on initially through an agency, and only once they had demonstrated a satisfactory work record did the company employ them directly.

Employment relations reflection 2.3   Flexibility and migrant labour

The experience of many migrant workers demonstrates that employment flexibil-ity is often synonymous with low pay, poor working conditions, and job insecurity. Competitive pressures in the food industry, and the demand for ever cheaper foodstuffs, work their way downwards through the supply chain, to affect the workers responsible for picking, processing and packaging the produce. The seasonal nature of the food business, as well as the short-term fluctuations in demand from the big supermarket chains, mean that it is advantageous for producers to make use of a source of labour that can be switched on and off as desired. 'The reaction of farmers, food packers and processors, and indeed the supermarkets themselves, to the intensification of competi-tion between the retail giants has been to reorganise labour in a drive to make it more flexible in the face of stop-start demand, and cheaper' (Shelley 2007: 50).

What does this flexibility entail? The agriculture and food processing industries make extensive use of migrant labour, often provided by local employment agencies, known as 'gangmasters'. The firms that produce and process the food that goes on the supermarket shelves are thus relieved of the obligation having to employ staff themselves, relying instead on using agency staff, sometimes on an hourly basis, in order to respond to fluctuations in demand from their supermarket customers. Migrant workers are often hired on so-called 'zero hours' contracts, meaning that while they are expected to be available for work when needed, they have no guarantee of receiving regular work themselves. For them, employment flexibility equates with irregular earnings and manifold insecurity.

Using agency labour may, however, present its own problems for managers. Beynon et al. (2002) examined the extensive use of agency workers in the Consumer Division of 'Telecomco', a provider of telecommunications services. Within the workplace divisions arose between those workers who were directly employed by the company and those hired as 'temps'. While organizations might aspire to relieve themselves of the respon-sibility of managing labour through the use of temporary staff, in practice managers are obliged actively to manage all of the workers under their control and differences in pay and conditions between groups of workers doing the same job can be disruptive.

What about the third proposition concerning flexible employment, that it is under-taken in a purposive, strategic manner, based on the use of separate core and peripheral workforces? The flexible firm model is an unsatisfactory means of analysing the labour management strategies of employers. For one thing, it assumes that there has been a rapid and substantial growth in the extent of flexible employment, when in fact change has been more gradual (Dex and McCulloch 1997; McGovern et al. 2007; Pollert 1988b).

Nor should one assume that ostensibly core workers are necessarily multi-skilled and functionally flexible in the positive manner implied by Atkinson's model since this ap-pears to be a characteristic of only a minority of workplaces (Ackroyd and Proctor 1998). Moreover, the flexible firm model presents an overly crude distinction between a core and periphery when, in reality, there is a considerable heterogeneity within these catego-ries (Gallie et al. 1998; Ward et al. 2001). For example, we have already highlighted the diversity of temporary work arrangements.

Despite receiving qualified support from some writers (Proctor et al. 1994), the flex-ible firm model has been criticized for exaggerating the degree of strategic intent that underpins employers' decisions about labour use. Employers generally use temporary staff not as part of an explicit strategy but in order to align the size of their workforce to meet short-term changes in the level of demand, to acquire specialist skills, to cover short-term absences or, as in the case of the public sector, because funding constraints mean they cannot increase their permanent headcount (Hunter et al. 1993; Kersley et al. 2006). Moreover, it is not clear whether Atkinson's model was advanced as a description of existing organizational practice, as a prediction of how organizations would change their practice, or as a programme for organizations that did wish to change—three conceptually distinct approaches (Pollert 1988a).

The initial popularity of the flexible firm model during the 1980s and 1990s was a function of the prevailing political and economic climate, one in which trade union power was in decline (Pollert 1988b). It reflects the increased concern with management as the primary actor in employment relations, and of how managers can use their enhanced prerogative to effect change. In doing so, it deflects attention from the most significant aspect of how companies have pursued greater employment flexibility. This is the way in which they have sought to render their workforces more pliable as competitive pressures impel them to manage labour more efficiently.

In their analysis of seven organizations from the private and public sectors, Beynon et al. (2002) show how flexibility in practice meant the erosion of established norms and practices as managers responded to market pressure to reduce costs. 'With the vagaries of the market behind them, HR managers have sent a clear signal to workers that they are disposable and that previous employment terms do not count' (Beynon et al. 2002: 248). In this interpretation, flexibility is less about operating more innovative employment arrangements that satisfy the interests of both workers and employers, and more concerned with the search for stronger managerial prerogative, weakened trade unions, and a more pliable workforce, who are expected to work more intensively. The economic recession of the late 2000s will, if anything, exacerbate such an approach (see Chapter 10).

SECTION SUMMARY AND FURTHER READING

- There has been no fundamental transformation of employment relations consistent with the notion of a 'new' economy. The number of people who are self-employed is a rather small proportion of the total workforce. Much self-employment, moreover, is disguised employment. Thus the employment relationship is still of fundamental importance to the functioning of the contemporary economy.

- Wage labour in Britain is dominated by routine manual and non-manual work, with both the growth and the significance of managerial and professional occupations being of rather less importance than is often assumed. Given the way in which workers are increasingly treated by organizations as commodities, and thus inherently disposable, the potential for conflict is an important feature of contemporary employment relations.

- It is important not to exaggerate the extent of the increase in flexible employment arrangements in Britain. Although many workers choose to take part-time or temporary jobs, often their choices are constrained by a lack of appropriate alternatives, especially among women who have childcare responsibilities. The use of temporary labour highlights the way in which employers are impelled, given pressure to reduce

> costs, to render their workforces more pliable, since competitive pressures impel them to manage labour more efficiently.
>
> See Bradley et al. (2000: Chapter 3) for a critical assessment of debates about 'non-standard' or 'flexible' working. McGovern et al. (2007: Chapter 2) demonstrate that where they have occurred, any employment changes have been gradual and complex. Both Nolan and Slater (2003), and Nolan and Wood (2003) draw on reliable data in respect of labour market developments and occupational change to challenge the notion of a 'new' economy. See Warhurst (2008) for a critical assessment of the 'knowledge economy'. Beynon et al. (2002: 151–8, 243–8) consider issues pertaining to the management of temporary labour.
>
> Visit our Online Resource Centre for web links to sites connected to this section. www.oxfordtextbooks.co.uk/williams_adamsmith2e

2.3 Employment relations in a global economy I: multinational companies and union responses

The growing degree of global economic integration, or economic 'globalization' as it is often called, is one of the most important contemporary influences on employment relations. What, then, do we mean by the currently fashionable concept of globalization? Although economic activity has long spread across national borders, it is suggested that since the 1980s, in particular, there has been a major increase in the extent of economic interconnectedness on a worldwide scale, facilitated by innovations in information technology and communication networks, and the break-up of the Soviet bloc (Castells 1996; Dicken 2003; Held et al. 1999). We start this section by examining the broad implications of globalization for employment relations. This is followed by a discussion of the significant role enjoyed by multinational companies (MNCs) in the globalization process, before we consider the ways in which the international union movement has responded to the challenges of globalization.

2.3.1 Globalization and employment relations

The globalization of economic and business activity has four key features: growing levels of international trade in goods and services; the increasing volume of international financial transactions and the transformation of world financial markets; an acceleration in the amount of foreign direct investment (FDI) in the global economy; and the enhanced importance and power of MNCs, often as sources of FDI themselves (see Bradley et al. 2000: 18–19; Dicken 2003; Held et al. 1999). Moreover, globalization is associated with an increase in the incidence of migration by workers around the world (see Box 2.4).

It is sometimes claimed that economic globalization, in so far as it enables the greater mobility of capital, places constraints upon the capacity of individual nation-states to regulate their economies (e.g. Gray 1998; Strange 1996), to support employment levels, for example. Yet the extent of economic globalization, and also the way in which it is held to constrain the policy options of national states, have been questioned. According to Hirst and Thompson (1999), the current level of openness in the world economy is

---

Employment relations reflection 2.4   Globalization and migration

Migration, the movement of people across regions, national borders, or even continents, is a phenomenon of long-standing historical significance. Along with political and cultural changes, economic globalization has facilitated an increase in the extent to which people are willing and able to migrate. The impact of migration on 'receiving' countries is a source of particular political controversy. In the UK, for example, the government has taken ever more severe measures to restrict the entry of unwanted 'economic migrants', people who travel in search of opportunities to improve their lives, without official sanction, as a way of demonstrating its toughness on immigration policy.

Yet without migrant labour key areas of the British economy would immediately run into trouble since such people frequently fill jobs that indigenous workers are unwilling to take. The presence of migrant workers is extensive in the agriculture and food-processing industries, for example, where they constitute a cheap source of labour for employers, enabling the major supermarket chains to keep prices low while at the same time improving their profitability. A 2003 report by the Trades Union Congress—*Migrant Workers: Overworked, Underpaid and Over Here*—revealed the extensive degree of exploitation experienced by many migrant workers, including extremely low levels of pay.

In March 2004, an investigation by The *Guardian* newspaper highlighted the gruelling conditions endured by Chinese workers who, organized by labour suppliers known as gangmasters, were hired by agencies to work in the food-processing factories of eastern England, and received half the wages of their indigenous counterparts. The existence of such people is rarely acknowledged except when a tragedy occurs, such as the deaths of twenty Chinese cocklepickers at Morecambe Bay in 2004. As a result of trade union campaigning efforts, legislation designed to regulate the affairs of unscrupulous gangmasters was enacted, including the establishment of a Gangmasters Licensing Authority (GLA). Although the GLA has taken action to clamp down on rogue gangmasters, accounts of life as a migrant worker demonstrate that low pay, insecurity, unpaid wages, and poor health and safety standards continue to be prevalent (e.g. Pai 2008).

---

not without precedent. Nation-states, moreover, retain considerable powers over economic decision-making (Held et al. 1999; Weiss 1997).

The concept of globalization, then, is often used rhetorically by national governments as a means of persuading people that, given the enhanced mobility of capital and the pressures of global competition, deregulated labour markets and weakened trade unions are essential attributes of a competitive economy. Thus globalization may be interpreted as a 'myth', developed in such a way that it 'exaggerates the degree of our helplessness in the face of contemporary economic forces' (Hirst and Thompson 1999: 6).

The process of global economic integration is not a neutral force, but one that is a feature of the development of capitalism (Bradley et al. 2000). Moreover, it has been fostered by influential international agencies like the International Monetary Fund (IMF) as a 'neo-liberal' project, based on what Stiglitz (2002) refers to as the 'Washington Consensus'. Thus governments, particularly those in developing countries, are pressured to liberalize markets, privatize state assets, and reduce taxation as a means of stimulating economic growth and competitiveness.

What are the implications for employment relations? In order to compete more effectively in a more globalized environment, the neo-liberal agenda determines that countries should seek to deregulate their labour markets and promote greater employ-ment flexibility (Debrah and Smith 2002; Leisink 1999), although, as Stiglitz (2002: 84) points out, when the promoters of the 'Washington Consensus' use the term 'labour market flexibility' they generally mean 'lower wages and less job protection'. Thus the process of economic globalization has been underpinned by a neo-liberal reform im-perative. It holds that deregulated labour markets, and greater employer flexibility over jobs, wages, and working conditions, are essential conditions for enhanced economic competitiveness. This threatens existing national systems of employment relations regu-lation and the role of trade unions (Eaton 2000).

The continuing erosion of economic barriers, symbolized by the 1995 establishment of the World Trade Organization (WTO), a body set up to promote and manage the liberaliza-tion of trade relations between nation-states, poses major challenges to workers and trade unions around the world. According to one interpretation, it 'will increase pressures to cut costs in order for businesses to stay competitive and, therefore, put still more downward pressures on labour costs and working-class incomes in particular' (Moody 1997: 134). Although proponents of free trade claim that economic globalization produces greater prosperity (Wolf 2004), as a process of capitalist restructuring along neo-liberal lines, it has the potential to erode workers' pay, rights, and conditions in a fundamental way.

Globalization may also contribute towards the growing 'convergence' of employment relations systems around the world. The concept of 'convergence' was originally used to re-fer to the way in which the process of industrialism, with its associated technical and insti-tutional arrangements, such as collective bargaining, for example, generated greater uni-formity in employment relations systems across nation-states (Kerr et al. 1962). The recent acceleration and intensification of global economic activity may, however, be responsible for accentuating pressures towards convergence around a new employment relations 'par-adigm' based upon deregulated labour markets, employment flexibility, weak or decentral-ized collective bargaining arrangements, and powerless trade unions (Eaton 2000).

In spite of the challenges posed by economic globalization, it is important to acknowl-edge the resilience of national systems of employment relations, something that is an obstacle to the convergence process and thus a source of divergence between nation-states (Ferner and Hyman 1998; Rubery and Grimshaw 2003). For example, Hall and Soskice (2001) distinguish between 'liberal market economies', such as Britain and the United States, and 'co-ordinated market economies', such as Germany. The former are characterized by the predominance of a neo-liberal policy agenda such that the 'result should be some weakening of organized labour and a substantial amount of deregula-tion, much as conventional views predict' (Hall and Soskice 2001: 57). However, among the 'co-ordinated market economies', deregulatory pressures are more likely to be con-strained, or at least moderated, by the presence of robust national-level employment relations systems. Here trade unions and centralized systems of collective bargaining are less brittle in the face of pressures for enhanced flexibility.

Some writers express the need to treat the concepts of 'convergence' and 'divergence' with caution. There are important sectoral differences across countries, for example (Katz and Darbishire 2000). Nevertheless, the employment relations effects of economic globalization are felt more acutely in those countries, like Britain and the United States, whose governments have been more favourable to neo-liberal policy imperatives.

2.3.2 Globalization and multinational companies

Multinational companies have long been a feature of the international business environment. Since the 1980s, though, the scale and scope of their activities have grown markedly and, as a result, they have contributed substantially to the process of economic globalization (Edwards and Ferner 2002; Muller-Camen et al. 2001). Investment flows from multinationals, rather than by patterns of trade between different countries, increasingly dominate international economic activity (Held et al. 1999; Hirst and Thompson 1999).

Companies including Coca-Cola, Microsoft, and IBM have been able to develop a massive worldwide presence, not only benefiting from the growing interconnectedness of the global economy, but also, through their activities, helping to stimulate it still further. The fast-food industry, in particular, is dominated by MNCs (Royle and Towers 2002).

While it is easy to cite examples of prominent multinationals, and industries in which they predominate, how can they be conceptualized? We use the term to refer to companies that invest in, and are thus directly responsible for, foreign subsidiaries beyond the boundaries of their national territorial base, although this underplays the increasing importance of cross-border mergers and acquisitions as a source of economic internationalization (Held et al. 1999). By the mid 2000s there were some 77,000 MNCs in existence, responsible for at least 750,000 foreign subsidiaries (UNCTAD 2006). The UK economy, in particular, is dominated by the activities of multinationals since it is a notably open, and attractive, venue for investment by overseas companies. At the start of the 2000s, 'over 18,000 foreign firms were operating in Britain, more than 5,000 of which had 1,000 or more employees' (Ferner 2003: 85).

Multinationals sometimes aim to integrate their operations on a worldwide scale, particularly through the use of global production chains (Hyman 1999). Kim Moody observes that the US car company General Motors can make use of improved transport facilities to 'use Mexican-produced parts in cars assembled in Michigan and sold throughout the USA or Canada, or Spanish-made body stampings and/or Czech-made engines in a car produced in eastern Germany and sold in western Europe' (Moody 1997: 69).

The greater the degree of integration, and in particular the standardization of products and services on a global basis, the easier it is for multinationals to undertake detailed scrutiny of, and thus be able to compare, the respective performance of each of their subsidiaries (Marginson and Sisson 1994). MNCs in this position enjoy the ability to make 'coercive comparisons' between plants operating in the same, or different, countries (Mueller and Purcell 1992). The concept of 'coercive comparisons' is used to refer to the way in which multinationals use intricate financial, productivity, and output data to make detailed comparisons of the performance of their respective plants. These can then be used to exert pressure on workers and unions in plants that are found to be under-performing to increase their work effort or accept more flexible working arrangements as a means of catching up.

Where the MNC is more globally integrated, then, it may be better able to challenge established national-level employment relations arrangements and resist unionization (Edwards et al. 1996). Multinationals often attempt to replicate employment relations techniques that prevail at home in their foreign subsidiaries, making as little attempt as possible to adjust them to the nature of environment they inhabit. The way in which

American multinationals operate in the UK, for example, is marked by efforts to develop distinctive and innovative approaches to managing employment relations (see Box 2.5).

Yet it is important not to exaggerate the implications of global integration for employment relations. By no means do 'all MNCs aim for, let alone have achieved, a globally-integrated production or operations strategy' (Rubery and Grimshaw 2003: 219). Moreover, the characteristics of the host country environment often exercise a profound influence upon the way in which employment relations is managed in multinational subsidiaries (Muller-Camen et al. 2001). In their study of an American multinational company, ITCO, Almond et al. (2005) discovered that it was able to implement its preferred non-union system of employment relations relatively easily in the UK and Ireland. Elsewhere in Europe, however, the presence of stronger national-level employment regulations meant that it was obliged to establish relationships with trade unions.

Nor should one assume that MNCs are supremely rational entities that are always capable of acting in a calculative and predictable manner. Just like any other organization, an MNC is characterized by the presence of power relations, something that may constrain its ability to secure the compliance of its foreign subsidiaries (Ferner and Edwards 1995). See, for example, the case study of the Scottish subsidiary of 'Cashco', a US-owned manufacturer of cash registers. While the company philosophy was marked by hostility towards trade unions, since the plant was successful local managers were able to forge a distinctive approach to employment relations, one that included a more consensual relationship with the unions (Martin and Beaumont 1999).

Nevertheless, the power of multinational firms has generated concerns about their ability to avoid, or subvert, national-level employment relations arrangements that obstruct their interests. In the fast-food industry, for example, companies like McDonalds often enjoy a level of power sufficient to enable them to avoid employment regulations, especially those governing collective bargaining and employee rights to information and consultation, that do not suit them (Royle and Towers 2002). Countries frequently offer MNCs incentives, including the relaxation of employment regulations, as a means of attracting investment (Leisink 1999), or of preventing it from going elsewhere. Multinationals can

INSIGHT INTO PRACTICE 2.5

American multinationals in the UK and Ireland

The importance influence of the country of origin on employment relations in multinationals is evident when we look at the experience of American firms in the UK and Ireland. Ferner (2003) points to the leading role of companies such as Ford in developing standardized mass-production techniques, and the elaboration of distinctive company-based personnel policies. American firms, such as Kodak and Heinz, eschewed multi-employer bargaining, preferring to bargain with unions over pay and conditions themselves. There is also a long history of attempts by American multinationals to exclude trade unions from their British subsidiaries (Gennard and Steuer 1971). American multinationals are particularly resistant to unionization, as demonstrated by the opposition of companies such as Amazon to union recognition.

shrewdly use the threat of withdrawal, of disinvestment, to secure government favour, or to control their employees' behaviour.

Thus writers have discussed the potential for MNCs to engage in 'regime competition' (Streeck 1997). This refers to the way that multinationals base decisions about investment, or disinvestment, on the relative attractiveness of a country's employment 'regime', that is, its set of employment laws and regulations. In order to attract investment in an increasingly internationalized economy, then, governments come under pressure to relax the supposed regulatory burden for fear that if they do not do so, MNCs will transfer their activities to countries that will. Thus the erosion of economic barriers, in a neo-liberal, deregulatory context, enhances the capacity of multinationals to operate in environments where labour costs are cheaper, employment regulation weaker, and workers more quiescent (Held et al. 1999: 255).

In the UK, government policy in this area has been dominated by a concern to promote the benefits to companies of its relatively deregulated labour market as a means of trying to attract inward investment by MNCs (Ferner 2003). Ironically, the weakness of its employment protection regime renders Britain more vulnerable to the negative effects of disinvestment than most of its European counterparts since multinationals can cease operations there more easily. Thus MNC investment in Britain has something of an 'easy come, easy go' character to it (Muller-Camen et al. 2001).

Yet for a number of reasons, it is, doubtful that 'regime competition' has been responsible for a significant worsening of employment conditions within developed countries (Debrah and Smith 2002). To multinationals, relative labour costs are rarely as important as easy access to consumer markets. Morerover, MNCs will often not only be concerned with how cheaply they can hire workers, but also with matters such as workforce skills and qualifications (Marginson et al. 1995). Nevertheless, competitive pressures, and the need to trim costs, mean that many British companies have increasingly looked abroad for cheaper sources of labour, such as in the call-centre market (see Box 2.6). This aspect of the globalization process, then, potentially renders many workers more insecure, vulnerable, and exposed.

2.3.3 Globalization and trade union internationalism

Any assessment of the implications of globalization for employment relations would not be complete without understanding how trade unions have responded to its challenges on an international basis. Historically, Cold War divisions impeded efforts to build solidarity between trade unions at an international level (Cohen 1991; Tsogas 2001). The foreign policy of American unions, in particular, was marked by a pronounced anti-communism which undermined relationships with organized labour in many developing countries. The collapse of the Soviet Bloc in the late 1980s meant the ideological divisions that had previously weakened the international union movement largely disappeared.

Globalization, however, has posed some major challenges to union movements around the world. The increased power enjoyed by multinationals has eroded the capacity of unions to effect the joint regulation of employment relations (Anner et al. 2006). The greater mobility of capital, and the ease with which MNCs can relocate their operations in search of cost savings, means that 'one of the fundamental goals of organized

INTERNATIONAL PERSPECTIVE 2.6

Globalization and the growth of the Indian call centre industry

One of the most prominent, and controversial, aspects of the way in which economic globalization affects employment concerns the growth of the call centre sector in India. Improvements in communication and information technologies enable companies to move jobs involving things like customer relations, telemarketing, payment processing, insurance claims, and credit card and loan applications to locations where labour is considerably cheaper. In India, wages are between 10 and 15 per cent of those offered in Britain. Moreover, firms can benefit from a highly educated and well-motivated pool of English-speaking labour. By 2004, the Indian call centre industry already employed 180,000 people and was growing at 20 per cent per annum. Many major companies, including BT, Norwich Union, Lloyds TSB, Prudential, and Abbey Bank, relocated some of their call centre and other customer service operations overseas, principally to India.

Companies tend to relocate operations that are high in volume and low in sophistication, resulting in very short job-cycle times for the Indian call centre operators. A study of Indian call centres found that they are geared towards undertaking 'standardized, low-value processes', resembling a 'mass production work model' (Taylor and Bain 2005: 269). Work is highly routinized, and involves rigidly adhering to prepared scripts when conversing with customers. The onerous nature of the work is exacerbated by long travelling times to and from work, and the nature of the night shifts. A further source of pressure for Indian call centre workers is the requirement that they conceal their location, and even their identities as Indians, by speaking with 'neutral' accents and taking on anglicized pseudonyms, in order to meet the expectations of western customers. The highly stressful nature of their jobs generates a high level of turnover among Indian call centre agents, something that runs counter to the picture of a well-motivated and highly satisfied workforce that is often portrayed in superficial accounts of working life in Indian call centres.

labour, taking workers' rights out of competition by establishing fundamental common standards, is under direct attack' (ICFTU 2004: 19).

Since unions are primarily national actors, whose power and capacity to influence employment relations stems from their ability to organize and mobilize workers within specific countries, and whose operations are to a large extent concerned with national-level employment regulation, the internationalization of economic activity has undoubtedly weakened them (Lillie and Martinez Lucio 2004).

Understandably, perhaps, a common trade union reaction to the challenges posed by globalization is to fall back on protectionist attitudes. This concerns the tendency for workers and their unions in specific countries to pursue policy goals that meet their particular needs, rather than those which would benefit the labour interest globally. Some American unions, for example, evince a concern with the need for improved labour standards in developing countries in order to pressurize policy makers to impose tariffs or restrictions on imported goods, thus protecting the jobs of their members. Protectionist attitudes among trade unions in some developed countries remain an enduring obstacle to the articulation of international union solidarity (Rubery and Grimshaw 2003). Workers' organizations in, and the governments of, developing nations perceive that the hostility towards globalization and free trade evinced by union movements in the rich countries stems from a concern to prevent the export of jobs, and thus protect living standards, at the expense of their workers.

Yet there are circumstances where workers and unions from around the world take action to demonstrate their support for, and sympathy with, workers in a different country who are engaged in a dispute over their terms and conditions of employment. Such activity has a particularly long history in the port transport industry. In 2002, for example, solidarity action by dock unions around the world helped American port transport workers involved in a dispute on the west coast of the United States (Lillie and Martinez Lucio 2004).

There are also signs that protectionist attitudes may have become a less important obstacle to the pursuit of effective trade union internationalism. For example, the run up to the 1999 world trade talks in Seattle, and its aftermath, saw new links being forged between trade unions and labour activists from developed countries in North America and Europe and their counterparts in the developing world, based on a shared understanding that the effective global regulation of labour standards was imperative to producing worldwide improvements in living standards and working conditions in a more globalized world economy (Compa 2001; Waterman 2001). Nevertheless, there remain some important obstacles to effective trade union internationalism (see Box 2.7).

INSIGHT INTO PRACTICE 2.7

The obstacles to effective labour internationalism

Based on his study of an international campaign event to challenge the employment practices of fast-food giant McDonald's, Ghigliani (2005) highlights some of the key problems and challenges that hinder the development of effective labour internationalism. His research involved studying a five-day 'meeting' held in Belgium and the Netherlands during October 2002. The event, which was organized by Dutch trade unions with the assistance of international union federations, brought together union bodies, sympathetic non-governmental organizations (NGOs), and representatives of anti-globalization social movements.

However, a number of problems emerged which adversely affected the outcomes of the event. For example, tensions arose between the international union federations involved, between the international union federations and national-level union bodies, and between the unions and the social movements. The international union federations expressed caution; they seemed reluctant to engage with the explicitly anti-McDonald's basis of the meeting, preferring to develop unionization through consensual methods, including a focus on establishing collective bargaining procedures as a means of improving pay and employment conditions. National trade unions were reluctant to engage in the struggle against McDonald's; because of their country-specific orientation, the significance of action against McDonald's on a global basis seemed of little direct relevance to them. Collaboration between the unions and the social movements and NGOs engaged in the struggle against neo-liberal globalization was also difficult. Campaigns based around consumer boycotts, a repertoire of action favoured by social movements and NGOs, may pose few problems for multinational companies like McDonald's who, through the judicious use of skilful public relations, are able to nullify their effect by demonstrating the depth of their commitment to corporate social responsibility.

Broadly speaking, there are three main approaches that have been used to foster greater trade union internationalism during the 2000s (Anner et al. 2006). First, one approach is for unions to combine on an international basis to regulate working conditions in one particular industry. This has been the case in maritime shipping, for example, where seafarers' unions have secured agreement from employers over certain minimum employment standards. However, there are special factors which apply in this sector, notably the longstanding influence over wages enjoyed by the global union federation that operates in maritime shipping, the International Transport Workers Federation (ITF), raising some important doubts about how far such an approach is capable of being effectively pursued elsewhere (Anner et al. 2006).

The second approach concerns the development of international links and networks between trade unions operating within the same company, something that has been particularly notable in the motor vehicle manufacturing industry, for example (Anner et al. 2006). However, such arrangements can be fragile. In 2000, for example, the German motor vehicle firm BMW controversially chose to sell its UK subsidiary Rover. While the UK trade unions were vehemently opposed to such a sale, since it would seriously jeopardize Rover's future, their counterparts in Germany, who were more concerned with the interests of the BMW group as a whole, implicitly supported it (Lillie and Martinez Lucio 2004).

The third approach involves the development of joint campaigning and mobilizing work between trade unions in developed countries and their counterparts in developing countries, often with the support of activist bodies, such as anti-sweatshop campaigning groups. The aim is to influence consumer behaviour, and use ethical arguments to put pressure on MNCs to improve labour standards and recognize unions within the factories that comprise their global supply chains in developing countries (e.g. in clothing manufacturing). For a number of reasons, though, this approach has so far been relatively unsuccessful on the whole. Although there have been some notable successes, where unions have won recognition, for example, multinational firms find it relatively easy to transfer production to other locations, leading to factory closures in some developing countries. Garment workers' unions now concentrate their energies on promoting international cooperation among developed countries (Anner et al. 2006).

In addition to these kinds of interventions, international union bodies, in the form of the Global Union Federations (GUFs) have increasingly tried to fashion a strategic response to the challenges of globalization (Croucher and Cotton 2009). Known until 2000 as international trade secretariats (ITS), GUFs operate, and represent the interests of their national-level union affiliates, on an industry basis. There are ten GUFs, including the International Transport Workers Federation (ITF), Public Services International (PSI), and the International Metalworkers Federation (IMF). Along with the umbrella union body, the International Trade Union Confederation (ITUC), the GUFs form the Global Unions network.

Perhaps the most significant activity undertaken by the GUFs concerns the role they have in concluding International Framework Agreements (IFAs) with multinational companies. IFAs are negotiated arrangements between GUFs and individual multinationals which establish a set of non-binding rules designed to govern employment relationships within the company on an international basis, in particular by establishing a set of minimum employment standards (Riisgaard 2005; Stevis and Boswell 2007). IFAs are important because they represent a new and innovative approach by the international trade union movement to regulating employment relationships above and beyond national borders (Hammer 2005).

While the first IFA covering the French multinational Danone was instituted during the 1980s, it is only in the 2000s that their number has really grown substantially, such that by the middle of 2008 there were 61 of them in existence, in companies such as the French retailer Carrefour, the Swedish retailer H&M, and the German motor vehicle manufacturer Volkswagen (Croucher and Cotton 2009). With few exceptions, most IFAs have been concluded between GUFs and European multinationals. The only American company to have signed an IFA is Chiquita, the banana firm.

There is some evidence that IFAs can help to promote stronger trade union activity. The agreement between the multinational hotel chain Accor and the IUF (International Union of Food, Agricultural, Hotel, Restaurant, Catering, Tobacco and Allied Workers' Associations), for example, has enhanced the effectiveness of union organizing efforts, thus helping to improve labour standards (Wills 2002). Set against this, however, where knowledge and awareness of the IFA is lacking, then its potential to deliver positive change is much reduced (Riisgaard 2005).

IFAs are relatively youthful structures. While their direct impact on employment relations has so far been somewhat limited, they are still the only directly negotiated international agreements between unions and multinationals in existence. This in itself is a positive development, one which the international labour movement can build upon (Stevis and Boswell 2007).

Globalization poses many problems for workers and trade unions. Yet in so far as it represents the development and expansion of a neo-liberal capitalist order on a massive scale, it may, given the pressure under which it puts workers, create the conditions for its own demise as they mobilize to challenge and contest it. There is already plentiful evidence from countries such as South Korea, Indonesia, and Brazil to suggest that economic development, and entry into the capitalist global system, generates the conditions that make the emergence of vigorous independent trade unionism viable (see Moody 1997). Thus it would be a mistake to assume that globalization will invariably weaken trade unionism around the world. Instead, it may prompt the emergence of a more progressive international union agenda, based on a common need to regulate effectively labour standards around the world.

SECTION SUMMARY AND FURTHER READING

- Although its extent and novelty has been questioned, the process of economic globalization has important implications for employment relations. In particular, the erosion of economic barriers between countries has been impelled by a neo-liberal ideology which holds that deregulated labour markets, and greater employer flexibility over jobs, wages, and working conditions, are essential conditions for improvements in competitiveness.

- Multinational companies have not only been an important catalyst of economic globalization but they are also among its principal beneficiaries. They may use their economic power to weaken national-level employment regulations as the price of investment. The effect on working conditions is, however, unclear given that multinationals' location decisions are based on a range of relevant matters and not solely labour force costs.

• Trade unions have long struggled to operate effectively at an international level. Globalization, moreover, presents workers and unions with a number of challenges. Some of the Global Union Federations (GUFs), though, have developed innovative new ways of regulating employment relationships internationally through the establishment of international framework agreements (IFAs).

The most rigorous and informative books on globalization are Dicken (2003) and Held et al. (1999). For a sceptical perspective on the significance of the globalization phenomenon, see Hirst and Thompson (1999). Bradley et al. (2000: Chapter 1) offer a brief and critical overview of globalization debates. For the employment relations implications of globalization, see Rubery and Grimshaw (2003: Chapters 8 and 9). For further information about the influences on the management of employment relations in multinationals, see Edwards and Ferner (2002), and Edwards (2004). Croucher and Cotton (2009) offer an excellent overview of contemporary efforts to promote trade union internationalism.

 Visit our Online Resource Centre for web links to sites connected to this section. www.oxfordtextbooks.co.uk/williams_adamsmith2e

2.4 Employment relations in a global economy II: regulating international labour standards

What effect does the activity of multinational companies (MNCs) have on jobs and employment relations in developing countries, given the attractiveness of such locations as a source of cheap labour costs? From the 1950s to the 1970s, East Asian countries such as Taiwan and Singapore were particularly popular as production locations. As wages and living standards there rose, however, countries such as China, Indonesia, and Cambodia, which offer extremely low labour costs, have become more popular investment locations. In this section, we consider whether or not there is a global 'race to the bottom' in respect of labour standards as multinationals, in search of lower production costs, look for cheaper sources of labour. We also consider the increasing interest in, and varieties of, international labour standards, and examine the extent to which they can help to regulate employment relationships on a global basis.

2.4.1 A global 'race to the bottom'?

There is a vigorous debate concerning the extent to which the activities of MNCs, whose supply chains stretch to poor countries, exploit workers there, and are thus undesirable. Wages are often very low, the hours long, and working conditions poor. It is sometimes asserted that the outcome is a global 'race to the bottom' when it comes to labour standards, as countries compete with one another to offer lower labour costs and weaker employment protections, in the contest to attract MNC investment. However, an alternative perspective holds that by investing in poorer countries, and creating jobs, MNCs create employment opportunities. This generates prosperity, and enables people who might otherwise be destitute to earn a living and improve their economic situation.

One would be mistaken in assuming that interest in the activities of MNCs in developing countries is of relatively recent origin. During the 1960s and 1970s, the 'New International Division of Labour' (NIDL) concept was advanced as a means of understanding the location decisions of multinational companies (Fröbel, Heinrichs, and Kreye 1980). This theory proposed that 'industrial capital from the core was moving to the periphery as "world-market factories" were established producing manufactured goods destined for export' (Cohen 1991: 125).

In other words, MNCs from the 'core' industrialized countries of Western Europe and North America actively sought out low-cost manufacturing locations in the 'periphery'—Brazil, Mexico and South Korea, in particular—taking advantage of relatively cheap and largely non-unionized, unskilled, and semi-skilled workforces to produce goods for world markets (Munck 1988). In these countries, production, typically of electric and electronic goods, toys, clothing, and shoes, became concentrated in special areas, sometimes known as 'free production zones' or, more popularly, 'export processing zones' (EPZs).

As a location incentive, manufacturers in these zones are often exempted from aspects of the country in question's employment, environmental, and taxation laws. In her book *No Logo*, Naomi Klein estimates that 124 export processing zones exist worldwide, with some 18 million workers employed within them (Klein 2000). Perhaps the best known is the 'maquiladora' system in Mexico along that country's long border with the United States. Established in the 1960s, it enables foreign companies, particularly those from the United States, to own and operate production facilities in Mexico, where labour costs are much lower, and export the finished goods back to their home country (Munck 1988). By the late 1990s over 3,500 maquiladora plants existed and some 900,000 workers were employed within them (Klein 2000).

Although the manufacture of textiles and electronics goods by a largely female workforce dominated at first, during the 1980s and 1990s the big US car-makers invested in new production facilities in Mexico, though not always in the maquiladora zone. Moody (1997) focuses on the 1986 establishment of a Ford/Mazda assembly plant. He observes that the 'workforce of 1,600, which proved to be as efficient as any in the US, cost about $2 an hour per worker in wages, benefits, and taxes, or about $7 million a year. A comparable workforce in a US Ford plant would have cost $30 an hour or nearly $100 million a year' (Moody 1997: 129). As Moody (1997) wryly notes, the cars sell for about the same price as if they were made in the United States.

The NIDL theory can be criticized in a number of respects. For example, investment flows tend to be predominantly between advanced industrialized societies (Marginson and Sisson 1994). Moreover, location decisions may be influenced more by the need to be close to key markets rather than by labour costs (Edwards et al. 1996). Nevertheless, the increasing internationalization of economic activity, facilitated by substantial improvements in information technology, transport links, and communications networks, provides MNCs with more favourable opportunities to relocate production in such a way that labour costs are substantially reduced. In 2003, for example, Proctor and Gamble closed its plant near Portsmouth, England, moving the production of female sanitary products to China. In the United States and Europe, major organizations, like aircraft manufacturer Boeing and the manufacturing conglomerate ABB, have relocated production to foreign locations where labour costs are lower, with the loss of thousands of jobs in their home countries (Held et al. 1999; Moody 1997).

To what extent has this trend affected jobs and employment relations in the advanced industrialized societies of Europe and North America? It has been suggested that the resulting decline in demand for labour, particularly unskilled labour, has kept wages in check and generated greater pay inequality (Wood 1994). However, while economic globalization has stimulated a shift in the balance of power between capital and labour in favour of the former (Held et al. 1999), its effects cannot be understood without reference to political factors. The policies that governments in the United States and Britain, in particular, have enacted to undermine trade unionism, and the anti-union ideology of many employers, have done more than globalization to challenge the established systems of employment relations in these countries (Hirst and Thompson 1999).

In respect of rich countries, then, evidence that globalization has induced a 'race to the bottom' in respect of labour standards is somewhat ambiguous. How, though, has it affected jobs in developing countries? On the one hand, globalization enthusiasts contend that workers in poor countries benefit from the prosperity generated by free trade and MNC investment. While the jobs they create are poorly paid by the standards of developed countries, the opportunities globalization gives to people, especially women, who would otherwise be entrenched in poverty, means that it should be welcomed. Moreover, MNCs, and their suppliers, tend to offer higher wages and better working conditions than do indigenous firms. In this interpretation, then, the proposition that globalization results in a 'race to the bottom' in respect of labour standards is nonsensical; rather, the investment it generates creates jobs, economic opportunities, and the potential for prosperity in places where they would otherwise be absent (Bhagwati 2004; Wolf 2004).

On the other hand, it is purported that the global sourcing strategies of many manufacturers have, as part of a 'race to the bottom', eroded labour standards (Tsogas 2001). Thus a considerable amount of controversy has arisen regarding the alleged 'sweatshop' conditions endured by workers in developing countries, particularly those employed by sub-contractors in one of the many EPZs, who make goods for famous global companies.

The giant US retailer Wal-Mart, for example, which owns the supermarket chain Asda in the UK, is well known for the effort it expends to find ever cheaper goods, something that has led it to source an increasing proportion of its wares from China, where wages are tiny relative to those in North America or Europe. A 2004 Oxfam report shows in some detail how the pressure Wal-Mart puts on its suppliers in developing countries squeezes workers' conditions and undermines their rights. It offers the example of a US-owned factory in Kenya that supplies Wal-Mart with jeans. The retailer 'pushes down the price it pays by getting quotations from several global sourcing agents and challenging the factory to match the lowest price'. Its buyers, moreover, closely monitor the production process, and suggest ways of reducing costs. The result is that the 'workers are left to face the squeeze. Excessive hourly production targets are almost impossible to reach. Few dare complain.' Although in principle the factory respects the workers' right to join a trade union, in April 2003, when there was a strike over pay, most of the union members were sacked (Oxfam 2004b).

Poor working conditions and labour rights abuses are especially prevalent in the increasing number of EPZs around the world (see Box 2.8). A 1996 report by the International

INTERNATIONAL PERSPECTIVE 2.8

Labour standards in Export Processing Zones

The Canadian writer Naomi Klein investigated EPZs in the Phillipines where workers making goods for the export market endure low pay and poor working conditions. She visited the Cavite free-trade zone that covers nearly 700 acres to the south of the capital Manila. Here, Klein discovered over 200 factories employing some 50,000 workers engaged in producing goods for IBM, Nike, and Gap, among others. She found that the 'management is military-style, the supervisors often abusive, the wages below subsistence and the work low-skill and tedious' (Klein 2000: 205). In one case, that of a factory making computer screens for IBM, overtime working was rewarded with a doughnut and a pen. Abuses of labour rights were commonplace. Any 'workers who do attempt to organize unions in their factories are viewed as troublemakers, and often face threats and intimidation' (Klein 2000: 213).

Perhaps most telling, however, was the prevailing climate of insecurity that characterized the zone. The government, factory owners, and workers were all aware of the inherently precarious nature of the jobs that multinational investment delivered and realized how easily they could be transferred elsewhere should multinationals find alternative, cheaper sources of production.

Confederation of Free Trade Unions (ICFTU 1996) highlighted the systematic violation of national labour laws evident within them, including the avoidance of minimum wage legislation, non-compliance with basic health and safety standards, and examples of child labour. The document cites numerous cases of anti-union repression in EPZs in such countries as Honduras and Guatemala in Central America, much of it undertaken with the implicit support of national governments. They accept violations of their own labour laws as part of the price to be paid for attracting foreign investment.

There are indications that some MNCs, such as Nike, for example, have responded to trade union and consumer campaigns against sweatshop labour by instituting codes of conduct, which establish minimum labour standards that their suppliers are obliged to respect (see Section 2.4.3). This has resulted in some improvements to working conditions (Connor 2002). However, MNCs are reluctant to submit themselves, and their supply chains, to independent scrutiny (Oxfam 2004b); and there is some doubt about the genuineness of their commitment to preventing abuses of labour rights. Despite its assertions to the contrary, Nike has been dogged by allegations that in Cambodia many of its products are made using child labour (BBC 2000), and there is also evidence that the production of sports shoes for Nike and Adidas in Indonesia is based on poverty wages and violent anti-unionism (Connor 2002).

In theory, as Stiglitz (2002) observes, economic globalization, by promoting freer trade and greater levels of FDI, has the potential to increase the standard of living of many of the poorest people on the planet. In practice, however, people in developing countries have received relatively little economic benefit from globalization; the countries of the industrialized world, and especially their companies, have profited the most. Multinationals vigorously manage supply chains in order to secure cheaper sources of production, something that results in considerable downward pressure on the pay and conditions of workers, and sustained union repression, among the myriad contractor and sub-contractor factories, often located in EPZs, that make the goods for relatively affluent western consumers.

2.4.2 Regulating international labour standards

Since the 1980s, there has been a marked growth of interest in the regulation of labour standards on an international basis. This has occurred for a number of reasons: the growing internationalization of economic activity, and the prominent role played by MNCs; concerns about the implications of a 'race to the bottom', particularly for jobs and working conditions in the developing world; and, related to this, the assertive campaigning by the American trade union movement against what it sees as the adverse social and employment consequences of global free trade (Compa 2001; Tsogas 2001).

In addition to these factors, international labour standards have become more imperative because of the failure of national governments to enforce their own labour laws (Kuruvilla and Verma 2006). In China, for example, regional and local administrations are often unwilling to effect compliance with minimum wage and other labour laws because of a concern that, if they were to do so, firms would move elsewhere. Ultimately, though, the question of international labour standards has arisen because of an increasing awareness that free trade under globalization needs to be balanced by effective employment regulation that prevents a race to the bottom (Hepple 2005).

The main body responsible for promoting labour standards on an international basis is the International Labour Organization (ILO). Founded in 1919, the ILO holds that economic growth should encompass 'the creation of jobs and working conditions in which people can work in freedom, safety and dignity … economic development is not undertaken for its own sake bit to improve the lives of human beings; international labour standards are there to ensure that it remains focused on improving human life and dignity' (ILO 2005: 7).

An agency of the United Nations, the ILO comprises representatives of governments, trade unions and employers' organizations from among its member states. The main instrument it uses to promote labour standards takes the form of conventions which its member countries are invited to ratify. By 2005, 185 conventions had been agreed. Among other things, they provide for the eradication of child labour (Convention 138, 1973), and the right of workers to enjoy freedom of association, by being able to organize in trade unions and bargain collectively with employers (Conventions 87, 1948, and 98, 1949).

Once a country has ratified a convention, it is obliged to uphold its provisions. However, countries are not obliged to ratify any of the conventions, and many do not do so (Kuruvilla and Verma 2006). About one-third have not ratified the convention outlawing child labour, for example. Moreover, the ILO lacks an effective means of ensuring that countries which ratify a convention actually comply with it in practice (O'Brien 2002).

Since the late 1990s the ILO has more actively propagated the need for effective international labour standards as a means of regulating employment relations at a global level (Elliott and Freeman 2003). In 1998, it published a Declaration of Fundamental Principles and Rights at Work, containing a number of 'core' conventions, which all member states

LEGISLATION AND POLICY 2.9

The ILO's Declaration of Fundamental Principles and Rights at Work

The ILO's Declaration of Fundamental Principles and Rights at Work consists of eight 'core' conventions covering freedom of association and the right to collective bargaining, the elimination of forced or compulsory labour, the elimination of workplace discrimination, and the abolition of child labour. All member states are required to comply with the obligations imposed by these conventions even if they have not ratified them.

- Freedom of Association and Protection of the Right to Organize Convention (Convention No. 87), 1948
- Right to Organize and Collective Bargaining Convention (98), 1949
- Forced Labour Convention (29), 1930
- Abolition of Forced Labour Convention (105), 1957
- Equal Remuneration Convention (100), 1951
- Discrimination (Employment and Occupation) Convention (111), 1958
- Minimum Age Convention (138), 1973
- Worst Forms of Child Labour Convention (182), 1999

are obliged to uphold (see Box 2.9). Yet the ILO possesses no sanctions to effect compliance with its conventions, apart from expulsion, and that is only ever used in extreme circumstances as a last resort. Instead, it seeks to 'promote labour standards through technical assistance and development policies, and to work with member states on how to implement the fundamental rights included in the declaration' (Rubery and Grimshaw 2003: 244).

There is some evidence that interventions by the ILO can help to improve labour standards. In the Middle East, for example, ILO technical assistance has helped to promote the independent representation of workers' interests even in countries where trade unions are banned (Kuruvilla and Verma 2006). The question of whether or not countries that violate agreed international labour standards should be penalized, perhaps through the imposition of trade sanctions, has influenced the policy debate in this area (see Section 2.4.3). The main problem with a more rigorous enforcement regime is that it would discourage countries from ratifying ILO conventions, or even cause them to quit the organization entirely (Hepple 2005).

The principal criticism of attempts to regulate labour standards on a global basis is that they are protectionist, and liable to hinder economic prosperity. Enthusiasts for globalization and free trade contend that setting international labour standards obstructs the efforts of developing countries that wish to use one of their key competitive advantages, low labour costs, to attract investment and pursue economic growth. By setting minimum employment rights, which developing countries are less likely to be able to meet, this hinders free trade and unfairly protects companies and workers in the developed world from the rigours of global competition, leading to fewer job opportunities, and reduced prosperity in poorer countries.

Jobs in EPZs might offer low pay and undesirable working conditions by the standards of rich nations, but the workers who undertake them are generally better off than if they had remained as agricultural or domestic labourers. Thus efforts to determine minimum international employment rights are misplaced and counterproductive (Bhagwati 2004; Wolf 2004).

However, the proposition that effective international labour standards prejudice economic competitiveness and prosperity has not gone unchallenged. On the contrary, their presence may contribute to, rather than hinder, economic growth in developing countries. The absence of international labour standards encourages countries to follow a 'low road' route to economic development, based on promoting export-led growth with competitive advantage gained through low pay and weak employment protections.

But such an approach is inimical to the long-term prosperity of developing countries. Instead, a more sustainable economic model is desirable, one that is contingent upon wage levels that are sufficient to boost demand-led growth and strong labour laws that encourage effective independent trade unions who can use their bargaining endeavours to raise wages (Palley 2004). The ILO claims that 'compliance with international labour standards often accompanies improvements in productivity and economic performance' (ILO 2005: 8).

It is important to recognize that labour standards can often be made context-specific. Freedom of association—the right of workers to organize and join trade unions—while ostensibly a universal standard, can be tailored to the circumstances and legal system of individual countries (Leisink 1999). ILO conventions do not cover minimum wages, meaning that countries can still maintain a competitive advantage in this key area of employment relations (Singh and Zammit 2004).

Globalization enthusiasts contend that since the presence of trade unions increases labour costs in developing countries, and thus impedes investment, restrictions on union activity are rational, and indeed desirable, if competitiveness and prosperity are to be advanced (Bhagwati 2004; Wolf 2004). But such an approach fails to appreciate that a union presence could work to the benefit of employers (Elliott and Freeman 2003). Unions may encourage firms to seek other, potentially more advantageous, ways of generating improvements in labour productivity rather than simply by exerting downward pressure on wages and conditions.

Countries like South Korea, for example, have experienced tremendous economic growth in recent decades, stimulated largely by capital investment and skills development, rather than by intensive, low-wage production techniques (van Roozendaal 2002). The presence of independent trade unions also helps to encourage better, and more transparent, corporate governance, helping to mitigate the corruption which often hinders a more equitable and efficient distribution of wealth in developing countries (Palley 2004).

Nevertheless, the case for international labour standards does not rest on economic grounds alone. Rather, they are often advanced as a means of stimulating social justice, including dignity at work, something that has informed the perspective of the ILO in particular (Leisink 1999). There are some interventions, such as the abolition of child labour, for example, which might be seen as basic, and thus universally applicable, human rights regardless of context. There is an argument that while child labour may be undesirable, it is nonetheless an indispensable feature of economic and social development in some societies because the additional wages are a vital contribution to family income. However, it is doubtful that economic development is contingent upon the practice of widespread child labour. Rather, its existence helps to keep wages low to the advantage of unscrupulous employers (Tsogas 2001).

The assumption that a system of international labour standards is inimical to globalization, free trade, and increased prosperity is far too simplistic. Indeed, in so far as it has the potential to raise living standards in poorer nations, and give the internationalization of economic activity greater support and legitimacy in richer ones, a system of international labour standards can be regarded as an integral feature of the globalization process (Elliott and Freeman 2003).

2.4.3 Approaches to international labour standards

There are a number of potential ways of regulating employment relationships through international labour standards. We have already considered the efforts made by the global union federations to conclude international framework agreements with multinational companies (see Section 2.3.3), and have examined the role of the International Labour Organization (ILO) (Section 2.4.2). Our concern here is to specify the main approaches to international labour standards: multilateral action by more than one country, including the ILO's efforts, the inclusion of so-called 'social clauses' in trade agreements that deal with labour rights issues, and the efforts of multinational companies themselves to develop voluntary codes of conduct (see Table 2.6).

The ILO is the most obvious expression of the multilateral approach in action. During the 1990s and 2000s, however, there have been calls from some quarters for a more rigorous multilateral regime, set against the pursuit of global free trade. Following years

Table 2.6 The main approaches to promoting international labour standards

Type of approach	Main features
International framework agreements	Negotiated, company-specific, and non-binding arrangements concluded between global union federations and leading multinational companies
Multilateral efforts through the ILO	A quasi-legal, non-company-specific approach to setting labour standards, based mainly on encouraging and supporting countries in their efforts to ratify and comply with ILO conventions
Social clauses in trade agreements	A non-company-specific approach which involves inserting binding clauses that deal with labour standards into unilateral, bilateral, or multilateral trade agreements between different countries
Multinational corporate codes of conduct	Unilateral, company-specific, and non-binding arrangements established by multinational companies designed to promote minimum labour standards in their supply chains

of negotiations, the World Trade Organization (WTO) was established in 1995 with the purpose of determining a global framework within which free trade could flourish.

In some quarters, within the United States labour movement for example, the formation of the WTO was viewed as an opportunity to enact a multilateral set of labour standards linked to free trade (Tsogas 2000; van Roozendaal 2002). The idea is that an obligation to uphold certain minimum labour standards, in the form of a so-called 'social clause', would be a condition of entry into the global free trade system ushered in by the WTO. Countries that failed to comply with the social clause, or failed to enforce it effectively, could thus face penalties in the form of trade sanctions.

Following sustained opposition from many developing countries, who were hostile to what they interpreted as blatant protectionism, the WTO, in its 1996 Singapore Declaration, rejected the idea of a social clause. Opposition stemmed from the belief that linking a country's ability to trade internationally to the operation of a minimum set of labour standards would put many developing countries at a competitive disadvantage. There are also doubts about whether the WTO is an appropriate vehicle for promoting labour standards given that its meetings are attended by trade ministers whose main concern is with promoting free trade, not employment rights and protections (Hepple 2005).

Nevertheless, labour activists, particularly those in the United States, continued to campaign for the inclusion of a social clause. The 1999 WTO meeting in Seattle, which was arranged to accelerate the liberalization of global trade, was the target of massive protests, not just by representatives of worldwide labour, but also from other groups opposed to the neo-liberal thrust of the globalization process. While the Seattle talks resulted in no further progress being made in respect of world trade liberalization, the activities of the protestors nonetheless ensured that debates about international labour standards received greater publicity (Tsogas 2001). So far, however, efforts 'to integrate labour rights into the multilateral world trading and financial systems have so far failed' (Hepple 2005: 128).

That said, though, labour standards have been linked to trade agreements concluded on a unilateral or bilateral basis, those reached between individual countries or groups of countries, and also at a regional level. Essentially, 'regional' arrangements to promote labour standards are linked to the development of free trade agreements between groups of countries, of which the EU's 'social dimension' (discussed in Chapter 3), and the North American Free Trade Agreement's (NAFTA) labour side agreement are the most prominent examples (see Box 2.10).

The bilateral approach involves including social clauses concerned with labour standards in trade agreements between individual countries or groups of countries; those between the United States and Jordan, and the United States and Singapore, for example (Kuruvilla and Verma 2006). The unilateral approach is marked by efforts by countries or groups of countries 'to secure compliance with specified labour standards by imposing trade and financial sanctions against countries that do not observe them, or by granting them trade or other preferences for doing so' (Hepple 2005: 89). Both the European Union (EU) and the United States, for example, operate Generalized System of Preferences (GSP) regimes whereby developing countries are given favourable trading rights in exchange for agreeing to abide by minimum labour standards. In respect of the US regime, there is some evidence that the GSP process may have had a positive impact on employment conditions. It led to the first union recognition agreement in Guatemala's EPZ factories, for example (Compa 2001).

The failure of the multilateral approach may have encouraged further activity of a bilateral and unilateral kind (Kuruvilla and Verma 2006). However, the GSP process is

INTERNATIONAL PERSPECTIVE 2.10

The North American Free Trade Agreement and labour standards

The North American Free Trade Agreement (NAFTA) was instituted in 1994 as a free-trade area incorporating the United States, Canada, and Mexico. As a result of pressure generated by American unions, the US government, under the presidency of Bill Clinton, insisted upon, and achieved, a side agreement governing labour conditions—the North American Agreement on Labor Cooperation (NAALC). It obliges the three governments to ensure that certain stated principles, such as the freedom of workers to organize in trade unions, are promoted within their own national-level employment regimes (Teague 2003). National Administrative Offices in each of the three countries deal with complaints that national labour laws have been transgressed in some way in one of the other countries.

There is evidence that the process has encouraged some slight improvements in employment rights in parts of the Mexican *maquiladora* sector. However, NAALC 'does not tie any of the participating countries to international labour standards. Nor does it have the capacity to make extra-national labour market rules' (Teague 2003: 441). In effect, all NAALC does, then, is offer a mechanism to ensure that the three governments comply with their own respective domestic labour legislation. Unlike the European Union's 'social dimension', which, as we see in Chapter 3, involves a degree of supranational regulation of employment relations, that is above the level of the nation-state, NAALC 'appears to have been deliberately designed to prevent supranational forms of regulatory or policy action on labour matters' (Teague 2003: 448). One should thus not put any faith in the capacity of this agreement to initiate substantial improvements in labour standards. Rather, it was established to overcome opposition to NAFTA, a free trade agreement that enormously benefits American multinationals operating in Mexico.

extremely susceptible to political interference. According to Tsogas (2001: 109), 'no close ally of the United States has ever been removed from the GSP programme'. Thus it would be unwise to expect that bilateral and unilateral approaches to promoting international labour standards will do much to improve employment conditions worldwide.

A further approach to promoting labour standards concerns the voluntary efforts of multinationals themselves to establish, and get their suppliers to abide by, corporate codes of conduct governing employment practices and working conditions. Such private regulation has become increasingly commonplace since the 1990s, particularly within the sportswear and fashion industries, as companies responded to trade union campaigns and consumer pressures for reform by instituting corporate codes which supposedly govern labour standards in their supply chains (Hepple 2005). A corporate code of conduct is 'a formal statement specifying the ethical standards that a [multinational] company holds and applies to the factories of its suppliers or to its trade partners' (Ngai 2005: 102).

The sportswear company Nike claims that its code dates back to 1991. In its current form, it obliges contractors not to employ workers aged below 18 in the production of footwear or below 16 in the production of clothing goods, accessories, and equipment. Nike is also a member of the Fair Labor Association (FLA), a body that also includes Puma and Reebok within its membership. The FLA publishes its own code of conduct which, as well as requiring member firms to ensure that their suppliers comply with local labour laws, also mandates them to respect workers' rights to organize in trade unions and bargain collectively.

In Britain, the Ethical Trading Initiative (ETI), which includes Tesco, Marks and Spencer, and WH Smith among its members, as well as the Trades Union Congress (TUC) and leading non-governmental organizations like Oxfam, fulfils a similar function. Its 'base code' requires its member companies to source their products from suppliers who, among other things, respect workers' rights to form trade unions and pay 'living wages', defined as 'enough to meet basic needs and to provide discretionary income'. See Box 2.11 for the key elements of the ETI's Base Code.

There is some evidence that the presence of a code, particularly where it is rigorously enforced, through some kind of independent verification arrangement for example, is associated with improvements in labour standards. Where codes based on the ETI's model exist there are signs of improved health and safety provision and better treatment of workers by local employers. In the Costa Rican banana industry, for example, the implementation of a corporate code of conduct led to a fall in the levels of sexual harassment and verbal abuse. However, codes have done little to challenge established discriminatory practices based on gender and ethnicity. Nor have they made much progress in helping workers to organize freely in trade unions (Barrientos and Smith 2006).

Yet the extent to which corporate codes of conduct, which of course have no legal force, can generate effective international labour standards is questionable. For example, we have already seen that, despite Nike's claims to the contrary and the provisions of its code of conduct, some of its suppliers appear to have still been using child labour in Cambodia (BBC 2000). Many US retailers instituted codes of conduct only because of consumer pressure, not from a genuine commitment to improving working conditions in the developing world (Compa 2001); they are sometimes established with the aim of improving a company's public relations image (O'Brien 2002). Trade unions often

LEGISLATION AND POLICY 2.11

Elements of the Ethical Trading Initiative's 'base code'

The ETI's 'Base Code' consists of nine sections which cover the following topics:

- the night for employment to be freely chosen (e.g. there is no forced labour);
- the rights of workers to freedom of association in trade unions and to bargain collectively;
- the provision of safe and hygienic working environment;
- the eradication of child labour;
- the payment of a living wage, enough to meet basic needs and to provide some discretionary income;
- working hours that are not excessive (e.g. workers shall not on a regular basis be required to work for more than 48 hours per week);
- the prohibition of discrimination on a number of grounds, including race, nationality, gender, and trade union membership;
- the provision of regular employment; and
- the prohibition of harsh and inhumane treatment of workers by employers, such as physical abuse and sexual harassment.

doubt the value of corporate codes, viewing them as a weak approach to promoting improvements in labour standards, particularly where there are no independent verification arrangements (Kuruvilla and Verma 2006).

Nevertheless, in the face of vigorous anti-sweatshop and other activist campaigns, which sometimes involve unions, companies such as Nike and Reebok have taken steps to strengthen their codes and subject them to a greater degree of independent scrutiny (Elliott and Freeman 2003). Since the late 1990s, many multinationals have responded to the criticism that their codes of conduct are ineffective by instituting improvements in monitoring arrangements, including opening them up to external scrutiny (e.g. Frenkel and Kim 2004; Locke et al. 2007).

However, there are a number of problems with monitoring arrangements in practice. In particular, suppliers have become adept at misleading auditors, giving the false impression that the code is being properly enforced, when the reality is rather different. Workers and managers in supplier factories report that codes are frequently violated in practice (Egels-Zendén 2007; Ngai 2005). In advance of inspection visits, workers are often coached by their employers to give positive answers to the auditors. Both the workers and their employers have a vested interest in asserting that the codes are being complied with; otherwise a multinational might change to another supplier, threatening the viability of the firm and putting jobs at risk. A Chinese worker was clearly aware of the danger:

> You know we are afraid of losing production orders. We also don't want to give wrong answers and get into trouble. (Ngai 2005: 107)

A further problem with corporate codes is that while they might promote improvements in labour standards, this often comes at a price. Take the case of a Chinese factory that makes sports shoes for Reebok, for example. The only way that the firm could afford to comply with the specifications of Reebok's code, while still being profitable, was by intensifying work and implementing a payment scheme that disadvantaged the workforce (Yu 2008). Multinational companies expect suppliers in developing countries to abide by the terms of their codes, but they rarely give them any money to do so. There is some hypocrisy here. MNCs expect suppliers to comply with their codes, but they also put pressure on them to produce goods at as low a cost as possible, with the threat to switch production to another firm hanging in the background if necessary. See Box 2.12 for details of allegations that leading UK retailers have violated elements of the ETI's Base Code.

Since they are private, voluntary arrangements there is a high level of variation in respect of both the content of codes (Hepple 2005), and also their effectiveness. The presence of an independent trade union, for example, can help to ensure that codes operate to the benefit of workers in a more sustained way (Frenkel and Kim 2004). We should recognize, though, that corporate codes of conduct are essentially managerial interventions, designed with managerial aims in mind; they are not put in place to foster the better representation of workers' interests (Ngai 2005).

The most effective way of improving labour standards would be to involve workers themselves, particularly by allowing them to organize in independent trade unions. But for the most part, this is the one thing that codes do not encourage. There is also little knowledge and awareness of codes among the workers they are intended to help (Kuruvilla and Verma 2006). All this suggests that we should be careful not to assume that the presence of corporate codes of conduct necessarily benefits workers in developing countries.

INSIGHT INTO PRACTICE 2.12

Flouting the code?

Leading UK retail chains like Primark, Asda, and Tesco, who are members of the Ethical Trading Initiative, have been accused of sourcing clothes from factories in Bangladesh with poor labour standards. An investigation in 2006 by the charity War on Want found numerous examples of labour practices that violated the ETI's Base Code. Among other things, its report accuses UK retailers of selling garments that have been made in factories where workers experience gross exploitation, for instance:

- extremely low wages, as little as five pence per hour in some cases, which are by no means enough for the workers to live on;
- excessive working hours, in some cases more than 80 hours per week;
- complaints that workers who complain that they have been sexually harassed are then sacked; and
- poor health and safety standards, such as inaccessible fire exits.

War on Want claims that pressure from retailers to keep the costs of production low, and thus ensure that the prices of items in their shops, such as jeans, t-shirts, and dresses, are cheap, mean that factories have no alternative other than to violate the terms of the ETI's Base Code. The retailers responded to the allegations by denying that pressure to cut production costs resulted in exploitation, emphasizing that their suppliers must comply with the appropriate ethical standards, and stressing that any violations of labour standards would be investigated.

Sources
The Guardian, 8 December 2006; BBC News website, 8 December 2006

SECTION SUMMARY AND FURTHER READING

- There is ample evidence that globalization has led to a 'race to the bottom' with respect to labour standards around the world. Multinational companies, particularly those responsible for clothing and sportswear brands, use their economic power to squeeze the margins of their suppliers, eroding pay and working conditions.

- This has generated renewed interest in the desirability of regulating labour standards on an international basis. Though open to criticism that they hinder economic growth in a way that unfairly protects jobs in developing countries, international labour standards can stimulate improved social and economic well-being.

- Voluntary efforts to promote improved labour standards by MNCs themselves, in the form of corporate codes of conduct, have a positive effect in some circumstances; however, weak compliance and enforcement arrangements mean that their overall impact is limited.

The Fair Labor Association (USA) and the Ethical Trading Initiative (UK) both promote good labour standards among their member companies (http://www.fairlabor.org; http://www.ethicaltrade.org). The International Labour Organization (ILO) is a key source of information on international labour standards (http://www.ilo.org). See Wolf (2004) for the economic case against international labour standards, and Palley (2004) for a contrary perspective. For further information about international labour standards, see the work of George Tsogas (1999, 2000, 2001), Bob Hepple (2005) and the overview provided by Rubery and Grimshaw (2003: Chapter 10).

 Visit our Online Resource Centre for web links to sites connected to this section. www.oxfordtextbooks.co.uk/williams_adamsmith2e

Conclusion

Perhaps the most notable theme to have emerged from our assessment of the implications of economic change for contemporary employment relations is the extent to which the competitive pressures associated with a capitalist market economy have impelled employers to find ever more efficient ways of managing labour, resulting in downward pressure on labour conditions. In the UK, this can be seen, for example, in the preference of employers for flexible working arrangements that make workers more 'disposable' (Beynon et al. 2002); see the introductory case study of BMW, for example. For workers, the outcomes of this intensification of market competition are greater job insecurity and higher workloads, matters we consider in Chapter 8, as employers seek to shift the terms of the wage-work bargain in a direction favourable to their own interests. On a global scale, the efforts of powerful multinational companies to undermine national systems of employment relations, and to shift production to locations where it is cheaper to employ staff, are major consequences of the process of economic globalization. Moreover, the erosion of labour standards in the developing world is further evidence of how the neo-liberal process of economic globalization, as an intensification of capitalist relations, often undermines workers' interests.

Economic change, then, far from inducing a more cooperative character to employment relations, has made the potential for conflict in the employment relationship more starkly apparent. For many workers in developing countries, who produce clothes, shoes, and other consumer items for western markets, conditions are often extremely poor, and their jobs precarious. The potential for conflict of interest that lies at the heart of the employment relationship is perhaps most readily apparent in the export processing zones and their like, which are increasingly dotted around the developing world.

Although the relentless process of capitalist restructuring and the associated intensification of competitive pressures described in this chapter would appear to be wholly advantageous to employers, one would be mistaken in assuming that they have made both national systems of employment relations and organized labour impotent. For one thing, we have established that, despite the convergence pressures associated with globalization, national-level diversity remains an important feature of contemporary employment relations. Furthermore, the conditions under which labour operates make the mobilization of workers, and their organization in trade unions, increasingly viable. As long as the exploitative capitalist employment relationship endures, workers will endeavour to combine and look to secure improvements by means of collective action.

Assignment and discussion questions

1   To what extent do people working as self-employed freelancers or sub-contractors have more control over their labour than would be the case if they were employees?

2   Discuss the proposition that part-time and temporary working arrangements benefit both employers and workers.

3   What are the main ways in which globalization has affected employment relations?

4   'Investment in developing countries by multinational companies leads to improvements in living standards by providing opportunities for paid employment that would otherwise not be available. Such investment should therefore be encouraged.' Discuss.

5   Critically assess the main strengths and weakness of voluntary codes of conduct as arrangements for delivering improvements in international labour standards.

 Visit our Online Resource Centre for web links to sites connected to this section.
www.oxfordtextbooks.co.uk/williams_adamsmith2e

Take your learning further: online resource centre

Visit the Online Resource Centre that accompanies this book to enrich your understanding of Chapter 2: Employment relations in the contemporary economy. Explore web links, test yourself using an interactive flashcard glossary, and keep up to date with the latest developments in the area.

  http://www.oxfordtextbooks.co.uk/orc/williams_adamsmith2e.

Chapter case study

Union organization of 'atypical' workers

One characteristic of contemporary employment is the number of workers employed on fixed-term and similar contracts. These include semi- and unskilled casual workers in industries such as hospitality and road haulage, and those with specialist technical skills, for example people working in journalism, and television and film production. The nature of such employment means that they may work for several different employers in the course of a relatively short period of time. This, then, is a very different relationship from that of the majority of employees, who have 'open-ended' contracts with one employer. While some may work alongside a substantial number of permanent staff, others, for example in film production, may comprise the majority, or even the whole of the workforce. For trade unions, such types of work pose particular challenges in respect of recruitment and representation and, in some cases, the type of service they provide.

Trade unions normally rely on local representatives, for example shop stewards, or work colleagues, to recruit new workers into membership. Such representatives may not exist where the majority of staff are on fixed-term contracts, or, where they do, they may focus on recruiting and representing permanent staff. Furthermore, workers may consider the costs of union membership not to be worthwhile if their period with any individual organization is relatively short. Even where unions succeed in recruitment, the intermittent nature of working arrangements often means that workers allow their membership to lapse when they stop working for that employer.

As well as finding alternative recruitment methods, unions may need to provide specific services that remain valuable to workers while they are between assignments. This might include a reduced level of subscription for these periods, access to training to maintain skills and knowledge which will continue to make them attractive to employers recruiting both temporary and permanent staff, and specific legal advice relevant to non-standard employment. Heery et al. (2004) point out that such services may provide a substitute to the benefits that would otherwise be available from employers. These include sickness and maternity benefits, health insurance, and pension advice. They also note that some unions provide information on job vacancies.

The possible absence of any existing workplace representatives, as noted above, raises questions about how unions can fulfil their traditional representational role on behalf of these workers, for example in grievance and disciplinary hearings. The appointment or election of a 'temporary representative' is one possibility, or full-time union officers might fulfil such a role. However, the former may not possess the depth of skills and knowledge needed to be fully effective, while full-time officers may have competing demands on their time. Where temporary workers are employed alongside permanent staff, shop stewards may not see the interests of mobile workers as a priority compared to their role in representing employees of the organization.

Sources: Adam-Smith (1997); Heery et al. (2004)

1. What are the problems faced by trade unions in representing the interests of atypical workers, and how might these be overcome?

2   Does this group of workers offer unions a means of increasing their membership, and of demonstrating the relevance of unionization to all categories of workers?

3

The politics of
employment relations

Chapter objectives:

The main objectives of this chapter are to:

* demonstrate the important influence which the political context exercises over employment relations;

* examine the main public policy developments in employment relations;

* assess and interpret the main features of Labour government policy towards employment relations after it was elected to office in 1997;

* explore the relationship between the Labour party and the trade unions; and

* consider the implications of European Union policy and the broader process of European integration for employment relations.

3.1 Introduction

In this chapter, the second of those that seek to contextualize contemporary employment relations developments, our concern is with the political dimension of the subject area. One of the most distinctive features of employment relations as a field of study is that it is highly politicized; in other words, employment relations arrangements, institutions, and processes are infused by, and cannot be understood without reference to, politics. The wage-work bargain itself is a political phenomenon since, as we saw in the introduction to this book, the employment relationship is a power relationship and thus cannot be understood simply as an economic process. Moreover, the state is an important employment relations actor, as we saw in Chapter 1.

In this chapter, we consider the implications of contemporary public policy developments, and explore the implications for employment relations of European integration, including the influence of the European Union's (EU) 'social dimension'. We start, in Section 3.2, by providing some historical context, outlining the main developments in public policy prior to 1997 when the Labour government under Tony Blair was first elected to office. We then examine,in Section 3.3, the main features of Labour policy towards employment relations, and look at aspects of the relationship between Labour and the unions. The implications of European integration for employment relations, and the impact of EU legislation, are then explored in Section 3.4. This chapter, then, aims to help readers more readily appreciate the importance of political developments to contemporary employment relations.

Introductory case study

The European Union's Agency Workers' Directive

In June 2008, European Union (EU) employment ministers agreed to enact legislation, in the form of an EU Directive, which would give workers employed through temporary agencies an entitlement to the same pay and holidays, among other things, as workers directly employed to do the same job. The agreement came six years after the legislation was first proposed. The lengthy delay was in large part due to the UK government's opposition to the proposed directive. It agreed with employers' bodies that such legislation would impede the UK's labour market flexibility and hinder competitiveness. Following pressure from the trade unions, which supported the legislation, the UK government convened talks between the Confederation of British Industry (CBI), on behalf of employers, and the Trades Union Congress. In May 2008 they agreed a compromise whereby agency workers would have to serve a qualifying period of 12 weeks before they were entitled to equivalent pay and conditions. With this deal in place, the UK government dropped its opposition to the agency workers directive, facilitating the following month's agreement between EU employment ministers.

The lengthy, tortuous progress of this piece of EU employment legislation is instructive for what it tells us about the politics of employment relations in a number of respects. First, it demonstrates the increasing influence of EU legislation on employment relations in the UK, particularly since the Labour government under Tony Blair signed up to the Social Chapter in 1997. Second, the case demonstrates that, despite signing the Social Chapter, during the 2000s Labour's policy approach in employment relations has become increasingly dominated by the need to respect employers' demands for flexibility, rather than improve protections for workers. Third, following on from this the case highlights the contrast that exists between the UK, with its emphasis on limiting legislative intervention in employment relations, and the more regulated approach favoured by other EU countries. Fourth, this case is also instructive for what it reveals about the influence of the trade unions over Labour. As the chapter demonstrates, the Labour party relies heavily on the trade unions for funds; for the most part, however, the unions get little in exchange for their support. The agreement on the agency workers' issue, however, indicates that while the unions may not enjoy a lot of influence, the pressure they exert on a Labour government cannot be entirely disregarded.

3.2 State policy and employment relations in Britain

In order to understand contemporary developments in employment relations policy properly, key elements of the historical background need to be examined. In this section, we consider developments in state policy up until the period of Labour governments under Tony Blair and Gordon Brown from 1997 onwards. Our starting point is to explain the concept of 'voluntarism' and the important influence it has historically exercised over employment relations policy. We then consider the growth of state intervention in employment relations during the middle part of the twentieth century, before examining the main features of Conservative policy towards employment relations under the governments of Margaret Thatcher and John Major between 1979 and 1997.

3.2.1 Voluntarism and employment relations in Britain

An appreciation of the importance of voluntarism is crucial to understanding the nature of employment relations in Britain. What, then, is meant by the term 'voluntarism'? In essence, it refers to the general absence of direct state intervention in employment relations and a preference for the terms of the employment relationship to be determined voluntarily by employers and trade unions, without state interference.

The roots of the voluntaristic tradition can be traced as far back as the seventeenth and eighteenth centuries. During this period, the development of capitalism in Britain was informed by the complementary ideologies of economic *laissez-faire* and market individualism within which the recognition of private property interests predominated (Fox 1985a; Hyman 1975). Nascent capitalist entrepreneurs were resistant to state intervention in their affairs and preferred, wherever possible, to handle their own affairs. Under the common law, with its emphasis on individual rights, the trade unions, as collective organizations of workers, were treated as criminal conspiracies acting in 'restraint of trade' (Clegg, Fox, and Thompson 1964). As well as 'master and servant' legislation that tied individual labourers to their employer, this made it very difficult for unions to operate without committing criminal or civil offences (Price 1986).

The dominance of market individualism and *laissez-faire* ideologies provided the foundation for the development of 'collective *laissez-faire*' as the dominant state approach to employment relations in Britain, a preference that employers should deal with employment relations matters, and with unions, themselves, without direct intervention by the state (Davies and Freedland 1993). The existing legal framework enabled employers to deal with union activities in ways that did not threaten their interests too severely, and thus obviated the need for more explicitly repressive measures.

Why, though, did the trade unions come to place so much faith in voluntarism? They were disinclined to look to the state for legislation that would enhance the labour interest and, suspicious of the pro-employer bias of state organs, especially the judiciary, were to develop a considerable attachment to the principle of 'free collective bargaining', based on the strength of their collective organization, as the most effective means of regulating the employment relationship (Flanders 1974).

The absence of state intervention in relationships between workers, unions, and employers is generally thought to have had a pronounced and long-standing influence on employment relations during the twentieth century (Kahn-Freund 1964). While some legislation was considered desirable, in the area of health and safety for example, unlike many other countries the regulation of the employment relationship in Britain came to be determined largely by a combination of collective bargaining and managerial prerogative, without the development of a comprehensive system of statutory employment rights (Fox 1985a; Hyman 2001b).

Howell (2005), though, contends that the state exercised a more profound influence over the development of employment relations in Britain than has hitherto been acknowledged, not so much through legislation, but rather by establishing and maintaining the conditions under which collective bargaining thrived. Moreover, during periods of sustained industrial unrest, such as in the years immediately following the conclusion of the 1914–18 war, the state acted promptly to take measures designed to repress trade unions and their ability to undertake strike action, including the enactment, in 1920, of an Emergency Powers Act which enabled the state to deal more effectively with large-scale industrial disputes, including the provision of troops as strike-breakers (Geary 1985).

This reminds us not to assume that the British state exercises neutrality in employment relations matters. Judicial hostility to organized labour—laws were interpreted in ways that benefited employers, for example (Fox 1985a)—frequently undermined unions' legitimacy. This demonstrates that the state's role in employment relations is far removed from being that of a neutral, disinterested observer. Rather, it is largely concerned with providing an environment in which businesses can thrive, something that in Britain has, for the reasons we have outlined above, generally implied limited direct state intervention in employment relations, but does not rule out a more coercive approach should it be dictated by circumstances (Hyman 1975).

3.2.2 Growing state intervention and employment relations

In the period after World War Two (1940s–1970s) there was a notable accentuation in the degree of state intervention in employment relations, something that posed a considerable challenge to the established voluntaristic system. For one thing, both Labour and Conservative governments supported full employment as the principal goal of economic policy. As part of the social-democratic post-war 'consensus', active government intervention to achieve this goal was deemed desirable (Crouch 1995). However, full employment caused upward pressure on wages, generated inflationary pressures in the economy, and consequently damaged economic competitiveness. Thus from the late 1940s onwards, governments sought union agreement, largely through the TUC, to restrain their wage-bargaining behaviour (S. Kessler 1994).

By the time of the 1964–70 Labour governments, these voluntary 'incomes policies' had developed from relatively short-term and *ad hoc* interventions designed to overcome short-term economic difficulties, becoming a characteristic feature of attempts to manage the economy (Crouch 1977). Given that they posed a major challenge to the principle of 'free collective bargaining', the development of incomes policies, which for a period of time during the late 1960s even had statutory force, helped to erode the hitherto dominant voluntarist system (Clegg 1979). Nevertheless, prompted by growing membership discontent, during the late 1960s the unions became more hostile to incomes policies, particularly statutory ones, something that impeded the ability of governments to incorporate and integrate the unions in processes of state economic management (Hyman 1975).

Alongside the development of incomes policies, during the 1960s and 1970s the development and evolution of tripartite arrangements for economic and industrial policy formulation was further evidence not only of greater state involvement in economic planning and management, but also of government efforts to incorporate, with business representatives, union leaderships and the TUC into state policy-making processes (Davies and Freedland 1993). Thus 'tripartism' refers to the participation of unions, employers, and government representatives in operating state institutions. In 1962, for example, the National Economic Development Council (NEDC) was established with government, business, and union participation. While it is important not to overstate the level of union influence during this period (Waddington and Whitston 1995), the trade union movement came to be characterized as a 'governing institution' (Middlemas 1979), or as an 'estate of the realm' (Taylor 1993).

Voluntarism was further eroded during the 1960s and 1970s by the growing statutory regulation of the employment relationship in areas such as redundancy payments, the dismissal of employees, equal pay, and sex and race discrimination. Hitherto, the prevailing assumption was that, apart from some exceptions like health and safety at work, individual employment rights were more effectively secured through collective bargaining. For a number of reasons, including economic efficiency, social change, and pressure from workers for improved rights, this period saw a substantial growth, which continues in the present period, in the 'juridification', that is the regulation of social and economic activity by the law, of the employment relationship (Davies and Freedland 1993).

The involvement of union leaderships and the TUC in the formulation of state policy marked a clear attempt to control the behaviour of the trade unions by involving and incorporating them into the machinery of the state. The success of such a strategy depended, however, upon the willingness of workers to accept it, something that could not be assumed (Hyman 1989).

In the area of employment relations policy, the 1974–79 Labour government was dominated by the experience of the so-called 'social contract'. In exchange for legislation designed to promote genuine social reforms, the TUC accepted the need for voluntary wage restraint as a means of reducing inflation and securing improvements in economic competitiveness (Davies and Freedland 1993). To what extent did the social contract resemble the corporatist arrangements characteristic of other European countries? By corporatism, or neo-corporatism as it is referred to in some accounts, we are referring to the way in which government intervention to manage the economy is achieved by integrating, or incorporating, employers' associations and trade unions into state policy-making processes (Davies and Freedland 1993). In particular, employers and trade unions agree to restrain their wage bargaining autonomy in the interest of long-term economic stability and consensus in return for influence in state policy formulation and, for the unions, favourable policy goals.

To a crucial extent, though, the British experience fell well short of genuine corporatism, although it is fair to suggest that corporatist 'tendencies' or 'pressures' were present during this period (Crouch 1977; Davies and Freedland 1993; Strinati 1982). The ethos of voluntarism proved to be rather too resilient to enable corporatism to prosper in Britain, not least because of the reluctance of the TUC and employers' groups to commit themselves to change, as well as their inability to control their affiliates and members. The extent of corporatism in Britain, then, was largely restricted to the institution of *ad hoc*, short-term efforts designed to relieve immediate economic crises, or as a means of conflict avoidance, for which the term 'bargained corporatism' has been deemed appropriate (Crouch 1977, 1979).

Despite its ambitious intentions, in practice the social contract ended up as little more than a conventional incomes policy since, after 1976, the government came under increasing pressure, not least from the International Monetary Fund, which made it a loan condition, to scale back its social policies in order to pursue austerity measures (Marsh 1992). Wage restraint policies provoked the wave of industrial action that affected Britain during 1978–79, a period which became popularly known as the 'winter of discontent' (see Box 3.1).

The development of corporatist 'tendencies' in the 1970s was part of an attempt by the state to accommodate trade union power, to shape and control it, in order to sustain economic growth and the long-term viability of the capitalist market economy. But it is important to acknowledge the repressive basis of this attempt to incorporate the union interest (Hyman 1989). Moreover, union leaders were also influenced by pressure from their members, which inevitably limited the extent to which a whole-hearted strategy of incorporation could ever be realized.

Perhaps the most notable trend of the second half of the twentieth century was the growth of state intervention and the concomitant erosion of voluntarism. How, though, did state policy evolve under the Conservative administrations of the 1980s and 1990s?

3.2.3 Public policy under the Conservatives: towards neo-liberalism?

On entering office in 1979, the Conservative government's economic policy was dominated by a concern to reduce inflation through tight control of the money supply, and an explicit abandonment of the objective of full employment. It placed a greater emphasis on the free play of market forces as a source of enhanced economic competitiveness, rejecting Keynesian methods of demand management as a tool of

HISTORICAL PERSPECTIVE 3.1

The 'winter of discontent' 1978–9

Whenever there is an increase in the level of strike activity in Britain, politicians and media commentators invariably speculate about the parallels with the industrial unrest of 1978–9 which popularly became known as the 'winter of discontent', a Shakespearean phrase in origin. So what was the 'winter of discontent'? The term is used to refer to the series of strikes which affected road haulage, transport, and public services during the winter of 1978–9. The industrial unrest of this period is often presented as the result of excessive union militancy; a sign that the trade unions had become too powerful. In reality, however, it expressed the profound discontent experienced by many workers, particularly in the public services, who were unhappy at the relative decline in their standard of living as a result of wage restraint policies. Nevertheless, the strikes, and particularly the way in which they were presented by the largely anti-union media, undermined the popularity and legitimacy of the Labour government under James Callaghan, helping to usher in a Conservative administration under the leadership of Margaret Thatcher in May 1979.

economic policy. Moreover, the Conservatives had little regard for tripartite methods of economic policy formulation and, over time, abolished most of the state institutions that exemplified tripartism (Crouch 1995). Thus there was a 'distancing of unions from the corridors of power' (Davies and Freedland 1993: 427).

The trend towards increasing juridification of employment relations did, however, continue under the Conservatives, although with a markedly different emphasis as they oversaw a large-scale programme of employment relations reform, by means of six major Acts of Parliament between 1980 and 1993, largely designed to weaken the trade unions. This constituted 'probably the most single-minded and sustained attack on the position of a major and previously legitimate social force to have been undertaken anywhere under modern democratic conditions' (Crouch 1996: 120). Excessive union power was perceived to be a major constraint on British economic competitiveness; thus the reform of employment relations was central to attempts to boost the economy.

Prior to entering office, the Conservatives had given little thought to the reduction of union power, beyond the desirability of doing so (Dunn and Metcalf 1996), though the lessons of the fate of Edward Heath's Conservative administration, which, in the early 1970s, had attempted to use the law to effect a wide-ranging transformation of employment relations, and failed, weighed heavily in Conservative thinking (Marsh 1992). What, then, were the Conservatives' principal aims in reforming the legislation governing unions and employment relations in Britain?

First, they wished to reduce the power of trade unions in the economy (Davies and Freedland 1993). Legislation was passed that severely restricted the ability of unions to undertake lawful industrial action, in particular by mandating that unions must win the support of a majority of members in a properly constituted postal ballot; see Chapter 9 for further details. The operation of closed shop arrangements (see Chapter 1) was also outlawed.

Second, Conservative governments were eager to diminish the scope for legitimate political activity by trade unions, something that involved attempts to challenge the links between the unions and the Labour party (Davies and Freedland 1993). Many unions, even those that were not affiliated to the Labour party, maintained political funds and used them for general campaigning purposes. The 1984 Trade Union Act obliged trade unions operating political funds to win the support of their members for such arrangements in a ballot at least once every ten years.

A third aim of the Conservatives' legislative programme was to promote greater internal democracy within trade unions, to restore membership control of union policies and leaderships, and thus, it was anticipated, instil greater moderation in union behaviour (Martin et al. 1995). For example, the Trade Union Act 1984 mandated that union general secretaries and executive bodies be subject to periodic election in a ballot. It was reinforced by the 1988 Employment Act, which made postal ballots mandatory in union elections.

The policy of 'giving unions back to their members' was based on an assumption that the moderate mass of trade union members was being led astray, or coerced, by militant union leaderships into taking unnecessary industrial action, and thus their voice needed to be heard, principally through a greater role for ballots (McIlroy 1991). However, the Conservatives' real aim seems to have been to use the rhetoric of individual member rights as a way of undermining collective union power, thus reducing the effectiveness of trade unionism (Martin et al. 1995). Legislative measures made it easier for individual members both to dissent from, and challenge, collective decision-making processes (McIlroy 1991). The scale of the Conservative governments' legislative reform of employment relations during the 1980s and 1990s is suggestive of a marked shift towards the repression of union activity by the state, something that also extended to the use of its powers to combat industrial disputes (see Box 3.2).

How should we interpret the Conservative's programme of legislative reform? What accounts for such a 'sustained assault' (Howell 2005: 133) on trade unionism in Britain?

Onc approach puts the onus on the ideological character of the Conservatives' programme (Wedderburn 1989). The important influence of the right-wing political

HISTORICAL PERSPECTIVE 3.2

The defeat of the 1984–5 miners' strike

Conservative governments of the 1980s and 1990s did not rely solely on the reform of employment law to suppress trade unionism, as the experience of the 1984–5 miners' strike demonstrates. In March 1984, the leadership of the National Union of Mineworkers (NUM), under Arthur Scargill, called for a national strike in order to defeat the National Coal Board's (NCB) plan, backed by the government, to close twenty pits with the loss of over 100,000 mining jobs. Miners in Yorkshire walked out and were followed by those in other regions, including Scotland and South Wales. The strike was to last for a year. Controversially, the NUM's leadership did not authorize a ballot, largely on the basis that the strike was underway anyway, and many miners in areas where the pits were not under immediate threat of closure, Nottinghamshire for example, only participated reluctantly.

Throughout the course of the dispute, the extensive powers of the state were deployed to ensure that the miners were defeated. In the years preceding the strike, the government had made arrangements for alternative energy supplies, and had built up coal stocks in preparation for a lengthy struggle. A special cabinet sub-committee was instituted, chaired by the prime minister, Margaret Thatcher, to oversee the state's response once the strike had started. Figures associated with the Conservative party, like businessman David Hart for example, helped to arrange support for miners who wished to return to work, and assisted the formation of a breakaway union, the Union of Democratic Mineworkers (UDM) in Nottinghamshire. They also backed legal actions by NUM members against their union for breaching its own rules by not holding a ballot. Eventually, in October 1984 the union had its assets seized, or 'sequestrated', by the courts.

The resources of the Security Service, MI5, were used to undermine the strike's effectiveness; it had an agent placed within the NUM's leadership. Extensive, military-style policing tactics, including the use of roadblocks on motorways, were deployed to prevent NUM pickets from travelling around the country blocking the supply of coal to electricity-generating plants, and obstructing efforts to return to work. Nearly 9,000 miners were arrested in 1984 as a result. In March 1985, after holding out for a year, the NUM called off the strike and organized a return to work, having failed in its attempt to use industrial action to prevent the pit closure programme.

Sources
Beynon (1985); Milne (2004)

scientist Friedrich Hayek is acknowledged. He viewed unions as coercive organizations that used their illegitimate collective power to put pressure on employers to concede improvements in pay and conditions that distorted the free operation of market forces, thus generating adverse economic outcomes, including higher inflation and greater unemployment.

Thus the Conservative legislative programme was underpinned by a coherent set of neo-liberal values and principles associated with the 'new right'. The reform of employment relations was based on a neo-liberal policy perspective which held, among other things, that free markets, deregulation, and weak trade unions were essential for economic competitiveness (Davies and Freedland 2007). See Box 3.3 for the details of how the neo-liberal reform agenda affected employment relations in New Zealand.

An alternative approach emphasizes the pragmatic and opportunistic aspects of Conservative policy-making during the 1980s (Auerbach 1990). Rather than reflecting a coherent neo-liberal ideology, the anti-union laws tended to be passed in response to particular events or were influenced by prevailing circumstances. For example, the measures designed to restrict 'unofficial' industrial action that were included in the 1990 Employment Act resulted from a series of industrial disputes in transport the previous year.

A reasonable conclusion is that the Conservatives' legislative programme was founded upon a combination of neo-liberal ideology and political opportunism (Davies

 INTERNATIONAL PERSPECTIVE 3.3

Neo-liberalism and employment relations in New Zealand

By no means was the UK government the most enthusiastic proponent of neo-liberal policies during the 1980s and 1990s. Prior to the 1980s, economic policy in New Zealand was dominated by the pursuit of full employment, and the use of Keynesian techniques of demand management with which to achieve it. The public policy environment was extremely favourable to trade unionism. Unions benefited from a system of 'compulsory unionism', and the existence of very centralized arrangements for collective bargaining. Following its 1984 election victory, the Labor government, in particular the finance minister Roger Douglas, who was supported by a cadre of enthusiastic and dedicated officials, forced through a series of free market reforms, including the dismantling of the welfare state, the privatization of state-owned industries, and labour market deregulation, to an extent unprecedented elsewhere among the advanced industrialized societies.

The neo-liberal reforms were extended by the right-wing National government, elected in 1990. The 1991 Employment Relations Act did away with the system of national-level collective awards and agreements, which had been the bases of union power, and encouraged employers to establish individual contracts with their staff. The result was a massive fall in the level of trade union membership, and a huge decline in the coverage of collective bargaining. More generally, the neo-liberal programme of reforms generated increases in poverty, inequality, and unemployment, and failed to improve New Zealand's economic performance. After 1999, a left-of-centre Labor/Alliance government halted, and partially reversed, the neo-liberal reforms, and enacted legislation more supportive of collective bargaining and trade unionism.

Sources
Harbridge, Crawford, and Hince (2002); Kay (2003); Kelsey (1995)

and Freedland 1993; Howell 2005). Some measures, though, such as the abolition of the closed shop, for example, do seem to have been driven more by ideology than others (Davies and Freedland 1993). Yet the opportunistic character of much of the Conservatives' later legislative interventions demonstrates that, while the policy regime had become much more repressive, the resilience of the unions compelled the state to respond to particular challenges to its authority as and when they arose (Davies and Freedland 1993).

What were the effects of the Conservative's legislative programme? To what extent did their reforms weaken union power in Britain? We should not ignore the possibility that Conservative governments were only able to enact such restrictive policies because of the degree to which the unions had been weakened by economic developments, such as job losses in manufacturing and increasing levels of unemployment (Dunn and Metcalf 1996).

Nevertheless, the sheer scale of state repression of the unions during this period, of which the legislation was but one part, significantly challenged the legitimacy of trade unionism in Britain. The restrictive legislation governing industrial action seems to have undermined the ability of unions to secure their objectives (see Chapter 9), reducing their power in the economy. The Conservatives were rather less successful in realizing their aim of challenging the political basis of trade union activity, for example by mandating political fund ballots (see Box 3.4).

Efforts to reform the internal government of the trade unions, by encouraging greater 'democracy' as a source of union moderation were similarly unsuccessful. Given the complexity of its demands, legislation stimulated greater centralization of authority in the unions, enhancing authority of union leaders, but reducing members' participation in union affairs (Undy et al. 1996).

There is no evidence that the balloting provisions encouraged moderation; in fact rather the opposite. In general, the obligation that union leaders be elected by postal

---

Employment relations reflection 3.4   The outcome of political fund ballots

Legislation enacted by the Conservatives during the 1980s obliges unions to win the support of a majority of their members in a postal ballot every ten years if they want to continue operating political funds. The Conservatives, who judged that members were opposed to the political activities of their unions and should be given an opportunity to halt them, expected that, when given the choice, they would vote against. However, the results from the first round of political fund ballots conducted in the mid 1980s were 'an outstanding success for the trade union movement' (Leopold 1986: 300). Not only did all the unions with political funds vote to keep them, often with very large majorities in support, but seventeen new ones were also established. In the second and third round of political fund ballots, undertaken during the mid 1990s and mid 2000s respectively, the retention of political funds once again received the strong support of members (Leopold 1997; Leopold 2006). This demonstrates that members support and value the political campaigning activities of their unions. The shopworkers' union USDAW, for example, stressed the importance of maintaining a political fund in order to finance its campaign against Christmas Day working.

ballot at least once every five years seems to have favoured radical challenges to more conservative general secretaries. The 2005 election of Matt Wrack, a left-winger, over the incumbent Andy Gilchrist to the leadership of the Fire Brigades Union (FBU), the result of widespread dissatisfaction with the terms of the settlement of the 2002–03 pay dispute, is a notable example. In thinking that more effective balloting arrangements would induce greater union moderation, Conservative politicians were, then, profoundly mistaken. If anything, union leaders tend to exert a moderating influence on a generally more militant membership.

Overall, then, the Conservative's programme of employment relations reform contributed to the diminution of trade union power in Britain, largely because of the severe constraints legislation imposed on strikes and other forms of industrial action. However, the Conservative's other aims—the depoliticization of the unions and the encouragement of greater union democracy and moderation—do not appear to have been so successful. We should also bear in mind that changes in the economy during the 1980s, such as the decline of manufacturing industry, had weakened the power of the trade unions already, reducing the strength of union opposition to the Conservatives' legislative programme.

SECTION SUMMARY AND FURTHER READING

- For many years, the principle of voluntarism, or collective *laissez-faire*, in which the state abstained from directly intervening in relations between employers, employees, and trade unions, characterized the role of the state in Britain. While it received the support of employers and unions, voluntarism should not be equated with neutrality on the part of the state. Abstentionism favoured the stronger party in the employment relationship, the employer.

- During the 1960s and 1970s, there was a marked increase in the degree of state intervention in employment relations. The imposition of incomes policies, the development of tripartite arrangements, and the growing statutory regulation of the employment relationship all eroded, but did not significantly undermine, the voluntarist ethos. Although the trade unions were given greater influence over state policy-making during this period, it fell well short of genuine corporatism and was largely designed to accommodate trade union power as a means of sustaining economic growth and the long-term viability of the capitalist market economy.

- During the 1980s and 1990s, Conservative governments used the machinery of the state, most notably through the enactment of repressive legislation, to undermine the power and legitimacy of the trade unions. Although it was informed by a neo-liberal ideological agenda, the opportunistic basis of the Conservatives' legislative programme is also evident.

For voluntarism in Britain, see Flanders (1974) and Hyman (2001b). S. Kessler (1994) examines the development of incomes policies. Davies and Freedland (1993) offer the best account of the growth of state intervention in employment relations during the 1960s and 1970s. For a critical overview of the Conservative's anti-union legislation, see McIlroy (1991). Howell (2005) offers a vigorous new approach to understanding the role of the state in employment relations in Britain.

 Visit our Online Resource Centre for web links to sites connected to this section. www.oxfordtextbooks.co.uk/williams_adamsmith2e

3.3 Labour and employment relations in Britain 1997–2009

The landslide election victory enjoyed by the Labour party in May 1997, and its sub-sequent re-election in the general elections of 2001 and 2005, raises two related ques-tions about the development of employment relations in Britain: to what extent did the nature of state policy shift away from the neo-liberal, anti-union approach of the Conservatives, and, following on from this, how far can 1997 be characterized as a 'turn-ing point' (R. Taylor 1998) in British employment relations? We begin by examining the main features of Labour's employment relations policy, supported by illustrative examples. We then interpret Labour's agenda, looking in particular at how far it can be said to have departed from neo-liberalism, before considering aspects of the relationship between Labour and the unions.

3.3.1 Labour's employment relations policies

Having originally opposed the Conservatives' legislative changes, during the early 1990s, the Labour party, following a string of election defeats, revised its employment relations policies, and came to favour retaining most of them. This formed part of a broader shift in Labour party policy towards the endorsement, and indeed the celebration, of a dynamic, free market economy (Coates 2000). In particular, Labour developed a notably enthusiastic acceptance of the desirability of a deregulated labour market as a source of economic competitiveness (e.g. DTI 2006), a marked convergence with the neo-liberal policies that had been followed by the previous Conservative governments. Labour's retention of the bulk of the anti-union legislation it inherited from its Conservative predecessors 'marked a shift in the political consensus of the most significant kind' (Davies and Freedland 2007: 111). Set against this, though, Labour has legislated in the area of employment relations quite extensively, offering working people new sets of rights, including wider protections against unfair discrimination and a minimum wage.

How, then, did state policy in the area of employment relations develop after 1997? Following the election of the Labour government some immediate and highly symbolic interventions were made that were favourable to the trade unions, including the restoration of union rights at the Government Communications Headquarters (GCHQ) (R. Taylor 1998). Although unions have enjoyed greater involvement in policy deliberations, over the level of the National Minimum Wage for example, by no means does this constitute a major revival of tripartism (Davies and Freedland 2007). Yet Labour's legislative programme, by increasing the juridification of employment relations (see Dickens and Hall 2003), held out the promise of a major expansion in the scope of employment rights, something that distinguishes its approach from that of its Conservative predecessors.

Labour's policy interventions in employment relations can be grouped under five main themes (see Box 3.5 for an overview of the relevant legislation).

- Labour has been concerned to encourage greater partnership between employers and trade unions (Brown 2000), something that informed the development of proposals, incorporated into the 1999 Employment Relations Act discussed in Chapter 5, oblig-ing employers to recognize a union for collective bargaining where this is wanted

LEGISLATION AND POLICY 3.5

The main elements of Labour's legislative programme

- Minimum Wage Act (1998): established the National Minimum Wage, and also a procedure for determining its level and scope (see Chapter 7 for further details)
- Employment Relations Act (1999): provided for a new statutory procedure whereby employers would be obliged to recognize a trade union for collective bargaining purposes where there is support from a majority of the workforce (see Chapter 5)
- Employment Act (2002): extended rights to paid maternity leave; introduced two weeks' paid paternity leave; gave parents of young children the 'right' to request flexible working arrangements (see Chapter 4); and provided for new 'three-step' grievance and disciplinary procedures designed to reduce the number of employment tribunal claims from aggrieved workers (see Chapter 9)
- Employment Relations Act (2004): effected revisions to the statutory recognition procedure introduced by the Employment Relations Act (1999)
- Work and Families Act (2006): extended the 'right' to request flexible working arrangements to workers who care for adults; and provided for the extension of paid maternity leave to a year, with the opportunity for some of it to be shared with fathers (see Chapter 4)
- Employment Act (2008): abolished the 'three-step' grievance and disciplinary procedures introduced by the Employment Act (2002)—see Chapter 9; and provided for measures to improve the enforcement of the National Minimum Wage

by a majority of the workforce. Labour's agenda, however, has been marked by an explicitly unitary perspective on social partnership, one that envisages employment relations as being about the development of a 'harmony of interests' (Howell 2004); a union presence is viewed as legitimate only in so far as it helps to enhance business competitiveness. Thus Labour's vision of employment relations partnership is one in which trade unions exist only as weak and powerless employment relations actors, dependent upon the goodwill of employers (Smith and Morton 2006).

- Labour has also articulated the need for greater 'fairness' in employment relations, particularly through the establishment of minimum employment standards that prevent workers from being overly exploited. One can point to important policy initiatives like the National Minimum Wage (NMW) as evidence of Labour's commitment to creating a more extensive system of individual employment rights (see Chapter 7). Labour has also introduced legislation which regulates the operation of labour providers, or 'gangmasters' as they are popularly known, in order to protect vulnerable migrant workers in some parts of the economy. Yet in articulating the benefits of Britain's 'flexible' labour market, the Labour government has been wary of the supposed threat to economic competitiveness of extending employment protection beyond a minimum floor of rights (DTI 2006).

- A further feature of Labour's employment relations programme has been the increased emphasis accorded to developing 'family-friendly' policies, designed to improve the balance between home and paid work responsibilities (Nash 2006), not least as a means of improving women's labour market prospects. For example, in its Employment Act 2002 Labour enhanced both maternity and paternity leave provisions, introducing paid paternity leave for the first time, and gave parents of young children the right to request flexible working arrangements. The Work and Families Act 2006 further extended some of these provisions (see Chapter 4). Yet the extent to which Labour was genuinely committed to securing change in this area, given its reluctance to legislate effectively against excessive working hours (see Chapter 7), is perhaps questionable.

- Labour has also extended both the breadth and depth of equality and anti-discrimination legislation (see Chapter 4). Before Labour entered office in 1997, legislation already outlawed employment discrimination on the grounds of sex, race, and disability. Subsequently, European Union (EU) legislation obliged the UK government to extend the scope of anti-discrimination legislation to cover sexual orientation, religion or belief (in 2003), and age (in 2006). With regard to the depth of equality and anti-discrimination legislation, in 2000 the Labour government introduced a requirement that public authorities (e.g. colleges, hospitals) take measures that positively encourage race equality, something since extended to gender and disability. Labour has also promoted greater gender pay equality by encouraging public sector organizations to conduct equal pay reviews as a means of eradicating discriminatory pay arrangements. While equality issues seem to have become an increasingly important priority for Labour, the government's reluctance to antagonize employers makes it reluctant to enact measures, like the proposed Agency Workers Directive for example, which could help to reduce employment discrimination and disadvantage (Bewley 2006).

- The final theme of the Labour government's approach to employment relations policy concerns its efforts to encourage people to move off welfare benefits and into paid employment, the so-called welfare to work agenda (Davies and Freedland 2007). Measures like the minimum wage should help to improve the attractiveness of work, and encourage people to leave welfare as a result. The centerpiece of Labour's welfare to work policy were the various New Deal programmes, offering skills training and employment advice to people who experience labour market disadvantage, such as young workers, for example. Between 1998 and 2006 some one million young people passed through the New Deal programme, making a substantial impact on reducing poverty (Brinkley, Coats, and Overell 2007). Critics of the government's approach argue that Labour puts too much of an emphasis on forcing people into work, by threats to withdraw benefits, and has given insufficient attention to the need to alter the perceptions of employers who are often prejudiced against people with little, or uneven, work experience.

You will already have noticed that some parts of Labour's employment relations programme have been influenced by the need to comply with European Union (EU) legislation. It is important to acknowledge the more supportive approach taken by Labour to the regulation of employment relations by the European Union (EU) than was the case with the Conservatives, the most evident feature of which was the government's signing of the 'social chapter' after entering office in 1997 (Dickens and Hall 2003). We consider the development of EU policy in the area of employment relations in Section 3.4 below. As later chapters will show in more detail, the result of this was to increase markedly the scope of juridification in employment relations with EU-derived legislation on such matters as parental leave, equality and discrimination in employment, information and consultation rights for employees, and new rights for part-time and fixed-term contract workers.

Yet Labour often introduced, or 'transposed', EU legislation reluctantly and, where possible, with opt-outs from key provisions, as in the case of the Working Time Directive, for example (see Chapter 7). The argument about the Agency Workers Directive, highlighted in the introduction to this chapter, demonstrates the Labour government's concern not to introduce employment legislation that would mitigate employment flexibility. This 'minimalist' approach to transposing EU directives accords with the emphasis Labour placed on the appropriateness of a flexible, deregulated labour market both as a means of sustaining economic competitiveness and maintaining the goodwill of employers (Howell 2005; Waddington 2003a).

3.3.2 Interpreting Labour's employment relations policy

How, then, can the nature of employment relations policy under the Labour governments from 1997 onwards be interpreted? Clearly, Labour's legislative programme constituted a marked shift in emphasis from the approach taken by the Conservatives (Dickens and Hall 2003). The introduction of the NMW, the encouragement of partnership in employment relations, and the greater engagement with the EU's social dimension would all have been inconceivable under the Thatcher and Major administrations. The breadth and depth of individual rights at work have been extended by Labour in ways that significantly benefit workers, the development of legislation dealing with equality and work–life balance issues for example, and the protection to vulnerable workers offered by policies such as the minimum wage (Bewley 2006; Brinkley, Coats, and Overell 2007).

This has provoked some harsh criticism from business organizations like the CBI, who contend that the increase in the amount of labour market regulation imposes too great a burden on businesses and thus damages economic competiveness. Nevertheless, Labour retained just about all of the Conservative's anti-union legislation; and the scope of the legal regulation of the trade unions means that their activities remain highly restricted (Smith and Morton 2006). Thus while important changes have undoubtedly occurred, these need to be set against a 'background of underlying continuity' (Hyman 2003: 55).

Continuity is particularly evident when we consider the importance Labour attaches to the desirability of maintaining a flexible, competitive market economy within which business can thrive, and thus generate jobs, unfettered by the activities of trade unions. In 2006 the government published a policy document, *Success at Work*, which proclaimed the success of its approach to employment relations matters, such as the increase in the number of people in employment and the advances made in developing work–life balance interventions. It articulated the importance of 'a labour market where adaptability and flexibility to promote employability and competiveness are combined with a commitment to fairness'. As well as this, there is 'no intention of changing industrial action laws or taking other measures that would damage employability or competitiveness in the UK' (DTI 2006: 5).

Labour contends that, given the pressures associated with globalization, it is essential that its employment relations policies help to support, rather than undermine, labour market flexibility and the advantages it produces (see Box 3.6). For some commentators, then, Labour government policy on employment relations, given its emphasis on promoting labour market flexibility while keeping the activities of the unions on a tight leash, can best be interpreted as a 'distinctive form of neo-liberalism' (Smith and Morton 2006). Although Labour has instituted policies ostensibly designed to support trade unions and to protect workers, 'their practical effect is rarely more than minimal' (Smith and Morton 2009: 221). Employment relations policy, then, continues to be informed by the dominant ideology of neo-liberalism (Daniels and McIlroy 2009).

However, we need to qualify this assessment in three important ways; and offer a more nuanced assessment of the Labour government's policy interventions. First, it is evident that the Labour's approach has changed over time. In its first term of office between 1997 and 2001, for example, the government favoured what Davies and Freedland (2007) call 'light regulation'. In other words, measures such as the minimum wage were introduced which, while offering important minimum employment standards, did not greatly undermine business flexibility. After 2001, though, Labour's policy stance became rather more incoherent, marked by a concern with further light regulation on the one hand (e.g. work–life balance legislation), and an outright deregulatory approach on the other (e.g. the concern with reducing the number of claims to employment tribunals).

Moreover, since 2005 Labour has placed the onus on the need to promote greater awareness of, and also enforce, already existing employment legislation (DTI 2006). The Employment Act 2008, for example, includes measures designed to improve the

LEGISLATION AND POLICY 3.6

A ministerial view

In a May 2008 speech to the left-of-centre Fabian Society John Hutton, the government minister then responsible for employment relations matters, outlined the key principles which informed Labour's policy approach. He emphasized the success of Labour's approach to employment regulation, pointing to the effectiveness with which the government has combined protection for workers with economic prosperity. Hutton stated his determination not to 'compromise' labour market flexibility, and declared his support for a framework of employment rights that 'continues to support the competiveness of our labour market, and advance the most important employment right of all—that is the right to work' (Hutton 2008). However, union leaders criticized Hutton's speech, especially his assumption that further employment laws to protect workers' rights were unnecessary, accusing him of being complacent and ignoring the persistence of injustice at work (http://www.guardian.co.uk 29 May 2008).

enforcement of the minimum wage following concerns about low compliance in some sectors of the economy, to the detriment of migrant and other vulnerable workers (see Chapter 7).

Second, it is also important to bear in mind that Labour has been keen to progress more change in some areas than it has in others. For example, the government seems to be more at ease promoting work–life balance policies, given the greater scope for employer engagement that exists, than it is with supporting better trade union rights (Dickens and Hall 2003).

Third, following on from this we should remember not to overstate the overall coherence of Labour's approach. It is partly to be understood as an 'amalgam of competing values' (Dickens and Hall 2006: 339). In other words, while neo-liberal ideology has undoubtedly been an important influence on policy outcomes, it sometimes conflicts with pressure coming from both inside and outside (e.g. trade unions, campaign groups) government for greater regulation of employment relations. A good example of this was the response to the tragic deaths of 24 Chinese cocklepickers who drowned while working in Morecambe Bay in 2004. Following pressure from the unions, and also some of its own supporters in Parliament, the government established the Gangmasters Licensing Authority (GLA), whose job is to regulate labour providers in employment sectors with large numbers of migrant workers (e.g. agriculture).

How, then, can we interpret the Labour government's approach to employment relations? Perhaps its main characteristic is the emphasis given to ensuring that employment regulation is progressed in a way that enhances, or at least does not damage, the competitive advantages held to result from labour market flexibility (Howell 2005). Historically, before the Conservative changes of the 1980s and 1990s, the primary purpose of employment regulation was to correct the imbalance of power in the employment relationship between a relatively powerless individual worker and a relatively powerful employer. Inspired by a neo-liberal ideology which held that the labour market needed to be deregulated, and the power of the unions tamed, if economic prosperity was to be increased, the Conservatives pursued a distinctively anti-union agenda.

Under Labour, however, the neo-liberal approach has been modified, rather than discarded. Rather than a wholesale emphasis on deregulation, as under the Conservatives, Labour has articulated a distinctive approach to employment relations policy which holds that the main purpose of regulation is to support and enhance economic competitiveness (Davies and Freedland 2007). In this way, then, aspirations towards fairness and better employment standards can be reconciled with, but are clearly subordinate to, the need to maintain labour market flexibility as a source of improved business performance. This explains the Labour government's opposition to EU measures, like the Agency Workers Directive, which are designed to improve workers' rights (see the Introductory Case Study).

Labour's approach to employment relations is based on an acceptance that economic globalization constrains the extent to which countries can regulate their own labour markets (Hay 1999). The Labour government's employment relations policy programme differs from the approach taken by its Conservative predecessors in some important respects. However, labour market regulation has been pursued only in so far as it does not challenge the prevailing neo-liberal assumption that deregulation is the most effective means of generating improvements in economic competitiveness. After 1997, the explicitly repressive approach to unions that was formulated under the Conservatives was modified, rather than reversed, making it difficult to see that year's election victory by the Labour party as a real turning point in employment relations.

3.3.3 The Labour party and the trade unions in Britain

Labour's reluctance to alter the anti-union legislation it inherited from its Conservative predecessors in government may appear surprising when we consider the historically close relationship it has enjoyed with the trade unions. Indeed, at the beginning of the twentieth century, the leading trade unions of the time, along with a group of prominent socialists, played a key role in establishing the Labour party in Britain to give working people a more effective political voice in Parliament.

In what came to be known as 'labourism', though, a rigid demarcation was established between the milieu of parliamentary politics, the arena for Labour politicians, and that of industrial affairs, in which the unions had a legitimate interest (Hyman 1989). Priority was accorded to parliamentary politics, and unions recognized the authority of the Labour party leadership in the House of Commons (Flanders 1975). Union leaders conceived of themselves as 'representatives of organized labour, involved in a bargaining relationship, notably over industrial and economic issues, with their political colleagues in the Labour party, and not in the least as political rivals' (Miliband 1972: 375).

The predominance of Labourism as an ideology, allied to the political conservatism of union leaderships, gave the Labour party's political programme a non-socialistic character in which radical ideas were generally downplayed in favour of incremental, pragmatic reforms, accommodating capitalism rather than seeking to challenge it (Hyman 1975).

For most of the twentieth century, then, the trade unions exerted a powerful, and moderating, influence over the politics of the Labour party. Even today 16 major unions, including Unison, Unite, and the GMB general union are affiliated to, and thus formally part of, the Labour party. Three features of the way in which the trade unions and the Labour party became 'symbiotically linked' (Thorpe 1999) are particularly worthy of attention:

- unions, their officials, and their members provided a considerable proportion of the necessary organizational activities essential to the effective functioning of the party;

- through their affiliation fees, the funding of election campaigning, and the sponsorship of Labour MPs, the unions provided much of the Labour party's funds (Alderman and Carter 1994); and

- the unions provided the Labour party with 'political ballast'; the leadership came to rely upon the support of the trade unions whenever it was necessary to defeat left-wing challenges to its policies (Minkin 1991).

The relationship between Labour and the unions has often been stormy, prompting Minkin (1991) to call it a 'contentious alliance'. The legacy of the 'winter of discontent' in 1978–79, a symbolic and highly charged manifestation of the breakdown of relations between the Labour government and the trade unions, endured for three decades. The Conservatives used it as a device to challenge the legitimacy of the unions' proximity to the Labour party; for the self-styled 'New' Labour 'modernizers', the winter of discontent signified the unelectability of a political party that was over-dependent on the trade unions.

Following the disastrous election performances of the 1980s, the Labour leadership tentatively began to distance the party from the unions, a process that accelerated after a fourth successive defeat in 1992. The union link was perceived to be unpopular with the electorate since it gave the impression that the Labour party was too beholden to one special interest group (Alderman and Carter 1994). For one commentator, 'ending the association, in the minds of voters and business, between the Labour party and organized labour . . . is *the* defining core of the modernization project for New Labour' (Howell 2005: 174).

Under the leadership of Tony Blair, Labour sought to reduce its dependency on the unions for financial support, and looked instead for donations from business and wealthy individuals (Leopold 1997; Osler 2002). Moreover, measures were taken to reduce the influence of the trade unions within the party's internal structures and decision-making processes; though the Labour leadership remained careful to avoid antagonizing the unions too much since they were still important as a source of funds and organizational support (McIlroy 1998).

What has happened to the relationship between Labour and the unions since 1997, when Tony Blair's first administration was formed? While their influence has been heavily diluted, the unions often play an important part in Labour's affairs. The Labour party remains heavily dependent on the unions for financial support, particularly as donations from wealthy individuals have dried up amidst controversies over political funding. Between 2001 and 2006 the unions gave some £56 million to Labour (McIlroy 2009). Labour victories at the 2001 and 2005 general elections depended on financial and organizational support from the unions; by 2008 the Labour party relied almost entirely on donations from key union affiliates in order to continue functioning.

In exchange for financial support, the unions have been able to extract some modest concessions from the government. In 2004, for example, a deal was struck at a University of Warwick policy forum. Under the terms of this 'Warwick Agreement', in return for union support at the forthcoming general election, Labour agreed to enact limited improvements in employment rights, including an extension to the statutory minimum annual leave entitlement. However, subsequent efforts to secure more union-friendly policies have largely been fruitless.

The Warwick Agreement notwithstanding, since 2001 the relationship between the trade unions and Labour has been increasingly strained. Much of the Labour government's policy programme is unpalatable to the unions, for example its concern to extend the influence of private sector businesses in the delivery of public services, through arrangements such as the Private Finance Initiative (PFI) (Waddington 2003a). The unions have also been frustrated by Labour's unwillingness to strengthen union rights, and by its support for the virtues of a deregulated labour market as a source of economic dynamism (Ludlum and Taylor 2003). During 2007 and 2008, government calls for pay restraint in the public sector also provoked sharp differences with some major unions. Yet while there has been internal pressure within many unions for the amount of money they give to Labour to be reduced, by 2008 only the Rail, Maritime and Transport union (RMT) and the Fire Brigades Union (FBU) had broken with the party entirely (McIlroy 2009) (see Box 3.7).

Employment relations reflection 3.7   The trade unions and the Labour party—a growing rift?

Since 2001, there have been signs of a growing rift between the Labour party and its affiliated trade unions as the latter became increasingly disenchanted with the Labour government's policy programme. During 2004, two unions disaffiliated from the Labour party. Having already reduced its financial support for the Labour party, in 2003 the Rail Maritime and Transport (RMT) union's annual conference voted to allow its branches to support other political parties, including the Scottish Socialist party (SSP), Plaid Cymru in Wales, and the Green party. Some of its Scottish branches subsequently chose to affiliate to the SSP—a breach of Labour's rules. Consequently, early in 2004, the RMT was expelled from the Labour party.

During 2002 and 2003, activist pressure to disaffiliate from the Labour party was evident within a number of other unions, though it was strongest within the Fire Brigades Union (FBU)—a reflection of membership discontent with the government's handling of their pay dispute (see Chapter 9). At the union's June 2004 annual conference, FBU delegates voted to sever its link with the party.

Many of the major union affiliates, including Unison and the GMB general union, reduced the level of their financial support. However, most union leaderships, including that of Unison, which represents workers in the public services, have strenuously resisted efforts to break with the Labour party, fearing that such an outcome would prejudice their political influence, and thus lose the unions a voice within government (Leopold 2006). The link with the Labour party is presented as an essential way in which workers, collectively through their unions, can influence government policy. That said, though, the benefits for the unions of the link appear to have diminished during the 2000s, as Labour's attachment to the virtues of a neo-liberalism has strengthened. The 'contentious alliance' between Labour and the unions still prevails, but it has come under increasing strain (McIlroy 2009).

SECTION SUMMARY AND FURTHER READING

- The Labour governments of Tony Blair and Gordon Brown instituted some important changes in employment relations policy, notably the development of new statutory protections in the area of individual employment rights, the minimum wage, for example. There was no extension of the programme of anti-union legislation that was enacted under the Conservatives.

- Labour did, however, retain the overwhelming bulk of the anti-union legislation it inherited from the Conservatives; and its employment relations policy interventions were designed not to upset employers. This reflects a largely uncritical acceptance of neo-liberal ideology: that economic competitiveness is contingent upon deregulated and flexible labour markets, making substantial improvements to union and workers' rights, through stronger employment regulation, undesirable.

- There is a long-standing, and frequently strained, relationship between the trade unions and the Labour party. Despite efforts by the Labour leadership to reduce the influence of the unions within the party, their financial and campaigning contributions were vital to Labour's general election campaigns. Although Labour's neo-liberal policy agenda, with its emphasis on the importance of deregulated labour markets as a source of economic dynamism, has caused relations with the trade unions to become increasingly strained, there is no sign as yet of a wholesale abandonment of Labour by the unions.

For an insightful analysis of Labour policy on employment relations, see Dickens and Hall (2006) in particular. You may find the book *Towards a Flexible Labour Market?* by Davies and Freedland (2007) a little hard-going, but it offers the most detailed account of Labour's policies. For a robust critique of Labour's neo-liberalism, see Smith and Morton (2006). The classic, and lengthy, account of the relationship between the trade unions and the Labour party is Minkin (1991). For a more concise historical perspective, and one that covers a shorter time period, Thorpe (1999) is recommended. Much of Ralph Miliband's *Parliamentary Socialism* (Miliband 1972), a robust critique of the reformist basis of Labour politics, is relevant today.

 Visit our Online Resource Centre for web links to sites connected to this section. www.oxfordtextbooks.co.uk/williams_adamsmith2e

3.4 Employment relations and the politics of European integration

In recent years, the influence of the European Union (EU) on employment relations has grown markedly, especially since 1997 when the newly elected Labour government under Tony Blair brought Britain under the auspices of the 'Social Chapter'. In this section we examine the progress of the EU's 'social dimension', which encompasses employment matters, since the Treaty of Rome established the original European Economic Community in 1957. The social dimension of the EU comprises four main elements: (1) legislation, largely in the form of directives which the governments of individual member states are required to implement in their own territories; (2) social programmes, including assistance and support to help unemployed people into work for example; (3) 'social dialogue', discussions between employers' bodies and trade union organizations; and (4) something called the 'open method of coordination' (OMC), which encompasses voluntary, non-binding measures to realize employment-related goals. In the material which follows we trace the origins and development of the EU's social dimension, paying particular attention to the way in which the popularity of legislative enactment has risen and fallen, and the growing preference for non-legislative interventions, in the shape of OMC and social dialogue. The role of the EU's social programmes is largely outside the scope of this book.

Before we proceed any further, there are two things that require attention. First, the respective roles enjoyed by the different EU institutions need to be understood. See Box 3.8 for details of relevant EU institutions. Second, you should be aware that the EU is based on a series of treaties which establish its powers, or competences, relative to those of its member states (Hepple 2005). One of the biggest sources of political conflict within the EU has been the resistance of the UK government to reforms that are perceived to weaken its national powers, and this includes powers to effect employment regulation. By the end of this section, you will have developed a better understanding of how European integration has affected employment relations.

INTERNATIONAL PERSPECTIVE 3.8

The institutions of the European Union

Employment relations in the UK is increasingly influenced by the policies of the European Union (EU). There are four principal EU institutions. The European Commission, comprising representatives of each of the 27 member states, is responsible for promoting and effecting legislation, and monitoring its progress. The European Court of Justice (ECJ) deliberates on matters of EU law, and on issues that are of EU-wide significance. The European Parliament, made up of directly elected members from all 27 EU countries, has traditionally lacked much influence, though it can now obstruct and amend legislation in some areas. Most power, however, rests with the Council of Ministers. It represents the interests of member state governments, comprises ministers from member states, and is the principal decision-making body of the EU.

In respect of employment relations, though, the role of the 'social partners', bodies representing the interests of employers and unions at EU level, must also be acknowledged. There are three main employers' organizations. Founded in 1958, the Union of Industrial and Employers' Confederations of Europe (UNICE) has since 2007 been called BusinessEurope (http://www.businesseurope.eu/). It acts on behalf of private sector employers. The Confederation of British Industry (CBI) is one of its 40 affiliates from 34 different countries. The European Association of Craft, Small and Medium-Sized Enterprises (UEAPME) represents the interests of small and medium-sized employers (http://www.ueapme.com/). The European Centre of Enterprises with Public Participation and of Enterprises of General Economic Interest (CEEP) acts on behalf of public sector employers in more than 20 countries (http://www.ceep.eu/).

The European Trade Union Confederation (ETUC) is the social partner that represents the interests of the trade unions (http://www.etuc.org/). Founded in 1973, it encompasses over 80 national union confederations, including the British TUC, from 36 different countries. The ETUC supports the activities of 12 European Industry Federations (EIFs), bodies that represent the interests of trade unions in specific industrial sectors, the European Metalworkers' Federation in the engineering industry, for example.

3.4.1 The 'social dimension' to European integration

The EU was instituted as the European Economic Community (EEC), or the 'Common Market', as it became popularly known, in 1957 when France, Italy, West Germany, as it then was, and the Benelux countries acceded to the Treaty of Rome. Britain joined the EEC sixteen years later. As its name suggests, the EEC was designed as a vehicle for greater economic cooperation across Western Europe, a means of promoting market integration. Apart from provisions designed to improve cross-border labour mobility and pay equality between men and women (Gold 1993), the Treaty of Rome covered social and employment matters relatively briefly. It mentioned improving working conditions, but this was considered relevant only in so far as it enhanced the operation of the common market and supported economic integration (Teague 1999). According to Hepple (2005: 199), the emphasis on economic cooperation meant that 'labour law and social protection were seen as almost exclusively national functions'.

In the early stages of the EEC's development, then, little attention was paid to the 'social dimension' of European integration, embracing employment-related matters, as well as social protection and benefits (Bridgford and Stirling 1994). Although the EEC was established in part from a desire to eliminate the possibility of armed conflict in Europe, it was advanced largely as a market-building project, designed to stimulate the economic capacities of Western European nation-states and thus help them to compete more effectively with the increasingly dominant United States economy (Hyman 2001a; Martin and Ross 1999).

By the 1970s, there was a greater concern to give the EEC a more active social and employment dimension. However, the 1979 election of Margaret Thatcher's Conservative government in Britain also posed an obstacle to the development of social and employment policy by the EEC, since at that time directives required the unanimous support of all the member states. Given its deregulatory policy agenda, the Conservatives were, unsurprisingly, opposed to extending the competence of the EEC in matters relating to employment relations on the basis that such interventions would damage economic competitiveness (Hepple 2005). Nevertheless, during the 1980s and 1990s Conservative governments were often frustrated by the obligation to adjust British law to comply with directives that had been enacted under the Social Action Programme, such as in the area of redundancy consultation, for example (Hall and Edwards 1999).

The British government's hostility notwithstanding, from the mid 1980s onwards the social dimension was revived, and indeed accelerated, under the auspices of then president of the European Commission, the former French finance minister Jacques Delors. The activities of the European Community were increasingly dominated by the prospect of the 1993 completion of the Single European Market. Thus a central motivating force underpinning the increased emphasis given to social and employment policy during this period was the need to secure support for, and the legitimacy of, further economic integration in Europe (Bridgford and Stirling 1994). Moreover, without the development of minimum labour standards the ability of multinational corporations to redirect investment, and therefore jobs, to locations where labour costs are lower, or 'social dumping' as it became known, would otherwise go unchecked (Adnett and Hardy 2005; Smith 1999).

The prospect of the single market inspired a major institutional innovation in European Community (EC) decision-making, one which was to have major implications for employment relations policy. The 1987 Single European Act (SEA) enabled the Council of Ministers to determine certain matters by 'qualified majority voting' (QMV), rather than a unanimous vote in favour. Individual member states were accorded a certain number of votes within the Council of Ministers—Britain now has 29, for example. Matters that were subject to QMV, those 'which have as their object the establishment and functioning of the internal market' (Bridgford and Stirling 1994: 77), needed to attract a certain number of votes in order to progress.

Although most employment matters remained subject to the need for unanimous agreement among the member states if they were to go forward, under the SEA, measures relating to improvements in the working environment, including health and safety at work, were covered by QMV. By the latter half of the 1980s, then, there was a growing acknowledgement that a more robust social and employment policy agenda was beneficial to the development and success of economic integration, and was not something that should be marginalized (Davies and Freedland 1993).

The adoption of the Social Charter, in 1990, and the enactment of a further programme of social action that accompanied it, demonstrates the extent of this increasing interest in the development of social and employment policy. The Social Charter, which Britain, alone among EC member states, refused to support was a declaration of intent, a political statement, rather than a concrete set of legislative proposals, and covered such areas as improvements in living and working conditions and information, and participation rights for workers (Martin and Ross 1999; Teague 1999). Moreover, it also provided the basis for a legislative action programme that encompassed 17 draft directives, mostly in the area of health and safety, including the regulation of working time (Bridgford and Stirling 1994), something to which Britain was deeply opposed (Davies and Freedland 1993; Hall 1992).

It would be a mistake, though, to overstate the significance of this activity in the area of social and employment policy. For one thing, as Mark Hall (1994: 297) contends, the proposed measures did not 'venture very far beyond the [European] Commission's longstanding social policy agenda'. Thus they did not presage a significant extension of EC intervention in the regulation of employment relations (Teague 1999). Moreover, the development of the social dimension remained subordinate to the process of market integration, and was articulated largely as a means of attracting support for it within European labour movements (Martin and Ross 1999).

Nevertheless, the British Conservative government was profoundly opposed to the expansion, however limited, of the European Community's competence in the area of social policy (Davies and Freedland 1993). As a result, the 1993 Treaty of European Union, agreed in 1991 in the Dutch town of Maastricht, in fact comprised two distinct documents. One included a new 'Social Chapter' that extended QMV to a range of social and employment matters, including information and consultation rights for workers, and was signed by all the member states except Britain. The other, which Britain signed, left it out.

The Maastricht Treaty also gave a major boost to another aspect of the developing social dimension—the process of 'social dialogue'. During the 1960s and 1970s, the European Commission supported various initiatives designed to facilitate discussion between trade union bodies and employers' organizations on matters of mutual interest, notwithstanding the suspicion of UNICE (Hall 1994; Waddington and Hoffman 2003). During the 1980s, though, under the presidency of Jacques Delors the European Commission took action to promote social dialogue as an integral part of the social dimension. The 1987 Single European Act obliged the Commission to encourage the development of social dialogue between the social partners at European level (Bridgford and Stirling 1994; Carley 1993). It was anticipated that legislative proposals in the field of social and employment policy would stand more chance of success if they already had the support of the trade unions and employers' organizations (Hall 1994; Teague 1989).

The 1993 Maastricht Treaty of European Union further encouraged the pursuit of social dialogue. It provided for the conclusion of 'framework agreements' between the social partners. In areas where directives had been proposed, trade unions and employers' organizations at EU level were given an opportunity to reach an agreement themselves which could then be taken forward and adopted as legislation.

The Maastricht Treaty also provided for 'framework agreements' between the social partners that could be implemented voluntarily across the EU member states without the need for legislative action (Keller and Sörries 1999). See Box 3.9 for details of how social dialogue has progressed.

Labour's 1997 election victory meant that the UK was brought under the aegis of the Social Chapter, something that was formally instituted by that year's Treaty of Amsterdam. Sex discrimination in employment had come within the purview of the EU since the Social Action Programme of the 1970s. Importantly, however, the Treaty of Amsterdam also extended the scope of the EU's competence in employment-related matters to cover matters relating to other aspects of discrimination, on the grounds of race and ethnicity, sexual orientation, religion or belief, and age (Davies and Freedland 2007). This resulted in two new directives being agreed in 2000: a framework directive covering equal treatment in employment and occupations, and a directive dealing with racial discrimination.

● INSIGHT INTO PRACTICE 3.9

The outcomes of social dialogue

Social dialogue operates in three broad ways. First, at EU-level the social partners (employers' organizations and trade union bodies) can reach their own negotiated 'framework' agreement on a proposal, which is then taken forward and enacted as EU legislation in the form of an appropriate directive. Although there was a failure to reach an agreement regarding European Works Councils, obliging the European Commission to intervene and take forward the relevant legislative proposals, directives regulating parental leave, and the rights of part-time and fixed-term contract workers were all enacted by QMV following agreement between the social partners (Keller and Sörries 1999). However, UNICE (now Business Europe) only participated reluctantly. Since the 1990s this element of social dialogue has produced rather little at EU level. In specific industries, however, some progress is evident. In 2008, for example, the social partners in the maritime industry struck a 'framework agreement', which was then enacted as a Directive, establishing minimum standards for seafarers in Europe.

Second, social dialogue at EU level can also lead to voluntary 'framework agreements' between the social partners, which do not have legislative effect. By the end of 2008 three such agreements had been reached: on telework (2002), workplace stress (2004), and harassment and violence at work (2007). A major problem with the voluntary approach is the difficulty of guaranteeing compliance across EU member states (Keller 2003). Moreover, employers' bodies can be reluctant to engage in meaningful dialogue because it is wary of encouraging cross-border bargaining with unions.

Third, social dialogue also operates at industry level between sector-specific employers' organizations and union federations. The European Commission has invested a great deal of effort encouraging dialogue between the social partners at industry level (Keller 2003). Overall progress, however, has been rather tentative, with notable achievements being evident only in the transport industry, where agreements regulating working time for specific occupations have been established, or in sectors where the implications of EU policy, such as the opening up of telecommunications markets, have been particularly important (Leisink 2002). Nevertheless, the European Commission remains committed to extending and strengthening the social dialogue process (European Commission 2002), seemingly at the expense of legislative action.

Since the mid 1990s a series of other directives designed to enhance gender equality at work (e.g. Parental Leave Directive) and promote information and consultation provision (e.g. European Works Council Directive) have been agreed. See Box 3.10 for details of the major EU directives in the area of employment policy that have been enacted since 1993.

How can we interpret the significance of the EU's social dimension? Business groups are often highly critical of the additional regulation created by EU legislation, citing the increased costs and inflexibility it generates. The Working Time Directive, which limits working hours (see Chapter 7), is seen as particularly harmful. Consistent with the neo-liberal, deregulatory ethos that informs its approach to employment relations

LEGISLATION AND POLICY 3.10

Major European Union directives in the area of employment relations since 1993

- The Directive on the Adaptation of Working Time (1993): provides for the regulation of working hours, rest breaks, and holiday periods (see Chapter 7)
- The European Works Council Directive (1994): provides for the establishment of transnational information and consultation arrangements in multinational companies operating in Europe (see Chapter 6)
- The Posting of Workers Directive (1996): gives workers who are posted abroad to another EU member state for a limited period of time the right to the same core pay and conditions enjoyed by local workers (see Section 3.4.3)
- The Parental Leave Directive (1996): provides for minimum standards of maternity and paternity leave provision within the EU, including the provision of at least two weeks of unpaid paternity leave (see Chapter 4)
- The Directive on Equal Rights and Treatment for Part-Time Workers (1997): prohibits employers from giving part-time workers less favourable pay and conditions than equivalent full-time staff (see Chapter 4)
- The Fixed-Term Contract Workers Directive (1999): prohibits employers from giving workers on fixed-term contracts less favourable pay and conditions than equivalent permanent staff (see Chapter 4)
- The Race Directive (2000): establishes minimum standards of Europe-wide legal protection for individuals on the grounds of racial or ethnic origins (see Chapter 4).
- The Framework for Equal Treatment in Employment and Occupations Directive (2000): prohibits direct or indirect discrimination on grounds of religion or belief, disability, age, or sexual orientation (see Chapter 4)
- The National Information and Consultation of Employees Directive (2002): provides for information and consultation arrangements among firms employing fifty workers or more (see Chapter 6)
- Proposed Directive on Temporary Agency Work: first proposed in 2002, and eventually agreed in 2008, provides for agency-supplied temporary workers to get pay and conditions that are comparable with those enjoyed by permanent employees—subject to certain conditions (see the introductory case study)

policy in general, the UK government has taken an increasingly business-friendly approach to the implementation of EU labour law, evident in its long-standing opposition to the Agency Workers Directive. Set against this, however, EU employment laws have generally been welcomed by the trade unions; they see the directives as a source of important new rights and protections for workers, and as an important counterweight to the more neo-liberal policy approach favoured by successive Conservative and Labour governments.

A more critical perspective suggests that the social dimension has not been a very effective means of enhancing workers' rights (Wedderburn 1995); EU legislation is often weaker than that which already exists in most member states. Moreover, key aspects of employment relations policy, such as collective bargaining and the right of workers to associate in trade unions for example, still come within the prerogative of individual member states. The limited progress of EU social and employment policy is, however, not particularly surprising when we consider the extent to which it has been subordinated to the process of market integration (Martin and Ross 1999). The EU is, then, as it always has been, primarily a vehicle for the promotion of market integration, an institution whose policies are favourable, in the main, to the large multinational corporations that have benefited from the removal of economic and other barriers within Europe (Hyman 2001a). The principal justification for the development of the social dimension rested upon the extent to which it could support, and add legitimacy, to the process of economic union.

3.4.2 The 'Lisbon agenda' and the erosion of the social dimension

By the late 1990s, the level of EU interest in social and employment policy initiatives seemed to have diminished markedly. The European Commission increasingly favoured 'relatively modest labour law proposals rather than the promotion of genuinely supranational initiatives', and demonstrates a preference for voluntary agreements, through a process of 'social dialogue' between employers and unions (see above) rather than legislative enactment (Teague 1999: 149).

During the 2000s, a number of other factors have contributed to the weakening of the social dimension of European integration. We consider the implications of EU enlargement in Section 3.4.3. Here, though, we examine the nature of the European Employment Strategy (EES) and highlight the increasingly neo-liberal character of EU policy as manifested by the so-called 'Lisbon agenda'.

The EES emerged in the mid 1990s, and was formally established by the 1997 Treaty of Amsterdam (Davies and Freedland 2007; Hepple 2005). The purpose of the EES is to tackle unemployment and social exclusion across EU member states through measures which promote not just more jobs, but also better quality jobs, and thus facilitate greater social protection. The scope of the EES includes guidelines which among other things encompass: measures to encourage job creation; efforts to improve the standard of vocational training; anti-poverty initiatives; and the promotion of gender equality. The development of the EES signals a shift in the EU's priorities, away from legislating to establish minimum labour standards, towards a greater emphasis on using labour market measures to improve economic competitiveness.

This emphasis on competiveness is symbolized by the so-called 'Lisbon agenda', which has dominated EU thinking during the 2000s. At the Lisbon summit of 2000 EU governments established the strategic aim that by 2010 Europe would 'become the most competitive and dynamic knowledge-based economy in the world, capable of sustainable economic growth with more and better jobs and greater social cohesion' (Adnett and Hardy 2005: 86–7). The Lisbon agenda portends a more neo-liberal emphasis on markets, competition, and flexibility. In this context, the EES has been increasingly favoured over legislation as a mechanism for realizing the EU's employment policy objectives.

Under the EES, the key mechanism for promoting change is not employment legislation in the form of directives, but rather something called the 'open method of co-ordination' (OMC). The OMC is an approach to realizing employment objectives, set out in the guidelines that determine the scope of the EES, which relies on targets and other non-legislative intervention, with the aim of coordinating measures across EU member states. Individual EU member states draw up 'national action plans' which indicate how they are realizing the objectives of the EES. The aim is that individual governments can share, and learn from, each other's experiences. Thus 'OMC is designed to assist member states in developing their own policies, whilst encouraging some element of coordination through peer pressure' (Adnett and Hardy 2005: 203).

Like much social dialogue, OMC is a way of realizing EU social and employment objectives through 'soft' regulation. There is no compulsion to ensure specific outcomes are achieved, or penalties for non-compliance. 'Hard' regulation involves using legislation to effect compliance with EU goals. Within the EU, there is an increasing preference for 'soft regulation' through social dialogue and the OMC, rather than 'hard regulation', in the form of directives (Hepple 2005; Hyman 2005).

On the one hand, the importance attached to the EES suggests that social protection, including measures to combat discrimination, for example, remains a major EU priority. On the other hand, the EES is a key part of the shift within the EU away from using legislation to improve labour standards, towards an approach that attempts to integrate the pursuit of economic competitiveness with the need to provide jobs of meaningful quantity and quality (Hepple 2005). The EU uses a rather ugly word—'flexisecurity'—to capture the reciprocity of efforts that promote business flexibility while at the same time giving workers more protection and security. Yet the onus is generally on diluting labour standards, at the expense of measures that help employers. As Hepple (2005: 228) observes, 'the balance between flexibility and security is weighted in the [EES] Guidelines against legal rights for workers'.

The most controversial element of this growing tendency towards a neo-liberal emphasis on flexibility and competitiveness concerns the arguments that raged during the mid 2000s over the EU's Services Directive, or the Bolkestein Directive as it was popularly known, after the name of the European Commissioner who was responsible for producing it. The aim of the legislation was to speed up progress towards a free market for the delivery of services within the EU; reducing the legal and administrative obstacles that obstruct businesses from offering services in different countries. The Bolkestein proposals embodied the increasingly neo-liberal thrust of EU policy-making during the 2000s, being primarily concerned with furthering market integration, at the expense of social and employment standards.

The most contentious part of the draft Directive, however, was the inclusion of something called the 'country-of-origin principle'. This would have allowed a business based in one member state (their country of origin) to employ people to deliver services in other member states, who would be subject to the employment regulations of the country of origin. In other words, an employer based in, say, Latvia, would have been entitled to employ people in the UK to deliver a service, but only have to pay them the Latvian minimum wage, one of the lowest in the EU, rather than the UK's National Minimum Wage, one of the highest.

Trade unions mounted a vigorous campaign against the proposed legislation, especially the 'country-of-origin principle'. They feared that it would cause a 'race to the bottom' in labour standards, as businesses would be encouraged to relocate to EU countries with relatively weak labour regulation, accelerating the process of social dumping. As a result of a major campaign led by the European trade union movement to oppose the directive, in 2006 the European Parliament voted to enact it without the controversial 'country-of-origin principle'.

Nevertheless, the Bolkestein Directive exemplifies an important shift in the EU's approach to labour standards that has occurred since the late 1990s. Until then, there was a general concern with what Hepple (2005) terms 'positive harmonization'. The aim was to promote a Europe-wide minimum level of labour standards, reducing the scope for social dumping by employers. 'Positive harmonization' embodied progress towards a European system of employment relations based on certain minimum standards.

During the 2000s, however, EU policy makers have made 'negative harmonization' more of a priority (Adnett and Hardy 2005; Hepple 2005). This encompasses policies to reduce the barriers to job creation, enacting measures that support business flexibility, and improve competitiveness. From this perspective, labour standards hinder economic prosperity, and should thus be weakened. Negative harmonization involves the freeing up of markets, including labour markets, on a Europe-wide basis, minimizing the effects of employment regulation, to give employers more flexibility. See Table 3.1 for the main differences between positive and negative harmonization.

To what extent could the Charter of the Fundamental Rights of the European Union, first published in 2000, reverse this trend of the negative harmonization of

Table 3.1 Positive and negative harmonization of labour standards

Positive harmonization	Negative harmonization
Preference for legal measures to promote employment protection ('hard regulation')	Preference for non-legal measures to improve the quantity and quality of jobs ('soft regulation')
Minimum employment standards	Improving labour flexibility
Active role for the social partners in advancing employment regulation	Reduced role for social partners, limited to social dialogue
Reducing social dumping	Promoting competitiveness
'Social Europe'	'Market Europe'

labour standards? The Charter contains 54 articles arranged in seven chapters, and was originally incorporated into the now defunct 2004 EU Constitutional Treaty. One of the chapters deals with the theme of 'solidarity', encompassing rights to fair and just working conditions, collective bargaining, and to take strike action (see Box 3.11).

Business groups in the UK expressed a great deal of concern about what they saw as the potential for the Charter to extend EU intervention to a range of employment relations matters that had previously come within the competence of individual member states, particularly a supposed new 'right' to take collective industrial action. As a result, the UK government has been determined to ensure that the Charter does not become legally binding. Yet Hepple (2005) observes that rights to collective bargaining and to take collective industrial action already exist within the Council of Europe's 1961 European Social Charter, which has been ratified by the UK, and also perhaps Article 11 of the European Convention on Human Rights, which has been incorporated into UK law.

Moreover, rules governing collective bargaining and the conduct of industrial action expressly remain matters that come within the jurisdiction of individual member states. As is evident from the examples in Box 3.11, many of the employment rights laid down by the Charter are provided strictly in accordance with 'Community law and national laws and practices'. This means that individual member states retain their control over matters like the laws governing strikes and other forms of industrial action. That said, 'the Charter gives the EU judges and institutions a clear and systematic statement of social rights which have been endorsed at the highest political level . . . ' (Hepple 2005: 245).

The Charter was originally intended to have been enacted as part of the EU Constitutional Treaty agreed by member states in 2004. The main purpose of the Treaty was to define the EU's powers, specify the scope of its activity, and consolidate existing

LEGISLATION AND POLICY 3.11

The Charter of Fundamental Rights of the European Union

Among other things the chapter on 'solidarity' contains these four articles:

Article 27. Workers or their representatives must, at the appropriate levels, be guaranteed information and consultation in good time . . . under the conditions provided for by Community law and national laws and practices.

Article 28. Workers and employers, or their respective organization, have in accordance with Community law and national laws and practices the right to negotiate and conclude collective agreements at the appropriate levels and, in cases of conflicts of interest, to take collective action to defend their interests, including strike action.

Article 30. Every worker has the right to protection against unjustified dismissal, in accordance with Community law and national laws and practices.

Article 31. (1) Every worker has the right to working conditions which respect his or her health, safety, and dignity; (2) Every worker has the right to limitation of maximum working hours, to daily and weekly rest periods and to an annual period of paid leave.

agreements and treaties. However, in order to come in to effect the Treaty needed to be ratified by all EU member states. In some countries, like Greece for example, the national parliament ratified it. Others, like the UK and France, promised to ratify the Treaty only if voters supported it in a referendum. In May 2005, the French voted to reject the Treaty by a margin of 55 to 45 per cent. A non-binding referendum in the Netherlands resulted in an even larger vote against the Treaty, an outcome which its government pledged to respect. Since the Treaty could not take effect, the UK government cancelled its own plans to hold a referendum.

Why was there so much opposition to the Treaty in France? One of the main reasons was a concern that EU policies were becoming too neo-liberal, prioritizing markets, free competition, and employment deregulation. The Charter of Fundamental Rights notwithstanding, opposition to the Treaty derived from a widely held and well-justified belief that European integration primarily serves business interests by eroding workers' rights (Syrpis 2008).

During 2006 and 2007 EU leaders fashioned a Reform Treaty, designed to replace the defunct Constitutional Treaty, which was agreed at the Lisbon summit of December 2007. In the negotiations over the new Lisbon Treaty, the UK government maintained its opposition to the inclusion of the Charter of Fundamental Rights. Along with Poland, it secured agreement over an opt-out protocol whereby nothing in the new Treaty could be used to challenge existing UK legislation, or introduce new rights into UK law. This opposition to the Charter has been roundly condemned by the trade unions, who see it as further evidence of the Labour government's neo-liberal employment relations values, notably the pursuit of flexible and deregulated labour markets.

By May 2009, 26 EU member states had ratified the Lisbon Treaty, including the UK, which did so by a Parliamentary vote rather than a referendum. The one exception was Ireland. In June 2008 the Irish voted against ratification in a referendum, leaving the status of the Lisbon Treaty, and the Charter of Fundamental Rights which it incorporates, in limbo. EU leaders hope that Irish voters will eventually support ratification, enabling the Lisbon Treaty to be enacted.

Yet the controversy over the UK's opt-out, and the problems encountered in ratifying the Treaty, perhaps deflect attention from the real significance of the Charter; this concerns how it is increasingly being drawn upon by the ECJ to inform its deliberations and judgments in employment-related cases (Syrpis 2008). The Charter of Fundamental Rights may come to exercise an ever greater indirect influence over EU employment relations, regardless of whether or not it is ever made legally binding by being incorporated within a fully ratified Lisbon Treaty. Under these circumstances, the status of the UK's opt-out may increasingly be immaterial.

3.4.3 European Union enlargement and employment relations

The significance of the Charter, and also what it portends for the social dimension of European integration, needs to be considered in the context of the process of EU enlargement and the pressures for negative harmonization which it has generated. Since 1957, when the Treaty of Rome was agreed, the European Union has expanded, from the six countries that originally comprised the EEC (West Germany, France, Italy, and the

'Benelux' countries—Belgium, the Netherlands, and Luxembourg) to 27 by 2007. Britain, for example, joined in 1973. During the 1980s and 1990s there was further expansion with the accession of countries such as Greece, Spain, Austria, and Sweden. In 2004, ten countries, including Poland, Hungary, and the Czech Republic, which until the 1990s had been part of the Soviet Bloc, joined the EU. Romania and Bulgaria acceded three years later (see Table 3.2). This process of enlargement has had major ramifications for employment relations, including the social dimension. The accession of the former Soviet Bloc countries may have helped to weaken the social dimension of the European Union in a number of ways.

Perhaps the most obvious impact of EU enlargement has been the increase in labour migration it has generated; people from Eastern European countries have more scope to travel to Western Europe in search of work. One of the key principles of the EU is free movement of workers between countries; in other words, the removal of barriers that prevent citizens of one member state from working in another. However, in the run up to the 2004 enlargement, there was some concern that the large disparity in pay and conditions between Western and Eastern Europe would prove overly disruptive. It was recognized that instituting the free movement of labour in a newly enlarged EU would need careful handling.

Thus existing EU member states (EU15) were given the right to operate transitional arrangements until 2011, enabling them to restrict the influx of migrant workers from the newly joined countries. Most have made use of such arrangements; although the UK, along with Ireland and Sweden, effectively relaxed all controls. However, the UK government did place a requirement on migrant workers from the so-called 'Accession 8' (A8) countries (Poland, Hungary, Latvia, Lithuania, Estonia, Czech Republic, Slovakia, and Slovenia) which joined in 2004 to have their intention to work in the UK approved under something called the Worker Registration Scheme. Nationals from Bulgaria and Romania, two countries which became part of the EU in 2007, face tighter restrictions.

Two of the countries most affected by the influx of East European migrants have been Ireland and the UK. Not only are migrants attracted by the wages on offer, often substantially higher than those available in their home countries, but also the economic boom

Table 3.2 Accession dates of EU countries

Countries	Date
Belgium, France, Italy, Luxembourg, Netherlands, West Germany	1957
Denmark, Ireland, UK	1973
Greece	1981
Portugal, Spain	1986
Austria, Finland, Sweden	1994
Cyprus, Czech Republic, Estonia, Hungary, Latvia, Lithuania, Malta, Poland, Slovakia, Slovenia	2004
Bulgaria, Romania	2007

which lasted until 2007 meant that there was a high demand for labour in the expanding service and construction sectors, much of which was met by migrants from Eastern Europe. Between May 2004 and June 2008 854,000 applications from A8 nationals were approved under the Worker Registration Scheme, the majority of whom came from Poland.

Labour migration, from Eastern Europe to Western Europe, has had major implications both for the migrants' home and host countries. Countries like Poland, and the Baltic States (Latvia, Lithuania, and Estonia) have suffered labour shortages as a result of the outflow of workers to Western Europe. In his study of Latvia, for example, Woolfson (2007) points to the adverse social consequences produced by widespread emigration, including disruption to family life.

While it is important not to over-generalize, many of the new accession states tend to be sympathetic to neo-liberal, deregulatory policies in the area of employment relations. This is particularly the case with the Baltic States. In Latvia, for example, neo-liberal market reforms have caused the erosion of employment standards; salaries are low, unions are weak, jobs are often marked by excessive working hours, and there is little protection for workers (Woolfson 2007). Deteriorating labour standards in their home countries, along with the opportunities available in Western European countries like the UK and Ireland, have been the major causes of emigration. Yet the neo-liberal policy approach favoured by many of the A8 countries is important for another reason. One of the effects of enlargement has also been to weaken political support for a rigorous social dimension, one that encompasses legislative interventions designed to enhance labour standards within the EU as a whole.

With regard to the effects of migration on host countries, the conventional view is that it benefits the economy. Business organizations, like the Confederation of British Industry, vociferously support the free movement of labour. They contend that labour migration improves the supply of labour, allowing businesses greater flexibility and adaptability, thus producing a more dynamic and competitive economy. Increased labour mobility from Eastern Europe has generally been beneficial; by helping to fill the gaps created by skills shortages, for example (Donaghey and Teague 2006), thus contributing to economic growth.

Critics, however, argue that the main benefit for employers is the flexibility to offer lower wages and weaker employment protections. Because migrant workers are willing to work for lower wages, and with less employment protection, the indigenous population comes under pressure to lower its expectations, and work for less reward. This results in downward pressure on wages and a lowering of labour standards. There is also a widespread popular belief that migrant workers take jobs that would otherwise have gone to the indigenous population.

Yet independent studies of the impact on employment levels and wages of migration from the A8 countries conclude that there is no evidence of any substantial negative labour market effects. The analysis by Reed and Latorre (2009), for example, suggests that while some groups of workers may have been disadvantaged as a result of migration from the A8 countries, overall there is no support for the proposition that the influx of workers from Poland and elsewhere in Eastern Europe has reduced employment opportunities for indigenous workers or significantly eroded wage levels. Thus 'the view of the tabloid press that migrants "take our jobs" and "cut our pay" is misplaced' (Reed and Latorre 2009: 34).

Nevertheless, in countries like the UK and Ireland there has been much discussion about the potentially adverse economic and social consequences of increased migration levels. In Ireland, for example, there is evidence that an influx of migrant workers has allowed employers to rely on a low-paid workforce who experience poor conditions and have little employment protection (Dundon, González-Pérez, and McDonough 2007). One of the main effects of labour migration from Eastern Europe, then, is the erosion of existing employment conditions and protections (Woolfson 2007). (See Chapter 2 for an extended discussion of the implications of globalization for labour standards.) In the UK, concerns about the adverse social consequences of increased migration from Eastern Europe, particularly the strain put on local public services, are widespread.

But there is no automatic link between migration and the dilution of labour standards. The onus is on governments to enforce existing employment protection, or to enhance it, so that migrant workers are not used by employers as a cheap and easily disposable workforce in a way that contributes to the deterioration of labour standards. In the UK the government has come under increasing pressure from trade unions and campaign organizations to enforce existing employment regulation, like the National Minimum Wage, more rigorously.

Generally, trade unions support the free movement of labour, and welcome migrant workers, because of the improvements in economic competitiveness it generates. However, they highlight the importance of improving, and rigorously enforcing, existing employment laws so that migrant workers are not exploited by employers and used as a cheap source of disposable labour. Unions are also keen to organize migrant workers, so that they are better placed to win better pay and conditions themselves, and promote solidarity with indigenous workers. For example, the GMB union launched a campaign to help unionize Polish migrant workers in two cities, Southampton and Glasgow. It worked with members of the local Polish communities to establish dedicated union branches specifically for Polish workers.

While much of the attention has been directed towards the impact of migration from Eastern Europe on employment relations, EU enlargement has posed the social dimension with other challenges too. The dismantling of economic barriers has enhanced the capacity of multinational companies to engage in social dumping; it has become easier for them to move production to Eastern European countries, where wages are lower and labour standards generally weaker. As a result, workers in Western Europe come under pressure to respond by moderating their wage demands, for example, or by accepting the deterioration of working conditions.

EU enlargement has also brought into sharper focus the contrast between 'positive' and 'negative' harmonization as competing visions of how labour regulation across Europe should operate (Hepple 2005). On the one hand, positive harmonization portends an interventionist role for the EU in setting or encouraging minimum employment standards to ensure that workers throughout Europe are adequately protected. On the other hand, however, the emphasis of negative harmonization is on creating a level playing field of employment standards through deregulation, allowing employers greater scope to benefit from an integrated and open market. For those, like the trade unions, for example, who want to maintain and improve upon existing employment standards, the increased mobility of businesses and workers in an enlarged EU poses a major threat. This is evident in some high profile industrial disputes. See Box 3.12 for the case of Irish Ferries.

The Irish Ferries dispute

The Irish Ferries dispute illustrates how EU enlargement potentially erodes labour standards since it allows companies wanting to pursue cost savings more scope to substitute their existing workforce with lower-paid workers from Eastern Europe. In 2004 Irish Ferries came into conflict with the Irish trade union SIPTU after it started replacing its existing Irish workforce with cheaper, non-Irish workers on some of its routes. However, matters were exacerbated the following year when the company announced it wanted over 500 'voluntary' redundancies from its unionized Irish staff, who would be replaced by non-union agency workers from Eastern Europe at much lower wages (Donaghey and Teague 2006: 658). While many staff accepted voluntary redundancy, a significant number did not and faced a huge pay cut when Irish Ferries instituted the lower rate of pay.

Following legal action in the Irish courts by SIPTU, and an intervention from the Irish Labour Court, which issued a non-binding recommendation that the company carry on employing Irish staff until 2007, the company took a harder line, which included sending replacement Eastern European workers on to the *Isle of Inishmore* vessel accompanied by security guards disguised as passengers. When crew members realized what was happening they seized control of the ship and instituted anti-piracy measures, some locking themselves in the boiler room. The dispute then escalated as port workers refused to handle any Irish Ferries vessels. Tens of thousands of workers also took to the streets in a number of Irish towns and cities to demonstrate their support for the beleaguered workforce as part of a 'national day of protest' (Woolfson 2007: 211).

In December 2005 a legally binding settlement allowed the company to continue with its plans to restructure its labour force, with a more generous redundancy package in place for existing staff who agreed to depart. Irish Ferries was also required to ensure that replacement workers were paid at least the Irish minimum wage, considerably more than the company had originally intended. A year after the dispute, just 12 members of the directly employed unionized workforce remained with the company out of the more than 500 who previously had jobs there. Given these events, Irish opposition to the EU's Treaty of Lisbon, particularly among workers, is perhaps easier to comprehend.

The most well-known legal case to have gone before the ECJ concerned a dispute over the employment of a relatively small number of Latvian workers on a construction project in Sweden. The Laval, or Vaxholm, dispute demonstrates the conflict that exists between the right of workers to take collective action like strikes and the right of businesses to benefit from the single market (Woolfson 2007). It also demonstrates the potential threat posed by EU enlargement to national-level employment regulation. The dispute involved a Latvian company, Laval un Partneri, which employed Latvian workers to refurbish a school in the Swedish town of Vaxholm on wages that were well below those set by collective bargaining in Sweden. The Swedish unions, which viewed this both as a threat to the wage levels agreed by collective bargaining within Sweden and also the effectiveness of collective bargaining itself, mounted industrial action against Laval, which was legal under Swedish law.

In December 2007 the ECJ ruled that although there was a fundamental right to undertake industrial action, it was outweighed by the even more fundamental right of business to operate freely within the single market, and found in favour of the company. The ECJ, in trying to strike a balance between the principle of upholding labour standards on the one hand, and the principle of supporting market integration on the other, seems increasingly to be coming down on the side of the latter.

Such decisions have raised questions about how effectively the EU's Social Dimension protects labour standards in an integrated Europe. The Posting of Workers Directive (1996) gives workers who are posted abroad to another EU member state for a limited period of time the right to the same core pay and conditions enjoyed by local workers. The aim is to combat social dumping, by preventing employers from bringing in workers from abroad to do jobs on lower rates of pay and with fewer conditions than indigenous workers. The January 2009 Lindsey oil refinery dispute, which involved walk-outs in protest against the use of Portuguese and Italian workers who had been brought in by the contractor to undertake construction work, arose in part because of a concern over the use of cheaper foreign labour.

Yet the ECJ's decision in the Laval case appears to validate the use of social dumping as a legitimate tool of labour management. While the Posting of Workers Directive was designed to help strike a balance between the desirability of a free market in the EU and the need to protect labour standards, in practice it has done little to prevent social dumping, suggesting that more needs to be done to make it an effective employment relations policy instrument (Cremers, Erik Dølvik, and Bosch 2007).

These disputes indicate the potential threat EU enlargement, in combination with a neo-liberal emphasis on free markets, poses to employment standards across Europe. They also point to the conflict that exists between the principle of market integration, whereupon the emphasis is given to the rights of businesses and workers to operate across the EU without hindrance, and the desirability of social and employment measures, which are increasingly seen as impediments to the effective functioning of the common market (Woolfson 2007).

EU enlargement has accentuated the potential for social dumping, exacerbating a 'race to the bottom' in labour standards (Donaghey and Teague 2006). For Woolfson (2007: 212), the most important challenge facing trade unions is that of 'preserving existing standards of employment in the altered context of the new Europe'. They should not place too much faith in the capacity of the Charter of Fundamental Rights to alter things, assuming it is ever formally enacted. The ECJ already draws upon the Charter, along with other relevant sources, to inform its judgements (Syrpis 2008).

The faltering EU social dimension is unlikely to be revived through judicial interventions. Rather, the actions of trade unions, and EU citizens themselves, offer the best chance of shifting the process of European integration in a more social direction. The campaigning efforts of the ETUC and other union bodies do much to ensure that workers' interests are heard at EU level. Moreover, the democratically elected European Parliament is increasingly acting as a bulwark against neo-liberal policies that would otherwise weaken the social dimension still further. For example, see Section 3.4.2 for the role played by the European Parliament in amending the Bolkestein Directive.

Nevertheless, despite much rhetoric about the EU's social dimension, our analysis has demonstrated the large extent to which it has been subordinate to powerful pressures of market integration. From this perspective, the social dimension has been a rather marginal aspect of the process of European integration. EU legislation in the area of social and employment policy has done little to counter the increased scope of multinational companies to benefit from the removal of economic and political barriers, including the use of social dumping as a way of reducing costs.

SECTION SUMMARY AND FURTHER READING

- During the 1980s and 1990s, the development of the 'social dimension', encompassing legislation in areas such as working time, and information and consultation rights for workers, became an increasingly important aspect of the process of European integration. Nevertheless, it remained subordinate to the process of market integration and was progressed largely in so far as it legitimized greater economic union.

- Since the late 1990s, the importance of the social dimension has declined, linked to the growing neo-liberal emphasis on free markets inspired by the Lisbon Agenda. EU policy-makers prefer to use 'soft' regulation, in the form of non-binding targets and guidelines, over 'hard' regulation, in the form of legislation, to realize social and employment goals. This is particularly evident in the measures that comprise the European Employment Strategy.

- The Charter of Fundamental Rights of the European Union would appear to portend a revival in the social dimension to European integration. While it has some symbolic importance, and is increasingly being used to inform judicial decisions, on its own the Charter is unlikely to reverse the neo-liberal trend towards free markets. The impact of enlargement demonstrates how the principle of market integration outweighs the desirability of social protection within the contemporary EU.

For the history of the 'social dimension' see Hall (1994), and the more critical analysis offered by Martin and Ross (1999). Both Adnett and Hardy (2005) and Hepple (2005: Chapters 8 and 9) are recommended sources of information on the employment relations implications of European integration. Each year one issue of the *Industrial Relations Journal* is devoted to European employment relations matters. The *European Journal of Industrial Relations* also contains relevant academic papers. For online sources of information, the following web sites are recommended:

The European Trade Union Confederation http://www.etuc.org/

The European Foundation for the Improvement of Living and Working Conditions http://www.eurofound.europa.eu/

The European Industrial Relations Observatory http://www.eurofound.europa.eu/eiro/

 Visit our Online Resource Centre for web links to sites connected to this section. www.oxfordtextbooks.co.uk/williams_adamsmith2e

Conclusion

This chapter has examined the highly politicized nature of employment relations. We have considered the influence of state policy, and the implications of greater European integration for employment relations. One thing that will be evident is the large extent to which both British governments and the EU have been concerned with developing and enacting policies that provide businesses with a supportive environment in which they can pursue growth more readily. The Conservatives' legislative reforms of the 1980s and 1990s, for example, were impelled by a belief that excessive union power was an obstacle to economic competitiveness, and that greater labour market deregulation was a necessary, and indeed desirable, component of wealth creation. During the late 1990s and 2000s

Labour has made some notable policy interventions ostensibly designed to favour workers and trade unions; yet in general they have been enacted in ways that ensure they do not conflict with the primacy of a neo-liberal belief that deregulated labour markets and weak trade unions are necessary components of a competitive economy. Looking beyond the UK, the impetus of the EU's 'social dimension' has dwindled markedly, a further reflection of its inferior status relative to the process of market integration, something that the process of EU enlargement has brought into particularly sharp focus.

It would be reasonable to suppose, therefore, that the nature of Labour and the EU's respective policy agendas is to maintain and extend the power of capital by accommodating, containing, and incorporating workers' and unions' interests, as opposed to the more obviously repressive approach taken by the Conservatives during the 1980s and 1990s. Yet it is important not to underplay the efforts expended by the trade unions in shaping the public policy agenda. Within the EU, for example, policy-makers are often sensitive to union activities and initiatives. Moreover, Labour's domestic programme of employment relations reform is strongly influenced by the efforts of the union movement to ensure that favourable policies were enacted. Thus it is important to recognize that the decisions made by state policy-makers, and those in supranational bodies like the EU, are not entirely concerned with supporting the aims of capital, but may also be disposed to the labour interest under some circumstances.

Assignment and discussion questions

1   What is voluntarism in employment relations? Why has its significance declined?

2   Identify the main implications of neo-liberal policies for employment relations.

3   Assess the extent to which the actions of the Labour governments of the 1990s and 2000s continued the public policy approach begun by preceding Conservative governments.

4   Discuss the view that trade unions would be more effective in achieving their aims if they were not so closely identified with the Labour party.

5   What is meant by the 'social dimension' of the EU? How successful has the EU been in achieving its social objectives?

6   What have been the main effects of EU enlargement on employment relations?

Visit our Online Resource Centre for answers to these questions.
www.oxfordtextbooks.co.uk/williams_adamsmith2e

Take your learning further: online resource centre

Visit the Online Resource Centre that accompanies this book to enrich your understanding of Chapter 3: The politics of employment relations. Explore web links, test yourself using an interactive flashcard glossary, and keep up to date with the latest developments in the area.

http://www.oxfordtextbooks.co.uk/orc/williams_adamsmith2e.

Chapter case study

Trade unions and the Euro

One of the key ways in which the 1993 Maastricht Treaty of European Union boosted the process of market integration was by setting out the convergence criteria for Economic and Monetary Union (EMU) and the adoption of the single currency—the Euro—though not as yet in the UK. In order to satisfy the conditions for EMU, member states were required to meet a rigid set of rules, or criteria, to facilitate the convergence of their economies. One of these was an obligation, supported by the 1996 Growth and Stability Pact, to keep budget deficits normally to within 3 percent or less of gross domestic product. Governed by a new European Central Bank, this policy was designed to impose strict price stability across Europe and thus keep inflation under control.

Progress towards EMU, with its priority of maintaining low inflation and controlling public expenditure to keep budget deficits within limits, has had a significant impact on the daily lives of workers and their families in those countries that have adopted the single currency—the Euro. The potential effect of EMU on their members has prompted trade unions across Europe to consider whether or not they should support entry into the Euro by their respective countries. Their response has been varied: no more so than among public sector unions whose members may bear the brunt of economic policies pursued by governments to maintain compliance with the Stability and Growth Pact's requirements on public sector borrowing.

Foster and Scott (2003) investigated the views of public sector unions towards EMU both in countries that had joined, and those that, to date, had not. They characterize union approaches under four broad headings. First, there are the 'Enthusiasts'. Public sector unions in Ireland are most typical of those holding this view. The country has received considerable benefits to its economy, and to the standard of living of the population, as a result of membership of the EU. It has developed a strong national-level social partnership in employment relations that has allowed the impact of economic controls to be mediated in terms of their effect on workers.

The second stance is labelled as the 'Altruists'. This tends to be the dominant position of public sector unions within the EU. It accepts that the impact of EMU will have short-term negative implications for the state sector. However, the belief here is that, in the longer term, EMU will deliver an improved economic situation, leading to greater prosperity, eventually benefiting those working in the state sector.

The 'Sceptics', at best, are resigned to the need for EMU, but have significant fears for the level of social provision that countries will be able to afford. Associated with this concern is the fear of job losses within the public sector. French unions are portrayed as most typical of the sceptical view, and the country has witnessed industrial action aimed at halting government proposals that could damage workers' employment terms, over reduced public sector pensions, for example.

The final approach identified by the authors is the 'Resisters'. This view can be seen within the UK public sector unions, where entry to EMU is opposed because of the claimed loss of national sovereignty over public spending. Resistance is deemed necessary so that control over welfare spending remains in the hands of national governments. From this perspective, EMU is part of a neo-liberal challenge to labour market regulation and trade unions.

Foster and Scott (2003) also highlight the large body of resistance to EMU that may exist among populations, including union members, throughout Europe. Even where union leaderships have been broadly supportive of EMU, many unionists have opposed entry. For example, the referendum in Denmark rejected adopting the Euro even though the public sector union supported the proposal. Unions should not assume members will unquestioningly follow their leaders' advice.

1. What are the implications of Economic and Monetary Union for employment relations in Europe?

2. What are the benefits and disadvantages to trade unions and their members of Economic and Monetary Union?

4

Social divisions and employment relations

Chapter objectives:

The main objectives of this chapter are to:

* explain the nature of employment disadvantage, and to consider the implications for employment relations;

* assess public policy and legislative developments designed to challenge disadvantage in employment;

* consider the extent, nature, and implications of employer-led initiatives designed to reduce disadvantage, including equal opportunity policies, the diversity management approach, and work–life balance initiatives; and

* examine the efforts made by trade unions to represent the interests of workers from disadvantaged social groups.

4.1 Introduction

Following on from Chapters 2 and 3, in which we examined employment relations in the contemporary economy, and the politics of employment relations respectively, this chapter, the third of those that aim to analyse contemporary employment relations' developments in a broader context, focuses on the influence of social divisions. By this we mean aspects of disadvantage and inequality that are socially constituted, that reflect people's shared social characteristics, such as gender, for example. The aim of this chapter is to provide you with a good knowledge of the nature, and principal features, of inequality and disadvantage in employment relations, and to enable you to develop a critical understanding of the main ways in which they have been addressed.

We start, in Section 4.2, by briefly assessing the dimensions of inequality and disadvantage at work, something which includes a discussion of divisions based on social class. Following on from this, in Section 4.3 we introduce and critically assess the evolving legal and policy framework governing equality and diversity issues, including family-friendly and work–life balance measures. The main focus of Section 4.4 is on understanding and interpreting employers' interventions, particularly equal opportunities and managing diversity policies, before Section 4.5 considers how the trade unions have attempted to promote greater workplace equality.

Introductory case study

Pregnancy discrimination at work

Despite being unlawful, studies show that each year tens of thousands of women workers are discriminated against on the grounds of their pregnancy. Between 2003 and 2005 the Equal Opportunities Commission (EOC) mounted a major investigation of pregnancy-related discrimination at work, including research with employers and a survey of 1,000 women who had worked during a recent pregnancy (EOC 2005). The EOC found that nearly a half (45 per cent) of the women they surveyed reported being discriminated against, which included being sacked in some cases. Other discriminatory practices included: failing to be get appropriate pay rises, and missing out on training opportunities. Young women, black and ethnic minority women, women who are relatively new to their jobs, and women on low incomes seem to be particularly prone to discriminatory treatment.

The issue of pregnancy-related discrimination highlights a number of important topics that we consider further in this chapter. One of these is the effectiveness of the law as a means of challenging employment disadvantage. Since discrimination on the grounds of pregnancy is unlawful, and has been since the mid 1970s, why is the law not a more effective instrument? Without effective enforcement the law can be a weak mechanism for protecting workers. A second topic concerns the role of managers in organizations. The EOC found that insufficient knowledge and understanding of maternity rights on the part of line managers, and a failure to manage pregnancy effectively, were among the main causes of pregnancy-related discrimination. As we see below, managerial commitment to anti-discrimination and equal opportunities provisions is sometimes found wanting. Third, how does pregnancy-related discrimination affect an employer's business? The EOC (2005: 7) observed that poor treatment of women during pregnancy 'makes it much less likely that they will return to their old jobs after maternity leave'. Employers who manage pregnancy effectively, however, are more likely to retain talented and more productive staff. The assumption is that where employers make a concerted effort to tackle discrimination and promote equality it can benefit their business. One of the main features of this chapter is to assess the extent to which there really is a strong 'business case' for equality and anti-discrimination action. Before we tackle such issues, however, we need to assess the nature of inequality and disadvantage at work, starting with the important, and often unjustifiably neglected, topic of social class.

4.2 **Workplace inequality and employment relations**

For many years, the principal focus of studies of workplace inequality concerned the so-called status divide between manual and non-manual workers. In this section, we consider the extent to which occupational and organizational changes have eradicated such inequality in British workplaces. We also direct our attention to the importance of other manifestations of inequality at work, those based on shared social characteristics such as gender. After reading this section, you will be better placed to appreciate the relevance of social divisions to employment relations in contemporary Britain.

4.2.1 Social class, inequality, and the status divide

Traditionally, the most fundamental divisions in society are those that are seen to arise from social class. The concept of class refers to hierarchical divisions in society which reflect differences in people's access to material resources. Social inequality and disadvantage are the consequences of differences in people's life chances, including access to education and employment opportunities, which reflect their class position. Generally, human resource management texts, while paying full attention to the employment implications of divisions created by gender, ethnicity, and disability, neglect to consider the effects of social class. Historically, though, class differences in society both reflected, and in turn exercised an important influence over, employment relationships. The concept of social class has long been the subject of much debate and controversy. One thing that is clear, however, is that someone's economic situation, in particular their occupation, is a major determinant of their class position. You need only think about how strongly the term 'working class' is associated with routine, manual labour in factory settings. Thus the concept of social class captures the way in which people have a sense of shared, collective identity based upon their work situation.

Traditionally, in employment relations, class divisions were manifest in the status divide that long existed between manual, blue-collar workers and their non-manual, white-collar 'staff' counterparts for much of the twentieth century. In manufacturing industry, for example, manual workers enjoyed the least favourable terms and conditions of employment, including a longer working week, shorter holidays, and fewer fringe benefits. Many firms had different canteen facilities for their manual and non-manual employees. Ninety per cent of manual workers were fined if they were late for work, whereas only a minority of non-manuals, and few managers, had to endure such a penalty (Wedderburn and Craig 1974). Non-manual work, largely undertaken in an office environment, was associated with higher status, better terms and conditions of employment, and greater job security. White-collar employees were more likely to benefit from sick pay arrangements, and enjoy longer holidays, a shorter working week, greater opportunities for promotion, and more autonomy at work (Price 1989).

What accounts for the higher status that was accorded to white-collar, non-manual staff? By virtue of the closer relationship they had with their employers, relative to manual workers, non-manual employees were considered to be more committed to the aims of the organization, possessed greater intrinsic motivation, generated by relatively high job security and career development opportunities in particular, and were thought to be more trustworthy as a result (Fox 1974; Lockwood 1958; Price and Price 1994). Detailed control of their work was largely unnecessary. Thus 'greater proximity to the functions of the employer brought with it higher social status and greater privileges in conditions of employment' (Price 1989: 277). Manual workers, however, were subject to a much more regimented employment regime, with strict controls over matters including working time, attendance, and discipline, since they were thought to exhibit less organizational commitment (Price 1989).

In the twenty-first century does the concept of social class, with all that it entails for employment relations, still have any relevance? Politicians often refer to the UK as a 'classless society', implying that the importance of social class as a source of disadvantage has diminished, and that it no longer acts as a barrier to individual self-advancement. It is often held that the salience of class has declined (e.g. Pakulski and Waters 1996), and that other sources of social identity, like gender or ethnicity, for example, have become more important sources of social inequality and disadvantage. Alternatively, inequality and disadvantage do not arise so much from differences in people's collective class position, but rather reflect variations in the talent and ability of individual workers, and thus their capacity to improve their livelihoods and advance their careers (see McGovern et al. 2007: 81–3).

The decline of the trade unions (see Chapter 6) is sometimes said to reflect the dwindling relevance of class, as the working class occupations on which many unions were founded, have become less prevalent. The supposed closing of the status divide at work, manifested by the supposed trend towards the 'harmonization' of employment conditions in Britain (Russell 1992), is a further reflection of the declining salience of class in employment relations. Organizational restructuring, in particular the demand for greater workplace flexibility, is held to have undermined traditional occupational patterns, and thus eroded the established distinction between manual and non-manual employees (Bradley et al. 2000).

Much of the impetus for reform came from the activities of foreign-owned multinationals in Britain, such as the American company Johnston and Johnston, for example. In their concern to enhance flexibility and employee commitment, and to generate a more cooperative employment relations environment, such firms have sought to extend the benefits traditionally enjoyed by non-manual employees to their manual counterparts (Price 1989; Price and Price 1994). In many cases, this has resulted in the conclusion of single-status agreements, where all employees, regardless of their job role, enjoy the same conditions of service and fringe benefits (Bassett 1987). Perhaps the best-known of these single-status agreements is that which was reached in local government in 1997. It established a single pay spine for manual, and administrative, professional, clerical, and technical (APC&T) staff, and it harmonized basic working conditions such as working time and holiday entitlement. The implementation of this agreement across the country, however, was rather difficult, not least because of insufficient funding (Bach and Winchester 2003).

While undoubtedly an important aspect of contemporary employment relations, overall harmonization has been of limited significance. Although occupational change has rendered the distinction between manual and non-manual employment less important than it once was, not least because of the growth of non-manual jobs in the economy, the status divide remains a durable feature of employment relations, and thus a source of workplace inequality. Access to a variety of benefits, including occupational pension schemes, paid holiday entitlement, and sick pay, is strongly linked to one's position in the occupational, and by implication, the class hierarchy (McGovern et al. 2007).

The enduring status divide at work is by no means the only evidence of the persistence of class-based inequality. Since the 1970s, for example, social mobility has been largely stable (Cabinet Office 2008); in other words, the class position of one's parents exercises as great an influence over one's own life chances as they did over a quarter of a century ago. As we see in Chapter 7, there has also been a notable growth in income inequality. All this indicates that UK society remains 'riven' by class divisions (Erickson et al. 2009).

Social inequalities based on class are an important feature of contemporary societies. Not only are class divisions still evident within the workplace, but work itself is an important source of the social class divide given the large extent to which one's occupation influences one's overall life chances (e.g. health, access to education, etc). Moreover, in the absence of any trend towards greater social mobility, the class position of one's parents, derived from their occupations, and the way in which they affect the life-chances of their children, continue to exercise a profound influence over employment outcomes in contemporary society.

4.2.2 Disadvantage at work: towards a broader agenda

Though important, on its own the persistence of class inequality insufficiently accounts for employment disadvantage in contemporary workplaces. Other sources of social identity, like gender or ethnicity, for example, also create divisions. If we take gender, for instance, one of the main weaknesses of the traditional, institutional approach to employment relations was its emphasis on arrangements in male-dominated manual work environments that were characterized by the presence of a strong trade union and collective bargaining (Greene 2003).

Consequently, the role of women workers, the relationship between men and women at work, and the ways in which these influenced employment relations have often been rather neglected (Wacjman 2000). Instead, 'there is a tendency to treat workers as homogeneous, with this homogeneity based around male experience' (Greene 2003: 308). But gender, the 'lived relationships between men and women through which sexual differences and ideas about sexual differences are constructed' (Bradley 1996: 82), exercises an important influence on the conduct of employment relations.

Although we focus on gender inequality at work in this section, this should not imply that other sources of disadvantage are less important. In spite of changing social attitudes and growing tolerance about people's sexual orientation, reports of discrimination against lesbian and gay workers persist (see Bairstow 2004). Widespread discrimination on the grounds of age has also been reported; according to a 2006 report from the Employers' Forum on Age, some three-fifths (61 per cent) of employees have witnessed manifestations of ageism (EFA 2006). A 2006 study by the Equal Opportunities Commission found that a fifth of mainly Muslim women of Pakistani and Bangladeshi origin had experienced negative attitudes to religious dress at work (EOC 2006). There is a long history of discrimination against disabled people in employment, who are especially prone to unemployment or segregation in poorly paid, low-skilled jobs as a result (Barnes 1992). Disadvantage on grounds of 'race' and ethnicity is also a feature of employment in Britain; generally black and minority ethnic workers are more likely to be unemployed, or work in low-paid jobs with few career prospects, than their white counterparts, and are markedly less evident in managerial roles (Bradley and Healy 2008).

For reasons of space, however, in this section we concentrate on the pattern of gender inequality and disadvantage at work. Historically, women were generally channelled by employers, often with the support of male-dominated trade unions, into poorly paid, low-skilled jobs that offered few opportunities for promotion (Bradley 1989), or were excluded from the workforce entirely. There is evidence of progress towards gender equality in contemporary Britain. For one thing, greater numbers of women now undertake paid employment; in 2006 women made up 46 per cent of the employed workforce (Bradley and Healy 2008). Moreover, growing numbers of women have secured entry to hitherto male-dominated professional and managerial jobs, in areas such as education (Crompton and Sanderson 1990; Walby 1997). As a result, 'women's over-representation in lower-grade and less well-paid occupations has been reduced, and their representation in professional and managerial occupations has increased' (Crompton 1997: 46). In 2004, for example, around a third of managers in British workplaces were female (Kersley et al. 2006).

Yet the progress towards gender equality at work should not be overstated. For one thing, although it has been eroded, the segregation of jobs and occupations based on gender remains a marked feature of contemporary employment relations. It is conventional to distinguish between 'vertical' and 'horizontal' gender segregation (Hakim 1979), although in practice the two are related (Bradley 1999). Vertical segregation refers to the over-representation of women in relatively poorly paid and low-skilled jobs at the bottom of organizational hierarchies, and their under-representation in executive and managerial roles. Horizontal segregation applies to the over-representation of women in particular occupations, such as that of supermarket cashier or nursing, for example, and their under-representation in others.

Contemporary employment relations is characterized by gender segregation in respect of work and occupations (Bradley and Healy 2008). Relative to males, female managers are under-represented in over two-thirds of workplaces (Kersley et al. 2006). In respect of manual jobs, horizontal segregation is pronounced, 'with men dominating, for example, in construction, transport and metalwork while women remain clustered in female specialisms as care assistants, hairdressers and cashiers' (Bradley et al. 2000: 83).

Although female participation in the labour force has grown, much women's employment is concentrated in poorly remunerated, part-time jobs in the service sector where opportunities for career progression are very limited (Women and Work Commission 2006), and which are often depicted as being less important than full-time ones. In the Royal Mail, for example, the male-dominated trade union sought to exclude the largely female part-time workforce from access to overtime arrangements, and thus better wages, on the grounds that their earnings were less important than those of full-time employees (Jenkins, Martinez Lucio, and Noon 2002).

The persistence of gender segregation at work is perhaps one of the main reasons why the gender pay gap has proved to be so resilient. This is the difference between the average earnings of men and those of women, and is a major aspect of gender disadvantage (see Box 4.1). In 2007, for full-time employees this gap was 17 per cent, meaning that average earnings for female employees are little more than four-fifths those of men. According to Hakim (1996: 150–1), studies of particular occupations 'indicate that vertical job segregation accounts for virtually all the difference'. In other words, women earn less on average than men because they are over-represented among poorly remunerated jobs at the bottom of organizational hierarchies. For Hakim (1996), the concentration of women

---

Employment relations reflection 4.1   The gender pay gap—an analysis

In February 2006, the UK government's Women and Work Commission published its report on gender pay inequality in Britain, *Shaping a Fairer Future*, and made a number of recommendations concerning how it could be reduced (Women and Work Commission 2006). The report shows that there is a mean average difference of 17 per cent between full-time hourly male earnings and those of female workers; the gap between full-time males and part-time females stands at 41 per cent. The 'gender pay gap' is a feature of most industries and occupations; but is particularly pronounced in some. The difference between full-time male and full-time female average hourly earnings in the financial services sector, for example, is 43 per cent. The gender pay gap in the United Kingdom is the largest in the European Union (EU).

   The report identifies two main causes of the gender pay gap. The first is occupational segregation; women's employment is concentrated in low-paying sectors of the economy where prospects for promotion are limited. The Commission highlights the high proportion of women's jobs that are located in the five 'c's of the labour market: cleaning, catering, caring, cashiering, and clerical work. In order to challenge such occupational segregation, education courses, vocational training provision, and careers literature should be redesigned to challenge traditional gender stereotypes that discourage girls and young women from entry into relatively well-paid male dominated occupations.

   The second main cause of the gender pay gap identified by the Women and Work Commission concerns the unequal burden of childcare and other domestic responsibilities. This often restricts women to part-time jobs, and other forms of flexible employment. Where women do make use of flexible working arrangements their career and salary prospects often suffer as a result. Among other things, the Commission urges employers to make more of an effort to recognize the contribution and potential of part-time workers.

   The Commission's report is imbued by a belief that, with sufficient encouragement, the voluntary efforts of employers, who are presented as largely blameless of any discrimination, and particularly women themselves, should be enough to effect positive change. The culpability for gender pay inequality is seen to rest with the education system for not doing enough to challenge traditional gender stereotypes. The Commission's report is largely exhortative. It calls for a culture change in respect of women's aspirations and employers' attitudes; but no sanctions are proposed if the latter fail to take action.

---

in low-paid, part-time jobs largely reflects women's own choices; many women choose not to pursue organizational careers to the same degree as men, but focus on their family responsibilities, perhaps combining them with part-time employment.

   Yet the existence of vertical segregation does not adequately explain the resilience of the gender pay gap. There is evidence that 'male-dominated jobs tend to be paid at a higher level than female-dominated jobs of an equivalent level of skill and qualification' (IDS 2003: 13). Thus those jobs that are largely undertaken by women are undervalued and not accorded as much importance as those that are primarily filled by men, even when, objectively, they appear to be equally, or perhaps more, demanding. Occupations and jobs that are primarily the preserve of women are treated as less important, not so highly skilled, and thus attract less pay than those that are largely filled by men (Dex, Sutherland, and Joshi 2000). Moreover, pay systems often operate in ways that disadvantage women at work, by linking earnings to length of service, for example (McColgan 1997).

A further, more fundamental problem with Hakim's notion that gender segregation at work, and thus the gender pay gap, reflect the choices exercised by many women (Hakim 1996) is that it pays insufficient heed to the structural constraints that inhibit women from advancing in organizations, in particular the ways in which men attempt to exercise power over, and exclude, them (Bradley 1999). The term 'glass ceiling' has been popularized to refer to the invisible barrier that seems to hinder women from getting to the top of organizations.

Gender disadvantage, as well as other forms of social inequality, is still a significant feature of contemporary employment relations in Britain. Yet different sources of social division are interconnected. If we take gender and ethnicity, for example, it is women of Pakistani and Bangladeshi origin who tend to experience the most disadvantage (Bradley and Healy 2008). Moreover, while looking at social class in isolation fails to recognize the importance of other sources of employment disadvantage, workplace inequality cannot be properly understood without reference to its interaction with other aspects of social identity, such as gender and ethnicity, for example. Although women increasingly occupy managerial and professional roles, many others lack access to such positions, and work in low-paid jobs with few opportunities for career progression, not just on account of their gender, but also because of their class position.

SECTION SUMMARY AND FURTHER READING

- Inequality at work has long been manifested in the status divide, reflecting divisions based on social class, something that harmonization initiatives have done relatively little to eradicate.

- Nevertheless, a broader conceptualization of social divisions at work is desirable, one that considers the implications for employment relations of disadvantage based on age, sexual orientation, disability, race and ethnicity, and gender. Gender inequality at work is reflected in the persistence of job segregation and the lower earnings of women, relative to those of men.

There are some good studies of developments in female employment; Bradley (1999), and Bradley et al. (2000: Chapter 4) are particularly recommended. See Erickson et al. (2009: Chapter 8) for an overview of the relevance of social class and other aspects of inequality.

 Visit our Online Resource Centre for web links to sites connected to this section. www.oxfordtextbooks.co.uk/williams_adamsmith2e

---

4.3 Public policy, anti-discrimination legislation, and equality at work

This section is concerned with examining the implications of the principal legislative interventions designed to challenge inequality and disadvantage at work, and the public policy assumptions that underpin them. Following an analysis of the way in which the legislation evolved between the 1970s and the 1990s, we consider the changes enacted since 1997 by the Labour administrations of Tony Blair and Gordon Brown, including the extension of protection from discrimination and the provision of rights to 'family-friendly' working arrangements. The legislative framework governing equality at work is then interpreted and assessed.

4.3.1 Public policy and the development of equality legislation

Since the 1970s the development of anti-discrimination and equality legislation has been a notable feature of employment relations in the UK. Initially, governments were concerned with discrimination on grounds of sex and race, though by the 1990s the need to challenge discriminatory treatment with regard to people with disabilities was also recognized. See Box 4.2 for details of the main pieces of anti-discrimination and equality legislation between the 1970s and 1990s.

During the 1970s, legislation designed to promote equality at work helped to erode the voluntarist basis of employment relations in Britain. The 1970 Equal Pay Act, which came into effect fully in 1975, provided for equal pay between men and women when engaged in 'like work'. Also in 1975, the principle that pregnant women be entitled to a period of paid maternity absence was established, alongside protection against discrimination on the grounds of pregnancy.

The 1975 Sex Discrimination Act made direct and indirect discrimination against women in employment unlawful. Direct discrimination refers to circumstances where a man or woman is not considered for employment, or for promotion, or a pay rise, among other things, purely because of their sex. The concept of indirect discrimination, however, concerns the situation where a condition of employment is applied 'to both sexes of a kind such that the proportion of one sex who can comply with it is considerably smaller. An example might be when a police force specifies that all candidates for the post of police officer must be two metres tall' (Cockburn 1991: 28–9). See Table 4.1 for key concepts related to the area of discrimination.

LEGISLATION AND POLICY 4.2

The main equality and anti-discrimination legislation of the 1970s–90s

Equal Pay Act (1970): provides for equal pay between men and women when engaged in 'like work'

Sex Discrimination Act (1975): prohibits direct and indirect discrimination in employment in relation to sex

Race Relations Act (1976): prohibits direct and indirect discrimination in employment in relation to race and ethnicity

Equal Pay (Equal Pay for Work of Equal Value) Regulations (1983): provide for equal pay between men and women when engaged in work of equal value

Disability Discrimination Act (1995): obliges employers to make 'reasonable adjustments' to ensure that a disabled employee, or potential employee, was not substantially disadvantaged; small firms were exempted

Table 4.1 Discrimination: key concepts

Concept	Definition
Direct discrimination	Unfair discrimination that arises where someone is treated less favourably in employment on account of their sex, race, etc
Indirect discrimination	Unfair discrimination that arises where a condition of employment is applied which results in a worker being treated less favourably on account of their sex, race, etc
Positive action	Measures designed to correct the under-representation of certain groups of workers through interventions which help their employment prospects (e.g. training and development)
Positive discrimination	Measures designed to correct the under-representation of certain groups of workers by giving them preferential treatment (e.g. quotas)—unlawful in the UK

Similarly, the 1976 Race Relations Act prohibited direct and indirect discrimination in employment on the grounds of race. Two state bodies, the Equal Opportunities Commission (EOC) and the Commission for Racial Equality (CRE), were established to promote, monitor, and provide guidance on the new anti-discrimination legislation.

Pressure from campaigning groups and trade union activists was an important impetus for the enactment of legislation covering equal pay and sex discrimination in particular (Cockburn 1991). Many of the more blatant discriminatory practices that had hitherto existed were eradicated as a result (Dickens 2000a). Nevertheless, the union movement's enthusiasm for equal pay was constrained by a desire not to upset existing pay structures, most of which operated largely to the benefit of men. While the equal pay legislation did cause the gender pay gap to close somewhat during the 1970s, its effect was rather short-lived (Dickens 1992; O'Donovan and Szyszczack 1988).

The development of anti-discrimination legislation was, and to a large extent continues to be, marked by a 'liberal' approach to securing greater equality (Dickens 2000a). This involves trying to ensure that people are accorded equal treatment regardless of their social characteristics (Jewson and Mason 1986). Progress towards equality is achieved by using formal procedures, covering recruitment, selection, and promotion decisions, for example, that encourage managers to treat people as if they are the same, reducing the salience of social differences (Liff and Wacjman 1996). The main instrument of redress for workers who claim to have experienced unlawful discrimination is to submit a claim to an employment tribunal, with an appropriate financial award the main form of recompense in successful cases (Dickens 2007). See Chapter 9 for more information about the system of employment tribunals.

With the 'radical' approach to securing greater equality, however, there is a greater emphasis on the importance of influencing outcomes directly, rather than on ensuring that processes are in place to treat people the same, regardless of their social characteristics. Radical measures encompass, for example, 'positive action' to deal with, say, the under-representation of particular categories of workers, such as women or black and minority ethnic workers, and can take the form of dedicated training interventions designed to increase their participation. While the law generally does not encourage positive action, unlike 'positive discrimination' it is not unlawful. Positive discrimination involves giving members of disadvantaged social groups preferential treatment in the jobs market or in promotion decisions. In the United States, affirmative action programmes are often used as a means of correcting the under-representation of black workers in certain jobs and occupations, and can be rather controversial.

As we saw in Chapter 3, the Conservative governments of the 1980s and 1990s favoured a deregulatory public policy approach, one based on the desirability of giving employers greater control over their own employment relations arrangements. In the area of equality, the Conservatives largely eschewed legislative interventions as a means of effecting change in favour of voluntary employer- and market-led efforts (Dickens 1997; Webb 1997). They promoted 'a privatized route to equality, with an emphasis on individual organizations deciding what is in their interests' (Dickens 1999: 11). The principal exception was the 1995 Disability Discrimination Act, which obliged large employers to make 'reasonable adjustments' to ensure that people with disabilities, encompassing both physical and mental impairments, were not substantially disadvantaged in employment, or experienced less favourable treatment without adequate justification, the result of many years of campaigning by pressure groups and disabled activists. It also established a Disability Rights Commission (DRC) whose activities included monitoring the implementation of the legislation and providing guidance to workers, employers, and other relevant parties.

The Conservative government's efforts at avoiding further state intervention in the area of equality were stymied by the obligations that went with Britain's membership of the European Economic Community (EEC) (Davies and Freedland 1993; Dickens and Hall 2003). During the 1980s and 1990s, the 'need for British law to give effect to European equality law and for judges to interpret national legislation in the light of such law protected this area of legislation from the Conservatives' deregulatory thrust and led to a strengthening of the national equality legislation in a number of areas' (Dickens 1997: 285).

One example in particular stands out. The 1976 Equal Treatment Directive obliged the Conservatives to amend the Equal Pay Act, which they eventually did in 1983, giving women workers the right to equal pay with men where they perform work of 'equal value'. This extended the scope for women workers to make equal pay claims since the basis of comparison was no longer whether or not they could demonstrate that their jobs were the same as those of men who were being paid more, something that could be difficult to establish in the many organizations where job segregation by sex was commonplace, but was based on the comparative value of what could be different jobs. It stimulated successful claims from, for example, female supermarket checkout operators who demanded equal pay with largely male warehouse workers in the same organization, who had hitherto earned more, on the basis that the skills demanded of their respective jobs were of similar worth.

4.3.2 The development of the legal framework during the 2000s

In Chapter 3 we saw that the extension of anti-discrimination legislation and the support given to 'family-friendly' working have been two key elements of Labour's employment relations policy since the 1990s. See Box 4.3 for details of the main legislative provisions. Any assessment of developments in public policy and legislation since Labour took office in

LEGISLATION AND POLICY 4.3

The development of equality and anti-discrimination legislation under Labour since 1997

Maternity and Parental Leave Regulations 1999: enacted in order to comply with the EU's 1996 Parental Leave Directive. Extended the minimum period of paid maternity leave from 14 to 18 weeks, established the right of parents to take up to 13 weeks of unpaid parental leave, and gave parents the right to unpaid time off work to attend to family emergencies.

Race Relations Amendment Act 2000: obliges public sector employers to promote positive race relations.

Part-time Workers (Prevention of Less Favourable Treatment) Regulations 2000: prohibit employers from treating part-time workers less favourably than a full-time equivalent. Enacted in order to comply with the EU's 1997 Directive on Equal Rights and Treatment for Part-Time Workers.

Fixed-term Employees Regulations 2002: prohibit employers from treating employees on a fixed-term contract less favourably than an equivalent permanent employee. Enacted in order to comply with the EU's 1999 Fixed-Term Contracts Directive.

Employment Act 2002: extends the minimum period of paid maternity leave to 26 weeks, introduces two weeks' paid paternity leave, and establishes a new right for parents to request flexible working arrangements.

Employment Equality (Sexual Orientation) Regulations 2003: give workers protection against discrimination on the grounds of sexual orientation. This legislation was enacted in order to comply with the EU's 2000 Equal Treatment Directive.

Employment Equality (Religion or Belief) Regulations 2003: give workers protection against discrimination on the grounds of religion or belief. This legislation was enacted in order to comply with the EU's 2000 Equal Treatment Directive.

Disability Discrimination Act 1995 (Amendment) Regulations 2003: among other things, it did away with the exemption for small employers, places an obligation on public sector employers to promote disability equality, and, in order to comply with the EU's 2000 Equal Treatment Directive, reduces the scope for employers to avoid making reasonable adjustments.

The Employment Equality (Age) Regulations 2006: prohibit age discrimination in respect of employment and vocational training, and introduces a new 'default' retirement age of 65; enacted in order to comply with the EU's 2000 Equal Treatment Directive.

Work and Families Act 2006: extends the right to request flexible working to carers of adults, provides for the extension of paid maternity leave to a minimum of 39 weeks along with the expectation that it would subsequently be increased to a year, and provides for the introduction of additional paternity leave, some of which could be paid.

Equality Act 2006: provides for the establishment of the Equality and Human Rights Commission; imposes a new duty on public bodies to promote gender equality.

1997 must also recognize the equality implications of the other strands to its employment relations agenda. In particular, the concern with promoting fairness at work mentioned in Chapter 3 has indirectly helped to alleviate disadvantage. The National Minimum Wage (NMW), for example, has particularly benefited low-paid women workers (see Chapter 7).

More significantly, though, the scope of anti-discrimination legislation has been extensively widened under Labour. In 2004, for example, disability discrimination was extended to cover all employers. Most of the impetus for reform has been stimulated by EU legislation (Dickens 2007), in particular a 2000 framework equality directive that prohibits discrimination in employment on the grounds of age, sexual orientation, and religion or belief. The 2003 implementation of legislation, in the form of regulations, to outlaw sexual orientation and religion or belief, aroused relatively little controversy. However, the government needed six years to implement regulations proscribing discrimination in employment on the grounds of age.

During the 1990s and early 2000s, discrimination against workers on the grounds of their age, or 'ageism' as it is popularly called, attracted an increasing amount of interest (see Glover and Branine 2001). Some organizations claimed to make effective use of older workers. The retail chain B&Q, for example, asserts that its policy of recruiting staff who are beyond the normal age for retirement led to reduced absenteeism, improved punctuality, and better customer service. Nevertheless, well-founded claims that older workers suffered from pervasive discrimination persisted (e.g. Taylor and Walker 1998).

Before taking office in 1997, Labour had promised to introduce legislation outlawing age discrimination. Once in government, however, it opted for a voluntary approach, publishing a code of practice, *Age Diversity in Employment*, in 1999. Among other things, the code urged employers not to use age as a criterion when advertising job opportunities. Yet voluntary methods were a rather ineffective way of preventing discrimination against older workers (Snape and Redman 2003). The charity Age Concern even claimed that age discrimination may have become more prevalent following the publication of the code of practice. Eventually, European Union legislation, in the form of a 2000 directive, obliged the government to eschew the voluntary approach.

As well as outlawing employment discrimination on the grounds of age, the Employment Equality (Age) Regulations 2006 removed the age limit for unfair dismissal claims and redundancy entitlement, established a new 'default' retirement age of 65, and made it potentially unlawful for employers to force an employee to retire below that age. Any employer operating a lower retirement age must be able to justify it. Once they reach 65, employees are entitled to request that they carry on working. While employers are obliged to consider any such requests, they are not compelled to uphold them, and can compulsorily retire people at or after the age of 65. Some pressure groups which campaign on age issues have criticized this element of the legislation, arguing that it effectively amounts to legalized discrimination against older workers.

European Union legislation has influenced the equality agenda in other respects. As we saw in Chapter 3, the EU has pursued non-legislative measures to promote equality; see Box 4.4 for details of its 'gender mainstreaming' policy. Moreover, directives establishing that part-time workers and employees on fixed-term contracts should not be less favourably treated than their full-time and permanent counterparts were enacted, and subsequently implemented in Britain in the early 2000s, because of a concern to

INTERNATIONAL PERSPECTIVE 4.4

Mainstreaming equality in the European Union

Equality action by the European Union (EU) is not confined just to legislative measures; it has also sought to promote greater equality in employment through 'mainstreaming' initiatives. What does the concept of equality mainstreaming mean? It 'can be summarized as the integration of equality considerations into all aspects of policy formulation, implementation and evaluation' (Bell 2004: 252). Mainstreaming implies the need for positive action to improve the employment position and prospects of people from disadvantaged social groups; that changes to institutions and practices are necessary in order to secure equality, even if this has been difficult to achieve in practice (T. Rees 1998). Since the 1980s, the European Commission has fostered the development of a number of action programmes designed to improve the labour market position of women and, in 1996, it mandated that a gender perspective should inform all EU decision-making. Although initially restricted to addressing gender-based inequality, mainstreaming has now been expanded to cover other forms of employment disadvantage, including race and disability (Bell 2004).

promote gender equality. The over-representation of women in part-time and temporary jobs meant that where employers treated people undertaking them less favourably than others, then this could amount to discriminatory treatment on the grounds of gender.

However, workers who believe they are disadvantaged as a result of their part-time status must identify appropriate full-time workers as comparators. The level of job segregation in Britain, though, which means that part-time workers generally do not undertake the same jobs as full-timers, makes such comparisons problematic (McKay 2001), resulting in few part-time workers being in a position to benefit from the legislation (McColgan 2000).

The strengthening of equality legislation has been a further aspect of change in the public policy framework during the 2000s, unrelated to Britain's membership of the EU. For example, the government responded to the report of the Macpherson inquiry into the murder of the black teenager Stephen Lawrence by enacting a new Race Relations Act 2000 that among other things obliges public sector employers to actively promote race equality (Fredman 2001). Subsequently, corresponding duties to promote disability equality and gender equality have also been enacted, though they do not apply to private sector firms.

The introduction of these positive duties to promote equality, a form of positive action, is rather significant. They represent a move, albeit limited, away from a liberal conception of achieving equality, based on treating everyone in the same way, to a situation where it is recognized that in order to alleviate inequality at work, employers need to do more to assist people from disadvantaged groups. These duties mark a shift in thinking, away from an approach dominated by an emphasis on reducing discrimination, towards a view that promoting equality is more desirable. However, the government is reluctant to extend these duties to private sector employers, limiting their overall impact. Here 'there is a continued reliance on benevolence or enlightened self-interest as the trigger for proactive measures—an inadequate basis for the pursuit of equality' (Dickens 2007: 474). Moreover, the public sector duties themselves are more concerned with instituting fairer procedures than dealing with unfair outcomes.

Finally, a major theme underpinning Labour's equality policies has been the encouragement given to promoting 'family-friendly' employment policies and a better 'work–life balance'; on giving as many people as possible, especially women and lone parents, the opportunity to reconcile their family responsibilities with undertaking paid employment, something that is presented as being advantageous to businesses because it helps them to attract and retain talented staff (McKay 2001).

The 'family-friendly' label is used to describe a wide variety of different practices that may assist parents and carers to reconcile their work with their domestic responsibilities, including, among other things, provisions for maternity, paternity, and parental leave (see Table 4.2), childcare facilities, job-sharing measures, and other forms of flexible working arrangements.

The term 'work–life balance' has increasingly been favoured over 'family-friendly', including by the British government, not least because it implies a focus on workers in general, not just those with family responsibilities. In so far as it assumes that workers should enjoy greater control over when, where, and how they undertake their jobs (Felstead et al. 2002), the work–life balance approach has some potentially far-reaching implications. The main problem with the concept, though, is the assumption that a distinction can easily be made between people's 'work' and 'lives' (Scholarios and Marks 2004). In reality, of course, they overlap and interact with each other in subtle, complex, and dynamic ways (Warhurst, Eikhof, and Haunschild 2008). As we will see below, moreover, it seems that people's duties at work increasingly affect, and constrain, the way in which they undertake the rest of their lives.

Labour's family-friendly policy agenda was initially stimulated by the need to comply with the EU's 1996 Parental Leave Directive. As a result, it enacted legislation in 1999 which raised the minimum period of maternity leave from fourteen to eighteen weeks, established a new entitlement for parents to take up to three months' unpaid parental leave up until a child's fifth birthday, and gave employees the right to take unpaid time off work in order to manage family crises, such as the sickness of a child.

During the 2000s, Labour further extended rights to family-friendly working, moving beyond what was required by the obligation to comply with EU legislation. The Employment Act 2002 included a number of relevant provisions that came into effect in April 2003. Among other things, it extended maternity leave provision to a minimum of 26 weeks, increased statutory maternity pay by a third, introduced two weeks' paid

Table 4.2 Parental leave: key concepts

Concept	Definition
Maternity leave	Leave taken by the mother before, during, and after the birth of a child
Paternity leave	Leave taken by the father after the birth or adoption of a child
Parental leave	Leave that can be taken by either parent in the first few years after the birth or adoption of a child

paternity leave, and provided for paid leave on the adoption of a child. It also established the right of parents of young, or disabled, children to have a request for flexible working arrangements, such as moving from full-time to part-time employment, taken seriously. Employers are entitled to refuse such a request on business grounds; if it would result in a substantial increase in costs, for example.

Since it is not a right to flexible working, merely a right to have any request to work flexibly taken seriously by an employer, the government was accused of enacting 'sound bite' employment legislation in this area. According to one commentator, the right to request flexible working was designed to attract a lot of favourable comment, but not to significantly change organizational practice (Anderson 2003). Nevertheless, the legislation has proved to be of some effect in provoking positive and constructive responses from employers when requests have been made.

According to one survey, one seventh (14 per cent) of employees (mainly women) had asked to work flexibly, by changing to part-time hours, for example, or working reduced hours for a limited period of time. Of those employees who had made a request to work flexibly, four-fifths (81 per cent) reported that it had either been fully or partly agreed by their employer. While most respondents reported that the change was largely beneficial—it gave them more time to spend with their families, for example—there were some disadvantages, such as the reduction in pay accompanying the shift from full-time to part-time working (Holt and Grainger 2005).

What explains the increased concern on the part of the government with developing a more family-friendly working environment in Britain? In one respect, it can be seen as an outcome of the increasing 'awareness of the difficulties in reconciling paid work and discharging family commitments [that] have helped to lead to a changing policy climate in the UK, where concerns about the effects of long working hours on parental responsibilities and relationships with children are being expressed' (Hyman et al. 2003: 220). But government policy has also been driven by other imperatives. One of these is to encourage workers with family responsibilities, especially women and lone parents, to take up paid employment, so that they are less dependent upon welfare benefits (Taylor no date). See Box 4.5 for a stimulating alternative perspective on the growth of the work–life balance movement.

Employment relations reflection 4.5   Accounting for the work–life balance movement

MacInnes (2008) offers a contentious interpretation as to why the work–life balance agenda has risen to prominence. He argues that governments are concerned that in the absence of effective family-friendly working arrangements increased levels of female employment may discourage women from having children, with adverse consequences for the future labour supply. However, he contends that the main factor stimulating demand for better work–life balance is not the so-called 'long hours culture'. Workers with parental and other caring responsibilities already make extensive use of flexible working arrangements which enable them to balance paid work with their family responsibilities. Instead, the principal reason why the work–life balance agenda has become increasingly prominent is linked to the profusion of leisure opportunities that now exist, and make demands on people's lives, creating a perception that there is an overall shortage of time.

During the second half of the 2000s, the UK government continued its efforts to encourage more family-friendly working arrangements. The Work and Families Act 2006 extended the minimum period of paid maternity leave to nine months, and provided for it to be increased to a year, something due to occur in 2010. It also provides for the introduction of a new right, also planned for 2010, for fathers to take up to 26 weeks' Additional Paternity Leave, some of which could be paid, if the mother returns to work. The legislation also extends the scope of the right to request flexible working to people who care for adults. In 2009 the Labour government extended the right to request flexible working still further, so that all parents of children aged under 17 can exercise it, despite calls from business groups for it to be postponed because of the recession.

Some concerns have been evinced that the family-friendly measures described above may accentuate, rather than diminish, gender disadvantage at work by reinforcing the presumption that it is largely the responsibility of mothers to adapt their employment arrangements, not fathers. As we have already seen, most requests for flexible working come from women, reflecting the gendered assumptions that govern the respective roles of mothers and fathers. Yet part-time working arrangements, and other forms of flexible employment, which are dominated by women, often provide limited opportunities for career development or progression. Moreover, the relatively long period of maternity leave available, compared to the provision for paternity leave, allied with feeble parental leave arrangements, potentially reinforce gender disadvantage by sustaining the belief that it is the job of the mother, rather than the father, to take time away from work to look after children (EHRC 2009). Thus too much family-friendly legislation reinforces the assumption that women's careers are of secondary importance, relative to those of men.

For Dickens (2007: 472) measures 'targeted at men may offer more in terms of gender equality'. While she acknowledges that some progress has been made to support fathers, the introduction of paternity leave, for example, most family-friendly legislation 'appears still to embody gendered assumptions about the nature of the father's role'. The way in which family-friendly measures, particularly flexible working arrangements, potentially reinforce, rather than diminish, gender disadvantage is explored further in Section 4.4.4 below, when we consider how employers operate them in practice.

4.3.3 The legal and policy framework: an assessment

In assessing developments in the legal and policy framework governing discrimination and equality at work, it is important to recognize the positive aspects of the Labour government's interventions. The scope of anti-discrimination legislation has been considerably widened; it is no longer lawful for an employer to discriminate against a worker on the grounds of his or her sexual orientation, for example. As we have seen, the right to request flexible working, while modest in its purpose, seems to have stimulated the greater use of flexible working arrangements, to the benefit of workers with caring responsibilities. In Section 4.4 we will see that the extension of anti-discrimination legislation has influenced employers' equal opportunities policies. These positive aspects of Labour's equality programme notwithstanding, there are three major problems with the current policy and legislative framework.

First, Labour's efforts to tackle discrimination and promote equality at work have been tempered by a desire not to overly disturb business interests (Dickens 2007). If positive duties to promote equality are a good thing, as the government appears to believe with regard to the public sector, why does it not extend them to private sector firms? If flexible working is so beneficial, why not give workers more than just simply a right to request greater flexibility? The government's approach subordinates equality considerations to the need not to antagonize powerful business interests which oppose any increase in employment regulation.

This has been particularly evident when it comes to implementing EU legislation, where the government has been concerned not to go beyond the minimum requirements of the relevant directives, or in some cases not even as far as that. In the case of parental leave, for example, the government's approach was imbued by the belief that legislation should prompt voluntary initiatives by employers who would recognize the business benefits of extending their provision (Hardy and Adnett 2002). However, in the absence of a trade union, which can exert pressure on an employer to make improvements, enhanced parental leave and other family-friendly measures may be more difficult to secure (Hyman and Summers 2004). Only pressure from unions and campaign groups resulted in the government going beyond what was required by the EU, by introducing paid paternity leave, for example. Parental leave, however, remains unpaid, a major disincentive to using it.

While the development of equality and anti-discrimination legislation has been a notable feature of employment relations policy in the 2000s, in general it has been enacted only to the extent that it does not require employers to do too much. As Dickens (2007: 468) notes, the prevailing assumption behind the approach taken by policy-makers is that voluntary interventions by employers are a more effective way of improving equality outcomes than legislative measures, and that equality action has to be 'justified in terms of promoting efficiency and competitiveness'. In other words, the pursuit of equality is desirable, but only in so far as it accords with the interests of employers. As we see below in Section 4.4, however, the notion that there is an unequivocal business case for promoting equality is dubious in the extreme.

A second problem concerns the liberal, equal treatment approach that underpins most of the legislative framework, something which leaves the structural causes of inequality at work largely unchallenged. Disadvantage is presented as a problem for the individual worker, rather than as something that stems from how the organization operates (see Box 4.6). Although the 2000s saw the introduction of some limited duties to promote equality in some areas, for the most part any kind of positive action designed to achieve greater equality has been eschewed by policy-makers. The emphasis on establishing a level playing field, upon which, in theory, people compete on the same terms, fails to appreciate the extent to which the rules of the game conform to the experiences of relatively privileged sections of the workforce, like men (Dickens 1992).

The third problem with the legal framework relating to equality and discrimination at work concerns the rather weak arrangements for enforcing rights. Two types of enforcement mechanism exist, administrative enforcement arrangements and legal enforcement arrangements (Dickens 2007). With regard to the former, until 2007 the EOC, CRE, and DRC covered the areas of gender discrimination, race discrimination, and disability discrimination, respectively. Although they were entitled to investigate employers suspected of operating discriminatory practices, these powers were only used sparingly; and enjoyed little scope to enforce changes.

In 2007, these bodies were then merged into a new Equality and Human Rights Commission (EHRC). The rationale for creating an all-encompassing equality body was

> ### INSIGHT INTO PRACTICE 4.6
>
> ## The individualized basis of responses to disability discrimination legislation
>
> The Disability Discrimination Act (DDA) 1995 obliges employers to make 'reasonable adjustments' to accommodate disabled workers, so that they are not put at a substantial disadvantage in employment, or when looking for employment. Based on interviews with disabled workers in the public sector, Foster (2007) demonstrates that the adjustment process is often damaging to the worker concerned, some of whom experience stress or ill-health as a result. Even when the process of adjustment produced a satisfactory outcome for the worker concerned, delays in implementation could cause difficulties. The most significant finding, however, concerns the informal, individualized basis of the adjustment process; much depended upon the disabled employee's relationship with their line manager. The problem with such a highly individualized approach, though, is that it lacks transparency, contributing 'nothing to the development of broader policy-making and practice' (Foster 2007: 81). Moreover, a worker's disability comes to be perceived as a problem for the individual, to be resolved through negotiation with his or her line manager, rather than a structural issue for the organization as a whole.

that with the introduction of new discrimination laws, covering age, sexual orientation, and religion or belief, it made sense to establish a single agency, one which would be a more effective guardian of equality than lots of smaller, issue-specific bodies. As we have already noted, moreover, in practice much employment disadvantage is multi-faceted, the product of an interaction between, say, gender and ethnicity (Bradley and Healy 2008). Thus a single equality body would be more effective in as much as it could develop a more integrated approach to tackling discrimination and promoting equality. The impact of the CEHR, and the extent to which it fulfils these expectations, remains to be seen.

The second type of enforcement mechanism concerns attempts by workers who have experienced unlawful discrimination to gain legal redress by submitting a claim to an employment tribunal (ET), which can award financial compensation to successful claimants. The weaknesses of ETs as vehicles for enforcing the legal rights of employees are considered in more detail in Chapter 9. Here, though, we focus on their limitations as arrangements for challenging unlawful discriminatory practices. One problem is that the onus is on an individual worker to take the appropriate action, when they might either lack knowledge about how to make a discrimination claim, or are anxious about the consequences of submitting one. Dickens (2007: 479) asserts that too much importance is placed 'upon awareness of rights and a capacity/willingness to enforce them'.

One way of resolving this problem would be to allow individual claimants to come together as a group to submit so-called 'class actions', since discrimination rarely affects just an individual worker, but is generally a collective experience (Bradley and Healy 2008). As Dickens (2007: 481) points out, class actions 'would allow discrimination to be challenged without a worker who has been affected having to be found or identified'. They could also allow 'embedded institutional practices to be challenged and can result in more substantial penalties for discriminators'. Currently, however, class actions are not permitted in the UK.

Even after submitting a claim, having to go through a tribunal hearing can be unpleasant for the workers involved. Interviews with black and minority ethnic workers who had brought race discrimination cases indicate that their experience of the tribunal process was generally a rather negative one (Aston, Hill, and Tackey 2006). Even in the small minority of cases where a discrimination claim is upheld, the remedy is usually in the form of financial compensation, generally less than £10,000. Moreover, employers are under no obligation to eradicate the discriminatory practice that prompted the claim in the first place (Dickens 1997). The emphasis is on 'compensating the individual rather than requiring unfairly discriminating employers to change their behaviour' (Dickens 2007: 480). As a mechanism for challenging discriminatory practices, the system of employment tribunals, the primary means by which workers enforce their right not to be unlawfully discriminated against, is marked by some serious flaws.

To conclude, the Labour government has generally favoured employer-led efforts when it comes to promoting equality at work, with legislative action treated as an undesirable last resort when voluntary efforts fail (Roper, Cunningham, and James 2003). Little has been done, then, to oblige employers to eradicate discriminatory practices at work. The system remains geared towards the readiness of individual workers who experience disadvantage to submit claims to employment tribunals, with little hope of adequate redress even if they win their case (Dickens and Hall 2003). The idea is that equality action is best fostered by a relatively light touch legislative regime within which employers are encouraged, because it is in their own interests, to take voluntary initiatives to promote equality (Dickens 2007). Further equality legislation (see Box 4.7), in the form of the Equality Bill which went through Parliament in 2008–9, is unlikely to alter things radically.

LEGISLATION AND POLICY 4.7

The 2009 Equality Bill

In April 2009, the UK government introduced equality proposals which it hopes to pass into legislation. The main purpose of the Equality Bill is to streamline existing equality and anti-discrimination laws, so that they are all incorporated into one single piece of overarching legislation. It would extend the existing duties on public bodies to promote equality on the grounds of gender, race, and disability to the areas of age, sexual orientation, and religion or belief. Following opposition from employers, initial proposals that these duties should be extended to the private sector came to nothing. In the Bill, the government also proposes, among other things, to

- oblige employers with 250 or more employees to report on the gender pay gap in their organization (not scheduled to take effect until 2013);
- prohibit secrecy clauses in pay arrangements, on the basis that greater transparency would help to tackle the gender pay gap;
- allow employers to take positive action and pick someone from an under-represented group when choosing between two or more equally suitable job candidates;
- strengthen enforcement action by employment tribunals, giving them the power to make recommendations to employers that would affect the whole workforce; and
- introduce a new duty on public bodies in England and Wales to tackle inequality resulting from social class, with the aim of reducing socio-economic disadvantage.

SECTION SUMMARY AND FURTHER READING

- Legislation prohibiting discrimination in work and employment on the grounds of sex and race developed during the 1970s. It was informed by a liberal conception of equality which holds that disadvantage is best alleviated by establishing measures which ensure that people are treated the same, irrespective of their gender or ethnicity. Conservative governments of the 1980s were ill-disposed towards further legislation. However, the need to implement EU directives and, in the case of disability discrimination, campaigns by activists, meant that some legislative intervention occurred.

- During the 2000s, Labour governments made some notable changes to the legal framework, including extending the scope of anti-discrimination legislation, for example, and establishing a range of policies designed to promote more family-friendly working arrangements. Much of this activity, however, was the result of having to comply with EU employment directives.

- While the changes Labour enacted have produced some positive benefits, public policy interventions in the area of equality and discrimination are nonetheless marked by a number of major weaknesses, including a reluctance to challenge the interests of employers, the predominance of a liberal, equal treatment ethos which fails to address the structural causes of employment disadvantage, and the presence of a weak enforcement regime which puts too much responsibility for tackling discrimination on to individual workers and not enough of an onus on employers.

For further information about the legislative and policy framework governing equality, see Kirton and Greene (2005: Chapter 6). The work of Linda Dickens on equality and anti-discrimination legislation is highly recommended (e.g. Dickens 1992; Dickens 2007). See Jewson and Mason (1986) for further details of the liberal and radical approaches to equality. The Equality and Human Rights Commission has a website: http://www.equalityhumanrights.com.

 Visit our Online Resource Centre for web links to sites connected to this section. www.oxfordtextbooks.co.uk/williams_adamsmith2e

4.4 Managing equality and diversity at work

In this section, we are concerned with organizational initiatives designed to challenge inequality and disadvantage at work. Equal opportunities policies are the main tool used by employers to promote equality in the workplace. How can such interventions be understood and why have they become so commonplace? There has been an increasing amount of interest in the concept of managing diversity as a means of challenging disadvantage at work. But how far does this approach differ from the more conventional equal opportunities approach, and is it more likely to promote equality in the workplace? Many organizations have also established policies dealing with work–life balance and family-friendly working issues. In the final part of this section we assess their effectiveness. As you read this section it will become evident that organizational initiatives on their own are unlikely to erode inequality and disadvantage at work in more than a minor way.

4.4.1 Understanding equal opportunities policies

Since the 1970s, employers have increasingly committed themselves to the pursuit of equal opportunities, in particular by styling themselves as 'equal opportunity employers', and enacting formal equal opportunities (EO) policies (Dickens 2000a; Jewson et al. 1995). This trend has continued in the 2000s. In 1998 under two-thirds (64 per cent) of workplaces with 10 or more employees were covered by a formal written policy covering equal opportunity or diversity matters. By 2004 the proportion had risen to nearly three-quarters (73 per cent). Much of the increase reflects the growing prevalence of EO policies in private sector workplaces (Walsh 2007).

Among larger organizations, the prevalence of EO policies is almost universal (IDS 2004). They are also particularly commonplace where there is a personnel or HR practitioner present in the workplace. The overwhelming majority of workplaces (92 per cent) with a personnel or HR specialist are covered by a formal EO or diversity policy, compared to less than half of those without one (Bradley and Healy 2008). Whereas in the past, EO policies were generally restricted to the areas of sex and race, there is evidence that, under the influence of legislation, their scope is widening to cover disability, and also age, religion, and sexual orientation too (Walsh 2007).

Under the influence of the legislative framework, organizational EO policies are characterized by a 'liberal' approach to tackling inequality at work (Jewson and Mason 1986). There is, therefore, an overwhelming emphasis on the development of a 'level playing field' (Webb 1997), so that workers are treated in the same way. As applied to the recruitment and selection of staff, for instance, the emphasis is on ensuring that procedures exist that enable employers to choose staff on the basis of their suitability for the job, irrespective of their social characteristics (Kirton and Greene 2005).

Why, though, have equal opportunities policies become so commonplace among organizations? Compliance with the law is the most significant influence on organizational practice (IDS 2004); equal opportunities policies are designed to ensure that the organization is less liable to actions on grounds of sex, race and, more recently, disability, religious belief, age, and sexual orientation. Bradley and Healy (2008: 81) acknowledge that concerns about the weakness of the legislation protecting workers from discrimination are well justified. Nevertheless, they maintain that legislative provisions 'may act as an incentive for good practice' in organizations. Employers have been encouraged to develop EO policies in order to avoid discrimination cases that could potentially damage their reputation.

The pursuit of equal opportunities in organizations has also been informed by a belief that inequality and unfair discrimination at work are inherently undesirable and, in the interests of social justice, should be eradicated (Davies and Thomas 2000). Since the 1980s, however, the social justice rationale for equality action has been eclipsed by the one that stresses the advantages to businesses of reducing inequality and disadvantage in the employment relationship (Dickens 1997, Glover and Kirton 2006).

There is no one business 'case' for equality action. Rather, it is proposed that the promotion of equality will, to varying degrees, generate certain business advantages (Dickens 1994; Liff 2003). These include being able to draw on a wider pool of talent when recruiting employees, retain important staff, benefit from the contribution of groups whose skills and potential contribution might otherwise have been neglected, match the characteristics of customers, and sustain a positive corporate reputation (Dickens 2000a; IDS 2004; Liff 2003).

Since the desirability of equality action is bound up with its potential contribution to improving organizational performance, business arguments may be more effective in generating positive reform, in particular by securing the commitment of managers, than the social justice rationale (Dickens 1994; Liff 2003). Employer-led bodies such as Opportunity Now (formerly Opportunity 2000), Race for Equality, and the Employers Forum on Age are at the forefront of articulating the business benefits of equality action, in the areas of sex, race and ethnicity, and age, respectively.

The adoption and development of organizational EO policies have made a positive difference to the position of some groups of workers, particularly relatively well-off women who are better able to gain access to managerial and professional jobs (Webb 1997). This is evident in the case of the airline company studied by Rutherford (1999). It was a founder member of Opportunity 2000 and, over a long period of time, had developed a range of sophisticated equal opportunities practices, job-sharing arrangements for example, designed to increase the number of women in management roles. Yet the proportion of women in senior management roles remained stubbornly low, largely, it seems, because of an assumption that such jobs required excessive working hours, something that was difficult to reconcile with women's family responsibilities.

4.4.2 Equal opportunities policies: a critical assessment

There are four main problems with equal opportunities policies as tools for challenging discrimination and disadvantage at work. The first is that they are often merely rhetorical statements of intent that help to conceal the presence of discriminatory workplace practices (Kirton and Greene 2005). In other words, the presence of a formal policy need not have much of an effect at all on employment relations processes and arrangements. Just because there is an equal opportunities policy in place should not be taken as a sign that unfair discrimination is absent (Aitkenhead and Liff 1991; Bradley and Healy 2008).

The experiences of the black trade union activists studied by Healy, Bradley, and Mukherjee (2004) were marked by incidents of racial discrimination, even in companies that were noted for their supposedly eager pursuit of equal opportunities. See Box 4.8 for evidence of the persistence of racist and sexist attitudes and behaviours in contemporary organizations.

In practice, equal opportunities policies are often just 'empty shells'. This means that in many workplaces covered by a formal equal opportunities policy, there are either few practices to support it or, if there are, they are restricted to certain groups of workers, such as the ability to undertake job-sharing, for example (Hoque and Noon 2004). Arrangements for monitoring the operation of equal opportunities policies tend to be rare. In barely more than one in ten workplaces do managers evaluate the impact of their organization's policy. Processes designed to identify potential indirect discrimination in organizational procedures are also somewhat uncommon, present in just a quarter of workplaces (Walsh 2007). While formal equal opportunities policies have become more prevalent in organizations, inadequate arrangements for monitoring and evaluating how

⊙ **INSIGHT INTO PRACTICE 4.8**

Racial disadvantage at work—the experiences of black and minority ethnic women trade unionists

Despite the growing use of equal opportunities policies, Bradley and Healy's (2008) study of the experiences of black and minority ethnic (BME) women trade union activists demonstrates that discrimination on grounds of race and ethnicity remains a prevalent feature of organizational life. Four aspects of discriminatory practice seem particularly noteworthy. First, the organizations in which the women worked were highly segregated on the grounds of both gender and race. Black women managers were rare. Second, racism was reportedly commonplace, albeit in a less explicit fashion than in the past. Bradley and Healy (2008: 146) point to the persistence of what they call 'everyday racism', meaning the 'remarks, actions and behaviours which, in a small way but persistently, emphasise difference from the majority . . .' Examples include the use of phrases such as 'you people' or 'you lot' when referring to BME staff. Third, racial stereotyping seemed to be a common feature of organizational life. The women were often made to feel as if they were inferior on the grounds that they were black. According to one woman, 'managers make us feel like as if we don' have brains, even if you do cleaning they say you are not doing it properly . . . This is the way they treat us . . .' (Bradley and Healy 2008: 148–9). Fourth, sometimes managers were accused of failing to take complaints of racial harassment seriously. The experiences of these women indicate that we should take care not to assume that the expansion of equal opportunities policies in organizations has necessarily eradicated racist and sexist attitudes and behaviours.

they operate limit the extent to which they can be used as effective tools for reducing discrimination.

A second problem with organizational equal opportunities policies is that their focus is often rather narrow, concerned with assisting women managers to break the 'glass ceiling' and secure more senior positions, for example. This was apparent in the case of the airline discussed above (Rutherford 1999). However, employers are often uninterested in developing interventions that would benefit the many more female workers who are employed in jobs characterized by low pay and poor working conditions, and whose prospects are obstructed more by the presence of a 'sticky floor' rather than a glass ceiling (Cockburn 1991; Dickens 1997). This is evident within the National Health Service (NHS). A member of Opportunity 2000, the NHS has pursued a gender equality agenda that prioritizes increasing the proportion of women in professional and managerial jobs. Such an approach, however, has 'little relevance to women in clerical and administrative grades, much less ancillary workers such as cleaners, catering staff and health-care assistants' (Richards 2001: 27).

The third obstacle to the progress of employer-led equality initiatives concerns the attitudes and behaviour of, often male, line managers. Equality initiatives are often treated as unimportant, or even resisted, by managers who see them as an infringement upon their prerogative (Kirton and Greene 2005). Collinson, Knights, and Collinson (1990), for example, discovered that when recruiting new employees line managers are reluctant to comply with procedures designed to secure equal treatment. This may be exacerbated during periods of organizational restructuring since equality initiatives can become marginalized.

This is apparent from a study of organizational change in a civil service agency that, among other things, gave line managers more discretion over equal opportunities. Although a minority of managers did take the opportunity to progress these issues, most had only a 'hazy perception of the role they were expected to play in maintaining and developing' equal opportunities (Cunningham, Lord, and Delaney 1999: 70), and some expressed downright hostility. According to one female employee, when equality issues are raised: 'The standard sort of reaction [in management meetings] is the raised eyebrows and an "Oh gawd, not this again, what a waste of time, here we go again with something else to complain about", you know' (quoted in Cunningham, Lord, and Delaney 1999: 71).

Linked to this, the fourth weakness of equal opportunities policies as devices designed to reduce unfair discrimination at work is that they generally fail to challenge those features of the cultures and structures of organizations that privilege men. This is evident in the case of a high street bank. The company had a longstanding formal commitment to equal opportunities and was a founder member of Opportunity 2000. In practice, however, major barriers to women's progress existed. Managers were expected to undertake excessive working hours, something of a problem for women with family responsibilities. Moreover, it was assumed that once they had children, women would lack the appropriate level of organizational commitment necessary for promotion. If a woman expressed an interest in flexible working, so as to combine work and family responsibilities more easily, this was taken as a sign that she was not interested in pursuing a career. Thus management in the organization, especially senior roles, was dominated by men. 'Formal equality statements expressed concern about this situation but there were far more powerful informal practices which reinforced it' (Liff and Ward 2001: 30).

It is important not to underplay the significance of equal opportunity initiatives in British workplaces. In some areas they have fostered a 'climate of equality', enabling women to challenge long-established structures of job segregation (Bradley 1999). By itself, though, employer-led equality action is a rather weak means of challenging such discrimination in employment (Dickens 2000a). A major source of this weakness is that it is underpinned by an assumption that equality is best promoted on the basis that it delivers important business benefits.

Yet there are a number of problems with this approach. For one thing, employers may focus their efforts on improvements in areas where it is easier to secure change, or where the business benefits are more easily identifiable (Dickens 1999). This explains the popularity of initiatives designed to erode the glass ceiling and increase the proportion of female managers in senior positions. Challenging long-established patterns of job segregation and low pay, which operate to the disadvantage of women workers in particular, is a much more complicated and difficult area and will not be in the interests of employers who secure important cost advantages by maintaining a pool of cheap, low-paid female labour (Dickens 1994). In such cases 'a business case can be articulated against [equal opportunities] action' (Dickens 1999: 10).

A further problem is that the supposed business benefits of equality action may be difficult to identify at an organizational level (Colling and Dickens 1998). They are also likely to be of a relatively long-term character, something that is problematic given the pressure on organizations to deliver short-term performance gains (Kirton and Greene 2005). Equality initiatives, then, are more likely to be perceived by employers as business costs, rather than as investments that can help to enhance organizational performance, and are liable to be withdrawn if no advantage is apparent (Dickens 2000a). As a result, employer-led efforts to challenge inequality at work are bound to be 'partial' and 'selective' (Dickens 1997), varying between organizations and over time according to managerial preferences, and not those of disadvantaged employees.

4.4.3 Towards managing diversity?

In contrast to the emphasis on equal treatment and fair procedures that characterizes the liberal model of equal opportunities approaches, interventions designed to produce equal outcomes are at the heart of the radical model. 'It seeks to intervene directly in workplace practices in order to achieve a fair distribution of rewards among employees, as measured by some criterion of moral value and worth' (Jewson and Mason 1986: 315). The radical model recognizes that structural factors particular to certain socially disadvantaged groups inhibit their participation in employment, for example women's greater share of domestic responsibilities (Webb and Liff 1988). Thus equality 'of access is an illusion while the white, male, full-time worker with few domestic responsibilities is seen as the norm' (Kirton and Greene 2005: 121). Positive action, then, such as the setting of employment quotas, for example, is necessary if equality at work is to be achieved.

The main problem with the radical approach is that it invites the complaint that certain groups of workers are the unworthy beneficiaries 'of special treatment', something that may erode support for equality initiatives. Nor does it 'promise any improvement *in the nature of the organisation itself*' (Cockburn 1989: 217, original italics). Instead, Cockburn (1989) proposes that it is more useful to distinguish between 'short' and 'long' equality agendas. Whereas the short agenda is concerned with rather superficial managerial interventions designed to improve equality of opportunity, at its longest the equal opportunities agenda should be a transformative programme, dedicated to challenging the power of privileged groups of white, male employees. It recognizes that 'disadvantage can be perpetuated through an organization's structure, culture and practices, rather than just through the biased decision-making of managers . . .' (Liff 2003: 440), and that it is these that should be reformed.

One of the claims made for the managing diversity approach is that it holds out the promise of transformative organizational change as a means of eroding disadvantage in employment (Blakemore and Drake 1996). The managing diversity approach has become increasingly influential, particularly in the United States, as a means of challenging discrimination and disadvantage in the employment relationship (Davies and Thomas 2000; Glover and Kirton 2006; Webb 1997). What, then, are the main assumptions that underpin, and the principal characteristics of, the managing diversity model?

Whereas the liberal equal opportunities approach emphasizes the importance of equal treatment and sameness as the best way of reducing disadvantage, the managing diversity model contends that equality is more effectively secured by acknowledging and lauding differences between employees (Kandola and Fullerton 1994). 'In contrast to equal opportunities approaches, which aim for workplaces where an individual's sex and race is of no greater significance than the colour of the eyes in determining the treatment they receive, the core idea behind managing diversity seems to encourage organizations to recognize difference' (Liff 1997: 13).

How might a managing diversity approach differ in practice from one based on equal opportunities? Liff (1999: 68) uses the example of employee appraisals. Managers operating within the confines of a liberal equal opportunities approach would seek to ensure that there is no bias in the assessment criteria for measuring employee performance that might disadvantage members of a particular social group. In an organization that focuses on managing diversity, however, managers would reconsider the very nature of the criteria used to establish effective performance. See Table 4.3 for the key characteristics of the equal opportunities and diversity management models.

Within the managing diversity approach, the emphasis on individual differences stands in marked contrast to the primacy of tackling group-based disadvantage that is central to liberal equal opportunities programmes (Liff 1997). Thus there 'is a move away from the idea that different groups should be assimilated to meet an organizational norm' (Kirton and Greene 2005: 124), one which is often, of course, based on the experiences of men (Liff and Wacjman 1996).

A further aspect of the managing diversity approach, which distinguishes it from an equal opportunities one, is that it is supposedly more attractive to managers (Liff 1997; Noon 2007). The emphasis on managing individual employees, and of realizing their potential in a way that benefits the business, is something that managers, who would otherwise be sceptical of the value of equal opportunity initiatives, are able to appreciate. In contrast to the equal opportunities approach, which is often perceived as an external imposition, managing diversity is more easily aligned with, and supportive of, the needs of the business (Ross and Schneider 1992; Glover and Kirton 2006). For example, the use of employee networks, or 'affinity groups' as they are sometimes called, is a feature of diversity management in the United States, and now appears to have spread to the UK (see Box 4.9).

The managing diversity approach would appear to constitute a firmer basis for managerial action to reduce disadvantage than traditional equal opportunities approaches; it may generate business benefits. The Guardian newspaper, for example, claims that its own commitment to managing diversity enables it to secure more advertising from

Table 4.3 The key characteristics of equal opportunities and diversity management approaches

Equal opportunities	Diversity management
A 'liberal' approach (sameness)	Recognizing and celebrating difference
Emphasis on the 'level playing field'	Attractive to managers
Equal treatment (group-based)	A more individualistic approach
The use of formal procedures (e.g.selection)	Emphasis on culture change

INSIGHT INTO PRACTICE 4.9

Affinity groups as a diversity management tool

The development of employee networks, or affinity groups as they are sometimes called, is an increasingly important feature of organizational efforts to manage diversity effectively, particularly in the United States, but also in the UK. They are managerially sponsored groups of employees based around some aspect of social identity, like sexual orientation, for example, which operate within a specific organization. The development of such employee networks has been particularly evident within the City of London. Between 2005 and 2007 Merrill Lynch established five employee networks, including a Women's Leadership Council, a black professional network, a lesbian, gay, bisexual, and transgender (LGBT) group, and a parents and carers' network with some 800 members. Deloitte & Touche has instituted, among other things, a disability group called Workability and a Globe (gay, lesbian, or bisexual employees) network (Smethurst 2007). These groups and networks are not just part of a broader attempt to recognize diversity, but are also viewed as a means of enhancing business performance, by helping firms to attract and retain talented staff, for example, and also because they help to make people feel more comfortable at work. Although they are becoming an increasingly important diversity management tool, and can also help to shape and influence the organizational diversity agenda, because they operate under the aegis of managers, employee networks rarely enjoy the power to challenge undesirable discriminatory practices (Healy and Oikelome 2007).

like-minded organizations (IDS 2004). The most profound claim for the approach, though, is that if organizations are to acknowledge and manage individual differences effectively, and thus realize the full potential of their employees, they should review the way they operate. Underpinning the managing diversity approach, therefore, is the assumption that an organization must 'recognize that *it* has to change to adapt to employee differences rather than simply expecting employees to fit in with its pre-existing practices' (Liff 1999: 68).

There is some evidence that where organizations take diversity seriously, and alter their practices accordingly, it can benefit employees. This is apparent from a study of the experiences of gay, lesbian, and bisexual (LGB) workers in 16 'good practice' case study organizations which had committed themselves to operating in ways that supported and enhanced diversity, by developing LGB networks, for example. Even though LGB staff were aware that the employers had not done all they could to recognize and promote the benefits of diversity, they recognized that their experience of employment had been enhanced by the adoption of a managing diversity approach (Colgan et al. 2007).

Managing diversity, then, appears to hold out the potential for a transformation in employer attitudes towards equality, consistent with the 'long' approach discussed above. In reality, however, it promises significantly more than it delivers. There are three major problems with the managing diversity model. First, in practice it is difficult to distinguish between equal opportunities and managing diversity approaches. In her study of BT, for example, Liff (1999) found evidence of managing diversity in action, including efforts to restructure jobs to make them more attractive to female graduates. But these co-existed alongside more conventional equal opportunities initiatives, including job-sharing arrangements. In this case, then, there was no 'radical separation between equal opportunities and managing diversity approaches' (Liff 1999: 72). The latter may involve little more than a simple re-labelling of conventional EO initiatives (Kirton and Greene 2005: 127), perhaps to make them more palatable to managers.

Second, the managing diversity approach has been criticized for offering a 'sanitized' and 'unthreatening' perspective on workplace differences (Webb 1997: 163). It is a model that is designed to be comfortable for managers, not to challenge their assumptions or prejudices (Noon 2007). The emphasis on individuals, moreover, means that pressure to change potentially discriminatory organizational practices is often absent, since they do not have the collective power to effect reforms enjoyed by socially disadvantaged groups (Webb 1997). As a result, understandings of 'differences', and of whether and how they should be valued, generally come within the prerogative of managers, who may support diversity only as long as it delivers explicit organizational benefits, or does not cost them anything (Glover and Kirton 2006; Webb 1997).

Third, although in theory the managing diversity approach holds out the promise of transformative organizational change in order to enable individual differences to be recognized and valued, in practice it generally leaves established beliefs and practices unchanged (Dickens 2000a). It is rarely used to challenge those long-standing features of organizations that systematically privilege white men, and thus contribute to employment disadvantage and inequality (Liff 1997). Despite a commitment to managing diversity, the international computer systems manufacturer studied by Webb (1997) continued to function in ways that disproportionately benefited male employees. Vertical job segregation was pronounced. Male managers simply assumed that women were uninterested in promotion; they did not recognize that the absence of facilities such as childcare arrangements, for example, hindered the advancement of women. Diversity, then, 'may have more to do with corporate image-building than with the kind of interventions designed to facilitate more egalitarian work organization and increased inclusion of women' (Webb 1997: 166).

Like conventional equal opportunities approaches, to which they often bear a marked resemblance, managing diversity policies, are, given their status as employer-led methods of generating change, somewhat weak interventions for challenging workplace inequality. As Noon (2007) observes, the rationale for the managing diversity approach is based on similar business case arguments that inform the development of equal opportunities initiatives more generally, and suffers from the same kind of problems. These include a tendency to focus solely on short-term performance improvements, which might not immediately be apparent, and a realization that there are often considerable benefits for employers of not taking action to deal with workplace disadvantage.

4.4.4 Managing work–life balance in organizations

As we have already seen in Section 4.3.2, since the late 1990s growing concerns about the need for more family-friendly working arrangements and better work–life balance have been a major influence over employment relations policy, evidenced by the establishment of the 'right' for some employees to request flexible working patterns, the extension of paid maternity leave, and the institution of new rights to paid paternity leave and unpaid parental leave. There is, as we saw, an emphasis on using legislation to prompt voluntary action on the part of employers, not least because of the resulting business benefits, like improved staff morale, reduced absenteeism, and easier recruitment (HM Treasury and DTI 2003).

There is evidence that employers accept the business rationale for family-friendly and work–life balance policies. A study of the Scottish oil and gas industry, for example, demonstrates that innovation is particularly evident in large multinational companies. These had developed job-sharing and flexible working arrangements, among other things, which helped them to compete for, and retain, skilled staff (McKee, Mauthner, and Maclean 2000). In the hospitality industry, recruitment and retention difficulties encouraged some major employers to invest in flexible working arrangements in order to hold on to women staff with young children (Doherty 2004).

Surveys point to the increasing prevalence of family-friendly working arrangements. Table 4.4 uses data from both the 1998 and 2004 Workplace Employment Relations Surveys to determine the proportion of workplaces which operate specific practices. It shows that during the late 1990s and early 2000s there was an increase, sometimes a marked increase, in the use of these family-friendly practices. For example, the proportion of workplaces that operate term-time working arrangements, whereby someone is employed only during school terms, enabling them to look after their children in the school holidays, doubled between 1998 and 2004, from 14 per cent to 28 per cent.

Some of the increase can be attributed to legislative change. For example, since 2003 fathers are entitled to a minimum of two weeks' paid paternity leave on the birth or adoption of a child; so we should expect 100 per cent of workplaces to operate such a practice. Nevertheless, the extent of the increase in the provision of flexible working and other family-friendly working arrangements seems to indicate that employers have embraced work–life balance measures, not least because of the espoused business benefits.

Table 4.4 The proportion of workplaces operating flexible working and leave arrangements for non-managerial employees, 1998 and 2004

	1998	2004
Switching from full-time to part-time hours	46%	64%
Flexitime	19%	26%
Job-sharing	31%	41%
Homeworking	16%	28%
Term-time working	14%	28%
Parental leave	38%	73%
Paid paternity leave/discretionary leave for fathers	48%	92%
Special paid leave in emergencies	24%	31%

Source: Kersley et al. (2005)

However, a certain amount of caution is needed when interpreting developments. Closer analysis of the relevant data suggests that the use of family-friendly working arrangements tends to be much more commonplace in organizations with some characteristics than it is in others. In particular, their use is concentrated among public sector employers, and in workplaces in the retail and hotel and catering sectors, generally where there are relatively high proportions of female and part-time workers (Kersley et al. 2006; Walsh 2005; White et al. 2004).

In some parts of the economy, like construction, for example, family-friendly working remains relatively uncommon. Many employers, moreover, have yet to be convinced of the business case for family-friendly and work–life balance policies, given the additional business costs they are seen to impose (Hyman and Summers 2004; Roper, Cunningham, and James 2003). There is a relatively low level of interest in introducing family-friendly working practices among firms that do not already operate them. That said, however, in general employers report the increased availability of family-friendly working arrangements. Between 2003 and 2007, for example, the proportion of employers offering staff the opportunity to undertake reduced-hours working for a limited period of time rose from two-fifths (40 per cent) to three-quarters (74 per cent) (Hayward, Fong, and Thornton 2007).

For a number of reasons, though, it is doubtful that voluntary action by employers alone will lead to the widespread adoption of robust family-friendly and work–life balance policies in a way that promotes gender equality at work. For one thing, despite all the rhetoric about supposed business benefits, survey evidence demonstrates that 'whilst demand for better balance by employees has grown, employers have yet to treat work–life balance as a priority' (Hyman and Summers 2004: 421). Those employers that have initiated changes, moreover, tend to restrict them to arrangements that enable workers to vary the times at which they start and finish work (Hyman and Summers 2004; Hyman et al. 2003).

Family-friendly and work–life balance policies are often presented by employers, and perceived by employees, as perks, additional benefits that may be, and indeed are, withdrawn, or at least not accorded as much importance, in periods of economic difficulty (Doherty 2004; Hyman and Summers 2004; Lewis 1997). If seen as perks, moreover, policies directed at workers with family responsibilities can be a cause of disaffection among staff who do not enjoy access to them in what has been termed a 'family-friendly backlash' (Walsh 2005).

Even when family-friendly working arrangements are operated, it cannot be assumed that they will promote equality between men and women at work. Indeed, they may reinforce disadvantage. Women who undertake flexible working, especially part-time employment, may be perceived by male managers as lacking the requisite commitment to the job and the organization necessary for promotion (Smithson et al. 2004). This was particularly evident in the firm of chartered accountants studied by Lewis (1997). She found that organizational commitment was largely equated with time spent at work. Female employees who were unable to match the number of hours at work put in by their male counterparts, or were on reduced hours, were seen as less promotable. Speaking of a female employee, one male senior manager commented that: 'She's a good manager, but she won't be promoted. She doesn' have the commitment . . . doesn' put in the time' (quoted in Lewis 1997: 16).

Unsurprisingly, then, there has been some reluctance on the part of employees to make use of family-friendly and work–life balance practices, resulting in a 'take-up gap' (Kodz, Harper, and Dench 2002). People sometimes shun them, reluctant to damage their careers by risking the appearance of being less committed to the organization. However, there is some evidence that the take-up gap has narrowed as demand from employees for more flexible working arrangements has increased (Holt and Grainger 2005; Hayward, Fong, and Thornton 2007).

Perhaps the biggest obstacle to the take-up of family-friendly and work–life balance practices is that they often come under the control of line managers who can be reluctant to allow employees to make use of them (Hyman and Summers 2004), in spite of what the organizational policy might say. This gap between the espoused policy of an organization and what managers actually allow to happen in practice has been identified as a considerable impediment to the take-up of family-friendly working arrangements (Visser and Williams 2006). See Box 4.10 for details of the experiences of professional women.

Increasing work demands are a further significant constraint on the effectiveness of policies designed to enable people to strike a better balance between the requirements of their job and their family lives. In the case of a local authority studied by Tailby et al. (2005) extensive work pressures had contributed to a growing 'work–life imbalance' as the increasingly demanding nature of people's jobs adversely affected their lives outside work. In call centres there is often a conflict between the flexibility demanded by managers, in particular the expectation that staff will work additional hours at short notice to cope with an unanticipated rise in calls, and the demand from workers for predictable working time arrangements so that they can plan their family responsibilities effectively (Hyman and Marks 2008).

● INSIGHT INTO PRACTICE 4.10

Family-friendly working; the experiences of professional women

Catherine Gatrell interviewed 20 working mothers, including teachers, architects, and lawyers for her book *Hard Labour: the Sociology of Parenthood*. Nearly all of them were either treated badly by their employer, or experienced discrimination, as a result of their pregnancy. On returning to work following maternity leave, moreover, these women often found that their managers were unsupportive, making it difficult for them to balance their careers with their child-rearing responsibilities, even in organizations that claimed to support equal opportunities and family-friendly working arrangements. Managers turned down requests for reduced hours, for example. There was also some evidence that mothers who switched to part-time employment experienced detriment because they did not conform to male-dominated career paths that put a premium on full-time employment. As a result, Gatrell (2005: 194) observes that 'organizations which claim to have put "family-friendly" policies in place may be paying lip-service to the idea, and might have no real intention of implementing or promoting the policies', like making sure that managers follow them, for example. While the business case for operating family-friendly working arrangements was recognized in some organizations, particularly those headed by working mothers themselves, for the most part it was not widely accepted.

Nevertheless, the campaigning efforts of trade unions and pressure groups, which have ensured that work–life balance and family-friendly working arrangements remain important aspects of the employment relations policy agenda, allied to demands from workers themselves for greater employment flexibility, mean that employers are under greater pressure than ever before to alter their practices and institute a more enlightened approach to managing this aspect of people's employment relationships.

SECTION SUMMARY AND FURTHER READING

- There has been an increase in the extent and coverage of equal opportunities policies among organizations in Britain. Such policies are characterized by a liberal approach to challenging disadvantage in employment, in which the importance of using formal procedures to ensure equality of treatment is emphasized, and they may have contributed to an increase in the number of women in professional and managerial jobs.

- However, since their rationale is largely one of business self-interest, employer-led equal opportunities policies are often restricted in their focus, and may help to mask discriminatory practices. They do little to assist women segregated in low-paid jobs, for example.

- The managing diversity approach is concerned with how organizations can manage and take advantage of individual differences. In practice there is often some overlap with traditional equal opportunities approaches. Moreover, the model does not challenge those aspects of organizational structure and culture that continue to privilege white males.

- During the 2000s the proportion of workplaces claiming to operate work–life balance and family-friendly practices has increased markedly, linked to the espoused business benefits that come from using them. However, there is some evidence that the reach of family-friendly working remains limited. The extent to which workers have benefited by achieving a better work–life balance is questionable, not least because of the reluctance of managers to apply organizational policies appropriately.

For an overview of the issues pertaining to managing equal opportunities and diversity in organizations, see Kirton and Greene (2005). Bradley and Healy's (2008) interviews with black and minority ethnic women trade unionists highlight some negative features of organizational practice. Linda Dickens outlines the weaknesses of business self-interest as a rationale for equal opportunities (see Dickens 1997). For critical perspectives on the managing diversity phenomenon, Liff (1997), Liff and Wacjman (1996), and Webb (1997) are especially recommended. See Hyman and Summers (2004) and Walsh (2005) for good insights concerning the management of work–life balance issues.

 Visit our Online Resource Centre for web links to sites connected to this section. www.oxfordtextbooks.co.uk/williams_adamsmith2e

---

4.5 Trade unions, collective bargaining, and the pursuit of workplace equality

As the previous section makes clear, managerial interventions are of limited effectiveness in challenging discrimination and disadvantage in employment. What difference, then, can trade union representation and collective bargaining make? In this section, we examine the extent to which equality considerations inform the contemporary bargaining agenda, and how far unions have progressed in recognizing and representing the interests of workers from disadvantaged social groups. The emphasis is largely on gender equality, which is where most union activity has been concentrated. Such efforts present major challenges for the unions, which have traditionally been reluctant to eschew the belief that workers in the same industry, occupation, or organization might have different interests based on their aspects of their social identity, such as gender, for example (Kirton and Greene 2005: 181). Should unions focus their efforts on representing their women members as *workers*, with their gender considered irrelevant, as *women workers*, who might have particular employment relations interests separate from those of men, or as *women*, addressing the multitude of concerns that affect their lives? To begin with, though, we consider the regressive role of trade unions in the area of equality and the factors that have compelled them to change.

4.5.1 Trade unions and the equality agenda

There is a long history of women's activity in trade unions. Between 1906 and 1926, for example, the National Federation of Women Workers 'organized more women, fought more strikes and did more to establish women trade unionists than any organization' (Boston 1980: 60). It challenged the low pay and poor working conditions that characterized female employment in parts of the clothing industry, for example. In general, though, the activities of the largely male-dominated trade unions supported and reinforced gender inequality and disadvantage at work. For one thing, during the nineteenth and early twentieth centuries unions often colluded with employers to exclude women from skilled, and therefore more highly paid jobs, helping to reinforce patterns of occupational segregation and a sexual division of labour that privileged the work of men over that of women (Bradley 1989). Union collective bargaining priorities, moreover, reflected dominant male assumptions concerning the inferior value of women's labour. Since men were presented as the principal family wage earners, or 'breadwinners', women's earnings were thereby considered less important, and thus only a 'secondary wage' or 'pin money'.

The extent of these assumptions was evident in a series of seven workplace studies undertaken in 1980. Union representatives commonly believed 'that most women who went out to work were earning a secondary wage and that therefore the fact that they were paid less than their male fellow workers was not a problem' (Charles 1986: 164). It is important to recognize, therefore, that historically the trade unions were largely uninterested in promoting gender equality at work. Indeed, their activities helped to support 'those very mechanisms in the organization of work which makes patterns of gender segregation so difficult to break down' (Rees 1992: 85).

One of the main reasons for the traditional conservatism of the unions in this area is that they are organizations whose decision-making structures were, and often still are, dominated by men (Cockburn 1991). What explains the under-representation of women within trade unions? The principal reason is that union organization and activity reflected the traditional dominance of men in paid work, in a way that led to the exclusion of women (Cunnison and Stageman 1993). Thus unions tended to operate in ways that privileged the interests of men, and developed an overly masculine culture within which women, and their interests, were marginalized.

The way in which trade unionism functions makes it difficult for women to pursue union careers, or to become active in decision-making structures. The rarity of child-care arrangements, for example, means that women's domestic responsibilities often preclude them from attending union meetings (Ledwith et al. 1990). Moreover, due to members' demands, union officials often have excessive workloads. The ways in which their jobs are structured, though, makes them difficult to combine with family responsibilities (Kirton 1999; Watson 1988). Thus there are a series of obstacles pertaining to the masculine norms and assumptions that govern how unions operate which inhibit the participation and representation of women in trade unions (Cockburn1991; Glover and Kirton 2006). Unsurprisingly, therefore, on the rare occasions when they did make an effort in this area, unions traditionally found it difficult to integrate and represent the interests of their female members effectively (Kirton 1999).

Whatever they might have said in their formal policy statements, until the 1970s the trade unions generally had a poor record on the issue of race. According to one commentator, 'history shows the record of the trade union movement to be characterized at worst by appalling racism and often by an indefensible neglect of the issues of race and equal opportunity' (Wrench 1986: 3). During the 1940s and 1950s, the increasing proportion of black migrant workers in the workforce, originating from places such as the Caribbean, for example, met with a hostile reception from many unions, who worried that immigrants would be used by employers as a cheap source of labour, and as replacements for striking workers (Wrench 1987). In many workplaces, white trade unionists often supported, or at least did not challenge, practices that excluded and disadvantaged black workers. Despite its formal denunciations of discrimination, until the 1970s the Trades Union Congress (TUC) opposed efforts to combat race-based disadvantage since these would 'discriminate against the white membership' (Wrench and Virdee 1996: 245).

However, trade union attitudes towards, and responses to, race-based disadvantage were rather complex (Lunn 1999). The unions came under increasing pressure from their own activists to improve their policies and practices, though discrimination against black workers was not entirely eradicated from the union movement (Phizacklea and Miles 1980; Wrench 1987). They continued to be under-represented in trade union decision-making structures, despite being more likely than white workers to be union members (Wrench 1987). Moreover, trade unions have experienced problems in trying to recruit and organize black and ethnic minority workers, largely because of the difficulties they have striking and sustaining relationships with community groups and activists (Wrench and Virdee 1996).

Historically, therefore, trade union practices and collective bargaining activity have often operated to the detriment of women and black workers. Since the 1980s, though, the unions have, albeit rather slowly and unevenly, sought to represent the interests of an increasingly diverse workforce more effectively, those of women in particular. They have done so for three related reasons. First, economic change has eroded the traditional heartlands of trade unionism in male-dominated manufacturing industry. Employment growth has been concentrated largely in the service sector, which is characterized by high levels of female employment. The unions have been compelled, therefore, to respond by re-orienting themselves as more female-friendly organizations (Liff 2003).

Second, with the decline of male-dominated manual industries, trade unionism, then, is increasingly concentrated in areas, such as public sector occupations like schoolteaching, that are disproportionately populated by female employees (Colling and Dickens 2001). Traditionally much lower, the proportion of women workers who are union members is now just about the same as it is for men. Between 1991 and 2001, the proportion of men who are union members fell from 41 to 29 per cent of the workforce; for women the fall was less marked, from 32 per cent to 28 per cent. During the 2000s, the proportion of women employees who are trade union members overtook that of male employees. In 2007, for example, 29.6 per cent of female employees were trade unionists, compared to 29.4 per cent of males (Mercer and Notley 2008).

Third, influenced by feminism, women themselves have challenged the male-dominated structures and decision-making processes of trade unions (Colgan and Ledwith 2002; Cunnison and Stageman 1993). 'If women's interests are better represented by trade unions today it has not been because of any natural trend but because of a concerted struggle by women themselves to defeat male self-interest' (Cockburn 1991: 111). In the sections that follow, then, we examine the effectiveness of union efforts to represent the interests of a diverse membership, beginning with the topic of equality bargaining.

4.5.2   Equality bargaining

Perhaps 'the most important indication of changed union behaviour . . . [is] an increased willingness to incorporate equality demands within collective bargaining' (Colling and Dickens 2001: 142). In a broad sense, we take equality bargaining to refer to initiatives undertaken by trade unions that are designed to reduce the employment disadvantage of particular groups, such as women workers, for example, through interventions directed at employers. An equality 'agenda' can be distinguished from an equality 'dimension'. The former refers to where unions develop a separate set of bargaining demands that are specifically designed to favour women workers, for example improved childcare arrangements. The concept of the equality dimension, however, seeks to ensure that the equality implications of all bargaining topics, including pay, for example, are recognized (Dickens 2000b).

We have already seen that in the past union bargaining priorities and activities discriminated against women at work by systematically undervaluing the contribution of their labour. Unions, moreover, often support pay structures, those that accord high value to length of service, for example, that disadvantage women. However, while collective bargaining has done much to sustain workplace inequality, it also has the potential to erode it (Cockburn 1991). Women who are in workplaces that are covered by collective agreements enjoy better pay and employment conditions, greater job security, and improved access to family-friendly working arrangements than those who are not (Bewley and Fernie 2003; Colling and Dickens 1998). Whereas under three-quarters (73 per cent) of all workplaces are covered by a formal equal opportunities or diversity policy, where there is a union recognized the proportion rises to 95 per cent (Kersley et al. 2006). The provision of family-friendly working arrangements is also more commonplace in workplaces with union recognition (Kersley et al. 2006; White et al. 2004).

In recent years, the concept of equality bargaining has attained greater significance as trade unions have sought to represent the interests of their women members more effectively (Colling and Dickens 1989). Unions may be more capable of securing equality action on the basis of social justice, rather than for narrow, insecure, and partial business reasons (Colling and Dickens 1998). Through trade union action, collective bargaining may give women workers greater influence over their pay and employment conditions. It 'provides a way of giving women a voice; an ability to define their needs and concerns and to set their own priorities for action' (Dickens 2000b: 197). Male and female workers enjoy many shared interests, such as a concern with securing pay rises, for example. Women, however, express a particular concern that issues such as job sharing be given greater priority on union bargaining agendas (Bradley 1999; Kirton 1999).

In recent years, many unions have been active in promoting and articulating equality issues as priorities for collective bargaining, including demands for pay equality between men and women, and greater access to family-friendly working arrangements (Bewley and Fernie 2003). See Box 4.11 for an assessment of union effectiveness in negotiating equality issues. Perhaps the most effective union action has been in the area of equal pay. Groups of largely female workers, such as speech therapists for example, have benefited from pay rises generated by successful union equal value campaigns (Bradley 1999). Trade unions, then, have sometimes been able to use legislative measures, and the threat of potential discrimination claims on a mass scale, to secure employer action (Colling and Dickens 1998). This has been evident in some parts of the public sector, the health service, for example, where, frustrated by the lack of progress made by employers on delivering equal pay, some unions have supported widespread tribunal claims by workers.

Yet unions have emphasized the pursuit of women's equality far more so than that of other groups, such as black workers, for example (Kirton and Greene 2005). Moreover, there is evidence that union representatives, particularly at the local level, do not recognize that issues that are of specific concern to women workers, such as childcare arrangements, are appropriate topics for collective bargaining. The bargaining agenda often fails

 INSIGHT INTO PRACTICE 4.11

Auditing union progress in the area of equality bargaining

In 2005, the Trades Union Congress (TUC 2005) published an equality audit which gives an indication of the areas where trade unions are making the most progress in negotiating with employers over equality issues:

- 67 per cent of unions reported some negotiating successes in the area of flexible working and work–life balance arrangements;
- 67 per cent reported having negotiated improvements in conditions for parents and carers;
- 54 per cent reported some negotiating success in the area of equal pay between men and women;
- 46 per cent reported negotiating improved rights for lesbian, gay, bisexual, and transgender workers; and
- 35 per cent reported successes negotiating improvements on age-related issues.

to incorporate an equality dimension. As a result, such a 'restricted agenda serves to promote lack of interest in unions, since they appear irrelevant to the experiences of workers and of the workplace' (Munro 1999: 196).

The presence of female union representatives, though, may ensure that women's issues are incorporated within a union's bargaining agenda. Female officials 'are more likely to make a priority of issues such as equal pay, childcare, maternity leave and sexual harassment in collective bargaining' (Heery and Kelly 1988: 502; see also Dickens 2000b). However, the greater incidence of female representatives in decision-making bodies in the public services union, Unison, does not appear to have markedly increased the extent to which issues relevant to women are promoted. Experienced men continued to dominate meetings, leading to equality issues often being marginalized (McBride 2001). This suggests that we need to assess how far unions have altered their representative structures, and the way in which their decision-making processes operate, to accommodate the interests of a diverse membership.

4.5.3 Representing diversity in trade unions

In assessing the extent and nature of changes to the unions' internal representative arrangements and structures, it is useful to employ, in modified form, the distinction between liberal and radical approaches discussed earlier in this chapter. The liberal approach is concerned with reducing the barriers that prevent people from disadvantaged groups participating in unions, or benefiting from their services; by seeking to remove discriminatory practices it seeks to establish a 'level playing field' (Kirton and Greene 2002). Certain measures, including the appointment of equality or women's officers and ensuring that union meetings are made more accessible, by offering childcare facilities, for example, have been taken in order to help promote equality of access (Colgan and Ledwith 2002). See Box 4.12 for details of how the unions have sought to represent the interests of their lesbian and gay members.

The liberal approach characterizes the approach of most trade unions to the way in which they promote internal equality, particularly with regard to gender. Its main weakness, however, is its failure to challenge male-dominated union power structures that often operate in ways that disadvantage women. There are two problems in particular. First, female union representatives can find it difficult to operate effectively in roles that are characterized by norms and assumptions derived from men's experiences. The excessive number of hours required by union work militates against the involvement of women who have childcare responsibilities, for example (Kirton 1999).

Second, there is some evidence that the male-dominated nature of trade unionism contributes to an environment in which women often face substantial obstacles when attempting to increase their participation (Bradley and Healy 2008). A study of the experiences of senior female representatives within the Manufacturing Science and Finance Union, now part of Unite, revealed that sexist attitudes and behaviour were commonplace. One female representative claimed that:

It's still a male culture, right from the top. There are too few women in positions of real power in unions. I think that most trade union meetings, if a new woman went along to one, she'd turn round and walk straight back out again—it's like a boys' club. (quoted in Kirton 1999: 216)

● INSIGHT INTO PRACTICE 4.12

Representing the interests of lesbian and gay members in British trade unions

Sam Bairstow studied the way in which trade unions in Britain represent the interests of their lesbian and gay members (Bairstow 2004). She found evidence of the existence of a dual approach in union practice. Some unions were characterized by bottom-up, activist-led efforts to secure change. This made for a more participatory, informal, and inclusive approach to the advancement of lesbian and gay interests. In others, though, the development of internal structures for lesbian and gay representation was a more top-down, leadership-driven affair. In these cases, links between lesbian and gay representative structures and mainstream union decision-making bodies seem to be more effectively realized. The problem here, however, lies in ensuring that centralized and bureaucratic union initiatives are sensitive to the particular needs of gay and lesbian members. Unions are also using their educational facilities and other programmes to build awareness of the issues facing lesbian and gay members, and to secure effective representation of their interests. There is little evidence of concerted resistance to these developments on the part of more conservative union members and officials. Most members, for instance, do not appear to be interested. Nevertheless, Bairstow (2004) does suggest that unions are sometimes uncomfortable with, or uncertain about, dealing with issues relating to sexual orientation.

Given the persistence of male-dominated decision-making processes and cultures, in recent years there has been a growing recognition that liberal measures are an ineffective means of securing the effective participation of under-represented groups, such as black and women members, in trade unions, and that more radical interventions may be necessary (Healy and Kirton 2000). The radical approach implies that positive action is required in order to enable union members from disadvantaged social groups to participate in trade unions and thus have their interests represented more effectively (Kirton and Greene 2002). It encourages the need for direct intervention 'in organizational practices to achieve fair representation and a fair distribution of rewards' across disadvantaged groups (Colgan and Ledwith 2002: 171). See Figure 4.1 for an illustration of how unions use liberal and radical interventions.

The most significant measures that come under the 'radical' label are, first, the provision of special seats, or 'reserved seats', for representatives from particular social groups, mainly women workers, on union decision-making bodies and, second, the establishment of internal structures that enable members from disadvantaged groups to organize and represent themselves through what is known as 'self-organization' (Virdee and Grint 1994). Both of these interventions challenge established assumptions about the nature of union democracy. Reserving seats for, say, women members goes against the tradition, central to the notion of representative democracy, that union representatives should be elected on behalf of the membership as a whole, and not owe their places to the electoral support of particular groups. Allowing some groups of workers to self-organize, on the basis of their social characteristics rather than their collective identity as workers, runs counter to traditions of participatory democracy in unions (McBride 2000; Terry 1996).

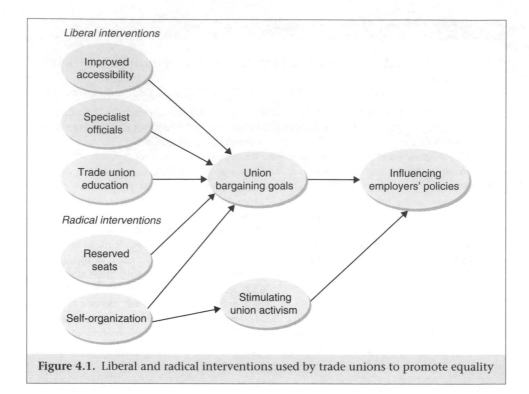

Figure 4.1. Liberal and radical interventions used by trade unions to promote equality

The presence of reserved seats on union decision-making bodies has become more common in trade unions, though they are still limited to a minority (Kirton and Greene 2005). The public services union, Unison, which has a very high female membership, is the most prominent example. Its emphasis on 'proportionality' in decision-making structures is designed to ensure that women are elected to representative positions in proportion to the number of female members. The principle of 'fair representation' in Unison takes proportionality a stage further, with the aim being to secure an appropriate number of elected representatives who are employed in low-paid jobs. One assessment indicates that proportionality 'has enabled women's systematic inclusion within' Unison and led to 'dramatic increases in women's access to the decision-making area' (McBride 2001: 69).

Nevertheless, the provision of reserved places in union policy-making bodies is not without its problems. Trade unionists, including some women, dislike its potential divisiveness (Bradley 1999: 186). This raises the question of how far women, and other socially disadvantaged groups, have specific interests that can only be articulated by representatives of their own kind. A further problem with reserved places is that those women who take them up are often made to feel inferior; they can be treated as second-class union representatives whose contributions should be limited to issues that specifically concern women members and thus can be easily marginalized (Colgan and Ledwith 2002; Kirton and Healy 1999). Conversely, women who have been elected to general, non-reserved seats often feel an obligation to speak on behalf of their entire constituency, male and female, leading them to play down the significance of issues that are specific to women (Healy and Kirton 2000; McBride 2000).

Perhaps the most fundamental criticism of reserved seats, though, is that although their presence advances the representation of individual women within trade unions, they are less effective in promoting the interests of women as a disadvantaged social group. In other words, tinkering with policy-making structures in a way that enables more women to participate as individuals does little to challenge the embedded, and collectively generated, male-dominated norms and assumptions that determine union action (McBride 2000, 2001).

Few unions have innovated with self-organization as a means of enabling disadvantaged social groups to participate and thus secure effective representation of their interests. Unison has the most sophisticated set of practices in respect of self-organization. Black, disabled, lesbian and gay, and women members all have the opportunity to self-organize (McBride 2000; Terry 1996). What, then, is meant by 'self-organization' in trade unions? It refers to arrangements that provide a separate space for collective organization and action by union members and activists, on the basis of their shared social characteristics. In order to secure more effective representation, it offers a means by which members from disadvantaged social groups can work together, separate from established union decision-making structures, to pursue their collective interests.

Whereas reserved seats focus on improving representative democracy in unions, self-organization is designed to enhance the participation of members from disadvantaged groups. It enables them to work together, constructing 'a sense of identity, political consciousness, confidence and solidarity and to develop and practice activist skills' (Colgan and Ledwith 2002: 178). Self-organization, therefore, explicitly challenges the notion that workers are a homogeneous group with a single set of common interests that can be articulated and represented by a trade union in an unproblematic manner. It recognizes that workers, by virtue of belonging to particular social groups, may have diverse interests, and that traditional approaches to participatory democracy in trade unions, which assumed a commonality of interest, are therefore inappropriate.

Studies of self-organization in practice show that, while it is still rare in British trade unions, it nonetheless gives members and activists a forum that they can use to develop participation, and to bring issues that specifically concern them on to the union agenda (Colgan and Ledwith 2000; Parker 2002). Black members' networks, for example, are not only an effective way of stimulating involvement and participation, but also serve to encourage greater discussion of race equality issues within a trade union context (Bradley, Healy, and Mukherjee 2002).

Self-organization arrangements may also serve to generate union activism, giving members a sense that they are able to effect changes that benefit their working lives. In her study of gay and lesbian self-organization in Unison, Colgan (1999) demonstrates how self-organization challenges discriminatory attitudes and practices within trade unions, producing a more inclusive union agenda. Interviews with black and minority ethnic women trade union activists demonstrate how getting involved in self-organized groups was a major stimulus to their participation in broader union affairs (Bradley and Healy 2008).

The positive effects of self-organization may, however, sometimes be limited in practice. For one thing, it relies upon the willingness of members to participate in union affairs, something that cannot be assumed. Moreover, apart from in Unison, separate organizing is generally limited to women (Kirton and Greene 2002). Where the links with established policy-making bodies are tenuous, self-organization can lead to the interests of disadvantaged social groups being marginalized. Autonomy, then, may foster exclusion (Colgan and Ledwith 2002), particularly if powerful union interests feel challenged. In Unison, for example, those policy issues discussed in the women's self-organized groups rarely made it on to the agenda of the powerful mainstream decision-making bodies (McBride 2000, 2001). Thus 'the predominant model of self-organization within Unison is of a pressure group whose comments are welcome but not necessarily taken into consideration' (McBride 2001: 172).

While there is some evidence that the relationship between the self-organized groups and established decision-making may improve over time (Colgan 1999), self-organization may reinforce, rather than ameliorate, the under-representation of disadvantaged groups within trade unions. That said, however, there is no doubting that the self-organizing approach has fostered greater trade union involvement among workers who belong to groups that often experience exclusion, like black and minority ethnic women, for example. Their enthusiasm for the self-organization approach indicates that despite the problems we have identified, it can be a valuable means of revitalizing union organization and of enabling trade unions to represent diversity in a more effective manner (Bradley and Healy 2008).

SECTION SUMMARY AND FURTHER READING

- Historically, trade unions have often supported employment arrangements and bargaining priorities that sustain and reinforce discriminatory employment practices to the disadvantage of women and black workers. Although the decline of the trade unions, their white, male-dominated heartlands in particular, has prompted a change of attitudes since the 1970s, much of the pressure for reform has come from union members and activists themselves.

- Collective bargaining has increasingly been used by the trade unions as a vehicle for advancing equality at work. How far the rise of equality bargaining has transformed union approaches is, however, questionable, since there is evidence of a more restricted trade union agenda sometimes existing in practice.

- Trade unions have undertaken efforts to improve the representation of members from disadvantaged social groups within their internal structures. Their initiatives have, however, been of a largely liberal kind, concerned with establishing equal treatment. The development of a more radical approach, incorporating the provision of reserved seats and, more rarely, arrangements for self-organization, faces certain obstacles, but may be a better means of enabling unions to represent diversity effectively.

For an overview of trade unions and equality at work, see Kirton and Greene (2005: Chapter 7). Cunnison and Stageman (1993) use a series of case studies to examine how unions have changed their policies and practices in order to respond to the demands of women members and activists. The most recent general study of equality bargaining issues is Colling and Dickens (2001). For details of practices in Unison, see McBride (2000). See Colgan and Ledwith (2002) for debates on reserved seats and self-organization in general. Bradley and Healy's (2008: Chapter 10) interviews with black and minority ethnic women trade unionists are highly illuminating.

 Visit our Online Resource Centre for web links to sites connected to this section. www.oxfordtextbooks.co.uk/williams_adamsmith2e

Conclusion

In this chapter, we have demonstrated that inequality and disadvantage, based on social divisions, are important features of contemporary employment relations. Like Chapters 2 and 3, the material discussed in this chapter shows the influence of environmental factors on employment relations. Thus relationships between employers and employees at work cannot simply be understood in the context of the workplace, but are informed by wider economic, political, and social influences that transcend particular employment situations. For example, although the practice of trade unionism is clearly founded upon collective values and the need for unity to combat hostile employers, it has also often been concerned with excluding groups of workers, such as women for example, in order to advantage a privileged male minority. Nevertheless, unions have come under pressure to operate more inclusively, not least because their traditional constituencies, male-dominated industries based on manual labour, have dwindled in significance. Thus unions have taken up the interests of women workers and other socially disadvantaged groups more readily, and have altered their structures to enable them to be more effectively represented.

Union activity in these areas, while not without its difficulties, is an important catalyst for greater equality in contemporary employment relations. Employer-led efforts, based on a rather narrow and insecure conception of the business advantages of equality action, can be of limited effectiveness. Equal opportunities policies, which emphasize the need to treat everybody the same regardless of their social characteristics, are strong on rhetoric, but often short on action. The managing diversity model, despite its ostensibly more transformative approach, does little to challenge socially generated disadvantage and inequality at work, and is often, in practice, little different from the more conventional equal opportunities agenda. A trade union presence, though, can exert pressure on employers to deliver a more effective set of equality policies, such as better family-friendly policies, for example.

Equality action at organizational level occurs within, and is informed by, a legislative framework. While Britain has had anti-discrimination and equality laws since the 1970s, in general they lack effectiveness; the liberal, equal treatment values that underpin the legislation largely preclude positive action, and employers are rarely obliged to undertake initiatives that promote equality, even if they are found to be operating discriminatory practices. During the 2000s, Labour governments extended the scope of anti-discrimination legislation and encouraged organizations to adopt family-friendly policies and work–life balance arrangements for their staff, although they were extremely reluctant to compel businesses to improve their practices. Robust equality action by employers is therefore dependent upon both a stronger legislative framework and the presence of a trade union that has made a commitment to effecting positive change in this area.

Assignment and discussion questions

1   What is meant by the concept of the 'status divide' at work?

2   Critically assess the main strengths and weaknesses of the legal framework relating to discrimination and equality at work.

3   Should employers have any concern with equal opportunities at work? Why?

4   Why might employers be more sympathetic to 'diversity management' than to the liberal equal opportunities approach?

5   Why might 'family-friendly' working practices accentuate, rather than diminish, gender disadvantage in employment?

6   Why have trade unions been slow to respond to the particular problems of disadvantaged groups at work?

 Visit our Online Resource Centre for answers to these questions. www.oxfordtextbooks.co.uk/williams_adamsmith2e

Take your learning further: online resource centre

Visit the Online Resource Centre that accompanies this book to enrich your understanding of Chapter 4: Social divisions and employment relations. Explore web links, test yourself using an interactive flashcard glossary, and keep up-to-date with the latest developments in the area.

 http://www.oxfordtextbooks.co.uk/orc/williams_adamsmith2e.

Chapter case study

Employer attitudes to employees' work–life balance

A growing body of legislation aims to allow employees to balance the demands of their paid work with that of their home and family responsibilities. However, the extent to which any additional provisions are available to workers depends upon the views that employers hold on the issue: are they seen as a burden, or things that can provide specific benefits to business through employees having greater job satisfaction?

One survey sought to identify how UK employers viewed this matter. The authors identified three phases in the approach taken by employers. Phase one is where organizations have given little or no thought to the matter, beyond normally adhering to legal requirements. In phase two, employers develop formal policies and practices to ensure that workers are more able to balance work–life demands. Organizations may obtain some business benefits as a result. Firms that have reached phase three strategically undertake a major change in their culture and employment arrangements. In such organizations, an employee's 'work' and 'life' are not seen as matters to be 'traded' against each other. Rather, full organizational and management support for a genuine work–life balance for employees is seen to add value to the business through the identification of work inefficiencies, and new and better forms of work organization.

The survey reported findings from 138 organizations, and the researchers estimate that the results covered over 650,000 workers. The findings suggest that there is little evidence of organizations moving towards a phase three approach. Over one-third of respondents were located in phase one: limited attention had been given to the issue beyond meeting provisions of the legislation. Almost half of the organizations saw work–life balance as a social issue and that any business benefits were a 'bonus'. Only around one-fifth of, typically large, employers saw the matter as a genuine business issue and could be classed as phase three organizations. Even among these, though, there was evidence that while employers believed benefits flowed to the firm, they were not able to identify any specific advantages.

In terms of the policies and practices that organizations had developed in this area, the majority focused on 'family-friendly' matters such as maternity leave and pay. The companies that had provisions beyond those required by law typically provided additional pay rather than longer leave, which would be important in balancing parental and work responsibilities. Only around 10 per cent of firms provided workplace nurseries or similar assistance with child care. Beyond family-related practices, over half offered an employee assistance programme or similar service concerned with confidential counselling for employees.

In many cases, these benefits were not a right for workers but subject to a manager's discretion, and there is evidence that managers were not readily willing to use such discretion in favour of the employee. In reviewing their evidence, the researchers conclude that 'achieving a work–life balance for the majority of employees in the UK is only likely if more comprehensive legislation is introduced' and that 'advocates of the business case (for work–life balance) have some way to go in convincing managers of the merits of their argument' (Adam-Smith and Copestake 2001: 8).

Source: Adam-Smith and Copestake (2001)

1. Why do managers appear reluctant to introduce comprehensive policies and practices to support the work–life balance of their employees?

2. What are the possible consequences for workers who are unable to effectively balance the demands of their work and non-work responsibilities and interests?

PART 3

Key Issues in Contemporary Employment Relations

5 Managing employment relations   169

6 Representation at work   211

7 Contemporary developments in pay and working time   255

8 Experiencing employment relations: involvement,
   insecurity, intensification   298

9 Conflict and employment relations   328

5

Managing employment relations

Chapter objectives:

The main objectives of this chapter are to:

∗ examine how the management role in employment relations developed in a context of growing unionization;

∗ examine how management has utilized the more favourable economic and social climate to challenge the role and influence of trade unions;

∗ consider the implications of the statutory procedure for union recognition;

∗ explore the extent to which the rise of human resource management has transformed the management of employment relations;

∗ analyse how employment relations is managed in firms that do not recognize trade unions; and

∗ consider the tensions inherent in management's need both to control employees' behaviour and performance, and to elicit their commitment and cooperation.

5.1 Introduction

In this chapter, we consider contemporary developments in the management of employment relations. Surprisingly, the management of employment relations used to receive very little attention from researchers and writers. Although the employment relationship must, by definition, comprise two parties—employer and employee—our understanding of how the former managed it was rather undeveloped (Clegg 1979). The principal areas of interest were the collective organization of employees in trade unions, and the features of the bargaining relationship that existed between employers' associations and trade unions. Since the 1980s, though, with changes in the economic and political climate having prompted union decline, there has been a much more sustained 'focus on management as the prime mover in industrial relations, both in terms of organizational practice and in the amount of academic research' (Marchington and Harrison 1991: 286). Rather than having to react to, and accommodate, trade unionism, managers would appear to enjoy an environment in which they are much better able to innovate in respect of employment relations.

We commence this chapter by investigating the historical development of employment relations management, and the important concern with managing trade unions that dominated the managerial agenda before the 1980s. In Section 5.3 we examine the nature, scope, and dimensions of the managerial challenge to trade unionism which dominated employment relations during the 1980s and 1990s, before considering the implications of legislation enacted in 2000 which compels employers to recognize a union where this is desired by a majority of the workforce. Union decline was, in part, influenced by the development of new techniques for managing employment relations associated with the development of human resource management (HRM). In Section 5.4 we investigate the main features of a sophisticated HRM approach to managing employment relations, and interpret its significance. This is followed, in Section 5.5, by an assessment of the main issues surrounding employment relations in the increasing number of firms without a union presence, before Section 5.6 considers the main challenges and tensions inherent in managing employment relationships.

Introductory case study

Engaging employees at McDonalds

One of the main themes of this chapter concerns the extent to which the management of employment relations has changed, away from a traditional focus on working with trade unions, and managing the implications of unionization, towards a more contemporary focus on improving business performance by engaging employees and securing their commitment to the organization, without the need for trade unions. The fast-food chain McDonalds is well known for its non-union status; but it is often portrayed as a low-wage employer, whose employment practices are based on securing employee compliance with organizational standards through rigorous control systems, resulting in low discretion. However, David Fairhurst, a senior McDonalds executive in the UK, asserts that such a stereotype is no longer appropriate. Rather, the need to improve customer service, and thus deliver better performance, has made jobs in the fast-food company more rewarding, increasing the commitment of employees. Since 2005, he claims, 'we have focused our efforts on engaging our people to deliver an outstanding experience for our customers by creating an outstanding employment experience for them' (Fairhurst 2008: 326).

Critics of McDonalds, however, point out that many jobs in the fast-food company still attract low rates of pay, at or just above the minimum wage, casting doubt upon its claim that employees are valued assets. In this chapter we question how far a concern with engaging employees, and securing their organizational commitment, linked to the development of sophisticated human resource management (HRM), has come to dominate approaches to managing employment relations. The twin aims of exercising control over employees, and resisting a trade union presence, continue to be managerial priorities in the area of employment relations.

5.2 **Managing with trade unions**

As we saw in Chapter one, a belief in managerial prerogative, or the right to manage, underpins management behaviour in employment relations. Historically, although managements vigorously attempted to exclude trade unions from their workplaces, in practice the strength of union organization in many areas of the economy obliged them to try to sustain their prerogative by accommodating workers' demands. During the twentieth century, employers often recognized unions for collective bargaining so as to mitigate disruption, and foster order and stability (Hyman 1975). This was, however, in large part a reaction by employers to the pressure coming from workers themselves to organize unions (Clegg, Fox, and Thompson 1964). Attempts to exclude unions caused too much disruption, given the collective power that workers were able to wield. Thus employers took a pragmatic approach, recognizing unions, but doing so in a way that disturbed managerial prerogatives as little as possible (Gospel 1992).

During the 1960s and 1970s, in a context of growing union power, companies that had hitherto not recognized a union found it advantageous to do so, in order to quell workplace militancy. For example, management in the biscuit works studied by Scott (1994) was aware of a growing union presence within the factory and chose to accommodate it by means of a centralized negotiating relationship with union full-time officers, from which workplace union activists were distanced. The company embraced collective bargaining with a recognized union, but did so in a way that upheld managerial rights and secured workplace order.

Although, for pragmatic reasons, employers may have chosen to recognize unions, by no means does this mean that they accepted their legitimacy and, indeed, made every effort to restrict union influence over employment relations within the workplace. For much of the twentieth century, many employers chose to try to exclude unions from their workplaces by dealing with them through employers' associations (see Chapter 1). However, the growth of workplace bargaining prompted employers to look for more sophisticated ways of managing employment relations in unionized environments.

5.2.1 Managerial innovation in employment relations: the pluralist agenda

Attempts to bargain with unions by means of employers' associations contributed to the widespread neglect of employment relations management in many firms, or what Hyman (2003) refers to as the 'tradition of unscientific management'. The historical weakness of the personnel management function in Britain has long been acknowledged (e.g. Flanders 1975). Writers point to the history of unsophisticated managerial control systems, the lack of complex managerial hierarchies within firms, and the slow, and indeed relatively late, diffusion of scientific management techniques (Gospel 1992; Tolliday and Zeitlin 1991). Employers exhibited a preference for *ad hoc*, informal, and unsophisticated ways of managing their workforces, such as a reliance on simple payment by results techniques.

What factors contributed to managerial neglect of employment relations matters? Clearly the externalization of relations with trade unions was one influence. Three other elements were also important: first, the process of industrialization in Britain, which started earlier than in other competitor economies, delayed the emergence of the modern corporate firm; second, diverse and fluctuating product markets and an ample labour supply were obstacles to modernization; and third, in some industries, a pre-industrial craft ethos, in which workers enjoyed a degree of control over the content of their jobs, prevailed (Gospel 1992). How realistic was it, then, to expect workplace unionism to be contained so easily, given the weakness of managerial control systems and the lack of attention given to employment relations by senior managers? Employers therefore found it increasingly hard to maintain managerial prerogatives within the workplace.

During the 1940s and 1950s, there was a marked growth in the incidence of workplace bargaining in Britain, particularly in the engineering sector (Gospel 1992). Not only did this reflect the increasing difficulty employers had in upholding managerial rights in the workplace, but the weakness of agreements reached by means of multi-employer bargaining, and a tight labour market created by full employment, which enhanced workers' bargaining power, were also contributory factors (Terry 1983). The reluctance of senior managers to take control over their own employment relations during this period in a resolute and strategic way, and to come to terms with, and accommodate the growth of, workplace unionism, rather than see it as a threat to be nullified, was seen by the pluralists as a major error, contributing to industrial disputes and workplace disorder (Flanders 1964, 1975).

Employers were encouraged to secure greater control over employment relations within the workplace by recognizing, formally, the legitimacy of shop floor unionism rather than by trying to extinguish it, something that would only cause greater disruption. Such a prescription characterized the findings and recommendations of the 1965–68 Royal Commission on Trade Unions and Employers' Associations, established under the chairmanship of Lord Donovan. It was set up to examine the system of employment relations in Britain, and to make proposals for its reform, given the detrimental effect aspects of it were held to have on British economic performance, in particular, 'wage drift', inflationary increases in earnings caused by workplace bargaining, and the associated high level of industrial conflict. Influenced by prominent pluralist writers such as Allan Flanders, Donovan identified managerial weakness as a prime source of Britain's employment relations problems and strongly recommended that, in order to rectify them, managers should secure greater control over workplace employment relations (Royal Commission 1968).

During the 1960s and 1970s, in a context of growing union militancy, managers adopted a notably more interventionist approach in respect of workplace employment relations anyway, in order to contain and accommodate trade union power, and thus exercise greater control. Employers were increasingly the 'main instigators in reshaping the system of industrial relations in Britain' (Gospel 1992: 140). Perhaps the most significant managerial intervention during this period was the rise of 'productivity bargaining', heralded as a major managerial initiative in the reform of employment relations. The theory and practice of productivity bargaining were popularized by Allan Flanders's celebrated study of the negotiation of a path-breaking collective agreement, known as the 'Blue Book', at Esso's Fawley oil refinery, near Southampton during the early 1960s (Flanders 1964).

What were the features of the Blue Book deal struck between management and unions at Fawley? Its major targets were the perceived 'under-utilization' of labour and excessive overtime working. The high level of overtime allowed workers to supplement low basic wages with premium payments for doing the extra work. This not only contributed to wage drift, since earnings became increasingly distant from formally negotiated pay rates, but it also encouraged workplace bargaining over overtime rates and allocation. Furthermore, the prospect of supplementing earnings through opportunities for overtime was detrimental to productivity since it gave workers an incentive to reduce their effort during their normal working time in the hope that this would make overtime necessary. The productivity agreement struck at Fawley, then, saw management 'buy out' overtime and other inefficient practices in return for higher basic earnings and a fixed working week. It was envisaged that such an approach would encourage order and stability, as well as generating productivity improvements (Flanders 1964).

Over and above the features of the agreement itself, the deal struck at Fawley was held to be significant in two important respects. First, it was an example of managerial innovation in employment relations, standing out from the hitherto *ad hoc*, unsophisticated, and reactive approach to employment relations exhibited within most British firms (Flanders 1964). Second, the agreement appeared to possess a 'higher order function', being the 'very embodiment of pluralist industrial relations' (Ahlstrand 1990: 61, 60). It represented an attempt by management to secure control of the workplace through cooperative means, by explicitly recognizing the legitimacy of the unions as the representatives of the workforce, rather than trying to marginalize or exclude them (Flanders 1964).

The Fawley experiment, then, appeared not only to be beneficial for the employer, in that it led to improved economic performance, but it also seemed to secure, and legitimize, the interests of employees through the establishment of a cooperative relationship with the unions. Ensuing productivity gains, though, were limited and largely the result of staffing cuts, rather than the more efficient utilization of labour, and overtime working remained commonplace. Managers, moreover, never eschewed their unitary beliefs; indeed, they used productivity agreements to undermine union power in the workplace, part of a long-term strategy to manage without unions altogether (Ahlstrand 1990).

During the late 1960s and early 1970s, there was a marked increase in the popularity of productivity agreements, though they varied considerably in their scope, detail, and outcomes. Perhaps their most important function, however, was to signal the growth of a more resolute and sophisticated approach to the management of employment relations within British firms (Clegg 1979), contributing to the declining incidence of multi-employer bargaining through employers' associations. In particular, employers increasingly sought to gain control of their own employment relations, encouraged by a process of corporate restructuring and rationalization which stimulated demand for greater managerial expertise and professionalism (Batstone 1988; Gospel 1992). Personnel policies were reformed. More sophisticated payment systems were introduced, for example, involving the introduction of new job evaluation techniques.

Moreover, workplace trade unionism, particularly the role of shop stewards (see below), became increasingly formalized as managers encouraged, or 'sponsored', them in an attempt to accommodate union power (Terry 1983). In the Cadbury's confectionery plant at Bourneville, for example, managers acceded to the operation of a closed shop arrangement (see Box 5.1) as part of an attempt to contain and accommodate the growing

HISTORICAL PERSPECTIVE 5.1

Managing with the closed shop

Union membership agreements, or 'closed shops' as they are more popularly known, were a major feature of British employment relations for many years. Under closed shop arrangements, union membership was a condition of employment. The 'pre-entry' closed shop restricted particular jobs to members of a specific union. The more commonplace 'post-entry' closed shop made union membership mandatory when a worker commenced employment. While union pressure was an important factor stimulating the growth of closed shop arrangements (McCarthy 1964), they became increasingly widespread in British industry during the 1970s, largely due to management acquiescence (Dunn and Gennard 1984; Gospel 1992; Marchington and Parker 1990). This was part of the broader concern of managers to accommodate and contain workplace trade unionism, to push it in a moderate and cooperative direction.

By 1980, some five million workers may have been covered by closed shop arrangements, mostly of the post-entry type (Millward et al. 1992). Margaret Thatcher's Conservative governments, however, made reform of the closed shop a key feature of their legislative assault on the trade unions until, with the enactment of the 1990 Employment Act, the operation of one was effectively made unlawful altogether. Perhaps a more influential factor contributing to the decline of the closed shop—by 1990 only about half a million workers were still covered by such an arrangement (Millward et al. 1992)—was the decline of employment in those industries, such as printing, for example, where it was prominent.

influence of the shop stewards, and to direct it in a 'responsible and realistic' direction (Smith, Child, and Rowlinson 1990: 195).

During the 1970s, shop steward structures were extended into areas, such as the public sector, where the presence of formal workplace unionism had hitherto been rare (Terry 1983). One should not disregard the extent to which the development of workplace union organization derived from the efforts of workers themselves to secure change. In practice, it 'is impossible to disentangle the influence of management acquiescence from that of worker pressure' (Marchington and Parker 1990: 208). Union activity was not always amenable to management objectives. In Cadbury's, for example, the Transport and General Workers' Union (TGWU) became rather more powerful in the workplace than managers considered desirable (Smith, Child, and Rowlinson 1990).

From this overview of how employment relations was managed in Britain before the 1980s, it should be clear that while employers accepted trade unionism, this reflected a pragmatic response to circumstances, notably union power, rather than a genuine belief in the virtues of a pluralist approach. If managers had to deal with trade unions, they tried to do so in such a way that it contained workplace militancy. Managers may have been obliged to respond constructively to the implications of growing union power, but their fundamentally unitary values generally remained constant.

SECTION SUMMARY AND FURTHER READING

- Employers have long played a leading role in employment relations by initiating union recognition, albeit under pressure from workers for union representation. In forming employers' associations and instituting multi-employer bargaining arrangements, employers sought to maintain managerial prerogative in the workplace by externalizing their relationship with trade unions.

- Among other things, this process of externalization contributed to a tradition of 'unscientific management', the weakness of managerial structures and systems in respect of employment relations. The growth of workplace bargaining and its effects encouraged firms to develop a more sophisticated approach to managing employment relations in the workplace, accommodating trade union power rather than attempting to repulse it.

- The reform of employment relations in the 1960s and 1970s, the conclusion of productivity agreements for example, while predominantly management led, was encouraged by the need to accommodate growing union power. There was no general shift in managerial philosophy away from unitary values, rather a pragmatic acceptance of pluralist approaches as the most effective means of ensuring stability in employment relations.

Gospel (1992) is the most authoritative study of the historical development of the management of employment relations. McIvor (1996) assesses the growth and development of employers' associations. Allan Flanders's classic 1964 account of the Fawley experiment, *The Fawley Productivity Agreements* (Flanders 1964), is seminal. It should be read in conjunction with Ahlstrand (1990).

 Visit our Online Resource Centre for web links to sites connected to this section. www.oxfordtextbooks.co.uk/williams_adamsmith2e

5.3 **Challenging unions**

Since the 1980s, the changes in the economic and political environment discussed in Chapters 2 and 3 have made it easier for employers to challenge the influence of trade unions, compounding the fundamentally unitary preferences of managers (Poole and Mansfield 1993). Managers no longer found it essential to reach pragmatic accommodations with the unions in order to contain their power. Given its well-known anti-union philosophy, the fast-food chain McDonalds is by no means representative of employers in Britain in general; however, the comment of one of its senior managers symbolizes the trend of increased 'employer militancy' (Kelly 1998).

> Unionization has risen its ugly head over the years, but you know, we feel that we don't need unions. I think we've seen that the unions' power within business has been eroded quite considerably over the last 15 years, we've managed to get rid of them. (quoted in Royle 2000: 110)

Even where they had hitherto encouraged a union presence, such as in the Cadbury's Bourneville plant, for example, managers attempted to undermine, and even extinguish, a formal union presence (Smith, Child, and Rowlinson 1990). In this part of the chapter, we examine the ways in which employers in Britain have sought to challenge trade unionism, and consider the implications of the statutory union recognition procedure introduced in 2000.

5.3.1 Union exclusion in Britain

Perhaps the most obvious measure of union exclusion in Britain is the substantial fall in the incidence of union recognition that occurred during the 1980s and 1990s, particularly in the private sector. As can be seen from Table 5.1, union recognition in the public sector generally held up rather well; the most significant falls occurred in the private sector, where, by the end of the 1990s, unions were recognized for collective bargaining purposes in just a quarter of workplaces.

Interestingly, Table 5.1 also shows that the decline in the incidence of union recognition in the private sector seems to have taken off not in the early 1980s, but in the latter half of that decade. This suggests that employers did not take immediate advantage of the more favourable political and economic climate to launch an assault on union power, but were rather more tentative in their approach, perhaps under the influence of the Conservative anti-union legislation.

For most of the twentieth century, an employer's decision to recognize a union, or not to recognize one, was a voluntary matter, influenced, of course, by the organizing efforts of workers and unions. In general, employers were never legally obliged to deal with a union. In theory, employers could withdraw recognition from, or 'derecognize', trade unions as they saw fit. Perhaps the most striking feature of the 1980s, then, was the somewhat limited extent of union derecognition (Claydon 1989, 1996; Gall and McKay 1994).

While outright union derecognition was rare, it was not unimportant, with incidents concentrated in certain sectors such as magazine and newspaper publishing and the maritime industry. One of the best-known examples in the newspaper industry was the withdrawal of union recognition by Rupert Murdoch's News International, owner of *The Times, The Sunday Times, The Sun*, and the *News of the World* titles, prompting a bitter industrial dispute in 1986–87 (Littleton 1992). In magazine publishing, the removal of union recognition rights was seen by managers as crucial since it gave them greater flexibility to cope with more competitive market conditions (Gall 1998). Although complete

Table 5.1 Percentage of workplaces with a recognized union, 1980–98

	All workplaces	Private manufacturing	Private services	Public services
1980	64	65	41	94
1984	66	56	44	99
1990	53	44	36	87
1998	42	29	23	87

Workplaces with 25 or more employees.
Source: Millward, Bryson, and Forth (2000: 96)

derecognition was rare, and where it did occur it was largely an opportunistic response by managers to declining union membership and organization, 'partial' derecognition, the withdrawal of collective bargaining rights from particular groups of workers, such as managers in the financial services industry for example, was perhaps more common (Claydon 1996; Gall and McKay 1994).

By the early to mid 1990s, though, it seemed that a 'cumulative trend towards derecognition might be emerging' (Claydon 1996: 163). Union derecognition became increasingly common in the oil and chemicals industries in particular, and even extended to the Fawley oil refinery, which, thirty years previously, had been celebrated as the epitome of pluralist employment relations (Smith and Morton 1994). Nevertheless, by the mid 1990s the derecognition trend appears to have been reversed; fewer instances of it arose and these were offset by an increasing number of new recognition agreements (Gall and McKay 1999).

By itself, the extent of union derecognition insufficiently accounts for the overall decline in union recognition in Britain during the 1980s and 1990s. A more significant factor was the increasing incidence of non-recognition by employers in new workplaces (Machin 2000). In 1998, 32 per cent of workplaces that had been in existence for twenty-five years or more recognized a trade union. Just 18 per cent of new workplaces, those that were under 10 years old, did so (Cully et al. 1999).

Newly established workplaces operating in growing sectors of the economy, such as high-tech industries, are unlikely to recognize unions in the first place (Findlay 1993; McLoughlin and Gourlay 1992). Thus the decline in union recognition can be ascribed to the policies of more assertive employers, who, aided by a supportive economic and political environment, were increasingly unwilling to countenance a union presence within their operations (Kelly 1998).

While not as prominent as the headline fall in union recognition, even where unions retained a formal workplace presence managers became keener to challenge their role. This was not in general by means of an outright, aggressive anti-union policy, as is commonplace in the United States (see Box 5.2). Rather, managers, tentatively at first, increasingly sought to erode the influence of unions in situations where, because of the size of union membership for example, outright derecognition was not feasible.

New methods of direct communications techniques (see Chapter 8), between management and employees, such as team briefings, for example, were designed to encourage greater organizational loyalty and commitment, and to foster among the workforce a sense of identification with the company (Storey 1992). Such innovations were a key feature of the shift towards greater employee involvement within the workplace, which, while perhaps not designed explicitly to undermine trade unionism, nonetheless contributed to its declining influence (Marchington and Parker 1990). However, it is doubtful whether management-controlled communications initiatives can offset the diminution of collective voice provided by robust trade unionism, and there is frequently a gap between formal policy and the reality of involvement, or rather the lack of it, on the ground (Marginson et al. 1988; Millward 1994).

Where union membership levels are high, it is likely to be more trouble than it is worth, in terms of potential disruption, to try to exclude unions entirely (Storey 1992). Added to which, many employers 'do not have an alternative set of employment relations policies that they can realistically hope to put in place of those agreed with trade unions' (Sisson

INTERNATIONAL PERSPECTIVE 5.2

Anti-unionism in the United States

Visceral hostility towards trade unionism and collective bargaining has been a long-standing feature of employment relations in the United States. Attempts by unions to gain recognition for collective bargaining purposes have generally been met by robust employer opposition, something that seems to have increased since the 1970s. Companies wanting to remain union-free frequently employ specialist anti-union consultants to advise on ways of resisting unionization efforts (Logan 2006)

Some insight into the kinds of problems encountered by workers when attempting to exercise their right to organize in trade unions can be gained from an examination of the fast-food industry where 'union-busting techniques'—sometimes illegal efforts to prevent unionization—are commonplace. In his book on the fast-food industry, *Fast Food Nation* (2002), Eric Schlosser details some of the methods used by McDonalds to remain free of the unions. It uses, for example, managerial 'flying squads', comprising experienced senior managers, who descend upon a restaurant to encourage the workforce to desist from unionization, by means of threats if other approaches fail to do the trick, as soon as a hint of union activity emerges (Schlosser 2002).

Perhaps the most infamous anti-union firm in the US is the giant retailer Wal-Mart, the owner of Asda in Britain. In the early days of the company, Wal-Mart's founder, Sam Walton, engaged a 'professional union-buster' in an effort to prevent unionization (Ortega 1999: 87). According to one worker, when the Teamsters union tried to organize a distribution centre Walton told the staff 'that if the union got in, the warehouse would be closed . . . people could vote any way they wanted, but he'd close her right up' (Ortega 1999: 107). Unsurprisingly, the union failed to get enough support to win recognition. Wal-Mart has fine-tuned its anti-union approach over the years, vigorously resisting any attempts by unions to organize its stores, often by means of heavy-handed tactics. When Ann Bertelli, a photo-processing clerk, tried to form a union at her store in Massachusetts she was dismissed (Ortega 1999: 354–5).

In his book on work and employment relations in the US, *The Big Squeeze*, Steven Greenhouse recounts similar stories of workers across a range of firms who have been fired, in violation of federal law, for supporting unionization efforts. Following years of struggle to resist union recognition, numerous legal challenges, and the use of specialist anti-union consultants, the EnerSys company eventually frustrated the stated wish of the majority of the workforce in its South Carolina battery factory for union recognition by closing it down (Greenhouse 2008). Managers in some firms are so opposed to unionization that they would prefer plants to close rather than have to recognize a trade union.

and Storey 2000: 193). Case study evidence from the food industry shows, moreover, that managers may not have the wherewithal to develop sophisticated new techniques of employment relations management in established workplaces, and are constrained by traditional arrangements (Scott 1994).

In situations where unions retain a formal presence, or where it is not practical to exclude them entirely, managers have sought to challenge their influence and marginalize their role (Marchington and Parker 1990), 'reducing the disadvantages' of a union presence in order to enhance managerial prerogative (Purcell 1991: 37). During the 1980s and 1990s, some employers looked to mitigate the perceived problems of multi-unionism, recognition of more than one union, by signing 'single union agreements', or 'sweetheart' deals, with unions that made a virtue of their cooperative approach. In 1985, for example, the Nissan car manufacturer chose, following a union 'beauty contest', to recognize the potentially more amenable engineering union, rather than a potentially more militant competitor (Garrahan and Stewart 1992). In Chapter 6, we examine the trend towards 'partnership agreements' between employers and unions, a further example, perhaps, of the way in which employers may, for pragmatic reasons, uphold union recognition, but seek to shape the relationship in a manner that better suits their interests.

5.3.2 Statutory union recognition in Britain

Except for the 1970s, when statutory procedures existed for a time (see Beaumont 1981), before 2000 employers were never under a legal obligation to recognize a union. The third statutory recognition procedure to be introduced in Britain was enacted by the 1999 Employment Relations Act (ERA 1999), and came into effect in June 2000. It was the outcome of the 1997 Labour government's commitment to introducing a measure that would oblige employers to recognize a union where the majority of the work-force wanted it (DTI 1998). The Trades Union Congress (TUC) anticipated that the new statutory recognition procedure could produce as many as a million new trade union members. For further details of how the procedure operates see Box 5.3; and also see Figure 5.1 for a diagrammatic representation.

The introduction of the new statutory recognition procedure would, at first glance, appear to be a distinctly union-friendly act; the principle underlying the policy is that union recognition should be granted where a majority of the workforce vote in favour of it. However, the procedure was enacted in a way that was largely favourable to employers (Wood and Godard 1999). For example, it does not apply where there are fewer than

LEGISLATION AND POLICY 5.3

The statutory recognition procedure in Britain

Under the procedure, if a union has a recognition claim for a particular group of workers dismissed by the employer it can make an application to a state body, the Central Arbitration Committee (CAC), which decides if the claim is a valid one for the purposes of the statutory procedure. It does not apply where fewer than 21 workers are employed. CAC must also determine whether there is sufficient support for unionization among the workforce; at least 10 per cent must be union members with the likelihood that a majority of the workforce would vote in favour of union recognition in a ballot. If these tests are met, and no other union is recognized for the group of workers in question, then CAC can mandate union recognition if 50 per cent or more of the relevant workers are in union membership, or it can order a ballot of the workforce. To secure recognition, a union must win approval from a simple majority of those voting, as long as this constitutes a threshold of 40 per cent of the relevant workforce. For example, in a workforce of 100 people if 39 people vote in favour of union recognition, and none vote against, then recognition would not be awarded because the 40 per cent threshold would not have been met. See Figure 5.1 for a diagrammatic representation.

A code of practice (DTI 2005) governs matters like union access to the workforce in the run-up to a recognition ballot. The Employment Relations Act (2004) made some changes to how the statutory union recognition procedure operates. In particular, employers and unions are prohibited from engaging in 'unfair practices', namely the use of incentives, threats, or some other kind of 'undue influence' to sway workers' votes.

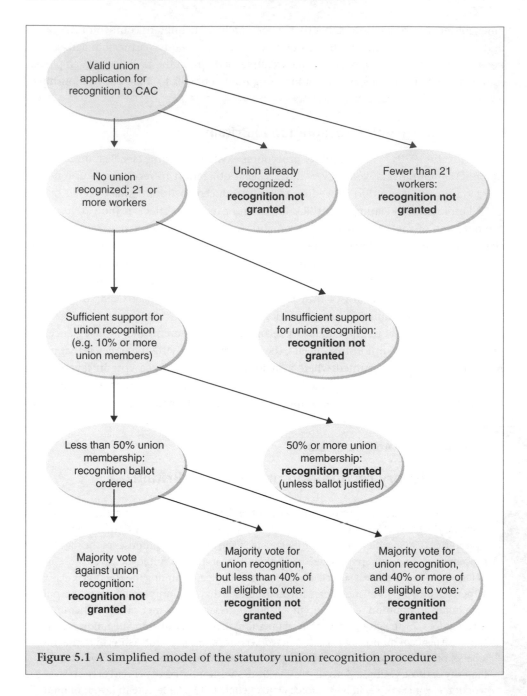

Figure 5.1 A simplified model of the statutory union recognition procedure

21 employees. Even if an employer is obliged to recognize a union by means of the statutory route, the scope of bargaining is limited to pay, hours, and holidays. There are also no guaranteed outcomes since the right to recognition is limited to the 'right to invoke a procedure' (Brown et al. 2001: 183).

As mentioned in Box 5.3, the principle of majority support for union recognition is qualified by the need for a union to win the support of at least 40 per cent of the relevant workforce, including non-voters. The government's aim was that the existence of the statutory procedure would encourage employers and unions to reach their own voluntary recognition agreement (Gall 2007; Oxenbridge et al. 2003). The statutory procedure was to prevail only if they were unable to reach a deal themselves.

What, then, have been the effects of the statutory union recognition procedure since it came into existence in 2000? Has it resulted in a surge of new agreements, reversing the decline in union recognition seen in the 1980s and 1990s? The first thing to appreciate is that the upsurge of new union recognition agreements dates from the mid 1990s, before the statutory procedure took effect (see Table 5.2). Knowing that legislation would soon compel them to recognize a union, some employers struck voluntary deals with trade unions beforehand. Table 5.2 shows the number of new recognition deals identified between 1995 and 2005. It indicates that the number of new agreements peaked in 2001, just after the statutory procedure was introduced. As can also be seen from Table 5.2, since 2000 there have been no more than a handful of cases of union derecognition each year.

The overwhelming majority of new recognition agreements since 2000 have been voluntary arrangements. By April 2008, the statutory recognition procedure had directly resulted in just 184 new agreements, 84 of them without a ballot, from 630 applications (CAC 2008). Among the companies that have signed recognition deals with trade unions as a direct result of the procedure are: Kwik Fit, the car repairer; Global Casinos; Xansa, the business services firm; and Honda, the car manufacturer. Yet in the period 2000–2005 alone, there were over two thousand new recognition agreements reported (Gall 2007).

Clearly, the main effect of the statutory procedure has been to stimulate voluntary union recognition by employers (Wood, Moore, and Ewing 2003). The preference for voluntary agreements demonstrates that in some cases unions have been successful in

Table 5.2 New cases of union recognition and derecognition, 1995–2005

Year	Number of new recognition deals	Number of cases of derecognition
1995	88	66
1996	86	54
1997	109	31
1998	128	7
1999	365	11
2000	525	4
2001	685	5
2002	388	9
2003	259	4
2004	239	2
2005	131	4
Total	3003	197

Source: Gall (2007: 83)

putting pressure on employers to concede recognition without needing to invoke the statutory procedure, though its existence is clearly an influence. There have been cases of employers initiating recognition themselves, in order to benefit from a 'sweetheart deal' with a moderate trade union (Gall 2003a). However, this has not been a major trend (Wood, Moore, and Ewing 2003).

There are two further details of union recognition trends that need to be appreciated. First, as can be seen from Table 5.2, since 2001 the number of new recognition agreements has declined. Unions initially targeted firms which they knew would be relatively easy targets for recognition claims, those with strong union support among the workforce. As the 2000s went on, though, these firms have been picked off, meaning that the unions have increasingly had to operate on 'harder terrain' (Gall 2007).

Second, recognition successes have largely come about in sectors of the economy where unions are already strong, particularly manufacturing industry (Blanden, Machin, and Van Reenan 2006). There is little sign that unions have been able to expand their influence by securing recognition agreements in key parts of the 'new economy', like the telecommunications and retail sectors (Gall 2007). Despite the number of new agreements, the overall level of union recognition has continued to fall during the 2000s (Kersley et al. 2006).

Table 5.3 details the main union recognition trends between 1998 and 2004, based on time-consistent data. Although the level of union recognition in the public sector was broadly unchanged, it fell markedly in the private sector, particularly among small workplaces, where it dropped from 28 per cent of workplaces in 1998 to 18 per cent in 2004. The number of new recognition deals has been outweighed by the growing number of new firms that do not recognize a trade union in the first place (non-recognition). Whereas unions were recognized in a quarter (26 per cent) of private sector workplaces that closed between 1998 and 2004, they only managed to secure recognition in just 10 per cent of new workplaces.

The extent to which some employers will go to resist unionization has impeded union recognition. Growing employer opposition to union recognition seems to have contributed to the declining number of new recognition agreements (Gall 2007). In one study, the researchers reported that half of the companies they visited had tried to prevent a formal union presence from becoming established, often because of the antagonism exhibited by senior managers towards unions (Oxenbridge et al. 2003). See Box 5.4 for the determination of Kettle Chips to avoid union recognition.

Table 5.3 Trade union recognition, 1998 and 2004 (% of workplaces with union recognition)

	1998	2004
All workplaces	33	27
Private sector	20	15
Public sector	83	82
Workplaces with 10–24 employees	28	18
Workplaces with 25 or more employees	41	39

Source: Workplace Employment Relations Survey, Kersley et al. (2006: 120)

INSIGHT INTO PRACTICE 5.4

Resisting union recognition at Kettle Chips

Kettle Chips is owned by the private equity firm Lion Capital and makes upmarket snacks and crisps at its factory in Norwich. In 2007 the Transport and General Workers' Union (TGWU)—now part of the Unite trade union—submitted a claim under the statutory union recognition procedure. Following an acrimonious battle between the union and employer, in October 2007 the workforce voted 206: 93 against union recognition. The firm claimed that its staff were relatively well paid, and enjoyed good benefits, including 25 days' holiday and comprehensive sick pay. Controversially, though, Kettle Chips hired the subsidiary of a prominent US union-busting firm, the Burke Group, to dissuade workers in the factory from voting for union recognition. Unite also claimed that managers had put undue influence on workers not to support unionization; one of its officials asserted that Kettle Chips had conducted a 'long and poisonous campaign' against the union. Nevertheless, because of a lack of evidence, CAC did not uphold Unite's complaint that Kettle Chips had engaged in 'unfair' practices through its anti-union threats and insinuations.

There are three broad ways in which employers can try and resist union recognition. First, some companies have adopted a hard-nosed, aggressive strategy of 'union suppression'. This is where managers use intimidatory tactics to forestall trade unionism, claiming, for example, that union recognition could threaten the viability of the workplace and thus cost jobs (Gall 2003a). The satellite broadcaster, BSkyB, for example, allegedly hinted that if its call centre workforce supported union recognition, this could undermine their competitiveness, particularly when set against the low costs of operating in India. Unsurprisingly, most workers voted against. One study found that some employers are prepared to 'invest whatever is necessary to defeat unions' (Moore 2004: 16). There are cases where employers have attempted to influence the outcome of the recognition ballot by threatening to close or relocate the workplace if the vote were to go in favour of the union. Although it is unlawful to dismiss workers for activities relating to union recognition, some employers have tried to resist unionization by firing union activists (Moore 2004).

Second, the purpose of the 'substitutionist' approach is to forestall unionization by providing employees with alternative, in-house methods of representation such as a company council, or by using rewards, like pay rises, to demonstrate that union recognition is unnecessary (Gall and McKay 2001). Companies like The Body Shop and Pizza Express have developed sophisticated employee involvement arrangements in an attempt to show that trade unions representation is not needed. In some cases, firms use a pragmatic mix of 'suppressionist' and 'subsitutionist' methods in order to remain union-free. The online retailer Amazon, for example, successfully resisted the unionization of its UK distribution warehouse through a combination of increased rewards, the establishment of a staff consultative forum, and threats against employees with strong union sympathies (Kelly and Badigannavar 2004).

The third way in which employers resist unionization is by refusing to engage meaningfully with the union even after recognition has been granted. This was the case in a marketing company's call centre. In the two years following the recognition agreement, the employer refused to bargain seriously with the trade union. As a result the workforce began to question the effectiveness of union representation, and support for it dwindled (Kelly and Badigannavar 2004).

Given such opposition to trade unionism, and the way in which the relevant legislation was designed not to antagonize employers, the direct impact of the statutory union recognition procedure on its own has been relatively limited. Nevertheless, indirectly it seems to have stimulated a substantial upsurge in voluntary recognition activity during the 2000s. Moreover, the procedure also has an important symbolic effect. It exemplifies the shift away from the overt anti-unionism of the Conservatives' legislative programme during the 1980s and 1990s, towards a more supportive policy environment in the 2000s. Nevertheless, the statutory recognition procedure is, like the rest of Labour's public policy agenda, imbued by a belief that robust, independent trade unionism is inimical to labour market flexibility and competitiveness, and should thus be kept in check (Smith and Morton 2006).

SECTION SUMMARY AND FURTHER READING

- Although some employers derecognized trade unions during the 1980s and 1990s, this form of union exclusion was rare. Newly established workplaces operating in growing sectors of the economy, such as high-tech industries, were unlikely to recognize unions in the first place.

- In organizations where unions retained a formal presence, managers tried to diminish their role and influence through the propagation of new direct communications techniques.

- In 2000 statutory union recognition procedure was introduced in Britain. It obliges an employer to recognize a union for collective bargaining purposes where the majority of the workforce want it. The procedure, however, was implemented so as not to antagonize employers, and its direct impact has been limited.

- Although the 2000s have seen an increase in union recognition activity, the number of new non-union workplaces means that union recognition levels have continued to decline. Moreover, resistance to union recognition among employers is a major constraint to unionization efforts.

For data on union recognition levels in Britain, see Kersley et al. (2006: Chapter 5). The best overview of union derecognition in the 1980s and early 1990s is Claydon (1996). For the impact of the statutory union recognition procedure in Britain, see Oxenbridge et al. (2003) and Gall (2007). Go to the CAC website—http://www.cac.gov.uk—for its annual report (CAC 2008), and also for details of specific cases under the statutory procedure. Moore (2004) is a study of employers' resistance to recognition claims.

 Visit our Online Resource Centre for web links to sites connected to this section. www.oxfordtextbooks.co.uk/williams_adamsmith2e

---

5.4 Human resource management and employment relations

Given the diminution of union recognition since the 1980s, to what extent have managements been able to develop new, more sophisticated techniques for managing employment relations? The terms 'personnel management' and 'personnel manager' have increasingly been replaced by 'human resource management' (HRM) and 'human resource manager' in organizational vocabularies. What are the implications of a sophisticated

HRM approach for employment relations, and how far has the rise of HRM changed the way in which employees are managed? There is an assumption that the rise of a sophisticated HRM approach is associated with a change in the focus of managing employment relations, away from a concern with exercising control over employees, and accommodating the potential for conflict in the employment relationship, towards an emphasis on securing their engagement, their cooperation, and their commitment to the organization. In this section, we consider the nature of sophisticated HRM as a managerial approach, account for its growing importance, and critically assess whether or not it has transformed the management of employment relations by raising organizational commitment and delivering better business performance.

5.4.1 HRM and the management of employment relations

An initial obstacle to be overcome when discussing the concept of HRM concerns its tendency to be used in different ways. On the one hand, 'HRM' is used as an umbrella label for managing people in organizations, being interchangeable with the term 'personnel management'. On the other hand, a second way of interpreting HRM, and the one we prefer here, is to view it as a particular approach to managing the workforce, based on engaging employees, winning their commitment to the organization, and thus driving improvements in business performance. We use the term 'sophisticated HRM' to refer to this second, narrower conceptualization, distinguishing it from the broader approach.

Whereas in the past the job of managing employment relations was dominated by the issues that arose from having to deal with unions, the focus now is on using effective people management skills to build relationships with, and engage, employees. 'In general, the agenda is no longer about trade unions. There is more emphasis on direct communication, managing organisational change and involving and motivating staff' (Emmott 2005: 3). Thus the principal concern of those responsible for managing employment relations in organizations is with developing and sustaining a climate in which employees feel valued, and are thus inspired to work more effectively and perform better to the advantage of the employing organization. As we saw in the introductory case study, even the fast-food chain McDonald's claims to be concerned with engaging its staff so that they can deliver improved customer service (Fairhurst 2008).

But we need to go beyond rather generalized statements about the importance of engaging staff, and specify the five main features of a sophisticated HRM approach to managing employees. The first of these features is the emphasis that is placed on aligning people management practices with the overall business strategy of the organization. What makes sophisticated HRM distinctive is that it puts a greater emphasis on the fit between employment policies and the overall business objectives of the organization. The management of employees is undertaken not for its own sake, but is carried out in a way that enables it to contribute to overall business goals.

Second, linked to this there is a concern with managing people in a way that helps to enhance business performance. Whereas in the past the principal managerial goals involved efforts to control staff, and to accommodate the power of trade unions, in contemporary employment relations employers use sophisticated HRM techniques to engage employees, and thus get better performance from them. The relationship between HRM and performance is considered in more detail in Section 5.4.3.

Third, there is a recognition that improvements in business performance can be secured by interventions designed to involve employees, and to increase their organizational commitment. This is based on the 'assumption that committed employees will be more satisfied, more productive and more adaptable' (Guest 1987: 513). There is a strong emphasis on ensuring that jobs are designed appropriately so that workers enjoy more autonomy and discretion, and that robust arrangements are in place to enable them to be involved in workplace decision-making, through sophisticated communication techniques, for example.

Fourth, in contrast to the traditional personnel management approach, which tended to rely upon bureaucratic methods, such as the provision of regular pay increments for example, to enforce control in the workplace, under a sophisticated HRM regime the emphasis is placed more on techniques for managing organizational culture (Legge 2005; Storey 1992). This is done through attempts to manipulate symbols, values, and beliefs in the workplace. Behaviour in organizations is increasingly guided, 'not by rules and structure, but by the bond of a strong corporate culture where employees love the company, the product and the customer. Employers are now engaging with hearts and minds and, some would say, souls as a means of harnessing employee commitment and gaining competitive advantage' (Bolton 2004: 47). In some call centres, for example, managers put a lot of effort into ensuring that, pressures of work notwithstanding, staff have opportunities to enjoy themselves. Activities such as piped music, dressing-up days, and social events help to build a convivial atmosphere which helps to improve workers' morale and positively affects customer service (Baldry et al. 2007).

The fifth feature of a sophisticated HRM approach to managing employment relations is a preference for weak or non-existent trade unions. It is marked by a unitary ethos; sophisticated HRM threatens unions by seeking to bind individual employees to the organization, and reduce the potential conflict of interest (Guest 1987). The onus is on the cooperative and harmonious nature of relations between managers and workers. Any conflict is either frictional, down to short-term, easily resolved problems, like personality differences for example, or is the product of external agitators, such as trade union activists.

Sophisticated HRM is not presented as an anti-union approach to managing employment relations, in the sense of seeking to drive unions out, or actively resisting them. Rather, the use of sophisticated HRM techniques for involving employees is claimed to make a union presence unnecessary. The management style of the multinational courier company studied by Dundon and Rollinson (2004) embodies such an approach. Characterized by an emphasis on developing a strong organizational culture, it was supported by the use of a range of sophisticated HRM interventions, including an extensive system of direct communication methods. There is a sharp contrast to be drawn between the unitary ethos of sophisticated HRM, where the role of unions is very much played down, and the purportedly more pluralist character of traditional personnel management in which the emphasis is on managing with, and accommodating the power of, trade unions. With sophisticated HRM, it would appear that managing employment relations is not so much about containing trade unionism, but rather is more concerned with managing employees in ways that help contribute to business performance. See Box 5.5 for an example of how managerial authority has increased in public sector organizations, through the development of the 'new public management' approach.

Employment relations reflection 5.5   Towards a new
public management?

For many years, the management of employment relations in public sector organizations
was characterized by the dominance of centralized, highly bureaucratic procedures,
which were determined from above, and national collective bargaining machinery.
Consequently, the role of the personnel management function was largely restricted to
the implementation of standardized procedures and national agreements, with very little
scope for discretion (Bach 1999b; Beaumont 1992; Farnham and Giles 1996). During
the 1980s, however, Conservative governments enacted policies that stimulated the role
and authority of managers in the public sector: the emphasis on better value for money
and customer service; the devolution of decision-making to smaller business units; and
the encouragement of a greater strategic awareness in a context of rigorous financial
targets (Winchester and Bach 1999). Such was the degree of apparent change in the
way in which public sector organizations were run, that a new term, the 'new public
management' (NPM), came to be used to refer to it (Hood 1991).

NPM comprises three key dimensions. First, it refers to the growth of a stronger, more
robust managerial function within public sector enterprises. Second, NPM is closely
associated with the devolution of managerial responsibility for decision-making to
business units. Third, it is characterized by the development of a more market-oriented
approach to the delivery of public services, based on an assumption that competitive
pressures can improve their quality (Bach and Della Rocca 2000). Thus the rise of NPM
is associated with an increase in managerial authority in the public sector, the
elaboration of more sophisticated managerial approaches, and the greater use of
management techniques imported from the private sector (Winchester and Bach 1999).

Evidently, NPM shares many of the characteristics of a sophisticated HRM
approach to managing employment relations in so far as the emphasis is placed upon
managing people in a more purposive way, with the aim of generating flexibility,
and enhancing commitment, in order to improve organizational performance (Bach
1999b). Yet it is important not to overstate the extent to which the management of
public sector employment relations has changed. There is evidence that, the NPM
agenda notwithstanding, management in public sector organizations continues to be
dominated by an administrative rationale, concerned with operating procedures rather
than contributing to business goals (Kirkpatrick, Ackroyd, and Walker 2004).

5.4.2 Interpreting HRM

What accounts for the development of a sophisticated HRM approach to managing
employees? Conceptually, it would appear to be based on two distinctive intellectual
approaches (Storey 1992). One is the growth of interest in the nature and dynamics of
corporate strategy, and of the way in which an organization's resources can contribute
to its objectives. Sophisticated HRM is also based on the revival of a human relations
approach to understanding organizational behaviour, one which emphasizes how sophisticated managerial techniques can enhance the motivation, commitment, and job satisfaction of workers to the benefit of the organization (Walton 1985).

During the 1980s and 1990s, the sophisticated HRM approach developed in a context of
changing markets and growing competitive pressures that affected business organizations.
Increasing competition obliged firms to find new sources of competitive advantage, the

knowledge, skills, and expertise of the people they employ in particular. In as much as they help to ensure these attributes are used effectively, the use of sophisticated people management practices is seen as an essential component of improved organizational performance. To a large extent, then, the rise of HRM was stimulated by a desire to ensure that the way in which people were managed at work was more supportive of business goals and competitive advantage (Kochan et al. 1986).

Another factor that has influenced the rise of sophisticated HRM is the important political and economic changes that have given organizations greater latitude when it comes to managing their staff. In the UK, for example, Conservative governments of the 1980s and 1990s sought to foster a business climate within which employers could reassert their 'right to manage', principally by weakening the power of the trade unions. The unitary ethos of sophisticated HRM accorded with the political climate of the time, one in which the trade unions, given the decline in their power, and the hostility exhibited towards them by the Conservatives, were on the retreat (Legge 2005).

As we saw in Chapter 3, while Labour has made some changes to the legislative framework that would appear to have partially ameliorated such a trend, its overall approach remains supportive of the need for businesses to have flexibility over how they manage their staff and of the desirability that unions should remain weak (Smith and Morton 2006).

To what extent has the development of sophisticated HRM transformed the main principles of the management of employment relations? While employers have no doubt taken the management of employment relations more seriously, the extent of any transformation is questionable. Organizations appear to have adopted particular elements of the sophisticated HRM approach, those that were most appropriate to their immediate needs, especially direct communications methods such as team briefings, in an *ad hoc* and opportunistic way (Legge 2005). Many employers, moreover, have eschewed a sophisticated HRM approach, finding it profitable to manage employment relations in a seemingly more cost-effective way. See Box 5.6 for the example of Ryanair.

Sophisticated HRM has always been characterized by an important ambiguity. On the one hand, it is portrayed as a way of managing employees centred on involving and developing

---

● **INSIGHT INTO PRACTICE 5.6**

Managing employment relations in Ryanair

The successful airline Ryanair takes an approach to managing employment relations that is consistent with, and indeed exemplifies, the low cost model on which it has based its business growth. It demonstrates not only that the sophisticated HRM approach is by no means universal, but also that there are alternative methods of managing human resources which may be as effective, if not more so, in business terms. Cabin crew staff are employed on short-term contracts, through agencies, not the airline itself, with pay, and other benefits, like holiday entitlement for example, that are low by industry standards. Ryanair's own staff handbook reveals that workers enjoy few opportunities to be involved in, or to influence, decision-making processes. Rather, the degree of involvement is minimal. Ryanair has become well-known for its prominent anti-trade union stance. In situations where its workers have asked for union representation, the company has vigorously opposed it.

them. Such a 'soft' approach to sophisticated HRM treats employees 'as valued assets, a source of competitive advantage through their commitment, adaptability and quality . . . ' (Legge 2005: 105). Thus the emphasis is placed on supporting employee well-being, through sophisticated stress management interventions and work–life balance policies, for example (Bolton and Houlihan 2007). The result is a more engaged workforce, whose high morale and organizational commitment drives improvements in business performance.

On the other hand, with the 'hard' approach to HRM, employees are treated as a resource, a factor of production, to be used, and discarded if necessary, in a way that supports organizational objectives. Performance improvements come, not from a more committed and engaged workforce, but from managers exercising greater control over, and intensifying, people's work activities. Whereas 'soft' HRM is driven by the aim of winning employee cooperation, 'hard' HRM is marked by a more coercive logic, akin to a traditional unitary style of management. The growing use of arrangements to monitor and manage the performance of staff testifies to the control-based dimension of HRM. In call centres, for example, workers are often subjected to a highly regimented pattern of work, including having to meet highly detailed targets governing call handling (e.g. number of calls per hour), with extensive monitoring of their activities by supervisors (Baldry et al. 2007).

Not only is the presence of 'soft' HRM somewhat rare, but it is also difficult to distinguish between 'soft' and 'hard' approaches in practice (Legge 2005). HRM practices sit easily alongside, and may even help to uphold, more traditional coercive management approaches (Bacon 1999). This is evident when we consider the management of culture, for example. In seeking to win the 'hearts and minds' of staff, and engage them with the values of the organization, managers use culture as a means of trying to control the behavior of workers (Willmott 1993). The promotion of workplace fun in some call centres, for example, is in part designed to obviate efforts by workers to contest aspects of their otherwise mundane and intensive jobs (Baldry et al. 2007).

Most of the 'Leading Edge' organizations studied by Gratton et al. (1999) claim to have adopted the 'soft' HRM approach. For example, they stressed the importance of developing employees as individuals, and of providing them with training opportunities. But the training was often related to the narrow, immediate requirements of the job, and not of much benefit to employees in the long term. Moreover, where the importance of individual development was attested, it was done in such way that it helped to legitimize increasingly limited employment and promotion opportunities. Thus the emphasis was placed on giving employees the necessary skills to self-manage their own careers in situations where the organization was, for financial reasons, less able to offer security of employment.

There may have been a lot of 'soft' rhetoric exhibited by the Leading Edge organizations, 'but the underlying principle was invariably restricted to the improvement of bottom-line performance' (Gratton et al. 1999: 56–7). While the 'soft' HRM model implies that business objectives can be more effectively realized if an emphasis is placed upon developing employees, and fostering their commitment, in practice the organizations predominantly viewed their employees as costs, and thus to be minimized. The language of 'soft' HRM was important since it helped to obscure the commodity status of employees. Thus 'even if the rhetoric of HRM is "soft", the reality is almost always "hard", with the interests of the organization prevailing over those of the individual' (Gratton et al. 1999: 57).

Based on such evidence, then, it would be unwise to claim that the development of sophisticated HRM has transformed employment relations. Competitive pressures, and the need to enhance short-term financial performance, preclude many organizations from investing in the kind of sophisticated, progressive management techniques necessary to foster greater organizational involvement and commitment. More fundamentally, perhaps, it is unclear how far managers are able to eschew a traditional concern with upholding their prerogatives in such a way that it enables a significant level of genuine employee involvement to become established (Scott 1994).

5.4.3 HRM and performance

As we have already seen, one of the most distinctive aspects of a sophisticated HRM approach is the emphasis on managing employees in a way that enhances business performance. This contrasts with the traditional approach in which the priority was to manage with, and accommodate the effects of, trade unionism and collective bargaining. Since the 1990s there has been a surge of interest in how the presence of so-called 'high commitment', 'high involvement', or 'high performance' practices has a positive impact on organizational performance (Godard 2004).

Why has there been such a growth of interest in the relationship between HRM and organizational performance in Britain? The quest for business credibility on the part of human resource practitioners is an important influence since, historically, this function was largely seen as a cost and not as a source of added business value. If the presence of sophisticated HRM practices can be demonstrated to have a positive impact on the financial bottom-line of organizations, then not only would this help to justify the existence of a specialist personnel or human resource function, but it would also enhance its credibility and status (Purcell and Kinnie 2007). Unsurprisingly, there has been much interest in 'the search for a Holy Grail of establishing a causal link between HRM and performance' (Legge 2001: 23).

What kinds of management practices are encompassed by the high commitment approach? One of the problems in demonstrating a link between commitment-based HRM and business performance is that there is no consensus about the practices that should be included under the 'high commitment' label (Purcell and Kinnie 2007). Different studies rarely rely on the same set of practices when assessing the impact of the high commitment management approach. Some consider the impact of a broad range of traditional personnel practices, including the formal selection procedures, grievance procedures and regular appraisals, on performance.

More justifiably, others work to a tighter, more restrictive definition of high commitment practices, focusing on those interventions that are specifically designed to motivate, involve, and reward employees in a way that increases their engagement with the business. This narrower interpretation suggests there are four main features of the high commitment approach in practice (Kersley et al. 2006; White et al. 2004):

- the presence of formal teamworking arrangements, particularly those which allow team members some responsibility for deciding how work should be done and who should do it;
- the existence of functionally flexible workforce, who are well-trained and have the necessary skills to be able to undertake a variety of jobs in their workplace;

- the use of employee involvement practices—Where staff are able to exercise some influence over managerial decision-making, by participating in problem solving groups for
example, this can be taken as evidence of a high commitment approach; and

- the use of sophisticated reward mechanisms which offer incentives to workers for
demonstrating commitment and performing well.

The increasingly precise way in which high commitment management is coming to
be defined is helping us to determine its overall significance in contemporary human
resource management.

The presence of high commitment practices is claimed to improve business performance by producing a better quality workforce who are more committed to, and engaged
with, business goals because they enjoy more fulfilling working lives. To the extent that
they develop a greater sense of identification with the organization, and are more involved in decisions that affect them in the workplace, employees will, it is assumed,
perform better and be more productive (Wood and de Menezes 1998). The high commitment management approach increases 'discretionary work effort' (Huselid 1995); people
who are managed well at work, and feel engaged, will contribute more (see Figure 5.2).

The positive impact of the so-called high commitment or high performance management
practices is, it is argued, more pronounced when they are used not in an idiosyncratic, *ad
hoc* way, but in a mutually supportive fashion, or in 'bundles' (MacDuffie 1995). Teamworking arrangements, for example, should produce better results where they are operated in
combination with appropriate recruitment and selection and reward practices. Research undertaken in the United States demonstrates that high commitment management practices,
particularly where they are used in bundles, and in combination with a flexible system of
work design, do have a positive impact on business performance (Huselid 1995).

There is some evidence that a high commitment approach to managing employees has
taken root in a substantial proportion of workplaces (White et al. 2004). Moreover, an
association has been identified between the use of high commitment practices and workplace

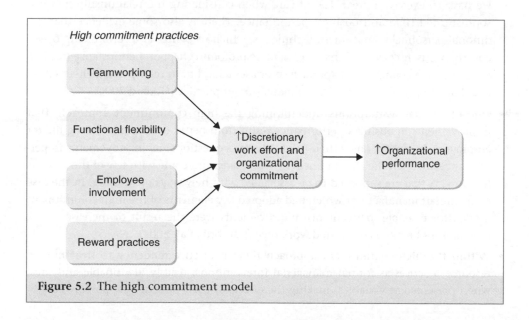

Figure 5.2 The high commitment model

financial performance in private sector companies (Guest et al. 2000; Ramsay, Scholarios, and Harley 2000). A major study of a number of large public and private sector organizations in the UK, including the Nationwide Building Society and Jaguar Cars, demonstrates that there is a connection between sophisticated HRM, organizational commitment, and business performance. However, the behaviour of line managers seems to be of crucial importance; a large part of the success of the high commitment approach depends on how effectively the practices are operated in particular workplaces (Purcell et al. 2003).

Unsurprisingly, personnel and HR practitioners welcome evidence that the presence of certain HRM practices is associated with better workplace financial performance, since it would appear to give them a more integral role within organizations. But how valid are the suppositions that, first, the use of high-commitment management practices has become more commonplace and, second, that their presence generates improved business performance? There are a number of difficulties in assuming that the high commitment paradigm has come to dominate the way in which employment relations is managed (Legge 2005). Six major problems are identified here.

- To begin with, the prevalence of high commitment practices remains rather low, relatively few UK workplaces making use of a substantial number of them as a coherent package. The high commitment approach to managing people at work is present in only a minority of workplaces, and does not appear to be becoming more widespread (Kersley et al. 2006).

- A second problem concerns the proposition that there is a link between high commitment HRM and business performance. Research studies in this area tend to exaggerate the extent of any association. Closer analysis of the relevant data reveals that the relationship between high commitment practices and business performance is often less clear-cut (Godard 2004; Wall and Wood 2005).

- As we have already seen, there is no consensus on what practices should comprise the high commitment management approach (Purcell and Kinnie 2007). This means that we have to exercise a great deal of care when considering the relationship between sophisticated HRM and business performance. There is also some evidence that traditional personnel management techniques, which recognize and reward employees' contributions, for example, may have a more profound effect on performance (see Box 5.7). The high commitment approach promises a lot, but in reality may deliver rather less than simply conventional good management practice (Godard 2004).

- One of the key assumptions underpinning the high commitment approach, that improvements in business performance result from better quality of working life for employees, because it raises their productivity, is questionable. Improvements in performance are often the result of heavier workloads, and come with few of the benefits for workers that are supposed to be associated with new ways of working. In the case of an aircraft manufacturer which had adopted key elements of the high commitment model, for example, performance improvements were the result of increased work pressures, not a more committed workforce (Danford et al. 2004).

- Within the high commitment approach there is often a tendency to treat human resource practices as formal managerial interventions, readily identifiable and thus, when presented as variables, making the effects of their presence supposedly easy to

High commitment working—the view from below

Undertaken over a period of four years, Sarah Pass's (2005) study of four manufacturing departments in a major healthcare company demonstrates some of the problems with the assumption that high commitment management practices cause performance improvements. As well as the interviews she undertook with workers, one of the strengths of her investigation is that she actually worked in a production capacity in the firm herself, and so is particularly well-placed to comment on its activities. Pass discovered that performance improvements came from the exercise of close managerial control over the workforce and heavy work pressures, not the kind of sophisticated HRM interventions that are supposed to engender greater organizational commitment. Increases in performance were also seen to result from the use of traditional personnel management practices which offered recognition and respect, and thus generated good relationships. When workers felt their contribution was recognized, were treated by managers with respect, and were able to form robust and supportive relationships, they responded more positively to managerial interventions.

measure. But the management of the employment relationship is a process; it possesses a dynamic, and should not be reduced to a set of formal practices. How these function in workplaces, where, for example, managers and workers contest their operation, or interpret them in different ways from those intended, is a much more complex and less easily measurable matter. In Hewlett-Packard, a firm characterized by an ostensibly sophisticated HRM approach, despite the presence of a formal system of measuring employees' performance against company set targets, informal methods, such as ensuring they got noticed, were more effective for people wanting to advance their careers (Truss 2001). As a result, studies of the relationship between high commitment management practices and business performance increasingly recognize the important role played by front-line managers in influencing the extent to which practices are actually put into effect (Purcell and Hutchinson 2007), and the responses of employees. When considering the effects of high commitment practices, a distinction should be made between 'intended' practices, those that the organization aims to enact, 'actual' practices, those that line managers actually do enact, and 'perceived' practices, those that are experienced by the workforce (Purcell and Kinnie 2007; Purcell et al. 2009).

- Finally, the research methodology that underpins studies of the relationship between sophisticated HRM and performance raise doubts about the high commitment paradigm (Legge 2001). We have already seen that there is no consensus on which practices constitute a high commitment approach; but the specification and measurement of business performance are also often somewhat rudimentary too (Purcell and Kinnie 2007). Research studies rely for their data on responses from managers who, unsurprisingly, offer a biased and partial perspective, and may know little of how the practices they identify are interpreted in the workplace (Godard and Delaney 2000; Legge 2001). While there may be an association between sophisticated HRM and business performance, it is not necessarily a causal one. Firms that are performing well may be in a better position to afford to implement expensive HRM interventions, suggesting that it may be difficult to disentangle cause and effect when it comes to measuring the impact of sophisticated HRM (Wall and Wood 2005).

There is an increasing recognition that in order to understand the relationship between sophisticated HRM and performance properly, the impact of management practices on workers, and how workers respond to them, needs to be considered (Purcell and Kinnie 2007; Purcell et al. 2009). As we have already seen, studies that draw on the experiences of workers tend to reveal that performance improvements are driven by more intensive managerial control and greater work pressures, rather than the presence of a more committed workforce.

However, it is not just workers' experiences that we need to consider, but also their interests. If we conceptualize the employment relationship as a wage-work bargain, marked by the potential for a conflict of interests, then it helps us to understand why the high commitment management approach, indeed any managerial interventions, will ultimately prove unsatisfying to managers. This is because workers have different interests to those of their employers, and will thus experience, and react to, management practices in ways that do not conform to managerial expectations. Teamworking arrangements, for example, may upset existing social relationships in an organization and thus damage morale, commitment, and, ultimately, performance (Jenkins and Delbridge 2007).

How, then, should sophisticated HRM, and its impact on employment relations, be understood? While it is clear that some changes have occurred, the growth of direct communications arrangements, for example (see Chapter 8), these hardly amount to a transformation of the way in which employment relations is managed in Britain. They occurred in part because the decline of trade unionism opened up opportunities for innovation, but, more commonly, have been elaborated because of a desire to challenge union influence.

The extent to which a sophisticated HRM approach has come to inform the management of employment relations should not be exaggerated. The case of a factory that makes sandwiches for high street retail outlets illustrates the contemporary relevance of a more traditional style of managing employment relations. The largely ethnic minority workforce, many of whom were migrants, had to put up with onerous working conditions and an uncaring management approach. The work was low-paid, boring, and hard. There was little, if any, concern on the part of management with securing the commitment of the workforce as a means of improving performance. Rather, workers were given little respect by the company, and sometimes endured treatment that could be construed as racist (Holgate 2005).

Even in situations where managers have been able to develop and sustain a sophisticated HRM approach, this does not necessarily mean that they are going to be effective in influencing and shaping employees' attitudes and behaviour. In the case of the multinational courier company mentioned in Section 5.4.1, despite the use of a high commitment approach, many staff remained unhappy about the lack of influence they had over decisions that affected them at work (Dundon and Rollinson 2004). The different interests of employees mean that the effectiveness of managerial interventions, of any kind, is always going to be partial and incomplete.

SECTION SUMMARY AND FURTHER READING

- Whereas traditional approaches to managing employment relations were dominated by a concern to manage the consequences of trade unionism, it is claimed that contemporary organizations are taking a more sophisticated HRM approach to managing employees. Rather than accommodating the potential for conflict, the prime focus of managerial endeavour in employment relations is concerned with building employee engagement, winning organizational commitment, and improving business performance.

- Yet the extent of change has been somewhat limited, and falls well short of being a genuine transformation. While elements of a 'soft' approach to HRM are increasingly evident, the management of employment relations is dominated by a concern to control employees, rather than use innovative new practices to encourage their commitment.

- There has been much recent interest in how the presence of sophisticated HRM, and so-called high commitment or high performance practices in particular, contributes to improvements in business performance. However, there are some major problems with the high commitment approach, not least a tendency to overlook the experiences and attitudes of employees.

Legge (2005) is the best critical assessment of the HRM phenomenon. Storey (1992) sensitively considers the emergence, characteristics, and implications of HRM based on case study research. For a general overview of developments, see Bach (2005). Gratton et al. (1999) use case study research to provide a splendid analysis of the limits and contradictions inherent within a commitment-based HRM approach. See Purcell and Kinnie (2007) for some of the problems inherent in drawing an association between HRM and business performance.

 Visit our Online Resource Centre for web links to sites connected to this section. www.oxfordtextbooks.co.uk/williams_adamsmith2e

5.5 Managing employment relations in non-union environments

For many years, the employment relations characteristics of firms without a formal union presence barely featured in studies of employment relations. There were some exceptions, such as the analysis of foreign-owned companies operating in Britain (e.g. Gennard and Steuer 1971). Until the 1980s, though, studies of employment relations were overwhelmingly dominated by analyses of the roles of trade unions, employers, and employers' associations, and the relationships between them. Companies without union recognition were, if they were large ones, treated as idiosyncratic and given some brief consideration (e.g. Clegg 1979), or, in the case of the many small firms where no formal union presence existed, largely ignored.

Since the 1980s, however, there has been something of a change in emphasis, not least because of the sharp decline in union recognition in Britain. Nevertheless, studies of employment relations in non-union environments, particularly in private services, remain far from commonplace. This reflects difficulties researchers have in gaining access to firms, especially smaller ones, in order to collect data, and the continuing emphasis in employment relations on developments in the unionized part of the economy. Nevertheless, the growing proportion of new workplaces without a formal union presence has provided the catalyst for a more considered appreciation of how employment relations is managed in non-union firms.

5.5.1 Sophisticated HRM and non-union firms

Perhaps the most important question about the employment relations arrangements of non-union firms, especially large ones, is the extent to which they exemplify a sophisticated HRM approach to managing employees. Given the absence of a formal union presence, how far, then, have managers been able to reshape the relationship with employees in such a way that commitment and cooperation have come to transcend conflict in the employment relationship? Notwithstanding the evidence that HRM practices are more commonly found in unionized, rather than non-unionized, workplaces, in some interpretations the rise of non-unionism in Britain 'has been closely linked with the emergence of new techniques of human resource management' (McLoughlin and Gourlay 1994: 23).

The association between HRM practices and non-unionism stems largely from the experience of companies like IBM, and its 'open' management style, single-status policy, robust communications, and emphasis on managing employees as individuals, and providing them with superior benefits (Bassett 1987). A study of an IBM plant in Greenock, Scotland, found that the company had 'erected a sophisticated system of industrial relations to enable it to function without the necessity of recognizing trade unions . . .' (Dickson et al. 1988: 510). During the 1970s and 1980s, the growing non-union sector in the United States became the focus of increasing attention, not least because it was thought that such companies embodied a superior, more enlightened way of managing their human resources (Foulkes 1980).

Two key features of employment relations in large non-union firms can therefore be identified. First, in so far as employees' pay, conditions, and benefits exceed those that could be won by union activity, the sophisticated HRM approach may be considered as a 'substitute' for trade union organization. Unions are therefore simply unnecessary, and indeed their presence would disrupt the cooperative and harmonious relationship between managers and workers that has been so carefully fostered.

The three case studies of non-unionism in the high-tech sector in Britain undertaken by McLoughlin and Gourlay (1994) illustrate these points. Although there were significant variations in the companies' approaches to managing employment relations, an overarching theme was the perceived irrelevance of trade unions. With the exception of manual staff in one of the firms, there was little evidence that workers were dissatisfied with their employment arrangements to the extent that a union presence would be considered desirable. According to one of the computer staff in one of the firms: 'The company has always challenged me and is a fun company with a very open management style. I have never considered the need for a trades union' (quoted in McLoughlin and Gourlay 1994: 115). What, then, would be the purpose of a trade union in such an environment?

Thus firms that operate sophisticated HRM policies in the absence of a formal union presence, often style themselves as 'non-union', rather than 'anti-union'. Managers claim not to oppose trade unions in principle, but simply cannot see any need for them given the favourable pay, conditions, and benefits enjoyed by employees.

The second key feature of employment relations in large non-union firms is held to be the emphasis on individualism; that members of staff are treated by managers as individuals, contrasting with the collective representation of employees in unionized environments, something which is thus rendered unnecessary. The computer firm IBM is often presented as the archetypal non-union firm in this respect. It 'refuses to recognize unions, not because of their potential nuisance value, but because their collectivism runs wholly counter to the company's fundamental individualist philosophy' (Bassett 1987: 164). According to a manager in another high-tech firm, 'the staff see it to their advantage to be treated as individuals . . . the type of work they do is such that it calls for an individual approach' (McLoughlin and Gourlay 1992: 680).

It would seem, then, that a combination of sophisticated HRM with an individualistic management style may not only provide workers with a superior quality of employment, but is also an effective way of preventing trade unions from gaining a foothold. The extent to which such an approach exists, beyond a small number of high-profile companies in high-tech industries is, however, questionable. It is striking how often the experience of IBM is cited by writers keen to demonstrate the advantages of the benefits of a non-union, sophisticated HRM approach. The reluctance of employees to embrace trade unionism is often not a reflection of progressive management policies, but more the result of an inability to see what value union membership could offer them or, in some cases, an aversion to trade unions (Dundon and Rollinson 2004; McLoughlin and Gourlay 1994).

It is also evident that an individualistic approach to managing employees is difficult to uphold in practice, not least because it is extremely costly to maintain. Much of the available evidence would suggest that while 'procedural individualization' is an important trend in British workplaces, 'substantive individualization' is much rarer (Brown et al. 2000). What, then, is the difference between 'procedural' and 'substantive' individualization? The former refers to the absence of collective procedures, generally involving trade unions, as a means of determining employment contracts, an increasing trend since the early 1980s. 'Substantive' individualization, however, 'the differentiation of contractual terms within the organization' (Brown et al. 2000: 627), is far from commonplace.

Indeed, there appears to be a 'high degree of standardization of employment contracts within British workplaces, so far as both pay and non-pay entitlements are concerned' (Brown et al. 2000: 620). This was evident in 'Knowco', a company specializing in the provision of IT skills training and consultancy which, while supposedly following a sophisticated HRM approach, nonetheless relied upon standardized contracts for employees. Substantive individualization, then, is 'potentially extremely expensive to pursue since, for it to be meaningful, it requires the management capacity to negotiate, monitor and review a portfolio of individual contracts' (Colling 2003: 387).

Employers' claims to be 'non-union', rather than 'anti-union', should be treated with caution given that 'professions of neutrality' towards unions may often mask a more oppositional and antagonistic approach (Clegg 1979: 102; Dundon and Rollinson 2004; Knox and McKinlay 2003). Marks and Spencer, for example, claims that it does not oppose unions, but that its staff do not need one. However, in the UK the company does its utmost to undermine any union-organizing efforts (Blyton and Turnbull 2004).

From our discussion of the implications of human resource management for employment relations, it should also be clear that 'sophisticated HRM' is often a benign façade obscuring the more authoritarian reality. In the steel company 'Ministeel', for example, the elaboration of HRM techniques was part of a policy designed to exclude the union from the workplace, and there were complaints from trade unionists of intimidation (Bacon 1999). In a study of a large retail store, the researchers discovered that the espoused sophisticated human relations policy obscured a more complex, and less benign, reality. They found evidence of, among other things, poor communications, low job satisfaction, and gender discrimination in respect of pay and promotion opportunities (Turnbull and Wass 1998: 108).

The difficulties inherent in sustaining a sophisticated approach to the management of employees are also evident from a case study of a non-union chocolate works. In the early

1980s, senior managers attempted to initiate a transformation in the way in which employees were managed, eschewing the traditional autocratic style in favour of a more sophisticated approach which, among other things, sought to give employees more responsibility over their work and to 'build a culture in which individuals felt responsible for contributing to the success of the wider organization' (Scott 1994: 122). This was not enough, though, to overcome the traditional character of employment relations, in particular the reluctance of managers to disavow authoritarianism, something that limited the propensity of workers to engage with the new approach. Even in situations where there is no union presence, important barriers hinder attempts by managers to engender a sophisticated HRM approach, not least the reluctance of managers themselves to embrace the implications of change.

5.5.2 Employment relations in small firms

It is rare to find a formal union presence within small firms. According to the 2004 Workplace Employment Relations Survey, just 11 per cent of private sector workplaces with between 10 and 24 employees have a recognized union present.

Two problems affect any assessment of employment relations in small firms. First, difficulties of access make it hard to obtain adequate data regarding employment practices and employees' attitudes. Nevertheless, we are now able to draw upon a range of high-quality research studies that illuminate our understanding of employment relations in small firms (e.g. Goss 1991; Holliday 1995; Marlow 2002; Moule 1998; Rainnie 1989; Ram 1994). Second, the diverse nature of the small business sector must be respected, even to the extent of questioning whether it is a discrete 'sector' in its own right at all (Scase 1995). We can, however, draw out some common themes.

Perhaps the most notable feature of the work undertaken on small firms has been to expose the myth that employment relations is inherently harmonious since, based on data used by the Bolton Committee of Enquiry on Small Firms in the early 1970s, for many years this was the accepted wisdom (Bolton 1971). The committee's report equated the low level of union activity within small firms with an absence of conflict. It also claimed that the low pay and inferior physical working conditions characteristic of small firms were more than made up for by the benefits that accrue to employees from being in close proximity to their employer (Bolton 1971). Thus arose the 'myth' that when it comes to employment relations small is beautiful, something that 'sunk deep into the consciousness of academics, government and media' (Rainnie 1989: 25).

While it became influential among policy-makers, the 'industrial harmony' thesis has now been subjected to a considerable amount of criticism by academic researchers (e.g. Goss 1991; Rainnie 1989; Ram 1994). Rather than seeing small as 'beautiful', given the relatively high level of worker dismissals and workplace accidents occurring in small firms, it is perhaps more appropriate to see it as 'brutal' (Rainnie 1989). Importantly, though, studies that question, and in effect demolish, the 'industrial harmony' thesis do not simply replace one over-simplistic view, that employment relations in small firms are inherently harmonious, with another, that management autocracy is unconstrained and that pay and conditions are poor (Goss 1991; Rainnie 1989).

Such investigations move away from a simple association between size of firm and employment relations characteristics, and incorporate other factors such as the influence of product and labour market factors. For example, Goss (1991: 73) suggests that the nature of employment relations in small firms can be understood with regard to two related dimensions: first, the extent to which the employer is dependent on his or her employees, and vice versa; and, second, the degree to which employees have the capacity, individually or collectively, to challenge the power of their employer. Using these two dimensions, it is possible to produce four distinct categories that 'reveal the complexity and diversity of employment relations in small businesses' (Goss 1991: 86). See Figure 5.3 for further details.

First, the term 'fraternalism' can be applied to situations where employers work with their employees and, principally because of tight labour market conditions, are highly dependent upon them. Such a situation 'gives all the appearance not only of industrial harmony but also of egalitarianism' (Goss 1991: 74), and is likely to be found in professional services where key employees enjoy generally favourable terms and conditions of employment.

Second, where 'paternalism' prevails there is a greater degree of difference between the employer and his or her employees than under fraternal arrangements, given the lower dependency of the former on the latter. Such 'differentiation of employer and employed is at the heart of paternalism' (Goss 1991: 76). At the same time, the employer attempts to generate among the workforce a sense of identification with the firm. The unequal nature of the employment relationship is legitimized by reference to the 'bonds of mutual duty and obligation' (Goss 1991: 77) held to exist between the employer and the workforce, and which frequently extend into the wider community.

Third, in situations where employers are relatively little dependent on their employees and where, partly as a consequence, the power of employees is somewhat constrained,

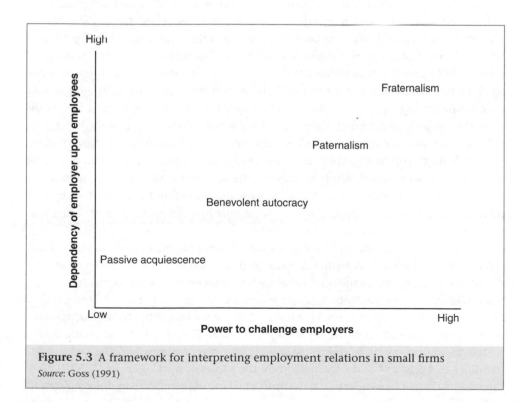

Figure 5.3 A framework for interpreting employment relations in small firms
Source: Goss (1991)

'benevolent autocracy' is the likely result, as in printing firms, for example. Without scarce skills, workers are more vulnerable to the actions of their employer, though this is unlikely to take the form of crude coercion since characteristics of the paternalistic approach can be an effective means of securing managerial legitimacy.

Fourth, where the emphasis is on workers as a cost, to be hired and fired according to the vagaries of the market, with no preference on the part of employers for stability, and with vulnerable, often female workers from ethnic minorities, who are highly dependent upon the employer for paid work, then 'sweating' is commonplace. In such environments, clothing manufacturing for example, 'passive acquiescence' is often the only tactic workers can pursue (Goss 1991: 84).

There can be little doubt that the work of Rainnie (1989) and Goss (1991) has greatly improved our understanding of employment relations in small firms, though by their nature typologies do not capture the dynamism of employment relations. An important study of employment relations in small Asian-owned firms in the West Midlands clothing industry, Monder Ram's (1994) *Managing to Survive*, focuses on the dynamic nature of the employment relationship, conceptualizing it as a 'negotiated order'. Ram (1994) discovered that to portray employment relations in these firms as autocratic was far too simplistic an approach. Rather, even in an environment where one might expect sweating to prevail, managerial authority was bounded by the need to construct and reconstruct bargains with workers over the pace of work tasks, and the wages payable for undertaking them. Space for 'informal accommodations' was created by the workers' intricate knowledge of the production process, given the imperative for a steady flow of output. Thus 'workers were not passive in the face of authoritarian managements; they would endeavour to alter the terms of the effort bargain if they felt that they were not "fairly" rewarded' (Ram 1994: 122).

Further studies demonstrate the broader relevance of the finding that the employment relationship in small firms is 'socially negotiated', though 'bound by market constraints' (Marlow 2002: 39). In their examination of 'WaterCo', a company that supplies water facilities to offices and other locations, Dundon and Rollinson (2004: 91) found that even in the absence of a trade union, 'workers were not passive recipients of the conditions they experienced. Rather, they exerted influence in return and, in so doing, partially shaped how management regulated the employment relationship'. Nevertheless, while it is important to highlight the limits of managerial control, bounded as it is by product and labour market factors and also by the accommodations that are required to elicit workers' cooperation within the workplace, one should not overlook the superior power of the employer in the employment relationship (Marlow 2002), something that is more obvious in the absence of a trade union.

Studies show that small firm employers have a pronounced hostility towards trade unions, seeing them as a potential obstacle to their ability to run the business as they like (Rainnie 1989). One of the owner-managers interviewed in a study of manufacturing businesses in the East Midlands told the researcher: 'I'll never be told what to do by a bloody trade unionist; this is my business . . .' (Marlow 2002: 33). Owner-managers often prefer to keep their employment relations informal. Thus employment arrangements within the firm come to be based 'mainly on unwritten customs and the tacit understandings that arise out of the interactions of the parties at work' (Ram et al. 2001: 846). Informality does not just refer to the unconstrained use of prerogative by the employer in the absence of joint regulation or statutory provisions. Instead, it is a process, one that is influenced by the ongoing mutual accommodations reached by employers and employed, and the characteristics of the product and labour market environments (Ram et al. 2001).

There is some evidence of a growing degree of formality in small firm employment relations. The 2004 Workplace Employment Relations Survey revealed, for example, that formal grievance and disciplinary procedures are commonplace in organizations with between 10 and 99 employees (Kersley et al. 2006). The existence of such procedures is one thing; how they are used is quite another. A study of small manufacturing firms re vealed a pronounced reluctance on the part of owner-managers to use formal procedures since 'they would disrupt the informal negotiated nature of the employment relationship' (Marlow 2002: 34).

There is also some evidence that ostensibly 'formal' procedures, such as in the area of discipline, for example, can be used in a somewhat 'informal' way, since managers use them simply as a way of 'going through the motions', having already decided the outcome in advance (Earnshaw, Marchington, and Goodman 2000). This demonstrates that while managerial prerogative in small firms is restricted by the need to reach accommodations with employees, and by product and labour market factors, it nonetheless exists, and is pronounced. While employment relations in small firms may not be wholly autocratic, by no means can it be said to be harmonious.

SECTION SUMMARY AND FURTHER READING

- Employment relations in large non-union firms would appear to be characterized by the presence of sophisticated HRM policies that focus on the effective management of individual employment relationships. In practice, though, there are limits to the individualization of employment relations, and such an approach may mask an anti-union philosophy.

- The widely held view that employment relations in small firms is inherently harmonious has been challenged by a number of authoritative studies. These have revealed the diversity of employment relations, and the factors, such as product and labour markets, that contribute to it.

- While a trade union presence is rare within small firms, and owner-employers often display a marked antipathy to unions, even here there are limits to managerial prerogative. Many employment relations arrangements are the outcome of an ongoing process of bargaining between managers and workers, though this should not lead one to disregard the superior power of the employer in the employment relationship.

There is still a limited amount of work available on non-unionism. The assessment by Blyton and Turnbull (2004) is highly recommended. Dundon and Rollinson (2004) provide four case studies of non-union employment relations in practice. For small firms, the overview provided by Scase (2003) is a good starting point. Beyond this, the work of Al Rainnie (1989), David Goss (1991), and Monder Ram (1994), respectively, has done much to improve our understanding of small-firm employment relations. For a good shorter study, see Marlow (2002).

 Visit our Online Resource Centre for web links to sites connected to this section. www.oxfordtextbooks.co.uk/williams_adamsmith2e

5.6 **Conceptualizing the management of employment relations**

Historically, a defining feature of the management of the employment relationship was its pragmatic or opportunistic character, typified by a preference for relatively unsophisticated personnel practices (Gospel 1992). The growing influence of management as an employment relations actor, however, has generated an increasing amount of interest in how its role should be understood, mainly through a consideration of management 'style'. This 'implies the existence of a distinctive set of guiding principles, written or otherwise, which set parameters to and signposts for management action regarding the way employees are treated and how particular events are handled' (Purcell and Ahlstrand 1994: 177).

The starting point for most analyses of management style in employment relations is the distinction between 'unitary' and 'pluralist' approaches made in the 1960s by Alan Fox (Fox 1966). The unitary style is characterized by an assumption that the employer and employees share common goals, and that the presence of unions would bring conflict and disorder to an otherwise harmonious workplace environment. The pluralist approach accepts that employers and employees may have different interests in the employment relationship, and that unions have a legitimate role in articulating them. As we have already established, though, employers often recognize trade unions for pragmatic reasons, in response to particular circumstances, notably union power, rather than from a genuine belief in the virtues of a pluralist approach.

In the period since Alan Fox articulated the distinction between unitary and pluralist approaches, a number of writers have refined the concept of managerial style. It is evident that the nature of the relationship between management and unions in unionized organizations may vary. In some organizations, the retail giant Tesco, for example, which has forged a 'partnership' agreement with the union (see Chapter 6), an explicitly cooperative relationship has been forged whereas in others, and here the Royal Mail comes to mind (Gall 2003c), relations are more adversarial.

5.6.1 **Management style in non-union firms**

Much of the recent interest in the concept of management style has centred on attempts to understand the diversity of employment relations approaches in non-union firms. By examining the extent to which employees are treated as individuals, and managed in a sophisticated way aimed at releasing their potential, Purcell and Ahlstrand (1994) were able to distinguish between three styles of management in non-union environments. Companies like IBM, which appear to use a range of personnel practices designed to promote the development of their employees as individuals, are typified by a 'sophisticated human relations' style.

In 'paternalist' firms, however, of which Marks and Spencer was traditionally held up as a leading example, there tends to be a history 'of welfare-based personnel policies which seek to emphasize loyalty on the part of employees, often by means of reasonably generous fringe benefits and pay levels' (Purcell and Ahlstrand 1994: 180).

'Traditional' firms follow a 'cost minimization' approach in which employees are essentially treated as commodities to be hired, and then discarded, according to the dictates of the market. Employment relations tend to be marked by the 'passive acquiescence' of workers to managerial dictates.

How appropriate is it to classify the management style in non-union firms in this way given the gap that exists, for example, between the espoused rhetoric of sophisticated HRM and the often less benign reality? In 'Ministeel', elements of a sophisticated human relations approach coexisted with more traditional coercive methods of managing the employment relationship (Bacon 1999). Styles of management should perhaps be seen, then, as characteristic tendencies, rather than as mutually exclusive approaches (Edwards 1987).

An alternative way of classifying non-union firms has been used in a study of new workplaces. The researchers examined whether or not firms had a clear HRM strategy, and also the take-up of HRM practices. From this, they were able to identify four management approaches (see Figure 5.4):

- 'good' firms, those which espoused a clear HRM strategy and made extensive use of a range of HRM practices;
- firms with no HRM strategy and a low uptake of HRM practices, the 'bad face of non-unionism';
- the 'lucky' firms, those that had no HRM strategy but, by chance, operated a large number of HRM practices; and
- 'ugly' firms, those that had a clear strategy but made little use of HRM practices and, being 'efficiency driven', must be 'bleak environments in which to work' (Guest and Hoque 1994).

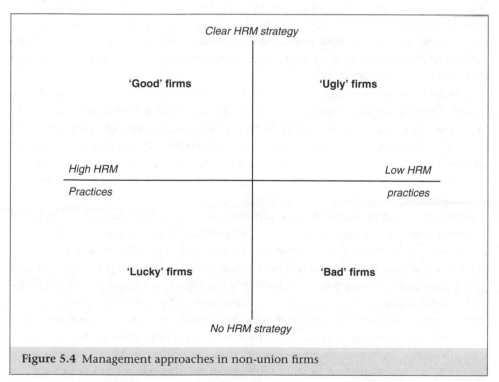

Figure 5.4 Management approaches in non-union firms

Although it is claimed that the 'good' firms, those that have a clear HRM strategy and make use of a wide range of supporting practices, and which were found to be the most common type, have better performance outcomes (Guest and Hoque 1994), there are a number of problems with this method of classifying non-union firms. For one thing, it comes from a very limited sample of firms in the manufacturing sector. Moreover, it is entirely based on the responses of managers (Kelly 1998), informants who are often unreliable when it comes to reporting workplace developments. It is unwise to assume that the reality of employment relations matches up with managerial rhetoric (Turnbull and Wass 1998).

5.6.2 Typologies of management style: a critique

Typologies have their uses in employment relations, to capture the diversity of small firms, for example (Goss 1991), but they tend to present a rather static picture of employment relations and, in respect of the management of the employment relationship, over-emphasize the degree of consistency evident in managerial approaches. Two features of how the employment relationship is managed which we identified in Chapter 1 hinder the capacity of managers to develop consistent approaches to the management of labour.

First, managers need to exercise control over employees while at the same time gaining their cooperation. Understandably, the ways in which managements exert control over their employees have been a long-standing feature of workplace studies. For example, a distinction has been made between two types of managerial control strategy: 'direct control', in which managers closely regulate and supervise the activities of workers; and 'responsible autonomy', where control is exercised by deliberately ceding to workers some degree of discretion over how they carry out their work tasks (Friedman 1977).

In order to sustain management prerogative, organizations have been compelled to design ever more sophisticated techniques; the growth of formal personnel policies and procedures can be seen as an attempt to secure 'bureaucratic control' (Edwards 1979). The rise of HRM, given the extent to which it is concerned with securing organizational culture change, is, in some interpretations, a more robust and, in so far as it is concerned with manipulating the meaning employees attach to their work, a more insidious way of securing managerial control (Willmott 1993).

In service industries, where the relationship between the employee and the customer is a key source of competitive advantage, managers have been obliged to develop novel techniques in an attempt to exercise control (see Box 5.8). This may, for example, involve using customers themselves (Korczynski 2002). Some companies use fake, or 'mock', customers. Their job is to establish that employees are fulfilling their role in the prescribed manner while pretending to be consumers (Fuller and Smith 1991). In some sectors, most famously the airline industry, but also in call centres, companies have attempted to control the operation of the service encounter through the manipulation of workers' feelings or emotions (Hochschild 1983; S. Taylor 1998). Delta Airlines, for example, used wide-ranging and sophisticated training methods to ensure that its

INSIGHT INTO PRACTICE 5.8

Tipping as a source of management control?

In some parts of the economy, restaurants for example, customer tips, as part of the 'total reward system' for front-line customer service staff, are viewed as an important component of workers' remuneration since they offset low rates of basic pay (Mars and Mitchell 1976). The practice of tipping, moreover, particularly where it has been 'institutionalized', that is has become a standard and accepted feature of workplace life, can serve to enhance managerial control of customer service workers, such as waiting staff, for example. In a study of the 'Central Restaurant Group', Ogbonna and Harris (2002: 730–1) noted that the use of tipping was an 'integral part of reward', and had 'a long history in the organization', a reflection of its founder's belief that 'the best way to generate enthusiasm, loyalty and the required customer service behaviour from front-line staff was in encouraging them to keep their own tips'. Three main reasons underpinned the institutionalization of tipping in Central Restaurant Group. First, as a motivational tool it helped to improve employees' performance. Second, it allowed the company to pay a low basic wage, helping to keep labour costs down. Third, it enabled management to maintain control, albeit indirectly, over employee behaviour during the customer service encounter.

The institutionalization of tipping in Central Restaurant Group served to reinforce managerial control over employee behaviour in three ways. First, competition for tips encouraged self-interest among the workforce, and thus impeded the development of a collective ethos which might challenge managerial standards. Second, by keeping basic pay low managers fostered among the waiting staff a sense of dependency on the tips. Third, the company used a number of means, including communications processes, to promote its approach to tipping.

Since tips comprised a substantial proportion of their earnings, workers were, understandably, supportive of the Central Restaurant Group's approach. Nevertheless, there was some dissatisfaction among workers over the behaviour it was felt necessary to produce in order to receive tips. Managers sometimes encouraged flirting, a form of potentially exploitative sexual labour, as a means of keeping customers happy. Ogbonna and Harris (2002: 742) suggest that such activity is a 'degrading and debasing' feature of front-line customer service work, and that workers may feel obliged to 'prostitute' themselves in exchange for the possibility of additional tipped income. They conclude, however, that despite the high level of management manipulation inherent in the institutionalization of tipping, and its potentially exploitative implications, workers nonetheless used the system for their own ends. They were not the passive dupes of managers, but rational and calculative actors aware of what they needed to do to maximize their earnings.

cabin crew acted appropriately, in particular by smiling, in all of their interactions with customers. Thus 'the emotional style of offering the service is part of the service itself' (Hochschild 1983: 5).

The importance of control notwithstanding, managers also need to secure the cooperation and consent of their staff. Thus 'management strategy is always a blend of consent and coercion, though the nature of that blend varies between companies and between the various levels within each company hierarchy' (Fox 1985b: 66).

Consent was traditionally secured by means of *ad hoc* accommodations with trade unions (Hyman 2003). Yet even in non-union environments, managers must operate in such a way as to gain the cooperation of, and thus secure legitimacy among, those they manage, as was evident in the firms studied by Ram (1994). Other studies demonstrate how workers, collectively, exert an influence over the way in which employment relations is managed even in the absence of a trade union (Dundon and Rollinson 2004; McLoughlin and Gourlay 1994). Typologies of management style, therefore, cannot adequately capture the complexity of how employment relations is managed in practice (Dundon and Rollinson 2004).

A second factor that hinders managerial consistency concerns the tension that is created by the dual function of labour in a capitalist market economy. The experience of Esso's oil refinery at Fawley, mentioned earlier in the chapter, illustrates the tension that can exist between an imperative to cut labour costs as a means of enhancing productivity, something that involves workforce reductions, and the need to secure greater employee commitment as a means of generating flexibility (Ahlstrand 1990). Thus the management of labour in a capitalist economy is beset by contradiction (Legge 2005). Managements have to reconcile two seemingly conflicting interests, 'to cut costs to the bone and yet at the same time promote the security, autonomy and teamwork, which are the conditions for innovation into new markets, products and services' (Sisson and Storey 2000: 29).

5.6.3 Managing employment relations in a market economy

Financial imperatives, and the need constantly to keep labour costs under control, are a major obstacle to the development of a sophisticated HRM approach within firms operating in Britain. The case of Hewlett-Packard, a firm with an espoused sophisticated HRM approach, is instructive. Intense competitive pressures compelled the firm to reduce its workforce, resulting in increased pressure and lower morale among those who remained. Inevitably, such feelings influenced the perceptions and behaviour of employees, thus ensuring that HRM techniques were rendered less effective (Truss 2001).

The dominance of short-term pressures on companies to improve their financial performance is particularly acute in Anglo-Saxon economies such as Britain, where firm performance is judged according to strict financial criteria. A study of British manufacturing firms revealed the importance of finance-based forms of control and how this encouraged a particular form of labour flexibility, one founded upon the intensive use of relatively unskilled workers, rather than contingent upon the use of a better developed, more committed workforce (Ackroyd and Proctor 1998). Thus the short-term nature of the capitalist market economy, reinforced by the widespread adoption of tight financial and accounting controls, is a key obstacle to the development of a high commitment management approach (Thompson 2003). See Box 5.9 for different interpretations of how private equity ownership affects employment relations.

The management of employment relations in market economies is marked by two contradictory tendencies: the need to exercise control over employees as well as to secure their consent and cooperation, and the desirability of treating employees as resources

Employment relations reflection 5.9 Private equity and employment relations

During the 2000s, the growth of private equity funds attracted a considerable amount of attention. Private equity funds borrow large sums of money from institutional investors, in combination with small amounts of their own, to buy out underperforming companies, taking their shares off the stock market. Through rigorous control over costs, and away from the public eye, the fortunes of the company are improved. This helps to service the repayments on the debt incurred and leads to handsome rewards for the members of the private equity fund. Among the companies taken over by private equity funds during the 2000s were Alliance Boots, Birds Eye, and the car park firm NCP. By 2008 some three million workers in the UK (10 per cent of the workforce) were employed in companies under the control of private equity.

The impact of private equity ownership on employment relations has prompted a lively debate. Critics contend that pressure to reduce costs has adverse consequences for staff employed in firms taken over by private equity. Not only do private equity funds look for efficiency savings through job cuts, but they also try to lower costs by eroding terms and conditions of employment and making remaining employees work harder. Legislation that exists to protect employees' pay and conditions when their business is sold doesn't apply to private equity takeovers (Clark 2008). In some cases, new private equity owners have terminated union recognition agreements. In 2004, for example, the private equity funds CVC Capital Partners and Permira took joint control of the car rescue firm the AA in a deal worth £1.75 billion. This resulted in a reported 3,400 job losses (from a total of 10,000) and the derecognition of the GMB trade union (Harris 2007).

However, others argue that the impact of private equity on employment relations is more positive. While job losses sometimes do occur, in general private equity ownership may help to stabilize and even raise employment levels. This is because previously under-performing companies are made more secure, thus supporting jobs. The emphasis on improving financial performance may even generate greater interest in using high commitment management practices. Moreover, for the most part private equity control seems to have no effect on union recognition (Brown and Wright 2008). The financial crisis of 2007–08, and the subsequent economic recession, means that while private equity is unlikely to disappear, its overall significance as a model of corporate ownership is likely to diminish. There is simply less money around to finance private equity buy-outs.

to be developed and the obligation to consider them as commodities to be discarded should it be necessary. They pose immense challenges to organizations which are keen to manage employment relations in a long-term, purposive, or 'strategic' way (Hyman 1987). In Section 5.2 we discussed the unsophisticated way in which employment relations was traditionally managed in Britain, influenced, as it was, by certain characteristics of the product and labour market environment (Gospel 1992). The contradictions in the management of the employment relationship we have highlighted here, though, point to the inevitability of opportunism. For Hyman (1987: 30), 'there is no "one best way" of managing these contradictions, only different routes to partial failure'. In other words, management can never enjoy complete control over employment relations, and the results of their interventions may differ substantially from the intended outcomes.

SECTION SUMMARY AND FURTHER READING

- The concept of 'management style' is a useful device for capturing the diversity of managerial approaches to employment relations, particularly among non-union firms. However, the main problem with the concept of management style is that it implies a consistent and long-term pattern of managerial action which may not be evident in practice.

- The nature of employment relations makes it difficult for managers to pursue effective long-term and strategic approaches. On the one hand, managers view their employees as valued assets whose cooperation and consent is deemed essential to achieving organizational objectives. On the other hand, managers also have to exercise control over the workforce, exploiting and discarding them as necessary.

For further insights on the managerial style concept, see Purcell and Ahlstrand (1994: Chapter 7). Hyman (1987) provides a thought provoking and sophisticated conceptualization of the management of employment relations.

 Visit our Online Resource Centre for web links to sites connected to this section. www.oxfordtextbooks.co.uk/williams_adamsmith2e

Conclusion

What, then, are the salient aspects of the way in which contemporary employment relations is managed? Clearly, pressures to sustain and expand the scope of managerial prerogative, and accommodate the influence of trade unions, are long-standing features of the management of employment relations. During the 1980s and 1990s, employers took advantage of a more favourable economic and political climate to challenge the influence of trade unions. Among newly established workplaces, union recognition is rare; where unions do retain a formal presence, managers have attempted to erode their influence, through the use of sophisticated HRM techniques. The way in which some employers have responded to the introduction of the statutory union recognition procedure demonstrates that anti-union values persist.

The development of sophisticated HRM, and the use of high commitment management practices, portends a transformation in the management of employment relations. Whereas in the past the managerial agenda was dominated by the need to deal with accommodating the trade unions, the key emphasis now, it is claimed, is concerned with engaging employees, and building their organizational commitment as a key source of improved business performance. As indicated in the introductory case study, McDonald's claims that employee engagement is a main priority. However, the extent to which the fundamental basis of managing employment relations has changed is questionable. There is little sign that the high commitment approach has become widespread. Moreover, the activities of those non-union firms that espouse a sophisticated HRM approach demonstrate their main concern is with preventing a union presence from becoming established, something that makes the distinction between 'non-unionism' and 'anti-unionism' approaches difficult to uphold in practice (Blyton and Turnbull 2004).

Although attempts to expand the scope of managerial prerogative are a defining feature of the way in which employment relations is managed, the very nature of the employment relationship, as a 'negotiated order', means that it is inevitably limited in practice. In order to realize the efficient production of goods and services, managers must not only seek to exercise control over their employees, but are also compelled to win their consent and cooperation. Even within small, non-union workplaces, where 'passive acquiescence' is all that might be expected from employees (Goss 1991), employers are obliged to secure a degree of legitimacy from them in order to operate efficiently. Thus the scope of managerial prerogative is inherently limited by the nature of the employment relationship as a wage-work bargain.

The need to exercise control over employees, as well as gain their cooperation, is an important contradictory feature of the management of employment relations. As such, it militates against consistency in managerial interventions, making the elaboration of a purposive, or strategic, approach difficult to pursue in practice. This is reinforced by a further contradictory feature of the way in which the employment relationship is managed in capitalist market economies, that which exists between the desirability of treating employees as resources, whose skill, commitment and dedication contribute to raising organizational performance, and the need to consider them as commodities, to be discarded should competitive pressures dictate it.

These contradictions render consistency in managerial approaches, such as the pursuit of HRM, difficult to achieve in practice. An espoused policy goal of high commitment may be undermined by the effects of more intense competitive pressures, leading to job cuts, insecurity, and a lowering of employee morale. Despite a more favourable climate, then, and the dramatic decline of trade unionism, it is clear that there has been no real transformation in the way in which employment relations are managed in contemporary Britain.

Assignment and discussion questions

1   Why and how do managers seek to retain their prerogative in employment relations?

2   Why and how have employers been able to weaken the influence of trade unions?

3   Discuss the view that employers should not be obliged to recognize a trade union under any circumstances.

4   In theory, why might 'high commitment practices' lead to improved business performance? What are the obstacles in practice?

5   How far do you agree with the view that in non-union firms management practices are aimed at preventing unions from gaining a foothold by providing a substitute for the role of a trade union?

6   What arguments have been put forward to support the view that employers cannot take a longer-term, strategic approach to the management of employment relations? Explain whether you agree or disagree with these arguments.

Visit our Online Resource Centre for web links to sites connected to this section. www.oxfordtextbooks.co.uk/williams_adamsmith2e

Take your learning further: online resource centre

Visit the Online Resource Centre that accompanies this book to enrich your understanding of Chapter 5: Managing employment relations. Explore web links, test yourself using an interactive flashcard glossary, and keep up to date with the latest developments in the area.

http://www.oxfordtextbooks.co.uk/orc/williams_adamsmith2e.

Chapter case study

Human resource management and the hotel industry

Human Resource Management (HRM) is claimed to offer organizations a new and improved approach to the management of the employment relationship. Through its 'key levers' of sophisticated recruitment and selection techniques, the appraisal of employees' performance linked to individualized payment strategies, and communication with workers, it offers a route to enhanced employee commitment to the organization's business objectives. The focus of HRM on delivering improved quality would seem to be particularly relevant to sectors such as the hotel industry that claim to rely on good customer service by employees as a means of securing competitive advantage.

Studies undertaken in the hotel sector paint very different pictures of the extent to which HRM, and its associated focus on techniques that enhance employee commitment, has replaced the traditional emphasis on managerial and cost control in the industry. Hoque (1999) compared large hotel companies with similar-sized manufacturing firms, where most research on the use of HRM has been undertaken, to identify whether any differences existed between them on the use of HRM. Based upon managers' replies to questionnaires, he notes a significant adoption by hotel companies of the principles of HRM. More of them, compared to manufacturing businesses, had developed a formal HR strategy that was integrated with their business strategy. Moreover, the key levers of HRM themselves were integrated with each other such that there was a clear link between, for example, performance appraisal and reward systems. Furthermore, the use of HR practices to support the strategy, such as selection criteria, terms and conditions, training, consultation, and communication, were as likely, and, in some cases, more likely to be found among hotel companies than in manufacturing firms.

Other studies, however, suggest a different reality. That by Adam-Smith, Norris, and Williams (2003) covered both large hotels, often part of a group, and smaller businesses, and examined the views not only of managers, but also the experience of workers in the industry. The researchers identified a largely reactive approach to the management of labour, aimed at meeting customer demands while also minimizing costs. Workers suffered from work intensification through the need to cover staff shortages, and through having to switch to other duties as required by managers. There was little evidence of flexibility derived from investment in training to multi-skill workers. Few organizations had introduced merit pay based upon employee performance: rather, most payment systems were unsophisticated. Pay enhancements, for example, to train new employees or to undertake some minor supervisory responsibilities, were often introduced in an ad hoc manner, rather than as the result of a planned employment strategy. The management of employment relations in many hotels is characterized by a considerable degree of informality, rather than by strategic intent.

1. Why might the HRM approach to managing the employment relationship be attractive to hotel companies?

2. What factors might inhibit its take-up in such firms?

6

Representation at work

Chapter objectives:

The main objectives of this chapter are to:

* consider the development of the trade unions;

* examine the ways in which trade unions represent the interests of workers;

* consider the effectiveness of non-union arrangements for the representation of workers' interests;

* assess the implications for employers and trade unions of 'partnership agreements'; and

* evaluate the extent to which organizing unionism can enhance workers' interests.

6.1 Introduction

In this chapter, we examine how the interests of workers are represented. Workers have traditionally had their interests represented by means of the 'single channel' of trade unionism. Therefore, we begin by tracing the development of the unions during the twentieth century, and consider how they represent workers' interests. However, declining unionization levels have reduced the extent to which workers enjoy effective representation of their interests. In order to understand developments in the representation of workers, we need to consider both how unions have sought to respond to the decline in membership, and alternative forms of worker representation.

What, though, are workers' interests? How can they be defined? In order for a union, or indeed any body, to represent the concerns of workers it helps to know what they are. This may seem obvious; surely workers want higher pay? But non-economic issues, such as job security for example, may sometimes be an equally, if not more important, demand. The concept of workers' 'interests' is extremely ambiguous, incorporating a potentially diverse and complex set of issues. Moreover, is it in the interest of workers to challenge, or to cooperate with, their employers? While there is always the potential for conflicting interests in the employment relationship, workers also have a concern with ensuring that their employer is successful, since their job and wages depend on it (Kelly 1998). When reading this chapter, then, it is important to recognize that workers' interests are rarely unambiguous.

Introductory case study

Revitalizing trade unions: the case of Community

One of the main themes of this chapter concerns how trade unions represent the interests of workers. Since the 1980s, however, union membership has declined, and the unions have had to explore innovative ways of demonstrating their value to working people. The Community union was formed in 2004 from a merger of two unions representing steel workers, and footwear and textile workers. In addition to the conventional functions that we would expect from a trade union—bargaining with employers, and providing members with employment advice, support, and representation—Community also emphasizes the importance of taking a broader, community-based approach to promoting the interests of its members, one which is not just restricted to the workplace. It provides members with lifelong learning opportunities, for example, and works to ensure that 'it is seen as a force for good in the communities in which [its] members live' (http://www.community-tu.org).

Trade unions have long been an integral part of many industrial communities, for example in coal mining areas. Yet the example of Community demonstrates that unions are exploring new ways of representing the interests of their members. In this chapter we consider the main approaches unions have developed to expand their representational capacities, through organizing new members, for example, or by instituting more cooperative partnership working with employers. By the end of this chapter you will be better placed to judge whether or not the unions do have a bright future when it comes to representing workers' interests, or if the growth of non-union forms of representation, or even the absence of any representation arrangements at all, are more likely outcomes of contemporary developments in employment relations.

6.2 Trade unions, worker representation, and the rise of a 'representation gap'

In Chapter 1, we examined the main functions of the trade unions, and provided an outline of their nineteenth-century origins. In this section, we consider the main ways in which trade unions represent the interests of workers, set against the development of the unions during the twentieth century, before focusing upon the union membership decline that commenced in the 1980s and assessing the factors that contributed to it.

6.2.1 The development of the trade unions in the twentieth century

In Chapter 1 we examined the origins of the trade unions among skilled craft workers during the nineteenth century. The period between 1880 and 1920 saw a major expansion of trade unionism in Britain. The development of 'general' unions, in industries such as the docks, transport, and gas, for example, in two waves, first during the 1880s, and second, during the 1910s, demonstrates how, under the influence of prominent leaders, many of whom were imbued with a socialist outlook, increasing numbers of semi- and unskilled workers became organized (see Hyman 2001b).

Unlike their skilled craft counterparts, most of the workers who unionized in this period looked to secure improvements in their pay and conditions through widespread collective organization, and a readiness to use strikes and political activity, including the formation of a dedicated parliamentary party to represent the labour interest (see Chapter 3). By 1910, trade union membership had reached over 2.5 million, albeit concentrated in certain areas such as coal mining—the Miners' Federation of Great Britain (MFGB) was the largest union in the country—engineering, railways, and cotton production. These were industries in which trade unionism had secured a foothold before the 1880s (Burgess 1980). The most sizeable occupation, domestic service, was almost entirely unorganized, however (Clegg 1985; Hyman 1975).

During the first half of the twentieth century union membership grew, to more than eight million in 1921, before falling back to under five million during the economic depression of the 1930s (see Table 6.1). Although trade union membership had already started to edge upwards during the late 1930s, the Second World War (1939–45), and

Table 6.1 Trade union membership and density in the UK, 1892–1979

Year	Union membership	Union density (%)
1892	1,576,000	10.6
1900	2,022,000	12.7
1910	2,565,000	14.6
1917	5,499,000	30.2
1920	8,348,000	45.2
1926	5,219,000	28.3
1933	4,392,000	22.6
1938	6,053,000	30.5
1945	7,875,000	38.6
1950	9,829,000	44.1
1955	9,741,000	44.5
1960	9,835,000	44.2
1965	10,325,000	44.2
1970	11,187,000	48.5
1975	12,026,000	51.0
1979	13,447,000	55.4

Source: Bain and Price (1983)

the political and economic climate of the post-war period, in which full employment predominated, were major sources of union growth.

Trade union membership reached 13 million by the 1970s (see Table 6.1). The development of trade unionism in Britain during this period was marked by a number of distinctive features, including the growing significance of shop stewards, the spread of unionization beyond its manual worker origins, and the increasing influence of the Trades Union Congress (TUC).

The post-war economic recovery was predicated upon the growth of manufacturing industry, the mass production of electrical goods and other standardized products such as motor vehicles, based on a narrow division of labour. Full employment encouraged greater shopfloor bargaining activity, creating the conditions that enabled trade unionism to flourish at the workplace level (Terry 1983). Moreover, the rather monotonous nature of the assembly-line work in large-scale factory environments, allied with the more vigorous exercise of managerial prerogative, generated increasingly adversarial and 'low-trust' relations between managers and workers (Fox 1974).

The role of shop stewards, unpaid union representatives based in the workplace, attracted greater attention. Although the shop steward position originated in the first two decades of the twentieth century (Hinton 1973), the growth of workplace bargaining saw a massive rise in their numbers, particularly in engineering and parts of manufacturing industry, thus generating a 'shift in authority' within the trade unions away from the salaried cadre of full-time professional officials (Royal Commission 1968; Terry 1983).

By the end of the 1970s, shop stewards had spread to the public sector, and there may have been as many as 250,000 of them active in Britain (Clegg 1979). Legislation of the 1970s, which obliges employers to give shop stewards of recognized unions reasonable paid time off work to undertake union activities, reflected the prevailing pluralist policy assumption that by accepting and integrating workplace unionism, rather than challenging it, managers could effectively contain industrial conflict.

During the 1960s and 1970s, the development of trade unionism in Britain was characterized by two notable trends. First, union membership and organization became more commonplace among non-manual, so-called 'white-collar' workers in both the private and public sectors (Blackburn and Prandy 1965). Much of the rapid acceleration in union membership during this period—by 1979 over half the British workforce were unionized—reflected the increased unionization of workers in office-based occupations in sectors such as central and local government administration. Much was made of the success of the Association of Supervisory, Technical and Managerial Staff (ASTMS), now part of the Unite trade union, in recruiting scientific, professional, and quasi-professional workers. By 'the end of the 1970s nearly 40 per cent of all trade unionists were in white-collar jobs' (Price 1983: 155).

The second development concerns the increasingly prominent role enjoyed by the Trades Union Congress (TUC) in British employment relations. As a trade union confederation, which spoke on behalf of its union affiliates, provided them with services, such as education and training, for example, and also attempted to regulate their behaviour, the TUC originated in the nineteenth century. During the 1960s and 1970s, however, the growth of state intervention in employment relations enhanced the stature of the TUC as a conduit to government.

By the 1970s, perhaps the most striking feature of employment relations in Britain was the strength of trade unionism. For example, the aggregate level of trade union membership, and membership density, a term used to refer to the proportion of the workforce who are union members, peaked in the late 1970s (see Table 6.1). From the 1980s onwards, though, a series of related political, industrial, and economic changes, which we examine below, significantly eroded the power of the unions in contemporary employment relations. First, however, we consider how trade unions represent workers' interests.

6.2.2 Trade unions and the representation of workers' interests

There are four main ways in which trade unions represent the interests of workers. First, unions insure workers against difficulties and problems that arise during the course of their working lives. We have already observed (in Chapter 1) that the provision of friendly benefits was a major function of the early unions of skilled workers (Webb and Webb 1920a). During the twentieth century, the importance of friendly benefits as a union function declined markedly, not just because collective bargaining became the principal way in which unions sought to regulate the employment relationship, but also because the state's role in providing welfare benefits, such as unemployment assistance, for example, expanded considerably.

Nevertheless, one of the defining features of union organization is that it reflects the wishes of workers collectively to insure, or protect, themselves against problems at work. This was evident from a study of public sector trade unionism in the north-east of England undertaken by one of this book's authors. Organizational restructuring in the health service and local government generated a more assertive style of management, increased pressure on employees, and produced a climate of job insecurity. Unsurprisingly, then, the need for protection at work was an important determinant of union membership. According to one member: 'It is a necessity to be a union member in today's economic climate as a safeguard against employers attempting hardline proposals which may be unreasonable—a safeguard against hardline tactics.' While union membership may be predicated on workers' demands for insurance against individual problems at work, it is something that is achievable only through robust collective organization (Williams 1997).

The second way in which unions represent the interests of workers is by bargaining on their behalf with managers over pay and other terms and conditions of employment. We considered the nature of collective bargaining in Chapter 1. Importantly, collective bargaining is not just an economic process, concerned with setting the terms on which workers are hired, but it is also a political activity since it enables workers, through their union representatives, to influence, and thus regulate jointly with managers, workplace decision-making (Flanders 1975). Contemporary trends in collective bargaining activity are discussed in Chapter 7.

We have already traced the evolution of the shop steward role in British employment relations. The third way in which unions represent the interests of workers concerns the activities of stewards and workplace union representatives. They are generally the first point of contact for union members, and act to advocate their interests to managers, supporting and standing up for them in the workplace (Coates and Topham 1980), sometimes as a safeguard against hard-line employers.

One problem is that stewards are essentially concerned with representing the (sometimes narrow and sectional) interests of their own members, hindering union efforts to expand their membership base. Moreover, the way in which stewards represent their members' interests is often shaped by their assumptions about the kinds of issue that are legitimate for union action. Munro's (1999) study of shop steward organization among ancillary staff in the health service demonstrates the influence of a relatively narrow 'trade union agenda' dominated by the concerns of male workers. This affects stewards' behaviour in that they ignore issues of particular importance to women workers, such as childcare provision.

Fourth, unions do not just represent the interests of their members in the workplace, but also in the broader political arena. Indeed, by seeking to advance the interests of workers in general, and not just those of their members, unions act as a 'sword of justice' (Flanders 1975), for example by campaigning for effective laws governing employment rights. In Chapter 3, we considered the influence of unions in the Labour party. The enactment of the National Minimum Wage in 1999 (see Chapter 7), the culmination of a successful campaign run within the party by some trade unions to secure a manifesto commitment to introduce it, demonstrates how unions can use political channels to advance workers' interests. Unions have increasingly looked to alternative, broader ways of representing workers' interests politically, other than through the Labour party. For example, in the 2000s the union movement has campaigned to improve the rights and employment conditions of mostly non-unionized 'vulnerable' workers, such as migrant workers (TUC 2008).

6.2.3 Declining unionization in Britain and the 'representation gap'

While trade unionism has traditionally constituted the 'single channel' by which workers have had their interests represented in Britain, declining levels of unionization mean that many people no longer enjoy effective representation at work. During the 1980s and 1990s, trade union membership fell by more than 5 million; by the 2000s, fewer than 30 per cent of employees were union members.

While the presence of a trade union does not guarantee that workers will have effective representation, the absence of the protection that a union can provide has diminished the extent of their 'representation security' (Burchell, Ladipo, and Wilkinson 2002). While there are signs that the decline in union membership may have bottomed out, some two-thirds of workers in Britain still have no access to independent means of representing their interests.

Although the decline in the level of union membership has attracted much attention, it has to be seen in the context of the broader diminution of joint regulation as a means of regulating the workplace. In Chapter 5, for example, we considered the falling incidence of union recognition since the 1980s. The decline in the level of collective bargaining coverage is discussed in Chapter 7. Union workplace organization has also been rendered less effective by the increased preference of managers to bypass shop stewards, and to communicate with workers directly (Marchington and Parker 1990; Storey 1992). In 1980, trade union representatives were present in 53 per cent of workplaces. By 2004, they were present in just 38 per cent (Kersley et al. 2006). Nevertheless, union representatives are

Employment relations reflection 6.1   Union Lear...

Employers who recognize a trade union are obliged to give union representatives shop stewards—a reasonable amount of time away from their work in order to undertake their union duties. A recognized union is also entitled to appoint safety representatives whose activities include investigating health and safety issues and making representations to managers. The 2002 Employment Act provided for the establishment of union learning representatives. Their role is designed to promote learning, training, and development activities, by raising awareness of the opportunities that are available to workers, for example, or by encouraging employers to improve their provision.

By 2005, one estimate put the number of union learning representatives at 6,500. An evaluative study found that union learning representatives make an effective contribution to widening participation in learning activities, and can stimulate positive action by employers. Not all employers, however, support the objective of enhancing opportunities for workplace learning, and some have failed to engage constructively with union learning representatives (Wallis, Stuart, and Greenwood 2005). Nevertheless, the union learning representative model has been taken forward as a useful way of achieving progress in other areas of employment relations. For example, some unions have appointed equality representatives; the UK government intends to give them a more formal role in challenging workplace discrimination and promoting equality. Some unions have also pressed for a new role of union environment representative to be recognized, helping managers in workplaces to develop greener ways of working. The role of the union representative is clearly changing in important ways.

taking on new roles (see Box 6.1). Successive Conservative governments reduced the influence of the unions over the formulation of public policy (Heery 1998c). Since 1997 Labour governments have kept the unions at a distance, tending to treat them as a liability, rather than as a partner in the labour movement (McIlroy 2009).

Nevertheless, membership decline is perhaps the starkest indication of the collapse of the union movement's fortunes (see Table 6.2). In 1979, there were over 12.5 million union members in Britain, some 53 per cent of the workforce. During the 1980s union membership fell by a third. Membership decline continued during the 1990s, albeit at a more gradual pace; by 2000 fewer than three in ten employees (29.8 per cent) were union members.

During the 2000s the drop in union membership levelled off, at around the seven million mark. Nevertheless, union density—the proportion of employees who are union members—continued to decline, suggesting that unions were not taking advantage of employment growth during the period. What caused the union membership decline of the 1980s and 1990s, and why has union density continued to drop? Seven possible factors are considered here.

First, it is sometimes suggested that social change, in particular the diminution of class as a source of social identity, and the rise of an ethos of individualism, has eroded the collectivism that traditionally underpinned people's motivation to unionize (Bassett and Cave 1993). Yet such a view is based on a profound misunderstanding of the basis of trade unionism. In particular, it ignores the large extent to

..2 Trade union membership and density, 1980–2008*

Year	Union membership	Density (%)
1980	12,239,000	54.5
1985	10,282,000	49.0
1990	8,835,000	38.1
1995	7,125,000	32.4
2000	7,120,000	29.8
2005	7,056,000	28.6
2008	6,883,000	27.4

* Great Britain (1980–90), UK (1995–2008).
Source: Barratt (2009); Waddington (2003b)

which union practice has always been informed by a complex mix of individualistic and collective orientations. Moreover, survey data suggest that collective reasons are important in influencing workers' decisions to join unions (Waddington and Whitston 1997).

A second, more persuasive explanation for union membership decline is not that workers have become more individualistic, but that the benefits of trade unionism are no longer as evident as they once were (Fernie 2005). In particular, there is strong evidence that a key incentive behind the decision to join a union, that it will help to raise a worker's wages, is no longer as compelling as it once was. The wage premium, the greater earnings that accrue to workers whose pay is set by union bargaining, declined during the 1990s from 14.2 per cent in 1993 to just 6.3 per cent in 2000 (Metcalf 2005).

A third factor concerns the changing composition of employment in Britain. The compositional approach asserts that, since the 1980s, employment has been contracting in areas where unions are strong and increasing in areas where unions are weak. Thus the number of full-time, male-dominated jobs in large manufacturing enterprises, where unionization tends to be commonplace, has dwindled considerably. Most employment growth has been in the private services sector, where jobs are often held by women on a part-time basis, and where unions are relatively weak.

The main problem with the compositional approach, though, is that many of the trends that supposedly weaken trade unionism, such as increasing levels of employment in the service sector, for example, or the rise in the number of part-time jobs, existed in the 1970s when union membership grew (Metcalf 1991). Moreover, the trend towards so-called flexible employment is much exaggerated, as we saw in Chapter 2; and workers in part-time jobs are by no means inimical to unionization (Walters 2002).

Fourth, to what extent have economic factors, in particular the incidence of unemployment, affected the level of union membership in Britain? During the early 1980s, the sharp fall in unionization coincided with a dramatic increase in unemployment. Not only are unemployed workers unlikely to maintain their union membership, but those still in employment may be wary of unionization if it is perceived as jeopardizing their jobs. The problem with this explanation for union membership decline, however, is that it continued, albeit at a slower rate, during periods when employment levels have been rising (Fernie 2005). Union density continued to fall during the 2000s despite substantial employment growth. This suggests that there is no straightforward relationship between the incidence of unemployment and the overall level of union membership (Waddington 2003b).

Fifth, increased employer hostility towards unions has also contributed to membership decline. In Chapter 5, we considered the efforts of employers to avoid unions, particularly in new workplaces, or, where this is not feasible, to weaken their influence by using techniques associated with sophisticated human resource management, for example.

The capacity of employers to undermine union power, though, was underpinned by a sixth factor, the hostility directed by successive Conservative governments towards the trade unions—what Waddington (2003b) calls a 'neo-liberal assault' on trade unionism. We considered the nature of Conservative policy on employment relations in Chapter 3. Although some writers argue that the anti-union legislation enacted by the Conservatives was largely responsible for union membership decline during the 1980s (Freeman and Pelletier 1990), much of it occurred before the changes in the law could take effect. The anti-union laws were introduced more easily because the unions had already been weakened by other factors (Waddington 1992, 2003b). Nevertheless, the Conservatives established a political climate that helped to undermine the legitimacy of the unions, giving managers more confidence to exclude them from workplaces. Trade unionism was rendered less effective, making union membership less attractive to workers. Thus 'the impact, either directly or indirectly, of the Conservative political project had a wide-ranging influence on the decline in unionization' (Waddington 2003b: 219).

The seventh and final factor we need to consider concerns the activities of the unions themselves. Much of the decline in the level of unionization can be attributed to the failure of unions to organize in new workplaces, and thus gain recognition from employers in expanding areas of the economy (Machin 2000). Clearly, the hostile industrial and political climate impeded the ability of the unions to expand their constituencies. But the unions themselves were reluctant to embark on vigorous recruitment and organizing drives, for reasons we will discuss later on in this chapter. Between the mid 1980s and mid 1990s, union efforts at dealing with the membership crisis were largely focused on improving individual membership benefits, or creating economies of scales through mergers (Heery 1996; Willman 1989), not with organizing new members.

In summary, then, the overall fall in the level of union membership during the 1980s and 1990s was the result of a complex combination of factors (Waddington 2003b). Although compositional changes and increasing unemployment levels caused a dramatic fall in union membership during the early 1980s, by the latter part of that decade the effects of the Conservative's legislative changes were beginning to take effect, fostering a climate within which the exercise of managerial prerogative was strengthened, and union confidence undermined. Moreover, the decline in the wage premium associated with union membership meant that workers had less of an incentive to join unions.

During the 2000s, the decline in the overall level of trade union membership largely stabilized. What caused the fall in trade union membership to level off? Clearly, Labour governments have offered a less hostile public policy climate than their Conservative predecessors, even if, as we saw in Chapter 3, it is far from being pro-union. Moreover, as we see later on in this chapter, some unions are devoting more resources to organizing workers. Employment growth in the public services, a sector where the level of unionization is robust, has also helped. It is important to bear in mind that union density varies markedly by sector and industry (see Table 6.3). In the public sector 57 per cent of employees are trade unionists, compared to just 15 per cent in the private sector. Over half (54 per cent) of employees in education are trade union members, compared to just one in twenty (5 per cent) in hotels and restaurants.

Set against these positive developments for the unions, however, there are a number of factors which continue to suppress union membership; the declining wage premium, for example. As we saw in Chapter 5, despite the increasing number of new union recognition agreements, the proportion of workplaces with a recognized union has continued to decline, reflecting ongoing compositional change unfavourable to the union movement and the failure of the unions to secure recognition in new and growing areas of the economy. The changing composition of employment also meant that the proportion of employees who are union members continued to decline during the 2000s.

The decline in union membership has prompted a considerable amount of interest in the implications for workers' interests and how they are represented. The diminution of trade unionism has, in some interpretations, generated a 'representation gap' (Towers 1997). Although the statutory union recognition procedure has generated an increase in

Table 6.3 Union density by sector and industry, UK 2008 (selected industries)

	Union density (%)
All	27.4
Private sector	15.5
Public sector	57.1
Education	54.1
Electricity, gas, and water	41.7
Health and social work	40.7
Transport, storage, and communication	39.2
Financial services	20.8
Manufacturing	20.4
Construction	14.5
Wholesale, retail, and motor trade	11.1
Hotels and restaurants	5.3

Source: Barratt (2009)

SECTION SUMMARY AND FURTHER READING

- For much of the twentieth century union membership increased; it became a particularly prominent feature of some industrial sectors, for example, manufacturing. By the 1960s and 1970s union membership among white-collar workers had become commonplace.

- Trade unions represent the interests of workers by providing them with protection, or insurance, against problems that affect them at work, bargaining collectively with employers on their behalf, acting as a workplace advocate, and in the broader, political arena.

- Since the 1980s, there has been a marked fall in the overall level of trade union membership in Britain. This has been caused by a combination of factors, including the changing composition of employment, employer policies of union exclusion, the hostile anti-union policy climate propagated by Conservative governments, and the perceived weakness of the unions themselves.

- While the fall in overall union membership is perhaps the starkest dimension of union decline, it is just one aspect of the broader diminution of union power, something that also includes the contraction of collective bargaining coverage and dwindling numbers of workplace union representatives. The result has been a growing 'representation gap' across British workplaces.

For an overview of union membership trends and the factors that influence them, see Waddington (2003b) and Fernie (2005). The UK's Department of Business, Enterprise, and Regulatory Reform produces an annual study of trade union membership data (see Barratt 2009). For a study of the rise of the representation gap in Britain and the United States, see Towers (1997).

 Visit our Online Resource Centre for web links to sites connected to this section. www.oxfordtextbooks.co.uk/williams_adamsmith2e

the number of recognition agreements (see Chapter 5), it has not reversed the declining trend of union recognition. In the rest of this chapter, we consider the implications for worker representation of three developments in contemporary employment relations, and whether or not they are likely to close the representation gap: the evolution of non-union systems of employee representation; partnership agreements between employers and unions; and the development of a more explicit concern with organizing new members evident in some parts of the trade union movement.

6.3 Non-union forms of employee representation

The scale of the crisis of union representation in Britain has raised questions about whether the 'single channel' of trade unionism and collective bargaining necessarily guarantees workers influence over their working lives (e.g. Frege 2002; Rogers and Streeck 1995). Would a system of works councils, as is found in many European countries, be an effective alternative? The German 'dual system' of employee representation (see Box 6.2), based on the formal separation of collective bargaining from

INTERNATIONAL PERSPECTIVE 6.2

The system of works councils in Germany

Collective bargaining in Germany is largely conducted at multi-employer level between trade unions and employers' associations. Works councils, however, which can be established in all private sector companies with five or more employees and which enjoy specific rights to information, consultation, and co-determination, are technically independent of the unions. Co-determination, which in effect allows the works council the right to reject management proposals, applies to 'social' issues, including payment methods, overtime arrangements, and the allocation of working hours. Works councils have information and consultation rights over matters pertaining to, among other things, the working environment, job design, and new technology; and information rights on financial issues.

Works councillors are elected by the entire workforce, have a term of office of four years, and are obliged by law to cooperate with management 'in a spirit of mutual trust' for the benefit of employees and the establishment. While the powers of works councils should not be overstated, their presence places considerable limits on the ability of managers unilaterally to reform working conditions (Hyman 1996: 71). Nevertheless, their formal separation notwithstanding, there is a strong 'mutual dependence' between the unions and the works councils (Jacobi, Keller, and Müller-Jentsch 1998: 212). Moreover, despite being prohibited from being involved in collective bargaining, in some instances works councils negotiate improvements to industry-level collective agreements (Tüselmann and Heise 2000).

participation rights, has received a considerable amount of attention as a result (e.g. Towers 1997). Within the trade union movement itself there has been some attention given to alternative ways in which employees can have their interests represented, not least because of the dwindling significance of the 'single channel' of trade union representation (Gospel and Willman 2003).

In this section we assess the phenomenon of non-union employee representation in Britain and explain why it has become such a relevant contemporary topic. This is in the context of a growing concern with understanding the operation of different arrangements that enable workers to express voice at work. We also consider the implications of relevant European Union legislation, particularly the Information and Consultation Directive and the European Works Councils Directive.

6.3.1 The development of non-union forms of employee representation

There is nothing new about non-union systems of employee representation. In Chapter 1 we examined the nature of joint consultation arrangements in Britain, acknowledging that they can exist in unionized and non-unionized firms alike. Historically, though, consultation was treated as inferior to, and less desirable than, collective bargaining as a method of articulating workers' interests, particularly by trade unions (Marchington 1994). This is because consultation managers retain the right to make the final decision, whereas bargaining entails that managers may have to compromise, and moderate their objectives, in order to produce a negotiated, and thus jointly agreed, settlement to a problem or dispute.

The decline of union representation highlighted in Section 6.2.3 has prompted a growing level of interest in the role of non-union systems of employee representation (Dundon and Gollan 2007; Gollan 2007; see Box 6.3). Generally, non-union employee representation arrangements are established by employers with the purpose of enabling managers to inform and consult with staff, often by means of elected or appointed employee representatives. Yet the most notable consequence of the diminishing significance of the 'single channel' of employee representation through collective bargaining by trade unions is that many employees go without any kind of representation at all.

Over four-fifths (83 per cent) of private sector workplaces do not have any arrangements, union or non-union, that enable employees to have their interests represented. Only just over a half of all employees (51 per cent) work in workplaces where representation, either through a union or some kind of non-union system, like a company council, for example, is available (Charlwood and Terry 2007: 323). Yet the use of non-union employee representation arrangements is far from common, suggesting that in the absence of unions employers generally prefer to establish more direct forms of dialogue, using communication methods such as team briefings, for example (see Chapter 8), or nothing at all.

Growing interest in alternative methods of representing employees' interests has generally taken the form of attempts to understand the different ways in which workers can express their voice at work. Essentially, 'voice can be described as methods that provide for employees to have a say in matters that affect them' (Dundon and Rollinson 2004: 56–7). Whereas employee voice has traditionally been associated with union representation, the concept has increasingly been stretched to encompass alternative ways in which employees can articulate their interests, like machinery for raising individual grievances, for example, or arrangements that allow staff to communicate their views to management. See Box 6.3 for details of how the activities of civil society organizations provide workers with voice. Managers in non-union firms generally interpret voice as

---

Employment relations reflection 6.3   Representing workers' interests beyond the workplace

Much of the interest in non-union forms of employee representation has justifiably been concerned with workplace-based arrangements, like systems for informing and consulting with staff, for example. However, bodies which operate outside the workplace, in society at a large, may also act in ways that help to protect and support the interests of workers. Civil society organizations (CSOs) include charities, pressure groups, and other non-governmental organizations. Some provide workers with advice, support, and legal representation. The gay rights organization Stonewall, for example, sometimes sponsors legal cases by workers who have been discriminated against on the grounds of their sexuality. CSOs lobby governments for legislative and policy changes that benefit workers, including better family-friendly working rights. They often work with employers to improve conditions for workers who often suffer from employment disadvantage, for example migrant workers. CSOs also sometimes campaign alongside trade unions to improve the pay and employment conditions of specific groups of workers, such as homeworkers (Heery, Abbott, and Williams 2009).

involving the 'transmission of ideas to managers in order to improve organizational performance' (Dundon et al. 2005: 312).

This is a unitary conceptualization of employee voice. The purpose of allowing employees to have a say over decisions that affect them at work is to help realize the goals of the organization more effectively, part of a 'sophisticated HRM' (see Chapter 5) approach to managing the workforce. This should be contrasted with union-based voice arrangements, which are rooted in the pluralist assumption that employees have different interests to those of their employers which may come into conflict and thus need reconciling.

Nevertheless, the diminution of trade unionism, and of collective bargaining (see Chapter 7), have focused attention on alternative means by which workers can express their voice at work, and ensure that their interests are represented. But what has prompted employers to consider non-union systems of employee representation, in the form of arrangements that enable managers to inform and consult with employee representatives, for example? It is worth emphasizing that non-union employee representation is generally restricted to arrangements that enable employees or their representatives to be informed and consulted about decisions; unlike collective bargaining they rarely encompass negotiation. Three main factors are evident.

First, non-union systems of employee representations are sometimes used as part of 'sophisticated HRM' approach (see Chapter 5), part of a range of techniques for managing people at work that helps to enhance business performance. Among other things, non-union systems of employee representation can be used to improve communications with staff, to enable employees to raise and articulate any grievances, or as a way of facilitating organizational change (Gollan 2007). Where employees have some influence, or 'voice', over decisions that affect them at work, it is thought that positive business benefits arise.

For example, the Pizza Express chain of restaurants established an employee forum in the aftermath of a damaging dispute concerning its failure to comply with the National Minimum Wage regulations governing tips. Management considered that a more open, transparent, and rigorous system of communications could be used to demonstrate to staff that Pizza Express was a good employer, improve levels of organizational commitment, and enhance business performance (Cooper 2001; IDS 2002).

The development of such a 'business case' for operating non-union systems of employee representation is a notable feature of contemporary employment relations since they are designed to influence the attitudes and behaviour of employees. This runs counter to the long-established assumption that 'the basis for employee participation lies in employee rights to have their views and interests taken into account in managerial decision-making; that is, the fundamental point of employee participation is to shape employer rather than employee attitudes and behaviours' (Hall and Terry 2004: 216). The outcome of employee representation arrangements that are driven primarily by a desire to improve organizational performance is a highly restricted form of employee voice, one over which management enjoys significant control (Hall and Terry 2004).

However, it is not clear that employers in general recognize the supposed benefits of operating non-union systems of employee representation. In the early 2000s, the proportion of workplaces where workers had no access to consultation arrangements increased, from just over a half to three-fifths of workplaces. Where unions are not recognized, the decline in the prevalence of workplace-based consultation arrangements was particularly notable, falling from an already low figure of 14 per cent of workplaces in 1998 to just 8 per cent in 2004 (Kersley et al. 2006). Non-union systems of employee representation are present in only a small—and declining—proportion of workplaces.

A second factor which explains managerial interest in non-union systems of employee representations concerns the desire to avoid, or discontinue, union recognition. In other words, they are designed to act as a substitute for union representation, helping to preclude an 'active union presence' (Gollan 2007: 104). Some of the enthusiasm for non-union systems of employee representation is linked to the introduction of the statutory union recognition procedure discussed in Chapter 5, and is best understood as an attempt to avoid unionization.

Gall and McKay (2001: 103) note that 'consultative' or 'representative' forums are more commonplace in situations where the employer is keen to resist a union presence. In the manufacturing company 'Aeroparts' an employee council was established 'explicitly as a mechanism for union substitution', after the trade unions there were derecognized following a change in company ownership (Lloyd 2001: 323). Although the principal stated objective of the 'employee forum' at Pizza Express was to improve internal communications, and thus increase employee commitment, it is evident that managers were also concerned that allowing employee grievances to go unvoiced might have provided a union with an opportunity to establish a presence.

The implementation of European Union (EU) legislation concerning information and consultation rights for workers is the third main reason why some employers have evinced an interest in non-union systems of employee representation. Before the 1990s obligations to inform and consult with staff with regard to redundancy situations and health and safety matters were generally restricted to unionized employers, who could make use of union representatives (e.g. health and safety committees). However, the UK government was required to extend the obligation to inform and consult with staff on these matters to non-union employers too.

The 1998 Working Time Regulations (see Chapter 7) established the concept of the 'workforce agreement' concept, something that was also a feature of legislation on parental leave (see Chapter 4). Workforce agreements 'are intended to offer employers without union recognition agreements the same flexibility in the application of the Regulations as that available through collective agreements with trade unions' (Hall and Terry 2004: 209). The idea is that non-union employers have a representative body of employees in place with whom they can negotiate.

In public policy terms these developments were rather significant (Dickens and Hall 2003; Hall and Edwards 1999). For one thing, under certain circumstances employers became obliged to establish formal information and consultation arrangements, involving elected employee representatives, a marked shift in emphasis away from the previously voluntarist approach. Second, although 'piecemeal' and 'issue-specific' (Dickens and Hall 2003), the legislation nonetheless started to erode the hitherto dominant single-channel system of employee representation in Britain. In later sections we consider the implications of two pieces of EU legislation brought in under the 'Social Chapter' which are specifically concerned with information and consultation arrangements, the Information and Consultation Directive (6.3.3) and the European Works Council Directive (6.3.4), respectively.

Changes in the law, and the encouragement given to non-union arrangements, mean that the pattern of employee representation has become increasingly complex and fragmented (Gospel and Willman 2003). While the single channel of union representation remains important in some areas, in the public sector, for example, and among large private employers, its significance has markedly waned. While around a half of employees have no access to representation at all, non-union arrangements, of the type we describe below, have attracted greater interest.

Charlwood and Terry (2007) point to the growing importance of hybrid approaches to employee representation. This is where some employees in the same firm have access to union representation, and others non-union arrangements, or no representation at all. The erosion of the single channel of representation even in unionized firms, and the rise of a hybrid approach, signal the 'gradual displacement of union by non-union forms as employers seek to persuade employees that they can enjoy the benefits of representation without the costs of union membership' (Charlwood and Terry 2007: 336). Evidently, non-union forms of employee representation are worthy of greater consideration.

6.3.2 Non-union systems of employee representation in practice

Studies of how non-union systems of employee representation operate in practice demonstrate that, while they can sometimes offer some limited benefits, overall they are inadequate substitutes for trade unions when it comes to articulating the interests of employees. This is primarily because they operate as managerial tools, lack the power to challenge managerial decisions, and are therefore not seen as representing the interests of employees effectively. Being too closely controlled by managers, non-union systems of employee representation thus lack legitimacy.

The case of manufacturing firm 'Aeroparts', which had derecognized its trade union and sought to replace it with an employee council, highlights some of the problems associated with non-union systems of employee representation (Lloyd 2001). Office workers were cautiously favourable about the employee council, because it made for better communications, and improved relations with management. This was largely due to the inactivity of their union when it had been recognized, or because workers had not been union members anyway. Any initiative, however modest, was considered to be an improvement.

Shopfloor workers, however, overwhelmingly wanted to see a return to union representation. The employee council did not have the power, the independent power free from managerial control, that the trade union had enjoyed. Thus it was not perceived as an effective constraint on managerial prerogative. As one front-line manager admitted, 'since the introduction of the EC [employee council] the company have managed to bulldoze through any policy they feel fit, with hardly any kickback from employees', and that the 'things I do now, I wouldn't have dreamt of doing in a trade union environment because I know I can get away with it' (quoted in Lloyd 2001: 322).

Non-union systems of employee representation, precisely because they are management tools, rarely have sufficient power to influence managerial decision-making, and are thus viewed by employees as ineffective arrangements for protecting and supporting their interests at work. In a study of non-union employee representation at the Eurotunnel call centre, Gollan (2003) discovered that managers largely saw the company council as a vehicle for communicating information to staff rather than giving them voice. Most employees surveyed 'stated that the company council was not effective in representing general employee interests' (Gollan 2003: 537).

In another case, that of 'Liftco', the non-union consultative committee was held up by the company as evidence of its participatory style of management. A large majority of employees voted against unionization in a recognition ballot. However, the economic recession of the early 1980s meant that 'Liftco' needed to cut costs. It proposed reductions in working time, redundancies, and a pay freeze, and sought employees' views on the latter directly, by-passing the consultative committee. The committee's employee representatives all resigned, claiming that it had been ignored. Systems of non-union representation may be feasible when business conditions are favourable, but lack the independent power to challenge the employer when people's jobs, pay, and conditions are threatened (Terry 1999).

For all these reasons, then, non-union employee representation systems are generally viewed as ineffective substitutes for a union presence. Based on research into non-union employee representation in a number of firms, Gollan (2007: 130) found that 'many employees felt their respective representation structures lacked the effectiveness and power required for effectively representing their interests' (Gollan 2007: 130). Thus they are not seen by the workforce as an effective substitute for union representation. In both Eurotunnel and South West Water, for example, attempts to replace unionized systems of employee representation with non-union arrangements proved to be unsuccessful, as unions regained recognition rights (Bonner and Gollan 2005; Gollan 2007). While non-union systems of employee representation might be appropriate arrangements for communicating with staff in firms where support for unionization is minimal, by no means can they be considered as an effective substitute for union representation.

Overall, it is evident that non-union systems of employee representation do not give employees effective representation at work. These forums are generally management devices to improve internal communications, rather than arrangements for giving employees genuine influence, in a way that enhances, rather than restricts, managerial prerogative. Nevertheless, we should not assume that dissatisfaction with non-union forms of employee representation necessarily equates to a demand for unionization. In the case of Eurotunnel, for example, some employees would have preferred a company council that had teeth to union representation (Gollan 2003).

6.3.3 The implementation of the Information and Consultation Directive

Along with the European Works Council Directive (see 6.3.4), the most significant piece of European Union (EU) legislation that deals with information and consultation matters is the Information and Consultation Directive, which was agreed in 2002 and implemented in the UK by means of the Information and Consultation with Employees (ICE) Regulations 2004. The purpose of the Directive was to ensure that employers have arrangements in place for informing and consulting with their staff. The legislation establishes the circumstances under which employers may be obliged to inform and consult with employee representatives over certain matters, including likely employment changes, for example, and to ensure that staff are kept informed about matters such as business performance (see Gollan and Wilkinson 2007: 1146).

For a number of years beforehand, the Labour government in the UK had strenuously opposed the Information and Consultation Directive. By 2002, however, it found itself unable to block the measure since, under the system of qualified majority voting (see Chapter 3), there was insufficient opposition on the EU's Council of Ministers to prevent it from being enacted. Nevertheless, lobbying from employers meant that one of the government's main objectives when designing the ICE Regulations was to ensure that firms were given a considerable amount of flexibility over their information and consultation arrangements (Hall 2006; Hall and Terry 2004). The government emphasized that legislation should focus on helping employers 'to develop their own arrangements tailored to their particular circumstances, through voluntary agreements' (DTI 2003: 5).

A further aspect of the government's approach to implementing the Information and Consultation Directive was to stress the positive contribution that employee involvement can make to business performance (Gollan and Wilkinson 2007). In other words, arrangements for informing and consulting staff should be viewed primarily as managerial tools, designed to help employers realize their business goals, not to enhance the representation of workers' interests in the employment relationship.

The implementation of the ICE regulations was staged. Initially, in April 2005 they applied to employers with 150 or more employees; coverage was extended to all employers with 50 or more employees in 2008. Their main features include:

- there is no automatic obligation on employers to establish arrangements for informing and consulting with employees or their representatives; at least 10 per cent of the workforce must submit a written request, either to the employer or to a state body—the Central Arbitration Committee (CAC);

- in the event of a valid request, arrangements must be put in place to enable appropriate employee representatives to be elected or appointed;

- the employer and employee representatives then have six months to reach a negotiated agreement governing the operation of information and consultation arrangements;

- in some circumstances an employer is entitled to claim that employees are already covered by appropriate information and consultation arrangements. So-called 'preexisting arrangements' must satisfy certain conditions (e.g. they have to be in writing and cover all employees);

- where there is a pre-existing arrangement in place, then any request to change it must be supported by a majority of employees in a ballot, and by at least 40 per cent of all those eligible to vote (including abstainers); and

- where a valid request is made, but is ignored by an employer, or where negotiations do not produce an agreement within the six-month time period, then a statutory model procedure for information and consultation, as prescribed by the Regulations, applies.

How likely is it that the ICE Regulations will help to enhance the representation of workers' interests by strengthening provisions for informing and consulting with employees in British workplaces? While it is too soon to determine the effects of the ICE Regulations with any degree of certainty, the government's emphasis on implementing the legislation in a way that prioritizes business flexibility means that we should not expect them to have a major impact. For one thing, the need for a written request from at least 10 per cent of the workforce before an employer is obliged to negotiate over information and consultation arrangements is a sizeable obstacle (Hall and Terry 2004).

Moreover, the ICE Regulations also permit employers to obtain their employees' agreement to 'direct' forms of information and consultation, that is directly between managers and staff, without the need for employees to have representatives to act on their behalf (Hall 2006). This is consistent with the government's view that informing and consulting with employees should primarily be seen as a means of involving staff, improving their commitment to organizational goals, and thus enhancing business performance, and not as a means of enabling them to have their interests more effectively represented.

Some initial work has been undertaken to assess the implications of the ICE Regulations, based on case study research (e.g. Hall 2006; Hall et al. 2007). A key finding is that the legislation has stimulated a limited amount of activity from employers to establish information and consultation arrangements, beyond that which already exists. The flexibility permitted by the ICE Regulations has prompted a 'risk assessment' rather than a 'compliance' approach (Hall 2006). In other words, some employers have been concerned to review, alter, and strengthen their existing information and consultation arrangements to ensure that they are in a robust position should a valid request from employees materialize. A good example of this concerns the non-union retail chain B&Q, which revised its 'Grassroots' system of employee consultation in the light of the ICE Regulations (Hall 2006).

Few employers anticipated that their employees would actually make a valid request; and there have been few moves to establish pre-existing arrangements (Hall 2006). Given the emphasis in the legislation on encouraging employers to improve their information and consultation arrangements voluntarily, there is considerable scope for them do very little, or even nothing at all. Therefore, it is inappropriate to refer to employers having to *comply* with the ICE Regulations, since the term implies that requirements that they are obliged to uphold actually exist, which is generally not the case.

While we may have to wait a little longer for the impact of the ICE Regulations to be properly evaluated, particularly as they were only fully implemented in 2008, on its own it seems unlikely that the ICE legislation will provide a major boost to information and consultation activity by employers. The trade unions have reacted to the legislation cautiously. On the one hand, it gives them an opportunity to secure a foothold in non-union firms by organizing a request for information and consultation arrangements, for example, or by using information and consultation machinery as a platform for union representatives. On the other hand, the legislation provides unionized employers with an opportunity to challenge existing union-based representation arrangements centred on collective bargaining (Hall 2006).

6.3.4 European Works Councils

European Works Councils (EWCs) are transnational arrangements for informing and consulting with employee representatives on a Europe-wide basis. In 1994 European Union (EU) legislation, in the form of the European Works Council Directive, provided for the establishment of transnational information and consultation machinery in 'community-scale undertakings'—multinational companies that employ at least 1,000 employees in the European Economic Area (EU member states plus Iceland, Norway, and Liechtenstein), including at least 150 in each of two or more of these countries. The purpose of the EWC directive was to promote more effective information and consultation arrangements in multinational firms operating within Europe.

EU policy-makers had long sought to enhance information and consultation arrangements in multinational firms operating within Europe. However, the completion of the Single European Market, and the process of internationalization it encouraged, meant that there was greater pressure to institute arrangements that would allow employees to influence corporate decisions increasingly being made at a European level (Hall and Marginson 2005). The aim of the EWC Directive was to ensure that worker representatives are informed and consulted about matters with a transnational bearing including, among other things, the economic and financial situation of the firm, likely employment trends, the implications of investment decisions, and substantial changes to working methods and production processes.

Article 13 of the EWC Directive gave multinational companies operating within Europe scope to develop their own machinery for informing and consulting with worker representatives. Until 1996, they were able to establish arrangements which could be 'tailored to the circumstances of the enterprise' (Carley and Hall 2000: 105). Some 400 'Article 13' agreements, as they became known, were eventually concluded, in firms such as Deutsche Bank and Unilever. Because the EWC Directive was enacted under the 'Social Chapter' (see Chapter 3), the UK did not come under its aegis until 2000, after the Labour government under Tony Blair reversed the 'opt-out' secured by John Major, his Conservative predecessor as prime minister. Nevertheless, a number of UK firms which had a substantial presence in other European countries, and were thus obliged to set up transnational information and consultation machinery for staff there, United Biscuits, for example, extended the coverage of their EWCs to the UK voluntarily.

After 1996, firms could no longer take advantage of 'Article 13' agreements; that route was closed. Instead, the mechanism for establishing EWCs is specified in Article 6 of the Directive, and involves the establishment of something called a 'Special Negotiating Body' (SNB). Firms that meet the definition of 'community-scale undertaking' are obliged to institute an SNB on receiving a written request from a hundred or more employees, or their representatives, in at least two EU member states; or they can set up one up voluntarily themselves.

The purpose of the SNB is to determine the constitution and procedure of the EWC, including its coverage (what areas of the firm and which employees it will cover), its scope (what issues it will handle), its composition (e.g. the balance between managerial and employee representatives, and the process for choosing employee representatives), and how it is intended to operate (e.g. the timing and format of EWC meetings), subject to certain minimum specifications set out in the Directive. Should the SNB process fail to reach agreement on how the EWC should operate, or where an employer ignores a valid request to establish an SNB, the EWC Directive lays down a default model, in the form of a set of 'subsidiary requirements' which have to be applied, such as a minimum of one meeting each year.

While there are no reported cases of the EWC's subsidiary requirements being put into effect, the content of so-called Article 6 agreements often resembles them in important respects (Hall and Marginson 2005: 206), suggesting that SNBs use them as a model when negotiating their own firm specific arrangements. See Box 6.4 for the details of an EWC agreement.

Consultation is limited by the directive to 'the exchange of views and establishment of dialogue' (Carley and Hall 2000: 105), and few companies went beyond this when instituting Article 13 EWCs (Marginson et al. 1998: 25). Panasonic, for example, emphasized that the scope of its EWC was strictly limited to 'consultation' as defined in the directive (Kalman 1999). Trade union bodies have criticized this element of the EWC Directive, contending that consultation obligations should be strengthened, something that has informed their approach to the revision of the EWC Directive. In particular, they argue that there should be a greater onus on firms to respond to proposals put forward by employee representatives in EWC meetings.

By 2004 around 1850 companies were estimated to be covered by the Directive (Hall and Marginson 2005); EU enlargement has increased this number. At the beginning of 2009, the European Trade Union Confederation (ETUC) claimed that some 2,300 multinationals were covered by the directive; and that 840 of them have EWCs in place (a 'strike rate' of 35 per cent). Remember that there is no obligation on eligible companies to establish EWCs without a valid request being made that triggers the SNB process.

Studies of EWCs show that they are marked by a high degree of variation. While most comprise both management and workers' representatives, some consist solely

---

⊙) INSIGHT INTO PRACTICE 6.4

The EWC agreement at Diageo

Diageo is a UK-based multinational drinks company whose brands include Baileys, Guinness, and Johnnie Walker. In 2002, it reached agreement with employee representatives on a revised EWC, known as the Diageo Europe Forum. The Forum, which meets once a year, comprises two senior management representatives and 35 employee representatives, drawn from across the company's European operations, though nearly half come from the UK (with ten representatives) and Ireland (seven). Half of the UK's representatives are trade union representatives, mainly from Diageo's Scottish operations, and half are non-union representatives, mainly from London. The Forum is designed to act as a vehicle by which Diageo can inform and consult with employee representatives on matters relating to, among other things, business performance, company strategy, the employment situation, organizational change, and the introduction of new working methods and production processes. While the approach to consultation is restricted to that laid down by the EWC Directive, namely the 'exchange of views and establishment of dialogue', the Diageo agreement specifies that the views of employee representatives must be heard, and that managers should respond to them in a timely fashion (EIRO 2002).

of workers' representatives. A typology of EWCs has been developed by Lecher et al. (2001) based on how active they are, as cited in Hall and Marginson (2005: 216):

- 'symbolic EWCs': are marked by a low level of information provision, with no formal consultation apparent;

- 'service EWCs': are marked by exchanges of information, without any sign that the EWC is developing its own distinct agenda;

- 'project-oriented EWCs': are marked by the tendency of workers' representatives to develop their own approaches relatively free from managerial control; and

- 'participatory EWCs': are marked by extensive and highly formalized consultation, and sometimes even negotiation, between workers' representatives and management.

There are a number of competing influences on how EWCs operate in practice. As we see below, a firm's product market strategy can exercise an important effect. EWCs tend to be more active in companies which have highly integrated, internationalized operations, relative to those whose product lines are more diverse and nationally oriented. The influence of the multinational's home country is also important; EWCs in UK-based companies, for example, tend to be less active than those whose headquarters are in France or Germany (Hall and Marginson 2005).

There are three major reasons why EWCs, as currently provided for by the EWC Directive, have been inadequate arrangements for improving the representation of workers' interests at a transnational level. First, they lack the power to influence managerial decisions effectively. This was evident in the case of the Swedish multinational companies studied by Huzzard and Doherty (2005), for example. Waddington (2006) surveyed EWC worker representatives in the engineering sector. In general, they did not consider that their respective EWCs had much of an influence over managerial decisions.

Second, linked to this the absence of a formal role for trade union representatives can contribute to the ineffectiveness of EWCs. One of the main weaknesses of the EWC Directive is that it does not provide for a formal trade union presence. Not only does this lead to a perception that EWCs are insufficiently powerful relative to management (Waddington 2006), but it may also help to legitimize union avoidance tactics. Panasonic, for example, needed to establish arrangements to select employee representatives to its EWC from its non-unionized sales company. Instead of extending union recognition, it chose to establish a new non-union consultative committee from which the EWC delegates could be nominated (Kalman 1999).

Third, studies of how EWCs operate indicate that in general they are seen by employers as a means of helping them realize their business objectives, rather than as arrangements that help to ensure that, through their representatives, workers have their interests protected. EWCs are used by senior managers as vehicles for communicating with staff, helping to disseminate information, and legitimize managerial decision-making (Redfern 2007). In the case of a UK-based manufacturing company, for example, interviews with worker representatives pointed to 'a concerted effort on the part of central management to use the EWC as a means by which to communicate the need for restructuring, to build company culture and to co-ordinate a Europe-wide strategic HRM policy' (Timming 2007: 255).

Article 13 agreements, in particular, tend to be used as managerially led devices to stimulate improved business performance through better communication with employees. In the case of the fast food chain McDonald's, for example, the EWC was used by the company as 'just another institution to be captured for management; another method of "getting the message across"' (Royle 2000: 193). In such cases, EWCs are primarily used as one of a range of techniques designed to improve the management of human resources in multinationals, rather than as arrangements for strengthening worker representation at a transnational level.

There are further factors, moreover, that limit the representational capacity of EWCs. Generally, there are few formalized arrangements that enable EWC representatives to forge effective relationships with national-level systems of information and consultation (Waddington 2006). Language barriers and national differences of interest inhibit collaboration between representatives from different countries (Wills 2000). The activity of worker representatives is often overly influenced by a national frame of reference, reflecting conditions in their home countries, rather than a genuinely transnational mode of understanding; though this may be changing as representatives develop a more 'European' outlook (Waddington 2006).

It is unlikely that, by themselves, EWCs can radically improve the prospects for worker representation at transnational level. This is clear from a case study of how the EWC in an unnamed multinational manufacturing and merchanting company operated. Genuine consultation was rare; managers came to EWC meetings to report on decisions that had already been made. Delegates had no opportunity to challenge managerial decision-making or to influence decisions. According to a frustrated British representative: 'We should be able to challenge things. What happens now is we are just told things. The unions put forward an alternative plan and the company ignores it. That surely isn' right?' (quoted in Wills 2000: 94).

It would be wrong, though, to imply that EWCs have made no contribution to enhancing the representation of workers' interests at transnational level. While the EWC Directive does not give the unions a formal role, the presence of union representatives on many EWCs gives these bodies some degree of independence from managerial control (Marginson et al. 1998). Moreover, in some cases union representatives have used EWCs as mechanisms for building networks of international cooperation and information-sharing (e.g. Huzzard and Doherty 2005).

It is also important to recognize that the effectiveness of EWCs varies according to the presence of specific factors, particularly the extent to which production and other operations are integrated transnationally (Hall and Marginson 2005). In his study of six UK-based multinationals, for example, Redfern (2007) found that EWCs were more active, in terms of networking and information-sharing between representatives, in unionized companies with a single product line and a Europe-wide management structure. In the highly internationalized and integrated vehicle manufacturing sector, the trade unions have used EWCs as the building blocks of a stronger, more transnational union movement (Greer and Hauptmeier 2008). According to two leading experts on EWCs, although few of them 'would appear to have developed into effective means of employee interest representation at a transnational, European level, they remain relatively youthful structures that are taking both management and employee representatives into uncharted territory' (Hall and Marginson 2005: 217).

The future of EWCs, and the extent to which they operate in ways that advance the interests of workers at a transnational level, largely depends on the capacity of trade unions to cooperate across national borders and use them as vehicles for enhancing international labour solidarity. Changes to the EWC Directive may help. Following a long period of consultation, and in the face of resistance from the employers' body Business Europe, in December 2008 the EU Council of Ministers and the European Parliament reached an agreement on the contents of a revised EWC Directive. Once it takes effect, the modified directive will give trade unions a stronger role in EWCs. It also specifies more clearly what is meant by 'information' and 'consultation'. Where relevant, for example, EWCs will be entitled to be consulted before a decision is taken, rather than just about how it is implemented.

SECTION SUMMARY AND FURTHER READING

- The decline in the 'single channel' of union representation has prompted an increased amount of interest in alternative methods of promoting worker voice, non-union systems of employee representation, such as information and consultation arrangements, for example.

- Although there is a business case for systems of non-union employee representation, union avoidance and changes in the legal framework appear to be more important reasons for the development of information and consultation arrangements. They are typically established in order to enhance managerial prerogatives and undermine trade unionism, not to give workers adequate independent representation of their interests.

- The Information and Consultation with Employees (ICE) Regulations implement an EU Directive which is designed to ensure that staff have access to information and consultation arrangements. However, the government transposed the Directive in a way that minimizes its impact, not least because of the requirement that at least 10 per cent of employees make a written request for information and consultation arrangements before an employer is required to do anything.

- While there are signs that in some cases EWCs have developed their own distinctive agenda, and can operate in ways that support the transnational representation of workers' interests, overall the experience of EWCs in this respect has generally been rather disappointing. Indeed, they are often used more as additional channels which multinational companies can use to communicate with staff.

Hall and Terry (2004) provide a useful guide to the evolving statutory framework of information and consultation rights in Britain. See Hall (2006) for an initial assessment of the implications of the ICE Regulations. The most comprehensive study of non-union systems of employee representation is Gollan (2007). For an overview of EWCs, see Hall and Marginson (2005).

 Visit our Online Resource Centre for web links to sites connected to this section. www.oxfordtextbooks.co.uk/williams_adamsmith2e

---

6.4 **Partnership agreements**

While there is nothing new about cooperative industrial relations (Kelly 1998), one of the most striking trends of the 1990s and 2000s has been the growth in significance of partnership agreements struck between employers and trade unions. One of the main reasons why the partnership approach has generated so much interest in Britain is the novelty of the concept. Elsewhere in Europe the term 'social partnership', while it is employed with some flexibility, is commonly used to refer to the relationship between employers and unions (Ferner and Hyman 1998). In this section, we identify the main characteristics of the partnership agreements, look at why the concept of partnership has become so popular, examine the outcomes of partnership, and critically assess the contribution partnership working has made to closing the representation gap.

6.4.1 Partnership agreements in Britain

The greater encouragement given to the development of partnership working between employers and unions is a major feature of contemporary employment relations (Stuart and Martinez Lucio 2005). As we see below, when we examine the main features of partnership agreements, under partnership the emphasis is on promoting cooperative relations between managers and unions, to the benefit of all parties, including workers. While there is nothing new about cooperation in employment relations, the emphasis that has been placed on partnership is notable, and reflects the difficulties that unions face when attempting to use adversarial methods to realize their objectives, such as strikes and other forms of industrial action (see Chapter 9). Therefore, the emphasis on partnership must be set against the underlying background of union weakness, something that has constrained a more militant agenda.

The 1990s and 2000s saw a large number of partnership agreements being struck between employers and unions, involving such well-known companies as Barclays Bank and Legal and General. Perhaps the most prominent agreement was the one signed in March 1998 by the leading supermarket chain Tesco, Britain's largest private sector employer, and the Union of Shop, Distributive and Allied Trades (USDAW). Tesco managers contended that employee representation methods in the company were no longer appropriate for the more competitive and dynamic environment in which the retailer operated, and which demanded greater employee flexibility and commitment. They were also concerned that the ritualized process by which the annual pay rise was agreed—it involved a ballot of union members—generated too much conflict, and that non-union members lacked an adequate voice. The company considered a range of options, one of which was to derecognize USDAW, even though more than a half of store staff were union members (IRS 1999).

The partnership agreement was developed over several months with the help of academics at Cranfield School of Management, and received the support of USDAW members in a ballot. The agreement comprised nine 'pillars of partnership', including 'effective representation', 'genuine consultation', 'reliable communication', 'sharing values and culture', and a 'sharp business focus' (IRS 1999). As part of the desire to allow all employees a voice, consultative staff forums were established in all Tesco stores, to which non-union employees could be elected, although each had to include a union representative. These workplace forums sent representatives to three regional forums which elected the national forum responsible for discussing the annual pay review and other major business issues (Tailby and Winchester 2000). Following the conclusion of the partnership agreement, USDAW benefited from an increase of nearly 20,000 in its Tesco membership, and a 20 per cent rise in the number of its workplace representatives (Haynes and Allen 2001).

This case study of a well-known partnership agreement is a useful starting point for an assessment of the components of partnership in practice. USDAW maintained its presence in the company, but lost its monopoly of employee representation, and gave managers more scope to secure employment flexibility. However, critics inside the union accused USDAW of being too cooperative with Tesco, and complained about the overly collaborative nature of the partnership agreement (IRS 1999). Studies of partnership deals indicate that they generally include:

- a shared commitment on the part of the unions and management to business success;
- employer guarantees about job or employment security;
- union agreement to more flexible working practices; and
- new forms of information and consultation arrangements, perhaps to the extent that unions are involved in strategic business decision-making (Kelly 2004; Terry 2004).

In general, partnership agreements involve trade unions agreeing to the establishment of new forms of employee involvement and representation, including the abandonment of the commitment to the 'single channel' of union representation, and accepting greater job flexibility. In exchange, employers offer employees enhanced employment security, a greater stake in the financial success of the company, and better information and consultation arrangements. However, the concept of partnership is rather ambiguous (Stuart and Martinez Lucio 2005). While we have looked in broad terms at the main features of partnership agreements in general, they are marked by a large degree of variation.

As we see below, at the heart of partnership working is the notion that it benefits the employer, the recognized union, and the workforce at large too. Nevertheless, there has been a particular emphasis on the capacity of partnership working to revitalize trade unions, and enhance their capacity to represent the interests of working people (Stuart and Martinez Lucio 2005). As we will see, however, it is doubtful that the development of partnership in employment relations has strengthened trade unionism, and it is more likely to have weakened it.

6.4.2 Why partnership?

Employers have largely generated pressure for partnership (Oxenbridge and Brown 2005), as the case study of Tesco demonstrates. Two main factors explain the interest in partnership among employers during the late 1990s and the 2000s. For one thing, the political climate has encouraged greater partnership working (see below). Second, more importantly, perhaps, employers and managers support partnership working because it is seen to benefit them.

In the United States the concept of the 'mutual gains enterprise' has been developed to capture the ways in which employers can benefit from instituting cooperative management–union relationships, in particular by easing the introduction of new working practices and helping to boost business performance (Kochan and Osterman 1994). Advocates of partnership working contend that it not only benefits the workforce, who enjoy greater job security, are better informed about decisions, and who maintain union representation, but that it also contributes to improved business performance. Thus partnership is mutually beneficial for employers and employees.

There are two related ways in which partnership working is seen to produce business benefits through the mutual gains approach. First, it can assist managerial efforts to secure, and gain support for, organizational change (Oxenbridge and Brown 2005). In the case of Barclays Bank, for example, senior managers viewed a partnership agreement as essential in order to retain the cooperation of the recognized trade union, and thus avoid potentially highly damaging industrial action during a period of intense restructuring (Wills 2004b). In his study of a financial services firm, Samuel (2007) observed that the main managerial motive for developing a partnership approach was the belief that securing support from the unions would help the company adapt more effectively to changing market conditions.

The second way in which partnership working is held to be beneficial for business, through the mutual gains approach, is by ensuring that workers feel more involved, secure, and trusted. There is a presumption that if organizations want greater effort and commitment from their staff, then, in the interests of 'mutuality', they should give them opportunities to express their views (Guest and Peccei 2001). As we see below, however, some critical interpretations of partnership working contend that the main objectives of managers when developing partnership arrangements are securing a quiescent workforce and reinforcing managerial control (e.g. Danford et al. 2005).

As we saw in Chapter 3, one of the key features of employment relations policy under the Labour government since the late 1990s has been an emphasis on partnership. It has made money available in a special fund to support partnership working (see Box 6.5). For Stuart and Martinez Lucio (2005: 1), partnership 'has formed a critical part of the Labour government's new employment policy and forms a key plank of its modernisation of employment relations'. Speaking in 2000 at the TUC's Partners for Progress conference, the former prime minister Tony Blair emphasized that partnership is 'about modernisation and getting rid of old class legacies, it's about trust and co-operation and it's about bringing employee relations into line with a company's business position' (Danford, Richardson, and Upchurch 2002: 1–2).

LEGISLATION AND POLICY 6.5

The Partnership Fund

Between 1999 and 2004 the UK government operated a Partnership Fund which provided money to support partnership working. Over the five years of its operation, the fund supported 249 workplace projects in total, at a cost of over £12m. Among the joint employer and trade union projects which attracted funding were: an initiative by St George's Healthcare NHS Trust in London and the trade union Unison to tackle bullying and harassment in the workplace; and a collaborative effort between the GMB union and the National Library for the Blind to develop flexible working practices for the latter's staff. Not all the money, though, went to support joint working between employers and unions. For example, some non-union firms, such as Pizza Express, drew on the Partnership Fund to help develop their own information and consultation arrangements.

As we can see, the government's approach to partnership is founded on the belief that its principal aim is to support businesses; helping them to 'modernize' their employment relations arrangements in a way that encourages greater cooperation between managers and workers. Partnership is conceptualized in an explicitly unitary fashion (Ackers and Payne 1998). If there is a role for the unions, it is a very restricted one, limited to working with businesses in a cooperative way in order to improve competitiveness.

Why, then, have the unions embraced the partnership approach so readily, since, at first glance, it does not appear to be a very attractive proposition for them? In the case of Tesco, the union was concerned to maintain a presence in a company that employed a large proportion of its members. The possibility of derecognition would have weighed heavily in influencing the union's policy. In an otherwise hostile environment, partnership appears to guarantee the unions a presence, a degree of institutional security, and some, however limited, influence over organizational decision-making. In the case of Barclays, for example, partnership meant that the company was better able to 'implement change through consultation with the union, so making better decisions and minimizing obstruction to change', while the recognized union maintained 'employer support for its role and activities in the bank' (Wills 2004b: 335).

According to a leading union representative working in a National Health Service hospital, partnership enhances union input to the benefit of employees:

> We've got an opportunity to go in and comment on and respond to policies even before they have been offered as a formal paper. We can contribute to drafting them and I think that's what partnership means. It means taking full account and giving full weight to the staff side and their views. (quoted in Danford, Richardson, and Upchurch 2002: 20)

For the unions, then, partnership working is attractive because it enables them to maintain an organizational presence, and may even give them more influence over decisions (Guest and Peccei 2001).

6.4.3 The outcomes of partnership

To what extent do the outcomes of partnership agreements in practice match the expectations outlined above? The espoused benefits of partnership appear to make it a very enticing prospect for all the parties to the employment relationship. For employers, partnership working has a positive impact on business performance (for example, see Knell 1999). Moreover, the unions maintain a presence and have enhanced opportunity to influence organizational decision-making.

There are some suggestions that partnership working can strengthen trade unionism. In the financial services firm Legal and General, for example, the partnership agreement meant that while the union lost influence over pay determination, it gained more involvement over a wider range of issues, such as staff training and development. The union gained members, and also benefited from the development of a stronger cadre of activists, as a result of partnership (Samuel 2005).

Advocates of partnership claim that it also produces important benefits for workers: they are better informed and consulted about decisions, enjoy greater job security, and are represented by a union which has become more influential. Yet when we examine the outcomes of partnership in practice, we find that it is often used to undermine trade unionism and reinforce managerial control, with no real benefits for workers, repudiating the assumptions of the mutual gains approach.

Proponents of partnership agreements claim that they do not threaten trade unionism (Knell 1999). A closer examination of the evidence indicates that this is far from the case. For one thing, the representational capacity of the unions is often weakened by partnership. The role of the unions under partnership regimes may be restricted to an entitlement to be consulted about developments, rather than a right to bargain over them (Terry 2004). Moreover, as has already been noted with regard to the case of Tesco, management almost always drives partnership, often with the threat of union derecognition, or of major workforce reductions, hanging in the background if the unions do not concur (Kelly 2005). This was the case at both United Distillers and Allied Domecq, where partnership was initiated by the respective companies 'as part of a restructuring and closure package' (Marks et al. 1998: 217).

Within the labour movement, support for partnership is strongest among union leaderships and full-time officers, who may sign agreements over and above the heads of shop stewards (e.g. Marks et al. 1998). While these deals give unions 'institutional security'—that is, they help to secure a formal presence for the union at an organizational level—they nonetheless shift the balance of power firmly in favour of management.

In the case of Barclays, for example, although the recognized union secured greater access to, and influence over, organizational decision-making, this generated its own tensions. From the point of view of its members and activists, senior union representatives were too closely identified with managerial decisions. Therefore the union did not seem to be fighting on behalf of its members' interests as strongly as it ought to have done; it appeared to have developed a relationship with the bank that was too cosy and cooperative. According to one union member:

> How it seems to be working is that the union hierarchy go and have their meeting and discussions with the bank, negotiate whatever and they come back to me as a union member and say, 'this is what's been offered to you, this is the option, how do you feel about it?' I don't think we're actually consulted when it comes down to making any sort of hard-and-fast decisions as to what our contracts are going to look like. (quoted in Wills 2004b: 340)

Thus, one of the main dangers of partnership for the trade unions concerns the distance that is potentially opened up between those union representatives who are party to managerial decision-making, and use their position to influence it, and the members, who may become disillusioned about the extent to which, as they view it, the union is really representing their interests in opposition to management (see Oxenbridge and Brown 2004).

Partnership agreements can also be used as instruments for reinforcing managerial prerogative, further weakening the influence of the trade unions. Advocates of partnership working contend that its appeal to employers and managers rests upon the business benefits of involving workers, and of building cooperative relationships with unions, because of the mutual gains that transpire. In practice, however, managers often have less alluring motives for instituting partnership working.

Danford et al.'s (2005) study of two aerospace firms suggests that the 'business case' for partnership rests not so much on the desirability of achieving mutual gains, but rather on the belief that partnership working could enhance managerial prerogative by weakening trade union power. Managers often 'demanded a strengthening of their prerogatives and came to regard partnership as a means of further reducing union influence rather than fostering independent union participation' (Danford et al. 2005: 166).

Partnership agreements, because they have been jointly concluded, even if it is by senior officials on the union side, have a level of legitimacy that makes them difficult to counter, even when they have detrimental results for the employees and undermine workplace unionism. When shop stewards in a supermarket chain tried to represent workers' grievances, they were rebuffed, and told by managers that their actions ran counter to the provisions of the partnership agreement. Trade unionism, 'in the short term, is acceptable as long as it does not interfere with managerial prerogatives on the shop floor' (Taylor and Ramsay 1998: 137). At United Distillers, a shop steward explained how partnership had strengthened management power:

> The people who work with us day in day out in the office or on the lines haven't changed, and these people are still going to manage us in the way that they always have, except now they have got an agreement which the union signed up to and they will beat us with it. (quoted in Marks et al. 1998: 221)

How committed are managers to genuine partnership with the trade unions anyway? Agreements are generally concluded on the terms of the employer who would, ideally, prefer to manage in a non-union environment, but is willing to make a pragmatic compromise (Kelly 1998). Indeed, it should not be assumed that 'partnership' entitles the union to a presence at all. The government has emphasized the desirability of building partnerships between employers and employees, not trade unions (Hyman 2001b); and managers' attitudes to partnership indicate that they do not envisage much of a role for the unions (Guest and Peccei 1998).

There have been rather few efforts to assess the implications of partnership working for employees (though see Box 6.6 for an exception). Although there are cases where partnership seems to have contributed to increases in union membership, in Legal and General and Tesco for example, the presence of one key purported benefit for workers, the development of more effective union representation, generally seems to be absent. There is little evidence that partnership arrangements provide workers with genuine employment security. Indeed, organizations with partnership agreements have a higher rate of job losses than those without them in place (Kelly 2005). It is widely acknowledged, moreover, that partnership delivers little real employment security (Oxenbridge and Brown 2002). The few studies which compare workers in partnership organizations with those in similar non-partnership organizations indicate that for the most part it is those working in the non-partnership organization who have the more positive experiences (e.g. Badigannavar and Kelly 2004).

The extent to which partnership arrangements can be used to engage staff, and to give them a more positive experience of employment relations, depends on the attitudes of

Partnership at Borg Warner

Studies of partnership agreements that consider how far they benefit employees are rare. Suff and Williams (2004), though, asked employees at Borg Warner in South Wales, a manufacturer of specialist components and systems for vehicles that has developed a celebrated partnership approach with the Amicus trade union, about whether or not they had benefited from it. The 1997 agreement, known as the 'Margam Way', after the location of the plant, comprises a ten-point plan that, among other things, emphasizes the importance of transparency and good communications. Managers and union representatives cited the positive impact of partnership, in particular the way in which the development of cooperative relations enabled the business to grow.

What were employees' views, though? How did they experience partnership in practice? Most of those surveyed (57 per cent) thought it had improved their working lives, and had enabled the union to participate more effectively in organizational decision-making. Thus there was general backing for the partnership approach. Nevertheless, despite the emphasis on communications many staff felt that they had limited influence over decisions that affected them at work. While partnership had increased their job security, in general people considered themselves to be insecure, a reflection of the competitive market environment and the history of job losses in the plant. Job satisfaction was high; generally employees did not see this as a product of the partnership agreement. Although partnership had clearly cemented the reputation of Borg Warner as a 'good' employer, employees nevertheless exhibited a low level of trust in management.

In this case, a partnership agreement had secured important benefits for employees, and the plant had remained open, ensuring that jobs were saved. However, the level of cooperation between management and employees was strictly bounded, and fell well short of that proposed by the 'mutual gains' model. In the context of a market economy, in which workers have to be treated as disposable, as well as dependable, it is doubtful whether genuine partnership can ever be realized in practice.

managers. One of the workers in the supermarket chain studied by Taylor and Ramsay (1998) was not particularly impressed by the way in which partnership operated: 'They [managers] are in a people-oriented business but they do not treat all the people they deal with equally. They bend over backwards for the customers but they treat us like shit!' (quoted in Taylor and Ramsay 1998: 131). Employers might espouse the rhetoric of partnership working which presents it in attractive terms, but the reality as experienced by the workforce is often not so pleasant.

Overall, there is little support for the proposition that partnership working is associated with the elaboration of an approach to managing employment relations marked by mutual gains (Guest et al. 2008). Rather, partnership has been advanced primarily as part of an employer's agenda to circumscribe the influence of recognized trade unions and enhance managerial prerogative, with few genuine benefits accruing to workers.

6.4.4 Partnership: an assessment

While partnership working generally operates to the benefit of employers and managers rather than unions and workers, it can nonetheless enhance the scope of employee representation in a limited way. Not only do partnership agreements offer recognized unions some security and help to stimulate membership growth, as at Tesco, but they may also encourage a broadening of the bargaining agenda, to include quality of working life issues such as 'family-friendly' working practices, for example (Heery 2002; Terry 2004).

Moreover, the inherent ambiguity of the partnership concept may provide the unions with an opportunity to extend their organizational capacity. In Barclays, for example, the union benefited from a greatly enhanced system of workplace representation that extended union organization to parts of the company from which it had hitherto been absent (Wills 2004b). There is no accepted definition of the 'partnership' term, and it can be used both in a pluralist sense, as the trade unions do, and a unitary one, as do the government and employers (Guest and Peccei 2001). For Ackers and Payne (1998: 546), such ambiguity could be an asset for the unions. They may even be able to use the notion of 'partnership' rhetorically, as a way of extending their organization in circumstances where it would otherwise be difficult.

There is some evidence that this may have happened. The public services union Unison has extended learning opportunities for its members as a result of 'partnership' with some employers, who contribute towards the costs. But this is explicitly not a form of cooperative unionism. The provision of learning opportunities has enhanced the attractiveness of the union to potential members, increased existing members' identification with the union, and strengthened collective organization (Munro and Rainbird 2000). In some circumstances, then, a partnership approach need not be inimical to effective trade unionism and the representation of workers' interests.

Nevertheless, the overall assessment must be a negative one. Since they are arrangements that are designed to alter existing management–union relations, partnership agreements do little for the millions of workers without access to union representation (Badigannavar and Kelly 2004). Kelly (2004) observes that union organizing campaigns resulting in new recognition agreements have been more effective than partnership in extending unionization, and thus eroding the representation gap. This suggests that an adversarial approach, based around contesting the way in which employers manage employment relationships, is a more effective method of strengthening trade unionism than a cooperative partnership-based orientation.

Generally, the partnership agenda is firmly under the control of managements, and has for the most part been elaborated under conditions of union weakness (Kelly 2005). Even though partnership agreements may acknowledge that legitimate differences of interest exist between an employer and union, 'that is about all they do say, and the language is otherwise overwhelmingly unitarist in flavour' (Terry 2004: 212). While it is important to recognize that it may at least help to secure a trade union presence, partnership is a largely managerial initiative, one that reflects the general weakness of the union movement (Terry 2004), and does little to close the representation gap in British workplaces.

As the limits of the partnership approach become increasingly evident, it is notable that support for it has dwindled among a new generation of trade union leaders who are more sceptical about the benefits of the cooperative approach. By the late 2000s, moreover, the government's enthusiasm for partnership also seems to have dissipated (Guest et al. 2008). The future prospects for partnership in employment relations, then, are somewhat unclear.

SECTION SUMMARY AND FURTHER READING

- The development of partnership has been a notable feature of employment relations during the 1990s and 2000s. In general, partnership agreements offer workers the promise of greater employment security and new forms of employee involvement and representation, in exchange for union agreement to greater job flexibility and a more cooperative stance.

- Encouraged by the government, which saw partnership as a means of modernizing employment relations, employers have been the main protagonists of partnership working. The concept of mutual gains which underlies partnership implies that employers, unions, and workers all benefit from partnership working. In practice, however, partnership agreements largely serve the interests of employers, and are used as instruments that enhance managerial prerogative.

- While partnership agreements may help to secure the position of a recognized union, which may also be allowed some limited influence over organizational decision-making, this comes at the expense of workplace trade unionism, which is weakened by the shift in the balance of power in favour of management. Nevertheless, the inherent ambiguity of the partnership concept may in certain circumstances be used by unions to secure greater influence.

For overviews of the partnership phenomenon see Tailby and Winchester (2005: 430–41) and Terry (2004). The book *Partnership and Modernisation in Employment Relations* is an edited collection dealing with various aspects of partnership; the introductory chapter by Stuart and Martinez Lucio (2005) is particularly useful. Kelly (2004) provides an in-depth critique of partnership in employment relations. There are a number of good case studies of partnership available, for example at Legal and General (Samuel 2005), United Distillers, and Allied Domecq (Marks et al. 1998), and Barclays Bank (Wills 2004b), respectively.

 Visit our Online Resource Centre for web links to sites connected to this section. www.oxfordtextbooks.co.uk/williams_adamsmith2e

6.5 Organizing unionism

In 1899, the Workers' Union's first full-time district organizer, Will Buchan, initiated a recruitment drive at Sir Thomas Lipton's City Road warehouses in London. The 1,300 workers were badly paid, and experienced poor working conditions. As Hyman (1971: 19) reports: 'Girls worked a 10-hour day with only one half-hour break, carrying heavy loads in unhealthy conditions; often they fainted, and the time lost was deducted from their wages.' Perhaps unsurprisingly, Buchan's attempts to organize these workers met with considerable success at first, and a new branch of the Workers' Union was established. As the union became more powerful, however, Lipton took measures to undermine its position, and dismissed many of the leading union activists among the workforce. By early 1900, union organization in the warehouses had collapsed (Hyman 1971).

The Workers' Union was to go on to become one of the most important general unions in Britain during the first two decades of the twentieth century, eventually to become a part of the Transport and General Workers' Union (TGWU), which is now Unite. Nevertheless, its failure to secure a presence, because of intense employer hostility, at Lipton's warehouses in 1899, demonstrates that the process of organizing workers into unions can be a daunting task.

6.5.1 Trade unions and recruitment

By the second half of the twentieth century, union organizing activity had dwindled markedly in Britain (Beaumont and Harris 1990). Since the overall level of union membership, which was rising in most years, appeared to be determined principally by extraneous factors such as the business cycle and the public policy climate, and not by trade union activities themselves (Bain and Price 1983), it is scarcely surprising in retrospect that unions marginalized recruitment activity, even though such a reactive approach may have encouraged membership passivity (Hyman 1989). Understandably, unions tended to focus on providing representational services to existing members, like collective bargaining. Such a 'servicing' approach to trade unionism, which focuses on supporting the current membership, is to be contrasted with an organizing approach, one concerned with pursuing membership growth by organizing workers in new areas.

Given that there was some evidence to suggest that a union's policies could positively influence its membership levels (Undy et al. 1981), the precipitous decline in union membership during the 1980s and 1990s encouraged some unions to pursue explicit growth strategies. While this mainly took the form of 'market-share' unionism, whereby unions sought to gain members through mergers and amalgamations, thus increasing their share of the existing 'market' for trade union members without actually extending it (Willman 1989), by the early 1990s recruitment activity was gaining a higher priority.

One of the few unions to experience membership growth during the 1980s was the shop-workers' union, USDAW. While this was partly a reflection of increasing retail employment, the union's own recruitment efforts were also important. USDAW officials were mandated to spend a certain proportion of their time on recruitment activity (Upchurch and Donnelly 1992).

Elsewhere, union efforts to recruit new members met with limited success. The TGWU's 'Link Up' campaign, for example, aimed to: increase membership in workplaces where the union already had recognition; prioritize the recruitment of categories of workers who had previously been neglected by unions, such as part-time and temporary workers; and to build stronger links between the union and the wider community. The TGWU made some important recruitment gains as a result. However, while recruiting new members was found to be relatively straightforward, retaining them proved difficult. There was also internal opposition to the increased emphasis on recruitment from some union officials who were resistant to change (Snape 1994). Traditionally, most union officials' expertise lay in supporting and providing services to existing members, not in going out and finding new ones. This is something that has long inhibited recruitment and organizing activity by unions (Kelly and Heery 1994).

During the 1990s and 2000s, however, in Britain and elsewhere, there has been an increased emphasis on how unions themselves can rebuild their strength, and expand their membership, through intensive and focused recruitment activity. They have also attempted to develop a more effective internet presence (see the end-of-chapter case study). The establishment of the statutory union recognition procedure (see Chapter 5) has been an important catalyst; it encourages unions to build up membership in firms in order to be in a position to submit a claim for recognition. Some writers (e.g. Kelly 2005) argue that such an approach is more likely than partnership working to revitalize the trade unions.

Sometimes union organizing campaigns are successful; in 2003, the telecommunications company Telewest (now part of Virgin Media) recognized the Communication Workers Union (CWU) after a successful campaign. However, strong opposition to recognition from employers often renders organizing initiatives unsuccessful (Gall 2005).

As we see below, another source of change has been the experience of trade unions in other countries, notably the United States, where there has been a renewed emphasis on organizing new members. In the remainder of this section we consider the main features of the organizing model of trade unionism, explain why it has increased in significance, and consider its implications for the representation of workers' interests.

6.5.2 The characteristics of organizing unionism

The origins of organizing unionism in Britain can be traced to the 1996 launch of the TUC's 'New Unionism' project, one of the objectives of which was to 'promote organizing as the top priority and build an organizing culture' (TUC 1997: 39). While it was considered important to build union membership among the 4 million workers in Britain based in unionized workplaces but who were not members themselves, particularly in the short term, the TUC considered that this would not be enough to revive trade unionism on its own. Rather, the unions needed to 'break into new jobs and industries' and 'sharpen unions' appeal to "new" workers, including women, youth and those at the rough end of the labour market' (TUC 1997: 39).

The adoption of the organizing approach recognized the limitations of servicing unionism as a source of union resilience. The TUC acknowledged that some unions had enhanced their recruitment activities. However, influenced by the development of the organizing unionism model in the United States and Australia (Bensinger 1998; TUC 1997), it argued that a more strategic, encompassing approach was needed if unions were to recapture their vitality. What, then, are the principal characteristics of organizing unionism?

First, it is necessary to distinguish 'organizing' from 'recruitment'. With the latter the recruiter simply enrols the worker into the union and leaves it at that; 'organizing', however, goes further and, recognizing that retaining existing members can often be more difficult for unions than recruiting new ones, involves an ongoing process of developing and strengthening workplace organization (Heery et al. 2000c). In the United States, the 'union building' approach, in which existing members play an active part in organizing initiatives, has been shown to be more effective in expanding trade unionism (Bronfenbrenner and Juravich 1998).

Organizing unionism has also spread to New Zealand, where it has enjoyed some initial success. Following the introduction of a new law that heavily circumscribed union activity, in 1994 the Service Workers' Union (SWU), which mainly represented workers in low-paying jobs in the healthcare, cleaning, and hospitality sectors, initiated an organizing approach. The adoption of this new strategy was not determined by the union's leadership in isolation, but in the context of a commitment to, and a history of, building unionism from the bottom-up and of actively involving members and union activists themselves in the process of organizing. As Oxenbridge (1997: 21) explains, 'SWU leaders' values centred around the political education of members and a belief in the power of grassroots organizing methods which translated into a commitment to resourcing organizing reform initiatives'.

Second, organizing unionism is characterized by an emphasis on the unionization of groups of workers that the unions have largely neglected in the past, and who frequently suffer from labour market disadvantage. In Britain, the TUC has emphasized improvements to the representation of part-time and young workers (Heery 1998b; TUC 1997). In the United States, though, the organization of immigrant workers, particularly those from Latin America, is seen as crucial to the revival of the trade unions (see Box 6.7), notwithstanding the poor historical record of American unions in this area (Milkman 2000; Moody 1997).

 INTERNATIONAL PERSPECTIVE 6.7

'Justice for janitors' in Southern California

Perhaps the most notable example of the efforts of American unions to expand their memberships through 'organizing' has been the campaign to build trade union strength among office cleaning workers, or 'janitors', in Los Angeles, popularized by Ken Loach in his film *Bread and Roses* (2000). In the 1980s, competitive pressures encouraged building owners to contract out their cleaning activities, increasingly to non-unionized operators who were able cut costs by undercutting union pay rates and worsening conditions. Even though the office-cleaning industry boomed in this period, union membership declined. Contractors preferred hiring cheaper and supposedly easy-to-control immigrant workers from Mexico and Central America.

   The Service Employees International Union (SEIU) launched the 'Justice for Janitors' campaign in Southern California in 1988. After two years, it had enjoyed considerable success, including a recognition agreement at the Century City office complex in west Los Angeles. How was this achieved? First, many of the largely immigrant workers themselves were favourable to trade unionism. Not only were they becoming acutely conscious of their disadvantaged labour market position, and wanted to do something about it, but many also had activist backgrounds in their home countries. Moreover, the presence of dense community networks allowed trade unionism, once introduced, to flourish. Second, the SEIU itself played a crucial 'top-down' role in strategically planning the organizing campaign. The union devoted a major proportion of its budget—up to 25 per cent—to recruitment activity, in effect using resources gained from its existing members to find new ones. Third, Justice for Janitors used innovative organizing techniques to forge unionization. Significantly, union organizers eschewed the traditional route to gaining union recognition in the United States—building up membership before workers are balloted, in a 'representation election', to determine whether or not they want a union to bargain on their behalf. Instead, they used public demonstrations and 'in-your-face' campaigns to call for 'justice' and 'dignity' for janitorial workers, causing embarrassment for the companies using the offices. Thus pressure was put on the contractors, and also the building operators, to recognize and bargain with the union.

   Following its initial success, during the 1990s the Justice for Janitors campaign stalled somewhat. The principal challenge that faced the union was whether to focus on consolidating its membership base or to concentrate on organizing new workers. Nevertheless, in 2000 the Justice for Janitors campaign secured another notable victory after mobilizing public opinion in support of a successful campaign for a pay rise.

Sources: Erickson et al. (2002); Fisk, Mitchell, and Erickson (2000); Waldinger et al. (1998)

During the 2000s some unions in Britain have made efforts to organize migrant workers, many of whom are often exploited by unscrupulous employers who fail to respect their employment rights. For example, the GMB general union developed an initiative aimed at organizing Polish workers in two cities, Southampton and Glasgow. The GMB worked with local Polish community organizations, and set up dedicated union branches solely for Polish workers. Union officials were struck by the level of support for unionization. For unions like the GMB, organizing migrant workers is not only important because they are a source of new members, but also because it helps to prevent exploitation and the erosion of labour standards.

Third, perhaps the most distinctive feature of organizing unionism is the use of a specialized cadre of officials, whose task is to build union organization. After investigating the operation of the Organizing Institute in the United States and the Australian Congress of Trade Unions' 'Organizing Works' programme, since the late 1990s the TUC has operated an 'Organizing Academy', the purpose of which is to give union-sponsored trainees a year-long training programme combining classroom-based learning and real-life organizing activity with their union sponsors. 'The intended result is to produce a cadre of "lead organizers" who can plan and manage organizing campaigns and promote the cause of organizing across the British trade union movement' (Heery et al. 2000b: 400).

The characteristics of the early participants differed somewhat from those of traditional union officers. Most initial trainees were women under 30 years of age, who had a broad range of campaigning experience outside the union movement, though the majority had been union members (Heery et al. 2000b: 404). On completing their training, participants are well-placed to become dedicated union organizers who are able to use their skills to expand union organization in Britain.

Fourth, following on from this, the use of trainees has been associated with innovative organizing tactics (Heery et al. 2000b). One of the most distinctive features of organizing unionism is the use of novel techniques to encourage unionization. These include 'mapping' the workforce in particular establishments, identifying those workers who are more susceptible to trade unionism, and the choice of particular 'levers' or grievances that 'lead' union organizers can use to build support (Heery et al. 2000a: 40). In the United States, there has sometimes been a moral dimension to organizing initiatives as unions campaign on the basis of giving workers 'justice' or 'dignity', as in the case of the Justice for Janitors example (see Box 6.7).

6.5.3 Organizing unionism: an assessment

The organizing unionism approach is now sufficiently well-established for us to be able to consider its effectiveness. There is some evidence that unions have used it effectively to secure recognition from employers. The Communication Workers Union (CWU), for example, was recognized by 'Typetalk', a not-for-profit call centre service operated as a joint venture between a charity and the telecommunications firm BT, following an intense organizing campaign. The language used to frame the campaign was carefully fashioned. A contrast was drawn between the progressive policies the organization pursued with regard to its client base and its opposition to unionization. Union organizers developed a 'language of "dignity", "fairness" and "respect", stressing union membership as a human right and emphasising that the rights of employees were as equally important as the rights of clients' (Simms 2007: 125). They also identified a series of specific grievances, health and safety problems, for example, which they could use to mobilize support from the workforce for union recognition.

The recognition campaign also involved the establishment of an organizing committee, comprising union activists, who took the leading role in recruiting new members and raising awareness of the union's activities. A key objective was to 'encourage activists to be independent of officials and to address their own problems' (Simms 2007: 127). As a result, the organizing campaign was rather successful, in the sense of securing the objective of union recognition, despite managerial opposition to unionization. That said, however, the emphasis in the Typetalk campaign of organizing in the workplace means that union activists there are not effectively integrated within the structures of the wider union (Simms 2007).

Elsewhere, the effectiveness of organizing unionism has often been hindered by a number of major constraints (see Heery and Simms 2008). Clearly, the most important external obstacle has been employer opposition to union organizing initiatives. Gall's (2005) study of organizing campaigns indicates that opposition from employers is commonplace. Employer hostility to unionization in the charity Scope, for example, was a major reason why the organizing campaign there did not result in union recognition (Simms 2007).

Opposition from employers is not the only obstacle impeding the effectiveness of the organizing model, by any means. There are also some notable internal constraints within unions themselves. Two of these are particularly important: the resource-intensive nature of organizing campaigns and the lack of enthusiasm towards organizing evinced among some union officials. Organizing unionism demands considerable investment on the part of the unions involved (Simms 2003), something which may be lacking.

Unsurprisingly, perhaps, internal union opposition to the development of an organizing approach is also relatively widespread (Heery and Simms 2008). Union officials whose expertise is based on servicing existing members have understandably felt threatened by the increased emphasis on organizing, perceiving it as an added burden on top of their already heavy workloads, and thus a form of work intensification. This was the case in the MSF union, now part of Unite, where the adoption of an organizing initiative, and the emphasis on recruitment, resulted in other aspects of union activity, which might also have contributed to the development of union organization, being sidelined (Carter 2000).

The take-up of the organizing model in Britain has been restricted to a relatively small number of unions (Heery 2002). Some of the leading British trade unions, the GMB general union, for example, have not been involved in the Organizing Academy, sometimes preferring to establish their own initiatives (Daniels 2009; Heery and Simms 2008). They have been wary of the enhanced role being carved out by the TUC in this area, seeing it is a potential threat to their autonomy (Heery et al. 2000b).

While unions are taking recruitment more seriously, by employing more specialized officials, for example (Heery et al. 2000c), the extent to which organizing unionism has been adopted remains questionable. There remains a tendency among unions to consolidate their existing membership bases, rather than attempt to take the resource-intensive step of seeking to organize workers in areas of the economy where their presence is weak (Daniels 2009). A good example of this is the attempt by a higher education union to organize contract research workers in universities (Badigannavar and Kelly 2005).

Even where the organizing approach is pursued, unions appear to use selected elements of it in their recruitment campaigns, those that are most appropriate to their particular circumstances, rather than adopt the entire model. Person-to-person recruitment has been the most popular method, while workforce mapping appears to be relatively rare. Some use of a moral discourse of 'dignity' and 'justice' has been reported. A union organizing drive among restaurants in London's Covent Garden district was accompanied by pressure to establish a 'Respect at Work Zone'. Nevertheless, British unions have blanched at the overly evangelistic tone of some American organizing campaigns (Heery et al. 2000b; Heery et al. 2000c).

Two other difficulties with the organizing unionism approach have also been identified. First, the underlying assumption that workers are relatively easily organized, especially where they have demonstrable grievances, is often mistaken (Heery and Simms 2008). As Badigannavar and Kelly (2005) show in their study of contract university researchers, a number of factors, including the extent to which workers blame their employers for their grievances, and the degree to which they expect a union to remedy them, help to explain why some organizing campaigns succeed whereas others fail.

Organizing campaigns may also stall because the workers concerned do not identify with the union. There are 'instances of women, members of ethnic minorities and younger workers proving difficult to recruit because unions were not perceived as "their" institutions' (Heery and Simms 2008: 35). Organizing campaigns sometimes fail because unions are insufficiently attuned to, and respectful of, workplace diversity. Holgate (2005) studied a union organizing drive in a factory that makes sandwiches for high street retail outlets. The low-paid workforce comprised a large number of black and minority ethnic staff, many of them migrants, who were treated in ways that suggest the presence of racial discrimination. Although the organizing campaign led to an increase in union membership in the factory, from 40 to 150, it was not enough to secure recognition from the employer.

The effectiveness of the initiative was undermined by language difficulties and the presence of ethnic divisions within the workforce. Union officials also played down the relevance of racism, declining to use it as an organizing tool. As a result, 'the opportunity to organize around issues that the workers felt to be most important to them was lost, and the failure to acknowledge the racialized nature of the employment practices at the factory did nothing to build trust and respect in the union' (Holgate 2005: 475). Perhaps one way of overcoming such difficulties is for unions to engage with, and build a more effective presence in, local communities (see the introductory case study). Box 6.8 concerns the current efforts to develop community unionism.

A second difficulty with the organizing unionism approach is the contradiction that exists between, on the one hand, the need for union officials to exercise some degree of control and, on the other hand, the emphasis on encouraging workers themselves to organize and pursue unionization. Although without some degree of coordination from above it is difficult to see how unions can mobilize effectively to improve people's

Employment relations reflection 6.8   Community unionism

There has been an increasing recognition among some unions that in order to organize workers who suffer from labour market disadvantage more effectively, and to improve their livelihoods, the focus of union activity needs to extend beyond the workplace to encompass the wider community. There are three main types of community unionism.

First, some unions have themselves tried to develop a more community-based orientation. In the UK two trade unions, representing iron and steel workers and garment workers, respectively, merged to form a new union which they actually called Community. Both predecessor unions had deep roots in specific industrial communities but, because of economic change, membership levels were dwindling. The focus on community was designed to stem this decline (see the introductory case).

A second type of community unionism has become increasingly commonplace in the United States. It takes the form of organizations that support and campaign on behalf of workers who experience labour market disadvantage. Perhaps the best-known examples of this type of community unionism are the immigrant worker centres, organizations that work to improve the prospects of poorly- paid, vulnerable, and disadvantaged workers (Fine 2006).

A third type of community unionism involves joint initiatives between traditional labour unions and community-based organizations, such as faith groups. The idea is that broad-based coalitions can raise awareness of labour market disadvantage, and campaign for effective ways of reducing it, more effectively. The London Citizen's group and its London living wage campaign has been one of the most effective of its type in the UK (see Wills 2004a).

A greater emphasis on operating in communities offers unions certain advantages. Their activities there are not impeded by employer opposition, for example. Moreover, a community focus enables unions to engage with, and potentially represent, a more diverse workforce, helping to combat labour market disadvantage. However, there are some problems. The strength of the unions traditionally rests upon their workplace organization. Existing union members may be unhappy with, and challenge, efforts to develop a community orientation. Added to which, the interests of communities, and particularly community bodies, and unions may come into conflict. There has been opposition in some unions to working with faith bodies, because of a perceived prejudice against gay and lesbian people.

working lives, initiatives designed by union leaderships to boost workplace unionism may be of limited effectiveness since they are perceived to be bureaucratic interventions and thus lack support on the ground (Carter 2000).

Perhaps the best way of characterizing organizing campaigns is to see them as involving a degree of 'managed activism' (Heery et al. 2000c). To be effective they require coordination from above and management by union officials; but they also depend on the participation and activism of the workers concerned for their success. Rather than seeing coordination from above and participation from below as mutually exclusive, the concept of 'managed activism' implies that both can be effectively integrated. In her study of union organizing campaigns in the not-for-profit sector, Simms (2007: 131) contends that effective organizing campaigns benefit from a degree of top-down coordination, as well as the participation of workers themselves.

What, then, are the implications of organizing unionism for the representation of workers' interests? The approach has an ostensibly inclusive character, given that a leading objective is to expand union organization into areas where it has hitherto been weak and thus offer representation to workers who would previously have lacked it. However, most British unions have been reluctant to adopt organizing unionism whole-heartedly and have preferred to concentrate on building membership in areas of existing strength (Heery et al. 2003: 61).

Perhaps the most notable effect of the unions' dalliance with organizing, then, has been to reinforce their 'institutional security', in much the same way as the partnership approach. This is not, of course, something that should be derided. Robust trade union-ism is vital to the effective representation of workers' interests, and those who accept that there is an inherent imbalance of power in the employment relationship should welcome anything that secures a union presence. The challenge for the unions is how they can expand their representative capacity to cover the millions of British workers without the means of independent and effective representation at work. While 'organiz-ing has risen up the list of many unions' agendas over the last decade ... it is no panacea. In and of itself, it cannot reverse the severe decline [in union membership] that has occurred over the last three decades' (Daniels 2009: 275).

SECTION SUMMARY AND FURTHER READING

- While the recruitment of new members has always been an essential feature of union activity, influenced by developments in the United States during the late 1990s, there has been a marked revival of interest among unions in organizing workers, associated with the concept of 'organizing unionism'.

- The organizing unionism model is held to differ from traditional union recruitment effort in a number of key respects. First, it is concerned with 'union building', that is the ongoing development of workplace organization, and not just recruitment on its own. Second, it is designed to attract into union activity workers who have previously been marginalized by the union movement. Third, it involves specially trained union organizers. Fourth, it uses novel organizing techniques such as 'workplace mapping'.

- The diffusion of organizing unionism in Britain has so far been somewhat limited. Most unions remain conservative in their recruitment priorities. Moreover, attempts to initiate novel organizing campaigns have come up against both external constraints, like employer opposition, and internal obstacles, such as a lack of commitment from officials.

The series of articles written by Heery and his colleagues (Heery et al. 2000a, 2000b, 2000c) is very useful for the characteristics of organizing unionism. See Gall (2003d) for some useful case studies of union organizing in practice. For an overview of union organizing initiatives, see Daniels (2009). Heery and Simms (2008) assess the constraints on union organizing. Part of the TUC's web site is devoted to recruitment and organizing, and you can get details of its Organizing Academy at http://www.tuc.org.uk/organisation

 Visit our Online Resource Centre for web links to sites connected to this section. www.oxfordtextbooks.co.uk/williams_adamsmith2e

Conclusion

In this chapter, we have focused upon how workers' interests are represented. For many years in Britain, the trade unions have been responsible for representing workers' interests. By virtue of their collective organization, unions can provide individuals with protection, or insurance, against problems at work. They also bargain with management on behalf of their members, seeking to alter the terms of the wage-work bargain in favour of their members. Unions operate in the workplace itself, where the union representative, or shop steward, not only negotiates with management, but also advises, supports, and represents his or her members. Finally, unions represent the interests of workers in the wider political arena, by influencing the legislative process for example.

Nevertheless, the complex nature of workers' interests poses considerable challenges for unions as they attempt to carry out their representative functions. Workers generally want protection for themselves as individuals, but this requires collective action to be effective. Unions must therefore demonstrate their relevance to individuals, while at the same time operating as a collective agency on behalf of what may be a considerably diverse membership. Thus effective trade unionism depends upon the extent to which the unions are able to translate diverse, individual interests into collective action (Hyman 1994b).

Moreover, unions frequently face difficulties when seeking to construct a broader representative agenda. Campaigning on political and social issues can lead to discontent among members who, understandably, would prefer their union to concentrate its resources on representing their 'sectional' interests in the workplace rather than waste money, as they see it, on irrelevant causes. Thus unions are caught between narrow and broad understandings of interest representation (Hyman 1994b).

Perhaps the most important implication of this overview of employee representation in the workplace is that it is not representation mechanisms, by themselves, that give workers influence over the decisions which affect their working lives, but those that are effective (Kelly 1998). In the UK non-union systems of employee representation are generally used as management tools to improve communications, or to avoid a union presence. They lack the power and legitimacy of agencies that are independent of the employer, like trade unions, and thus do not help to offer workers adequate representation of their interests.

Although a trade union presence is a necessary condition of effective representation, it is not a guarantee. Invariably unions must strike a cooperative relationship with employers, if only to secure a presence, while at the same time acting to challenge their interests. The concept of 'partnership' has become popular among union leaderships specifically because, in a hostile environment, cooperation with employers is seen as the only way of guaranteeing 'institutional security'. But is this in the interests of their members? Clearly a union presence, however constrained, is important. Without it, workers would have little protection against threats to their pay and employment conditions. However, partnership agreements may not only damage workplace union organization, but also do not seem to provide workers with any real job security.

Finally, workers' interests are not constant, but are fluid, and subject to ongoing adjustments as the characteristics of their environments change. The process of interest representation does not simply mean that trade unions act on behalf of, or 'for', their members. Unions themselves play an active part in shaping, influencing, and controlling the interests of workers and thus exercising power 'over' them (Hyman 1975). In one sense, organizing unionism may be viewed as a kind of 'managed activism' (Heery et al. 2000c), something that enhances the power of union leaderships. Unions are to a large extent, however, agencies that embody the collective power of their members. Not only does this limit the authority of union leaderships, since policies depend for their effectiveness on mobilization from below, but it also highlights the tension that exists in all unions between the desirability of coordination from above by union leaderships and the pressure for democratic control from below.

Assignment and discussion questions

1   Critically assess the proposition that 'workers no longer need to be represented at work by a trade union or other body since, in the twenty-first century, management fully take account of the needs and views of workers when making decisions that affect them'.

2   What factors accounted for the decline in union membership in the UK during the 1980s and 1990s?

3   What are the main strengths and weaknesses of non-union employee representation?

4   Why do employers support partnership working? What do workers and unions gain from partnership agreements?

5   You have been asked to advise a trade union on how it might go about recruiting younger workers into membership. In small groups, or by talking to friends, identify what younger people want from employment, and explain what unions could do to meet these needs.

 Visit our Online Resource Centre for web links to sites connected to this section. www.oxfordtextbooks.co.uk/williams_adamsmith2e

Take your learning further: online resource centre

Visit the Online Resource Centre that accompanies this book to enrich your understanding of Chapter 6: Representation at work. Explore web links, test yourself using an interactive flashcard glossary, and keep up to date with the latest developments in the area.

 http://www.oxfordtextbooks.co.uk/orc/williams_adamsmith2e.

Chapter case study

e-unions

In common with many commercial and other voluntary organizations, trade unions at both national and local levels have developed websites to publicize their activities to members, non-members, and the wider public. The relative cheapness of communication offered by the web provides unions with an additional means of attracting members to complement existing recruitment methods. However, the web may offer unions the opportunity to improve and increase services, and indeed some have suggested that it could herald the advent of 'virtual unions'. During the 2000s, the unions improved their web presence. The TUC, for example, has developed a number of sites, like Worksmart, for example, which is designed to keep working people informed about their rights at work (http://www.worksmart.org.uk).

Two immediate advantages of the web to unions concern recruitment, and organizing in small and/or non-union workplaces. The average age of union members continues to increase, and they find it difficult to reach out to younger workers. However, these workers are more likely than their older colleagues to use the internet and be more comfortable with using it. To attract such workers, unions will need to identify issues that are relevant to them to encourage access to union sites. For existing union members, the web offers them a route to discover information about both union activities, and those of their employer. In those firms where membership is insufficient to achieve employer recognition, the web provides a means of establishing a permanent presence for workers that would otherwise be difficult and expensive for unions to maintain. Bulletin boards, chatrooms, and online question-and-answer pages, free of any possible victimization from management, may offer an effective, low-cost alternative to direct personal contact in these companies. Only a small number of committed activists are needed to set up and maintain these pages.

The provision of these services can be developed by trade unions at the national level. E-mail offers members a convenient way of requesting expert advice unconstrained by 'office hours'. Specific information can be made available to local workplace representatives rapidly. For example, the TUC and the union for building workers have weekly e-bulletins and forums for health and safety representatives on risks to workers. Services can be differentiated to appeal to non-members with further 'password-protected' information available only to existing members.

Two further organizational benefits are claimed for unions using the web. First, it can enhance internal democracy by disseminating information and improving communication between the union's leadership and members. Following the tentative steps being taken in the UK for national and local government elections, the web could also be used for union ballots on industrial action and leadership elections. Second, in industrial disputes, unions could use their web sites to present their case to members, the media, and the public, and to engender support from other unions, both nationally and internationally. More tantalizingly, the web can be used as a weapon in disputes, for example by flooding an employer's web site with messages in support of the union's case: so-called 'cyber-disruption'. While the unions have adapted relatively slowly to the opportunities provided by the web, there is increasing evidence of innovative approaches to the development of e-unions.

Sources: Diamond and Freeman (2002); Freeman (2005); Greene, Hogan, and Grieco (2003)

1. Can the virtual union become a reality?

2. What are the possible limitations and disadvantages to unions that become increasingly reliant on the internet to extend their organizing capacity?

7

Contemporary developments in pay and working time

Chapter objectives:

The main objectives of this chapter are to:

* provide an overview of the development and contraction of collective bargaining;

* assess the extent to which greater managerial freedom to determine pay arrangements has produced more innovative wage payment techniques;

* explore the reasons for the resilience of collective bargaining as an influence on the terms of the wage-work bargain in the public sector;

* assess the main effects of the introduction of the National Minimum Wage;

* consider the main developments in working time and the implications of the Working Time Regulations.

7.1 Introduction

The concept of the wage-work bargain, as we demonstrated in Chapter 1 of this book, is central to understanding the nature of the employment relationship. In exchange for the promise of wages, workers agree to engage in productive labour. This is not a one-off transaction, though. The terms of this open-ended bargain are subject to an ongoing process of adjustment and contestation. Since an employer does not pay for a worker's labour, but rather his or her capacity to labour, or potential labour power, the job of managing employment relations is invariably characterized by contradictory tendencies. As we saw in Chapter 5, managers must not only secure employees' compliance, but also elicit their cooperation, in order to realize the production of goods and services. Moreover, the wage-work bargain is as much a struggle over working time, and how it is used by employers to secure productive effort from workers, as it is over pay.

In this chapter we explore how contemporary developments in employment relations have influenced the terms of the wage-work bargain, with regard to pay and working time issues in particular. In Section 7.2 we start by examining pay-setting trends, tracing the evolution, development, and decline of collective bargaining, before considering the implications of this decline for how pay is determined. The focus of Section 7.3 is devoted to pay inequality and the regulation of low pay, with a particular emphasis on the impact of the National Minimum Wage introduced in 1999. In Section 7.4 we turn our attention to the topic of working time, and examine the main working time trends and how they are regulated.

Introductory case study

The 'fair tips' campaign

For many years collective bargaining was the main pay-setting arrangement in the UK. As we demonstrate in this chapter, though, its importance has waned, particularly in the private sector. For low-paid workers in the service sector, where collective bargaining has never been very commonplace anyway, the protection provided by the National Minimum Wage (NMW), which since 1999 has set a legal minimum floor of wages, is a more important consideration. As we see in Section 7.3, in general most employers in low-paying sectors of the economy have complied with the NMW relatively easily. However, some restaurant chains, like Café Rouge and Strada for example, took advantage of a loophole in the minimum wage legislation which allowed them to pay their waiting staff an hourly rate of pay that was less than the NMW, and use revenue taken from service charges to top up wages to the legal minimum. Only tips left for waiting staff directly on the table could not be counted towards the NMW. In May 2008, the trade union Unite launched a 'fair tips' campaign to draw attention to this loophole in the NMW legislation whereby money taken from customers in the form of service charges, supposedly to reward good service, was actually being used to supplement staff wages so that they reached the legal minimum. Leading newspapers like the *Daily Mirror* and the *Independent* supported the campaign to stop revenue from tips being used to make up the minimum wage. As part of the campaign, Unite published a 'Fair Tips Charter' which it invited employers to support. One of its clauses was a commitment to 'pay all employees at least the minimum wage with 100 per cent of tips added on top as a bonus with no hidden charges'. Some restaurant chains, like Pizza Hut and TGI Fridays, signed up to the Charter.

As a result of the campaign, and lobbying by trade unions, in July 2008 the government announced that it would close the legal loophole which allows employers to use tips and service charges to count towards the NMW. According to Unite's joint general secretary Derek Simpson, the decision to close the loophole 'means that unscrupulous employers will no longer be able to use the tips left for staff to subsidise low wages. Workers in restaurants, hotels and bars across the country have waited a long time for what they deserve' (http://www. unitetheunion.org.uk).

7.2 **The changing pattern of pay determination in Britain**

In this section, we examine contemporary trends in pay determination in Britain. Historically, most employees had their pay set through collective bargaining between employers, or employers' associations, and trade unions. One of the most notable recent developments in employment relations has been the diminished importance of collective bargaining as a pay-setting tool, and the resulting increase in the level of managerial discretion over pay. To what extent have managers been able to innovate in methods of pay determination? Performance-based approaches have become increasingly popular. Nevertheless, there is little evidence to suggest that managers have used the greater latitude they enjoy over pay determination very effectively. We finish the section by examining the resilience of collective bargaining, including multi-employer arrangements, in the British public sector. While the importance of collective bargaining as a means of determining pay has declined, it continues to influence earnings for millions of workers across many organizations.

7.2.1 The evolution and development of collective bargaining in Britain

Collective bargaining in Britain emerged during the nineteenth century as craft societies, the forerunners of the trade unions, in industries such as printing and engineering for example, eschewed their traditional reliance on trying to regulate employment conditions unilaterally in favour of joint regulation with employers. Initially, bargaining took place at a local or district level but, by 1910, following the path-setting 1898 national agreement in engineering, unions in the shipbuilding, printing, building, and footwear industries, among others, secured national recognition agreements (Clegg, Fox, and Thompson 1964), frequently as a result of industrial action.

In general, collective bargaining found favour among employers, as well as among cautious union leaders, because it enabled industrial conflict to become 'institutionalized', accommodated, and contained within the bargaining relationship. The alternative was continuing instability and disorder as unions struggled to secure a presence. Thus the decision to recognize and bargain with unions reflected an acceptance on the part of employers that a union presence was inevitable—as the 'lesser of two evils' (Blyton and Turnbull 2004: 228).

The implications of the 1914–18 war, in particular the growth of union bargaining power, compelled the British government to intervene in employment relations and, in 1917, a committee of inquiry was established under the chairmanship of J. H. Whitley. Its remit, part of broader governmental concern with the conditions for post-war reconstruction, was to examine ways in which relationships between managers and workers could be improved. Five reports were published over a period of two years. The most well-known recommendation was that collective bargaining arrangements, in the form of Joint Industry Councils (JICs), should be established at a national level across all industries, supplemented by joint committees at lower levels.

Even though many of the new JICs soon became moribund, government intervention had nonetheless accentuated the trend towards industry-wide bargaining (Hyman 1975). During the inter-war years, economic depression meant that the development of collective bargaining was gradual, but the 1939–45 war provided a further stimulus. The maintenance of orderly and stable employment relations was considered to be an important contribution to the war effort.

By the 1950s, multi-employer, industry-wide bargaining arrangements dominated the formal system of employment relations in Britain. Of the estimated 80 per cent of employees whose pay was set by collective bargaining, three-quarters were covered by multi-employer agreements either at national or sometimes regional level (Brown, Marginson, and Walsh 1995). Multi-employer bargaining became increasingly common in the public sector; during the 1950s, for example, national bargaining spread to the health service (Carter and Fairbrother 1999). Often these arrangements were called 'Whitley Councils', named after the chairman of the above-mentioned committee.

However, the predominance of multi-employer bargaining increasingly obscured workplace developments. The main advantage of multi-employer arrangements for employers was that they could be used to exclude union influence from the workplace. However, the inadequacies of industry-level collective agreements enabled more localized bargaining to flourish (Hyman 1975; Royal Commission 1968). During the 1950s and 1960s, in a climate of full employment, shop stewards in the engineering industry were able to negotiate with local managers over bonuses, overtime arrangements and incentive payments, and reach settlements that were outside, and in addition to, the industry agreements. Thus 'many managements tended increasingly to settle matters in their own workplace by negotiating through shop stewards rather than through multi-employer bargaining involving their employers' organisation' (Sisson and Brown 1983: 138).

The influence of multi-employer bargaining was inevitably eroded, and there were concerns about the consequences. The increasing gap between the rates agreed by means of industry-level bargaining and the actual earnings of workers, augmented by locally negotiated supplements, or 'wage drift' as it became known (Brown 1973; Royal Commission 1968), was perceived to have inflationary consequences. Added to this, informal workplace bargaining tended to 'sap management control over work' (Brown, Marginson, and Walsh 2003: 200), and generated a multitude of small-scale, often short industrial disputes which, taken together, were deemed by policy-makers to be detrimental to British economic performance.

Although dominated by the experience of the engineering sector, the Donovan Royal Commission (1965–68) found, as we have already observed, that much of the blame for the problems outlined above could be laid at the door of management who, it was asserted, should take a greater degree of responsibility for shaping their own employment relations arrangements (Royal Commission 1968). While the extent of Donovan's influence is questionable—single-employer bargaining was rising in popularity anyway as employers sought to develop organization-specific arrangements—the 1970s saw a diminution in the incidence of multi-employer bargaining.

A study of manufacturing industry undertaken in the late 1970s revealed that while multi-employer agreements continued to be commonplace, in textile production for example; yet their effectiveness was much diminished (Brown and Terry 1978). While single-employer bargaining had grown rapidly in significance, it had come about not as a result of the 'deliberate rejection of established multi-employer arrangements' but as a 'largely unplanned consequence of piecemeal reform' (Brown 1981: 24).

By the early 1980s, collective bargaining remained the predominant method of pay determination in Britain, with over 70 per cent of employees covered by collective agreements (Daniel and Millward 1983). Although single-employer bargaining had become more common, particularly in manufacturing industry, in large parts of the economy, including the food retail and banking sectors, multi-employer arrangements prevailed. Moreover, employment relations in the public sector were dominated by national, multi-employer collective bargaining based on Whitley principles. Though some criticism of these latter arrangements had been expressed, no fundamental reforms were initiated (Bailey 1996), and generally single-employer bargaining was restricted to a small number of local authorities (Beaumont 1992).

7.2.2 The contraction of collective bargaining in Britain and the rise of managerial discretion over pay

Two major trends characterized the development of collective bargaining in Britain between the 1980s and the 2000s: first, a substantial decline in the coverage of collective bargaining; and second, the almost complete disappearance of multi-employer bargaining from the private sector. Taking the diminution of collective bargaining coverage for a start, whereas in 1980 some two-thirds of employees had their pay set by collective bargaining, by the 2000s the proportion had fallen to some 40 per cent of employees. While much of the decline occurred in the 1980s and 1990s, the erosion of collective bargaining coverage continued during the 2000s, albeit at a slower rate (Brown and Nash 2008; Kersley et al. 2006).

While there is no collective bargaining in three-quarters (73 per cent) of workplaces, Table 7.1 shows that collective bargaining coverage varies extensively by industry sector. Perhaps the most obvious variation is that which exists between the private and public sectors. Among private sector firms, collective bargaining is present in just 14 per cent of workplaces, and covers around a quarter (27 per cent) of employees. This indicates that

Table 7.1 Collective bargaining coverage by industry sector, 2004

	Workplaces with any collective bargaining (% workplaces)	Employees covered by collective bargaining (% employees)
All workplaces	27	40
Private sector	14	26
Public sector	83	82
Manufacturing	20	39
Electricity, gas, and water	96	87
Construction	17	26
Wholesale and retail	9	17
Hotels and restaurants	2	5
Transport and communication	43	63
Financial services	63	49
Public administration	93	90

Source: Kersley et al. (2006: 180)

workplaces with collective bargaining tend to be larger, with more staff, than those without (see below). In the public sector, however, collective bargaining occurs in over four-fifths (83 per cent) of workplaces, and covers a similar proportion (82 per cent of employees). The decline in collective bargaining coverage has been particularly marked in the private sector.

There are also further variations in collective bargaining coverage which are worth noting. On the one hand, in some industry sectors it is very high. In the electricity, gas, and water industry, for example, just four per cent of workplaces have no collective bargaining. On the other hand, in some industries the presence of collective bargaining is rare indeed. Just five per cent of hotel and restaurant employees, for example, are covered by collective bargaining.

Collective bargaining coverage also varies according to both the size of the workplace, and also the wider organization of which the organization is a part (see Table 7.2). There is a notable association between workplace size and collective bargaining coverage. Collective bargaining is present in just 19 per cent of small workplaces (those with between 10 and 24 employees), compared to two-thirds (65 per cent) of very large workplaces (those with 500 or more employees). The presence of collective bargaining in a workplace is also associated with the size of the organization of which it is a part; in general, the larger the organization, the more likely it is that collective bargaining will occur within the workplaces within it. Just one in twenty employees in small organizations, those with between 10 and 99 staff, are covered by collective bargaining, compared to well over a half (56 per cent) of employees in very large organizations, those with 10,000 or more staff.

Table 7.2 Collective bargaining coverage by workplace size and organization size, 2004

	Workplaces with any collective bargaining (% workplaces)	Employees covered by collective bargaining gaining (% employees)
All workplaces	27	40
Workplaces with 10–24 employees	19	17
25–49 employees	33	26
50–99 employees	31	27
100–199 employees	48	42
200–499 employees	57	52
500 or more employees	65	68
Organizations with 10–99 employees	6	5
100–999 employees	26	29
1,000–9,999 employees	40	55
10,000 or more employees	53	56

Source: Kersley et al. (2006: 180)

These variations show that, while its coverage has clearly diminished substantially, collective bargaining continues to be present in many parts of the economy. The giant retailer Tesco, for example, has a formal bargaining relationship with a trade union, one that, as is shown in Chapter 6, has been reconstructed as a 'partnership agreement'. Moreover, as we see below, collective bargaining remains an important feature of employment relations in the public sector. The 'wide variation in the coverage of collective bargaining at workplace level is an important feature of pay setting in Britain, one that is often overlooked by those who simply dismiss joint regulation over pay and conditions as a thing of the past' (Kersley et al. 2006: 181).

Its declining coverage is not the only measure which we can use to examine the erosion of collective bargaining in contemporary employment relations. The nature of collective bargaining also seems to have changed in important ways, becoming less about hard negotiation, and more likely to take the form of managers sharing information with union representatives, or consulting with them, rather than actually negotiating. There is a growing trend for some private sector workplaces, while formally recognizing a union for collective bargaining over pay, not to engage in any bargaining activity (Millward, Bryson, and Forth 2000). Particularly in the private sector, collective bargaining is marked by 'a lack of confrontation and by a more consultative style over a relatively wide range of issues' (Brown and Nash 2008: 102).

While the role of collective bargaining is most evident when it comes to pay-setting, it is also important to remember that the scope of bargaining can cover a potentially wide range of other employment issues, like holiday entitlement, for example, or grievance and disciplinary procedures. Not only has the coverage of collective bargaining declined, but, where it remains, its scope has often been narrowed (Brown and Nash 2008). What this means is that often the range of issues subject to joint regulation has diminished (Brown et al. 2000).

Why, then, has the extent and coverage of collective bargaining declined so precipitously since the 1980s? A number of factors have been at work. During the 1980s and 1990s, Conservative governments discouraged collective bargaining, a reflection of their espoused belief in individualism. Collective bargaining was portrayed as an archaic process that, in so far as it restricted managerial flexibility, undermined business performance. There was also a compositional effect. The changing composition of the workforce, in particular the increasing proportion of employees working in the private services sector, where collective bargaining had never been widespread anyway outside a few sectors such as food retailing, contributed to the diminution of collective bargaining. Moreover, collective bargaining is much rarer in newer workplaces, those established since the 1980s, than it is in older workplaces.

The most important cause of the overall fall in collective bargaining coverage, though, has been the diminution of union power. Not only have unions been increasingly unable to secure bargaining arrangements in new workplaces, but employers have also attempted, often successfully, to exclude them from existing ones, in an effort to forge more individualistic relations with their staff. It should not be forgotten that collective bargaining has always been something that managers were willing to accept, often reluctantly, as a way of avoiding disruption. Thus the decline in collective bargaining coverage reflects the determination of managers to extend their prerogative to the area of pay determination, something that was enabled by, and further contributed to, the frailty of the union movement.

The second major collective bargaining trend to have occurred since the 1980s concerns the decentralization of pay bargaining activity. During the 1980s and 1990s, for example, multi-employer bargaining in the private sector almost disappeared, except for a few industries like electrical contracting (see Box 7.1). In 2004, just 4 per cent of private sector employees had their pay set in this way (Brown and Nash 2008). Where collective bargaining prevails in the private sector, it is now much more likely to be undertaken at single-employer level. Although the importance of multi-employer bargaining had been dwindling well before the 1980s, that decade saw the termination of national agreements across a range of sectors, including retail banking, engineering, and food retailing (Brown and Walsh 1991; Brown, Marginson, and Walsh 1995). This trend continued into the next

---

INSIGHT INTO PRACTICE 7.1

The survival of national bargaining in the electrical contracting industry

Although increasingly rare, national-level, multi-employer bargaining has survived in some parts of the private sector, for example the electrical contracting industry. The sector encompasses firms and self-employed contractors that install and wire electrical systems in homes and businesses. During the 1960s, the Electrical Contractors' Association (ECA), the employers' association for the industry, and the leadership of the electricians' union, now a part of the Unite trade union, established a close working relationship borne out of a mutual concern to purge workplace union militancy. Set up in 1966, the Joint Industry Board (JIB), made up of an equal number of employers' and union representatives, not only regulated pay, hours, and holidays, but also certified training and provided insurance cover and other benefits.

During the 1980s and 1990s, increasing competitive pressures, and the growth in the numbers of self-employed, challenged the 'viability of national regulation' (Gospel and Druker 1998: 257). Nevertheless, the JIB system has survived. Why was this? The nature of the industry, comprising a large number of small firms, is one factor. Multi-employer bargaining ostensibly allows employers to save on much of the cost of dealing with unions. It can also help to take wages out of competition, an important consideration given that the skills profile of the workforce could result in pay leapfrogging as firms compete with each other for qualified staff. The leaders of the electricians' union, too, favoured national bargaining, since it facilitated widespread recognition from employers and 'further reinforced their central control', thus helping to 'contain political challenges mounted by disaffected members' (Gospel and Druker 1998: 262).

These reasons have not been enough on their own, however, to sustain national bargaining. The most important factor is that many employers continue to welcome the stability and predictability in employment relations engendered by the JIB system. Moreover, the presence of the JIB itself, given that it developed an increasingly important role in the electrical contracting industry, particularly over matters relating to training, further helps to maintain joint regulation. Thus for relatively small firms in competitive product markets, who rely on a skilled workforce, multi-employer bargaining, in so far as it engenders stability in employment relations, may continue to be attractive in some sectors. (The Joint Industry Board for the Electrical Contracting Industry: http://www.jib.org.uk)

decade in such a way that multi-employer bargaining 'which had greatly diminished in importance in the 1980s, became even more of a rarity in the 1990s' (Cully et al. 1999: 228).

Although the Conservatives disliked the perceived rigidity and inflexibility of multi-employer bargaining, the principal cause of its decline was the ambition of firms to align pay more closely with business performance, and to exert greater control over pay outcomes in a more competitive environment. Without control over their own bargaining arrangements, firms found it difficult to secure increasingly necessary flexibility over pay (Brown and Walsh 1991; Brown, Marginson, and Walsh 2003).

In the publicly owned water industry, for example, until the late 1980s multi-employer bargaining was preferred since it helped to counterbalance union power, preventing 'leapfrogging' in pay settlements. In other words, the unions were unable to move from organization to organization bidding up pay rates. However, in the period leading up to privatization of the water industry in 1989, national bargaining arrangements were terminated. The ostensible cause was the withdrawal of Thames Water from the industry agreement. Across the sector, however, there was a growing realization that as private sector organizations, operating in a more commercial environment, and governed by the imperative for profitability, the new water companies would need to secure greater control over their own employment relations and, in particular, arrangements for managing pay and performance (Ogden 1993).

What, then, are the implications of the contraction of collective bargaining in Britain? How do employees have their pay determined, if not through the process of collective bargaining? In the private sector the most notable trend has been the growing extent to which pay is subject to unilateral regulation by management (Brown and Nash 2008; Brown, Marginson, and Walsh 2003; Millward, Bryson, and Forth 2000). Table 7.3 shows the proportion of employees covered by specific pay-setting measures. Whereas collective bargaining, through multi-employer arrangements, dominates the public sector, in the private sector a substantial majority of employees have their pay set unilaterally by managers, either at workplace level (45 per cent of employees) or

Table 7.3 Pay determination methods (employees), 2004

	All workplaces	Private sector	Public sector
Multi-employer bargaining	18	4	58
Single-employer bargaining	11	10	16
Workplace bargaining	6	7	2
Set by management at the workplace	35	45	5
Set by management at a higher level	22	27	8
Individual negotiation	4	5	0
Set by some other method	4	1	10
Pay review body	3	0	10*

Workplaces with ten or more employees. * Also counted as 'some other method'.
Source: Kersley et al. (2006: 186)

a higher level in the organization (27 per cent). During the early 2000s, there was a marked increase in both the proportion of employees whose pay was set unilaterally by management, and the proportion of workplaces where all pay was set by management at workplace level (Brown and Nash 2008: 96; Kersley et al. 2006: 184-5).

Since the diminution of collective bargaining means that managers now appear to enjoy more latitude over pay-setting arrangements, how have they used this greater freedom? And how far have they been able to eschew the apparent rigidities of collective bargaining, and thus design innovative pay systems that enhance flexibility, commitment, and performance?

7.2.3 Managerial innovation in pay-setting arrangements

There has been a growing level of interest in how pay can be used as part of a sophisticated human resource management (HRM) approach (see Chapter 5) to managing employees. The term 'reward', rather than pay, is often used to refer to innovative methods of remunerating employees that assist the achievement of organizational goals. Rather than basing pay on relatively unsophisticated criteria, such as the number of hours employees spend at work each week, for example, or their length of service, reward schemes may offer employees greater flexibility over their methods of remuneration, or align wages with their performance at work, individually, or sometimes as members of a team. The decline of collective bargaining, with its common rate for the job, supposedly gives managers greater scope to implement more variable arrangements for determining pay, enhancing their flexibility when it comes to rewarding individual staff (Kersley et al. 2006).

For Druker and White (1999:13), the management of reward 'is one of the key levers to be deployed in the pursuit of effective HRM. If pay is to "deliver the goods" in terms of HR strategy, then it must be structured ... in order to meet HR objectives.' Thus the way in which pay is managed must not only be aligned with, and supportive of, broader HRM objectives, but also be integrated with the overall strategic goals of the organization. Should this be the case, then, one would expect pay to be more closely aligned with the characteristics of individual employees, or contingent on business performance.

Given the lack of progress made towards sophisticated HRM in general (see Chapter 5), it should come as no surprise that management-inspired innovations in respect of pay arrangements have been somewhat limited. Even PRP, despite its attractiveness to managers, not least as a way of undermining collectivism, is far from common, as is the individualization of pay more generally (Arrowsmith and Sisson 1999). One overview of developments in the management of pay suggests that the decline of collective bargaining failed to encourage much in the way of innovation, 'and certainly the absence of any daring new departures' (Kessler 2000: 283).

While high-profile instances of innovations such as competency or team-based pay have been reported, their overall significance appears to be limited. Managers have been reluctant to make substantial reforms to pay systems. They prefer to tread carefully, restricting their efforts to instituting incremental, minor adjustments (Kessler 2000). Thus managers have 'not taken advantage of the demise of collective bargaining to implement new integrated systems of individualised employee relations and pay determination' (Charlwood 2007: 43). Generally, the decline of collective pay-setting arrangements has produced 'procedural individualization' rather than 'substantive individualization' when it comes to determining pay. In other words, while the decline of collective bargaining means that procedures for determining pay have become increasingly decollectivized, managers still prefer to operate standardized arrangements for rewarding staff (Charlwood 2007).

What, then, explains the absence of significant innovation in the way in which pay is managed, despite the apparently increased freedom of managers to effect change? Three factors would appear to be important. First, managers are reluctant to bear the risks of innovation. Attempts to reform pay arrangements can disrupt employment relations, by undermining established norms of fairness and the legitimacy they offer. Managers are wary about making changes to existing payment systems. The 'tried and tested nature of arrangements, it seems, invests them with a high degree of legitimacy in the eyes of managers and employees' (Arrowsmith and Sisson 1999: 66).

Second, external pressures limit the capacity of managers to innovate in respect of pay arrangements. Although profitability is an important determinant of pay settlements, the significance of two long-standing influences—cost of living and comparability—persists, despite the diminution of collective bargaining (Ingram, Wadsworth, and Brown 1999). In other words, firms' decisions over pay settlements are constrained by the need to offer rises that are in line both with inflation, and with what other, comparable, groups of workers have been awarded.

Third, following on from this, there is evidence of a sector effect in respect of pay. What this means is that similarities between firms operating in the same industry sector can be identified. Arrowsmith and Sisson (1999) found this to be the case after examining arrangements and trends in two sectors—printing and the NHS—where multi-employer bargaining prevailed, and two others—engineering and retailing—where it did not. Although pay was determined within the firm in the latter two sectors, this did not seem to have resulted in organizational outcomes that were noticeably different. Employers 'in each of the four sectors ... continue to move like ships in a convoy' (Arrowsmith and Sisson 1999: 63). Managers may aspire to freedom in determining pay, but they do not appear to have made much use of it (Arrowsmith and Sisson 1999: 70).

7.2.4 The implications of performance-related pay

Perhaps the most notable type of variable pay arrangement involves attempts to link some element of an employee's reward to their performance in some way. By examining in detail how performance-related pay (PRP) operates, we are better placed to understand some of the difficulties and challenges that apply when trying to innovate in respect of pay-setting arrangements.

First, we need to distinguish between two different types of performance-related pay systems. Incentive-based payment systems, those that link an element of workers' pay to a measure of their output, have a long history in employment relations. Managers are often attracted to payment by results schemes since they seem to be a relatively straightforward way of securing more effort from workers without the need for close supervision (Brown and Walsh 1994). In practice, though, such arrangements rarely operate as effectively as managers anticipate. Workers, for example, may restrict their output, in order to maximize the earnings of them all as a group, and not go flat out in pursuit of a higher individual wage. Moreover, the effect of incentive payments on motivation is rarely unambiguous (Brown, Marginson, and Walsh 2003); the demotivation resulting from a failure to be awarded an expected wage bonus, for example, may outweigh any motivational advantages.

Nowadays, the term PRP is more conventionally associated with arrangements for determining pay that links an element of a worker's wages to some assessment of their worth, or merit. Under PRP, or individual PRP as it is sometimes called, an element of an employee's remuneration is based, over a given period of time, upon an often subjective assessment of the quantity and quality of his or her work, normally by an immediate manager, set against a series of targets. Its use in white-collar jobs in particular represents a shift away from pay based on job grade or length of service 'towards relating pay more directly to individual characteristics' (Kessler and Purcell 1995: 350), particularly in the public sector where PRP schemes have become somewhat popular (Bach 2002; White 1999), though they are more commonly found in the private sector. While some PRP schemes fell into disrepute during the 1990s, largely because of operational problems, they seem to have become more popular during the 2000s (Kersley et al. 2006).

What is the purpose of PRP? Why have managers been so concerned to relate pay more directly to employees' performance? Kessler and Purcell (1995) suggest that three sets of managerial goals provide the rationale for PRP. First, managers use it as a way of stimulating pay flexibility. PRP ostensibly gives them greater latitude to restructure pay systems so that they support organizational objectives, though this is rarely done in a strategic way. The second set of goals relates to the desirability of enhancing employee motivation, commitment, and loyalty. If pay is made more contingent upon their performance, then it is presumed that employees will identify with, and become more attached to, managerially determined organizational goals.

In his study of PRP in four local authorities, Heery (1998a) identified a contradictory rationale underpinning the decision to adopt PRP. On the one hand, managers sought to use it to gain greater employee compliance; PRP could help to reduce shirking and augment management control. On the other hand, the implementation of PRP was also seen as a way of generating culture change, towards a climate in which an ethos of flexibility and commitment predominated. Perhaps this should not be surprising given that the management of the employment relationship is driven by the need to secure employee compliance, as well as elicit their commitment, as we saw in Chapter 5.

The third set of managerial goals concern the use of PRP as a way of challenging collective bargaining arrangements and marginalizing the influence of trade unions. In some cases, such as with the derecognition of unions for managerial grades at British Telecom, there was 'an unambiguous attempt by management to use performance pay to undermine the collective dimension of industrial relations' (Kessler and Purcell 1995: 358–9). Evidence from a study of new workplaces in Ireland demonstrates that PRP schemes, in so far as they marginalize collective bargaining and individualize pay-setting arrangements, undermine joint regulation, thus 'posing an explicit challenge to collectivism in employment relations' (Gunnigle, Turner, and D' 1998: 574).

Yet the existence of PRP is not incompatible with a trade union presence. While a desire to reduce the influence of trade unions and collective bargaining is a major rationale for the adoption of PRP schemes, there is evidence that a union presence can help to regulate how they are implemented, and shape the details (Heery 1997). In the case of 'PharmCo', a pharmaceutical company that until privatization in the 1980s had been in the public sector, the unions jointly regulated the implementation of PRP with management. The effect was to dilute the initial aim of management for a scheme in which pay progression was determined solely by performance, and most staff continued to receive annual increments (I. Kessler 1994).

When implementing PRP, managers must take into account the reactions of employees. Heery (1998a: 85), in his study of local government, considers that 'PRP has been the subject of a tacit exchange between managers and employees, in which managers have refrained from an exacting application of formal procedures for fear of alienating employees'. This helps to explain, for example, the reluctance of managers to give employees low performance ratings. The experience of PRP schemes suggests that the need to win the consent of employees places important constraints upon managerial discretion over how pay is determined. Like any management initiative in employment relations, then, the implementation of PRP is conditioned by the need to elicit employees' cooperation as well as their compliance.

To what extent, though, is PRP effective, in managerial terms, as a way of increasing employees' motivation, and thus their levels of performance? Key features of PRP schemes, such as the manipulation of performance targets, the subjective evaluation of performance by managers, and the fact that the performance element to pay is generally a very small proportion of overall earnings, conspire to reduce their effectiveness (Kessler 2000). Added to which, PRP, given that it generates variations in earnings between employees, has the potential to create jealousies and erode staff morale.

If anything, then, in practice PRP schemes may have a greater demotivating effect than a motivating one, as can be seen from the experiences of two government agencies, the Inland Revenue and the Employment Service (Marsden and French 1998). Although most employees supported the principle of PRP, in general they were highly critical of the way in which the respective schemes operated in practice. In the Employment Service, for example, the individual performance targets were a source of discontent since it was difficult for employees, given that they had insufficient control over their workloads, to attain them. It was widely felt, moreover, that managers manipulated the performance review process to give higher ratings to favoured employees. In both organizations, PRP appears to have led to a significant decline in morale, caused jealousies, and reduced the level of cooperation between managers and employees.

There are two further aspects of how PRP schemes operate. First, in the public sector it would seem that the introduction of performance pay has been driven not so much by a concern with improving employees' motivation, commitment, and loyalty, but by a need to cut wage bill costs. PRP is associated with a significant increase in workloads as fewer staff are required to take on more tasks and work harder (Foster and Hoggett 1999; Marsden and French 1998). Thus it can be seen as a way of attempting to secure greater work effort in a context of staff reductions.

Second, as the cases of the Inland Revenue and the Employment Service show, PRP is often implemented in such a way that it is perceived by employees to be unfair. The principle of PRP is widely understood to be fair; in practice, however, it is bound to disrupt established pay arrangements and, in doing so, upset existing norms of fairness and the sense of legitimacy that they create, something which forms the basis of workplace order. Thus any alterations to pay-setting arrangements, particularly those that link an element of pay to performance in some way, unless handled very carefully and with due sensitivity, seem likely to have a demotivating effect (Brown and Nolan 1988; Brown and Walsh 1994; Brown, Marginson, and Walsh 2003). While the use of merit-based PRP has grown during the 2000s, it is still only present in a sixth of all workplaces; whereas traditional incentive-based payment schemes, in the form of payment by results, exist in two-fifths of workplaces (Kersley et al. 2006).

7.2.5 Pay determination in the public sector

While the extent of unilateral regulation of pay by managements has undoubtedly risen, by no means does this imply that collective bargaining in Britain has become extinct. We have already seen that there is a widespread variation in the incidence of collective bargaining arrangements throughout the economy. In the public sector, collective bargaining, often of the multi-employer type, continues to exert a powerful influence over the determination of pay.

The resilience of national bargaining in the public sector (Corby 2000), despite the efforts of Conservative governments during the 1980s and 1990s to challenge it, is striking. Decentralized bargaining was seen as complementing the devolution of operational decision-making to local managers, hence making employment relations more 'responsive to the needs of managerial efficiency and labour market conditions, and more sensitive to employee performance' (Winchester and Bach 1999: 45). The restructuring of many public services, such as the 1991 creation of NHS trust hospitals, was designed in large part to stimulate local bargaining, and also to undermine the national power bases of the major public sector trade unions.

However, with the exceptions of the Civil Service, where responsibility for pay determination has been devolved to individual executive agencies, such as the Benefits Agency for example, and further education colleges, where national bargaining has been eroded (see Box 7.2), significant decentralization has been limited. 'Across the public services, more decentralized and flexible arrangements for pay determination ... have developed but in a piecemeal, uneven and often inconsistent way' (Bach and Winchester 2003: 299). Why, then, have attempts to decentralize bargaining in the public sector been largely unsuccessful, and why have national bargaining arrangements proved to be so resilient? In some areas, structural factors have impeded decentralization. Schools, for example, are generally too small to be able to handle their own employment relations effectively (Ironside, Seifert, and Sinclair 1997).

Despite attempts in the 1990s to stimulate local bargaining in the NHS, it was challenged by a combination of management ambivalence and union opposition (Carr 1999; Thornley 1998). The Treasury, moreover, was reluctant to cede control over pay outcomes. Thus a tension exists between the objective of devolving decision-making and the necessity of maintaining central control over the public sector paybill (Carter and Fairbrother 1999; Winchester and Bach 1999). In the health service, the 2004

The erosion of national bargaining in the further education sector

Apart from the civil service, where the more direct role of government as employer appears to have been critical, the only other part of the public sector in Britain where national bargaining has been significantly eroded is the further education sector in England and Wales. Until 1993, further education colleges came under the control of their respective local authorities, which were the employers of college staff. Pay rates were negotiated nationally between representatives of the local authorities and the appropriate trade unions. Conditions of service were also determined by multi-employer bargaining at national level. The national 'Silver Book' agreement—as it was called because of the colour of its cover—among other things set upper limits on the number of teaching hours that lecturers could work on a weekly and annual basis. In 1993, the colleges were taken out of local authority control and, in a process called 'incorporation', became employers of college staff in their own right. Although the arrangements would change, there was no expectation that national bargaining would cease. It was anticipated that the newly established College Employers' Forum (CEF), an employers' association which took on the job of representing the colleges' employment relations interests, would continue to negotiate agreements with the unions which would then apply throughout the sector. The CEF's leadership, however, developed an ambitious reform agenda. Since college budgets were to be squeezed, it proposed replacing the Silver Book with a 'flexible' contract that placed no specific limitations upon college lecturers' workload. This provoked a lengthy and bitter industrial dispute as the main lecturers' union tried to resist the imposition of new contracts. While some colleges were able to impose the CEF's contract, many introduced, either unilaterally or after negotiations with local union representatives, a version of their own which included some workload limits. By the end of the 1990s, then, a large variety of different contractual arrangements existed in the sector. Pay remained formally subject to national bargaining, although the inability, or reluctance, of many colleges to implement annual recommended awards in full, or at all in some cases, because of purported financial difficulties, led to an increasingly disparate set of pay rates across the sector, as well as a number of industrial disputes. During the 2000s, attempts have been made by the employers and the unions to reinforce the authority of national agreements linked to the availability of more funds for the sector. It has proved difficult, though, to reinstate their influence given the diversity of employment arrangements present in the college sector.

Source
Williams (2004)

'Agenda for Change' agreement, which established a national pay and grading system in the health service, constitutes a further obstacle to decentralization.

Furthermore, the operation of pay review bodies has 'contributed to the resilience of national systems of pay determination' (Bach and Winchester 1994: 273). What, though, are pay review bodies? Briefly, they are ostensibly independent institutions, whose members are appointed by the government, which, after evaluating appropriate data and submissions from interested parties such as trade unions, make non-binding recommendations to the government on pay increases, and any other relevant matters within their remit. Since the 1960s, pay review bodies have covered some groups of public sector employees, such as doctors and dentists and senior civil servants, and also members of the armed forces. However, their remit subsequently widened to encompass nursing staff and 'professions allied to medicine', including midwives and health visitors and schoolteachers, in 1983 and 1991, respectively. In 2001, prison officers were also given a pay review body. Linked to the Agenda for Change agreement, during the 2000s the scope of the pay review body for nursing staff and professions allied to medicine was widened to encompass all NHS staff, with the exception of doctors and senior managers, and renamed the NHS Pay Review Body. In 2008, the pay of some 1.8 million public sector workers was set by pay review body recommendation.

The key thing about pay review bodies is that generally their pay recommendations apply nationally, restricting the ability of managers to secure local pay flexibility. Why, then, have governments favoured them as a pay-setting tool in the public sector? Pay review bodies were preferred to traditional collective bargaining arrangements because they helped to mitigate industrial conflict in key public sector occupations. The pay review body process, with its ostensibly rational, ordered, and consensual approach to determining pay outcomes, seemed less likely to cause disputes than traditional collective bargaining, with its more adversarial dynamic, and would help to reduce the power of the public sector unions.

Pay review bodies were introduced for nurses and schoolteachers in the aftermath of large-scale industrial disputes. In the case of nurses, the then Conservative government was shaken by industrial action in the NHS during 1982. By establishing a pay review body, it anticipated nurses and other related groups of workers 'would never again join other health-service workers in a sector-wide pay campaign' (Bach 1999a: 107–8). The government abolished collective bargaining arrangements for schoolteachers in 1987 as a 'punishment for extensive industrial action in the mid 1980s' (Bailey 1996: 137), and despite promising to restore them, instead made teachers' pay subject to pay review body recommendations (Ironside and Seifert 1995). For the government the two main attractions of pay review bodies are, first, that they offer a 'more stable and less conflictual system of pay determination than existed previously' (White 2000: 94), and second, that they give the impression that the government is an indifferent bystander, allowing it to avoid being drawn into potentially messy employment relations issues.

As can be seen from Box 7.3, during the mid 2000s there was a wave of increased militancy among groups of public sector workers, mainly on the grounds of pay. As a result, the pay review body process seemed to lose some of its effectiveness as a way of preventing disputes, mainly in the context of government efforts to keep public sector pay rises in check as an anti-inflation measure. In 2007, for example, the government chose to implement the recommended annual pay rise of 2.5 per cent for nurses and other health professions in England in two stages, 1.5 per cent in the spring, and the other 1 per cent in the autumn, giving an overall rise of 1.9 per cent for the year as a whole. In Scotland and Wales, though, the recommended 2.5 per cent pay rise was implemented in full. The following year, one of the leading teachers' unions, the National Union of Teachers, held a national one-day strike in England and Wales in pursuit of a four per cent pay claim, following a recommendation by the review body of a three-year pay deal, with a rise of 2.45 per cent in the first year.

How, then, is one to interpret the implications of the pay review bodies? Their presence has undoubtedly hindered the development of local bargaining arrangements since pay

Employment relations reflection 7.3 Pay disputes in the public sector

There was a wave of industrial militancy during the mid 2000s as a result of government efforts to restrict public sector pay rises. In 2007–08, for example, civil servants, local government workers, prison officers, and schoolteachers all took strike action over pay. The April 2008 one-day strike by schoolteachers in England and Wales was the first national teachers' strike in over two decades.

Even the police, not noted for being a very militant occupation, were moved to take action. Police pay is determined by negotiation through a Police Negotiating Board, which comprises representatives of the police staff associations (police officers are not allowed to join unions) and employers, and makes recommendations to the government, in the form of the home secretary. Where negotiation fails to produce an agreement, arbitration machinery exists to facilitate a mutually acceptable deal. In 2007–08, the process of arbitration resulted in a recommendation that police pay in England and Wales should rise by 2.5 per cent. However, instead of backdating the award from 1 September 2007, which is when it should have come into effect, the government chose to implement the pay rise from 1 December 2007, meaning that the overall pay increase for the year as a whole was 1.9 per cent. Forbidden by law from undertaking industrial action, many thousands of police officers protested by marching through London. The association for rank and file police officers, the Police Federation, organized a ballot which showed that an overwhelming majority of its members wanted to see the law that prevents them from engaging in strikes and other forms of industrial action overturned. It also fought, and lost, a legal battle to overrule the home secretary's decision.

recommendations generally apply across the board. In respect of pay outcomes, it would seem that public sector occupations whose pay awards are the outcome of pay review body recommendations do better than those who are covered by traditional bargaining arrangements. Moreover, the review body process can boost the legitimacy of trade union arguments, implying that losing the right to traditional collective bargaining may not be all that damaging. Perhaps the biggest losers are public sector employers, who have to bear the cost of implementing pay awards but have little influence over the process by which they are enacted (Bach and Winchester 2003). While the pay review body process has generally helped to reduce the number of national pay disputes in the public sector, government efforts to restrict public sector pay rises, manifest in the guidance given to the review bodies, mean that they have become a less effective tool for moderating industrial conflict.

But how should the pay review body process itself be understood? In some interpretations, it is treated as a form of pay determination that is distinct from collective bargaining (e.g. Kersley et al. 2006). More plausibly, pay review body arrangements should be viewed as a 'particular type of collective bargaining' (Brown and Nash 2008: 95). Rather than being a 'substitute' for the collective bargaining process, pay review bodies, as a kind of third-party intervention, are in fact 'part of it' (Burchill 2000: 155). In other words, the review bodies mediate between the claims of the unions, representing the collective interests of their members, and the counter-claims of the employer representatives; recommendations 'may be more or less favourable to one or other of the two main groups but are generally not too distant from either', and are implemented by the government with due regard to the unions' bargaining power, with the possibility of industrial action should the unions be dissatisfied with the outcome (Burchill, 2000: 152).

Just because the parties do not meet with each other directly over a single negotiating table does not invalidate the status of the pay review process as a form of bargaining. The concept of 'arm's length bargaining' would therefore appear to be the most appropriate way of classifying the review body process (Winchester and Bach 1995).

Finally, it is important to be aware that the resilience of formal national bargaining arrangements across most of the public sector has disguised significant changes within many workplaces. Faced with pressures to improve service delivery, make cost savings, and improve efficiency, public sector managers have been able to secure some degree of flexibility by altering the composition of their workforce. One popular way of re-profiling the workforce has been to use greater proportions of auxiliary staff, whose pay and conditions, unlike those of teachers, are not subject to determination at national level.

In the health service, for example, the employment of health-care assistants (HCAs) enabled managers to gain much sought-after flexibility; their pay and conditions were set locally, often unilaterally by management, though sometimes with union involvement (Grimshaw 1999). Since 2004, though, health service employers have lost this method of securing flexibility, since HCAs now come under the national Agenda for Change pay and grading agreement. Elsewhere in the public sector, however, workforce re-profiling initiatives continue to be a popular way of promoting employment flexibility and realizing efficiency savings. Increasing numbers of classroom assistants and police community support officers testify to the attractiveness of this approach for employers (Bach, Kessler, and Heron 2006; Loveday, Williams, and Scott 2008).

Moreover, the opening up of public services to private sector providers increasingly undermines national pay and conditions of service agreements. In education, for example, the operators of city academies, new types of school partially funded and run by private companies, are, in principle, able to set their own terms and conditions of employment for schoolteachers. While national, multi-employer bargaining in the public sector has proved to be remarkably resilient, increasing private sector involvement in the delivery of public services may erode it in future.

SECTION SUMMARY AND FURTHER READING

- For much of the twentieth century, collective bargaining, often in the form of multi-employer arrangements, was the principal pay-setting method in employment relations.

- Since the 1980s, multi-employer bargaining in the private sector has become a rarity. In order to secure greater flexibility over their own employment relations, employers increasingly prefer to bargain with trade unions themselves. Moreover, the contraction of collective bargaining coverage in general in the private sector means that the majority of employees in Britain have their pay determined unilaterally by management.

- Though it may not be all that common, a large amount of attention has been devoted to PRP and its implications. Managers find arrangements that associate pay with performance attractive; they help to secure the commitment of employees to business goals. While sometimes designed to undermine collectivism, PRP is not inimical to joint regulation and trade unionism. Nevertheless, despite the apparently greater freedom they enjoy to reform pay systems and influence pay settlements, managers have been reluctant to upset existing, 'tried-and-tested' arrangements.

- In the public sector, formal multi-employer bargaining arrangements have been somewhat resilient, despite attempts to challenge them. The operation of pay review bodies for key groups of workers, a form of 'arm's length bargaining', is an important contributory factor. The apparent resilience of formal machinery at national level may, however, disguise important changes in the workplace, such as 're-profiling' and 'skill-mix' initiatives, designed to alter the wage-work bargain in favour of the employer.

Collective bargaining trends are amply covered by Brown and Walsh (1991), and Brown, Marginson, and Walsh (1995, 2003). For data on pay-setting arrangements in contemporary employment relations, see Brown and Nash (2008) and Kersley et al. (2006). Marsden and French (1998) report on the findings of a study of PRP in the public services; Heery's (1998a) careful and sophisticated analysis of PRP in local government is also recommended. Charlwood (2007) demonstrates the continuing relevance of standardized pay-setting processes. See Bach and Winchester (2003) for an overview of employment relations developments in the public sector, and White (2000) for the role of pay review bodies. More information about the operation of pay review bodies can be found at the website of the Office for Manpower Economics http://www.ome.uk.com.

 Visit our Online Resource Centre for web links to sites connected to this section. www.oxfordtextbooks.co.uk/williams_adamsmith2e

7.3 Pay inequality, low pay, and the National Minimum Wage

One of the main implications of the diminution of collective bargaining as a pay-setting mechanism in Britain, and the consequent increase in managerial discretion, has been the growth of pay inequality. There is a strong relationship between low pay and gender, with women concentrated in low-paying occupations. In this respect, the 1999 introduction of the National Minimum Wage (NMW) as a means of regulating low pay was undoubtedly a significant development. Following an opening section in which we consider the growth of wage inequality and the problem of low pay, we assess the means by which low pay has been regulated from a historical perspective, before focusing on the details of the NMW and its effects.

7.3.1 Pay inequality in Britain

During the 1980s and 1990s there was a marked growth of pay inequality in Britain. By this we mean that the gap between high earners and low earners widened considerably, 'reaching the highest levels experienced in the twentieth century' (Machin 1999: 185). Between 1979 and 1996, the earnings of the bottom 25 per cent of male wage earners fell from 80 per cent to 73 per cent of median average earnings, while for the top 25 per cent they rose from 125 per cent to 138 per cent (Kessler and Bayliss 1998: 227). Increased inequality, then, was largely fuelled by the trend for pay rises of high and relatively high earners to far outstrip the increases for people on more modest earnings. With the exception of Ireland, where wage inequality also rose, in the rest of the European Union it largely remained stable or even diminished (Machin 1999).

The growth of pay inequality slowed during the 1990s (Machin 2003), before going into reverse during the first half of the 2000s. Overall, the 10-year period from 1996–97 to 2006–07 was a time when incomes grew relatively evenly, in contrast to the rapid rise in inequality that preceded it. Nevertheless, this general trend towards greater income equality, the result of people on middle incomes doing rather better, masks a couple of key details: the rise in incomes was fastest for those at the top of the income distribution scale, and lowest for those at the very bottom, despite the introduction of the NMW (see below).

Moreover, in 2005–06 and 2006–07 the trend towards greater overall income inequality resumed, largely because the incomes of a small minority of people at the very top of the income distribution scale were 'racing away' from the incomes of people further down (Brewer et al. 2008). Very high earners, those at the very peak of the income distribution scale, like boardroom directors, for example, have been able to secure ever higher levels of remuneration relative to others (see Box 7.4).

But the rising level of boardroom pay is only part of the story, albeit a very important one. Economic and labour market trends, in particular the development of new technology and increased wage premiums that can be attracted by more highly qualified workers, are also important factors. More importantly, however, employment deregulation (see below), the diminution of trade union power, and the fall in collective bargaining coverage also contributed to the growth of earnings inequality during the 1980s and 1990s (Brown, Marginson, and Walsh 2003). Where collective pay-setting institutions are robust, and particularly where they are centralized, they can act to compress pay differentials, especially if the unions are strongly committed to the pursuit of equality, as in Scandinavia, for example (Robson et al. 1999; Rubery and Edwards 2003). Thus the presence of powerful trade unions, and strong, centralized collective bargaining arrangements, can act to lessen the problem of low pay, though not so much for women (Dex, Robson, and Wilkinson 1999).

For some people, pay inequality is relatively unimportant. As long as there is no decline in the income of those at the bottom of the earnings hierarchy, it does not matter if there is an increasing gap between their income and that of those at the top. The Labour politician Peter Mandelson famously once confessed to being 'intensely relaxed about people getting filthy rich'. Yet there is a powerful body of evidence which demonstrates that the size of the gap between high and low earners matters in some very important ways. In their book *The Spirit Level*, for example, Wilkinson and Pickett (2009) show that countries with relatively high levels of income inequality (e.g. US, UK) suffer from greater social problems, higher crime rates and poorer health outcomes, than those which are more equal. Obesity, for example, is more prevalent in the UK than it is in countries with less inequality, such as Sweden.

7.3.2 The regulation of low pay

The growth of pay inequality during the 1980s and early 1990s meant that the issue of low pay, and how it could be regulated, became a priority for policy-makers. How, though, is low pay defined? Is there a particular level below which we can say pay is low? Or is low pay a relative concept, something that can only be measured in relation to the general level of earnings characteristic of a particular society? For example, a British worker earning £5.70 per hour may consider herself to be low-paid; an Indonesian worker on the same rate might think herself somewhat well off.

Employment relations reflection 7.4   Directors' pay and the growth of pay inequality

One of the contributory factors to the growth of pay inequality in Britain has been the ever increasing level of remuneration enjoyed by the directors of public limited companies. In 2002, for example, average boardroom pay rose by 23 per cent, some seven times greater than the growth in average earnings for all employees. In 2006, the pay of directors in top British companies increased by 37 per cent. In 2007, Bob Diamond, the head of Barclay's investment banking arm took home some £18m. Much of the increased remuneration for directors has come in the form of bonuses—after clinching deals for example.

Business groups, such as the Institute of Directors, claim that companies are operating in a global market for talent, and thus need to offer high basic salaries, and also the prospect of share options and generous bonuses, in order to attract key executives. Nevertheless, since the size of a director's remuneration package signals their importance relative to others, status, rather than the market, would appear to be the foremost influence on boardroom pay. One feature of executive pay that has caused widespread concern is that directors frequently receive large pay-offs on leaving their companies, regardless of their performance. During the 2000s, for example, the top executives of British banks benefited from massive bonuses, despite presiding over a banking system which almost collapsed in 2008, and was only kept afloat with the infusion of billions of pounds of taxpayers' money. In early 2009 there was a public outcry when the pension arrangements of Sir Fred Goodwin, the former chief executive of banking group RBS came to light. Despite presiding over what were perhaps the largest corporate losses in UK history—RBS lost £24 billion in 2008—Goodwin managed to secure a lifetime annual pension payment of nearly £700,000 at the age of fifty.

In the past, the government has been reluctant to legislate to regulate boardroom pay. During the 1990s, both Conservative and Labour administrations encouraged self-regulation, in particular the adoption of the Cadbury, Greenbury, and Hampel codes of practice which, among other things, recommended the establishment of dedicated remuneration committees made up of non-executive directors, and greater transparency and disclosure of directors' pay arrangements. The presumption was that it was for the shareholders of companies to challenge excessive and unjustified pay awards.

Some controversial pay deals did, however, prompt the Labour government to introduce legislation. Shareholders were given the opportunity to vote on directors' remuneration arrangements at company annual general meetings. In 2003, shareholders of the pharmaceutical firm Glaxo-SmithKline voted down the £22 million pay-off due to chief executive Jean-Pierre Garnier should his contract be terminated. Such votes, though, are merely voluntary, and companies can ignore them if they wish. Yet despite occasionally hinting at the need for further action, the government has been unwilling to intervene directly, stressing that the responsibility for directors' remuneration should rest in the hands of the company's shareholders. The economic slowdown of the late 2000s led to a sharp fall in the rate at which boardroom pay increased. Yet it remains to be seen if the government will take the opportunity presented to legislate to curb the pay excesses of the boardroom. Many experts believe that the City of London's profligate bonus culture, by encouraging executives to behave imprudently, was a significant cause of the banking system's failure, and thus a major contribution to the economic recession which it spawned.

Studies of low pay prefer to treat it as a relative concept (e.g. Rubery and Edwards 2003). What measure, then, should be used? The Organization for Economic Cooperation and Development (OECD) defines low pay as a level of earnings that falls below two-thirds of median average full-time earnings. The profusion of different measures can sometimes make international comparisons difficult, especially if they restrict the analysis to full-time earnings, since low pay is often a feature of part-time jobs (Rubery and Edwards 2003), which are largely populated by women. Low pay is also more common in small businesses than in larger ones, and also in certain occupations, such as hospitality, private social care, retail, clothing, and textile manufacturing, and hairdressing.

Broadly speaking, there are two main ways in which low pay is regulated in modern economies: by collective agreements, or by means of a statutory minimum wage (Rubery and Grimshaw 2003). In the case of the first of these arrangements, a floor of wages is generally set by collective bargaining on an industry-by-industry basis, such as in Germany, for example, with governments sometimes having the power to extend the settlement to all employers in the sector, even those that are not directly party to the agreement. Centralized systems of bargaining can often be quite effective ways of regulating low pay, and of impeding the growth of wage inequality, especially for men (Bazen and Benhayoun 1992; Robson et al. 1999). The second type of arrangement, a statutory minimum wage, exists in countries such as France, Spain, Portugal, and, since the late 1990s, in Ireland and Britain too.

But the NMW, which took effect in Britain from April 1999, is by no means the first way in which the British state has acted to regulate low pay. Fair Wages Resolutions, for example, which originated in 1891, meant that employers had to respect minimum standards when working on government contracts, largely to prevent unfair competition arising from the undercutting of wages (Bercusson 1978; Coats 2007). In the early 1980s, the Conservative government repealed them. In 1993, the Conservatives also abolished all bar one of the remaining wages councils, which, for a large part of the twentieth century, had fixed wage rates, and sometimes employment conditions, in a range of low-paying sectors. They were seen as outdated and anachronistic institutions which inhibited labour market flexibility, ineffective at tackling poverty and, given the claim that they priced workers out of jobs, impediments to employment growth (Dickens et al. 1993; Rubery and Edwards 2003).

Research into the impact of the abolition of the wages councils found evidence of widening pay distribution, and an absence of any positive impact on employment. According to Coats (2007: 17), the 'effect of wages councils abolition was significantly to increase the number of low paid workers in the UK'. A study of the hospitality industry found that abolition caused pay to fall in a third of establishments; nevertheless, one employer welcomed the greater 'flexibility' that the removal of the wages councils had brought, meaning that he could 'get away with paying lower wages' (Lucas and Radiven 1998: 11).

Thus we are presented with a stark indication of how the weakening of the institutions of labour market regulation, driven by Conservative governments of the 1980s and 1990s, contributed to increasing wage inequality (Coats 2007). The Labour government elected in 1997, however, initiated an important change of direction by establishing, for the first time ever, a National Minimum Wage, 'belatedly bringing Britain in to line with the rest of the industrialized world' (Brown 2000: 309). Over the following pages, we examine the main features of the NMW and assess its effects, including its impact on inequality.

7.3.3 The National Minimum Wage in Britain

Labour's commitment to an NMW was the outcome of protracted debates and struggle within the party as supporters of the policy, particularly within some trade unions, tried to overcome the traditional ambivalence towards statutory wage-fixing that had characterized attitudes within much of the labour movement (see Coats 2007).

Following its victory at the 1997 general election, the Labour government set up a Low Pay Commission (LPC), comprising employers' and union representatives, as well as academic experts. The LPC's initial role was to make recommendations to government over such matters as the coverage of the minimum wage (i.e. to whom would it apply?), the elements of pay that could be counted towards the minimum wage (e.g. what should happen to tips—see the introductory case study), and the minimum wage rates themselves.

Once the NMW came into effect, the LPC continued in existence with its role largely devoted to investigating the effects of the minimum wage, and with making recommendations to the government over changes to the minimum wage rates (or 'upratings') and other relevant matters. The operation of the LPC, in particular the high level of consensus that informs its recommendations, has been praised (e.g. Brown 2000). For Coats (2007: 46), a former LPC member, one of its main achievements has been to win round sceptical employers, helping to establish a 'consensus that the NMW should be a permanent feature of the labour market'.

Once it had determined what aspects of pay could be counted towards the NMW (tips left on the table by customers are excluded, for example), perhaps the most significant tasks which faced the LPC were to recommend a minimum rate, and to determine which workers would be entitled to receive it. The LPC proposed that all workers aged 21 and over should be covered by the full NMW rate, at a 'deliberately prudent' (Metcalf 1999) £3.60 per hour. It also recommended a lower 'development' NMW rate of £3.20 per hour which should be paid to workers aged between 18 and 20. The government accepted these recommendations, but made two adjustments. First, the lower NMW rate was introduced at £3.00 per hour for young workers. Second, it was extended to cover 21-year-olds. Since their introduction in 1999, the NMW rates have been changed, or 'uprated', several times, as can be seen from Table 7.4.

There was a considerable amount of discussion within the LPC about the provision of a lower, or 'subminimum', NMW rate which would apply to younger workers. What was the rationale for the differential rates? Although it was expected that in the longer term the youth development rate should be linked to a programme of relevant skills training (LPC 1998, 2000, 2001a), it was introduced largely because of a concern that if young workers were to be covered by the main NMW rate it would make them too expensive for employers to hire, thus significantly damaging their labour market prospects (Coats 2007; Metcalf 1999). Research on the effects of minimum wages in the United States demonstrates, however, that subminimum rates of pay for young

Table 7.4 National Minimum Wage rates, 1999–2009

	Workers aged 22 and over	Workers aged 18–21	Workers aged 16–17
April 1999	£3.60	£3.00	
June 2000	No uprating	£3.20	
October 2000	£3.70	No uprating	
October 2001	£4.10	£3.50	
October 2002	£4.20	£3.60	
October 2003	£4.50	£3.80	
October 2004	£4.85	£4.10	£3.00
October 2005	£5.05	£4.25	No uprating
October 2006	£5.35	£4.45	£3.30
October 2007	£5.52	£4.60	£3.40
October 2008	£5.73	£4.77	£3.53
October 2009	£5.80	£4.83	£3.57

workers are not only unpopular among employers, largely based on the belief that they would not be able to attract workers at such low wages, but that they also appear to have no discernible positive impact on employment (Card and Krueger 1995; Katz and Krueger 1992).

Initially, the use of the youth development rates was far from extensive. In a study of the textiles industry, Heyes and Gray (2001) found that forty-eight out of the fifty-three workplaces they studied paid 18–21 year olds an hourly rate that was greater than the development rate. The reluctance of employers to use the lower rate for young workers is something that has been identified elsewhere (e.g. Langlois and Lucas 2005). There are difficulties recruiting, motivating, and retaining younger workers at rates of pay that are below the main 'adult' NMW level; many managers view it as unfair to discriminate against them on the grounds of age (Williams, Adam-Smith, and Norris 2004). However, as the main NMW rate has increased, some employers have reintroduced age-based differentials as a way of managing the extra costs of compliance.

Originally, the NMW did not cover workers aged below 18. The LPC and the government did not want to encourage teenagers to leave full-time education. However, in October 2004 the government introduced a new, lower rate of £3.00 per hour that applies to 16 and 17 year olds. This was done because of concerns raised by trade unions that some young workers were being exploited by unscrupulous employers who were paying them very low rates of pay, less than £2.00 an hour in some cases (LPC 2004).

The LPC and the government attracted criticism from some quarters for coming up with a main initial NMW rate which, at £3.60 per hour in 1999, was set at far too low a level. Based upon her experiences of a series of low-paying jobs, including cleaning hotels and working in a care home, the journalist Fran Abrams challenged the assumptions upon which the introduction of the minimum wage was based. She referred to the NMW as 'an old-fashioned political stitch-up, set at a level which would ensure the lowest possible level of protest from employers without enraging the unions sufficiently for them to cause real trouble' (Abrams 2002: 170). In some parts of Britain, notably London, pressure for a higher, 'living' wage has grown (see Box 7.5). While the NMW policy is clearly a marked contrast with the deregulatory labour market approach followed by the Conservatives during the 1980s and 1990s (see Chapter 3), it has been implemented in a way that is deliberately designed not to inconvenience employers too greatly.

Yet such criticisms have been challenged by former members of the LPC. Coats (2007), for example, points to the notable annual increases in the NMW, particularly between 2002 and 2006, when they exceeded both inflation and rises in average earnings. He defends the deliberately cautious stance initially followed by the LPC, which favoured introducing an NMW at a relatively low level, just in case there were any adverse effects on the economy, and, through regular upratings, building from there. Coats (2007: 49) maintains that once 'it was clear that there were no negative effects on employment ... the LPC had scope for somewhat greater ambition in testing the boundaries'.

7.3.4 The impact of the National Minimum Wage

In considering the impact of the NMW we first need to ascertain who has benefited from it; and second, to assess what, if anything, it has done to alleviate the above-mentioned growth of wage inequality. Some 1.1 million workers gained directly from the 1999 introduction of the NMW. Later upratings have benefited between 1 and 1.25 million

---

Employment relations reflection 7.5   Campaigning for a 'living wage'

During the 2000s the focus of many campaigners against low pay shifted away from the need for a minimum wage towards greater advocacy of a 'living wage', particularly in the United States (Luce 2004). The living wage movement has spread to the UK, particularly in London, where the community organization London Citizens has won the backing of both the Mayor of London and the Greater London Authority for a living wage—£7.45 per hour in 2008–09—well above the statutory NMW. What is a living wage? London Citizens states that it is the amount of pay necessary for a worker to be able to enjoy a proper standard of living both for themselves and their family. In collaboration with some trade unions, London Citizens has campaigned vigorously to get employers to agree to pay all their staff a living wage, including those employed indirectly by contractors to undertake cleaning and catering duties among other things. Among the employers that support the London Living Wage are Barclays, KPMG, and Hilton Hotels (http://www.livingwageemployer.org.uk). Coats (2007), however, is sceptical about the living wage concept, arguing that since the needs of households and families vary so widely, it is inappropriate to specify a rate of pay which encompasses them all.

workers. Most of the beneficiaries, some two-thirds, are women workers, especially those employed in part-time jobs. Workers in low-paying sectors of the economy—notably hairdressing, hospitality, retail, and social care—have benefited disproportionately from the presence of the NMW.

There is some evidence that the NMW may have contributed to the decline in income inequality during the first half of the 2000s, in particular by helping to increase the income of the poorest working households (see Coats 2007: 57; Metcalf 2008). The NMW also seems to have contributed to a reduction in the gender pay gap (Coats 2007; Metcalf 2008). Nevertheless, while annual increases in the NMW rates have matched, and sometimes exceeded rises in average earnings and prices (Metcalf 2008), helping low-paid workers to catch up, they are considerably outstripped by the growth in earnings enjoyed by those at the very top.

Prior to the implementation of the NMW, there were some well-informed, and many not so well-informed, predictions of its likely effects both on employment in low-paying sectors of the economy and also on the economy in general. Before, during, and after the 1997 general election, both the Conservative party and many business organizations opposed the minimum wage policy (though the Conservatives now support it), claiming that it would push up inflation, and would have such an adverse impact on employment that hundreds of thousands of jobs would be at risk.

The simple economic reasoning behind these claims is that any rise in the price of labour—wages, that is—will, without a corresponding increase in productivity, reduce employers' demand for it. Alternatively, firms will pass on the higher costs of adapting to the NMW to customers in the form of higher prices. Such problems would be exacerbated if, as critics of the minimum wage expected, other groups of workers were to secure corresponding increases in their wages in order to preserve their relative position in the pay hierarchy or, in other words, restore their existing pay 'differentials'.

Yet contrary to these expectations, the introduction of the NMW appears to have had little adverse effect on the British economy; it arrived with a 'whimper rather than a bang' (Dickens and Manning 2003: 202). The impact on inflation was negligible, and employment levels in many low-paying sectors of the economy, such as hospitality and retail, for example, rose, rather than fell, once the minimum wage took effect (LPC 2001a).

The low level at which the NMW was initially set meant that most firms, even in low-paying sectors of the economy, were unaffected directly by its introduction; and many of those that were found the necessary increases in wage rates easily affordable. Moreover, the NMW was introduced in a period of robust economic growth. Increasing demand for hospitality services, for example, led to a tightening of the labour market, often pushing up wages to well above the NMW rate (Adam-Smith, Norris, and Williams 2003). There has also been little pressure from workers higher up the earnings hierarchy to maintain their differentials. The economic recession of the late 2000s may cause this picture to change, of course.

Overall, neither the introduction of the NMW, nor its subsequent upratings, seems to have had a detrimental impact on employment levels (Coats 2007; Metcalf 2008). Machin and Wilson (2004) surveyed care homes before and after the NMW came into effect. Despite having a substantial impact on wage rates in the sector—nearly a third (32 per cent) of care workers employed by firms in the survey earned less than £3.60 per hour before the NMW came into effect in 1999—the minimum wage had few adverse consequences for employment, and no establishments were forced to close as a result.

What explains the absence of a negative impact on employment? Metcalf (2008) considers the strengths and weaknesses of a range of explanations, some of which he rejects. Based on a rigorous assessment of the available data, he posits five plausible reasons for the relatively muted employment effects of the NMW:

- employers have coped with the increased costs of the NMW by raising productivity, rather than reducing employment;
- some of the increase in costs has been passed on to consumers in the form of higher prices;
- firms have coped by taking a smaller share of profits;
- employers have reduced hours of work rather than cut jobs; and
- employers have a degree of market power and thus some flexibility when determining wages; this means that they did not necessarily react to the NMW by cutting jobs.

This last point is important for understanding why the NMW has not created a 'labour market shock', and reduced employment levels, in the manner expected by some (e.g. Brown and Crossman 2000). Studies of the impact of the NMW in low-paying sectors of the economy generally show most firms to have been unaffected directly by the introduction of the statutory floor of wages (Adam-Smith, Norris, and Williams 2003; Heyes and Grey 2001; Undy, Kessler, and Thompson 2002).

They also demonstrate that even where firms were required to raise wages in response to the NMW, there was generally little impact on employment levels. For many firms, frequently small businesses operating on tight margins, there is no further scope to reduce their workforce since they already operate with the minimum number of staff necessary to function. In the clothing and knitwear industries employment was falling, but this was largely a consequence of greater foreign competition (Undy, Kessler, and Thompson 2002).

Among firms that have been directly affected by the minimum wage, perhaps the most noticeable way in which they have attempted to recoup the costs of higher wages, particularly in clothing manufacturing where piecework incentives have been eroded, has been through increased workloads and greater supervision (Heyes and Grey 2001; Undy, Kessler, and Thompson 2002). The minimum wage also appears to have caused some firms to invest in new technology as a way of boosting productivity and thus recouping costs. But this has been rare. Indeed, the most striking feature of firms' responses to the NMW has been the absence of any pattern other than that its introduction does not appear to have been overly traumatic. How, then, did the minimum wage come to be accommodated so relatively easily?

The key to understanding the relatively muted impact of the NMW rests upon an appreciation that firms in low-paying sectors of the economy, where formal arrangements for determining pay are uncommon, have the ability to respond to changes in their environment, such as the introduction of a minimum wage, in a dynamic way

(Edwards and Gilman 1999). In other words, the high level of informality that characterizes the management of employment relations in small firms means that employers
enjoy considerable freedom to juggle the terms of the wage-work bargain in order to
respond to external challenges.

In the hospitality industry, for example, employers are well used to operating with
less than a full complement of staff, not least because of high turnover levels and the
need to keep costs under control. The introduction of the NMW, insofar as it raises costs,
has not transformed this situation, but merely encouraged employers to tinker with it
(Adam-Smith, Norris, and Williams 2003). Many employers in low-paying sectors of the
economy have adapted to the increased costs of the NMW simply by 'muddling through'
(Metcalf 2008).

Thus, far from being a shock to firms in low-paying sectors of the economy, the minimum wage is simply a further influence among the many that shape the employment
relationship. It is unlikely that a consistent pattern of responses to the NMW will be
identified, particularly with it being set at such a low level. Rather, affected firms will
react in idiosyncratic and diverse ways, influenced by the characteristics of their product
and labour market environments (Gilman et al. 2002; Ram et al. 2001). A study of the
impact of the NMW in small firms demonstrated that, while the establishment of a statutory floor of wages often raised their costs, its arrival 'did not provide a shock sufficient
to jolt employers or workers out of their customary practices and habits' (Arrowsmith
et al. 2003: 451–2).

Of course, another way in which employers in low-paying sectors of the economy can
avoid the consequences of the NMW legislation is by failing to comply with it. How
much of a problem is non-compliance? And what are the main methods used to effect
enforcement with the NMW? While the extent of non-compliance is difficult to measure, overall it seems to be quite rare. Nevertheless, concerns have been expressed that
the level of non-compliance in the informal economy, particularly among migrant workers, may be rising (Croucher and White 2007). Some unions claim that the practice of
employers providing opportunities for unpaid work experience should be more closely
scrutinized (see Box 7.6). Generally, though, it is the technical aspects of the NMW regulations that cause the biggest problems, such as ensuring tips are handled correctly, for
example, suggesting that much non-compliance is done inadvertently.

Principal responsibility for enforcing the NMW rests with HM Revenue and Customs
(HMRC). Each year, enforcement officers make some 5,000 visits to employers, sometimes in response to complaints from workers. On average, each year HRMC enforcement action results in workers receiving some £3 million in pay arrears. However, the
system of enforcement has been criticized for being inadequate. Metcalf (2008) calculates that on average an employer can expect a visit from an enforcement officer once
every 320 years.

Employers found to have paid workers less than the minimum wage are typically
not penalized. Generally they are only obliged to make up any arrears; even then
there are no specific methods to make sure that employers actually do pay up, apart
from the threat of criminal proceedings—which have never been instituted (Croucher
and White 2007: 155). Given the feebleness of the enforcement arrangements,

---

Employment relations reflection 7.6   Unpaid work experience: opportunity or exploitation?

In some areas of work, particularly the media industry, it has become increasingly commonplace to find menial, entry-level tasks being undertaken by a cadre of young and unpaid 'volunteer' staff—often known as 'interns'—who agree to work for no wages in exchange for training, work experience, and the chance to develop contacts—perhaps with the chance of securing a glamorous, well-paid job on a newspaper or in television as a result. While much of their work involves running errands, or procuring refreshments, it can also encompass reception duties. However, some trade unions claim that employers use unpaid work experience as a way of reducing costs, and of avoiding having to pay the minimum wage, with little benefit for the workers involved. The National Union of Journalists, for example, asserts that few interns receive proper training or end up securing employment at the end of their period of work experience. The media and broadcasting union BECTU also claims that any training element is largely absent, and that the use of volunteer labour in this way 'amounts to the exploitation of young people desperate to gain a foothold in the film/TV sector' (TUC 2008: 121).

---

the really remarkable thing is 'that so many employers *do* comply with the NMW' (Metcalf 2008: 499).

Such a 'soft' enforcement regime was designed on the basis that workers themselves could also pursue their right to be paid the minimum wage by instituting legal action against employers (Croucher and White 2007: 155). In 2006–07 there were some 800 complaints about non-payment of the NMW made to employment tribunals. However, there are three problems with this method of effecting compliance with the NMW. First, workers may lack the appropriate knowledge of their rights under the NMW legislation; and so may not be aware that they have a justified complaint.

Second, even if they do have adequate knowledge, workers may be reluctant to complain about underpayment of the minimum wage; with good reason, since there is some evidence that employers victimize workers who make their voice heard.

Third, workers may be discouraged from making a complaint against their employer because of a fear that it would jeopardize their jobs (Croucher and White 2007).

Since 2005, as a result of LPC recommendations and pressure from trade unions and campaign groups for the low-paid, the government has taken steps to improve the enforcement of the NMW. This includes better targeted enforcement activity by HMRC officers, particularly in the hospitality sector, where there are large numbers of migrant workers. Responding to calls for further improvements, the government has taken steps to reform the NMW's enforcement regime. For example, the Employment Act 2008 establishes a new procedure under which employers who fail to comply with the minimum wage could face civil penalties.

SECTION SUMMARY AND FURTHER READING

- During the 1980s and 1990s, wage inequality in Britain grew markedly, caused by labour market changes, the erosion of collective bargaining coverage, and soaring pay rises for high earners. During the 2000s, the inequality trend appears to have stabilized; although as the decade went on there were signs that it had begun to take hold again.

- There are two broad ways in which low pay can be regulated, either by some form of statutory minimum wage, or by means of comprehensive collective agreements which provide a floor of wages on an industry basis. The latter appears to be a more effective way of tackling wage inequality, especially among men.

- The first National Minimum Wage (NMW) was introduced in Britain in 1999. The main NMW rate was initially set at a rather low level, something which attracted a large amount of criticism, though it has since been substantially increased.

- The NMW has not had any adverse consequences for employment, and has been accommodated by firms in low-paying sectors of the economy with relative ease. Nevertheless, there are growing concerns about non-compliance in some parts of the economy.

Machin (2003) provides a good overview of trends in wage inequality in Britain up to the early 2000s. The Institute for Fiscal Studies is a good source of up-to-date material on inequality and related matters (http://www.ifs.org.uk). The best analysis of low pay, attempts to regulate it, and the implications of the NMW is offered by Rubery and Edwards (2003). Coats (2007) offers a very lucid and readable assessment of the background to, and details of, minimum wage policy. For an account of the way in which the Low Pay Commission handled its task from a notable advocate of a cautious and prudent approach to the NMW, see Metcalf (1999). Croucher and White (2007) deal with compliance and enforcement issues. The Low Pay Commission produces regular reports, available online, which contain masses of detail about the operation of the NMW (http://www.lowpay.gov.uk). Finally, for studies of the impact of the NMW in particular sectors, see Adam-Smith, Norris, and Williams (2003), and Arrowsmith et al. (2003).

 Visit our Online Resource Centre for web links to sites connected to this section. www.oxfordtextbooks.co.uk/williams_adamsmith2e

7.4 Developments in working time

Working time—its length, its pattern, and its use—is a central concern of employment relations, although it is often overlooked in textbooks (Sisson and Storey 2000). This is somewhat odd since, as was discussed in chapter 1 of this book, the principal feature of the employment relationship is the exchange of wages for latent labour power—an employee's capacity to work. When a job is started it is not the worker's labour that an employer is buying, but, in effect, his or her time. It is then the task of the employer to ensure that this time is used productively (Arrowsmith and Sisson 2000: 303). Moreover, working time has long been an issue on which trade unions have campaigned, for a shorter working week in particular. In order to understand contemporary employment relations properly, then, it is essential to consider trends in working time, and also how it is regulated.

The issue of working time has recently attracted an increasing amount of interest, to such an extent that it may even have become as important as pay as an employment relations topic. There are three reasons for this. First, because of claims employers are seeking innovations in how working time is organized as a way of generating efficiencies. Second, concerns have been expressed about the harmful effects of excessive working time in Britain, or what has popularly become known as the 'long hours culture'. Third, in 1998 the British government introduced the Working Time Regulations (WTR), as a result of a European Union (EU) directive, which ostensibly places legal limits upon the number of hours that can be worked. Before we consider these developments, it is necessary to consider working time and employment relations in general.

7.4.1 Working time and employment relations

The organization of working time by employers was critical to the development of capitalist industrialization during the late eighteenth and nineteenth centuries. Since it helped employers to develop a new ethos of factory discipline, the clock was a crucial component of the rise of the factory system (Pollard 1968; Thompson 1967). Although workers did not submit meekly to the new industrial capitalist order, attendance at work, for a specified period of time governed by the clock, became the norm.

Like any other aspect of the employment relationship, attempts by employers to control working time have always been challenged. One way in which employees can appropriate working time is by absenting themselves (Ackroyd and Thompson 1999)—see Chapter 9. But there are also other ways in which workers have manipulated working time to suit their interests.

In particular, in workplaces based around production lines workers have opportunities to exert control over their working time, by working 'back up the line', for example. This refers to the process, commonplace in vehicle manufacturing at one time (e.g. Turner, Clack, and Roberts 1967), by which an increase in the pace of work enables workers to generate short, informal rest breaks as the production line catches up. This is particularly effective in situations where workers are able to manipulate job timings set through work study techniques. If workers can slow a job down and make it look difficult when it is being measured, this is likely to result in a 'loose' rate, making it easier to accumulate informal rest periods if they revert to their normal, faster pace or, alternatively, allowing them to work more leisurely, at the pace set for the work study engineers, without any loss of pay (Roy 1952). While it may have become harder for workers to manipulate working time to their advantage, attempts to do so remain an important feature of the employment relationship.

Not only is working time an important feature of the employment relationship, but it is also one that is contested between the employer and employee. This can be seen in the long-running attempts by workers, collectively through trade unions, to shorten the length of both the working day and the working week. Although nineteenth-century campaigns by prominent liberal philanthropists helped to secure reduced working hours for women and child workers, it is important to recognize that legislation was largely the outcome of working-class pressure for reform (Arrowsmith 2002). The reduction of working time has been an aim of organized labour ever since, if not always a central one.

Working time has long been a key source of contestation between unions and employers, and campaigns to reduce its length were 'fundamental to the organization of the working class and the development of labour solidarity' (Arrowsmith 2002: 114). During the 1980s and 1990s, for example, engineering unions in Germany and Britain successfully used industrial action to reduce the length of the working week, to thirty-five hours in the case of the former. However, this often came at a price as employers conceded lower hours in return for greater flexibility over the utilization of working time (Hyman 2001b; McKinlay and McNulty 1992). Nevertheless, trade unions have an important role in successfully campaigning for, and wresting from employers, reductions in working time, and also paid holiday entitlement (Green 1997).

7.4.2 Trends in working time

Having considered the importance of working time in employment relations, and the way in which trade union efforts have been directed at reducing it, what, then, have been the main trends? Historically, the overall trend in Britain, at least until the 1990s, was towards the reduction in the average number of weekly working hours for full-time employees. Nevertheless, reflecting the large extent to which working time reductions were the outcome of struggles and campaigns by organized labour, it was 'manifested in sporadic discrete jumps punctuated by long periods of stability' (Green 2001: 58).

During the 1990s, however, this trend came to an end, and may even have been reversed, resulting in British full-time employees achieving the dubious distinction of having the longest average working week in the EU; raising significant concerns about the rise of a so-called 'long-hours culture' (Arrowsmith 2002). While working hours for full-time employees in the UK are relatively high, contrary to popular perception they are no longer the highest in the EU (see Table 7.5).

Table 7.5 Number of hours usually worked each week by full-time employees in their main job, selected EU countries 2008

Austria	42.9
Czech Republic	42.3
Greece	42.2
Germany	42.1
Poland	41.8
The Netherlands	41.1
United Kingdom	41.0 (42.0 in 1999)
Spain	41.0
Belgium	40.9
Italy	40.4
France	39.5

Source: Eurostat

Taken as a whole, the average length of the working week in Britain is unremarkable relative to other EU countries. Moreover, the high number of part-time jobs in Britain means that there is a notable 'dispersion' of working hours (Green 2001): some work many hours in an average week, whereas others may only work on a part-time basis for a few. Moreover, as can be seen from Table 7.5, during the 2000s the average weekly hours worked by full-time employees fell; see below for an explanation.

Before we examine the Working Time Regulations, and consider whether or not they have made any impact on working hours, we first need to consider the factors responsible for the lengthening of the average working week for full-time employees during the 1990s. Four factors seem to have been significant. First, greater competitive pressures encouraged many businesses to find ways of increasing output while freezing, or even reducing, staff numbers. Thus employees, particularly those in white-collar jobs like professionals and managers, were obliged to work more hours, usually unpaid, to make up the slack (Beynon et al. 2002).

Second, unlike other EU countries, where statutory limits on working time are commonplace (see Box 7.7 on France), before the advent of the Working Time Regulations in 1998 (see below) there was little statutory regulation of working time in Britain (Arrowsmith and Sisson 2000).

Third, the trade unions which, through their collective bargaining endeavours, had been a major influence on the shortening of the working week, suffered a significant reduction in their power during the 1980s and 1990s.

Fourth, employment relations in Britain was, and still is, characterized by a remarkably high incidence of overtime working, paid, usually at a higher, premium rate, or unpaid work undertaken in excess of the 'normal' working day or week.

Data from the 2004 Workplace Employment Relations Survey indicate that so-called 'long-hours working', held to mean in excess of 48 hours per week, is concentrated in certain areas of the economy (see Kersley et al. 2006: 266–7):

- 11 per cent of employees usually work more than forty-eight hours a week (13 per cent in 1998); 31 per cent of employees working in transport jobs usually work more than 48 hours a week;

- 9 per cent of employees reported having worked more than 48 hours a week every week for the preceding year; 54 per cent never work more than 48 hours a week;

- 20 per cent of transport employees and 15 per cent in education reported having worked more than 48 hours a week every week over the previous 12 months;

- 18 per cent of managers, 13 per cent of supervisory staff, and 6 per cent of other non-managerial employees said that they had worked for more than 48 hours a week every week for the preceding year; and

- 36 per cent of men and 70 per cent of women reported never working more than 48 hours a week.

The data indicate that so-called 'long-hours working' is concentrated among certain groups of workers (e.g. male workers, managers) and within particular industries (e.g. transport). It is worth bearing in mind that the Working Time Regulations (see below), which were introduced to combat excessive working hours by setting an upper limit of

INTERNATIONAL PERSPECTIVE 7.7

The 35-hour working week in France

The regulation and control of working time has long been a central concern of trade unions in France, and a prime source of contestation in employment relations. For much of the twentieth century, reductions in working hours, either through legislation or employer concessions, were the outcome of intense periods of mobilization and struggle by organized labour (Jefferys 2000). Following the 1981 election of François Mitterrand as president of France, and the establishment of a coalition government of socialists and communists, a 1982 law fixed the maximum working week, before overtime payments apply, at 39 hours, with the progressive reduction to 35 hours as a longer-term aim, and increased the minimum period of paid annual leave to five weeks.

Although a 1996 law provided employers with incentives to shorten the working week voluntarily, realization of the 35-hour limit had to await the 1997 election of a Socialist government under the premiership of Lionel Jospin. While it had never really disappeared from the political agenda, working time 'was now back with a vengeance' (Jefferys 2003: 141–2). The first 'Aubry' law of 1998, named after its ministerial sponsor, offered incentives for employers who negotiated 35-hour agreements that created jobs. The second 'Aubry' law of 2000 made the maximum 35-hour week mandatory for all those working in firms with more than 20 employees.

The ostensible aim of the legislation was to create job opportunities, and thus reduce the level of four million unemployed. Perhaps some half a million new jobs were generated between 1997 and 2001. By 2001, full-time employees in France worked an average of 38.3 hours per week including overtime, the lowest of any EU country. But the legislation was also driven by another imperative, 'that of a continuing process of state modernization of industrial relations in which working time was held out as bait' (Jefferys 2003: 142). The aim, then, was to encourage firms to negotiate workplace agreements with local union representatives over the more flexible use of working time. This would, it was hoped, not only stimulate workplace bargaining, and thus challenge the authority of the unions and their national power bases, but also enhance productivity through the more intensive use of working time.

Understandably, therefore, many manual workers, who bore the brunt of such flexibility initiatives, were rather restrained in their support of the 35-hour week. However, the main challenge has come from the right-wing presidency of Nicolas Sarkozy, who was elected in 2007 on a platform which included a pledge to loosen the 35-hour limit. Reforms introduced in 2008 allow employers to reach agreements with unions and employees which provide for greater flexibility over working hours. While the 35-hour limit has not been abolished, the reforms have moderated its effectiveness.

48 hours on the length of the working week, initially did not cover jobs in transport, and still do not apply to senior managers.

The preponderance of overtime working in Britain has long been criticized. Flanders (1975) viewed the existence of 'systematic overtime' as a sign of managerial irresponsibility; it was an inefficient, albeit relatively easy, way of securing increases in output without hiring new staff or, more importantly, investing in capital machinery, and thus stifled innovation. Workers welcomed the opportunity to undertake overtime since it enabled them to supplement their low basic wages. In the 1950s and 1960s, then, overtime working became 'institutionalized', particularly among male manual workers (Arrowsmith 2002). This refers to the way in which overtime came 'to be accepted as a habit—as a way of life in industry—for which all kinds of justifications are then invented'. It gained 'a self-perpetuating character' (Flanders 1975: 56).

Overtime working remains commonplace in Britain (Arrowsmith and Sisson 1999), and has had a major influence on the length of the working week. On average, employees undertake 3.6 hours of overtime each week (Kersley et al. 2006). An over-reliance on overtime working can be a source of disruption for employers (see Box 7.8). It is also a potentially very inefficient way of organizing working time. Workers may work more slowly during their normal contractual working hours in order to ensure that overtime—paid at a premium rate—is needed to complete their tasks.

One notable working time trend concerns the rising incidence of unpaid overtime—some two-thirds of managers and professionals who undertake overtime receive no reimbursement for the additional hours worked. However, the most widely cited reason why workers undertake overtime working is that they need the additional earnings in order to supplement their regular wages (Kodz et al. 2003).

There has also been a marked trend towards greater diversity in working time arrangements as the hitherto 'standard' working week of 9.00 to 5.00, Monday to Friday working becomes less commonplace. While some industries, such as transport, for example, have long been marked by the presence of shift-working arrangements, which require staff to attend work outside of the weekday norm, patterns of working time have become more complex and fragmented (Walsh 2005). Increasing numbers of people work what used to be called 'unsocial hours', in the evening or at weekends, as competitive pressures oblige businesses, particularly in the expanding service sector, to open for longer periods. Many large supermarkets, for example, open until late in the evening, and sometimes all night; Sunday opening has also become the norm.

Moreover, while part-time working arrangements have long been commonplace in many areas of economy, especially parts of the service sector like the retail and hospitality industries, as we saw in Chapter 4 there has been a substantial growth of interest in how flexible working time arrangements can be used to promote more 'family-friendly' employment. This has encouraged a certain amount of innovation in working time arrangements. Some employers, like the Foreign and Commonwealth Office, for example,

INSIGHT INTO PRACTICE 7.8

The disruptive potential of overtime working

The following example demonstrates how an over-reliance on overtime working can, when handled badly, create disruption. In December 2005, Central Trains, one of the UK's passenger rail operators cancelled all of its services on the Sunday before Christmas because too few train drivers had reported for work. Sunday working was undertaken on the basis of voluntary overtime. In other words, drivers worked on Sundays in return for a premium payment. Most of the time this meant that Central Trains had sufficient drivers to maintain its Sunday timetable. In this instance, though, the failure of enough drivers to report for work was intensely damaging for the business.

have established compressed working weeks, which enable staff to work the same number of hours in a week, or fortnight, as before, but over fewer days.

Another way in which working time can be organized on a more flexible basis is through the use of so-called 'zero-hours contracts'. Under these arrangements, the employer is not obliged to provide work to an employee; nor is there any obligation on the employee to accept work from their employer. Thus the number of working hours to be worked, and when they are to be worked, are not specified in the employment contract. Employees are only paid for the hours that they work. Supporters of zero-hours contracts claim that not only do they give employers flexibility to adjust working time in response to patterns of demand in a very cost-effective way, but that they also benefit workers, who benefit from the flexibility to work when it is suitable for them to do so, enabling them to accommodate family responsibilities more easily. While some retailers (e.g. Boots) have used zero-hours contracts for shop staff, overall they are not very common, being present in just 5 per cent of workplaces (Kersley et al. 2006). Concerned about their potential to cause exploitation, by not providing workers with any guaranteed earnings, some unions have campaigned against zero-hours contracts, and have called for them to be banned.

One of the most innovative forms of flexible working time arrangement is 'annualized hours'. While they vary in their detail, the main feature of annualized hours arrangements is the specification of a certain number of hours to be worked by an employee in any given year, in exchange for a guaranteed wage. Among the companies that have instituted annualized hours schemes for some of their staff are RAC Motoring Services and Siemens (Arrowsmith 2007). The main benefit of annualized hours for employers is that it enables them to manage peaks and slumps in demand for a product over a year without having to resort to the use of expensive overtime when it is high, or having workers sitting around idle when it is low.

Given that, for the employer, the aims of introducing annualized hours are to secure greater flexibility and eliminate overtime, employees are, understandably, often wary about it, even though their overall working time may fall and basic earnings rise (Arrowsmith 2007). Managers may pledge that the average guaranteed wage will leave most employees better off, but the loss of overtime may have a significant negative impact on the income of some (see Heyes 1997); and a greater likelihood of 'unsocial hours' working under annualized hours arrangement may prove to be difficult for people, usually women, who have childcare responsibilities (Rubery and Grimshaw 2003).

Given that annualized hours offer employers some major benefits, including reduced overtime payments, enhanced flexibility, and greater control over how working time is used, why is it not more commonplace? Fewer than one in twenty employees (some 4.6–4.7 per cent) work under annualized hours contracts. Arrowsmith (2007) posits two reasons why annualized hours arrangements have not become more widely used. First, employers are satisfied with the flexibility offered by other types of working time arrangement, such as part-time working in areas like retail, for example, or shift-working in manufacturing industry. Moreover, there remains a strong preference for using overtime as a source of working time flexibility, in order to respond to fluctuations in demand for products and services, despite its expense and inefficiency.

Second, instituting annualized working arrangements demands a high degree of strategic management commitment, not least because of the need to overcome potential resistance from employees, something that is often absent. It is no coincidence that most annualized hours schemes operate in workplaces where there is a formal union presence, enabling the employer to negotiate their introduction in a way that helps to satisfy the interests of the workforce (Arrowsmith 2007). The rarity of annualized hours schemes suggests that many employers are either incapable of, or unwilling to bear the risks of, innovating when it comes to managing working time arrangements. The preponderance of overtime working indicates a preference on the part of employers for relatively simple and familiar methods of securing working time flexibility. Despite its association with weak and ineffective management (Flanders 1975), the institutionalization of overtime working continues to be a commonplace feature of contemporary employment relations.

7.4.3 The legal regulation of working time

As was mentioned above, in Britain, unlike elsewhere in the EU, the legal regulation of working time was traditionally very limited, except for legislation restricting the working hours of women and children. By the end of the 1980s, though, there was increasing concern within the European Commission that the regulation of working time needed to be addressed across the EU as a health and safety measure (Bridgford and Stirling 1994). Membership of the EU, then, obliged the British government to implement the 1993 Directive on the Adaptation of Working Time (the 'Working Time Directive'), something that was done by means of the 1998 Working Time Regulations.

John Major's Conservative government tried to obstruct its implementation, arguing that, as a 'social' measure, it could only be enacted through the so-called 'Social Chapter', from which Britain, because of its Maastricht 'opt-out', was exempt (see Chapter 3). In 1996, the European Court of Justice (ECJ) ruled that the directive was, as the European Commission maintained, a 'health and safety' measure and thus fell outside the 'Social Chapter', was subject to Qualified Majority Voting and, having thus been enacted, had to be extended to Britain. Nevertheless, Tony Blair's Labour government, which took office in 1997, was able to win some significant concessions when the WTR were implemented in 1998, notably the right of workers to choose whether or not they want to work for more than 48 hours a week.

The WTR provide for:

- a limit of 48 hours that a worker is required to work (including overtime), normally averaged out over a 17-week reference period;
- workers to have at least 11 consecutive hours of rest in any 24-hour period;
- workers to have a minimum rest period of at least 24 consecutive hours in any 7-day period, or 48 hours in a 14-day period;
- workers to have at least a 20-minute unpaid rest break if the working day is longer six hours;

- nightworkers, who are defined as workers who normally work at least 3 hours between 11.00pm and 6.00am, to be limited to an average of 8 hours of work in any 24-hour period; and

- a minimum of 4 weeks' paid annual leave.

There are additional restrictions that apply to workers aged below 18; they are limited to an 8-hour working day and a 40-hour working week, for example.

Some groups of workers, junior doctors and workers in transport, for example, were originally excluded from the scope of the 48-hour maximum working week, as were senior managers, and others whose working time is said to be 'unmeasured'. Employers can reach a collective agreement with a recognized trade union, or by means of a 'workforce agreement' with elected employee representatives in the absence of a recognized union, to benefit from certain flexibilities; for example, the 17-week reference period over which the 48-hour maximum limit is calculated can be extended to up to a year. The most controversial aspect of the WTR, and something that the British government fought hard to include, and even harder to retain (as we see below), is the provision that workers can, by virtue of an 'individual agreement' with their employer, exceed the 48-hour average weekly limit.

The enactment of the WTR in 1998 was a momentous event. Regulating working time by means of legislation, while commonplace in the rest of Europe, had previously been extremely limited in the UK. For the first time in the UK, workers were given a legal entitlement to paid annual leave, a provision that benefited perhaps as many as 1.5 million workers. But the enactment of the WTR was not the end of the matter. During the 2000s, the legal regulation of working time has developed and evolved in three broad ways, as we now see.

The first thing to be aware of is that working time legislation has been extended to cover groups of workers who were excluded from the WTR. For example, the EU's Horizontal Amending Directive (2000)—what a charming name!—extended the scope of the Working Time Directive to cover, among others, non-mobile workers in the road transport industry and rail workers. Implemented in the UK in 2003, the legislation also required that health service employers reduce the maximum weekly working hours of junior doctors in stages, to an upper limit of 48 by the middle of 2009. The EU's Road Transport Directive (2002) took effect in 2005; it restricts drivers' weekly hours to 48, averaged over a four-month reference period, with an absolute upper limit of 60 hours in any one week.

Second, the UK government has altered the regulations governing paid holiday entitlement in two important respects. When the WTR were enacted the entitlement to four weeks' paid annual leave was subject to a 13-week qualifying period, and did not include bank holidays. Some employers included the eight bank holidays as part of the four-week entitlement, meaning that a full-time worker could be left with just 12 days of paid leave. However, following legal action from the trade unions, in 2001 the European Court of Justice (ECJ) ruled that the qualifying period did not comply with the Working Time Directive, and was thus unlawful. Workers are entitled to start accruing annual leave entitlement from the time they start a job. As part of the 2004 'Warwick Agreement' (see Chapter 3), the trade unions secured a further alteration, the exclusion of bank holidays from the four-week entitlement to paid annual leave. As a result, paid holiday entitlement increased to 4.8 weeks (24 days for people working a five-day week) in 2007, and to 5.6 weeks (28 days) in 2009.

Third, there have also been some important case law developments, with the provisions of the WTR being subject to close scrutiny by the ECJ. Perhaps the most important topic concerns what is actually meant by 'working time'. In a 2003 judgment the ECJ ruled that the period of time when doctors in a hospital are 'on-call', that is available on the employers' premises to work if required, should be counted as working time, even if the workers concerned use it to rest or sleep. This potentially resulted in a considerable amount of difficulty for employers across Europe who operate 'on-call' arrangements, particularly in the health sector.

By far the most controversial feature of the WTR, though, concerns the 'individual agreement' derogation, under which workers can choose to work for longer than an average of 48 hours per week. The Trades Union Congress (TUC) claims that in many cases employers put pressure on employees to 'agree' to opt out. Studies of the effects of the WTR show that some employers use the individual agreement derogation automatically, obliging new employees to sign opt-out clauses when they commence employment (Barnard, Deakin, and Hobbs 2003; Neathy and Arrowsmith 2001). Many workers, it is argued, have very little real 'choice' about whether or not their working week is limited to an average of 48 hours.

Employers' bodies, like the Confederation of British Industry (CBI) vigorously support the opt-out provision, claiming it is a necessary element that allows businesses much-needed flexibility in managing their working time arrangements. Indeed, both workers and their employers have a vested interest in ensuring that the opt-out remains, and that excessive working hours continue (Barnard, Deakin, and Hobbs 2003). Workers either need the additional income provided by paid overtime or, where it is unpaid, do the extra work in order to ensure that they keep their jobs, or are well regarded for promotion purposes. Employers, as we have seen, are reliant on overtime working as a key means of securing workplace flexibility. The widespread use of opt-outs is suggestive of a certain amount of 'pragmatic collusion' between workers and their employers (Goss and Adam-Smith 2001).

Nevertheless, the opt-out provision means that the effects of the WTR have been less marked than might have been expected—in three specific ways. First, they appear to have had little impact on working time patterns. As we have already observed, during the 2000s, average weekly hours of work for full-time employees have fallen. Yet this is more likely to have been the result of workers demanding, and employers instituting, more family-friendly working arrangements, and the growth of a broader concern with securing a better work–life balance (see Chapter 4), rather than the existence of the WTR.

Second, remember that the Working Time Directive was introduced as a health and safety measure. The widespread use of opt-outs will have rendered it less effective in this respect.

Third, we have already established the limited degree of innovation by employers when it comes to arrangements for managing working time. In theory, the WTR, by restricting the use of overtime as a means of securing working time flexibility, could have prompted employers to develop other, more efficient ways of organizing working time, perhaps by investing in production methods or reorganizing work. However, the ease with which employers can secure opt-outs means that they have less of an incentive to undertake such changes (White et al. 2004). As a result, 'it seems unlikely that … the WTR will initiate a radical break with the UK's established practice of working time' (Goss and Adam-Smith 2001: 207).

How long is the individual opt-out likely to remain though? In 2003, the European Commission launched a review of the individual agreement provision. On the one hand, the British government and CBI have lobbied vociferously for its retention on the grounds that, without it, employers would enjoy less flexibility over working time arrangements, and thus be rendered less competitive. On the other hand, the TUC wants to see the opt-out abolished. Between 2004 and 2008, various attempts to reach a compromise were blocked, as EU member states failed to agree on an approach that satisfied all their interests. Whereas some countries—France and Spain, for example—have on occasion demanded the eradication of the opt-out entirely, the UK government has consistently vowed to ensure that it stays in place.

In June 2008, the EU's Council of Ministers finally reached an agreement under which the individual opt-out would remain, albeit subject to certain conditions: that workers should not be asked to sign an opt-out agreement during the first month of their employment; that workers who do not sign, or repudiate, an opt-out agreement should not be victimized; and that a new, absolute upper limit of 60 hours in any one week should be instituted. The Council of Ministers also secured a deal on how to deal with on-call time.

However, in December 2008 the European Parliament voted overwhelmingly for the opt-out to be scrapped. Indeed, it had already voted to get rid of it three years previously; so the outcome shouldn't have come as too much of a surprise. Subsequently, further efforts were made to reach another, more acceptable compromise. However, in April 2009 these negotiations failed to secure an agreement on what to do about the opt-out. It remains in place, though its future is uncertain.

SECTION SUMMARY AND FURTHER READING

- Working time, and its regulation, is a key issue in employment relations, being a central feature of the employment relationship. It has long been a prime source of contestation between employers and unions.

- The historical trend towards the reduction in the length of the working week, in large part the result of union struggle, appeared to be reversed for full-time employees during the 1990s as the average number of weekly working hours began to rise. During the 2000s, though, there was a slight decline in the average length of the working week.

- Overtime working is the principal reason why some people work excessive hours in Britain. Perhaps as a result, employers have been somewhat reluctant to innovate in the area of working time arrangements.

- Given that working time has generally not been subject to legal regulation, the implementation of the 1998 Working Time Regulations represent a marked departure from established practice. However, the impact of the maximum working week has been limited because of the ease with which employers can secure opt-outs from their staff.

Two good overviews of working time as an employment relations issue are Arrowsmith (2002), and Arrowsmith and Sisson (2000). The former concentrates on the historical evolution of working time as a source of contestation between employers and unions; the latter focuses on the how working time is managed in modern organizations and, in particular, suggests a lack of innovation. See Arrowsmith (2007) for more details of annualized hours arrangements. Barnard, Deakin, and Hobbs (2003) and Goss and Adam-Smith (2001) examine the impact of the Working Time Regulations.

 Visit our Online Resource Centre for web links to sites connected to this section. www.oxfordtextbooks.co.uk/williams_adamsmith2e

Conclusion

One of the most important aspects of contemporary employment relations in Britain is the diminished significance of collective bargaining in the private sector. Nevertheless, collective bargaining, at multi-employer level, remains commonplace in the public sector, especially if the pay review body system is considered as a form of 'arm's length bargaining' (Winchester and Bach 1995). What have been the main implications of the contraction of collective bargaining coverage in Britain? This chapter considered three particularly note-worthy developments. First, the increased extent of unilateral regulation of the terms of the wage-work bargain by management was identified. However, managers do not appear to have used their apparent new-found freedom to innovate very much in pay and working time arrangements. Rather, they prefer to rely on established, tried-and-tested approaches, such as the reliance on overtime for example. In attempting to pursue changes in employment relations, managers are constrained by the need to secure their legitimacy among the workforce. This is very important since it demonstrates that, even though the power of the trade unions has declined substantially, the wage-work bargain remains relevant as a way of conceptualizing the employment relationship, and that limits to the exercise of managerial prerogative exist.

Second, although other factors have played a part, the decline of collective bargaining as a means of determining pay in Britain has contributed to the growth of pay inequality since the 1980s. Moreover, as we established in Chapter 1, collective bargaining is not just a pay-setting mechanism; its presence also allows workers a say, or voice, over decisions that affect them at work. The diminution of trade union power has enabled managers to secure changes to the wage-work bargain in ways that are to the advantage of the employer. In particular, the lengthening of the working week for full-time workers has been caused in part by the erosion of joint regulation in the workplace. In Chapter 8, we will examine the implications for work effort and intensity.

Third, the implementation of the Working Time Regulations and the National Minimum Wage in Britain are significant developments as statutory interventions designed to regulate low pay and working time. Such regulation of the employment relationship by statute is a weak substitute for collective bargaining. The minimum wage was set at a deliberately low, or cautious, level that was designed to alleviate the most extreme cases of low pay in a way that would not be disruptive to employers. Given the scope for opt-outs enjoyed by employers, it seems unlikely that the Working Time Regulations have, until now, done much to challenge excessive working hours in Britain. Thus statutory regulation of the employment relationship is, by itself, not an adequate replacement for joint regulation as a means of securing improved pay and conditions for workers.

Assignment and discussion questions

1   Identify the reasons for the decline in collective bargaining coverage in Britain since the 1980s.

2   Why did British private sector firms withdraw from multi-employer bargaining? Why has it remained significant in the public sector?

3   What are the advantages and disadvantages of performance-related pay for employers?

4   Why have employers not been more innovative in devising new pay and working time arrangements?

5   Does pay inequality between the highest and lowest paid reflect an abuse of power by those at the top of organizations, or simply the market rate for different jobs?

6   In your view, are the current NMW rates set too high, too low, or about right? Or would you get rid of the NMW entirely? Justify your answer.

7   Why have the Working Time Regulations not had a major impact on the typical working hours of British workers?

 Visit our Online Resource Centre for web links to sites connected to this section. www.oxfordtextbooks.co.uk/williams_adamsmith2e

Take your learning further: online resource centre

Visit the Online Resource Centre that accompanies this book to enrich your understanding of Chapter 7: Contemporary developments in pay and working time. Explore web links, test yourself using an interactive flashcard glossary, and keep up to date with the latest developments in the area.

 http://www.oxfordtextbooks.co.uk/orc/williams_adamsmith2e.

Chapter case study

The National Minimum Wage and the hairdressing industry

The British hairdressing industry employs some 100,000 staff, of whom two-thirds are female and a half work on a part-time basis. The hairdressing sector comprises many small firms; 80 per cent of the workforce is employed in firms with fewer than 10 staff (Druker et al. 2005). It is also marked by a high proportion of young workers. These characteristics are typical of low-paying industries in general. In 1998, the year before the NMW took effect, the average pay was £3.56 per hour, just below the new statutory floor of wages. Hairdressing, then, is a low-paying industry. Consequently, many employers report difficulties in filling vacancies from suitably qualified applicants, particularly for junior positions. However, once staff qualify as stylists earnings can be relatively high. Moreover, the fairly lengthy entry period on low pay does not seem to deter those who have firmly decided on a career in the sector. Nonetheless, younger workers do feel that their pay should be higher, particularly in relation to what their friends earn in other occupations (Druker et al. 2002). The introduction of the National Minimum Wage (NMW) in 1999, and its subsequent upratings, had a major effect on wages in the hairdressing sector. Between 1998 and 2003 average pay for female full-time hairdressing staff rose by 44 per cent, compared to 28 per cent for female full-time staff in general (Druker et al. 2005). The group of workers most dramatically affected by the introduction of the NMW was younger workers, typically employed as shampooists, trainee stylists, and receptionists (Druker et al. 2005).

There is little evidence that hairdressing employers have not complied with the NMW. While there were a varied range of responses to the minimum wage, two main patterns stood out. First, some salons responded to the minimum wage by purposely adopting innovative approaches to cope with any rise in wage costs. For example, in some cases firms had made an effort to improve training and development provision for their staff, particularly younger employees. The idea was that this would result in higher levels of service quality, and better productivity from the workforce, thus compensating for the NMW. These firms tended to have a formalized approach to managing staff which pre-dated the introduction of the minimum wage, and generally operated pay rates that were above the NMW minima. The second, more common pattern was a reactive approach. Salons responded to increases in wage costs as a result of the NMW either by taking a short-term cost-cutting approach (e.g. reducing training) or, more commonly, by raising their prices by an appropriate amount to compensate. Growing demand for hairdressing services enabled the salons to raise prices without adversely affecting their trade.

1. What does this case study show us about the impact of the NMW on both employers and workers?

2. In what other ways might employers have responded to the introduction of the NMW?

8

Experiencing employment relations: involvement, insecurity, intensification

Chapter objectives:

The main objectives of this chapter are to:

* examine some key features relating to how workers experience employment relations;

* assess the extent to which management policies of employee participation and involvement allow workers to influence workplace decisions;

* develop an understanding of the nature of the redundancy process and its implications for workers' feelings of job insecurity; and

* examine the reasons why workers in Britain are working harder, and to consider the implications of this process of work intensification.

8.1 Introduction

Managerial accounts of workplace life change increasingly dominate the contemporary employment relations agenda, linked to the emergence of human resource management (HRM) as an area of study. Accounts of HRM that consider the implications of managerial interventions for workers are somewhat rare. Yet the employment relationship is not only something that is regulated by employers, it is also experienced by workers. A proper assessment of developments in contemporary employment relations must acknowledge that the employment relationship *is* a relationship and that it is characterized by the potential for conflicting interests as well as by cooperation. In this chapter, then, we draw upon a range of up-to-date quantitative and qualitative research findings to demonstrate both the extent to which an understanding of workers' experiences of the employment relationship is a relevant matter for investigation, and also how they can differ markedly from those of their employers. We start in Section 8.2 by considering the degree of employee involvement and participation in workplace decision-making. In

Section 8.3 we examine the nature of redundancy in employment relations, and consider the implications for job insecurity among workers. Finally, in Section 8.4 we identify a notable trend of work intensification: what are the causes of increased work pressures? And what have been their main effects?

Introductory case study

Employment relations in a recession

During 2008 many leading economies, including the UK and the US, experienced a significant downturn, linked to the financial crisis arising out of the so-called 'credit crunch'. There has been a big impact on jobs. Firms have gone out of business, resulting in job losses. In September 2008, for example, the holiday airline XL went bust with the loss of some 1,700 jobs. Alternatively, in order to maintain their competitiveness, and remain solvent, firms have sought to cut costs, often by shedding labour. In October 2008, JCB, a company that makes construction and agricultural equipment, announced 150 job losses; a further 350 jobs were saved only because the rest of the workforce agreed to work fewer hours. The early months of 2009 saw further large-scale job losses, at firms including BT, BMW, and Royal Bank of Scotland. The parlous economic situation will affect people's experience of employment relations in important ways. The fear of losing one's job, and the income that goes with it, leads to increased perceptions of insecurity. In such circumstances, many workers will be anxious for information about the security of their employment, putting a premium on effective communication and information-sharing arrangements. Perceptions of insecurity may also contribute to greater work pressure. Workers who feel that their jobs are under threat will work harder, to demonstrate their contribution, and thus hope to avoid being made redundant. Thus the main themes of this chapter—the involvement of employees in workplace decision-making, redundancy and insecurity, and work intensification—are brought into sharp relief during times of economic difficulty.

8.2 Developments in employee involvement and participation

We have already examined the nature of employee involvement and participation (in Chapter 1), indicated that the use of direct communication techniques is held to be integral to the sophisticated HRM approach (in Chapter 5), and considered the way in which trade union representation enables workers to exercise voice over workplace decisions (in Chapter 6). Here, though, we investigate workers' experiences of involvement and participation in contemporary employment relations.

Our starting point is the increasingly espoused managerial concern to communicate directly with their employees, and to involve them more in workplace decision-making. The aim is to enhance employee motivation and commitment, thus realizing improvements in business performance (see Marchington and Wilkinson 2005). Together with the diminution of union voice arrangements (Millward, Bryson, and Forth 2000), it means that employee involvement and participation 'are increasingly characterized by being management rather than union driven and by the underlying aim of increasing commitment and seeking competitive advantage' (Sisson and Storey 2000: 93).

8.2.1 Employee involvement: communicating with employees

Since the 1980s there has been a substantial increase in the use of employee involvement techniques by employers, notably arrangements for communicating information between managers and staff, and vice versa (Kersley et al. 2006; McGovern et al. 2007; Storey 1992). The 'cascading' of information downwards through the management hierarchy has become a more commonplace feature of workplace life. Moreover, regular workforce meetings, newsletters, and team briefings have become increasingly popular methods for communicating information to employees. There has also been a less pronounced increase in the incidence of arrangements that enable staff to communicate their views 'upwards' to managers. Nearly a third of workplaces operate suggestion schemes, which allow employees to communicate information, in the form of ideas for improving how products are made or services delivered, to managers.

Data from the Workplace Employment Relations Survey shows the proportion of workplaces that used specific direct communication techniques in 2004 (see Table 8.1). Workforce meetings and team briefings, which involve the verbal communication of information between a line manager or supervisor and his or her work group, exist in the overwhelming majority of workplaces. We can also see the extensive use that is made of the management chain to cascade information downwards to employees (64 per cent of workplaces. In two-fifths (42 per cent) of workplaces employee surveys are used as a form of upward communication, allowing managers to gauge the views and attitudes of their staff. While traditional methods of disseminating information are still popular—noticeboards are used in three-quarters (74 per cent) of workplaces, for example—Table 8.1 also indicates that newer information-sharing techniques, electronic mail (38 per cent) and intranet facilities (34 per cent), exist in over a third of workplaces. With the exception of suggestion schemes, used in equal proportions of public and private sector workplaces, all of the communications methods listed are more commonplace in the public sector.

Table 8.1 Percentage of workplaces with direct communications methods, 2004

	Public sector	Private sector	All workplaces
Meetings with entire workforce or team briefings	97	90	91
Systematic use of the management chain	81	60	64
Regular newsletters	63	41	45
Noticeboards	86	72	61
E-mail	48	36	38
Intranet	48	31	34
Suggestion schemes	30	30	30
Employee surveys	66	37	42

Workplaces with 10 or more employees.
Source: Kersley et al. (2006)

The increasing incidence of downwards and upwards communications arrangements in British workplaces would, then, appear to signal a significant change in employment relations, given that before the 1980s communication channels, largely in the form of consultation machinery, were dominated by the unions. But the evidence on direct communications and employee involvement must be handled with some care. For one thing, while the presence of direct communication arrangements has undoubtedly increased, there is plenty of evidence to suggest that the largely top-down way in which information flows from managers to staff—limits the degree to which employees are able to influence decisions that affect them at work, and thus precludes genuine involvement.

'Downward' communications arrangements, those that refer to the flow of information from managers to employees, predominate. A study of a group of 'Leading Edge' companies, including Citibank, Hewlett-Packard, and WH Smith, found that while many employees felt well informed about their company's objectives, and the ways in which it was attempting to achieve them, few considered they had any influence themselves. Opportunities for employees to communicate their ideas, concerns, and suggestions upwards were scarce (Gratton et al. 1999). There is plenty of case study evidence that the flow of information is generally one-way, from managers to workers, with the latter afforded few opportunities to express their voice.

In the non-union chocolate works studied by Scott (1994), for example, managers considered that the regular bi-monthly 'job involvement meetings' (JIs) not only gave them the opportunity to keep the workforce informed about the company's performance, changes in company practice, and other relevant matters, but also enabled the workers to communicate their feelings and views. In reality, however, most workers did not believe that the JIs served this dual purpose, and saw them as a one-way, top-down method of delivering messages. Some workers, moreover, were worried about the consequences of communicating their views. One of them, for example, emphasized that he worked for a 'good company', but

> . . . I haven't got long to go and I don't want any trouble. Once at a JI I spoke my mind to the manager. Two weeks later I found myself being transferred to another job and I reckon that speaking out cost me £50 a week in wages that I could have earned. Some managers are alright [*sic*], but others you've got to watch. (quoted in Scott 1994: 116)

Unsurprisingly, there is little evidence that, as a form of employee involvement, direct communications initiatives, despite their prevalence, impact much on employees' organizational commitment, or their performance at work (Marchington 2001), though there is a suggestion that they may be effective as a means of influencing management behaviour (Bryson 2004). Managers prefer to restrict communication to sharing information with employees, and are reluctant to respond positively to their suggestions (Gallie et al. 1998).

Moreover, there is evidence that communications techniques can be used to enhance managerial control, rather than involve employees (see Box 8.1). A Japanese-owned plant manufacturing televisions used its extensive communications arrangements to influence workers' behaviour so that it conformed to managerial expectations, particularly in matters pertaining to quality (Delbridge 1998). In so far as managers use communication techniques to influence workplace behaviour in ways that they deem desirable, such as the need to prioritize quality, for example, it is inappropriate to characterize such employee

> **INSIGHT INTO PRACTICE 8.1**
>
> ## Communication practices in two aerospace firms
>
> Both of the two aerospace firms studied by Danford et al. (2005) made use of an extensive range of communications methods, including newsletters, bulletins, annual workforce meetings, and, in particular, team briefings. However, the experiences of the workers indicate that genuine involvement was limited, and that the communications arrangements were used largely as a means of maintaining managerial control. Most workers thought managers were poor at keeping them informed about developments. Moreover, there was little scope for workers to be involved in decisions that affect them at work. According to an engineer in one of the firms: 'There is a lot of potential for two-way communications but a lot of the time you don't get the opportunity to communicate properly . . . a lot of the time it's more a process of management telling you what's relevant to them at a higher level' (Danford et al. 2005: 176).

involvement initiatives as interventions that widen the scope of workers' influence over decision-making. Rather, they are better envisaged as a means of enabling managers to uphold their prerogatives, and to restrict the influence of employees, especially where they are organized in trade unions.

8.2.2 Employee participation and the reorganization of work

Having considered downward and upward forms of direct communications, as measures designed to give employees more involvement in decisions that affect them at work, we now assess the extent to which they benefit from greater participation over the way in which their jobs are undertaken. As mentioned in Chapter 1, the concept of participation is often used to refer to union-based efforts to enhance the influence of workers, through collective bargaining activity in particular. Trade union representation and collective bargaining are dealt with in Chapters 6 and 7, respectively. In this section, though, we focus on relevant innovations in the organization of work—in particular quality circles and problem-solving groups, teamworking arrangements, and empowerment initiatives—and judge how far their presence provides employees with greater participation with regard to how their jobs are undertaken.

It has been suggested that giving employees greater influence and voice over the organization of work, and changes in work processes, are essential if companies are to secure the levels of commitment necessary for the production of high-quality goods and services, and thus thrive in increasingly competitive global markets (see Boxall and Purcell 2007). As discussed in Chapter 5, forms of task-based participation, teamworking arrangements in particular, are among the major best practice HRM interventions that are thought to deliver improvements in business performance (Marchington and Wilkinson 2005).

Organizations have increasingly recognized the importance of quality as a source of competitive advantage, and instituted more rigorous systems of quality management, often associated with the concept of Total Quality Management (TQM) (Hill 1991; Wilkinson et al. 1997). The characteristic feature of a TQM approach is that quality is something that is built into all aspects of the process of production or service delivery.

Consequently, all workers should take responsibility for the quality of their own contribution, and constantly seek ways of improving it.

Despite its managerial emphasis, effective quality management is associated with greater employee participation. It is 'supposed to place a greater emphasis on self-control, autonomy and creativity, expecting active cooperation from employees rather than mere compliance' (Wilkinson et al. 1992: 5). In a study of four organizations that were 'pioneers' of TQM, for example, Hill (1995) observed that employees enjoyed greater influence over their work tasks as a result.

One of the most notable features of a quality management approach is the presence of 'problem-solving groups', sometimes known as quality circles, in which employees come together, sometimes alongside managers, to discuss and resolve specific issues and concerns affecting quality or performance. According to Gallie et al. (1998), quality circles are a particularly effective means of stimulating employee participation. The authors of one major study of changes in the organization of work suggest that quality circles, or 'work improvement groups' as they call them, have become a prominent feature of the organization of work. They are portrayed as a form of 'intelligent' workplace flexibility; participating employeess 'must draw on their job experience and use it creatively to identify and solve problems' (White et al. 2004: 46). The 2004 Workplace Employment Relations Survey indicates that problem-solving groups are present in about a fifth of UK workplaces.

Teamworking can also be viewed as a manifestation of 'intelligent flexibility' (White et al. 2004). One of the main ways in which organizations have sought to enhance the quality of their employees' contributions is by instituting some form of teamworking arrangement. Teamworking potentially enables workers collectively to organize and manage part of the process of production or service delivery without the need for direct supervision by management. In so far as it holds out the promise of a significant increase in the degree to which employees are able to exercise an influence over the organization of their work, self-managed teams are often portrayed as the 'ultimate in direct participation' (Marchington and Wilkinson 2005: 406).

In his study of organizational change in one of Pirelli's plants, for example, Clark (1995) found that the overwhelming majority of employees enjoyed greater job satisfaction and more autonomy at work as a consequence of the establishment of self-supervised teams. The benefits of teamworking were also evident to one white-collar worker in a utilities company: 'Business improvement teams/working groups ...have expanded my awareness of other business unit issues. I've gained problem-solving experience, and also job satisfaction, that you are achieving something in the short term, fixing it in the short term' (quoted in Hudson 2002: 54). As a manifestation of 'intelligent flexibility', teamworking is claimed to have become a prominent feature of contemporary work organization (White et al. 2004).

TQM and teamworking complement one another in so far as improvements in the quality of production, or the delivery of services, may be associated with innovative work practices that enhance employee involvement and participation. This has prompted consideration of whether or not such developments have enabled employees to become 'empowered'. What, then, is meant by the concept of 'empowerment' in the workplace? It comprises two related aspects. First, empowerment is held to involve the devolution to workers of some supervisory responsibilities that hitherto would have come under the auspices of managers. Second, following on from this, the presumption is that workers will enjoy greater autonomy at work and, in particular, more discretion over the way in which their jobs are performed (Cunningham and Hyman 1999).

What is the overall significance of these innovations in the organization of work, and to what extent have they generated greater worker participation? Have workers really become more empowered? On the positive side, it is evident that during the 1990s there was a substantial increase in the presence of 'intelligent flexibility' in UK workplaces, evidenced by the growing incidence of problem-solving groups and teamworking arrangements, for example (White et al. 2004). On a more pessimistic note, though, this growth appears to have stalled in the 2000s; the incidence of teamworking arrangements and problem-solving groups is little changed since the 1990s (Kersley at al 2006). The use of 'intelligent flexibility' is still only evident in a minority of workplaces, contributing to a widespread perception among workers that they should have more influence over issues that affect them at work (McGovern et al. 2007).

More fundamentally, perhaps, it would appear that initiatives which are ostensibly designed to enhance the participation of workers, giving them greater autonomy and discretion over their work as a result, may in fact be used to reinforce managerial control. If we look at the implications of TQM, for example, there is evidence that organizations use quality management systems to secure the subordination of workers, and thus extend managerial control (Delbridge 1998; McArdle et al. 1995). In these critical perspectives, TQM, as an explicitly management tool, is portrayed as a means of enforcing employee compliance with corporate policies and of stifling their independent collective organization, rather than as a means of enhancing involvement and participation.

Quality management initiatives rarely increase worker participation beyond a modest degree. As part of its efforts to establish a greater customer orientation, the supermarket chain 'Shopco', for example, used its 'Service Excellence' programme to extend the discretion of its front-line employees. Although staff welcomed the changes, the extent of their autonomy was nonetheless rather limited, to decisions on customer refunds, for example (Rosenthal, Hill, and Peccei 1997). More generally, it is apparent that TQM initiatives, while they may slightly increase employee involvement and participation over the performance of job tasks, do so within boundaries set firmly by management and are associated with the stricter imposition of managerial control, in particular over discipline and standards of performance (Edwards, Collinson, and Rees 1998).

Critical interpretations of teamworking arrangements suggest that they are interventions designed to serve the interests of management, rather than increase employee participation. In their study of work organization and employment relations in the Nissan car plant near Sunderland in north-east England, Garrahan and Stewart (1992) observed that the peer pressure to fulfil production quotas evident among the factory's teams could be interpreted as 'management by stress'.

But what do we mean by 'teams' anyway? In the service sector, for example, teams are often no more than 'administrative work groups of individual workers under the jurisdiction of one supervisor' (Korczynski 2002: 134), with no element of self-supervision. There is little in such an arrangement that fosters worker participation. The form of teamworking most likely to generate genuine worker participation occurs where team members are allowed to appoint their own leader; but this is rare indeed. See Box 8.2 for details of how teamworking arrangements, and the level of participation they engender, vary. Therefore, we cannot equate teamworking with worker participation in an overly straightforward manner.

> **Employment relations reflection 8.2**   Varieties of team
>
> Data from the 2004 Workplace Employment Relations Survey indicate that formally designated teams are present in nearly three-quarters (72 per cent) of workplaces. Nevertheless, by no means do teams always function in the same way:
>
> • in 83 per cent of workplaces with teams, a team was given responsibility for a specific product or service;
>
> • in 81 per cent, team members depended upon each other when undertaking their jobs;
>
> • in 66 per cent, job tasks were rotated among members of the team;
>
> • in 61 per cent, team members jointly decided how work was done; and
>
> • in 6 per cent, team members were responsible for appointing their own team leaders (Kersley et al. 2006).

There is also evidence that managers use teamworking initiatives as a means of extending their control over labour. In his study of a plant manufacturing car components, Danford (1998) shows that the company introduced teamworking in order to undermine workers' influence over the production process. The new arrangements enabled management to institute flexibility on its terms, rather than those of the workers, exercise greater control over the way in which work tasks were undertaken, and raise effort levels. According to one of the workers:

> As I see it, the management have bought in all these fancy new ideas but they're all the same really. Every one is about squeezing more work out of less men. You can forget all the pretty words, they're about making you work harder it's as simple as that. (quoted in Danford 1998: 421)

In respect of empowerment, there is now a widespread body of research evidence suggesting that real power is seldom transferred from management to workers (e.g. Danford et al. 2005). Rather, workers are generally given a relatively small amount of additional discretion, such as in the case of 'Shopco', for example, within boundaries that are tightly regulated by managers (Beynon et al. 2002; Rosenthal, Hill, and Peccei 1997). In a study of the restaurant chain TGI Fridays, for example, Lashley (2000) discovered that waiting staff were encouraged to accept customer requests for variations to standard menu products, deal with, and rectify, customer complaints themselves, and to customize their uniforms. Nevertheless, such discretion was constrained by the existence of tightly prescribed rules governing service delivery, such as maximum waiting times between courses, for example.

Workers, then, are often sceptical about the prospects for empowerment. According to an office worker in a utilities company:

> Empowerment it . . . empowers you to do what you think you should do after you've been asked to do it . . . It's a load of rubbish. It's OK when you're there [at the training centre], but as soon as you get back you realize that you are not empowered at all. It's different for the top bosses. (quoted in Hudson 2002: 55)

The concept of empowerment is rather misleading in that it suggests that workers enjoy greater power over workplace decision-making when often all it involves is a relatively minor expansion in people's job tasks.

Unsurprisingly, then, workers do not seem to have benefited from greater discretion and autonomy at work. Indeed, the evidence indicates that, on this measure, the degree of worker participation has declined, with adverse consequences for the quality of jobs. In general, during the 1990s and early 2000s '. . . British workers experienced a fall in their perceived influence over their daily work tasks. They reported less choice over the way they did their jobs, and less personal influence over what tasks they did, how they did them, how hard they worked, and to what quality standards. This decline in influence has had substantial, unambiguously detrimental effects on the satisfactions that British workers experienced in their jobs' (Green 2006: 173–4).

In general, participation initiatives appear to have had little, if any, positive impact on workers' discretion and autonomy at work. Despite the evidence that it generates greater job satisfaction, improved levels of commitment, and better business performance, the principal obstacle to worker participation, and the transfer of real power from managers to workers, is the concern of the former with upholding their prerogatives, and their unwillingness to cede control to the latter (Geary 2003). In his study of a frozen food factory that had hitherto been characterized by a rather authoritarian style of management, Scott (1994) accounts for the failure of an initiative designed to give part of its workforce more autonomy. When the workers failed to behave in ways that entirely accorded with management's expectations, the latter quickly reverted to a less participatory approach.

During the 1990s and 2000s, moreover, the development of new, more sophisticated methods of monitoring and recording the activities of employees intensified the potential for managerial control over labour. Performance management arrangements, for example, have become a commonplace feature of workplace life. The widespread use of information and communications technology (ICT) to record what workers do, and how quickly they do it, has strengthened the potential for managerial control. Electronic point of sale (EPOS) technology, for example, and electronic time recording techniques can be used by managers to monitor, and control, the behaviour of their staff. In call centres managers use surveillance technology to 'spot hour-by-hour or even minute-by minute anyone who is dallying between calls or is lavishing too much time on a customer' (White et al. 2004: 85). For many workers in contemporary employment relations, the experience is not one of greater discretion and autonomy, brought about through increased opportunities to participate in workplace decisions, but one of greater subordination to managerial control. In Section 8.4.2 we examine how ICT-based monitoring and surveillance techniques contribute to work intensification.

Work reorganization initiatives of the kind we have discussed here have, then, largely failed to transform employment relations in Britain, not only because of an ongoing managerial concern with the control of labour, and the development of new, more sophisticated arrangements for monitoring employee performance, but also due to a failure on the part of management to ensure that reforms are pursued in a consistent and coherent manner (Edwards, Geary, and Sisson 2002). Where significant change has occurred, such as in the case of an aluminium plant operated by Alcan, for example, it is as a result of certain conditions being present, such as a consensual employment relations climate, a genuine management commitment to reform, and the process-based nature of the industry which, since it gave workers space and time to collaborate, made teamworking arrangements viable (Edwards and Wright 1998; Geary 2003). Not even in this case, though, were managers able to secure high organizational commitment.

Overall, then, while new methods of work organization do seem to have stimulated greater employee participation in some cases, they are often accompanied by tighter managerial control of performance and discipline, and greater pressure on workers to work harder (Edwards, Collinson, and Rees 1998), limiting the extent to which they can stimulate genuine autonomy and discretion. Thus the employment relationship, and the balance of control and consent that characterizes it, has been not been transformed by new working practices.

SECTION SUMMARY AND FURTHER READING

- The extent to which employers communicate with their workers has risen markedly in recent years, though it tends to be limited to keeping them informed of developments. Not only do workers appear to have few opportunities to influence organizational and workplace decisions, but communication techniques, as explicitly managerial interventions, are also used to uphold managerial prerogative.

- Innovations in work organization, such as quality management techniques and teamworking arrangements, for example, do not seem to have led to increases in the autonomy and discretion which workers exercise in their jobs.

- It would be a mistake to assume that employee participation arrangements have brought about a genuine shift in power, away from managers and towards workers, since the extent of the latter's discretion is generally quite narrow, and exists within a framework of more intensive forms of managerial control over performance.

For an overview of developments in employee participation and involvement, see Marchington and Wilkinson (2005). Geary (2003) is particularly good on task-based participation. See Gratton et al. (1999) for case study evidence of the preference of managers for downward communications, and Danford et al. (2005) for an illustration of the limitations of employee involvement methods. Lashley's (2000) case study of empowerment at TGI Friday's is also recommended.

 Visit our Online Resource Centre for web links to sites connected to this section. www.oxfordtextbooks.co.uk/williams_adamsmith2e

---

8.3 Redundancy and insecurity

Losing one's job, or the threat of losing one's job, is perhaps the most unsettling of experiences for workers in contemporary employment relations. It also demonstrates in a stark fashion the difference of interest that marks the employment relationship, between an employer, whose decision it is to terminate someone's employment, and the employee, who has to bear the consequences of losing a job. In this section, we consider the functions and process of redundancy, and its implications for workers, before assessing the dynamics of workplace insecurity.

8.3.1 Redundancy and employment relations

First of all, what is meant by 'redundancy'? It refers to situations where, in return for financial compensation, it is deemed justifiable for an employer to dismiss employees because fewer of them are needed to undertake a specific set of work activities. Legally, employers only have to demonstrate that changing business circumstances mean that fewer employees are required, not that there has been a reduction in the amount of actual work. They can claim that a redundancy situation arises when there is no change, or even an increase, in the amount of work required, should the needs of the business mean that job losses are needed to produce efficiency savings.

Prior to the 1960s, the concept of redundancy scarcely registered in employment relations. Nevertheless, the term started to become more widely used as some employers, who wanted to reduce employment levels, offered financial payments to compensate workers for the loss of their jobs (Fryer 1981; Mukherjee 1973). Unions often strongly opposed management proposals to discharge employees and, in situations where dismissals appeared to be unavoidable, insisted on 'last-in, first-out', or 'LIFO', as the principal selection criterion. In other words, those who had the least length of service with the firm would be chosen to go first.

Policy-makers increasingly viewed the strength of union opposition to such dismissals as an obstacle to the efficient functioning of the economy since something needed to be done to encourage workers in declining industrial sectors to move to parts of the economy that were experiencing growth. In the 1960s legislation was introduced to make it easier for employers to institute redundancies. It recognized that workers hold property rights in their jobs, stipulating that cash compensation, in the form of severance payments based on age and length of service, be awarded to those made redundant by their employer (Anderman 1986). But the main aim was to promote economic efficiency by enabling the more rational use of labour in a climate of full employment (Mukherjee 1973).

Although redundancy legislation appeared to satisfy the twin rationales of stimulating greater economic efficiency, while at the same time providing displaced workers with cash compensation for the loss of their jobs, it was nonetheless infused by 'a clear managerial agenda' (Turnbull and Wass 1997: 30). The legislation was underpinned by a desire to make it easier for employers to dismiss employees, in that it was designed to reduce both union opposition to dismissals, and the workplace disputes that they often provoked, thus strengthening managerial prerogative (Fryer 1973; Fryer 1981).

Having outlined what redundancy means, and examined some key elements of the public policy background, we now need to consider the principal causes of redundancy situations in employment relations. Managers often justify the need for job losses with reference to vague assertions about the need to cut costs and improve efficiency. Yet in practice six main causes of job losses can be identified:

- industrial decline (e.g. during the 1980s and 1990s hundreds of thousands of jobs were eliminated as the importance of traditional industries like coal mining dwindled);

- declining demand for an organization's products or services;

- new technology is often introduced in a way that displaces jobs;

- organizational restructuring (e.g. where employers transfer functions to overseas locations, causing job losses at established sites);

- business insolvency: unless a new buyer is found quickly, job losses ensue when a firm goes out of business (e.g. XL Airlines in 2008); and

- demands from shareholders and senior executives for greater profitability through efficiency savings.

This last point highlights an increasingly important aspect of how redundancies are used as a cost-cutting measure, not as a way of responding to poor performance, but rather as a means of improving performance by enhancing competitiveness. In further education colleges, for example, teaching staff employed on permanent contracts have been made redundant, and then re-engaged through an employment agency on a cheaper, part-time basis. We should not be surprised that redundancies are commonplace among financially successful firms (Blyton and Turnbull 2004).

Redundancy has become a convenient way for managers to dismiss staff. Judicial interpretations of the relevant legislation largely support the supremacy of managerial prerogative over redundancy decisions (Turnbull 1988; Turnbull and Wass 1997). The concept of redundancy, moreover, has been treated increasingly loosely, to such an extent that it is taken to apply to an employer's decision that fewer employees are required to undertake particular work, without any obligation to demonstrate that the amount of work has in fact diminished (Lewis 1993: 72).

The up-front financial costs of making severance payments are rarely onerous for employers (Turnbull 1988); in 2008, the maximum statutory payout that an individual could receive was £9,300. Redundancy has therefore become a popular means of instituting efficiency savings, through cuts in labour costs, and has become far removed from its original stated purpose of improving the economy-wide supply of labour.

The process of redundancy also enables managers to restructure their workforces in ways that benefit the employer's interest. It 'is a time when new standards can be laid down as the organization gears up to operating in a changed environment' (Lewis 1993: 39). In particular, management exercises control over the redundancy selection criteria and can use them to streamline their workforces in a desirable manner through the use, for example, of supposedly more objective factors, such as performance, ability, skills, and disciplinary and attendance records, rather than LIFO. Redundancy provisions, then, are used to enhance organizational flexibility and competitiveness, and do little to provide workers with job security. That said, the decision to make redundancies, and also the terms on which those redundancies are then put into effect, do not go unchallenged by workers (see Box 8.3).

Employment relations reflection 8.3   Challenging redundancies

We should acknowledge that redundancy can be a major source of conflict in organizations. Workers and unions often challenge redundancy decisions. In 2006, for example, the car parts manufacturer Dura Automotive Systems announced that its plant in Llanelli, South Wales would close by the end of that year. The company claimed that rising costs, competitive pressures, and over-capacity had combined to make the plant uneconomic. The workforce, unhappy about the low level of proposed redundancy payments, took strike action which resulted in management having to increase the compensation on offer by some £4 million. During 2009 there were some notable instances of redundancy-induced conflict, including workplace occupations, as the economic recession caused job losses to mount.

8.3.2 **The process and experience of redundancy**

In this section we consider the contemporary salience of redundancy in employment relations, since it 'is probably the most evocative and fear-inducing form of organizational change for many workers' (Worrall, Cooper, and Campbell 2000: 648). In particular, we examine the implications for workers of the substantial discretion enjoyed by managers over the decision to shed labour, who should be dismissed, and how and when they should go.

Redundancies have become an established part of the employment relations landscape, linked in particular to the economic recessions of the early 1980s and early 1990s when millions of workers lost their jobs as a result of business closures and rationalization programmes (Gallie et al. 1998). Although the incidence of redundancies in Britain diminished during the late 1990s and 2000s, linked to the growth of the economy, since 2008 there has been a marked increase in the number of people being made redundant as a result of the economic recession. Table 8.2 shows changes in both the level and the rate of redundancies over the 10-year period 1999–2008 for the UK. The redundancy rate (the number of redundancies per 1,000 employees) fluctuated around the 7.5 mark in the early 2000s, before falling to 5.0 in 2007. The onset of the recession, though, prompted a rise in the number of redundancies during 2008. Table 8.3 uses quarterly data to demonstrate how both the level and rate of redundancies increased during 2008. In the final quarter of 2008 (October to December), the redundancy rate was 10.2, more than twice that of the year before.

Redundancy may have more of an impact on some groups of workers than others. The Trades Union Congress reported that the beginning of the economic recession during 2008 impacted heavily upon sectors dominated by female employment, retail for example, meaning that women were particularly affected by redundancy (TUC 2009). It is

Table 8.2 The level and rate of redundancies in the UK, 1999–2008

	Redundancy level*	Redundancy rate**
1999	178,000	7.6
2000	169,000	7.1
2001	177,000	7.4
2002	185,000	7.6
2003	158,000	6.4
2004	141,000	5.7
2005	143,000	5.7
2006	138,000	5.5
2007	127,000	5.0
2008	163,000	6.4

* Quarterly averages.

* The number of redundancies per 1,000 employees.

Source: Labour Force Survey, http://www.statistics.gov.uk

Table 8.3 The level and rate of redundancies in the UK, 2008

	Redundancy level	Redundancy rate
January–March 2008	111,000	4.4
April–June 2008	127,000	5.0
July–September 2008	156,000	6.1
October–December 2008	259,000	10.2

Source: Labour Force Survey, http://www.statistics.gov.uk

also important to bear in mind that the official redundancy figures do not include other measures used to reduce staff numbers, such as so-called early retirement, for example, which may be a form of disguised redundancy (Worrall, Cooper, and Campbell 2000).

Even before the recession commenced, there was plenty of evidence that redundancy, and the threat of being made redundant, was salient to the experience of workers. Seventeen of the twenty organizations studied by Burchell et al. (1999) had instituted redundancy programmes in the preceding five-year period, with several having done so more than once.

In their study of the aerospace industry in south-west England, Danford, Richardson, and Stewart (2003) demonstrate the extent to which large-scale redundancies, linked to rationalization initiatives following changes of ownership, decimated employment levels in many workplaces across the region. During the 1990s, the number of skilled manual workers employed by BAE Systems, for example, was more than halved.

Major reductions in employment are not confined just to the manufacturing sector. Rationalization initiatives in financial services, for example, including the slimming down of branch networks, appears to have also generated significant numbers of job losses (Hudson 2002).

Perhaps the most striking aspect of redundancies is the way in which they are now used by organizations to shed labour even when they are performing relatively successfully (Blyton and Turnbull 2004). You will recall that in public policy terms the ostensible aim of redundancy was to encourage the movement of workers from declining industrial sectors of the economy to new, expanding ones. Increasingly, however, redundancy programmes seem to be initiated not because there has been a diminution in what workers are expected to do, but as a means of generating cost savings, or of instituting greater workplace flexibility (Hudson 2002; Worrall, Cooper, and Campbell 2000).

We have already observed that the decision to make redundancies is generally one that is in the prerogative of managers. Key features of the redundancy process, moreover, are also subject to managerial control, often to the detriment of certain groups of workers. In the case of the docks, for example, Turnbull and Wass (1994) observed that older workers, those who were medically restricted in some way, and thus unable to undertake a full range of tasks, and union activists were over-represented among those selected for redundancy.

In respect of the redundancy selection criteria, there is evidence that managers may override supposedly objective scoring systems in order to exercise discretion over who stays and who goes. In their study of redundancies among defence-related firms in

Scotland, Donnelly and Scholarios (1998) found that in one case, workers were awarded points based on their performance. Other criteria, however, appeared to influence the selection process in a way that was perceived as unfair. According to one former employee:

> 'The selection method was sick to say the least. I was picked out for one and a half days ill in seven years with the company, the same week I got my assessment sheet and my total points were 28 out of 30' (quoted in Donnelly and Scholarios 1998: 332).

One of the ways in which management can intensify their control over redundancy exercises is to encourage workers to depart voluntarily with the promise of an enhanced cash payment if they agree to go of their own volition. This must seem odd. One would assume that voluntary redundancy, as opposed to being made compulsorily redundant, at least gives workers some discretion. In reality, however, it is not as simple as that; voluntary redundancy is marked by the combination of managerial control and employee choice which varies from situation to situation (Clarke 2007) (see Box 8.4).

There is evidence from the coal-mining industry that ostensibly voluntary redundancy programmes are subject to extensive managerial influence over selection (Wass 1996). Furthermore, managers enjoy the right to refuse applications for voluntary redundancy from people whom they would prefer to stay on, particularly if they have 'certain skills, knowledge or capabilities deemed essential to the firm' (Turnbull and Wass 1997: 33).

As opposed to this, they may actively encourage, and indeed impose, voluntary redundancy on people they do want to be rid of. Thus it is not inappropriate to refer to the concept of 'forced' voluntary redundancy in many cases (Turnbull 1988). Donnelly and Scholarios (1998) encountered a number of instances where simply enquiring about the possibility of voluntary arrangements resulted in the workers concerned being targeted for compulsory redundancy. In some cases, the alternative to voluntary redundancy is the acceptance of new terms and conditions of employment that provide for more flexible working and limit pay increases (Hudson 2002).

In the docks, for example, in the aftermath of a major strike called against the government and employers' decision to terminate a national agreement covering conditions of

---

(•) **INSIGHT INTO PRACTICE 8.4**

Voluntary redundancy—managerial control or employee choice?

Clarke (2007) identifies two features of voluntary redundancy, distinguishing it from a compulsory approach: employees supposedly exercise choice over whether or not they leave the organization; and enhanced severance payments are used as an incentive to encourage people to volunteer. Her study of the voluntary redundancy experiences of Australian workers found that the extent of genuine employee choice varied considerably. Some workers resented the way in which they were effectively forced out, with little alternative but to leave. Others, however, offered a more positive assessment of the voluntary redundancy process. This was particularly the case among workers who, realizing that alternative positions were unavailable, welcomed the opportunity to 'escape' demanding jobs with an enhanced severance payment.

service, many workers felt that the onerous terms of their new contracts made it impossible for them to remain. According to one worker:

'The amount of money was irrelevant really. For me it didn't matter if it was £10,000, £20,000 or £30,000. The choice was something or nothing, because there was nothing for me in the docks after the strike' (quoted in Turnbull and Wass 1994: 497).

In practice, then, there is often little to distinguish voluntary from compulsory redundancy (Burchell et al. 1999). Indeed, the term 'voluntary redundancy' may be 'something of a misnomer' (Turnbull 1988; Turnbull and Wass 1997), in so far as it communicates the misleading impression that workers can exercise much choice over whether they go or not.

Evidently, redundancy exercises offer managers an opportunity to strengthen their prerogative and, moreover, institute efficiency gains at the expense of workers' jobs. This is largely unaffected by the obligation to consult with representatives of the workforce (see Box 8.5). In a review of practice in three sectors, the docks, steel industry, and coal mining, Turnbull and Wass (1997) demonstrate that redundancy exercises enabled managers to secure work effort at less cost to the employer. In particular, workers who had been made redundant were then re-hired, on a self-employed, contract, or casual basis on drastically inferior conditions of service. In these cases, then, redundancy exercises were used to alter the terms of the wage-work bargain in a way that was advantageous to employers.

Those who have been made redundant often face a period of unemployment or are forced to accept jobs that offer worse pay and conditions than those to which they are accustomed (Donnelly and Scholarios 1998; Harris 1987; Turnbull and Wass 1997,

IINSIGHT INTO PRACTICE 8.5

Redundancy consultation

Where employers propose to dismiss twenty or more employees they are obliged to consult with union representatives if the organization recognizes a trade union, or, if it does not, with elected employee representatives. The consultation should, according to government advice, 'be in good faith with a view to reaching an agreement, ought to encompass ways of avoiding dismissals, any means of reducing the number of people due to be dismissed and alleviating the consequences of the redundancies' (see Hall and Edwards 1999: 312–13). Although in theory organizations are liable to financial penalties if they do not engage in adequate consultation, in practice the obligation to consult is rarely an obstacle to the management of redundancy (White 1983).

There is some evidence that appropriate consultation, especially where union representatives are involved, may encourage managers to reform their proposals. In one case, for example, following a consultation exercise, the company made voluntary arrangements available having initially decided upon a compulsory redundancy programme (Hall and Edwards 1999). Nevertheless, the decision to make redundancies is generally taken before any consultation commences (Turnbull and Wass 2000). Consultation rarely results in fewer redundancies (Kersley et al. 2006). Moreover, firms often avoid their obligation to consult and 'operate outside the law by using voluntary severance arrangements and offering enhanced severance payments' (Turnbull and Wass 1997: 32), in lieu of consultation.

2000). Generally, the people who are most likely to be made redundant, older workers for example, or those with health problems, are those who have relatively greater difficulty in finding new ones (Turnbull 1988; Turnbull and Wass 1997). Understandably, then, the ease with which employers can make people redundant in Britain, relative to other European countries, and the large extent to which managers enjoy prerogative over the redundancy process, shapes the experience of workers in important ways and is, it would seem, a major source of job insecurity.

8.3.3 Job insecurity

A high level of job security is often cited as one of the most important features of jobs in so far as it enables people to carry on with their working lives without the fear of redundancy and its adverse consequences (i.e. loss of income). Historically, though, the jobs of manual workers were often far from secure. Employers frequently used fluctuations in the level of demand for their products as a reason for suspending production and sending staff home—laying them off—without pay. This worker at Ford's Halewood plant on Merseyside in the late 1960s protested about the uncertainty that this generated:

> 'Look, we've been laid off this afternoon and we haven't even been told that officially. They tell you nothing. All your pay can be stopped and they tell you nothing. That's typical of this firm' (quoted in Beynon 1973: 156).

Since the mid 1990s, however, there has been a marked increase of interest in the extent to which employment in Britain has become more insecure (Burchell et al. 1999). The insecurity thesis holds that jobs are becoming short-term in nature, a function of the increasing reluctance of employers to contemplate long-term employment relationships, leaving workers more disposable. Furthermore, the thesis holds that widespread redundancy exercises during the 1990s, which often affected people in middle-class jobs—managers and professionals—meant that insecurity increasingly affected people who had previously considered their employment to be secure.

Proponents of the insecurity thesis claim that two developments in particular have rendered workers more vulnerable. First, pressures generated by the process of neo-liberal economic restructuring associated with globalization have generated a heightened level of insecurity (see Elliott and Atkinson 1998). Richard Sennett, for example, proposes that the ascendancy of a system of flexible capitalism, in which companies are exposed to more sustained competitive pressures, and are expected to produce ever faster returns for their shareholders, means that they are increasingly unable to offer long-term security to their employees, eroding trust, loyalty, and commitment. Given its short-term nature, then, neo-liberal capitalism creates vulnerability and undermines the features of working life that once enabled people to fashion careers and structure their lives (Sennett 1998).

Second, the rise in perceptions of job insecurity is also associated with the growth of non-standard, or flexible, employment patterns (see Chapter 2). Since these arrangements are often intended to make the workforce more disposable, it is unsurprising that workers are rendered more vulnerable and insecure. Conley (2002) examined the job insecurity experienced by care workers and newly qualified teachers who were employed by local authorities on temporary contracts. According to Max, a temporary local authority care worker:

> If you have a family you can't plan long term. You can't plan a holiday, you can't plan what is going to happen six months down the road. You can't plan whether you are going to have a job tomorrow. It is just a nightmare. (quoted in Conley 2002: 730)

While the attention accorded to job insecurity ensures that the experience of workers receives due emphasis (Heery and Salmon 2000b), considerable scepticism has been evinced about its significance in contemporary employment relations. For one thing, there has been no real change in the number of people working in the kind of non-standard, flexible employment arrangements (e.g. temporary jobs) that are often claimed to signify insecurity. At 5 per cent of the workforce, the proportion of workers in temporary jobs is relatively low, and has not been rising (McGovern et al. 2007). Moreover, the assumption that non-standard employment arrangements are an inherent source of insecurity is also questionable; people working in part-time jobs often perceive themselves to be rather secure (Charles and James 2003).

A further problem with the so-called 'insecurity thesis' is the assumption that employers have retreated from long-term employment relationships. The evidence demonstrates this to be mistaken. This is evident when we look at the proportion of the workforce who have spent ten or more years with the same employer. In 1994 it was 31.4 per cent; ten years later the proportion was 30.5 per cent (McGovern et al. 2007: 56). This is hardly evidence of greater insecurity.

Related to this, studies of job tenure, that is the length of time people stay in their jobs, reveal that generally it has been rather stable (McGovern et al. 2007). Although since the 1980s men have experienced a slight fall in the average length of time they spend in their jobs, women's job tenure has increased, perhaps because they are more likely to return to work after taking maternity leave (Gregg, Knight, and Wadsworth 2000). By this reckoning, the whole 'Insecurity thesis' has been rather exaggerated; the 'degree of change is nowhere near the somewhat hyperbolic claims of ever greater insecurity and instability that have been sold to the general public' (McGovern et al. 2007:56.

Why has there been so much interest in 'insecurity' then? The most convincing argument is that insecurity, manifested through job losses, and the threat of job losses, permeated hitherto relatively comfortable middle-class occupations, including managerial and professional employment (McGovern et al. 2007). The early to mid 1990s saw a rise in perceptions of job insecurity in the UK, linked to the high unemployment of that period.

From the late 1990s onwards, though, as unemployment fell, there was an associated decline in perceptions of insecurity. This suggests that insecurity, in the sense of the perceived risk of job loss, and the perceived consequences of losing one's job (e.g. the ease of finding another one), reflects the business cycle (Green 2006). On this basis we would expect the economic recession of the late 2000s, and the job losses and threats to jobs it produces, to raise perceptions of insecurity once more. The sacking of 850 agency staff from BMW's Cowley car plant in February 2009, with just one hour's notice (see Chapter 2), demonstrates just how insecure some people's jobs are in a market economy. Moreover, as unemployment climbs above the two million mark, there are considerably fewer alternative jobs available, meaning that the consequences of losing one's job become much more serious.

Perhaps, though, we also need to refine our understanding of insecurity. Tenure, for example, may not be a very good measure of job security. In a more uncertain environment workers may prefer to hang on to their current job, rather than look to change it and thus expose themselves to greater risk (Burchell 2002). A more refined approach to understanding job insecurity would adopt broader measures than the proportion of workers in temporary jobs, the incidence of simply job tenure, and incorporate the subjective feelings of employees themselves, in particular the prospect of losing their jobs, and the consequences of job loss for their livelihoods (Burchell 2002; Burchell et al. 1999). The perceived cost of losing one's job is a major source of insecurity, given the resulting likelihood of worse employment conditions in a new one, or even unemployment (Turnbull and Wass 2000).

Thus insecurity can be understood as a 'property of jobs', linked to matters such as job tenure and the risk of losing one's job, and as a 'property of the subjective experience of employees'. In order to appreciate the insecurity phenomenon properly, however, it is also necessary to consider it as a 'property of the environment' (Heery and Salmon 2000b: 12–13). In other words, we need to examine the way in which changes in the broader economic, political, and institutional contexts have contributed to greater job insecurity. In particular, higher levels of job insecurity can be explained by the greater exposure of organizations and their employees to market forces, which is a consequence of the rise of a neo-liberal capitalist order, with its preference for deregulated labour markets as a means of delivering improvements in economic performance. Rising insecurity, then, is not a function of jobs, or even of labour market restructuring. It 'is the outcome of a conscious strategy of government that arises from attempts to increase the productivity and competitiveness of the economy' (Doogan 2001: 439). See Box 8.6 for details of endemic job insecurity, and the problems it creates, among migrant workers.

The extent to which exposure to market forces has contributed to greater job insecurity is particularly evident within the British public services. Since the 1980s, in many areas, especially in local government and the health service, the delivery of public services has been subject to the processes of competitive tendering and market testing, often resulting in them being operated by private sector contractors. While not all workers have been disadvantaged by a change in their employer (Foster and Scott 1998), there is plenty of evidence to suggest that, given the need to secure efficiency gains, contracting out and market testing lead to reductions in employment levels, and erode people's terms and conditions of employment (Allen and Henry 1996; Colling 1999; Morgan, Allinton, and Heery 2000).

More generally, restructuring initiatives in the public sector have contributed to workers' insecurity, as one civil servant observed:

Like everybody else, in the back of your mind, worries about the future, redundancies. At one time the Civil Service was considered the most secure job, once you were in you were in for life, but like everything else that's changing. (quoted in Bradley 1999: 123)

Employment relations reflection 8.6   Migrant workers—a disposable workforce?

While some aspects of the so-called 'insecurity thesis' can justifiably be criticized, we should not ignore the fact that many workers in the UK are treated as easily disposable commodities, capable of being hired and fired at whim, with little expectation of stable and well-remunerated employment. According to a trade union official, much employment in the cleaning, catering, and care sectors is marked by a 'hire and fire culture'. As a result, workers 'don't belong to the organization, don't feel valued. They' disposable' (TUC 2008: 17). In the agriculture and food-processing sectors, migrant workers are often recruited through employment agencies on a day-by-day basis, with no guarantee of future work, creating much anxiety and indebtedness (Shelley 2007).

The experiences of Hsiao-Hung Pai, recorded in her 2008 book *Chinese Whispers*, demonstrate the extreme insecurity and vulnerability generated by the irregularity of work. Pai recounts how one branch of Pertemps, the employment agency which supplies workers to Grampian Country Park's plant in East Anglia, the largest poultry and meat manufacturer in Britain, operates. Newcomers are guaranteed work for one day only; and 'have to turn up each morning looking for work'. Pai eventually secured work by bribing the agency's staff, something Pertemps denies. As well as the irregularity of work, which of course made their already low earnings unpredictable, workers were also disadvantaged by extensive non-payment and under-payment of wages.

Relative to the private sector, the level of job insecurity in the public sector is still rather low. Nevertheless, restructuring initiatives, and the growth of private sector involvement in service delivery in particular, given its potential to erode pay and employment conditions, have generated greater insecurity for public sector workers (Morgan, Allinton, and Heery 2000).

By adopting a broader perspective on job insecurity, one that both examines workers' subjective experiences and stresses the important influence of changes in the wider environment, we have seen that it has become an increasingly pertinent feature of contemporary employment relations (Burchell et al. 1999; Heery and Salmon 2000b). Not only does insecurity damage the psychological health and well-being of workers, but there is evidence that, in so far as morale suffers, it may also undermine organizational effectiveness too (Mankelow 2002; Wichert 2002).

SECTION SUMMARY AND FURTHER READING

- Redundancy is a salient feature of contemporary employment relations given the extent to which organizations use it as a means of shedding jobs and thus delivering efficiency gains. For those workers who have been made redundant, the aftermath is often characterized by periods of unemployment, or employment in jobs that offer worse pay and conditions to which they had hitherto been accustomed.

- Managers have considerable scope to exercise their prerogative during redundancy programmes. Not only do they enjoy discretion over the decision to shed labour, who should be dismissed, and how and when they should go, but they also are rarely hindered by the obligation to consult with trade union or employee representatives.

- Claims that job insecurity, measured by job tenure, for example, has become an increasingly salient part of day-to-day experience of workers have been subjected to valid criticism. A broader view of insecurity, though, one which views it in the context of the development of a more neo-liberal, market-based economic climate that renders workers more disposable, demonstrates its relevance as a feature of contemporary employment relations.

For a managerial perspective on redundancy, see Lewis (1993). Based on industry studies, Turnbull and Wass (1997) provide a more critical interpretation of management's control of the redundancy process, situating it within an assessment of the public policy framework. Donnelly and Scholarios (1998) offer a rare study of workers' experiences of redundancy. For job insecurity, see the collection of essays in Heery and Salmon (2000a), and also the findings of the Joseph Rowntree-funded research study of twenty case study organizations (Burchell 2002). The best critical overview of the 'insecurity thesis', based on extensive empirical data, is McGovern et al. (2007: Chapter 2).

 Visit our Online Resource Centre for web links to sites connected to this section. www.oxfordtextbooks.co.uk/williams_adamsmith2e

8.4 **The intensification of work**

Having discussed trends in pay and working time in Chapter 7, developments in one further feature of the wage-work bargain remain to be assessed—how is working time utilized by employers? What do workers do when they are at work, and how intensively, or with how much effort, do they perform their jobs? This is an important area of analysis since the concept of 'effort' is critical to employment relations. Employers, when they hire workers, as we now know, buy their potential labour power, or their capacity to engage in productive effort. How this latent effort is then used is subject to an ongoing process of negotiation and renegotiation between managers and workers.

8.4.1 **Work intensification in Britain**

Problems of measurement render judgements of work effort difficult to calculate with any degree of certainty (Green 2001; Nichols 1986). While one can attempt to measure the speed at which a job is undertaken, its physical and mental intensity is personal to the individual performing it, and is thus an inherently subjective phenomenon (McGovern et al. 2007). Work effort, then, is an ambiguous concept (Green 2006).

Nevertheless, studies of work effort tend to demonstrate that during the 1980s and 1990s work in the UK became more intensive, before stabilizing at a relatively high level during the 2000s (Green 2006). See Box 8.7 for European data. During the 1980s, for example, both survey and case study evidence highlighted the importance of work intensification linked to demands from employers for improved flexibility in the utilization of labour (Elger 1990). Based on interviews with workers in four case study companies, Edwards and Whitston (1991) detected evidence of some work intensification—the jobs of railway platform staff, for example, demanded greater effort.

The trend of work intensification continued throughout the 1990s (Green 2001; Green 2006), as is clear from a number of relevant research studies. In 1992, for

---

⊕ INTERNATIONAL PERSPECTIVE 8.7

European data on work pressures

Two surveys of employee perceptions of work pressure across 15 European countries were undertaken in 1996 and 2001, respectively. While overall work pressure declined over the five-year period, substantial cross-country differences were identified. In the UK and Ireland, work pressure was found to be particularly high; in some other countries, notably Italy, Spain, Belgium, and Portugal, work pressure was relatively low. The main cause of falling work pressure was the overall reduction in people's working hours during this period. In the UK, however, not only are working hours generally higher, for full-time workers anyway, but also managerial prerogative tends to be stronger than elsewhere. This means that there are fewer obstacles to the introduction of practices that intensify work (Gallie 2005).

---

example, 31 per cent of employees strongly agreed that their jobs required them to work very hard; this had risen to 40 per cent of employees by 2000 (McGovern et al. 2007). Gallie et al. (1998: 223) discovered a 'marked increase in the intensity of work effort over the last decade'. While this was most likely due to a rise in the level of skill required in carrying out certain jobs, the resulting work intensification was nonetheless a source of work strain.

The most substantial case study evidence we have about work intensification in 1990s' Britain comes from research undertaken in twenty workplaces from both the private and public sectors funded by the Joseph Rowntree Foundation (Burchell 2002; Burchell et al. 1999). The researchers asked employees whether the speed of their work, and the effort they expended in undertaking it, had increased or decreased. Sixty-four per cent of employees reported an increase in the speed of their work; 61 per cent claimed an increase in effort. Only 5 per cent of employees thought the speed of their work had decreased; and just 4 per cent reported a reduction in the effort required by their jobs.

Data from the 2004 Workplace Employment Relations Survey enables us to identify the types of jobs where high work effort is particularly marked (see Table 8.4). The researchers asked employees to respond to two statements concerning the perceived intensity of their work. Overall, three-quarters (76 per cent) of employees agreed with the proposition that their job required them to work very hard; and two-fifths (40 per cent) agreed that they never seemed to have enough time to get their work done. Based on these measures of work effort, some notable occupational variations can be identified. Managers and professionals appear to experience greater intensification than employees in unskilled, elementary jobs. Moreover, there is an association between work effort and hours worked per week. People who work the longest tend to report greater intensification. Table 8.4 also shows a marked difference between the public and private sectors. Jobs in the public sector employees are marked by greater intensity than those in the private sector (Kersley et al. 2006).

Although levels of work effort appear to have stabilized during the 2000s (Green 2006), albeit at a relatively high level, work intensification seems to be particularly marked in some areas. See Box 8.8 for evidence from the airline industry.

Table 8.4 Work intensity, by selected job and workplace characteristics

	My job requires that I work very hard (% of employees agreeing)	I never seem to have enough time to get work done (% of employees agreeing)
All	76	40
Occupation		
Managers and senior officials	86	58
Professionals	84	60
Administrative and secretarial	74	39
Elementary occupations	71	25
Sector of ownership		
Private	75	36
Public	80	51
Hours worked per week		
Less than 16 hours	66	24
16–29	72	34
30–38	75	39
39–48	79	44
More than 48	84	51

Source: Kersley et al. (2006: 100)

8.4.2 The causes of work intensification

But what has caused greater work pressures? Perhaps jobs have become more intrinsically satisfying, with workers more willing to exert additional effort as a result? Work intensification is linked to increasing skill levels (Gallie et al. 1998). Some employees now enjoy greater responsibility and discretion in their jobs, making them harder, yes, but also more challenging (see Beynon et al. 2002: 280–1).

The importance of such 'supply-side' factors—that greater work pressures are the result of workers supplying more effort—should not be entirely discounted. However, work intensification seems to have mainly been demand-driven (Gallie 2006), with three interrelated sources of added work pressure being particularly evident, along with organizational restructuring in the public sector (see Table 8.5). First, increasing competitive pressures have led employers to pursue greater flexibility, and ruthlessly manage costs in such a way that the same number of employees, or fewer, are obliged to produce ever greater quantities of work (Burchell 2002).

In their study of seven private and public sector case study organizations, Beynon et al. (2002) note the large extent to which demands for enhanced organizational competitiveness and efficiency savings drove managers to intensify the labour of their staff.

INSIGHT INTO PRACTICE 8.8

Work intensification in the airline industry

The airline industry is intensely competitive, and prone to major fluctuations in demand that can lead to problems of over-capacity. Moreover, so-called 'low-cost' providers such as EasyJet and Ryanair increasingly threaten established operators like British Airways. Boyd (2001) surveyed over 900 cabin crew from scheduled and charter airlines based in the UK. She discovered that intense competitive pressures encouraged operators to adopt an approach to managing staff that was so dominated by the imperative to reduce costs that it intensified workers' labour, damaged their health, and potentially undermined safety standards. Boyd's respondents reported that the pursuit of efficiency savings dominated the way in which companies managed cabin crew numbers and their shift patterns. Airlines may choose to operate services with fewer cabin crew, for example, and sometimes just with the minimum legal requirement. The work of cabin crew is very intensive, and contributes to numerous health problems, including fatigue, backache, and stress. According to one worker: 'Every year we are expected to carry out more services, more flights with less crew, minimum hours off in between—how long do management expect us to continue working to a high standard of service without cracking up?' (quoted in Boyd 2001: 448).

On short-haul routes in particular, brief turnaround times between incoming and outgoing flights, often less than thirty minutes, create added strains for cabin crew. Pressure to sell products to passengers also contributes to their workload: '. . . we spend eight out of ten services running around like headless chickens. During turnaround we are treading on cleaners and caterers while getting the aircraft ready for the next sector. Our endeavour to satisfy the passengers means that we compromise safety' (quoted in Boyd 2001: 447).

For the private sector companies, the obligation to satisfy the expectations of financial institutions, and thus enhance shareholder value, resulted in pressure to prune staff numbers as a means of taking out costs.

Although the public sector organizations were not subject to the disciplines of the stock market, budget cuts compelled them to manage their employment relations in an overly commercial manner. Indeed, the researchers 'were struck by the way managers at the two public sector organizations were often more concerned about performance pressures than were their private sector counterparts' (Beynon et al. 2002: 266). As we have already seen, work intensification is particularly marked in the public sector, often linked to the pressures associated with organizational change (see the-end-of chapter case study).

Competitive pressures mean that managers are often impelled to try and increase the work effort of their staff as a means of realizing short-term improvements in organizational performance. Job cuts can result in the workload having to be shared out between the remaining employees. When, for example, managers in a further education college were made redundant, lecturers were obliged to take on their public relations and marketing duties (Hudson 2002).

Notwithstanding some evidence of an increase in job discretion and responsibilities (Beynon et al. 2002; Gallie et al. 1998), Hudson (2002) discovered that in most

Table 8.5 The potential sources of work intensification

Supply-side factors	Demand-side factors
Greater job satisfaction	Greater competitive pressures
More highly skilled jobs	More sophisticated information and communication technologies (ICT)
Greater discretion and responsibility	Rigorous performance management arrangements
	Organizational restructuring (public sector)

cases when workers' jobs are expanded, they are expanded in a 'horizontal' rather than a 'vertical' direction. In other words, workers are expected to take on more tasks at a similar level of skill rather than benefit from an enhancement of their skills base. According to a customer assistant in a supermarket: 'My job title changed from cashier to customer assistant . . . it just means that we can do the packing role as well if we see the red light go; cashiers and packers all have the same name now' (quoted in Hudson 2002: 45).

In front-line service work, moreover, where people have responsibility for dealing with customers, managers may use this relationship as a means of extracting greater work effort from staff. The telecommunications company studied by Beynon et al. (2002), for example, had given greater priority to service quality considerations, and expected its workers to be more sensitive to customer needs—an added source of pressure.

A second source of added work pressure is the use of increasingly robust performance management systems (McGovern et al. 2007). In a study of two financial services companies and two public sector organizations, Poynter (2000) demonstrates how managers use sophisticated performance management techniques to increase the work effort of their staff, and to enhance their own control. Within financial services, for example, the use of performance targets is an effective means of generating faster work rates, not least because in some areas employees faced the threat of disciplinary action should their output be deemed unacceptable.

According to Shona, a mortgage processor working for a financial services company in Glasgow: 'There is so much pressure with the phone calls from the branches . . . In a way the real pressure comes from the daily statistics sheet. They can not measure how much we work from the screens but they can from the daily statistics sheets' (quoted in Baldry, Bain, and Taylor 1998: 173).

Third, the effectiveness of performance management systems is often based on the use of information and communication technology to monitor workers', so-called ICT-based monitoring techniques. Electronic Point of Sale (EPOS) arrangements can be used to monitor the performance of checkout staff in retail stores, for example. In call centres and other office-based environments, ICT monitoring systems can be used to record the number and length of telephone calls, and even the keystrokes on a computer. By 2000 over a half of employees (52 per cent) in one survey reported that their work activities were recorded in some way by a computer system; nearly a quarter (23 per cent) indicated that information gathered in this way was used to monitor their performance (McGovern et al. 2007: 170).

In office-based environments, ICT allows managers greater freedom to organize the flow of work in a way that reduces the ability of workers to manipulate their effort. According to a union representative in a financial services company:

> Instead of you picking and choosing which bit of work you want to do, when you finish the piece of work and you press a button to say I have finished this piece of work, it just brings up the next bit. There's no question of you having a break . . .
> (quoted in Danford, Richardson, and Stewart 2003: 107)

Call centres are environments where the use of ICT enables managers to control the pace of work and monitor staff with particular ease, a source of work intensification. According to one worker:

> The major pressure is . . . the calls . . . and that is understandable because we work in a call-centre environment, and you also get the pressure . . . because you haven't got time to literally stand up and do what you need to do or take two minutes. You feel as though you're under pressure by taking the calls because it [the indicator] could be flashing 'there's eight minutes of calls waiting' which is quite regular in the evening. (quoted in Beynon et al. 2002: 289)

What Green (2006) calls 'effort-biased technological change' has been a major source of increased work pressures. In other words, ICT helps managers to secure extra effort from their subordinates, because their activities are more easily monitored and recorded. Evidently, innovations 'like the mobile phone and the laptop computer—devices that enable work to be carried out at what, previously, had been idle times—are only the most tangible signs' of how technology can be used to increase work effort (Green 2006: 174). More importantly, the profusion of ICT-based monitoring systems, and the way in which they are used to inform performance management arrangements, allows managers to secure greater employee compliance with organizational norms, standards, values, and targets.

However, we should be careful not to exaggerate the capacity of managers to secure control over, and extract more effort from, their staff. As we see in Chapter 9, workers are capable of challenging the encroachment of managerial control initiatives in rather imaginative ways. Moreover, there is evidence that employers have had to pay a price for increases in work effort; in particular, the use of financial incentives, in the form of increased wages, to encourage higher effort. 'Additional earnings provide employees with the motive to increase effort, and employers have developed methods of monitoring and control to ensure that effort is increased' (McGovern et al. 2007: 186).

While the weakness of the trade unions means that workers are less defended from work intensification, increases in work effort are nonetheless accompanied by higher earnings, suggesting that managers cannot simply impose higher workloads, but rather have to bargain over them with employees.

8.4.3 The effects of work intensification

What, though, are the effects of work intensification? For organizations, it seems that the conditions for increases in the levels of trust and cooperation necessary to stimulate long-term, real improvements in economic performance are unlikely to exist. The evidence, on both working time, which we considered in Chapter 7, and work effort, examined here, indicates that many employers prefer to 'sweat' their staff, generating short-term improvements in output by intensifying workloads or using overtime.

While pressure is an aspect of all work, and can have an important part in stimulating and maintaining motivation, excessive workloads not only undermine performance at work, but can also make people ill. To have situations where, as observed by some researchers, workers are unable to leave their desks to take refreshments, cannot be healthy (Baldry, Bain, and Taylor 1998).

Work pressures are a major source of stress-related ill-health. In 2006–07 some 455,000 people were thought to suffer from ill-health as a consequence of work-related stress, anxiety, or depression. Each year, over thirteen million days are not worked because of stress-related illnesses; work-related stress accounts for one in three new incidents of ill-health. For workers who experience it, stress can seriously compromise their health and well-being. It 'can lead to heart disease, back pain, gastrointestinal disturbances, anxiety and depression' (Boyd 2003: 46).

The following quotations, the first from a call-centre operator, and the second from a further education lecturer, encapsulate the psychological and physical damage of excessive work pressures on individuals.

> I know a lot of people are off with stress. Because you get customers on the telephone and I have seen women sit there and cry because of the calls they are getting . . . In this job women get sworn at and cry. (quoted in Beynon et al. 2002: 281)

> So many people are going home with work to do that they haven't really got time to do. I find myself going home feeling physically exhausted, although I've hardly done anything physical. (quoted in Nolan 2002: 122)

The experience of the ill-fated Child Support Agency (CSA) in the UK demonstrates how excessive workloads can damage employee well-being. Until 2008 it was responsible for assessing and collecting child maintenance payments from non-resident parents. Delays in processing claims became a matter of particular concern; and the CSA was widely castigated for its ineffectiveness. However, restructuring initiatives designed to resolve these problems were undertaken with little regard for their effects on staff, and seemed to make matters worse. Pressures of work, those associated with performance targets in particular, adversely affected the workforce in terms of generating excessive stress, something which compromised operational efficiency. Staff morale was extremely low. There was a high incidence of long-term sickness absence, largely due to stress-related complaints. According to one member of staff, 'every single day someone in their office would be crying through stress and frustration' (Atkinson and McKay 2005: 75).

It is rare for textbooks on employment relations and human resource management to consider the topic of work intensification, its causes, and its effects. The material reviewed here, however, demonstrates that it is an integral feature of contemporary employment relations and is central to the day-to-day experience and job quality (see Box 8.9) of many workers. The evidence of a 'widespread intensification of work effort and its detrimental impact on well-being is unambiguous' (Green 2006: 174).

Employment relations reflection 8.9   Job quality

What makes for a good quality job? Is it simply one that is relatively well-paid? Or are there other, more qualitative indicators which determine whether or not a job is of good or bad quality, like matters relating to employee well-being? Green (2006) uses five criteria—wages, skill, the extent of workers' discretion and control, effort, and job security—to evaluate what has been happening to job quality. Overall, with the exception of the United States, wages have risen across the advanced industrialized societies, though this has sometimes been accompanied by greater inequality. While skill is an ambiguous concept, and thus difficult to measure, the growing complexity of jobs, linked to the increased use of information and communication technologies, suggests that skill levels have been gradually rising. Set against this, however, in the UK there has been a marked diminution in the perceived influence enjoyed by workers in their jobs. Work intensification, moreover, has been widespread. Job security, and its converse, job insecurity, tend to be more cyclical, and rise and fall depending upon the state of the economy and the level of unemployment. On some measures (e.g. wages, skill levels) the overall quality of jobs appears to have improved. On other measures, particularly those linked to employee well-being (e.g. discretion, effort), job quality has markedly declined. Overall, though, the lack of any evidence that job satisfaction has been rising suggests that workers' experiences of contemporary employment relations are far from being positive.

SECTION SUMMARY AND FURTHER READING

- Although there are difficulties associated with measuring how much effort people expend in their jobs, there is nonetheless overwhelming evidence that employment relations in the 1980s and 1990s were marked by work intensification, after which effort levels stabilized at a high level during the 2000s.

- While an increase in their job responsibilities may in part have led some people to work harder, the principal causes of increased work pressures are the growing competitive pressures upon organizations that have compelled them to increase staff workloads, the extensive use of new systems for managing performance, linked to developments in information technology, and, in the public services, myriad organizational restructuring initiatives.

- It is unlikely that the increases in work effort seen in the UK will generate long-term improvements in economic performance. Moreover, there is increasing evidence of the adverse consequences for workers' morale, health, and well-being at work.

For data on work effort, and explanations of why it has increased, see Green (2006: Chapters 3 and 4) and McGovern et al. (2007: Chapters 5 and 6). For case study research see Beynon et al. (2002), Burchell (2002), and Hudson (2002).

 Visit our Online Resource Centre for web links to sites connected to this section. www.oxfordtextbooks.co.uk/williams_adamsmith2e

Conclusion

In this chapter, we have examined three important aspects of contemporary employment relations—employee involvement and participation, redundancy and job insecurity, and work intensification—in order to consider the experiences of employees. In general, people are better informed about organizational and workplace decisions, and sometimes enjoy a limited degree of increased discretion over how they undertake their jobs, albeit within strict boundaries. They have, however, little genuine influence over decisions that affect them at work, and there is evidence that managerial control over the wage-work bargain has intensified.

Management control over the decision to make redundancies, and the means by which they are undertaken, are also prominent features of contemporary employment relations. In a context of greater competitive pressures, which oblige organizations to search continually for efficiency savings, redundancy exercises are used largely as a means of cutting costs through the shedding of labour. One of the main consequences is a marked increase in the level of job insecurity in Britain. This is amplified by the neo-liberal character of contemporary capitalism, and its preference for deregulated labour markets, something that enhances the disposability of the workforce. Redundancies, and job losses in general, are a function of the pressure on organizations to operate in a leaner, more efficient manner with an emphasis on the need to make cost savings on an ongoing basis. For many workers the result is that they are expected to work harder. Work intensification is one of the most salient features of contemporary employment relations in Britain, given growing competitive pressures on organizations that cause them to increase staff workloads, the extensive use of new systems for managing performance, linked to developments in information technology, and, in the public services, major restructuring processes.

In general, then, the experience of employees in contemporary Britain is marked by an increased exposure to work intensification, insecurity, and a tightening of managerial control over their behaviour, with limited opportunities to influence decisions that affect them at work. The economic and political circumstances outlined in Chapters 2 and 3 of this book give employers greater opportunity to shift the terms of the wage-work bargain in their favour, to the detriment of employees' interests. The latter are not passive actors, though, as the material on work intensification demonstrates. Work pressures have increased, yes, but at the cost to employers of higher earnings. This highlights the basic antagonism that marks the relationship between an employer and employee as a wage-work bargain. How the potential conflict this generates manifests itself in practice is the subject of the next chapter.

Assignment and discussion questions

1 Why do managers prefer downward forms of communication to other forms of employee involvement?

2 How do workers experience teamworking and empowerment initiatives? What can managers do to make such processes more effective?

3 In what ways do redundancy exercises potentially strengthen managerial control of the workplace?

4 How relevant is the concept of job insecurity in contemporary employment relations?

5 What is meant by 'work intensification'? What are the main causes of increases in work effort?

  Visit our Online Resource Centre for answers to these questions.
www.oxfordtextbooks.co.uk/williams_adamsmith2e

Take your learning further: online resource centre

Visit the Online Resource Centre that accompanies this book to enrich your understanding of Chapter 8: Experiencing employment relations: involvement, insecurity, intensification. Explore web links, test yourself using an interactive flashcard glossary, and keep up to date with the latest developments in the area.

 http://www.oxfordtextbooks.co.uk/orc/williams_adamsmith2e

Chapter case study

Work intensification in the public sector

As we have noted in the main part of the chapter, work intensification in the public sector is particularly marked. This is evident from studies of employment relations in public sector organizations. Harriet Bradley interviewed workers in a hospital for her book *Gender and Power in the Workplace* (1999). At the time of the research the hospital was preparing a bid to become a self-governing trust. The process appears to have increased concern to reduce costs in a way that generated work intensification. According to a male charge nurse:

> **The workload's too much, staffing loads are deplorable. I personally feel as though that money is the name of the game . . . being just out to cut costs at all costs. I know I could be doing a better job if I had the resources . . . It's beyond a joke, you're just pushed and pushed and pushed.** (quoted in Bradley 1999: 118)

A further aspect of the restructuring of the public sector in Britain, the contracting out of some services, such as schools meals provision and refuse collection, to the private sector has also intensified the effort of many of the workers involved in delivering them. In order to increase productivity, and thus generate profitability in what are labour-intensive activities, private sector providers may reduce the numbers of staff employed, and raise the number of job tasks of those who remain (Colling 1999).

The reform of management in the public sector, and the introduction of techniques associated with the 'new public management', which were discussed in Chapter 5, also appears to have been a cause of work intensification. Research studies demonstrate that performance targets are used intensively in the public sector, perhaps more so than in private companies, constituting a significant source of pressure on staff (Beynon et al. 2002; Poynter 2000).

In the Benefits Agency, a civil service executive agency in the UK responsible for welfare payments, researchers discovered that the implementation of teamworking and performance-related pay, based on the subjective appraisal of staff by managers, had caused profound changes in two of the three offices they studied: 'It is difficult to convey fully the atmosphere of intense stress and low morale caused by an acute intensification of workloads and individual appraisal uncovered by our interviews within the [Benefits Agency] . . . [the] overriding impression was of an organization at breaking point' (Foster and Hoggett 1999: 30–1, 31).

Work intensification has been particularly marked in the public sector, a function of the restructuring of the public services, enhanced performance pressures, and the development of new management techniques. It is clear that changes in the public sector, most notably a more market-based approach to the delivery of services, have, in a context of tight budgetary constraints imposed by the Treasury, been a major source of increased work intensity.

1. Why do you think work intensification has been such a prominent feature of public sector occupations?
2. What are the likely implications of work intensification for employment relations in the public sector?

9

Conflict and employment relations

Chapter objectives:

The main objectives of this chapter are to:

∗ examine the nature of strikes, and their significance as a form of industrial conflict;

∗ consider recent strike trends, and discuss their implications for employment relations;

∗ assess the nature and significance of forms of industrial conflict other than strike action; and

∗ examine the ways in which workplace disputes are resolved in employment relations.

9.1 Introduction

In the introductory chapter, we observed that the employment relationship, given that it is a wage-work or effort bargain, is characterized by a basic antagonism between an employer and employee. It is misleading only to refer to the existence of a conflict of interest; cooperation is also an important feature of employment relations. Nevertheless, there is always the potential for conflict in employment relations (Edwards 1986). Industrial conflict, however, is often overlooked, particularly in the growing number of texts devoted to human resource management. This is often justified with reference to the virtual disappearance of strike activity in the private sector. In this chapter, we demonstrate that conflict in employment relations is about much more than strikes; it can occur in a variety of forms. We examine the main influences on strike levels and the main features of the legal framework governing industrial action by trade unions. We also consider the processes used to resolve disputes when they arise, including the use of negotiation to reach agreements, the role of the Advisory, Conciliation, and Arbitration Service (ACAS), and the main characteristics of the system of employment tribunals, used for handling individual disputes at work.

The use of several key terms needs to be outlined. The concept of 'industrial conflict' is used to refer to a variety of behaviours undertaken by employees, such as sabotage, for example, that potentially reflect the basic antagonism underlying the employment relationship. Instances of conflict at work may be translated into a 'dispute'. Thus conflict generated by an employee grievance, for example, or a union pay claim, is articulated and formalized in a manner that enables it to be addressed. We use the term 'industrial action' to refer to those manifestations of industrial conflict that take the form of explicitly collective behaviour by workers and which are usually organized by a trade union. A strike is an example of industrial action.

Introductory case study

The US writers' strike

Between November 2007 and February 2008 members of the Writers Guild of America union, who write the scripts for film and television shows, stopped work in a dispute over payments for internet downloads and DVD sales. The strike had a major impact on the US entertainment industry. Production on films and hit television shows, such as Desperate Housewives, Grey's Anatomy, and House, came to a halt. The strike was ended after union leaders negotiated an agreement with the owners of the major Hollywood studios which gave the writers a larger share of the profits from television programmes and films sold through the internet and other new media. This case is important for a number of reasons. First, it demonstrates the way in which the withdrawal of labour by workers—a strike—can be used as an effective means of achieving their demands. Second, the case shows us that conflict in employment relationship is a global phenomenon; strikes are a feature of employment relations around the world. Third, it demonstrates that strikes, and industrial conflict more broadly, are not just restricted to traditional industries dominated by manual labour, like coal mining for example. Strikes can occur whenever workers who are organized in a trade union have a grievance which, to them, is sufficiently serious to warrant action.

9.2 Strikes and employment relations

Understandably, strikes, the withdrawal by workers of their labour, dominate analyses of conflict in employment relations. They are the 'most obvious manifestation' of industrial conflict (Hyman 1975: 186). But, as we shall see in later sections, strikes and industrial conflict should not be treated as if they are synonymous; other forms of industrial action and types of behaviour may express conflict in the employment relationship. First, though, we examine the nature of strikes, consider the main strike trends in Britain, and assess the principal explanations for the level of strike activity, in particular the impact of the law.

Although the level of recorded strike activity has fallen to historically low levels in recent years, this does not imply that strikes, and their causes, are unimportant. From a global perspective, for example, it is by no means clear that the strike is an extinct social phenomenon. Moreover, mobilization theory contributes to our understanding of why employee grievances translate, or do not translate, into industrial action (see Section 9.2.5).

9.2.1 Strikes: meanings and measurement

What is a strike? It can be defined as 'a temporary stoppage of work by a group of employees in order to express a grievance or to enforce a demand' (Griffin 1939, cited in Hyman 1977: 17). There are three aspects of this definition that demand further attention:

- first, the strike is designed to be a temporary act; employees withdraw their labour based on the understanding that work will be resumed once the dispute that has caused the strike is resolved;

- second, the strike involves a stoppage of work; as a manifestation of conflict in employment relations, it can therefore be distinguished from other forms of industrial action, such as the overtime ban, for example, which we consider later on in this chapter; and

- third, strikes are forms of behaviour that are undertaken by workers with a specific purpose in mind: to get a dismissed colleague reinstated, for example, or to secure an increase in pay.

Strikes, then, generally have a calculative, purposive character (Hyman 1977, 1989). They rarely arise without a reason, even if it is implicit. Conventionally, a distinction is drawn between official and unofficial strikes. Official strike activity is that which, once it has been approved by their appropriate decision-making machinery, has the formal, or official, backing of a trade union. Unofficial strikes, however, occur when employees withhold their labour, perhaps by walking off the job, without receiving the formal support of their union.

Since unofficial strike action is often of rather a short duration, involving relatively few workers, it is sometimes portrayed as being largely spontaneous behaviour undertaken in order to redress an immediate grievance (Knowles 1952), hence the popularity of the term 'wildcat strike' to describe such activity (Gouldner 1955). However, unofficial strikes cannot be treated as if they are spontaneous; their occurrence reflects the ongoing efforts of employees to resist potentially damaging changes to their working conditions, or to improve their position and power, in the context of the wage-work bargain (Cronin 1979). Such activity demands organization, and hence calculation.

The preponderance of unofficial strikes in the Royal Mail reflects the efforts of workers to resist managerial attempts to realize efficiency gains, through the implementation of new working methods among other things. Such activity is generally organized by local union representatives, with or without the knowledge of the formal union hierarchy, who use it to challenge management initiatives. Thus 'unofficial strikes in [Royal Mail] are predominantly organized, premeditated and not spontaneous' (Gall 2003c: 168). A further example of the organized basis of unofficial action came in January 2009 when union activists helped to coordinate the apparently spontaneous walk-outs around the country in support of workers at the Lindsey oil refinery in their dispute over the use of foreign labour (see Chapter 1).

Two implications arise from the purposeful and organized nature of strike activity. First, the notion sometimes advanced by governments and employers that strikes are abnormal, a deviation from the normal character of stable, ordered, and peaceful employment relations, cannot be upheld. In the context of an exploitative employment relationship, the withdrawal of their labour by employees is a rational form of behaviour designed to achieve a particular purpose, to alter the terms of the wage-work bargain in a way, or ways, favourable to them (Hyman 1977). Nevertheless, it is important not to present strikes as examples of rational, purposive activity simply in the context of collective bargaining; they also reflect the capacity of workers to act collectively, to mobilize in pursuit of their interests through the vehicle of a trade union (Cronin 1979; Hyman 1989).

This highlights the second main implication of the strike being an activity that is both purposeful and organized, that is the importance of the collective organization of workers in trade unions. Without the presence of a strong union that is able to mobilize workers, organize the action, and coordinate resistance to employer efforts to defeat it, effective strike activity is hard to uphold (Edwards 1983; Hyman 1989).

Strikes are often taken as a measure of the level of industrial conflict because they are apparently easy to quantify. There are three main ways of ascertaining the level of strike activity in any given period, usually over the course of a year:

- the duration of strike activity is measured by calculating the numbers of working days not worked due to strike activity;
- the breadth of strike activity is calculated by measuring the number of workers involved; and
- the frequency of strike activity is determined by totalling up the number of strikes, or stoppages, in any given year.

In Britain, unless the total number of days not worked amounts to 100 or more, stoppages involving fewer than ten workers, or lasting less than one day, are excluded from official data (Hale 2008).

The measure of strike activity used can influence one's perception of trends in strike levels. In 1996, for example, a national dispute in the Royal Mail contributed to a threefold increase in the number of working days lost due to strike activity over 1995. The number of recorded stoppages, however, barely rose. Thus, measured by frequency, the level of strike activity in 1996 was similar to that of the previous year. However, the duration, and also the breadth, of strike activity were very different. While official strike data can be used constructively to map trends in strike activity over time (Edwards 1995), they should nonetheless be treated with caution (Hyman 1977). Managers sometimes do not record strikes, for example (Batstone, Boraston, and Frenkel 1978).

9.2.2 The declining level of strike activity in Britain

A prominent feature of recent employment relations in Britain has been the diminution in the level of strike activity since the 1970s. While the 1980s were characterized by occasional large-scale strikes, in industries such as steel making and coal mining, as workers and their unions fought rationalization initiatives that threatened their jobs, livelihoods, and communities (Gilbert 1996), by the 1990s the amount of strike activity had fallen to very low levels indeed (Edwards 1995). See Table 9.1 for historical data on the level of strike activity in the UK.

Since the 1980s, the trend of declining strike activity has broadly continued. See Table 9.2 for further details. 2005 saw the lowest recorded number of working days not worked due to strike activity–157,000–while the lowest number of strikes–just 116–was recorded

Table 9.1 The level of strike activity in Britain, 1946–1989

	Strikes	Workers involved (000s)	Days not worked (000s)
1946–52	1,698	444	1,888
1953–59	2,340	790	3,950
1960–68	2,372	1,323	3,189
1969–73	2,974	1,581	12,497
1974–79	2,412	1,653	12,178
1980–85	1,276	1,213	9,806
1986–89	893	781	3,324

Annual averages.

Source: Edwards (1995)

in the same year. Despite the low level of strike activity, it is important to realize that notable annual fluctuations do occur. In some years, there is a marked upsurge in strikes. In 2002, for example, over 1.3 million working days were not worked largely as a result of two major public sector strikes involving local government workers and firefighters. 2007 saw a marked increase in recorded strike activity, mainly as a result of disputes in the public sector (e.g. local government). The decline in the level of strike activity is an international phenomenon. Nevertheless, it has been more pronounced in Britain than elsewhere (Waddington 2003b).

Table 9.2 The level of strike activity in Britain, 1990–2008

	Strikes	Workers involved (000s)	Days not worked (000s)
1990–94	334	223	824
1995–99	193	180	495
2000	212	183	499
2001	194	180	525
2002	146	943	1,323
2003	133	151	499
2004	130	293	905
2005	116	93	157
2006	158	713	755
2007	142	745	1,041
2008	144	511	756

Annual averages 1990–94; 1995–99.

Source: Office for National Statistics, http://www.statistics.gov.uk

What factors have caused the incidence of strike activity to fall to such low levels in contemporary Britain? Clearly, the changing composition of employment has been influential. Levels of employment in traditionally strike-prone industries, such as coal mining and the docks, for example, have fallen considerably. Job growth has been concentrated in private sector service industries where trade unionism is weaker and strike action less commonplace. That said, the idea that workers in certain occupations and industries are particularly 'strike-prone' (e.g. Kerr and Siegel 1954) often fails to stand up to critical scrutiny (Edwards 1977). Strike levels may vary considerably from workplace to workplace even within the same industry.

There is also some evidence that economic factors have contributed to the declining level of strike activity. During the 1980s, for example, a combination of relatively low inflation and high unemployment appears to have reduced the number of strikes (Edwards 1995). The former reduces the incentive for strike action, since employees do not feel that their standard of living is threatened by rising prices, whereas the latter invokes a greater fear of the consequences of losing one's job as a result of going on strike.

What, though, has been the effect, if any, of the way in which employment relations is managed? Given the limited impact of human resource management techniques (see Chapter 5), and also considering the nature of people's experiences of contemporary employment relations (see Chapter 8), it seems doubtful that the level of strike activity has diminished because workers are more contented. The potential for conflict in contemporary employment relations is as pronounced as it ever has been, if not more so. What does seem to have changed, though, is that many employers are managing employment relations more assertively. They are fostering a workplace climate in which it is made apparent to employees that, given greater competitive pressures, their cooperation is essential in order to prevent job losses, and the erosion of pay and working conditions (Edwards 1992).

The level of strike activity has fallen as a consequence of the changing balance of power between organized labour and capital. The decline in their membership and organizational capacities has rendered the union movement less capable of undertaking effective industrial action. Many union leaders have placed their faith in partnership and cooperative employment relations as the route to greater influence largely, as we saw in Chapter 6, because they are operating from a position of weakness.

Much strike activity now occurs in the public sector, where union organization continues to be somewhat robust (Mathieson and Corby 1999), something which helps translate workers' grievances into tangible industrial action. During the 2000s, public sector disputes, among post office workers, college lecturers, local government workers, and firefighters in particular, increasingly dominated the strike statistics. Much of their action, moreover, was often relatively short, or discontinuous, in nature, such as a series of one- or two-day strikes, for example, something which increases the pressure on the employer while reducing the costs to the employee of striking, in particular loss of wages.

Finally, perhaps the most important constraint on the power of unions to organize effective strike action is the highly restrictive legal framework, something we consider below (see Section 9.2.4).

9.2.3 Strikes: a global phenomenon

While the amount of recorded strike activity is at historically low levels in Britain, from a global perspective we can see that strikes continue to be an important feature of contemporary employment relations. In a review of strike levels in Western Europe, Gall (1999) suggests that although during the 1980s and 1990s overall strike activity was, relative to the previous two decades, somewhat low, cross-national differences in the way in which data are collected mean that official statistics under-represent the real level of conflict. Moreover, his careful analysis of strike data demonstrates that the level of strike activity is prone to fluctuations and that strikes are therefore not going to vanish.

Nevertheless, the overall level of strike activity across advanced, industrialized countries has considerably declined. Particularly where unions are relatively weak, globalization seems to have been a major cause of the diminution in strike levels, given its tendency to erode the power of organized labour (Piazza 2005). Yet in so far as it threatens people's working conditions, the process of economic globalization may stimulate the extent, and extend the dimensions, of industrial conflict. In countries that have been subject to 'structural adjustment' programmes imposed by global financial institutions, such as Argentina, for example, the implementation of neo-liberal policies has generated considerable labour unrest (Silver 2003).

Since the 1980s, strikes and protests have occurred in response to the enactment of neo-liberal economic policies, including wage restraint and privatization, in countries such as South Korea, France, and Bolivia, some of which have informed, and developed connections with, the growing worldwide anti-globalization movement, exemplified by the demonstrations at the 1999 World Trade Organization meeting in Seattle (Kingsnorth 2003; Silver 2003).

From a global perspective, it is apparent that strike activity and other forms of labour unrest have not disappeared. One of the major challenges facing the rulers of Dubai, part of the United Arab Emirates, for example, is how to deal with the widespread labour unrest evident among its largely migrant construction workforce (see Box 9.1). The development of export-oriented manufacturing industries in countries such as China, and the concomitant need for cheap labour on a massive scale, generates an environment in which the growth of industrial conflict is a likely development (Silver 2003).

There are strong indications that the economic reforms, which are designed to create a capitalist market economy in China, are stimulating widespread worker unrest in many parts of the country, over matters such as unpaid wages, for example, and employer violations of labour regulations (Cooke 2008). Conflict encompasses everything 'from everyday worker resistance, petitions, work stoppages and strikes to public protests, violence, independent unionism and political movements' (Taylor, Chang, and Li 2003: 158). Not only has the recorded number of official labour disputes in China risen, but there is also strong evidence that they constitute just the 'tip of the iceberg of the true level of discontent in China' (Cooke 2008: 112–13). These examples suggest that in the twenty-first century, labour unrest, including strikes, will in all likelihood remain an important feature of employment relations around the world.

INTERNATIONAL PERSPECTIVE 9.1

Strikes and labour unrest in Dubai

During the 2000s, the emirate of Dubai in the Middle East was one of the fastest growing places in the world, with scores of new hotel complexes, luxury apartments, and shopping centres going up to service a growing tourism and leisure industry. The construction industry is booming. With 160 storeys, one building, the Burj Dubai Tower, will be the tallest in the world when it is completed. The construction workforce is overwhelmingly made up of migrant labourers from countries such as India, Pakistan, and Bangladesh who travel to Dubai under the belief that finding work will make them prosperous. The reality is often excessive working hours, under oppressive conditions, in temperatures that sometimes reach 50 degrees. Low and unpaid wages often leave many of the workers, who share rooms in concrete barrack compounds, heavily in debt. They are often required to surrender their passport, so are not free to leave.

Any form of industrial action by workers is illegal in Dubai; and there is no right to join a trade union. Workers who do make a fuss are treated as troublemakers and deported. During 2006 and 2007, however, some major instances of industrial conflict were reported as construction workers took strike action and protested over low pay, inadequate accommodation, and poor working conditions. This demonstrates that even where the odds are heavily stacked against it, industrial action by workers who want to improve the conditions under which they labour is always possible.

9.2.4 The legal regulation of industrial action in Britain

Unlike many other European countries, in Britain workers have never enjoyed a 'right' to go on strike. Under the common law, based on the notions of freedom of contract and the importance of property rights, workers who strike, or undertake any form of industrial action, generally act in breach of their employment contracts. Trade unions that organize industrial action potentially transgress the common law in a range of areas; most notably they commit the offence of inducing workers to breach their contracts.

During the late nineteenth and early twentieth centuries, legislation was enacted that gave unions and their officials immunities from criminal prosecution for organizing industrial action, and from civil proceedings for damages by employers, as long as the action was 'in contemplation or furtherance of a trade dispute' (Wedderburn 1986). The concept of 'immunities' gave the misleading impression that trade unions were above the law, and attracted much judicial hostility (Wedderburn 1991). In practice all they did was ensure that the common law of contract and property rights did not make the conduct of employment relations impossible to uphold in practice (Davies and Freedland 1993).

Without these immunities, trade unions would have been in no position to bargain effectively on behalf of their members. The only alternative was a system of positive rights for workers and their unions, something that was contrary to the preference for voluntarism and autonomous self-regulation that characterized employment relations in Britain.

However, during the 1980s and 1990s, the Conservative governments enacted six major pieces of legislation restricting the capacity of trade unions to undertake lawful industrial action. The main focus of their interventions was to reduce the scope of the immunities that enabled unions to organize industrial action within the boundaries of the law (Dickens and Hall 2003; Dunn and Metcalf 1996). Among other things, legislation was enacted that:

- obliged unions to win majority support for industrial action from the workers concerned in a properly constituted secret postal ballot;
- prohibited any form of 'secondary' industrial action, meaning that it is only lawful when it involves a 'primary' dispute between workers and their own employer;
- enabled employers, and other aggrieved parties, to sue a union for damages arising out of unlawful industrial action; and
- gave employers greater scope to dismiss workers taking industrial action.

The legislation was a major element of the Conservatives' efforts to challenge the power of the unions in Britain. Since 1997 Labour governments have introduced some relatively minor changes to the statutory framework governing strikes and industrial action. For example, it effectively became unlawful for an employer to dismiss employees undertaking lawful industrial action; and some of the balloting requirements were made less onerous for the unions. Nevertheless, Labour retained the bulk of the anti-strike legislation it inherited from its Conservative predecessors in government, and has shown no inclination to repeal any of it despite representations by union leaders (Davies and Freedland 2007).

The extent to which the restrictive legal framework weakened the capacity of trade unions to mount effective strikes was evident in a number of high-profile disputes, particularly in the newspaper publishing and transport sectors, during the 1980s and 1990s (Gennard 1984; McIlroy 1991). For the most part, though, employers have been reluctant to invoke the law when facing industrial action by trade unions (Undy et al. 1996). In the Royal Mail, for example, managers generally prefer to avoid the courts when faced with unlawful, unofficial industrial action on the basis that legal action would only inflame disputes, making them harder to resolve (Gall 2003c).

Nevertheless, some employers have been prepared to request interim labour injunctions, judicial orders temporarily preventing trade unions from undertaking industrial action. Most applications from employers for an injunction are successful, often on very thin, or sometimes no, legal grounds, and few are ever pursued to a full court hearing (Gall and McKay 1996; Wedderburn 2001). Generally, employers apply, or threaten to apply, for injunctions in order to put pressure on unions to settle disputes, or to delay impending industrial action in the hope that the workforce's support for it will dwindle because of the wait (Elgar and Simpson 1993; Evans 1987).

The complex legislation governing industrial action ballots gives employers plenty of scope to challenge, and thus delay, any planned action, even if their substantive case turns out to be weak. Such legal cases cost unions a great deal of money. Moreover, 'they reiterate the limits of permissible industrial action; keep unions under pressure; engage the energies of officers and officials; divert attention from organizing effective action; and, where injunctions are granted, dislocate it' (McIlroy 1999: 528–9).

The impact of the legal restrictions on union behaviour is by no means straightforward though. Where workplace union organization is relatively strong, the obligation to hold a ballot before taking industrial action can work to a union's advantage. A large vote in favour, for example, can be used to exert pressure on employers to grant concessions. In situations where they are confident that they have the support of the workforce, canny union officials sometimes use ballots to strengthen their bargaining power in negotiations with employers (Undy et al. 1996).

Nevertheless, the constraints the law imposes on industrial action have contributed to a general strengthening of managerial prerogative. In his study of employment relations in an autocomponents factory in South Wales, Danford (1999) demonstrates the large extent to which the legal restrictions on industrial action eroded union resistance to managerial initiatives, and enhanced the capacity of management to secure workplace changes unfavourable to the interests of employees.

It is difficult to quantify the contribution of the restrictive legislative framework to the declining level of strike activity in Britain. Many other European countries have also seen falling strike levels, suggesting that broader economic and industrial trends, the changing composition of the workforce, and the reduction of the number of people employed in 'strike-prone' industries in particular, have exercised more influence (Dunn and Metcalf 1996). Yet the indirect effects of the law, in particular the large degree to which it restricts the capacity of the unions to challenge employers' actions, have certainly contributed to the decline in the incidence of industrial action in Britain over recent decades. Unions are much more hesitant about calling industrial action now than would have been the case before the 1980s.

By retaining the majority of the Conservatives' anti-strike legislation, Labour has ensured that Britain remains in contravention of international conventions that deal with rights at work. In recent years, for example, various International Labour Organization (ILO) committees, as well other international bodies, have expressed concern that Britain's extreme anti-strike legislation negates workers' freedom of association, and undermines the ability of unions to organize workers and bargain effectively (see Ewing and Hendy 2004).

British law fails to comply with international norms in a number of potential respects. For example, the capacity of employers to impose sanctions upon employees undertaking industrial action, up to and including dismissal, is one notable failing. Any employee engaged in unofficial action is not covered by unfair dismissal legislation, and employers also enjoy considerable freedom to dismiss strikers once a 12-week protected period expires (see Box 9.2). Moreover, the prohibition on all forms of secondary action 'is contrary to international law which stipulates that industrial action is not to be confined to disputes with employers and is, in particular, to be permitted on matters of economic and social policy' (Ewing and Hendy 2002: 91). Although the British government is under no obligation to amend legislation to comply with the ILO's recommendations, interventions by international bodies are likely to stimulate further debates about the appropriateness of the current legal framework governing industrial action in Britain.

9.2.5 Conflict at work in contemporary employment relations: insights from mobilization theory

While broader industrial, economic and political factors clearly affect the level of strike activity, it is important to recognize that the causes of strikes are rooted in the dynamics of the relationship between managers and workers in particular workplace

> **● INSIGHT INTO PRACTICE 9.2**
>
> ## Sacking employees who are taking lawful strike action
>
> In 1999, Labour made it unlawful for an employer to dismiss employees undertaking lawful industrial action during the first eight weeks of a dispute. Once the eight-week 'protected period' was over, dismissals are lawful only if an employer has made an effort to resolve the dispute. This 'protected period' has since been extended to 12 weeks. The experience of Friction Dynamics, an American-owned car parts plant based in North Wales, demonstrates how the odds are stacked against workers taking strike action, even when it has been lawfully organized by a trade union. In 2001, members of the Transport and General Workers Union (TGWU) employed at the plant went on strike over the employer's proposals to change shift patterns and institute a temporary pay cut. After exactly eight weeks, the employer dismissed the 86 strikers. They mounted a picket outside the firm's premises that was to last for two-and-a-half years.
>
> In 2002, the strikers won their employment tribunal claim for unfair dismissal, and waited for the company to pay the compensation they were due. In August 2003, though, the American owner put the company into liquidation, claiming that the size of its recent losses meant that it could not continue in business. The remaining workers were dismissed. Two weeks later, a new company, called Dynamex Friction, and under the same ownership, took over the business and re-engaged 40 workers. Since the company that had been found to have unfairly dismissed the 86 workers technically no longer existed, their compensation would have to be provided by the government. Speaking in August 2003, the TGWU's former general secretary, Bill Morris, claimed that the company's closure, and its reappearance under a new name, was 'a tactical manoeuvre designed to avoid making the compensation payments to the eighty-six unfairly dismissed workers and to put the financial burden on to the taxpayers of this country'. Despite winning £750,000 in a compensation award, the workers have yet to receive a payment.

environments. Strikes, then, are both social and political phenomena (Batstone, Boraston, and Frenkel, 1978; Hyman 1989). They occur primarily because workers mobilize collectively, in order to resist or influence decisions made by their employers. Thus, their existence constitutes a political challenge to the established order of the organization.

In order to understand why strikes occur, then, attention must be directed at the way in which workers, organized in trade unions, perceive the need to undertake industrial action, and the effectiveness with which they are able to do so (Shorter and Tilly 1974). Broader structural factors clearly exercise an influence on strike levels in as much as they generate grievances or a more general sense of disaffection, but whether or not such discontent produces a strike in a particular organization or workplace depends upon the mobilizing capacity of the workers involved, as well as their willingness and opportunity to take action (Batstone, Boraston, and Frenkel 1978).

Three implications follow from this understanding that strikes are social and political phenomena, whose manifestation is contingent upon the capacity of workers, organized in trade unions, to mobilize and defend their conditions or challenge their employer, albeit within particular contexts. First, it helps to explain variations in strike activity between different organizations and workplaces. For example, between 1993 and 2002 the further education sector in England and Wales was greatly disrupted by industrial action, but the level of strike activity varied considerably between colleges, reflecting the different mobilizing capacities of the union at different sites (Williams 2003).

Second, since strikes reflect the mobilizing capacity of the workers involved, in the context of antagonistic relations that always have the potential to generate conflict, it can be difficult to identify the causes of a particular dispute (Hyman 1989). In Royal Mail, although strikes are generally called in response to particular incidents, such as the suspension of union representatives, for example, their provenance tends to reflect the 'underlying discontent' caused by commercialization pressures and workplace restructuring (Gall 2003c).

Third, the rationale for, and the meaning of, strike action sometimes changes during the course of a dispute. One of the best examples of this was the firefighters' dispute in 2002–03. Although the strikes ostensibly concerned the Fire Brigades Union's (FBU) demand for a full-time annual salary of £30,000, the Labour government, which undermined early efforts to reach a settlement, increasingly saw the dispute as a means of securing far-reaching changes to the organization of the fire service and the nature of its operations. Thus over a period of some months, the basis of the FBU's action changed from a principal concern initially with attaining a hefty pay rise, to a determination to resist major encroachments on firefighters' working conditions and changes to their duties (Seifert and Sibley 2005).

A focus on the capacity of workers to organize themselves collectively in response to problems at work, and engage in some form of industrial action to redress them, is central to the contribution that mobilization theory makes to an understanding of changes in the level of strike activity in Britain. The fall in the level of strike activity does not reflect greater contentment at work, and thus a diminution of industrial conflict; rather, in the absence of trade unions, discontent is expressed in different forms, as exemplified by the sharp rise during the 1990s and 2000s in the number of complaints made by aggrieved employees to employment tribunals, concerning matters such as unfair dismissal and discrimination, for example (see below).

In the largely non-union hotel industry, the unilateral exercise of managerial authority is the source of numerous grievances among employees concerning their perceived unfair treatment, many of which are submitted to tribunals (Head and Lucas 2004). Far from declining, the potential for conflict in employment relations has been increasing. Given evidence that people are willing to act collectively to pursue their interests in society (Kelly 1998), how, then, can the decline in the level of strike activity be explained?

Mobilization theory helps us to understand the social processes that enable, and constrain, the development of collective industrial action. It 'directs our attention to the social relations of the workplace and the processes by which employees perceive and respond to injustice and assert their rights' (Kelly 1998: 51). Mobilization theory holds that it is not enough for workers just to hold a grievance for industrial action to arise. Rather, the workers concerned must hold a collective sense of injustice, recognize that their interests are different from those of their employer (agency), and attribute the source of their grievance to the actions of their employer. Moreover, a mechanism needs to exist, in the form of union activists, that channels the discontent into collective action (see Figure 9.1). Thus mobilization theory seeks to explain the circumstances under which

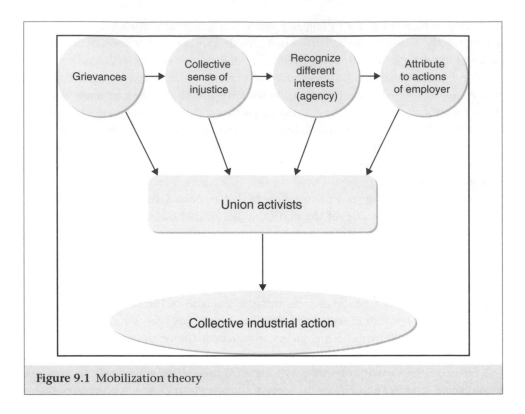

Figure 9.1 Mobilization theory

individual grievances take on a collective dimension, inform the collective organization of workers, and result in collective industrial action (Kelly 1998: 24).

What, then, is the relevance of mobilization theory to understanding the levels of industrial conflict and strike activity in contemporary employment relations? First, it suggests that the absence of strikes does not imply that industrial harmony prevails in British workplaces. Mobilization theory shows that effective collective action by workers is a highly contingent process, something that takes root in particular circumstances, and often in the face of determined employer opposition, even where a demonstrable conflict of interest exists.

Given a supportive political context and legislative framework, employers enjoy plenty of scope to counter-mobilize, and thus impede the capacity of workers to engage in collective action. In the case of Japanese manufacturer 'Nippon CTV', for example, this was done by developing a cooperative relationship with a moderate trade union. Despite the manifest discontent experienced by workers, the company's approach effectively stifled the emergence of any collective action to improve working conditions. Although workers engaged in individual acts of resistance–some refused to wear the company's blue jackets, for example–they rarely took on a collective dimension (Delbridge 1998).

The second contribution of mobilization theory is its emphasis that collective action by workers can take a variety of forms and is thus not just restricted to strikes. In non-union environments, for example, where the organization of strikes faces insuperable difficulties, there is evidence that collective action by workers, such as protests over changes to people's jobs, for example, may impel managers to rethink their proposals, or even back down entirely (see Dundon and Rollinson 2004; Scott 1994). One of the most striking examples of the use by workers of alternative forms of collective industrial action as a means of winning improvements in pay and conditions concerns the Justice for Janitors campaign in the United States (see Chapter 6). Erickson et al. (2002) demonstrate the respective contributions made by street protests, petitions, and the mass picketing of company premises to raising public awareness, and the eventual success of the largely immigrant cleaning workers. See Box 9.3 for a case in Britain.

The third way in which mobilization theory enhances our understanding of industrial conflict is the importance it attaches to leadership: the role activists play in using the existence of grievances to mobilize workers, and to encourage them into taking collective action in opposition to their employer. This is evident from studies of the call-centre sector that highlight the vast range of grievances and simmering discontent characterizing much of its employment relations. In 'Telecorp', for example, some key activists built on workers' concerns over a number of issues, in particular the poor quality of customer service (the centre dealt with calls to the emergency services), to develop union organization (Bain and Taylor 2000). In the face of management opposition, though, activists often find it difficult to sustain the level of mobilization in a way that enables workers to feel confident that unionization is effective (Bain et al. 2004).

By highlighting the potential constraints on collective action in workplaces, as well as pointing to the features that make it possible, mobilization theory makes an important contribution to our understanding of contemporary employment relations and the nature of industrial conflict. It recognizes that the potential for conflict exists in all employment relationships. Yet the extent to which this latent conflict is expressed, and also the means of its expression, is contingent upon the pattern of relationships between workers and their managers in particular workplace settings, albeit within particular contexts. This is a theme that informs our discussion of non-strike manifestations of industrial conflict in the next section.

INSIGHT INTO PRACTICE 9.3

'Living wage' campaigns in London

In Britain, innovative forms of collective action have been pioneered by The East London Communities' Organization (TELCO) in partnership with the Unison trade union. As part of its 'living wage' initiative, TELCO campaigns on behalf of low-paid cleaning and catering staff who are employed by contractors on the premises of major organizations like banks and hospital trusts. Its activity, which has involved demonstrations, picketing, and the mass occupation of a branch of the HSBC bank in one instance, is designed to embarrass organizations, since public attention is drawn to the low pay and poor conditions endured by many of the people who, indirectly, work for them. While such tactics are as yet rare in Britain, the experience of TELCO highlights the potential way in which community-based initiatives can mobilize around employment issues, and inspire collective action among groups of workers whom trade unions find difficult to organize.

Source
Wills (2004a)

SECTION SUMMARY AND FURTHER READING

- Given the inherent potential for conflict that characterizes the employment relationship, it is understandable that strikes, the collective withdrawal by workers of their labour, are a feature of employment relations. They are the most obvious and visible manifestation of industrial conflict. Strikes, whose occurrence generally depends on the existence of union organization, are types of purposive, calculative behaviour in employment relations, designed to pursue a demand, or express a grievance.

- There are a number of ways in which the level of strike activity can be measured, though the accuracy of the data should be treated with caution. Nevertheless, the amount of strike activity in Britain has fallen to very low levels. A number of factors appear to be responsible, including the decline in union bargaining power associated with a more restrictive legal framework. However, the process of economic globalization appears to be intensifying labour unrest in many parts of the world.

- It is important to understand the causes of strikes with reference to the mobilizing capacity of workers and their unions. Mobilization theory can be used to understand the circumstances which generate strikes. Moreover, it also demonstrates that collective action by workers is not just confined to strike action.

The classic introduction to the topic is Hyman's book on *Strikes* (Hyman 1977 and other editions). For strike trends in Britain, see Edwards (1995), Gilbert (1996), and Waddington (2003b). The government publishes an annual survey of the level of strike activity in *Labour Market Trends* (e.g. Hale 2008). See Silver (2003) for the implications of globalization for labour unrest. Kelly (1998) considers the relevance of mobilization theory. For further information about changes in the legal framework see Davies and Freedland (2007: 110–14), Dickens and Hall (2003), and McIlroy (1991, 1999). Seifert and Sibley's (2005) detailed account of the 2002–03 firefighters' strikes is recommended.

 Visit our Online Resource Centre for web links to sites connected to this section. www.oxfordtextbooks.co.uk/williams_adamsmith2e

9.3 Other forms of industrial conflict

While strikes are the most conspicuous form of conflict in employment relations, by no means are they the only one. In this section, then, we broaden our examination of industrial conflict to examine other manifestations of conflict. Following Scott et al.'s (1963) study of the coal mining industry, it is conventional to distinguish between 'organized' and 'unorganized' forms of conflict in the workplace. The latter is distinguished by its spontaneous, individualistic character, and sometimes goes under the label of 'organizational misbehaviour' (Ackroyd and Thompson 1999). Workers respond to the demands of the work environment through some form of resistance, by undertaking actions that allow them to express their frustration, through committing sabotage, for example, or by distancing themselves from the causes of their problems, like going absent, or by quitting their jobs.

Organized forms of conflict, though, are imbued with a more formal, collective, and purposeful character, undertaken in order to challenge and change managerial decisions, not merely to enable workers to cope with them. Such conflict is 'far more likely to form part of a conscious strategy to change the situation which is identified as the source of discontent' (Hyman 1977: 53). Although a strike is the most obvious manifestation of organized conflict, other forms of collective industrial action short of a strike, including overtime bans and work-to-rules, for example, are used by workers collectively, usually in trade unions, to influence organizational decision-making. See Table 9.3 for the main forms of 'organized' and 'unorganized' industrial conflict.

We begin this section by examining forms of organized industrial conflict other than strikes, before moving on to explore the various manifestations, and significance, of unorganized conflict. Our discussion will demonstrate that not only is the conventional distinction between organized and unorganized conflict often rather difficult to make in practice, but also that the term industrial conflict itself needs to be used with a considerable degree of caution.

9.3.1 Forms of organized industrial conflict

Forms of organized industrial conflict other than strikes are often referred to as 'action short of a strike', or as 'cut-price' (Flanders 1975) methods of industrial action. While they are types of behaviour designed to disrupt an employer's ability to produce goods and services, as a strike does, they do not involve a complete withdrawal of labour. These are forms of action in which workers mostly continue to undertake their duties. There are three main types of cut-price industrial action:

- the 'go-slow' occurs in situations where workers carry on performing their jobs, but do so at a much slower pace than normal. In 2003, for example, in a dispute over safety London Underground train drivers threatened to limit their speeds to 25 miles per hour, well under normal;

- the 'work-to-rule' generally involves a refusal by workers to undertake some aspect or aspects of their job in order to disrupt the normal production of goods, or delivery of a service. In 2008, for example, industrial action over pay by staff of the UK's Coastguard Service included a work-to-rule which involved responding only to emergencies; and

- since many organizations rely on their workers undertaking overtime in order to maintain production levels, or to ensure that services are maintained, overtime bans,

Table 9.3 The main forms of 'organized' and 'unorganized' industrial conflict

'Organized' conflict	'Unorganized' conflict
Strikes	Fiddles
Protests, demonstrations, boycotts	Sabotage
'Cut-price' industrial action	Absenteeism
Working-to-rule	Quitting
Go-slows	
Overtime bans	

where workers collectively refuse to take on overtime, can be extremely disruptive to the organization. This was the case in June 2008 when, as part of a pay dispute, Shell tanker drivers instituted an overtime ban in addition to strike action.

Like strikes, these forms of industrial action are designed and undertaken with a purpose, to challenge managerial decisions, for example, or to put pressure on the employer to adjust the terms of the wage-work bargain in a way that benefits the workforce. With the possible exception of a refusal to undertake voluntary overtime, like strike action these types of behaviour almost certainly constitute a breach of workers' employment contracts (Wedderburn 1992).

Nevertheless, they are seen as less risky forms of action than strikes. Moreover, workers do not lose as much in wages as they would if they were to go on strike. Like strikes, though, go-slows, working-to rule, and overtime bans require organization and coordination, generally through the activities of a trade union (Edwards 1995).

While there is some evidence from manufacturing industry of the popularity of overtime bans relative to strike action (Milner 1993), data from successive Workplace Employment Relations Surveys demonstrate that the incidence of organized forms of industrial action short of a strike has substantially declined. For example, in 1980 some 10 per cent of workplaces reported the occurrence of at least one overtime ban in the year preceding the survey. By 1990, this had fallen to 7 per cent of workplaces. Only 2 per cent of workplaces reported the occurrence of a work-to-rule (Millward et al. 1992). By the end of the 1990s, non-strike forms of industrial action were, like strikes, rare indeed, and were reported in only about 1 per cent of workplaces (Cully et al. 1999). The most recent survey, undertaken in 2004, points to a modest resurgence of cut-price action, with its occurrence reported in 5 per cent of workplaces (Kersley et al. 2006).

While its incidence may be rare, cut-price industrial action is nonetheless an effective means by which organized groups of workers can challenge managerial decision-making, express a grievance, or enforce a demand in contemporary employment relations. In 2003, for example, lecturers at London Metropolitan University refused to divulge exam marks to students, or to participate in exam boards, as part of a campaign to improve London weighting allowances. Schoolteachers sometimes enforce effective work-to-rules by refusing to provide cover for absent colleagues, or by refusing to help undertake tests, among other things. While they may be relatively uncommon, not least because managers have taken a more assertive approach to dealing with cut-price industrial action, by deducting wages for 'partial performance', for example, instances like these demonstrate that organized industrial conflict should not be equated simply with strike activity.

9.3.2 Forms of unorganized industrial conflict

Clearly, levels of strike activity and also other forms of organized industrial action are, compared to the past, relatively uncommon in contemporary employment relations. Yet the concept of industrial conflict needs to be broadened, to encompass forms of unorganized conflict and organizational misbehavior which, given the diminution of trade union power in Britain since the 1970s, and the concomitant reduction in significance of organized types of action, may be of more relevance.

We consider fiddling, sabotage, absenteeism, and quitting, four types of employee behaviour that are often held to exemplify unorganized conflict in employment relations in as much as they are spontaneous or unconsidered acts undertaken by individual workers in order to enable them to cope with the frustrations and pressures of the working environment. Before we do this, however, some initial questions arise that will help to inform the reader's understanding of the nature and dimensions of unorganized industrial conflict.

First, to what extent do the types of worker behaviour considered here conflict with managerial objectives? Can they really be interpreted as industrial conflict, along with more purposeful and organized activities such as strikes and overtime bans, for example?

Second, how far are the behaviours associated with so-called unorganized forms of conflict spontaneous, lacking in purpose, and thus distinct from organized activity? Is it wise, therefore, to make a rigid distinction between organized and unorganized forms of conflict?

Third, unorganized types of industrial conflict are often portrayed as alternatives to strikes or other manifestations of organized action (Knowles 1952), the implication being that if conflict in the employment relationship is not expressed by means of, say, a strike, it will simply take another form. Are different manifestations of conflict to be regarded as alternatives? Or do they act in concert, complementing one another?

Fiddles

Fiddling can encompass a wide range of illicit activities ranging from employee theft to actions that alter the terms of the wage-work bargain to the benefit of the workers. Much of the early interest in fiddles focused on the latter. Roy (1952) and Lupton (1963) examined the way in which workers, through the process of 'making-out', collectively manipulated piece-rates, that is the amount they were paid per item of production, by regulating their effort. In as much as it influences the wage-work bargain, in a way that runs counter to the interests of the employer, such activities are unambiguously an expression of conflict at work (Edwards 1992).

The term 'fiddling' is also used to describe more illicit behaviours at work. McIntosh and Broderick (1996) examine the practice of 'totting' among refuse collectors, something that was commonplace before the increased work pressures created by the contracting out of the collection service rendered it more difficult to operate. It involved 'sifting through bags and bins in search of "valuables" or "sellables" which were then either kept or sold—many refuse collectors regularly took part in car boot sales' (cited in Noon and Blyton 2007: 249).

The most well-known account of employee fiddles is contained in Mars's book *Cheats at Work* (Mars 1982). He examines the way in which the characteristics of particular jobs encourage certain types of employee fiddle to emerge. Supermarket workers, for example, being closely supervised and monitored, tend to be opportunistic in their fiddling behaviour, making the most of opportunities, such as the chance to secure a free bar of chocolate, as and when they arise. Other groups of workers, sales staff for instance, tend to have developed well-articulated and sophisticated fiddling techniques, often collectively, for example, the manipulation of expenses claims.

Many fiddles, then, are underpinned by a collective ethos and cannot be seen simply as a spontaneous reaction on the part of an individual worker; they are often informed by collectively generated norms and assumptions that govern the limits of what is acceptable, and what is not. Hence there is a difficulty with seeing fiddles as an unambiguously unorganized form of conflict; many of the most effective workplace fiddles are the product of the collective effort by workers to secure for themselves a more favourable working environment, or to increase the rewards from employment.

To what extent, moreover, can fiddling be conceptualized as a form of industrial conflict? Workers who participate in fiddles are engaged in activities that would appear to run counter to the interests of their employer, but 'making-out' sometimes operates in ways that support managerial objectives (Edwards 1986). Moreover, one of the most prominent features of studies of workplace fiddling is the often high level of managerial toleration of, or indulgence towards, such behaviour.

Why should managers tolerate such activities? For one thing, fiddles help to sustain employee morale in an otherwise mundane working environment, and thus help make the task of supervision less burdensome. In some industries, like hospitality, for example, toleration of fiddles enables managers to keep wages low. They can also be extremely difficult to eradicate. As long as fiddling is kept within what managers consider to be appropriate limits, and does not overly damage the interests of the business, it is often tolerated on the basis that if challenged it would only reappear in another, perhaps more damaging, guise elsewhere (Edwards 1988; R. Wood 1992).

Sabotage

One of the main difficulties presented by employee sabotage is defining what it is. Sabotage at work, which has been the subject of a number of academic studies (e.g. Brown 1977; Taylor and Walton 1971), is often portrayed rather narrowly as involving the deliberate vandalism or breaking of machinery. The term 'often conjures up the image of people engaged in wilful acts of destruction' (Noon and Blyton 2007: 264).

Some writers, however, prefer a broader, more inclusive definition, such that the term 'sabotage' can be used to refer to any type of employee behaviour that does not comply with managerial objectives, such as the fiddles discussed above. By this reckoning, incidents of sabotage cannot just be seen as the product of individual frustration with the pressures of work, but may also, in some circumstances, have a collective dimension, being used by organized groups of workers to alter the terms of the wage-work bargain in their favour (Dubois 1979).

Rather than acting as an alternative to more conventional forms of industrial action, sabotage may complement them. During 1999, for example, incidents of sabotage were a feature of industrial disputes in Spain. They included 'the cutting of electric cables during a rail dispute, engine drivers destroying the safety mechanism in their cabs, and striking shipyard workers immobilizing the bridge giving access to the Bay of Cadiz' (Rigby and Marco Aledo 2001: 291).

Given its association with the breaking and destruction of machinery, sabotage is sometimes thought to be something that is specific to manufacturing industry and thus, given the diminution of manufacturing employment in countries like Britain and the United States, of little importance now. Nevertheless, reports of alleged sabotage still occur. In 2001, for example, the US Federal Bureau of Investigation (FBI) was called in to investigate a suspected incident of sabotage involving damaged wiring at Boeing's

---

◉ INSIGHT INTO PRACTICE 9.4

Employee sabotage in the contemporary service sector

The most extensive analysis of sabotage in the contemporary service sector is Harris and Ogbonna's (2002) study of four firms in the hospitality industry. They use the term 'service sabotage' to refer to behaviours by workers and managers 'that are intentionally designed negatively to affect service', and report that over 85 per cent of the customer service employees they interviewed admitted to having committed 'some form of service sabotage behaviour' in the preceding week (Harris and Ogbonna 2002: 166, 168). One waiter explained how he might deal with a rude customer: 'There are lots of things that you do that no one but you will ever know—smaller portions, dodgy wine, a bad beer—all that and you serve it with a smile! Sweet revenge!' (quoted in Harris and Ogbonna 2002: 169).

The researchers encountered examples of service sabotage behaviour involving hygiene issues: 'ranging from spitting in consumables to adding dirt to food to spoiling guest rooms in a discreet fashion (an unpleasant example including the wiping of a used tissue around the rim of a drinking glass)' (Harris and Ogbonna 2002: 171). While some of these activities were the product of an attempt on the part of the individual worker concerned to deal with the pressures of the working environment, such as the demands of rude customers, for example, others were far from spontaneous affairs, with employees collectively complicit in such behaviours, sometimes with the tacit approval of their managers.

Renton plant in Washington state, which manufactures the 737 series aircraft. Workers at the plant faced an uncertain future since the company had announced its intention to relocate some production and other activities away from the state.

Incidents of sabotage, broadly defined, can be found in many parts of the service sector and, in so far as they cause the quality of service offered to customers to deteriorate, potentially damage the interests of the business (see Box 9.4). In his study of employment relations in McDonald's, Royle (2000) discovered employees engaged in competitions to see which of them could perspire the most over the company's food products. Even the reluctance of customer-facing staff to relate to customers in the approved manner, for example by not smiling when they are supposed to do so (see Fuller and Smith 1991), can be interpreted as a form of sabotage.

Absenteeism

Dealing with absenteeism appears to be a much greater challenge for managers in contemporary employment relations than confronting strikes. In 2007, over 30 million working days in the UK were not worked due to sickness absence. According to one study, over one-third of days not worked because of sickness absence is not due to ill-health at all, amounting to an average of three days off each year for every worker in the country (*The Guardian*, 15 May 2000). The survey of nearly 1,700 organizations found that the main reasons given by employers for increases in absenteeism were 'changes in workforce morale' and 'workloads'. In 2004, annual sickness absence among employees working for Birmingham City Council, for example, amounted to more than 10 days for each worker on average. Some departments were particularly susceptible to absenteeism; in social services the annual rate was in excess of 16 days on average for each worker (*The Guardian*, 18 February 2004).

These data highlight some important features concerning the role of absenteeism in employment relations. It often reflects workers' dissatisfaction with the conditions of their labour, and can thus constitute a form of withdrawal from work (Hill and Trist 1953, cited in Nichols 1997). The frustrations, pressures, and tensions that confront individuals in the working environment are relieved through the taking of an occasional spontaneous 'sickie'. In this way, absenteeism may be viewed as the archetypal form of unorganized industrial conflict.

Yet the observation that absence rates vary, according to sector, organization, and department, suggests that, as a form of industrial conflict, absenteeism cannot be understood purely in individualistic terms. For one thing, studies of absenteeism indicate the presence of absence 'norms', tacitly accepted, perhaps even institutionalized, and collectively held assumptions concerning acceptable levels of attendance. This was traditionally the case in the docks, for example (Turnbull and Sapsford 1992). Moreover, perspectives that treat absenteeism as a means by which individuals withdraw themselves from work generally ignore the powerful influence of structural factors, such as the nature of the work environment, or the incidence of injuries and ill-health at work (Nichols 1997). Where the work process is organized in such a way that workers enjoy little autonomy or control over their labour, or where the pace of work is intense and relentless, such as in some call centres, for example, it can damage people's physical and mental well-being (Taylor et al. 2003).

Absenteeism may be used as a tactic by organized groups of workers to alter the terms of the wage-work bargain or to resist managerial challenges to jobs and working conditions (see Box 9.5). For example, in his study of a plant manufacturing agro-chemicals and dyestuffs, Heyes (1997) demonstrates how the introduction of an annualized hours system undermined the practice of 'knocking'. In one of its manifestations, knocking would involve a worker reporting sick in order to generate lucrative overtime opportunities for a colleague. At a later date, the roles would be reversed and the joint proceeds shared. The end-of-chapter case study demonstrates the significance of mass absenteeism as an effective form of industrial action in British Airways.

INSIGHT INTO PRACTICE 9.5

Worker resistance and industrial conflict in a call centre

The case of 'PhoneCo', a call centre located in Northern Ireland, indicates the degree to which workers are able to collectively resist managerial control, and the endemic state of industrial conflict, even without the presence of a strong trade union. In a highly pressurized and demanding working environment, sales workers cheated the system by engaging in the activity of 'slammin'—that is, pretending to be involved in sales encounters; going absent while actually at work. Workers also challenged managerial control by avoiding work—'scammin'; absenting themselves on smoking breaks, for example, regardless of whether or not they smoked. Efforts by managers to clamp down on unauthorized absence simply exacerbated the shared sense of grievance felt by the workers. Ostensibly unorganized forms of behaviour were in fact underpinned by a strong collective identity which enabled the workforce to challenge managerial control more effectively.

Source
Mulholland (2004)

There are, however, some problems with viewing absenteeism as a manifestation of industrial conflict. For one thing, in the majority of cases, absenteeism is the product of ill-health, and not a reaction to unpleasant working conditions, or part of a protest against management decisions. Moreover, the extent to which absenteeism can be conceptualized as a form of industrial conflict often depends upon the context in which it occurs. For the poorly organized women workers in the clothing factories studied by Edwards and Scullion (1982), for example, absenteeism was an 'escape valve', giving them the opportunity to relieve the tensions associated with an authoritarian working environment and the tedium of their jobs, while posing little challenge to managerial control. Within the engineering factories in the study, though, the well-organized male workforce enjoyed an important degree of collective control over the pace of their work, and thus had less of a need to use absenteeism as a means of escaping their jobs.

Quitting

Perhaps the most unambiguously unorganized and individualistic expression of industrial conflict, and the most explicit manifestation of withdrawal from work, is the practice of leaving, or quitting, one's job as a result of unpleasant working conditions. Thus high levels of labour turnover are often interpreted as evidence of a conflict-ridden working environment.

In one of the call centres studied by Beynon et al. (2002), managers reported that in the preceding three months 300 staff had resigned, suggesting an annual turnover rate of some 130 per cent. The causes were obvious. For one thing, working conditions were exceptionally onerous. 'Managers talked of "burn-out" and frequently expressed scepticism over whether anyone could effectively perform the job for an extended period' (Beynon et al. 2002: 152). Workers also found the unsocial working hours distinctly unappealing. A further factor was the organization's reliance on large numbers of agency-supplied temporary workers, many of whom left because it was unlikely that they would be offered a permanent contract.

For many workers, particularly those based in industries where unions are weak, and thus more organized forms of conflict inappropriate, resigning from one's job is one of the few ways of expressing one's grievances. In the US fast-food industry, for example, young 'workers generally do not see fast-food work as a long-term career, so quitting is a more common response to dissatisfaction with wages, working conditions, or management than is a collective effort to improve the work' (Leidner 2002: 18).

But there are problems in equating quitting with conflict in an over-deterministic way. For one thing, many workers voluntarily resign their jobs not out of dissatisfaction with the conditions of their labour, but because of superior employment opportunities elsewhere (Edwards 1995; Edwards and Scullion 1982). A high turnover rate may operate to the benefit of management since it gives them greater flexibility to adjust staff numbers to meet fluctuations in demand, and thus secure control over costs, particularly in labour-intensive customer service industries, such as hospitality (Adam-Smith, Norris, and Williams 2003).

A study of the hospitality industry demonstrates that turnover levels are contingent upon the characteristics of the workforce. Whereas turnover among the bar workers was very high, as businesses competed to recruit a mainly young, student labour force, it was much lower among hotel housekeeping staff. Workers in these positions were mostly mature women whose employment was structured around childcare responsibilities. They enjoyed fewer opportunities to find alternative jobs, had established relatively stable working arrangements, and were thus less likely to consider quitting, even though the conditions of their jobs were no better, and often somewhat worse, than those of the bar workers (Adam-Smith, Norris, and Williams 2003).

9.3.3 'Unorganized' industrial conflict: an assessment

Having considered the main types of so-called unorganized industrial conflict, what conclusions can we draw about the nature of conflict at work? Five points are particularly worthy of note.

First, in order to understand the significance of conflict in contemporary employment relations we need to look beyond the level of strike activity, and other cut-price forms of industrial action, and consider the implications of fiddles, sabotage, absenteeism, and quitting. The fall in the number of strikes in Britain cannot therefore be equated with a decline in industrial conflict. Moreover, the internet gives workers scope to develop innovative new ways of challenging and contesting managerial decision-making (see Box 9.6).

Second, the analytical distinction between so-called organized and unorganized forms of industrial conflict is rarely so clear-cut in practice (Blyton and Turnbull 2004). Seemingly spontaneous and individualistic behaviour, such as absenteeism, for example, is often underpinned by collectively established norms governing appropriate levels of absence.

Third, the types of behaviour we have considered as examples of unorganized conflict often appear to operate in ways that benefit managers. They may tolerate a certain amount of fiddling, for example, or some relatively minor sabotage, if it helps them to

---

Employment relations reflection 9.6 Virtual industrial conflict

The growth of the internet has enabled workers to engage in new and innovative forms of industrial conflict both individually and collectively. On an individual level, anonymous personal web logs (or 'blogs') can be used by workers to mock, criticize, and challenge aspects of how their organization operates, and are thus to be viewed as an expression of industrial conflict (Richards 2008). One relatively mild example of the genre is the blog maintained by someone working for Pizza Hut: http://pizza-hut-team-member.blogspot.com. Bloggers need to be careful though, else they could end up losing their jobs. In 2005, for example, Joe Gordon, who worked for the bookseller Waterstone's, was sacked after the company claimed his blogging had brought the company into disrepute.

Trade unions have tentatively begun to see the potential of the internet as a tool for challenging employers. In 2007, IBM attracted a considerable amount of negative publicity after members of its Italian workforce organized a 'virtual strike' in the online community Second Life. The protest arose after IBM Italy withdrew a pay benefit worth some $1000 per year. Instead of using conventional industrial action to try and get the decision changed, the Italian union representing the workers opted to disrupt IBM's area on Second Life. Workers from 23 countries joined the action, using their online representations of themselves, or 'avatars' as they are called, to protest and picket against IBM within the firm's own 'virtual world'. While the exact impact of the dispute is hard to judge, soon afterwards the head of IBM Italy left his post, and a new pay agreement was negotiated which restored the workers' pay benefit.

secure control over the workplace. That such activities occur cannot be taken as evidence of conflict since the way in which they function may not hinder, and can even act to support, management objectives. Moreover, in so far as they enable people to cope more easily with the pressures, demands, and frustrations of their jobs, these activities help to reconcile workers with the exploitative nature of the system of wage labour. Thus a 'given form of behaviour can, then, involve aspects of accommodation and adaptation to a system of work relations as well as being in conflict with or a form of resistance against it' (Edwards 1986: 76). Whether or not a particular type of behaviour can be labelled as conflict depends upon the particular context in which it exists, and the meanings which workers and managers attach to it (Edwards and Scullion 1982).

Fourth, what is meant by the concept of industrial conflict? Quitting one's job because the working environment is particularly unpleasant, for example, or behaving towards customers in a way that does not comply with managerial wishes because one is dissatisfied with one's working conditions, both reflect the antagonism that characterizes the employment relationship. But in general these are expressions of frustration; they are not intended to challenge managerial decisions or to influence the terms of the wage-work bargain in the purposeful manner of a strike or an overtime ban. Thus when referring to the term 'industrial conflict' one needs to be careful to ensure that its meaning is clear.

Fifth, it is clear that rather than acting as alternatives, different manifestations of industrial conflict often complement one another (Turnbull and Sapsford 1992). This can be seen in the case of sabotage incidents, for example, which are sometimes used by groups of workers to supplement other forms of industrial action during the course of a dispute.

SECTION SUMMARY AND FURTHER READING

- Strikes are not the only manifestation of collective industrial action by workers. Industrial conflict can take the form of so-called 'cut-price' forms of industrial action, such as overtime bans, for example, or the range of different behaviours that come under the label of 'unorganized' conflict, including fiddling and sabotage, among other things.

- The conventional distinction made between 'organized' and 'unorganized' forms of industrial conflict is hard to uphold in practice. Seemingly spontaneous and individual behaviour, such as sabotage is often underpinned by collective norms and expectations. Moreover, it frequently exists in conjunction with, rather than as a substitute for, more ostensibly collective and organized activities.

- One must be cautious about ascribing the label of 'conflict' to behaviours such as fiddling, sabotage, absenteeism, and quitting. They may operate to the advantage of managers. Whether or not such types of behaviour can be classified as conflict depends upon the context in which they occur, and the meanings which the participants attach to them.

For discussions of industrial conflict, how it can be understood, and the various examples of behaviour that constitute it, see Edwards (1988, 1992). Mars's *Cheats at Work* (Mars 1982) is an engaging analysis of various types of fiddling behaviour. Good overviews of industrial conflict can also be found in Blyton and Turnbull (2004) and Noon and Blyton (2007).

 Visit our Online Resource Centre for web links to sites connected to this section. www.oxfordtextbooks.co.uk/williams_adamsmith2e

9.4 **Resolving disputes in employment relations**

It would be inappropriate to discuss industrial conflict without considering the means by which disputes are resolved in employment relations. It can be helpful to distinguish between individual and collective disputes. The former involves the grievances of individual employees, whereas the latter concerns conflict between trade unions and an employer. However, ostensibly individual disputes often have a collective dimension (Dickens 2000c), since the grievances that cause them may be widely expressed in the workforce as a whole.

In this section, following a discussion of the characteristics and process of negotiating agreements, we examine collective disputes procedures, look at how procedures are used to resolve individual disputes at work, and consider the activities of state bodies in helping to resolve workplace conflict, focusing in particular on the respective roles of the Advisory, Conciliation and Arbitration Service (ACAS) and the system of employment tribunals.

9.4.1 **Negotiating agreements in employment relations**

Attempts to resolve disputes in employment relations generally involve some form of negotiated settlement. Negotiations, then, are an important feature of the collective bargaining process; by enabling disputes to be resolved, they help to ensure that industrial conflict is contained, institutionalized, and thus prevented from causing too much disruption. One should not assume that negotiation is appropriate only in situations where there is a collective dispute, that is, one between an employer and a trade union. The resolution of individual grievances at work is often achieved by means of a negotiated compromise. This demonstrates the relevance of power to the bargaining process. In a non-union environment, without union representation the aggrieved employee enjoys little power to influence the terms of the eventual settlement; where an effective union is present it is more likely that management will be obliged to make concessions.

For present purposes, our analysis of the process of negotiation will focus on its role in resolving collective disputes. Walton and McKersie (1965) distinguish between two broad types of negotiation. Employers and unions sometimes use negotiations in order to address and deal with problems, for example, improvements to the workplace environment. This is known as 'integrative bargaining', akin to a joint problem-solving exercise. 'Distributive bargaining', though, is designed to resolve an outstanding issue, such as a union pay claim, for example, where there is an explicit dispute.

Staying with distributive forms of bargaining, then, what does negotiation actually involve? In essence, it is a means of resolving disputes by concluding a mutually acceptable agreement. It is a social process in which the parties argue with one another, try to convince each other of the merits of their respective cases, come to appreciate the virtues of their opponent's position, and thus draw closer together so that a settlement is made possible (Martin 1992; Torrington 1991). Without compromises, or 'trade-offs', in which a party will offer to back down in one area in return for a perhaps more important concession from their opponent, negotiation will not resolve a dispute. But each side will attempt to wrest more concessions from its opponents than that which it is obliged to concede in return. As well as being a social process, then, the practice of negotiation exemplifies the struggle for power that characterizes relations between employers and unions.

What determines the extent to which an employer or trade union emerges victorious from a negotiation event? Clearly, the expertise and skills of the participants exercise an influence on the outcome of negotiations, particularly their knowledge of relevant issues, how effectively they can process and handle information, and their ability to persuade their opponent of the strengths of their case. Preparation is also important. Not only do effective negotiators rigorously plan the issues on which they are prepared to trade, in exchange for something more worthwhile, and those they are not, but they also consider the likely arguments and negotiating position of their opponents. The negotiating event itself is characterized by the efforts of each party to influence the attitudes of the opposing sides; adjournments are often useful in helping a party to discuss and, if necessary, adjust its position, and can also help to maintain unity among the negotiating team (Walton and McKersie 1965).

Yet the main factor that influences the outcome of negotiation is the prevailing balance of power between the parties. The concept of bargaining power refers to the ability of a party to induce its opponent to make concessions it would otherwise not entertain. Clearly, the skills and expertise of a negotiating team, and the extent to which they are able to control a negotiation event, are important sources of power (Martin 1992). But the nature of the environment also influences negotiation outcomes. For example, if an employer is struggling to increase capacity to meet a rapid influx of orders, other things being equal, it will be less capable of resisting a union pay demand, given the importance of avoiding potentially disruptive industrial action. Thus environmental variables provide employers and unions with latent bargaining power, influencing their capacity to secure negotiation outcomes (see Box 9.7). But the extent to which this latent bargaining power is translated into the ability of a party to wrest concessions from their opponents depends upon how effectively they can use it, in other words their mobilizing capacity (Martin 1992).

Employment relations reflection 9.7 Negotiating power in action

Government intervention in industrial disputes can have a crucial influence on the bargaining power of the parties to a negotiating exercise. In the case of the UK firefighters' dispute 2002–04, over their claim for a £30,000 per annum pay deal, the willingness of the Fire Brigades Union (FBU) to take strike action put the employers' side in a rather weak position. Extensive governmental efforts to defeat the FBU, however, strengthened the employers' bargaining position, prolonging the dispute, and eventually concluded it in a way that satisfied the union's leaders, and could be interpreted as qualified success, but caused a lot of grassroots discontent among the FBU's activists (Seifert and Sibley 2005).

In a study of a dispute over contracts of employment in the further education sector, Williams (2004) demonstrates the way in which environmental change, the removal of colleges from local authority control in particular, weakened the bargaining power of the main trade union relative to that enjoyed by the college employers. But the main cause of the union's difficulties, and a factor prolonging the dispute, was the superior mobilizing capacity of the employers' leaders, the way that they used the characteristics of the more commercial environment in which the colleges operated, to resist union demands. In this case, initial efforts to achieve a negotiated settlement proved fruitless; the parties were too far apart. But what happens when negotiations fail? How are procedures used to resolve disputes between employers and unions?

9.4.2 Collective disputes procedures

Procedures for resolving collective disputes, between unions and employers, are a long-standing feature of employment relations in Britain (see Hyman 1972). The 1970s saw a rise in the incidence of disputes procedures (Kessler 1993), a reflection of the pluralist character of reform in employment relations during that period. There is evidence that formal disputes procedures remain an important feature of employment relations in Britain. In 2004, 43 per cent of all workplaces, and 74 per cent of workplaces with 500 or more employees, operated a procedure for dealing with collective disputes (Kersley et al. 2006).

Such procedures are generally formal arrangements that set out the method for resolving disputes and, as such, 'provide a framework within which workplace industrial relations are conducted' (Brown 1981: 42). Procedures often provide for some sort of third-party intervention in circumstances where a dispute cannot be settled internally, through conciliation, mediation, or arbitration. What, then, is meant by these terms?

With conciliation, the 'aim is to bring the parties to agreement' (J. Wood 1992: 250). The conciliator works to bring the sides closer together, enabling them to bargain more productively, and thus reach their own agreement. Mediation is a relatively rare form of dispute resolution in Britain. It is similar to conciliation, but differs in that the third-party has a more active role, with the scope to make recommendations in particular (J. Wood 1992).

With arbitration, the dispute is submitted to a third party, an individual arbitrator, or sometimes an arbitration board, who, after weighing up the arguments of the two sides, and taking into account any other relevant information, decides the issue. It is often used where negotiation and conciliation have both failed to resolve a dispute, particularly in the area of pay. In general, arbitration awards are not legally binding; like collective agreements in Britain, they are binding in honour only. Disputes procedures that make reference to arbitration will specify whether it can be invoked unilaterally, that is by just of one of the parties, or jointly, that is with the necessary agreement of both.

Governments in the UK have long recognized the advantages to be gained by facilitating machinery for resolving disputes. State intervention in this area, which dates from the late nineteenth century, was predicated on the need to ensure that potentially harmful industrial action could be resolved without it causing the country too much economic disruption (J. Wood 1992). The use of state-supported conciliation and

CONFLICT AND EMPLOYMENT RELATIONS

arbitration facilities for resolving disputes was envisaged as a last resort, to be initiated only with the agreement of both parties once all other methods had been exhausted. The 'emphasis was placed on providing a non-legalistic, flexible system based on voluntarism' (Mumford 1996: 292). (See Box 9.8 for details of how arbitration arrangements are developing in China.)

9.4.3 Resolving individual disputes at work: grievance and disciplinary procedures

On the face of it, grievance and disciplinary procedures ostensibly exist to provide a formal means for resolving individual disputes that have arisen from breaches of organizational rules or acceptable standards of conduct. Disciplinary procedures set out the arrangements for dealing with employees who are suspected of contravening organizational rules in some way, by being persistently late for work, for example. Employees may also have cause to complain about the managerial interpretation of organizational rules, particularly if they feel they have been treated unfairly in some way, by being denied access to promotion opportunities, for example. Therefore, grievance procedures are designed to offer a formal means of resolving a dispute that arises when an individual employee has a complaint regarding their treatment at work.

Before the 1960s few organizations had their own written procedures for dealing with grievances and disciplinary issues (Edwards 2005). Since then, though, there has been a remarkable increase in the growth of formal grievance and disciplinary procedures in the UK. In 2004, 88 per cent of workplaces had a formal procedure for dealing with individual employee grievances, and 91 per cent had one covering discipline (Kersley et al. 2006).

Grievance procedures establish a process which aggrieved employees can use to express their complaint. They usually specify the need for a statement from the individual concerned outlining their grievance, make provision for a hearing at which the employee can discuss their complaint with one or more managerial representatives, and state what happens (e.g. any right to appeal) if the outcome of the hearing does not satisfy the complainant.

 INTERNATIONAL PERSPECTIVE 9.8

The development of labour arbitration in China

As we have already noted above, employment relations in China is marked by extensive and rising levels of industrial conflict as workers combine to challenge the adverse consequences of economic reforms on their jobs and livelihoods. As a result, the Chinese authorities have tried to develop new methods of resolving labour disputes, including arbitration arrangements, in order to keep labour unrest under control. Between 1996 and 2004 there was a more than five-fold increase in the number of labour disputes dealt with by arbitration, from 47,591 to 260,471. Evidently, 'arbitration has become increasingly popular . . . as the preferred mechanism for resolving labour disputes in China' (Shen 2007: 536). The effectiveness of existing arbitration arrangements, however, is limited by their lack of independence from government control, something which reduces their legitimacy as employment relations institutions.

Generally, disciplinary procedures set the appropriate standards of conduct expected from employees and delineate areas of unsatisfactory activity, provide a process that managers should use to investigate allegations of offending behaviour, outline the constitution of any disciplinary hearing, including the right of employees to voice their response to any allegations made against them, and indicate the relevant sanctions to be used in the event of a confirmed breach of discipline. For minor offences, such as a small number of illegitimate absences, the penalty might be a verbal warning by an employee's immediate supervisor. Where the offence is repeated, or in instances of gross misconduct, which can include matters such as sexual harassment, for example, the disciplinary procedure might provide for instant dismissal.

Why have formal grievance and disciplinary procedures become so commonplace in organizations? One key influence has been the need for employers to provide a defence against employment tribunal claims. The introduction of unfair dismissal legislation in the 1970s was a particularly important catalyst for change. The use of an appropriate, formal procedure to discipline, or dismiss, employees, and a formal grievance procedure to enable staff to raise complaints, and have them resolved, enabled employers to defend tribunal claims more effectively.

Second, formal procedures help to define the authority of managers, and thus enhance managerial control. Grievance machinery, for example, enables employee complaints to be dealt with in a seemingly fair and consistent manner. Formal disciplinary procedures have a number of managerial benefits. They allow managers to establish expected standards of performance and conduct among their staff; and demonstrate that the punishment of an employee, by dismissing them, for example, is a fair outcome, the result of following due process, and not an arbitrary decision.

Thus it is important to see grievance and disciplinary procedures less as arrangements for dispute resolution, and more as methods of maintaining managerial control over employment relations in organizations. Grievance procedures, for example, rarely seem to lead to issues being handled in a way that satisfies aggrieved workers (Abbott 2007).

Disciplinary procedures, in particular, are explicitly managerial tools. By giving legitimacy to disciplinary and dismissal decisions, their existence buttresses managerial authority rather than erodes it (Fenley 1986). Disciplinary procedures largely reflect managerial aspirations and, by formalizing the application of workplace discipline, help persuade employees that the rules elaborated within them should be obeyed. In his study of a British-based Japanese television plant, 'Nippon CTV', Delbridge (1998) demonstrates the effectiveness of disciplinary rules in regulating workplace order. During induction, new recruits are instilled with the need to comply with the firm's rules, particularly those concerning absenteeism and punctuality.

It would be wrong to assume that the formalization of disciplinary practice in Britain has provided workers with added protection against arbitrary discipline. Managers frequently fail to follow their own procedures. In their study of how workers experience discipline, Rollinson et al. (1997) encountered among their respondents a strong sense that managers had assumed their guilt even before any disciplinary hearing had commenced, and paid little attention to anything they said in mitigation. In small firms managers may make up their minds to dismiss an employee before any disciplinary hearing takes place (Earnshaw, Marchington, and Goodman 2000); while a study of workplace discipline among nurses identified numerous procedural irregularities, including reports that managers were prepared to lie during disciplinary cases (Cooke 2006).

Moreover, the exercise of discipline continues to be marked by a 'punitive' rather than a 'corrective' ethos. In other words, the emphasis is on getting workers to obey management's rules for fear of the punishment, such as dismissal, that would result from any failure to comply (Fenley 1998), rather than helping them to identify any failings and thus improve their behavior. Studies which consider the experience of workers tend to bear this out. 'For a large proportion of those formally disciplined, the process was not seen as a persuasive one designed to get them to observe rules, but as an event which gave the manager an opportunity to take retribution, or administer a deterrent to limit future transgressions' (Rollinson et al. 1997: 298). Cooke's (2006) study of nursing demonstrates not only that disciplinary action against staff was commonplace, but also that it was undertaken largely for punitive reasons, whatever managers said about the need to improve performance or protect patient care.

9.4.4 The work of ACAS

The establishment of ACAS in 1974 signalled the rise of a more interventionist approach to dispute resolution by the state. ACAS is a tripartite body, independent of government, and is overseen by a council comprising employers, trade unionists, and academic experts. On its formation, ACAS 'was given the general duty of promoting the improvement of industrial relations, and in particular of encouraging the extension of collective bargaining and the development and, where necessary, the reform of collective bargaining machinery' (Kessler 1993: 220). In particular, it was empowered to provide conciliation facilities, to make any necessary arrangements for mediation and arbitration, and to provide advice on effective personnel and employment relations practice.

Perhaps the most impressive achievement of ACAS is the way in which, as a tripartite body, it managed to endure the period of Conservative rule between 1979 and 1997. As we saw in Chapter 3, not only were Conservative governments hostile to tripartism, but they were also keen to encourage the exercise of greater managerial prerogative, to undermine the power of trade unions, and to challenge the significance of collective bargaining. Thus the pluralist ethos, which during the 1960s and 1970s had encouraged greater state involvement in resolving disputes through procedures (Kessler 1993), was supplanted by a more unitary emphasis on the primacy of employer action.

Three factors contributed to the resilience of ACAS, its tripartite character notwithstanding. First, it has effectively demonstrated its independence, from government, employers, and the unions alike (J. Wood 1992). Second, ACAS attracts the continued support of many employers. Third, the main priorities of ACAS have changed in important ways, from an early focus on the improvement of collective employment relations, and a duty to promote collective bargaining, to a greater concern with resolving individual disputes, providing advice about workplace problems, and with working to stop problems from arising in the first place (Dix and Oxenbridge 2004; Hawes 2000). ACAS affirms that its role is to 'help prevent disputes and, when they do occur, to help resolve them' (ACAS 2007: 7).

The organization's duty to promote collective bargaining was revoked in 1992. The extent of its collective conciliation activity, working to resolve collective disputes between an employer and trade union, has declined markedly (Goodman 2000). Nevertheless, in 2006–07 ACAS still received over 900 requests to provide collective conciliation (ACAS 2007). It usually gets closely involved in attempts to resolve high-profile national industrial disputes, such as the one involving the firefighters, their employers, and the government between 2002 and 2004 (Seifert and Sibley 2005). ACAS does not mediate or arbitrate in disputes; rather, it refers disputes for mediation or arbitration where appropriate. ACAS also oversees certain standing arbitration bodies in the public sector, such as in the police service, for example (Corby 2003).

How, then, does collective conciliation work? It is, above all, a voluntary process; ACAS cannot compel the parties to cooperate (Goodman 2000). Once underway, the integrity, and therefore the effectiveness, of conciliation work is predicated upon the impartiality of the conciliator, and the need to secure the trust and confidence of both parties (IRS 2001). ACAS conciliators often become involved in a dispute before the formal reference to conciliation is made. By 'running alongside' the dispute, they are able to understand its dimensions, and thus consider potential aspects of a settlement, more quickly (Dix and Oxenbridge 2004). Most conciliation work progresses in a series of so-called 'side meetings', during which the respective parties discuss, hone, and adjust their positions separately in response to the contributions of the conciliator, before they are subject to further bargaining at the negotiating table (IRS 2001).

Conciliators work with each of the parties in order to help them to strike their own agreement. They do this:

> by acting as an intermediary in the exchange of information and ideas, by keeping the parties communicating, clarifying issues, establishing common ground, identifying barriers to progress, eroding unrealistic expectations, pointing to the costs and disadvantages if the dispute is not settled, developing possible solutions and creating confidence that an acceptable solution will be found. The conciliator has no powers other than those of reason and persuasion. (Goodman 2000: 38)

Employers and unions generally appreciate the way in which ACAS conciliators are able to explain, challenge, and test their negotiating positions and thus open up potential areas of agreement (Dix and Oxenbridge 2004). It should not be assumed, however, that the conciliator makes no contribution to the terms of a deal. In the 2002 local government pay dispute, for example, the principal conciliator produced a number of proposals that ended up forming a major part of the eventual settlement (ACAS 2003).

Stimulated by a considerable increase in statutory individual employment rights (e.g. anti-discrimination laws, minimum wage, etc), much of the work of ACAS now involves disseminating advice and handling disputes between an individual employee and his or her employer (Sisson and Taylor 2006). In particular, it is under a statutory duty to offer conciliation when an employee makes a complaint against his or her employer to an employment tribunal. ACAS intervention operates as an 'effective filter', reducing the number of cases dealt with by tribunals (Dickens et al. 1985).

About 80 per cent of tribunal applications do not reach a hearing, at least a quarter directly because of ACAS involvement. ACAS may resolve a dispute at the conciliation stage by passing on to the complainant an employer's offer of a financial settlement, for example, or by highlighting the potential weaknesses of a case. Among other things, ACAS conciliators discuss the features of the case with the parties, point out how tribunals have dealt with similar cases in the past, and act as an intermediary between the sides in the production of a settlement. Moreover, they 'often try to get the parties to critically examine their own cases; to consider weaknesses as well as strengths' (Dickens 2000c: 76).

As we see below, the growth in the number of tribunal applications has been a source of increasing concern for employers and the government. Since it makes a major contribution to reducing their workload, individual conciliation activity helps to keep the costs of running the system of employment tribunals under control (Hawes 2000). The main criticism of individual conciliation is that, by encouraging the parties to reach their own settlement before a dispute gets as far as a tribunal, or by encouraging people to withdraw their complaint, it militates against effective justice. In other words, there is 'a conflict between the search for compromise, which is at the centre of conciliation, and the pursuit of rights' (Dickens 2000c: 80). Nevertheless, the skill, sensitivity, and competence of ACAS conciliators tend to be highly regarded by others (Latreille, Latreille, and Knight 2007).

During the 2000s, the work of ACAS has come to be increasingly focused not on resolving disputes, but on preventing them from arising in the first place (Dix and Oxenbridge 2000). ACAS is frequently used as a source of employment relations advice. See Box 9.9 for details of the help line service it operates. ACAS also works in an advisory capacity with employers and trade unions on projects designed to improve the quality of employment relations, such as the operation of a joint working party on developing effective bullying and harassment procedures in a health service trust, for example (Dix and Oxenbridge 2004; Purcell 2000).

A growing aspect of ACAS's work involves supporting 'workplace effectiveness', by taking action to demonstrate that 'good' relations between employers and employees can boost business performance, through lower absenteeism, for example. It is also

Employment relations reflection 9.9 The ACAS help-line service

The provision of information and advice about employment matters has become one of ACAS's most important activities. Much of the information is available in publications, many of which can be accessed by going to the ACAS website: http://www.acas.org.uk. However, a growing amount of advice and information is being disseminated through its telephone help-line service. The help line is open to, and used by, both workers and employers. There has been a growing demand for the impartial and confidential information and advice offered by the service. In 2006–07 it received nearly 840,000 calls. Disciplinary and dismissal matters are the topics on which advice and information are most frequently sought— 24 per cent of calls (ACAS 2007). The complex nature of the help-line adviser role has come in for praise. 'The skill of the help-line advisers is key in disentangling the various problems, identifying the key point, providing the relevant information and, where appropriate, pointing them towards other sources of help and advice . . .' (Sisson and Taylor 2006: 29).

concerned to promote the value of its work among small businesses, overcoming the 'hard-to-shift perception that ACAS is all about dispute resolution' (ACAS 2007: 22).

Despite the decline in the level of industrial action in Britain, the inherent potential for conflict in the employment relationship means that the process of dispute resolution, and hence the work of ACAS, remains an important feature of contemporary employment relations. Moreover, its conciliation work in individual disputes, and the advice it provides through its publications and the help line, mean that the demand for the services of ACAS remains high. Importantly, ACAS now places a particular emphasis on the contribution its activities make to improving 'workplace effectiveness', an indication of how far it has moved away from a pluralist approach of promoting collective bargaining, towards a more unitary concern with supporting harmonious employment relations climates.

9.4.5 Resolving individual disputes: the system of employment tribunals

Since the 1960s, employment tribunals, which were called industrial tribunals until 1998, have dealt with individual disputes between an employee and his or her employer, with the number of their jurisdictions having increased markedly over time. Tribunals were originally established to adjudicate disputes over the payment by employers of training levies. In 1965, their scope was extended to cover disputes over redundancy payments. The 1971 introduction of an employee's right not to be unfairly dismissed, though, ensured that the tribunals would secure a long-lasting place in Britain's system of employment relations. The 1968 report of the Donovan Commission had envisaged that a system of labour tribunals, which would adjudicate individual disputes between employees and employers, could provide an 'easily accessible, informal, speedy and inexpensive' means of settling them (Hepple 1992: 92; see also Dickens et al. 1985).

Tribunals, which comprise a legally qualified chair and two lay members, were designed to be free of the perceived encumbrances of conventional legal environments. Applicants are not entitled to legal aid. The 'emphasis on informality and official encouragement to tribunals to eschew legalism is part of the distinguishing of tribunals from the ordinary courts and of promoting simple informal justice' (Dickens et al. 1985: 83).

Reflecting the growth in the scope of employment legislation, over the years tribunals have accumulated an increasing number of jurisdictions: claims relating to sex, race, and disability discrimination; the non-payment of wages; and complaints about the failure of employers to pay the National Minimum Wage. The most common type of complaint, though, still concerns unfair dismissal.

By the late 1990s, there was growing concern on the part of employers and also the government that tribunals were attracting an excessive number of complaints. In 1980 41,000 people made a tribunal claim; by 2000–01 the number had reached 105,000. Although the number of claims subsequently fell for a time, during the mid 2000s the upward trend resumed such that in 2007–08 the number reached a record high of nearly 190,000 claimants. Note that many claims involve more than one jurisdiction (e.g. a claim that involves allegations of unfair dismissal and race discrimination).

Table 9.4 Employment tribunal claims by jurisdiction, selected jurisdictions

Nature of claim	2004/05	2005/06	2006/07	2007/08
Unfair dismissal	39,727	41,832	44,491	40,941
Unauthorized deductions from wages	37,470	32,330	34,857	34,583
Breach of contract	22,788	26,320	27,298	25,054
Sex discrimination	11,726	14,250	28,153	26,907
Working Time Directive	3,223	35,474	21,127	55,712*
Redundancy pay	6,877	7,214	7,692	7,313
Disability discrimination	4,942	4,585	5,533	5,833
Redundancy: failure to inform and consult	3,664	4,056	4,802	4,480
Equal pay	8,229	17,268	44,013	62,706
Race discrimination	3,317	4,103	3,780	4,130
National Minimum Wage	597	440	806	431
Discrimination: religion or belief	307	486	648	709
Discrimination: sexual orientation	349	395	470	582
Discrimination: age	n/a	n/a	972	2,949

* Includes a series of multiple claims from airline pilots.
Source: Tribunals Service (2008)

Table 9.4 shows that the rise in the number of ET claims has been especially marked in the areas of sex discrimination (up from 11,726 claims in 2004–05 to 26,907 in 2007–08) and equal pay (up from 8,229 claims in 2004–05 to 62,706 in 2007–08). The rapid growth in the number of sex discrimination and equal pay claims has largely come about as a result of actions initiated by female staff who work in local government and the health service, who are seeking financial restitution after years of inequality.

Employers often claim that excessive and unwarranted complaints to tribunals impose a heavy burden since, in contesting them, they incur significant costs in terms of the amount of management time needed to prepare a case, and in securing legal representation (Emmott 2001). There is some evidence that tribunals may not sufficiently take into account the circumstances of small firms in particular when adjudicating cases; and that judgements do not reflect their preference for managing staff in flexible and informal ways (Earnshaw, Marchington, and Goodman 2000).

There is also concern that disgruntled employees use the tribunal system to claim unwarranted monetary compensation. Business leaders sometimes claim that the number of tribunal applications reflects a growing 'compensation culture' in Britain in which people are increasingly prone to 'have a punt', and thus secure financial awards to which they are not entitled (EIRO 2001; Shackleton 2002). The intervention of 'no-win, no-fee' lawyers is particularly resented.

Right-wing critics of tribunals, and especially the growth in the number of jurisdictions, contend that the regulatory burden they impose on businesses damages economic competitiveness. It is claimed that the 'tribunal system has grown piecemeal to a size where it now imposes significant costs on the economy as a whole—in terms of uncertainty, tension and stress at work, erosion of trust, addition to business costs and, most importantly, discouragement of job creation' (Shackleton 2002: 113).

Governments have tried to reduce the number of complaints to employment tribunals by giving ACAS greater scope to resolve disputes before they reach tribunal, for example. The Conservatives introduced a system of pre-hearing reviews in the 1980s, arrangements designed to filter out weak cases before they reach the tribunal proper. Labour has tightened the pre-hearing review process in a number of ways, with the aim of reducing the alleged burden on the tribunal system by disposing of weaker, supposedly 'misconceived' claims, before the hearing (Colling 2004; Pollert 2007).

Labour has also sought to put more of an onus on discontented employees to use their employer's internal grievance machinery before making a complaint to a tribunal. In the early 2000s it enacted the so-called 'three-step' approach. This obliged an employee to (1) put their grievance to the employer in writing, (2) stipulated that the employer should hold a formal grievance hearing, and (3) provided for the employee to have the right to appeal against the outcome of the grievance hearing. A similar model disciplinary procedure was the minimum to be applied when an employer wanted to dismiss an employee. However, the 'three-step' approach led to grievance procedures becoming overloaded (DTI 2007); and following complaints from employers it was shelved.

From 2009 onwards tribunals have the power to reduce by up to 25 per cent the compensation for successful claimants who are judged to have acted 'unreasonably' in relation to the relevant ACAS code of practice. Yet the main problem with encouraging the internal resolution of complaints is not that it puts too much of a burden on employers' grievance procedures, but that it potentially restricts employees' access to justice, by giving managers too much control over the resolution of legitimate employment disputes (Colling 2004).

One of the most prominent charges levelled at the tribunal system is that it is characterized by an excessive amount of legalism, that the tribunals have departed from their original purpose of resolving disputes in a speedy, relatively informal, and non-expensive manner without the formalism of courts of law, the legal arguments that dominate them, and the participation of lawyers. Yet legalism can be interpreted in a positive way in as much as it captures the importance tribunals attach to legal standards, rules, and consistency in their decisions (Macmillan 1999). Perhaps, then, some degree of legalism is inevitable (Dickens et al. 1985), and even desirable. It is somewhat ironic that complaints about excessive legalism in tribunals come from employers since they are more likely to have legal representation than complainants (Dickens et al. 1985; Hayward et al. 2004).

The notion that the rise in the number of tribunal cases reflects the emergence of a 'compensation culture' in which large numbers of employees are willing to 'take a punt' in pursuit of financial gain at the expense of virtuous and over-burdened employers is superficially attractive, but far from the truth, and conceals a more complex set of contributory factors. One, no doubt, is the increasing number of jurisdictions for which tribunals enjoy responsibility (Pollert 2007). But the growth in the number of tribunal claims also reflects rising levels of discontent at work, and that employees have more grievances (Kelly 1998). Only a small fraction of the grievances that could potentially result in a claim to a tribunal actually do so; of those that do, less than a quarter get to a hearing—most are settled or withdrawn beforehand. According to the TUC's Brendan Barber:

> I am fed up listening to employers griping about a so-called compensation culture. Tribunal claims do not arise because sacked workers are 'having a punt'. Only around 30,000 claims a year go to a full tribunal hearing. Meanwhile, as many as three-quarters of a million times a year employers get away with actions that could land them in a tribunal. That is the real scandal. (quoted in EIRO 2001)

Linked to this, the rise in the number of applications to tribunals also reflects the growth in the number of people employed in those parts of the private services sector, where the management of employment relations is often conducted in a harsh and arbitrary manner by small employers, and unions are weak, thus generatating more claims (Dickens 2000c). The presence of trade unions is associated with lower rates of complaints to tribunals (Kersley et al. 2006); unions are often able to resolve grievances collectively within the workplace, rendering applications to tribunals unnecessary (Knight and Latreille 2000).

The decline in the level of unionization, then, and the increasing proportion of employment in sectors of the economy where unions are weak have been partly responsible for the upsurge in the number of tribunal claims (Hawes 2000). Even right-wing critics of the tribunal system concede that the rise in the number of applications to tribunals partly reflects the decline in unionization (Shackleton 2002: 45).

We should be wary of exaggerated claims from employers about the alleged burden of the employment tribunal system. Rather than complain about the time and energy that has to be expended in defending a claim, employers might be better off ensuring that their staff have as few grounds as possible for complaint in the first place, by taking a less punitive approach to discipline, for example, or by handling equality and diversity issues more effectively. They might also consider strengthening employee representation arrangements, for example by recognizing a trade union, allowing grievances to be resolved internally more readily.

Barely more than one in five applicants ever gets as far as a tribunal hearing; the rest either withdraw their claims, or reach a settlement with the employer as a result of ACAS intervention, or have them discontinued prior to the hearing, because of the perceived weakness of their claim. For the 12–13 per cent of all claimants who actually win their case at a tribunal, restitution is often limited. Even when complainants win their case for unfair dismissal, the tribunals' power to order their re-employment is rarely used; financial compensation is the most common form of restitution.

Contrary to the impression one might have gained from accounts of isolated, but high-profile, sex discrimination cases, which have resulted in professional women receiving large financial settlements, most awards are relatively modest. In 2006–07 three-fifths (59 per cent) of all compensation awards for successful claims involving

Employment relations reflection 9.10   The obstacles to effective workplace justice

In 2008 the TUC's (Trades Union Congress) Commission on Vulnerable Employment reported its findings. It found that some two million people in the UK work in low-paid, insecure, and 'vulnerable' employment, often migrant workers in industries such as cleaning, catering, and social care. Many vulnerable workers are unaware of their employment rights and, given the low level of trade union membership among such workers, generally have little access to sources of advice. Vulnerable workers may be reluctant to institute tribunal claims against employers because of the consequences. According to an employment rights adviser: 'They are stopped by the fear that even though they might have the strongest case in the world, once the next employer who they go to finds out they took the previous employer to the tribunal, the chances of getting a job go out of the window' (TUC 2008: 132).

The Commission also discovered that many vulnerable workers face difficulties obtaining their rightful compensation even after winning a tribunal case because of the employer's refusal to pay. In England and Wales, a tribunal award can only be enforced by obtaining a County Court or High Court judgment, a complex and expensive procedure. Citizens' Advice Bureaux report dealing with between 650 and 700 cases of non-payment each year. The Commission called for more effective enforcement arrangements, including giving tribunals the power to enforce their own awards (TUC 2008).

unfair dismissal were for less than £5,000; half of all awards for successful claims involving sex discrimination come to less than £6,700. Moreover, the unwillingness of some employers to pay compensation awards appears to be a growing problem (see Box 9.10).

Studies demonstrate that many workers face substantial obstacles to bringing tribunal claims, let alone winning them, even when they have legitimate cause for dispute. In her study of non-union workers, Pollert (2005) found that people with employment problems generally did nothing about them. Either they had little awareness of their employment rights, or the prospect of the financial costs involved in bringing the claim acted as a deterrent. The legal aid system in England and Wales does not cover employment tribunals; without union support, or the help of under-funded and over-stretched law centres and Citizens' Advice Bureaux, claimants have to bear their own costs.

The main problem with the tribunal system is not that it places a costly burden on hard-pressed and blameless employers, but rather its failure to deliver effective industrial justice to the thousands of employees who have legitimate grievances each year, but who rarely gain adequate redress (Colling 2004; Pollert 2005). The Labour government's efforts to reduce the number of claims to employment tribunals, and thus weaken employees' access to justice, reflects a neo-liberal belief that economic competitiveness is best achieved by diluting employment regulation (Pollert 2007). However, there are growing calls for more effective enforcement of individual employment rights; moving away from an approach where the onus is on the aggrieved individual to make a complaint, towards a system marked by greater proactive enforcement by state agencies (TUC 2008).

SECTION SUMMARY AND FURTHER READING

- Attempts to resolve disputes in employment relations generally involve some kind of negotiated settlement. The nature of any settlement is strongly influenced by the extent of the respective parties' bargaining power. The characteristics of the environment give the parties a degree of latent power, but the outcome of negotiations is largely determined by how effectively they mobilize to make use of it.

- Employers commonly use procedures for resolving collective disputes with trade unions, and, in the form of grievance and disciplinary arrangements, for handling individual problems and complaints at work. Grievance and disciplinary procedures are used to maintain managerial control, rather than as impartial methods of resolving legitimate disputes and problems.

- There is a long history of state support for third-party dispute resolution machinery in Britain, in order to ensure that potentially damaging disputes can be settled without causing too much disruption. ACAS provides collective conciliation, and arranges access to mediation and arbitration arrangements in disputes between employers and trade unions. It also offers individual conciliation before complaints by individual employees progress to an employment tribunal hearing. The work of ACAS is increasingly concerned with preventing disputes from arising, in addition to helping to resolve them when they do occur.

- Employment tribunals were conceived as relatively quick, informal, inexpensive, and accessible forums for delivering industrial justice in respect of disputes between an individual employee and his or her employer. The number of jurisdictions has expanded markedly. The government is concerned with reducing the number of complaints that reach tribunals. Business complaints that the tribunal system imposes an excessive burden on employers are misplaced. Rather, the main weakness is its failure to provide justly aggrieved employees with adequate redress.

For perspectives on negotiations and the skills needed for effective negotiation, see Torrington (1991). The historical evolution of third-party arrangements for dispute resolution is covered by Hawes (2000), and J. Wood (1992). The best overview of workplace discipline is Edwards (2005). ACAS annual reports (e.g. ACAS 2007) describe its activities in detail. See Sisson and Taylor (2006) and Towers and Brown (2000) for the work of ACAS. The most extensive study of the employment tribunal system is Dickens et al. (1985). Recent issues and developments can be gleaned from Colling (2004) and Pollert (2005).

 Visit our Online Resource Centre for web links to sites connected to this section. www.oxfordtextbooks.co.uk/williams_adamsmith2e

Conclusion

Industrial conflict is a major feature of contemporary employment relations. Since the employment relationship is characterized by a 'basic antagonism' between the employer and the employee there is always the potential for conflict to arise (Edwards 1986). The fall in the level of strike activity cannot be equated with a decline in the level of industrial conflict. The low amount of strikes in contemporary employment relations is the product of a number of factors: restrictive government legislation; industrial change, and lower levels of employment in 'strike-prone' industries; a more assertive and interventionist manage-rialism; and the declining level of unionization. Some of these developments, industrial change, for example, are an international phenomenon; others, like the restrictive legislative framework, are peculiar to Britain. Thus the declining level of strike activity has not come about because the potential for conflict has diminished in importance, but rather it is the expression of a number of political, economic, and industrial developments.

From a global perspective, strikes remain a central feature of contemporary employment relations. Strike activity has not vanished. Instead, it has been subject to a process of relocation so that it is increasingly evident in emerging economies, such as China. Moreover, there is evidence that economic globalization is a major source of labour unrest around the world. Therefore, the need to understand strikes, how they occur, and how they are resolved, remains of pressing importance in contemporary employment relations. Mobilization theory is an important tool for identifying the factors that contribute to, and also those that constrain, strikes. It also contends that industrial conflict should not be equated with strikes. Other forms of collective labour protest, such as petitions and demonstrations, for example, are perhaps more effective ways of redressing grievances for workers in sectors where there is little tradition of robust trade unionism. Moreover, industrial conflict expresses itself in a range of different forms, including so-called 'unorganized' behaviours, such as sabotage and quitting, for example.

The significance of conflict in employment relations can be gauged from the large number of employee grievances, very few of which ever become the subject of a formal complaint to an employment tribunal. Given the potential for the employment relationship to generate disputes, knowledge of how arrangements to resolve them operate is of central importance to understanding contemporary employment relations. Although employers complain about the supposed burden of the employment tribunal system, by keeping the potentially damaging consequences of industrial conflict in check, tribunals, and other methods for resolving disputes, contribute to the maintenance of order and stability in employment relations. While the potential for conflict is an inherent feature of the employment relationship, the process of negotiation, and the interventions of third parties, limits its capacity for disruption (Hyman 1975).

Assignment and discussion questions

1 Discuss the view that: 'the decline in strike activity means that conflict between employers and workers is not an important feature of contemporary employment relations'.

2 Why has the incidence of strike activity in Britain fallen since the 1970s?

3 How does mobilization theory explain why strikes occur?

4 Is it sensible to distinguish between 'organized' and 'unorganized' forms of industrial conflict? Why?

5 Should it be compulsory for all disputes to be referred to arbitration, thus making strikes unnecessary? Give reasons for your view.

6 Why has the number of claims to employment tribunals risen? What are the main strengths and weaknesses of the system of employment tribunals?

 Visit our Online Resource Centre for web links to sites connected to this section.
www.oxfordtextbooks.co.uk/williams_adamsmith2e

Take your learning further: online resource centre

Visit the Online Resource Centre that accompanies this book to enrich your understanding of Chapter 9: Conflict and employment relations. Explore web links, test yourself using an interactive flashcard glossary, and keep up to date with the latest developments in the area.

 http://www.oxfordtextbooks.co.uk/orc/williams_adamsmith2e.

Chapter case study

A British Airways case

Faced with increasing competition on its long-haul flights, by companies such as Virgin Atlantic, and on its domestic and European routes, by EasyJet and Ryanair, over the last decade British Airways (BA) has sought ways of reducing its costs. With employment accounting for about 30 per cent of operating costs, reductions here offered the company a means to increase its profitability. Proposed changes to workers' terms and conditions of employment led to a number of disputes over this period. One famous case in 1997 involved cabin crew staff. The company planned to make changes that would substantially reduce their earnings, and, in response, one of the unions representing employees called them out on strike. On the first day, only 330 workers went on strike. However, over 1,000 telephoned in sick, with a further 1,000 reporting sick during the next two days. The dispute was settled several weeks later, and it was estimated that it had cost the company £124 million in lost revenue.

Following the 11 September attacks in 2001, and with the downturn in the global economy leading to a reduced demand for flights, the company instigated a programme of change that would eventually lead to the loss of 13,000 jobs. In order to meet its need to improve the deployment of staff as a consequence of reduced staffing levels, in 2003 the company linked its annual 3 per cent pay offer to its 2,500 check-in staff to new 'signing-in' procedures, a system used by some 20,000 other BA workers.

Check-in staff are the first contact passengers have with the airline, and are often the ones who bear the brunt of any customer dissatisfaction, for example over flight delays. Their basic rate of pay was £14,000 per annum, and the company estimated that average earnings, including shift payments, were around £19,000. Staff record their shift arrival and departure by signing a paper attendance sheet. A majority of the staff are women, and a substantial number work part-time, most with families. In order to meet domestic commitments, by custom and practice, there is some degree of 'self-rostering', whereby staff swap shift times with colleagues and thus are able to balance home and work commitments. The company claims that the system is abused, with staff leaving early, and colleagues forging their signatures. However, BA was unable to confirm that any staff had been disciplined for the offence.

The company proposed to replace the paper-based system with an electronic swipe card. Negotiations with the unions over the proposal and pay offer broke down and the company unilaterally imposed the new system. On 18 July 2003, around 250 check-in staff spontaneously, and to the surprise of the union, and without its backing, stopped work. Further walk-outs occurred the following day, stranding 80,000 passengers, and requiring the cancellation of over 400 flights in total.

British Airways stated that the new system, common throughout industry, was an attempt to simplify the procedure, and would help in the deployment of staff. However, employees claimed that it was being introduced as a precursor to annualized hours, and pointed out that if no changes to staffing arrangements are planned, then they could see no reason for implementing the system in the first place. An annualized hours system would allow the company to send staff home at quieter times, and require longer working when the airline is busier. Rather than allow staff to balance work and home, the new system would place total discretion over working hours with management, and possibly lead to further redundancies. Unions representing the workers believed the company should have clarified what it intended to use the new system for, should not have imposed it, and should have consulted more with staff and unions. They also point to the reduction in staffing levels through the redundancy programme, which they believed had left BA without sufficient staff to run the airline, and had lowered morale. Employees' fears may be well-founded since the company supplying the system claims that it can increase workforce flexibility, individualize rosters to suit operational requirements, and reduce overtime payments.

1. Was the 'swipe card' issue the cause of the dispute or the trigger for underlying conflict to become overt?

2. Would you have advised BA to do anything differently?

PART 4

Conclusion

10 Employment relations: regulating,
    experiencing,and contesting the employment
    relationship   371

Employment relations: regulating, experiencing, and contesting the employment relationship

The principal aim of this book has been to demonstrate the significance of employment relations in contemporary societies, particularly Britain. In Chapter 1 we examined the nature of employment relations as a field of study, with specific reference to understanding the characteristics of the employment relationship, in particular the way in which it should be conceptualized as a wage-work, or effort, bargain. This captures the struggle over the terms and conditions of employment that characterizes relations between employers and workers. Consequently, employment relations cannot simply be understood as the study of how jobs are regulated, since such an approach does not adequately capture the dynamic nature of the employment relationship.

This book is informed by a view that the subject matter of employment relations must comprise not only how workers experience their employment relationship, but also how they contest and challenge its terms. The purpose of this short, concluding chapter is to draw together some of the main themes of the book to establish the contemporary relevance of employment relations based on the premise that, as a field of study, it is concerned with ways in which the employment relationship is regulated, experienced, and contested. We also take the opportunity to consider the future prospects for employment relations.

Regulating the employment relationship

In an important sense, employment relations concerns the means by which the employment relationship is regulated. It is about understanding how the rules that govern employment relationships originate. To a large extent, then, employment relations is the study of job regulation (Flanders 1975). In the past, this approach was characterized by an understandable emphasis on the institutions of job regulation (Clegg 1979): the activities of employers, employers' associations, and trade unions; the structure and operation of collective bargaining machinery and consultation arrangements; all within a largely voluntarist public policy framework.

To a very large extent, the study of employment relations used to be devoted to the joint regulation of the employment relationship, by collective bargaining between employers and employers' associations, and trade unions. One of the most prominent trends since the 1980s has been the diminution of joint regulation in Britain as union membership and collective bargaining coverage have both declined. But employment relationships still have to be regulated somehow. Here, drawing on the material presented in earlier chapters, we consider three main developments.

First, as already noted, the decline of joint regulation has been an important feature of employment relations in Britain. In Chapter 7, we considered the contraction of collective bargaining coverage as a means of determining pay, especially in the private sector. This is associated with declining levels of unionization (see Chapter 6), the falling incidence of union recognition during the 1980s and early 1990s (see Chapter 5), the changing composition of industry, such that employment growth has been concentrated in sectors where joint regulation is relatively scarce, and a hostile public policy climate.

Nevertheless, one should not underplay the contemporary significance of collective bargaining as a means of regulating the employment relationship. The introduction of a statutory procedure (see Chapter 5) has stimulated a modest increase in union recognition agreements, notwithstanding the opposition of many employers, though the proportion of workplaces with union recognition has continued to fall. In Chapter 7, we observed that a number of major private sector employers, such as Tesco and Barclays Bank, for example, have revised their relations with trade unions as partnership agreements, although generally these weaken union organization in practice. Collective bargaining is an important means of determining pay and conditions in the public sector, even more so if the operation of pay review bodies is considered as a form of 'arm's length' bargaining (Burchill 2000; Winchester and Bach 1995).

Second, there has been a pronounced increase in the extent to which managements attempt to regulate employment relationships unilaterally. This is evident in the area of pay determination, for example. In Chapter 7, we noted that greater managerial attempts to exercise control over pay is a prominent feature of contemporary employment relations. Managers have taken advantage of a public policy climate unsympathetic to strong trade unionism and collective bargaining (see Chapter 3) to challenge the influence of the unions, and sometimes exclude them from their workplaces entirely (see Chapter 5). Yet for the most part joint regulation has not been superseded by a more individualized approach to managing employment relations. While collective regulation may have diminished in importance, standardized terms and conditions of employment predominate (Charlwood 2007).

We have been careful to assert that managements have *attempted* to regulate the employment relationship unilaterally. Yet the nature of the employment relationship as a wage-work bargain implies that their efforts are invariably influenced by the need to respond to their employees' interests, or to secure their consent and cooperation. Custom and practice expectations remain an important feature of employment relations. In Chapter 9, for example, we observed that managers may be willing to tolerate a certain amount of fiddling activity, or even sabotage, as long as it does not exceed tacitly understood boundaries.

The exercise of managerial prerogative, then, is always an aspiration and, given that the employment relationship *is* a relationship in which managers must, to some degree, gain workers' cooperation, can never be fully realized in practice. Nevertheless, there is some evidence, in the area of workplace discipline, for example, that managers are more able to manipulate custom and practice understandings to suit their interests better (Edwards 2000).

The third main development concerns the increasing degree of statutory regulation of the employment relationship in contemporary employment relations. This is not just the product of national-level legislation, like the National Minimum Wage (see Chapter 7) and the statutory union recognition procedure (see Chapter 5). European Union (EU) legislation increasingly affects employment relations in Britain, especially since the Labour government signed up to the EU's 'Social Chapter' in 1997 (see Chapter 3). The EU's 'social dimension' has, among other things, generated legislation regulating equality at work (see Chapter 4), information and consultation arrangements for employees (see Chapter 6), and working time (see Chapter 7). As we saw in Chapter 2, there are even calls for more rigorous regulation of labour standards on an international basis in order to ameliorate some of the exploitative effects of economic globalization on workers in developing countries.

While the growth in the level of state intervention has been a long-term trend (see Chapter 3), the increase since the 1980s in the quantity of legal regulation has had a marked effect on employment relations in contemporary Britain. The work of the trade unions is increasingly concerned with campaigning for better legal rights for workers, with ensuring that existing statutory protections are upheld, and with using them as a base from which to bargain improvements. In Chapter 4, for example, we examined the way in which some unions have used equal pay legislation to bargain for increases in women's pay (Colling and Dickens 1998).

There are three important features of this growth in the quantity of legal regulation that needs to be drawn out. First, in some respects, legislation that ostensibly favours the interests of workers and trade unions is enacted to benefit capital in the long term. In Chapter 3, we saw that the EU's 'social dimension' has been progressed largely as a means of giving the process of market integration, and thus enhanced economic competitiveness, greater legitimacy.

Nevertheless, it is important to recognize that pressure for legal enactment also comes from workers, trade unions, and other campaigning groups to which policy-makers are obliged to respond. This was the case with the establishment of the National Minimum Wage in Britain, for example (see Chapter 7). It is therefore unwarranted to treat interventions by the state, and by supranational bodies like the EU, as automatically benefiting the business interest, since policy-makers must accommodate the interests of labour as well as secure the conditions under which capitalism can thrive (Edwards 1986).

The second point concerns complaints from employers that greater legal regulation in employment relations is inimical to business competitiveness; but these do not have much credibility. For one thing, greater regulation can enhance competitiveness by encouraging innovation. Robust regulation of working time, for example, by reducing employers' reliance on overtime, could encourage them to make more effective use of people's normal working hours. Moreover, a significant part of the legal regulation of employment relations in Britain is concerned with undermining the power of the trade unions. In Chapter 9, for example, we highlighted the restrictive legislation governing strikes and industrial action.

Third, although the law supposedly protects working people to a greater degree, arrangements for enforcing people's legal rights at work are weak. Workers are obliged to exercise their statutory employment rights mainly by making a complaint to an employment tribunal. Yet as we have seen on a number of occasions, the system of employment tribunals is an ineffective means of providing aggrieved workers with effective justice. See Chapter 4 for the ineffectiveness of tribunals as a means of challenging discriminatory treatment. Workers may be unaware of their legal rights, or be unwilling to enforce them, for fear that they will be victimized by their employer. Current arrangements of enforcing individual employment law depend too much on the preparedness of the worker concerned to exercise his or her rights, with all the risks that entails.

Nevertheless, as we have already observed unions can use legislation as the basis for more robust joint regulation of the employment relationship. The effectiveness of the statutory union recognition procedure, for example (see Chapter 5), depends more on the extent to which unions can use it as a basis for expanding their organizational capacities than its own intrinsic merits. As we saw in Chapter 4, a union presence tends to enhance the scope and effectiveness of so-called family-friendly policies (Hyman and Summers 2004). Thus the outcomes of greater legal regulation in employment relations are contingent, varying according to the organizational context.

While there has been a considerable increase in the quantity of legal regulation, its overall significance for employment relations should not be overstated. Labour governments have implemented EU directives in a 'minimalist' way, so that they impose as few constraints on business as possible. This is consistent with the neo-liberal assumptions that characterize Labour's policy framework, in particular the importance of deregulated labour markets as a source of economic competitiveness in a more integrated global environment (Favretto 2003). The extent to which the financial crisis of the late 2000s, and the economic recession it spawned, marks the end of neo-liberalism as the predominant economic perspective, and the emergence of a new consensus about the desirability of greater regulation, remains to be seen.

Experiencing the employment relationship

One of the main features of this book has been a concern with examining workers' experiences in contemporary employment relations. The employment relationship is not just something that is regulated, but is also experienced by workers. Moreover, their experiences influence regulation. For example, increasing pay inequality during the 1980s and 1990s, and growing concerns about the effects of low pay on workers in Britain, stimulated campaigning for the National Minimum Wage. In Chapter 4, we demonstrated that the government has tentatively improved the statutory provisions relating to family-friendly working arrangements, partly because of increasing concern that workers were experiencing difficulties combining paid employment with family responsibilities.

We have examined the experience of workers in contemporary employment relations in a number of chapters. In Chapter 2, for example, we considered the working arrangements of self-employed freelance workers. Claims that such groups of workers benefit from greater freedom, autonomy, and control over their work, relative to employees, are rather exaggerated. We also demonstrated the poor working conditions that are often experienced by homeworkers and migrant labourers in Britain. In Chapter 4, we drew on the experiences of workers to show the limited effectiveness of equal opportunities and work–life balance policies in practice. The section on ostensibly 'unorganized' forms of industrial conflict in Chapter 9 was also informed by accounts of workers' experiences.

But our principal assessment of workers' experiences in contemporary employment relations came in Chapter 8. We demonstrated that their interests often differ markedly from those of their employers. Genuine employee involvement and participation tends to be rather limited in practice; workers have few opportunities to influence workplace or organizational decision-making. Job insecurity is an outcome of the way in which the neo-liberal character of contemporary capitalism, and ever-increasing competitive pressures, render workers more disposable. A further outcome is work intensification, something that has also been accentuated by technological developments.

One of the main contributions of this book, then, has been to offer a perspective on contemporary employment relations that differs from conventional human resource management (HRM) texts. These rarely, if at all, consider the experiences of workers and, as a result, often present a rather anodyne and insufficiently complex understanding of what happens in the workplace. But it is important to recognize that employers are not driven solely by a concern with intensifying labour, upholding control, and making workers more easily disposable. The employment relationship is, as we observed in the introductory chapter, inherently exploitative, but it is also characterized by a degree of cooperation. In Chapter 5, we noted that the management of employment relations in market economies is marked by contradiction (Hyman 1987). On the one hand, managers seek to control workers, ensure they comply with instructions, and, should competitive pressures harden, dispose of them if necessary. On the other hand, managers must acquire the consent of the workforce, and accommodate pressures from workers, individually and collectively, if goods are to be produced, or services delivered, efficiently.

Contesting the employment relationship

It is impossible to consider employment relations properly without an adequate assessment of how workers contest the employment relationship. As we have seen, the employment relationship, as a wage-work bargain, is imbued by a struggle over its terms and conditions. Our focus on the experiences of workers demonstrates that, whatever its other characteristics, the employment relationship is marked by a basic antagonism between a relatively powerful employer and a largely powerless employee. Moreover, both individually and, more importantly, collectively, workers have the capacity to challenge and contest the terms of their employment. Thus there is always the potential for conflict in employment relations (Edwards 1986).

This is evident at a number of points in this book. In Chapter 2, for example, we point to a major flaw in the argument that economic globalization, and the activities of multinational companies and their suppliers, invariably give rise to a 'race to the bottom' in terms of labour standards, as workers in developing countries see the conditions of their labour eroded. This is not because multinational investment generates greater prosperity, and thus improves living standards, though this is a popular proposition, especially among advocates of free markets (Bhagwati 2004; Wolf 2004). Rather, globalization, and its implications for poorer countries, may stimulate demand among workers for effective union representation and lay the foundation for a more vigorous labour internationalism (Silver 2003).

Our discussion of organizing unionism in Chapter 6 demonstrates the potential for unionization among groups of workers, who often have considerable and well-justified grievances about the way in which they are treated at work, but yet have traditionally not been attracted to trade unions. As we saw in Chapter 5, even in small, non-union firms, where one might expect managerial authority to be absolute, managers must accommodate the demands of workers. They are obliged to negotiate informally with workers over such matters as the organization and pace of work (Dundon and Rollinson 2004; Ram 1994). Workers, then, are never entirely passive actors; they always enjoy some, however limited, capacity to challenge and contest the terms of their employment relationships.

We dealt with the nature of industrial conflict in contemporary employment relations more substantially in Chapter 9. Clearly, the strike is the most visible manifestation of industrial conflict (Hyman 1975). Among the reasons for the decline of strike activity in Britain since the 1970s are: the diminishing proportion of employment in 'strike-prone' industries; the contraction of trade union organization; the articulation of a more assertive management style that aims to make strikes superfluous; and, in particular, the enactment of a whole raft of restrictive legislation. The legal framework places numerous obstacles in the way of trade unions hoping to undertake industrial action, including opportunities for employers to apply to the courts for injunctions that prevent it (Ewing and Hendy 2002).

In Chapter 9 we argued that just because there has been decline in the level of strike activity it does not follow that conflict is no longer an important feature of employment relations. For one thing, there are a variety of behaviours at work that can be encompassed under the umbrella of industrial conflict, including sabotage and absenteeism. Whether or not a type of behaviour is classified as evidence of conflict or not, though, depends upon the context in which it arises and the meanings attached to it by participants (Edwards and Scullion 1982).

The extent of workplace discontent and the rising number of complaints to employment tribunals substantiate the existence of conflictual relations at work. Mobilization theory, by focusing on how employees acquire a sense of grievance, and the way in which grievances are translated into collective action, suggests that the capacity of unions to organize workers, and mobilize around their discontents, is a crucial determinant of whether or not industrial action occurs (Kelly 1998). Finally, in an international context, strikes and other manifestations of labour unrest remain important features of contemporary employment relations.

Since it is an exploitative relationship, which is marked by a basic antagonism between employer and employee, the potential for conflict is an inherent feature of the employment relationship. Nevertheless, this conflict can be contained, by managerial action, jointly agreed procedures, such as negotiations, for example, and state policies, in particular legislation governing industrial action. For strikes, or some other form of collective industrial action, to occur depends upon the capacity of unions to respond to grievances and discontent at work by effectively mobilizing workers to challenge their employer.

Future prospects for employment relations

Writing in the Spring of 2009, in the midst of the biggest economic downturn in a generation, it is difficult to assess the future prospects for employment relations. As this chapter is being written, the so-called G20 world leaders are meeting in London with the purpose of reaching an agreement over how to rebuild the global financial system and deal with the economic crisis. That said, however, drawing on current and recent trends, it is possible to contemplate likely developments concerning the way in which employment relationships are regulated, experienced, and contested.

To some extent, the future prospects for the regulation of employment relationships in Britain depend upon the outcome of the general election due by May 2010 at the latest. The re-election of a Labour government may see further legal regulation of the employment relationship, albeit of a 'light' kind (see Chapter 3), not least because of calls for greater employment protections from the unions, the main source of financial support for the Labour Party. The publication of the Equality Bill in 2009, which among other things provides for the introduction of equal pay audits in large firms (see Chapter 4), suggests that there is support for continued light regulation in some parts of government.

More effort has also been put into raising awareness and promoting compliance with employment legislation, like the National Minimum Wage. That said, though, Labour's employment relations policy continues to be marked by a deregulatory, neo-liberal ethos. In April 2009, for example, the government battled hard to maintain the opt-out from the maximum 48-hour working week in the face of considerable opposition from the trade unions, the European Parliament, and some other EU member states.

Having opened up a consistent lead over Labour in the opinion polls, the Conservative Party looks well set to form a government following the next general election. Under the leadership of David Cameron, the Conservatives have made strenuous efforts to distance themselves from the neo-liberal policies followed by the Thatcher and Major administrations during the 1980s and 1990s. In particular, they now apparently believe that more effective interventions to help working people reconcile the demands of their jobs with their caring responsibilities are desirable, a marked contrast with their previous position.

Yet a closer examination of its policies shows that the Conservative Party's approach to employment relations is still marked by a pronounced neo-liberal character, something that includes a concern with diluting employment protection in the interests of business flexibility (Williams and Scott 2008). Perhaps the Conservative's main achievement has been to avoid any real amount of critical scrutiny from a largely supine media who are more concerned with detailing the problems of Gordon Brown's Labour administration than with holding up the policies of the opposition to critical scrutiny.

The Conservatives have vowed to repudiate the EU's Social Chapter should they form the next government. While they are unlikely to realize this goal in practice—the agreement of all the other EU member states would be required—a Conservative election victory would mean that the current trend towards 'soft', rather than 'hard', regulation (see Chapter 3) is accentuated. However, countervailing pressures for more rigorous regulation of employment relationships are growing at EU level. Consider the controversy over the future of the working time opt out, for example. An alliance of European Parliamentarians and trade unions have fought to abolish it. In future, the UK government, whether Labour or Conservative, may find it less easy than it thinks to avoid EU-level employment regulation and its consequences.

The future prospects for the joint regulation of employment relations appear to be somewhat dim. Enthusiasm for partnership working has diminished, the effectiveness of the organizing approach has been limited, the number of new union recognition deals has tailed off, and union density has continued to decline during the 2000s, albeit gradually. The trade unions are running very hard simply to stay still. That said, however, there are signs that the union movement is evolving increasingly innovative ways of demonstrating its effectiveness in the twenty-first-century labour market, including the use of the internet (see Chapter 6). There are also signs that the unions are beginning to forge a more effective international dimension to their activities (see Chapter 2).

Trade unions are also working more closely with other campaigning organizations, social movements, and community groups in order to achieve their goals. While unions remain vital and necessary institutions for protecting and advancing the interests of working people, perhaps in the future they will operate more closely alongside, and in coalition with, other sympathetic civil society organization; as key elements of a broader progressive movement devoted to combating poverty, reducing inequality, and promoting a fairer society. While the decline of joint regulation has given employers more opportunities to regulate the employment relationship on a unilateral basis, the inherent potential for conflict it contains means that workers will always need, and demand, independent means of expressing their interests.

This is particularly apparent when we consider the future prospects for the experience of workers. During the 2000s, the trend of work intensification levelled off, job insecurity fell as employment levels rose, and average weekly working hours also declined, linked to demands from workers for more flexible, 'family-friendly' working arrangements. At the same time, though, the trend towards the increased use of employee involvement techniques was countered by a reduction in the level of discretion and autonomy enjoyed by workers. The use of sophisticated information and communication technologies by employers enables managers to monitor and control the activities of workers to a much greater degree than before.

The economic recession is likely to accentuate the trend of falling working hours. One of the ways in which some firms have tried to respond to lower demand for their products has been to institute short-time working; reducing the working hours of their employees, and also their pay, in order to see out the downturn. Alongside this, however, workers may come under pressure to work harder in order to ensure that their employer remains competitive, particularly in situations where redundancy exercises have reduced the number of staff employed. Growing job losses, and the rising level of unemployment, may revive the insecurity trend that marked employment relations during the 1990s. For many workers who keep their jobs, further developments in technology may exacerbate the extent to which their activities are monitored by, and thus open to the control of, their employers.

All this suggests, then, that in future the employment relationship will remain a source of potential conflict. We have already seen that workers and unions have been experimenting with innovative forms of industrial action, the 'virtual strike' which affected IBM in Italy during 2007, for example (see Chapter 9). Moreover, the economic recession is likely to be a source of further disputes as workers struggle to retain their jobs, seek to improve the terms on which their employment is terminated, or protest against government and employer policies that threaten their livelihoods.

In April 2009, former employees of the US car parts firm Visteon, who had previously been employed by the giant car manufacturer Ford, occupied Visteon's Enfield and Belfast sites, after the company went into administration, to demand better redundancy terms; they had been dismissed with barely any notice and offered just the legal minimum severance pay. As a result of their actions, the workers' union Unite, was able to secure a much improved redundancy package. While the workers would not get their jobs back, their willingness to challenge the terms on which they had been dismissed ensured that at least they got increased financial compensation for losing their employment. This case illustrates, once more, the rational basis of industrial action by workers.

The January 2009 walk-out at the Lindsey oil refinery (see Chapter 1), and those which followed elsewhere, were ostensibly over the issue of foreign labour. Yet the main underlying cause of the dispute was anxiety about fewer job opportunities, against a background of rising unemployment. In France, workers are taking a particularly innovative form of action to challenge job cuts by their employers (see Box 10.1).

 INTERNATIONAL PERSPECTIVE 10.1

The 'bossnapping' phenomenon

During 2008 and 2009, there was a spate of incidents in France which involved workers holding their senior managers captive for short periods of time. The 'bossnapping' phenomenon is not new to France. However, factory closures, exacerbated by the economic recession, have prompted workers to take direct action to protect their jobs or improve their redundancy settlements. In 2008, for example, Mike Bacon, the head of car parts firm BRS, was held captive by workers over a weekend. Their action was prompted by the company's decision to move production from its factory in France to a plant in Slovakia. In the first few months of 2009, there were further incidents of bossnapping. Senior managers of multinational companies including Sony and Caterpillar, were temporarily held captive following the announcement of plant closures or job losses. As a specific type of industrial action, bossnapping is a rational form of behaviour. Workers use direct action of this kind in an effort to prevent job losses, or to improve their severance terms. In March 2009, the French head of office equipment firm 3M, Luc Rousselet, was released following two days and nights of captivity after the company agreed to renegotiate redundancy terms for its staff, to the disgust of many workers who felt that more concessions could have been extracted. One French trade union leader claimed that holding bosses captive in this way was often the 'only remaining bartering tool' workers have.

During periods of economic difficulty, the potential for conflict of interest that lies at the heart of the employment relationship is starkly evident. While some firms have clearly tried to reduce the scope for job losses, by using short-term working or temporary lay-offs to cope with falling demand, ultimately workers are disposable. How many otherwise profitable companies have used the economic recession as an excuse to cut jobs? For all the supposed efforts by employers to 'engage' staff, to secure their cooperation with, and commitment to, organizational goals, the terms of people's employment relationships are, and will remain, contested.

The potential for conflict lies at the heart of employment relations. The legal regulation of employment relationships (e.g. anti-strike laws, minimum wages), joint regulation (union recognition agreements), and unilateral regulation by employers (e.g. employee involvement techniques like company councils) can all help to contain it. They prevent the basic antagonism that marks the employment relationship from manifesting itself in the form of disputes, industrial action or other kinds of conflictual behaviour. Ultimately, though, the imbalance of power that exists between a relatively powerful employer and a relatively powerless employee, and the different interests that they have, means that employment relations have to be concerned with the ways in which employment relationships are contested, as well as how they are experienced and regulated.

GLOSSARY

Agenda for Change: a national pay and grading scheme that covers employees in the UK's National Health Service.

Annualized hours: arrangements that specify the number of hours to be worked by employees over a year, in return for a guaranteed wage.

Arbitration: a process of resolving disputes in which an independent third party proposes a settlement based on information supplied by, and the arguments of, the respective parties.

Coercive comparisons: a process used by multinational companies to compare the performance data of plants in different countries in order to exert pressure on under-performing plants to improve.

Collective agreements: agreements that are the outcomes of collective bargaining exercises.

Collective bargaining: the term used to refer to the process by which pay, and other conditions of employment, are regulated jointly by an employer, or employers' association, and one or more trade unions.

Conciliation: a process of resolving disputes in which an independent third party helps the parties to reach their own settlement.

(Joint) consultation: a form of workplace and organizational decision-making under which managers submit their proposals to employees, or their representatives, to gauge their views, but retain the right to make the final decision.

Convergence: an approach to understanding the impact of globalization which emphasizes the growing degree of uniformity in employment relations arrangements around the world.

Corporate codes of conduct: voluntary arrangements under which multinational companies agree to bind themselves and firms in their supply chains to upholding certain specified labour standards.

Corporatism: a term that refers to the incorporation of employers' and trade union representative bodies into state policy-making processes; often used as a means of moderating the wage demands of the latter.

Custom and practice: tacit and informal expectations and understandings that govern behaviour at work.

Divergence: an approach to understanding the impact of globalization which emphasizes the persistence of national-level diversity in the employment relations arrangements of different countries.

Diversity management: an approach to reducing employment disadvantage which is concerned with recognizing and celebrating individual differences between employees.

Employee involvement and participation: arrangements that enable workers to exercise influence over organizational or workplace decisions, or that allow managers to communicate with their staff.

Employers' association: a body that represents the employment and employment relations interests of a collective group of employers, often on an industry-wide basis.

Employment tribunal: a quasi-judicial body that deals with complaints from workers that employers have failed to uphold their employment rights.

Empowerment: the devolution of supervisory responsibilities from managers to workers, with greater autonomy and discretion for the latter.

Equal opportunity: an approach to reducing employment disadvantage which focuses on the use of formal procedures to ensure that people are treated the same regardless of their social and personal characteristics.

Equality bargaining: trade union initiatives that are designed to reduce disadvantage at work through interventions targeted at employers.

European Employment Strategy: an EU-level initiative designed to tackle unemployment, social exclusion, and labour market disadvantage by promoting employability and better quality jobs.

European Works Councils: arrangements that exist in multinational companies for informing and consulting with employee and trade union representatives at a European level.

Flexible specialization: a method of enabling specialized goods to be produced in a flexible manner based on the use of sophisticated new technology and a highly knowledgeable workforce.

Franchise: a form of organizing economic activity under which a self-employed person pays a fee in return for the right to operate a pre-packaged business format.

Globalization: refers to the growing interconnectedness of economic activities across and beyond national borders.

Hard regulation: the use of legally binding methods to secure policy objectives.

Harmonization: a process whereby any differences in non-wage terms and conditions of employment between different groups of staff in the same organization are reduced and eradicated.

Horizontal segregation: the over-representation of a specific category of workers in some occupations, and their under-representation in others.

Industrial action: a term that is generally used to refer to more 'organized' manifestations of industrial conflict, such as working to rule, and the strike.

Industrial conflict: a term that is generally used to refer to the broad range of behaviours, both 'organized' and 'disorganized', that express the antagonistic basis of the employment relationship.

Interim labour injunction: a judicial order temporarily restraining a union from holding industrial action.

International labour standards: arrangements for regulating the terms and conditions of employment relationships above and beyond individual nation states.

Job tenure: the length of time people stay in their jobs.

Joint consultation: a form of workplace and organizational decision-making under which managers submit their proposals to employees, or their representatives, to gauge their views, but retain the right to make the final decision.

Joint regulation: a term that is used to refer to the process by which terms and conditions of employment are determined jointly, as a result of bargaining between employers, or employers' associations, and one or more trade unions.

Juridification: a term used to refer to the way in which aspects of economic and social policy are regulated by the law.

Management style: the set of underlying principles that govern how employees are managed in particular organizations.

Managerial prerogative: managers' belief that they should exercise unilateral control over workplace relations.

Mobilization theory: a theoretical perspective used to explain why individual grievances are translated into collective action against employers.

Multi-employer bargaining: this term applies to situations where collective bargaining takes place between a collective group of employers, usually in the form of an employers' association, and one or more trade unions.

Multinational company: a firm that invests in, and is responsible for, subsidiaries located in territories beyond its home country base.

Neo-liberalism: a political and economic perspective which holds that economic prosperity is best achieved through deregulated markets, privatization, and weak trade unions.

Neo-unitary: a variant of the unitary perspective in which the emphasis is placed on the use of sophisticated human resource management practices to elicit employees' commitment.

New Public Management: an approach to managing public sector organizations based on greater managerial authority in a more commercialized environment.

Open Method of Coordination: a means of realizing the social and employment objectives of the European Union through voluntary, non-legally binding methods.

Partnership agreement: a term used to describe a formal relationship between an employer and a union that is based on the importance of cooperation and shared interests, rather than conflict.

Pay review body: independent bodies whose purpose is to make non-binding recommendations to government concerning the pay of particular groups of public sector workers.

Performance-related pay: an arrangement for determining pay that links an element of a worker's reward to some measure of their performance at work.

Pluralist: a perspective on employment relations that recognizes that employers and employees may have conflicting interests, but that these can be resolved to the mutual benefit of both by means of formal procedures, bargaining relationships with trade unions in particular.

Positive action: measures designed to correct the under-representation of certain groups of workers through interventions which help their employment prospects.

Positive discrimination: measures designed to correct the under-representation of certain groups of workers by giving them preferential treatment—unlawful in the UK.

Post-fordism: a model of organizing the production and consumption of goods and services based on fragmented and differentiated markets.

Procedural agreement: a type of agreement that sets out the rules, or procedure, governing the relationship between the parties to it; such as the issues to be determined by collective bargaining, for example.

Procedural individualization: a term that is used to refer to the absence of collective procedures, generally involving trade unions, as a means of determining employment contracts.

Protectionism: a political and economic perspective which holds that jobs in one's own country should be given priority over those in other countries.

Race to the bottom: an escalating process of weakened labour protections, caused by the tendency for multinationals to prefer investing in locations with low employment costs.

Radical: a perspective on employment relations that recognizes that employers and employees have potentially conflicting interests, which are so deep-rooted that when disputes arise they are incapable of being resolved to the mutual satisfaction of both parties.

Redundancy: a term used to refer to the dismissal of workers on the grounds that the number of workers required has diminished.

Regime competition: the process by which multinational companies use investment and disinvestment decisions in order to encourage countries to dilute their labour regulations.

Secondary industrial action: sometimes referred to as 'sympathy' action, the term used to describe action undertaken by one group of workers, who are not involved in a dispute with their own employer, to support another group of workers who are engaged in a dispute with their employer.

Self-employment: a form of employment under which an individual worker works for him- or herself, and not under the control of another employer.

Shop steward: a term that is often used in the UK to refer to unpaid union representatives in the workplace.

Social class: hierarchical divisions in society which reflect differences in people's access to material resources and that influence their life chances.

Social clause: the part of a trade agreement that deals with non-economic matters, such as employment standards.

Social dialogue: a term that is used particularly by the European Union to refer to discussions, consultations, exchanges of information, and negotiations between the social partners.

Social dumping: a term that is used to refer to situations where multinational corporations redirect investment, and therefore jobs, to locations where the costs of employment are lower.

Social partners: a term that is commonly applied by the European Union to the representative bodies of employees, trade unions, and employers.

Soft regulation: the use of non-legally binding methods to secure policy objectives (e.g. guidelines, targets).

Sophisticated human resource management: an approach to managing people at work based on engaging employees, and winning their commitment to the organization, as a means of driving improvements in business performance.

Status divide: refers to the differential treatment in respect of non-wage terms and conditions of employment accorded to different groups of workers in the same organization.

Statutory union recognition procedure: a legislative basis for establishing union recognition under certain defined circumstances.

Strike: the temporary withdrawal of labour by a group of workers, undertaken in order to express a grievance or to enforce a demand.

Substantive agreement: a type of agreement that covers the substance, or the outcomes, of a collective bargaining encounter.

Substantive individualization: a term that is used to refer to the differentiation of contractual terms between workers in the same organization.

Team briefing: a form of employee involvement and participation which involves front-line managers or supervisors sharing information with, and sometimes responding to queries from, their immediate staff.

Teamworking: a form of employee involvement and participation under which workers are organized collectively into specific groups for the purposes of making a product or delivering a service, sometimes with a degree of autonomy and self-management.

Total quality management (TQM): an approach to producing goods or delivering services in which quality is built into all stages.

Trade union: a collective organization of working people which works to improve their terms and conditions of employment.

Tripartism: a term used to refer to arrangements that facilitate the involvement of three parties—the government, unions, employers—in economic and social policy-making.

Union derecognition: the act of an employer who decides not to maintain union recognition.

Union recognition: the act of an employer who agrees to enter into a formal relationship, usually involving collective bargaining, with a trade union.

Unitary: a perspective on employment relations that emphasizes the harmony of interests that exists between employers and their employees.

Vertical segregation: the over-representation of a specific category of workers in low-paid and poorly skilled jobs, and their under-representation in managerial roles.

Voluntarism: a term that is used to describe the absence of state intervention in relations between employers and their employees, and between employers and trade unions.

Voluntary redundancy: a form of redundancy whereby workers supposedly put themselves forward for dismissal, in return for an enhanced severance payment.

Work intensification: a term that is used to describe the process of greater work effort.

Work-to-rule: a form of industrial action where the workers involved refuse to carry out a part, or parts, of their normal duties while continuing to attend work.

BIBLIOGRAPHY

Abbott, B. (2004). 'Worker representation through the Citizens' Advice Bureaux', in G. Healy, E. Heery, P. Taylor, and W. Brown (eds.), *The Future of Worker Representation*. London: Routledge, 245–63.

Abbott, B. (2007). 'Workplace and employment characteristics of the Citizens Advice Bureau clients'. *Employee Relations*, 29/3: 262–79.

Abrams, F. (2002). *Below the Breadline: Living on the Minimum Wage*. London: Profile Books.

Ackers, P. (2002). 'Reframing employment relations: the case for neo-pluralism'. *Industrial Relations Journal*, 33/1: 2–19.

Ackers, P. and Payne, J. (1998). 'British trade unions and social partnership: rhetoric, reality and strategy'. *International Journal of Human Resource Management*, 9/3: 529–50.

Ackers, P. and Wilkinson, A. (2003). 'Introduction: the British industrial relations tradition—formation, breakdown and salvage', in P. Ackers and A. Wilkinson (eds.), *Understanding Work and Employment: Industrial Relations in Transition*. Oxford: Oxford University Press, 1–27.

Ackers, P. and Wilkinson, A. (2005). 'British industrial relations paradigm: a critical outline history and prognosis'. *Journal of Industrial Relations*, 47/4: 443–56.

Ackers, P., Marchington, M., Wilkinson, A., and Goodman, J. (1992). 'The use of cycles? Explaining employee involvement in the 1990s'. *Industrial Relations Journal*, 23/4: 268–83.

Ackroyd, S. and Proctor, S. (1998). 'British manufacturing organization and workplace industrial relations: some attributes of the new flexible firm'. *British Journal of Industrial Relations*, 36/2: 163–83.

Ackroyd, S. and Thompson, P. (1999). *Organizational Misbehaviour*. London: Sage.

Adam-Smith, D. (1997). 'Atypical workers—typical expectations: on temporary work, temporary workers and trade unions'. *Employee Relations Review*, 3: 3–9.

Adam-Smith, D. and Copestake, Y. (2001). 'Tipping the scales? The business case for work–life balance'. *Employee Relations Review*, 7: 3–9.

Adam-Smith, D., Norris, G., and Williams, S. (2003). 'Continuity or change? The implications of the National Minimum Wage for work and employment in the hospitality industry'. *Work, Employment and Society*, 17/1: 29–45.

Adnett, N. and Hardy, S. (2005). *The European Social Model: Modernisation or Evolution?* Cheltenham: Edward Elgar.

Advisory, Conciliation and Arbitration Service (ACAS) (2003). *Annual Report 2002/03*. London: ACAS.

Advisory, Conciliation, and Arbitration Service (ACAS) (2007). *Annual Report and Accounts 2006/07*. London: ACAS.

Ahlstrand, B. (1990). *The Quest for Productivity: A Case Study of Fawley after Flanders*. Cambridge: Cambridge University Press.

Aitkenhead, M. and Liff, S. (1991). 'The effectiveness of equal opportunities policies', in J. Firth-Cozens and M. West (eds.), *Women at Work*. Buckingham: Open University Press, 26–41.

Alderman, K. and Carter, N. (1994). 'The Labour party and the trade unions: loosening the ties'. *Parliamentary Affairs*, 47/3: 321–37.

Allen, J. and Henry, N. (1996). 'Fragments of industry and employment: contract service work and the shift towards precarious employment', in R. Crompton, D. Gallie, and K. Purcell (eds.), *Changing Forms of Employment: Organisations, Skills and Gender*. London: Routledge, 65–82.

Allen, V. (1954). *Power in Trade Unions*. London: Longmans.

Almond, P., Edwards, T., Colling, T., Ferner, A., Gunnigle, P., Müller-Camen, M., Quintanilla, J., and Wächter, H. (2005). 'Unravelling home and host country effects: an investigation of the HR policies of an American multinational in four European countries'. *Industrial Relations*, 44/2: 276–306.

Anderman, S. (1986). 'Unfair dismissals and redundancy', in R. Lewis (ed.), *Labour Law in Britain*. Oxford: Basil Blackwell, 415–47.

Anderson, L. (2003). 'Sound bite legislation: the Employment Act 2002 and the new flexible working "rights" for parents'. *Industrial Law Journal*. 32/1: 37–42.

Anner, M., Greer, I., Hauptmeier, M., Lillie, N., and Winchester, N. (2006). 'The industrial determinants of transnational solidarity: global interunion politics in three sectors'. *European Journal of Industrial Relations*, 12/7: 7–27.

Arrowsmith, J. (2002). 'The struggle over working time in nineteenth and twentieth century Britain'. *Historical Studies in Industrial Relations*, 13: 83–117.

Arrowsmith, J. (2007). 'Why is there not more "annualised hours" working in Britain?'. *Industrial Relations Journal*, 38/5: 423–38.

Arrowsmith, J. and Sisson, K. (1999). 'Pay and working time: towards organization-based systems?'. *British Journal of Industrial Relations*, 37/1: 57–75.

Arrowsmith, J. and Sisson, K. (2000). 'Managing working time', in S. Bach and K. Sisson (eds.), *Personnel Management* (3rd edn). Oxford: Blackwell, 287–313.

Arrowsmith, J., Gilman, M., Edwards, P., and Ram, M. (2003). 'The impact of the National Minimum Wage in small firms'. *British Journal of Industrial Relations*, 41/3: 435–56.

Aston, J., Hill, D., and Tackey, N. (2006). *The Experience of Claimants in Race Discrimination Employment Tribunals*. DTI Employment Research Series No. 55.

Atkinson, A. and McKay, S. (2005). *Child Support Reform: the Views and Experiences of CSA Staff and New Clients*. Department for Work and Pensions Research Report No. 232, London: Department for Work and Pensions.

Atkinson, J. (1984). 'Manpower strategies for flexible organisations'. *Personnel Management*, August: 28–31.

Auerbach, S. (1990). *Legislating for Conflict*. Oxford: Clarendon.

Bach, S. (1999a). 'From national pay determination to qualified market relations: NHS pay bargaining reform'. *Historical Studies in Industrial Relations*, 8: 99–115.

Bach, S. (1999b). 'Personnel managers: managing to change?', in S. Corby and G. White (eds.), *Employee Relations in the Public Services*. London: Routledge, 177–98.

Bach, S. (2002). 'Annual review article 2001: public-sector employment relations reform under Labour: muddling through on modernization?'. *British Journal of Industrial Relations*, 40/2: 319–39.

Bach, S. (2005). 'Personnel management in transition', in S. Bach (ed.), *Managing Human Resources* (4th edn). Oxford: Blackwell, 3–44.

Bach, S. and Della Rocca, G. (2000). 'The management strategies of public service employers in Europe'. *Industrial Relations Journal*, 31/2: 82–96.

Bach, S. and Winchester, D. (1994). 'Opting out of pay devolution? The prospects for local pay bargaining in UK public services'. *British Journal of Industrial Relations*, 32/2: 263–82.

Bach, S. and Winchester, D. (2003). 'Industrial relations in the public sector', in P. Edwards (ed.), *Industrial Relations* (2nd edn). Oxford: Blackwell, 285–312.

Bach, S., Kessler, I., and Heron, P. (2006). 'Changing job boundaries and workforce reform: the case of teaching assistants'. *Industrial Relations Journal*, 37/1: 2–21.

Bacon, N. (1999) 'Union derecognition and the new human relations: a steel industry case study'. *Work, Employment and Society*, 13/1: 1–17.

Bacon, N. and Wright, M. (2008). 'Private equity: friend or foe? The case for'. *People Management*, 21 August: 21–2.

Badigannavar, V. and Kelly, J. (2004). 'Labour-management partnership on the public sector', in J. Kelly and P. Willman (eds.), *Union Organization and Activity*. London: Routledge, 110–28.

Badigannavar, V. and Kelly, J. (2005). 'Why are some union organizing campaigns more successful than others?'. *British Journal of Industrial Relations*, 43/3: 515–35.

Bailey, R. (1996). 'Public sector industrial relations', in I. Beardwell, (ed.), *Contemporary Industrial Relations: a Critical Analysis*. Oxford: Oxford University Press, 121–50.

Bain, G. and Price, R. (1983). 'Union growth: dimensions, determinants and destiny', in G. Bain (ed.), *Industrial Relations in Britain*. Oxford: Basil Blackwell, 3–33.

Bain, P. and Taylor, P. (2000). 'Entrapped by the "electronic panopticon"? Worker resistance in the call centre'. *New Technology, Work and Employment*, 15/1: 2–18.

Bain, P., Taylor, P., Gilbert, K., and Gall, G. (2004). 'Failing to organise—or organising to fail? Challenge, opportunity and the limitations of union policy in four call centres', in G. Healy, E. Heery, P. Taylor, and W. Brown (eds.), *The Future of Worker Representation*. Basingstoke: Palgrave Macmillan, 62–81.

Bairstow, S. (2004). *'Outing the Unions': Sexual Identity, Membership Diversity and the British Trade Union Movement*. Unpublished PhD thesis, University of Portsmouth.

Baldamus, W. (1961). *Efficiency and Effort*. London: Tavistock.

Baldry, C., Bain, P., and Taylor, P. (1998). '"Bright satanic offices": intensifcation, control and team Taylorism', in P. Thompson and C. Warhurst (eds.), *Workplaces of the Future*. Basingstoke: Macmillan, 163–83.

Baldry, C., Bain, P., Taylor, P., Hyman, J., Scholarios, D., Marks, A., Watson, A., Gilbert, K., Gall, G., and Bunzel, D. (2007). *The Meaning of Work in the New Economy*. Basingstoke: Palgrave Macmillan.

Barley, S. and Kunda, G. (2004). *Gurus, Hired Guns, and Warm Bodies*. Princeton NJ: Princeton University Press.

Barnard, C., Deakin, S., and Hobbs, R. (2003). 'Opting out of the 48-hour week: employer necessity or individual choice? An empirical study of the operation of article 18(1)(b) of the Working Time Directive in the UK'. *Industrial Law Journal*, 32/4: 223–52.

Barnes, C. (1992). 'Disability and employment'. *Personnel Review*, 21/6: 55–73.

Barratt, C. (2009). *Trade Union Membership 2008*. London: Department for Business Enterprise and Regulatory Reform.

Barrientos, S. and Smith, S. (2006). *The ETI Code of Labour Practice: Do Workers Really Benefit?* University of Sussex: Institute of Development Studies.

Bassett, P. (1987). *Strike Free*. London: Papermac.

Bassett, P. and Cave, A. (1993). *All For One: the Future of the Unions*. London: Fabian Society.

Batstone, E. (1988). *The Reform of Workplace Industrial Relations: Theory, Myth and Evidence*. Oxford: Clarendon.

Batstone, E., Boraston, I., and Frenkel, S. (1978). *The Social Organization of Strikes*. Oxford: Basil Blackwell.

Batstone, E., Ferner, A., and Terry, M. (1983). *Unions on the Board*. Oxford: Basil Blackwell.

Bazen, S. and Benhayoun, G. (1992). 'Low pay and wage regulation in the European Community'. *British Journal of Industrial Relations*, 30/ 4: 623–38.

BBC (2000). *Gap and Nike: No Sweat?*. Panorama, 15 October.

Beaumont, P. (1981). 'Trade union recognition: the British experience 1976–1980'. *Employee Relations*, 3/6: 2–39.

Beaumont, P. (1992). *Public Sector Industrial Relations*. London: Routledge.

Beaumont, P. and Harris, R. (1990). 'Union recruitment and organising attempts in Britain in the 1980s'. *Industrial Relations Journal*, 21/4: 274–86.

Behrend, H. (1957). 'The effort bargain'. *Industrial and Labor Relations Review*, 10/4, 503–15.

Bell, M. (2004). 'Equality and the European Union constitution'. *Industrial Law Journal*, 33/3: 242–60.

Bensinger, R. (1998). 'When we try more, we win more: organizing the new workforce', in J. Mort (ed.), *Not Your Father's Union Movement*. London: Verso, 27–41.

Bercusson, B. (1978). *Fair Wages Resolutions*. London: Mansell.

BERR (2008). *Agency Working in the UK: a Review of the Evidence*. Employment Relations Research Series No. 93. London: Department for Business, Enterprise, and Regulatory Reform.

Bewley, H. (2006). 'Raising the standard? The regulation of employment, and public sector employment policy'. *British Journal of Industrial Relations*, 44/2: 351–72.

Bewley, H. and Fernie, S. (2003). 'What do unions do for women?', in H. Gospel and S. Wood (eds.), *Representing Workers*. London: Routledge, 92–118.

Beynon, H. (1973). *Working for Ford*. Harmondsworth: Penguin.

Beynon, H. (ed.) (1985). *Digging Deeper: Issues in the Miners' Strike*. London: Verso.

Beynon, H. (1997). 'The changing practices of work', in R. Brown (ed.), *The Changing Shape of Work*. Basingstoke: Macmillan, 20–54.

Beynon, H., Grimshaw, D., Rubery, J., and Ward, K. (2002). *Managing Employment Change*. Oxford: Oxford University Press.

Bhagwati, J. (2004). *In Defense of Globalization*. Oxford: Oxford University Press.

Blackburn, R. and Prandy, K. (1965). 'White-collar unionisation: a conceptual framework'. *British Journal of Sociology*, 16/2: 111–22.

Blakemore, K. and Drake, R. (1996). *Understanding Equal Opportunity Policies*. Hemel Hempstead: Harvester-Wheatsheaf.

Blanden, J., Machin, S., and Van Reenen, J. (2006). 'Have unions turned the corner? New evidence on recent trends in union recognition in UK firms'. *British Journal of Industrial Relations*, 44/2: 169–90.

Blyton, P. and Turnbull, P. (2004). *The Dynamics of Employee Relations* (3rd edn). Basingstoke: Palgrave Macmillan.

Bolton, J. (1971). *Report of the Committee of Enquiry on Small Firms*. London: HMSO.

Bolton, S. (2004). *Emotion Management in the Workplace*. Basingstoke: Palgrave Macmillan.

Bolton, S. and Houlihan, M. (2007). *Searching for the Human in Human Resource Management*. Basingstoke: Palgrave Macmillan.

Bonner, C. and Gollan, P. (2005). 'A bridge over troubled water: a decade of representation at South West Water'. *Employee Relations*, 27/3: 238–58.

Boston, S. (1980). *Women Workers and the Trade Union Movement*. London: Davis-Poynter.

Boxall, P. and Purcell, J. (2007). *Strategy and Human Resource Management* (2nd edn). Basingstoke: Palgrave Macmillan.

Boyd, C. (2001). 'HRM in the airline industry: strategies and outcomes'. *Personnel Review*, 30/4: 438–53.

Boyd, C. (2003). *Human Resource Management and Occupational Health and Safety*. London: Routledge.

Bradley, H. (1989). *Men's Work, Women's Work*. Cambridge: Polity.

Bradley, H. (1996). *Fractured Identities*. Cambridge: Polity.

Bradley, H. (1999). *Gender and Power in the Workplace*. Basingstoke: Macmillan.

Bradley, H. and Healy, G. (2008). *Ethnicity and Gender at Work*. Basingstoke: Palgrave Macmillan.

Bradley, H., Erickson, M., Stephenson, C., and Williams, S. (2000). *Myths at Work*. Cambridge: Polity.

Bradley, H., Healy, G., and Mukherjee, N. (2002). *Inclusion, Exclusion and Separate Organisation—Black Women Activists in Trade Unions*, ESRC Future of Work Programme, Working Paper No. 25.

Brannen, P. (1983). *Authority and Participation in Industry*. London: Batsford.

Brewer, M., Muriel, A., Phillips, D., and Sibieta, L. (2008). *Poverty and Inequality in the UK: 2008*, IFS Commentary No. 105. London: Institute for Fiscal Studies.

Bridgford, J. and Stirling, J. (1994). *Employee Relations in Europe*. Oxford: Blackwell.

Brinkley, I., Coats, D., and Overell, S. (2007). *7 out of 10: Labour under Labour*. London: Work Foundation.

British Universities Industrial Relations Association (BUIRA) (2008). *What's the Point of Industrial Relations?* A statement by the British Universities Industrial Relations Association.

Bronfenbrenner, K. and Juravich, T. (1998). 'It takes more than house calls: organizing to win with a comprehensive union-building strategy', in K. Bronfenbrenner, S. Friedman, R. Hurd, R. Oswald, and R. Seeber (eds.), *Organizing to Win: New Research on Union Strategies*. Ithaca: ILR Press, 19–36.

Brown, D. and Crossman, A. (2000). 'Employer strategies in the face of a national minimum wage: an analysis of the hotel sector'. *Industrial Relations Journal*, 31/3: 206–19.

Brown, G. (1977). *Sabotage*. Nottingham: Spokesman.

Brown, W. (1973). *Piecework Bargaining*. London: Heinemann.

Brown, W. (ed.) (1981). *The Changing Contours of British Industrial Relations*. Oxford: Basil Blackwell.

Brown, W. (1993). 'The contraction of collective bargaining in Britain'. *British Journal of Industrial Relations*, 31/2: 189–200.

Brown, W. (2000). 'Putting partnership into practice in Britain'. *British Journal of Industrial Relations*, 38/2: 299–316.

Brown, W. and Nash, D. (2008). 'What has been happening to collective bargaining under New Labour?' *Industrial Relations Journal*, 39/2: 91–103.

Brown, W. and Nolan, P. (1988). 'Wages and labour productivity: the contribution of industrial relations research to the understanding of pay determination'. *British Journal of Industrial Relations*, 26/3: 339–61.

Brown, W. and Terry, M. (1978). 'The changing nature of national wage agreements'. *Scottish Journal of Political Economy*, 25/2: 119–33.

Brown, W. and Walsh, J. (1991). 'Pay determination in Britain in the 1980s; the anatomy of decentralization'. *Oxford Review of Economic Policy*, 7/1: 44–59.

Brown, W. and Walsh, J. (1994). 'Managing pay in Britain', in K. Sisson (ed.), *Personnel Management* (2nd edn). Oxford: Blackwell, 437–64.

Brown, W., Marginson, P., and Walsh, J. (1995). 'Management: pay determination and collective bargaining", in P. Edwards (ed.), *Industrial Relations: Theory and Practice in Britain*. Oxford: Blackwell, 123–50.

Brown, W., Marginson, P., and Walsh, J. (2003). 'The management of pay as the influence of collective bargaining declines', in P. Edwards (ed.), *Industrial Relations* (2nd edn). Oxford: Blackwell, 189–213.

Brown, W., Deakin, S., Nash, D., and Oxenbridge, S. (2000). 'The employment contract: from collective procedures to individual rights'. *British Journal of Industrial Relations*, 38/4: 611–29.

Brown, W., Deakin, S., Hudson, M., and Pratten, C. (2001). 'The limits of statutory union recognition'. *Industrial Relations Journal*, 32/3: 180–94.

Bryson, A. (2004). 'Managerial responsiveness to union and nonunion worker voice in Britain'. *Industrial Relations*, 43/1: 213–41.

Budd, J. (2004). *Employment with a Human Face: Balancing Efficiency, Equity, and Voice*. Ithaca NY: Cornell University Press.

Burawoy, M. (1979). *Manufacturing Consent*. Chicago: University of Chicago Press.

Burchell, B. (2002). 'The prevalence and redistribution of job insecurity and work intensification', in B. Burchell, D. Ladipo, and F. Wilkinson (eds.), *Job Insecurity and Work Intensification*. London: Routledge, 61–76.

Burchell, B., Lapido, D., and Wilkinson, F. (eds.) (2002). *Job Insecurity and Work Intensification*. London: Routledge.

Burchell, B., Day, D., Hudson, M., Ladipo, D., Mankelow, R., Nolan, J., Reed, H., Wichert, I., and Wilkinson, F. (1999). *Job Insecurity and Work Intensification*. York: Joseph Rowntree Foundation.

Burchill, F. (2000). 'The pay review body system: a comment and a consequence'. *Historical Studies in Industrial Relations*, 10: 141–57.

Burgess, K. (1980). *The Challenge of Labour*. London: Croom Helm.

Cabinet Office (2008). *Getting On, Getting Ahead. A Discussion Paper: Analysing the Trends and Drivers of Social Mobility*. London: Cabinet Office.

Card, D. and Krueger, A. (1995). *Myth and Measurement: the New Economics of the Minimum Wage*. Princeton: Princeton University Press.

Carley, M. (1993). 'Social dialogue', in M. Gold (ed.), *The Social Dimension: Employment Policy in the European Community*. Basingstoke: Macmillan, 105–34.

Carley, M. and Hall, M. (2000) 'The implementation of the European Works Councils Directive'. *Industrial Law Journal*, 29/2: 103–24.

Carr, F. (1999). 'Local bargaining in the National Health Service: new approaches to employee relations'. *Industrial Relations Journal*, 30/3: 197–211.

Carter, B. (2000). 'Adoption of the organising model in British trade unions: some evidence from Manufacturing, Science and Finance (MSF)'. *Work, Employment and Society*, 14/1: 117–36.

Carter, B. and Fairbrother, P. (1999). 'The transformation of British public-sector industrial relations: from "model employer" to marketised relations'. *Historical Studies in Industrial Relations*, 7: 119–46.

Castells, M. (1996). *The Rise of the Network Society*. London: Routledge.

Castells, M. (2001). *The Internet Galaxy*. Oxford: Oxford University Press.

Central Arbitration Committee (CAC) (2008). *Annual Report 2007–08*. London: Central Arbitration Committee.

Certification Officer (2008). *Annual Report of the Certification Officer 2006–07*. London: Certification Officer, http://www.certoffice.org/

Chamberlain, N. and Kuhn, J. (1965). *Collective Bargaining*. New York: McGraw-Hill.

Charles, N. (1986). 'Women and trade unions', in Feminist Review (ed.), *Waged Work: a Reader*. London: Virago, 160–85.

Charles, N. and James, E. (2003). 'The gender dimensions of job insecurity in a local labour market'. *Work, Employment and Society*, 17/3: 531–52.

Charlwood, A. (2007). 'The de-collectivisation of pay setting in Britain 1990–98: incidence, determinants and impact'. *Industrial Relations Journal*, 38/1: 33–50.

Charlwood, A. and Terry, M. (2007). '21st-century models of employee representation: structures, processes, and outcomes'. *Industrial Relations Journal*, 38/4: 320–37.

Clark, I. (2008). 'Private equity: friend or foe? The case against'. *People Management*, 21 August: 18–20.

Clark, J. (1995). *Managing Innovation and Change*. London: Sage.

Clarke, M. (2007). 'Choices and constraints: individual perceptions of the voluntary redundancy experience'. *Human Resource Management Journal*, 17/1: 76–93.

Claydon, T. (1989). 'Union derecognition in Britain during the 1980s'. *British Journal of Industrial Relations*, 27/2: 214–23.

Claydon, T. (1996). 'Union de-recognition: a re-examination', in I. Beardwell (ed.), *Contemporary Industrial Relations: a Critical Analysis*. Oxford: Oxford University Press, 151–74.

Clegg, H. (1975). 'Pluralism in industrial relations'. *British Journal of Industrial Relations*, 13/3: 309–16.

Clegg, H. (1976). *Trade Unionism under Collective Bargaining*. Oxford: Basil Blackwell.

Clegg, H. (1979). *The Changing System of Industrial Relations in Great Britain*. Oxford: Basil Blackwell.

Clegg, H. (1985). *A History of British Trade Unions since 1889. Volume II, 1911–1933*. Oxford: Oxford University Press.

Clegg, H., Fox, A. and Thompson, A. (1964). *A History of British Trade Unions since 1889. Volume I, 1889–1910*. Oxford: Clarendon.

Coates, D. (2000). 'New Labour's industrial and employment policy', in D. Coates and P. Lawler (eds.), *New Labour in Power*. Manchester: Manchester University Press, 122–35.

Coats, D. (2007). *The National Minimum Wage. Retrospect and Prospect*. London: Work Foundation.

Coates, K. and Topham, T. (1980). *Trade Unions in Britain*. Nottingham: Spokesman.

Cockburn, C. (1989). 'Equal opportunities: the short and long agenda'. *Industrial Relations Journal*. 20/3: 213–25.

Cockburn, C. (1991). *In the Way of Women*. Basingstoke: Macmillan.

Cohen, R. (1991). *Contested Domains*. London: Zed Books.

Colgan, F. (1999). 'Recognising the lesbian and gay constituency in UK trade unions: moving forward in UNISON'. *Industrial Relations Journal*, 30/5: 444–63.

Colgan, F. and Ledwith, S. (2000). 'Diversity, identities and strategies of women trade union activists'. *Gender, Work and Organization*, 7/4: 242–57.

Colgan, F. and Ledwith, S. (2002). 'Gender and diversity: reshaping union democracy'. *Employee Relations*, 24/2: 167–89.

Colgan. F., Creegan, C., McKearney, A., and Wright, T. (2007). 'Equality and diversity policies and practices at work: lesbian, gay, and bisexual workers'. *Equal Opportunities International*, 26/3: 590–609.

Colling, T. (1999) 'Tendering and outsourcing: working in the contract state?', in S. Corby and G. White (eds.), *Employee Relations in the Public Services: Themes and Issues*. London: Routledge, 136–55.

Colling, T. (2003). 'Managing without unions: the sources and limitations of individualism', in P. Edwards (ed.), *Industrial Relations: Theory and Practice* (2nd edn). Oxford: Blackwell, 368–91.

Colling, T. (2004). 'No claim, no pain? The privatization of dispute resolution in Britain'. *Economic and Industrial Democracy*, 25/4: 555–79.

Colling, T. and Dickens, L. (1989). *Equality Bargaining—Why Not?*. London: HMSO.

Colling, T. and Dickens, L. (1998). 'Selling the case for gender equality: deregulation and equality bargaining'. *British Journal of Industrial Relations*, 36/3: 389–411.

Colling, T. and Dickens, L. (2001). 'Gender equality and trade unions: a new basis for mobilisation?', in M. Noon and E. Ogbonna, (eds.), *Equality, Diversity and Disadvantage in Employment*. Basingstoke: Palgrave Macmillan, 136–55.

Collinson, D., Knights, D., and Collinson, M. (1990). *Managing to Discriminate*. London: Routledge.

Commons, J. (1924). *Legal Foundations of Capitalism*. New York: Macmillan.

Compa, L. (2001). 'Free trade, fair trade and the battle for labor rights', in L. Turner, H. Katz, and R. Hurd (eds.), *Rekindling the Movement: Labor's Quest for Relevance in the Twenty-first Century*. Ithaca: Cornell University Press, 314–38.

Conley, H. (2002). 'A state of insecurity: temporary work in the public services'. *Work, Employment and Society*, 16/4: 725–37.

Connor, T. (2002). *We are not Machines: Indonesian Nike and Adidas Workers*. Oxford: Oxfam.

Cooke, F-L. (2008). 'The changing dynamics of employment relations in China: an evaluation of the rising level of labour disputes'. *Journal of Industrial Relations*, 50/1: 111–38.

Cooke, H. (2006). 'Examining the disciplinary process in nursing: a case study approach'. *Work, Employment, and Society*, 20/4: 687–707.

Cooper, C. (2001). 'Talking Italian'. *People Management*, 14 June: 38–41.

Corby, S. (2000). 'Employee relations in the public services: a paradigm shift?'. *Public Policy and Administration*, 15/3: 60–74.

Corby, S. (2003). *Public Sector Disputes and Third Party Intervention*. ACAS research paper 02/03, London: ACAS.

Creegan, C. and Robinson, C. (2008). 'Prejudice and the workplace', in A. Park, J. Curtice, K. Thomson, M. Phillips, M. Johnson, and E. Clery (eds.), *British Social Attitudes: the 24th Report*. London: Sage, 127–38.

Cremers, J., Erik Dølvik, J., and Bosch, G. (2007). 'Posting of workers in the single market: attempts to prevent social dumping and regime competition in the EU'. *Industrial Relations Journal*, 38/6: 524–41.

Crompton, R. (1997). *Women and Work in Modern Britain*. Oxford: Oxford University Press.

Crompton, R. and Sanderson, K. (1990). *Gendered Jobs and Social Change*. London: Unwin Hyman.

Cronin, J. (1979). *Industrial Conflict in Modern Britain*. London: Croom Helm.

Crouch, C. (1977). *Class Conflict and the Industrial Relations Crisis*. London: Heinemann.

Crouch, C. (1979). *The Politics of Industrial Relations*. London: Fontana.

Crouch, C. (1995). 'The state: economic management and incomes policy', in P. Edwards (ed.), *Industrial Relations: Theory and Practice in Britain*. Oxford: Blackwell, 229–54.

Crouch, C. (1996). 'Review essay. Atavism and innovation: labour legislation and public policy since 1979 in historical perspective'. *Historical Studies in Industrial Relations*, 2: 111–24.

Croucher, R. and Cotton, E. (2009). *Global Unions, Global Business*. Hendon: Middlesex University Press.

Croucher, R. and White, G. (2007). 'Enforcing a National Minimum Wage'. *Policy Studies*, 28/2: 145–61.

Cully, M., Woodland, S., O'Reilly, A., and Dix, G. (1999). *Britain at Work*. London: Routledge.

Cunningham, I. and Hyman, J. (1999). 'The poverty of empowerment? A critical case study'. *Personnel Review*, 28/3: 192–207.

Cunningham, R., Lord, A., and Delaney, L. (1999). '"Next Steps" for equality? The impact of organizational change on opportunities for women in the civil service'. *Gender, Work and Organization*, 6/2: 67–78.

Cunnison, S. and Stageman, J. (1993). *Feminizing the Unions*. Aldershot: Avebury.

Danford, A. (1998). 'Teamworking and labour regulation in the autocomponents industry'. *Work, Employment and Society*, 12/3: 409–31.

Danford, A. (1999). *Japanese Management Techniques and British Workers*. London: Mansell.

Danford, A., Richardson, M., and Upchurch, M. (2002). '"New unionism", organising and partnership: a comparative analysis of union renewal strategies in the public sector'. *Capital and Class*, 76: 1–27.

Danford, A., Richardson, M. and Stewart, P. (2003). *New Unions, New Workplaces*. London: Routledge.

Danford, A., Richardson, M., Stewart, P., Tailby, S., and Upchurch, M. (2004). 'Partnership, mutuality and the high-performance workplace: a case study of union strategy and worker experience in the aircraft industry', in G. Healy, E. Heery, P. Taylor, and W. Brown (eds.), *The Future of Worker Representation*, Basingstoke: Palgrave Macmillan, 167–86.

Danford, A., Richardson, M., Stewart, P., Tailby, S., and Upchurch, M. (2005). *Partnership and the High Performance Workplace*. Basingstoke: Palgrave Macmillan.

Daniel, W. and Millward, N. (1983). *Workplace Industrial Relations in Britain*. London: Heinemann.

Daniels, G. (2009). 'In the field: a decade of organizing', in G. Daniels and J. McIlroy (eds.), *Trade Unions in a Neo Liberal World: British Trade Unions under New Labour*. Abingdon: Routledge, 254–82.

Daniels, G. and McIlroy, J. (eds.). (2009). *Trade Unions in a Neo Liberal World: British Trade Unions under New Labour*. Abingdon: Routledge.

Davies, A. and Thomas, R. (2000). 'Gender and human resource management: a critical review'. *International Journal of Human Resource Management*, 11/6: 1125–36.

Davies, P. and Freedland, M. (1993). *Labour Legislation and Public Policy*. Oxford: Clarendon.

Davies, P. and Freedland, M. (2007). *Towards a Flexible Labour Market*. Oxford: Oxford University Press.

Debrah, Y. and Smith, I. (2002). 'Globalization, employment and the workplace: diverse impacts?', in Y. Debrah and I. Smith (eds.), *Globalization, Employment and the Workplace: Diverse Impacts*. London: Routledge, 1–23.

Delbridge, R. (1998). *Life on the Line in Contemporary Manufacturing*. Oxford: Oxford University Press.

Department of Trade and Industry (DTI) (1998). *Fairness at Work*. London: HMSO.

Department of Trade and Industry (DTI) (2003). *High Performance Workplaces: Informing and Consulting Employees*. London: DTI.

Department of Trade and Industry (DTI) (2005). *Code of Practice: Access and Unfair Practices during Recognition Ballots*. London: DTI.

Department of Trade and Industry (DTI) (2006). *Success at Work*. London: DTI.

Department of Trade and Industry (DTI) (2007). *Better Dispute Resolution: A Review of Employment Dispute Resolution in Great Britain*. London: DTI.

Dex, S. and McCulloch, A. (1997). *Flexible Employment*. Basingstoke: Macmillan.

Dex, S., Robson, P., and Wilkinson, F. (1999). 'The characteristics of the low paid: a cross-national comparison'. *Work, Employment and Society*, 13/3: 503–24.

Dex, S., Sutherland, H., and Joshi, H. (2000). 'Effects of minimum wages on the gender pay gap'. *National Institute Economic Review*, 173: 80–8.

Diamond, W. and Freeman, R. (2002). 'Will unionism prosper in cyberspace? The promise of the internet for employee organization'. *British Journal of Industrial Relations*, 40/3: 569–96.

Dicken, P. (2003). *Global Shift* (4th edn). London: Sage.

Dickens, L. (1992). 'Anti-discrimination legislation: exploring and explaining the impact on women's employment', in W. McCarthy (ed.), *Legal Intervention in Industrial Relations: Gains and Losses*. Oxford: Basil Blackwell, 103–46.

Dickens, L. (1994). 'The business case for women's equality: is the carrot better than the stick?'. *Employee Relations*, 16/8: 5–18.

Dickens, L. (1997). 'Gender, race and employment equality in Britain: inadequate strategies and the role of industrial relations actors'. *Industrial Relations Journal*, 28/4: 282–91.

Dickens, L. (1999). 'Beyond the business case: a three-pronged approach to equality action'. *Human Resource Management Journal*, 9/1: 9–19.

Dickens, L. (2000a) 'Still wasting resources? Equality in employment', in S. Bach and K. Sisson (eds.), *Personnel Management* (3rd edn). Oxford: Blackwell, 137–69.

Dickens, L. (2000b). 'Collective bargaining and the promotion of gender equality at work: opportunities and challenges for trade unions'. *Transfer*, 6/2: 193–208.

Dickens, L. (2000c) 'Doing more with less: Acas and individual conciliation', in Towers, B. and Brown, W. (eds.), *Employment Relations in Britain: 25 Years of the Advisory, Conciliation and Arbitration Service*, Oxford: Blackwell, 67–91.

Dickens, L. (2007). 'The road is long: thirty years of equality legislation in Britain'. *British Journal of Industrial Relations*, 45/3: 463–94.

Dickens, L. and Hall, M. (2003). 'Labour law and industrial relations: a new settlement?', in P. Edwards (ed.) *Industrial Relations* (2nd edn). Oxford: Blackwell, 124–56.

Dickens, L. and Hall, M. (2006). 'Fairness—up to a point. Assessing the impact of New Labour's employment legislation'. *Human Resource Management Journal*, 16/4: 338–56.

Dickens, L., Jones, M., Weekes, B., and Hunt, M. (1985). *Dismissed: a Study of Unfair Dismissal and the Industrial Tribunal System*. Oxford: Basil Blackwell.

Dickens, R. and Manning, A. (2003). 'Minimum wage, minimum impact', in R. Dickens, P. Gregg, and J. Wadsworth (eds.), *The Labour Market under New Labour*. Basingstoke: Palgrave Macmillan, 201–13.

Dickens, R., Gregg, P., Machin, S., Manning, A., and Wadsworth, J. (1993). 'Wages councils: was there a case for abolition?'. *British Journal of Industrial Relations*, 31/4: 515–29.

Dickson, T., McLachlan, H., Prior, P., and Swales, K. (1988). 'Big Blue and the unions: IBM, individualism and trade union strategy'. *Work, Employment and Society*, 2/4: 506–21.

Dix, G. and Oxenbridge, S. (2004). 'Coming to the table with Acas: from conflict to co-operation'. *Employee Relations*, 26/5: 510–30.

Doherty, L. (2004). 'Work–life balance initiatives: implications for women'. *Employee Relations*, 26/4: 433–52.

Donaghey, J. and Teague, P. (2006). 'The free movement of workers and social Europe: maintaining the European ideal'. *Industrial Relations Journal*, 37/6: 652–66.

Donnelly, M. and Scholarios, D. (1998). 'Workers' experiences of redundancy: evidence from Scottish defence-dependent companies'. *Personnel Review*, 27/4: 325–42.

Doogan, K. (2001). 'Insecurity and long-term employment'. *Work, Employment and Society*, 15/3: 419–41.

Druker, J. and White, G. (1999). 'Introduction: the context of reward management', in G. White and J. Druker (eds.), *Reward Management: A Critical Text*. London: Routledge, 1–24.

Druker, J., Stanworth, C, and White, G. (2002). *Report to the Low Pay Commission on the Impact of the National Minimum Wage on the Hairdressing Sector*. London: University of Greenwich.

Druker, J., White, G., and Stanworth, C. (2005). 'Coping with wage regulation: implementing the National Minimum Wage in hairdressing businesses'. *International Small Business Journal*, 23/5: 5–25.

Dubois, P. (1979). *Sabotage in Industry*. Penguin: Harmondsworth.

Dundon, T. and Gollan, P. (2007). 'Re-conceptualizing voice in the non-union workplace'. *International Journal of Human Resource Management*, 18/7: 1182–98.

Dundon, T. and Rollinson, D. (2004). *Employment Relations in Non-Union Firms*. London: Routledge.

Dundon, T., González-Pérez, M-A., and McDonough, T. (2007). 'Bitten by the Celtic Tiger: immigrant workers and industrial relations in the new "glocalized" Ireland'. *Economic and Industrial Democracy*, 28/4: 501–22.

Dundon, T., Wilkinson, A., Marchington, M., and Ackers, P. (2005). 'The management of voice in non-union organisations: managers' perspectives'. *Employee Relations*, 27/3: 307–19.

Dunleavy, P. and O'Leary, B. (1987). *Theories of the State: the Politics of Liberal Democracy*. Basingstoke: Macmillan.

Dunlop, J. (1958). *Industrial Relations Systems*. New York: Holt.

Dunn, S. and Gennard, J. (1984). *The Closed Shop in British Industry*. London: Macmillan.

Dunn, S. and Metcalf, D. (1996). 'Trade union law since 1979', in I. Beardwell (ed.), *Contemporary Industrial Relations: A Critical Analysis*. Oxford: Oxford University Press, 66–98.

Earnshaw, J., Marchington, M., and Goodman, J. (2000). 'Unfair to whom? Discipline and dismissal in small establishments'. *Industrial Relations Journal*, 31/1: 62–73.

Eaton, J. (2000). *Comparative Employment Relations*. Cambridge: Polity.

Edelstein, J. and Warner, M. (1975). *Comparative Union Democracy*. London: George Allen and Unwin.

Edwards, P. (1977). 'The Kerr-Siegel hypothesis of strikes and the isolated mass: a study of the falsification of sociological knowledge'. *Sociological Review*, 25/3: 551–74.

Edwards, P. (1983). 'The pattern of collective industrial action', in G. Bain (ed.), *Industrial Relations in Britain*. Oxford: Basil Blackwell, 209–34.

Edwards, P. (1986). *Conflict at Work*. Oxford: Basil Blackwell.

Edwards, P. (1987). *Managing the Factory*. Oxford: Basil Blackwell.

Edwards, P. (1988). 'Patterns of conflict and accommodation', in D. Gallie (ed.), *Employment in Britain*. Oxford: Basil Blackwell, 187–217.

Edwards, P. (1992). 'Industrial conflict'. *British Journal of Industrial Relations*, 30/3: 361–404.

Edwards, P. (1995). 'Strikes and industrial conflict', in P. Edwards (ed.), *Industrial Relations: Theory and Practice in Britain*. Oxford: Blackwell, 434–60.

Edwards, P. (2000). 'Discipline: towards trust and self-discipline?', in S. Bach and K. Sisson (eds.), *Personnel Management* (3rd edn). Oxford: Blackwell, 317–39.

Edwards, P. (2003). 'The employment relationship and the field of industrial relations', in P. Edwards, (ed.), *Industrial Relations* (2nd edn). Oxford: Blackwell, 1–36.

Edwards, P. (2005). 'Discipline and attendance: a murky aspect of people management', in S. Bach (ed.), *Managing Human Resources* (4th edn). Oxford: Blackwell, 375–97.

Edwards, P. and Gilman, M. (1999). 'Pay equity and the national minimum wage: what can theories tell us?'. *Human Resource Management Journal*, 9/1: 20–38.

Edwards, P. and Scullion, H. (1982). *The Social Organisation of Industrial Conflict*. Oxford: Basil Blackwell.

Edwards, P. and Whitston, C. (1991). 'Workers are working harder: effort and shop-floor relations in the 1980s'. *British Journal of Industrial Relations*, 29/4: 592–601.

Edwards, P. and Whitston, C. (1993). *Attending to Work*. Oxford: Blackwell.

Edwards, P. and Whitston, C. (1994). 'Disciplinary practice: a study of railways in Britain, 1860–1988'. *Work, Employment and Society*, 8/3: 317–37.

Edwards, P. and Wright, M. (1998). 'HRM and commitment: a case study of teamworking', in P. Sparrow and M. Marchington (eds.), *Human Resource Management: The New Agenda*, Harlow: Pearson Education Limited, 272–85.

Edwards, P., Armstrong, P., Marginson, P., and Purcell, J. (1996). 'Towards the transnational company? The global organisation and structure of multinational firms', in R. Crompton, D. Gallie, and K. Purcell (eds.), *Changing Forms of Employment: Organisations, Skills and Gender*. London: Routledge, 40–65.

Edwards, P., Collinson, M., and Rees, C. (1998). 'The determinants of employee responses to Total Quality Management: six case studies'. *Organization Studies*, 19/3: 449–75.

Edwards, P., Geary, J., and Sisson, K. (2002). 'New forms of work organization in the workplace: transformative, exploitative, or limited and controlled?', in G. Murray, J. Bélanger, A. Giles, and P-A. Lapointe (eds.), *Work and Employment Relations in the High-Performance Workplace*. London: Continuum, 72–119.

Edwards, R. (1979). *Contested Terrain: the Transformation of the Workplace in the Twentieth Century*. London: Heinemann.

Edwards, T. (2004). 'The transfer of employment practices across borders in multinational companies', in A-W. Harzing and J. Van Ruysseveldt (eds.), *International Human Resource Management* (2nd edn). London: Sage, 389–410.

Edwards, T. and Ferner, A. (2002). 'The renewed "American challenge": a review of employment practice in US multinationals'. *Industrial Relations Journal*, 33/2: 94–111.

Egels-Zandén, N. (2007). 'Suppliers' compliance with MNCs' codes of conduct: behind the scenes at Chinese toy suppliers'. *Journal of Business Ethics*, 75: 45–62.

Elgar, J. and Simpson, B. (1993). 'The impact of the law on industrial disputes in the 1980s', in D. Metcalf and S. Milner (eds.), *New Perspectives on Industrial Disputes*. London: Routledge, 70–114.

Elger, T. (1990). 'Technical innovation and work reorganisation in British manufacturing in the 1980s: continuity, intensification or transformation?'. *Work, Employment and Society*, special issue: 67–101.

Elliott, K. and Freeman, R. (2003). *Can Labor Standards Improve under Globalization?* Washington DC: Institute for International Economics.

Elliot, L. and Atkinson, D. (1998). *The Age of Insecurity*. London: Verso.

Emmott, M. (2001). 'Tribunals are judged wanting'. The *Guardian*, 12 March.

Emmott, M. (2005). *What is Employee Relations?* London: CIPD.

Employers Forum on Age (EFA) (2006). *Ageism is Rife in UK companies*. EFA press release. http://www.efa.org.uk

Equal Opportunities Commission (EOC) (2005). *Greater Expectations: Summary Final Report of the EOC's Investigation into Pregnancy Discrimination*. London: EOC.

Equal Opportunities Commission (EOC) (2006). *Moving on up? Bangladeshi, Pakistani, and Black Caribbean Women at Work*. London: EOC.

Equality and Human Rights Commission (EHRC) (2009). *Working Better. Phase 1 Report*. London: EHRC.

Erickson, C., Fisk, C., Milkman, R., Mitchell, D., and Wong, K. (2002). 'Justice for Janitors in Los Angeles: lessons from three rounds of negotiation'. *British Journal of Industrial Relations*, 40/3: 543–67.

Erickson, M., Bradley, H., Stephenson, C., and Williams, S. (2009). *Business in Society*. Cambridge: Polity.

European Commission (2002). *The European Social Dialogue: a Force for Innovation and Change*. Brussels: EC.

European Industrial Relations Observatory (EIRO) (2001). 'Employers and unions argue over "compensation culture"', http://www.eiro.eurofound.eu.int/2001/10/inbrief/uk0110106n.html

European Industrial Relations Observatory (EIRO) (2002). 'Diageo Concludes Innovative EWC Agreement', http://www.eurofound.europa.eu/eiro/2002/11/feature/ie0211204f.htm

Evans, S. (1987). 'The use of injunctions in industrial disputes May 1984–April 1987'. *British Journal of Industrial Relations*, 25/4: 419–35.

Ewing, K. and Hendy, J. (eds.) (2002). *A Charter of Workers' Rights*. London: Institute of Employment Rights.

Ewing, K. and Hendy, J. (2004). *Submission by the Institute of Employment Rights to the Joint Committee on Human Rights Inquiry into the Concluding Observations of the UN Committee on Economic, Social and Cultural Rights*. London: Institute of Employment Rights.

Fairbrother, P. (1984). *All those in Favour: the Politics of Union Democracy*. London: Pluto.

Fairhurst, D. (2008). 'Am I "bovvered?" Driving a performance culture through to the front line'. *Human Resource Management Journal*, 18/4: 321–6.

Farnham, D. and Giles, L. (1996). 'People management and employment relations', in D. Farnham and S. Horton (eds.), *Managing the New Public Services* (2nd edn). Basingstoke: Macmillan, 112–36.

Farnham, D. and Pimlott, J. (1995). *Understanding Industrial Relations* (4th edn). London: Cassell.

Favretto, I. (2003). *The Long Search for a Third Way: the British Labour Party and Italian Left since 1945*. Basingstoke: Palgrave Macmillan.

Felstead, A. (1991). 'The social organization of the franchise: a case of controlled self-employment'. *Work, Employment, and Society*, 5/1: 37–57.

Felstead, A. and Jewson, N. (1999). 'Flexible labour and non-standard employment: an agenda of issues', in A. Felstead and N. Jewson (eds.), *Global Trends in Flexible Labour*. Basingstoke: Macmillan, 1–20.

Felstead, A. and Jewson, N. (2000). *In Work, at Home*. London: Routledge.

Felstead, A., Jewson, N., Phizacklea, A., and Walters, S. (2002). 'Opportunities to work at home in the context of work–life balance'. *Human Resource Management Journal*, 12/1: 54–76.

Fenley, A. (1986). 'Industrial discipline: a suitable case for treatment'. *Employee Relations*, 8/3: 1–30.

Fenley, A. (1998). 'Models, styles and metaphors: understanding the management of discipline'. *Employee Relations*, 20/4: 349–64.

Ferner, A. (2003). 'Foreign multinationals and industrial relations innovation in Britain', in P. Edwards (ed.), *Industrial Relations* (2nd edn). Oxford: Blackwell, 81–104.

Ferner, A. and Edwards, P. (1995). 'Power and the diffusion of organizational change within multinational corporations'. *European Journal of Industrial Relations*, 1/2: 229–57.

Ferner, A. and Hyman, R. (1998). 'Introduction: towards European industrial relations?', in A. Ferner and R. Hyman (eds.), *Changing Industrial Relations in Europe* (2nd edn). Oxford: Blackwell, xi–xxvi.

Fernie, S. (2005). 'The future of British unions: introduction and conclusions', in S. Fernie and D. Metcalf (eds.), *Trade Unions: Resurgence or Demise?* London: Routledge, 1–18.

Findlay, P. (1993). 'Union recognition and non-unionism: shifting patterns in the electronics industry in Scotland'. *Industrial Relations Journal*, 24/1: 28–43.

Fine, J. (2006). *Worker Centers: Organizing Communities at the Edge of the Dream*. Ithaca NY: ILR Press.

Fisk, C., Mitchell, D., and Erickson, C. (2000). 'Union representation of immigrant janitors in Southern California: economic and legal challenges', in R. Milkman (ed.), *Organizing Immigrants: the Challenge for Unions in Contemporary California*. Ithaca: Cornell University Press, 199–224.

Flanders, A. (1964). *The Fawley Productivity Agreements*. London: Faber and Faber.

Flanders, A. (1974). 'The tradition of voluntarism'. *British Journal of Industrial Relations*, 12/3: 352–70.

Flanders, A. (1975). *Management and Unions*. London: Faber and Faber.

Flanders, A. and Clegg, H. (eds.) (1964). *The System of Industrial Relations in Great Britain*. Oxford: Basil Blackwell.

Fleming, P., Harley, B., and Sewell, G. (2004). 'A little knowledge is a dangerous thing: getting below the surface of the growth of "knowledge work" in Australia'. *Work, Employment, and Society*, 18/4: 725–47.

Forde, C. (2001). 'Temporary arrangements: the activities of employment agencies in the UK'. *Work, Employment and Society*, 15/3: 631–44.

Foster, D. (2007). 'Legal obligation or personal lottery? Employee experiences of disability and the negotiation of adjustments in the public sector workplace'. *Work, Employment, and Society*, 21/1: 67–84.

Foster, D. and Hoggett, P. (1999). 'Change in the Benefits Agency: empowering the exhausted worker?'. *Work, Employment and Society*, 13/1: 19–39.

Foster, D. and Scott, P. (1998). 'Competitive tendering of public services and industrial relations policy: the Conservative agenda under Thatcher and Major, 1979-97'. *Historical Studies in Industrial Relations*, 6: 101–32.

Foster, D. and Scott, P. (2003). 'EMU and public service trade unionism: between states and markets'. *Transfer*, 9/4: 702–21.

Foster, J. and Woolfson, C. (1986). *The Politics of the UCS Work-in*. London: Lawrence and Wishart.

Foulkes, F. (1980). *Personnel Policies in Large Non-union Companies*. Englewood Cliffs, NJ: Prentice Hall.

Fox, A. (1966). *Industrial Sociology and Industrial Relations*. Research Paper No. 3, Royal Commission on Trade Unions and Employers' Associations, London: HMSO.

Fox, A. (1974). *Beyond Contract: Work, Power and Trust Relations*. London: Faber and Faber.

Fox, A. (1985a). *History and Heritage: the Social Origins of the British Industrial Relations System*. London: Allen and Unwin.

Fox, A. (1985b) *Man Mismanagement* (2nd edn). London: Hutchinson.

Fraser, J. and Gold, M. (2001). '"Portfolio workers": autonomy and control among freelance translators'. *Work, Employment and Society*, 15/4: 679–97.

Fredman, S. (2001). 'Equality: a new generation?'. *Industrial Law Journal*, 30/2: 145–68.

Freeman, R. (2005). 'From the Webbs to the web: the contribution of the internet to reviving union fortunes', in S. Fernie and D. Metcalf (eds.), *Trade Unions: Resurgence or Demise?* London: Routledge, 162–84.

Freeman, R. and Pelletier, J. (1990). 'The impact of industrial relations legislation on British union density'. *British Journal of Industrial Relations*, 28/2: 141–64.

Frege, C. (2002). 'A critical assessment of the theoretical and empirical research on German works councils'. *British Journal of Industrial Relations*, 40/2: 221–48.

Frenkel, S. and Kim, S. (2004). 'Corporate codes of labour practice and employment relations in sports shoe contractor factories in South Korea'. *Asia Pacific Journal of Human Resources*, 42/1. 6–31.

Friedman, A. (1977). *Industry and Labour: Class Struggle at Work and Monopoly Capitalism*. London: Macmillan.

Fröbel, F., Heinrichs, J., and Kreye, O. (1980). *The New International Division of Labour*. Cambridge: Cambridge University Press.

Fryer, R. (1973). 'Redundancy, values and public policy'. *Industrial Relations Journal* 4/2: 2–19.

Fryer, R. (1981). 'State, redundancy and the law', in R. Fryer, A. Hunt, D. McBarnet, and B. Moorhouse (eds.), *Law, State, and Society*. London: Croom Helm, 136–59.

Fuller, L. and Smith, V. (1991). 'Consumers' reports: management by customers in a changing economy'. *Work, Employment and Society*, 5/1: 1–16.

Gall, G. (1998). 'The changing relations of production; union derecognition in the UK magazine industry'. *Industrial Relations Journal*, 29/2: 151–61.

Gall, G. (1999). 'A review of strike activity in Western Europe at the end of the second millennium'. *Employee Relations*, 21,4: 357–77.

Gall, G. (2003a). 'Employer opposition to union recognition', in G. Gall (ed.), *Union Organizing*. London: Routledge, 79–96.

Gall, G. (2003b). 'Marxism and industrial relations', P. Ackers and A. Wilkinson (eds.), *Understanding Work and Employment: Industrial Relations in Transition*. Oxford: Oxford University Press, 316–24.

Gall, G. (2003c). *The Meaning of Militancy: Postal Workers and Industrial Relations*. Aldershot: Ashgate.

Gall, G. (ed) (2003d). *Union Organizing: Campaigning for Union Recognition*. London: Routledge.

Gall, G. (2005). 'Union organizing in the "new economy" in Britain'. *Employee Relations*, 27/2: 208–25.

Gall, G. (2007). 'Trade union recognition in Britain: an emerging crisis for trade unions?' *Economic and Industrial Democracy*, 28/1: 78–109.

Gall, G. and McKay, S. (1994). 'Trade union derecognition in Britain 1988–1994'. *British Journal of Industrial Relations*, 32/3: 433–48.

Gall, G. and McKay (1996). 'Research note: injunctions as a legal weapon in industrial disputes'. *British Journal of Industrial Relations*, 34/4: 567–82.

Gall, G. and McKay, S. (1999). 'Developments in union recognition and derecognition in Britain, 1994-1998'. *British Journal of Industrial Relations*, 37/4: 601–14.

Gall, G. and McKay, S. (2001). 'Facing "fairness at work": union perception of employer opposition and response to union recognition'. *Industrial Relations Journal*, 32/2: 94–113.

Gallie, D. (2005). 'Work pressure in Europe 1996–2001: trends and determinants'. *British Journal of Industrial Relations*, 43/4: 351–75.

Gallie, D., White, M., Cheng, Y., and Tomlinson, M. (1998). *Restructuring the Employment Relationship*. Oxford: Clarendon.

Garrahan, P. and Stewart, P. (1992). *The Nissan Enigma*. London: Mansell.

Gatrell, C. (2005). *Hard Labour: the Sociology of Parenthood*. Maidenhead: Open University Press.

Geary, D. (1985). *Policing Industrial Disputes, 1893 to 1985*. Cambridge: Cambridge University Press.

Geary, J. (2003). 'New forms of work organization: still limited, still controlled, but still welcome?', in P. Edwards (ed.), *Industrial Relations: Theory and Practice* (2nd edn). Oxford: Blackwell, 338–67.

Gennard, J. (1984). 'The implications of the Messenger Newspaper Group dispute'. *Industrial Relations Journal*, 15/3: 7–20.

Gennard, J. and Steuer, M. (1971). 'The industrial relations of foreign-owned subsidiaries in the United Kingdom'. *British Journal of Industrial Relations* 9/2: 143–59.

Ghigliani, P. (2005). 'International trade unionism in a globalizing world: a case study of new labour internationalism'. *Economic and Industrial Democracy*, 26/3: 359–82.

Gilbert, D. (1996). 'Strikes in postwar Britain', in C. Wrigley (ed.), *A History of British Industrial Relations 1939–1979*. Cheltenham: Edward Elgar, 128–61.

Gilman, M., Edwards, P. K., Ram, M., and Arrowsmith, J. (2002). 'Pay determination in small firms in the UK: the case of the response to the National Minimum Wage'. *Industrial Relations Journal*, 33/1: 52–67.

Glover, I. and Branine, M. (eds.) (2001). *Ageism in Work and Employment*. Aldershot: Ashgate.

Glover, J. and Kirton, G. (2006). *Women, Employment, and Organizations*. London: Routledge.

Godard, J. (2004). 'A critical assessment of the high-performance paradigm'. *British Journal of Industrial Relations*, 42/2: 349–78.

Godard, J and Delaney, J. (2000). 'Reflections on the "high performance" paradigm's implications for industrial relations as a field'. *Industrial and Labor Relations Review*, 53/3: 482–502.

Goldthorpe, J. (1977). 'Industrial Relations in Great Britain: a critique of reformism', in T. Clarke and L. Clements (eds.), *Trade Unions under Capitalism*. Glasgow: Fontana, 184–224.

Gollan, P. (2003). 'All talk but no voice: employee voice at the Eurotunnel call centre'. *Economic and Industrial Democracy*, 24/4: 509–41.

Gollan, P. (2007). *Employee Representation in Non-union Firms*. London: Sage.

Gollan, P. and Wilkinson, A. (2007). 'Implications of the EU Information and Consultation Directive and the Regulations in the UK—prospects for the future of employee representation'. *International Journal of Human Resource Management*, 18/7: 1145–58.

Goodman, J. (2000). 'Building bridges and settling differences: collective conciliation and arbitration under Acas', in B. Towers and W. Brown (eds.), *Employment Relations in Britain: 25 Years of the Advisory, Conciliation and Arbitration Service*. Oxford: Blackwell, 31–65.

Gospel, H. (1992). *Markets, Firms and the Management of Labour in Modern Britain*. Cambridge: Cambridge University Press.

Gospel, H. and Druker, J. (1998). 'The survival of national bargaining in the electrical contracting industry: a deviant case?'. *British Journal of Industrial Relations*, 36/2: 249–67.

Gospel, H. and Willman, P. (2003). 'Dilemmas in worker representation: information, consultation and negotiation', in H. Gospel and S. Wood (eds.), *Representing Workers*. London: Routledge, 144–63.

Goss, D. (1991). *Small Business and Society*. London: Routledge.

Goss, D. and Adam-Smith, D. (2001). 'Pragmatism and compliance: employer responses to the Working Time Regulations'. *Industrial Relations Journal*, 32/3: 195–208.

Gouldner, A. (1955). *Wildcat Strike*. London: Routledge and Kegan Paul.

Gratton, L., Hope-Hailey, V., Stiles, P., and Truss, C. (1999). *Strategic Human Resource Management: Corporate Rhetoric and Employee Reality*. Oxford: Oxford University Press.

Gray, J. (1998). *False Dawn: the Delusions of Global Capitalism*. London: Granta Books.

Green, F. (2001). 'It's been a hard day's night: the concentration and intensification of work in late twentieth century Britain'. *British Journal of Industrial Relations*, 39/1: 53–80.

Green, F. (2003). 'The demands of work', in R. Dickens, P. Gregg and J. Wadsworth (eds.), *The Labour Market under New Labour*. Basingstoke: Palgrave Macmillan, 137–49.

Green, F. (2006). *Demanding Work*. Princeton NJ: Princeton University Press.

Greene, A-M. (2003). 'Women and industrial relations', in P. Ackers and A. Wilkinson (eds.), *Understanding Work and Employment*. Oxford: Oxford University Press, 305–15.

Greene, A-M., Hogan, J., and Grieco, M. (2003). 'Commentary: e-collectivism and distributed discourse: new opportunities for trade union democracy'. *Industrial Relations Journal*, 34/4: 282–9.

Greenhouse, S. (2008). *The Big Squeeze: Tough Times for the American Worker*. New York: Alfred Knopf.

Greer, I. and Hauptmeier, M. (2008). 'Political entrepreneurs and co-managers: labour transnationalism at four multinational auto companies'. *British Journal of Industrial Relations*, 46/1: 76–97.

Gregg, P., Knight, G., and Wadsworth, J. (2000). 'Heaven knows I'm miserable now: job insecurity in the British labour market', in E. Heery and J. Salmon (eds.), *The Insecure Workforce*. London: Routledge, 39–56.

Griffin, J. (1939). *Strikes: A Study in Quantitative Economics*. New York: Colombia University Press.

Grimshaw, D. (1999). 'Changes in skill mix and pay determination among the nursing workforce in the UK'. *Work, Employment and Society*, 13/2: 295–328.

Grimshaw, D., Earnshaw, J., and Hebson, G. (2003). 'Private sector provision of supply teachers: a case of legal swings and professional roundabouts'. *Journal of Education Policy*, 18/3: 267–88.

Guest, D. (1987). 'Human resource management and industrial relations'. *Journal of Management Studies*, 24/5: 503–21.

Guest, D. and Hoque, K. (1994). 'The good, the bad and the ugly: employment relations in new non-union workplaces'. *Human Resource Management Journal*, 5/1: 1–14.

Guest, D. and Peccei, R. (1998). *The Partnership Company*. London: IPA.

Guest, D. and Peccei, R. (2001). 'Partnership at work: mutuality and the balance of advantage'. *British Journal of Industrial Relations*, 39/2: 207–36.

Guest, D., Brown, W., Peccei, R., and Huxley, K. (2008). 'Does partnership at work increase trust? An analysis based on the 2004 Workplace Employment Relations Survey'. *Industrial Relations Journal*, 39/2: 124–52.

Guest, D., Michie, J., Sheehan, M., and Conway, N. (2000). *Employment Relations, HRM and Business Performance*. London: CIPD.

Gunnigle, P., Turner, T. and D'Art, D. (1998). 'Counterpoising collectivism: performance-related pay and industrial relations in greenfield sites'. *British Journal of Industrial Relations*, 36/4: 565–79.

Hakim, C. (1979). *Occupational Segregation by Sex*. Department of Employment Research Paper No. 9, London: HMSO.

Hakim, C. (1988). 'Self-employment in Britain: recent trends and current issues'. *Work, Employment and Society*, 2/4: 421–50.

Hakim, C. (1996). *Key Issues in Women's Work*. London: The Athlone Press.

Hale, D. (2008). 'Labour disputes in 2007'. *Economic and Labour Market Review*, 2: 18–29.

Hall, M. (1992). 'Behind the European Works Councils Directive: the European Commission's legislative strategy'. *British Journal of Industrial Relations*, 30/4: 547–66.

Hall, M. (1994). 'Industrial relations and the social dimension of European integration: before and after Maastricht', in R. Hyman and A. Ferner (eds.), *New Frontiers in European Industrial Relations*. Oxford: Blackwell, 281–311.

Hall, M. (2006). 'A cool response to the ICE Regulations? Employer and trade union approaches to the new legal framework for information and consultation'. *Industrial Relations Journal*, 37/5: 456–72.

Hall, M. and Edwards, P. (1999). 'Reforming the statutory redundancy consultation procedure'. *Industrial Law Journal*, 28/4: 299–318.

Hall, M. and Marginson, P. (2005). 'Trojan horses or paper tigers? Assessing the significance of European Works Councils', in B. Harley, J. Hyman, and P. Thompson (eds.), *Participation and Democracy at Work*. Basingstoke: Palgrave Macmillan, 204–21.

Hall, M. and Terry, M. (2004). 'The emerging system of statutory worker representation', in G. Healy, E. Heery, P. Taylor, and W. Brown (eds.), *The Future of Worker Representation*. Basingstoke: Palgrave Macmillan, 207–28.

Hall. M., Hutchinson, S., Parker, J., Purcell, J., and Terry, M. (2007). *Implementing Information and Consultation: Early Experience under the ICE Regulations*, Employment Relations Research Series No. 88. London: Department for Business, Enterprise, and Regulatory Reform.

Hall, P. and Soskice, D. (2001). 'An introduction to varieties of capitalism', in P. Hall and D. Soskice (eds.), *Varieties of Capitalism: the Institutional Foundations of Comparative Advantage*. Oxford: Oxford University Press, 1–68.

Hammer, N. (2005). 'International framework agreements: global industrial relations between rights and bargaining'. *Transfer*, 4/5: 511–30.

Handy, C. (1994). *The Empty Raincoat*. London: Hutchinson.

Harbridge, R., Crawford, A., and Hince, K. (2002). 'Unions in New Zealand: what the law giveth …', in P. Fairbrother and G. Griffin (eds.), *Changing Prospects for Trade Unionism*. London: Continuum, 177–99.

Hardy, S. and Adnett, N. (2002). 'The Parental Leave Directive: towards a "family-friendly" social Europe?'. *European Journal of Industrial Relations*, 8/2: 157–72.

Harris, C. (1987). *Redundancy and Recession*. Oxford: Basil Blackwell.

Harris, J. (2007). 'In need of assistance'. The *Guardian*, 2 March.

Harris, L. and Ogbonna, E. (2002). 'Exploring service sabotage: the antecedents, types and consequences of frontline, deviant, antiservice behaviors'. *Journal of Service Research*, 4/3: 163–83.

Hawes, W. (2000). 'Setting the pace or running alongside? ACAS and the changing employment relationship', in B. Towers and W. Brown (eds.), *Employment Relations in Britain: 25 Years of the Advisory, Conciliation and Arbitration Service*. Oxford: Blackwell, 1–30.

Hay, C. (1999). *The Political Economy of New Labour: Labouring under False Pretences?*. Manchester: Manchester University Press.

Haynes, P. and Allen, M. (2001). 'Partnership as union strategy: a preliminary evaluation'. *Employee Relations*, 23/2: 164–93

Hayward, B., Peters, M., Rousseau, N., and Seeds, K. (2004). *Findings from the Survey of Employment Tribunal Applications 2003*. Employment Relations Research Series No. 33, London: Department of Trade and Industry.

Hayward, B., Fong, B., and Thornton, A. (2007). *The Third Work–Life Balance Survey: Main Findings*, Employment Relations Research Series No. 86. London: Department for Business, Enterprise, and Regulatory Reform.

Head, J. and Lucas, R. (2004). 'Employee relations in the non-union hotel industry: a case of "determined opportunism"?'. *Personnel Review*, 33/6: 693–710.

Healy, G. and Kirton, G. (2000). 'Women, power and trade union government in the UK'. *British Journal of Industrial Relations*, 38/3: 343–60.

Healy, G. and Oikelome, F. (2007). 'Equality and diversity actors: a challenge to traditional industrial relations?' *Equal Opportunities International*, 26/1: 44–65.

Healy, G., Bradley, H., and Mukherjee, N. (2004). 'Individualism and collectivism revisited: a study of black and minority ethnic women'. *Industrial Relations Journal*, 35/5: 451–66.

Heery, E. (1996). 'The new new unionism', in I. Beardwell (ed.), *Contemporary Industrial Relations: A Critical Analysis*. Oxford: Oxford University Press, 175–202.

Heery, E. (1997). 'Performance-related pay and trade union de-recognition'. *Employee Relations*, 19/3: 208–21.

Heery, E. (1998a). 'A return to contract? Performance related pay in a public service'. *Work, Employment and Society*, 12/1: 73–95.

Heery, E. (1998b). 'Campaigning for part-time workers'. *Work, Employment and Society*, 12/2: 351–66.

Heery, E. (1998c). 'The relaunch of the Trades Union Congress'. *British Journal of Industrial Relations*, 36/3: 339–60.

Heery, E. (2002). 'Partnership versus organising: alternative futures for British trade unionism'. *Industrial Relations Journal*, 33/1: 20–35.

Heery, E. and Fosh, P. (1990). 'Introduction: whose union? Union power and bureaucracy in the labour movement', in P. Fosh and E. Heery (eds.), *Trade Unions and their Members*. Basingstoke: Macmillan, 1–28.

Heery, E. and Frege, C. (2006). 'New actors in industrial relations'. *British Journal of Industrial Relations*, 44/4: 601–4.

Heery, E. and Kelly, J. (1988). 'Do female representatives make a difference? Women full-time officials and trade union work', *Work, Employment and Society*, 2, 4, 487–505.

Heery, E. and Salmon, J. (eds.) (2000a). *The Insecure Workforce*. London: Routledge.

Heery, E. and Salmon, J. (2000b). 'The insecurity thesis', in E. Heery and J. Salmon, (eds.), *The Insecure Workforce*. London: Routledge, 1–24.

Heery, E. and Simms, M. (2008). 'Constraints on union organising in the United Kingdom'. *Industrial Relations Journal*, 39/1: 24–42.

Heery. E., Abbott, B., and Williams, S. (2009). *Worker Representation through Civil Society Organizations*. Paper presented to the annual conference of the British Universities Industrial Relations Association, Cardiff University, 2–4 July.

Heery, E., Simms, M., Simpson, D., Delbridge, R., and Salmon, J. (2000a). 'Organizing unionism comes to the UK'. *Employee Relations*, 22/1: 38–57.

Heery, E., Simms, M., Delbridge, R., Salmon, J., and Simpson, D. (2000b). 'The TUC's Organising

Academy: an assessment'. *Industrial Relations Journal*, 31/5: 400–15.

Heery, E., Simms, M., Delbridge, R., Salmon, J., and Simpson, D. (2000c). 'Union organizing in Britain: a survey of policy and practice'. *International Journal of Human Resource Management*, 11/5: 986–1007.

Heery, E., Simms, M., Delbridge, R., Salmon, J., and Simpson, D. (2003). 'Trade union recruitment policy in Britain: form and effects', in G. Gall (ed.), *Union Organizing: Campaigning for Union Recognition*. London: Routledge, 56–78.

Heery, E., Bacon, N., Blyton, P., and Fiorito, J. (2008). 'Introduction: the field of industrial relations', in P. Blyton, N. Bacon, J. Fiorito, and E. Heery (eds.), *The SAGE Handbook of Industrial Relations*. London: Sage, 1–32.

Heery, E., Conley, H., Delbridge, R., and Stewart, P. (2004). 'Beyond the enterprise: trade union representation of freelances in the UK'. *Human Resource Management Journal*, 14/2: 20–35

Held, D., McGrew, A., Goldblatt, D., and Perraton, J. (1999). *Global Transformations*. Cambridge: Polity.

Hepple, B. (1992). 'The fall and rise of unfair dismissal', in W. McCarthy (ed.), *Legal Intervention in Industrial Relations: Gains and Losses*. Oxford: Blackwell, 79–102.

Hepple, B. (2005). *Labour Laws and Global Trade*. Oxford: Hart Publishing.

Herod, A., Peck, J., and Wills, J. (2003). 'Geography and industrial relations', in P. Ackers and A. Wilkinson (eds.), *Understanding Work and Employment: Industrial Relations in Transition*. Oxford: Oxford University Press, 176–92.

Hewitt, P. (1993). *About Time*. London: Rivers Oram Press.

Heyes, J. (1997). 'Annualised hours and the "knock": the organisation of working time in a chemicals plant'. *Work, Employment and Society*, 11/1: 65–81.

Heyes, J. and Gray, A. (2001). 'The impact of the National Minimum Wage on the textiles and clothing industry'. *Policy Studies*, 22: 83–98.

Hill, J. and Trist, E. (1953). 'A consideration of industrial accidents as a means of withdrawal from the work situation'. *Human Relations*, 6/4: 357–80.

Hill, S. (1991). 'How do you manage a flexible firm? The total quality model', *Work, Employment and Society*, 5/3: 397–415.

Hill, S. (1995). 'From quality circles to Total Quality Management', in A. Wilkinson and H. Willmott (eds.), *Making Quality Critical*. London: Routledge, 33–53.

Hinton, J. (1973). *The First Shop Stewards' Movement*. London: Allen and Unwin.

Hirst, P. and Thompson, G. (1999). *Globalization in Question* (2nd edn). Cambridge: Polity.

HM Treasury and Department of Trade and Industry (DTI) (2003). *Balancing Work and Family Life: Enhancing Choice and Support for Parents*. London: HM Treasury/DTI.

Hochschild, A. (1983). *The Managed Heart*. London: University of California Press.

Holgate, J. (2005). 'Organizing migrant workers: a case study of working conditions and unionization in a London sandwich factory'. *Work, Employment, and Society*, 19/3: 463–80.

Holliday, R. (1995). *Investigating Small Firms. Nice Work?*. London: Routledge.

Holt, H. and Grainger, H. (2005). *Results of the Second Flexible Working Employee Survey*. DTI Employment Relations Research Series No. 39. London: DTI.

Hood, C. (1991). 'A public management for all seasons?'. *Public Administration*, 69/1: 3–19.

Hoque, K. (1999). 'New approaches to HRM in the UK hotel industry'. *Human Resource Management Journal*, 9/2: 64–76.

Hoque, K. and Noon, M. (2004). 'Equal opportunities policy and practice in Britain: evaluating the "empty shell" hypothesis'. *Work, Employment and Society*, 18/3: 481–506.

House of Commons Employment Committee (1994). *The Future of the Unions*. Third Report Volume II, Minutes of Evidence, London: HMSO.

Howell, C. (2004). 'Is there a third way for industrial relations?'. *British Journal of Industrial Relations*, 42/1: 1–22.

Howell, C. (2005). *Trade Unions and the State*. Princeton NJ: Princeton University Press.

Hudson, M. (2002). 'Flexibility and the reorganisation of work', in B. Burchell, D. Ladipo, and F. Wilkinson (eds.), *Job Insecurity and Work Intensification*. London: Routledge, 39–60.

Hunter, L., McGregor, A., MacInnes, J., and Sproull, A. (1993). 'The "flexible firm": strategy and segmentation'. *British Journal of Industrial Relations*, 31/3: 383–407.

Huselid, M. (1995). 'The impact of human resource management practices on turnover, productivity, and corporate financial performance'. *Academy of Management Journal*, 38/3: 635–72.

Hutton, J. (2008). 'Next steps in fairness at work'. Speech to the Fabian Society, 29 May. http://www.berr.gov.uk/aboutus/ministerialteam/speeches/page46408.html

Huzzard, T. and Docherty, P. (2005). 'Between global and local: eight European Works Councils in retrospect and prospect'. *Economic and Industrial Democracy*, 26/4: 541–68.

Hyman, J. and Marks, A. (2008). 'Frustrated ambitions: the reality of balancing work and life for call centre employees', in C. Warhurst, D. Eikhof, and A. Haunschild (eds.), *Work Less, Live More: Critical Analysis of the Work–Life Boundary*. Basingstoke: Palgrave Macmillan, 191–209.

Hyman, J. and Mason, B. (1995). *Managing Employee Involvement and Participation*. London: Sage.

Hyman, J. and Summers, J. (2004). 'Lacking balance? Work–life employment practices in the modern economy'. *Personnel Review*, 33/4: 418–29.

Hyman, J., Baldry, C., Scholarios, D., and Bunzel, D. (2003). 'Work–life imbalance in call centres and software development'. *British Journal of Industrial Relations*, 41/2: 215–39.

Hyman, R. (1971). *The Workers' Union*. Oxford: Clarendon Press.

Hyman, R. (1972). *Disputes Procedure in Action*. London: Heinemann.

Hyman, R. (1975). *Industrial Relations: a Marxist Introduction*. London: Macmillan.

Hyman, R. (1977). *Strikes* (2nd edn). Glasgow: Fontana/Collins.

Hyman, R. (1987). 'Strategy or structure? Capital, labour and control'. *Work, Employment and Society*, 1/1: 25–55.

Hyman, R. (1989). *The Political Economy of Industrial Relations*. Basingstoke: Macmillan.

Hyman, R. (1991). '*Plus ça change*? The theory of production and the production of theory', in A. Pollert (ed.), *Farewell to Flexibility?*. Oxford: Blackwell, 259–83.

Hyman, R. (1994a). 'Introduction: economic restructuring, market liberalism and the future of national industrial relations systems', R. Hyman, A. Ferner (eds.), *New Frontiers in European Industrial Relations*. Oxford, Blackwell, 1–14.

Hyman, R. (1994b). 'Changing trade union identities and strategies', in R. Hyman and A. Ferner (eds.), *New Frontiers in European Industrial Relations*. Oxford: Blackwell, 108–39.

Hyman, R. (1996). 'Is there a case for statutory works councils in Britain?', in A. McColgan (ed.), *The Future of Labour Law*. London: Cassell, 64–84.

Hyman, R. (1999). 'Imagined solidarities: can trade unions resist globalization?', in P. Leisink (ed.), *Globalization and Labour Relations*. Cheltenham: Edward Elgar, 94–115.

Hyman, R. (2001a). 'The Europeanisation—or the erosion—of industrial relations?'. *Industrial Relations Journal*, 32/4: 280–94.

Hyman, R. (2001b). *Understanding European Trade Unionism: Between Market, Class and Society*. London: Sage.

Hyman, R. (2003). 'The historical evolution of British industrial relations', in P. Edwards (ed.), *Industrial Relations* (2nd edn). Oxford: Blackwell, 37–57.

Hyman, R. (2005). 'Trade unions and the politics of the European Social Model'. *Economic and Industrial Democracy*, 26/1: 9–40.

Incomes Data Services (IDS) (2002). 'Company Councils'. *IDS Study*, 730.

Incomes Data Services (IDS) (2003). 'The gender pay gap'. *IDS Report*, 873: 11–16.

Incomes Data Services (IDS) (2004). 'Diversity at work 2004'. *Diversity at Work*, 1: 6–13.

Industrial Relations Services (IRS) (1998). 'What do employers' associations offer to members?'. *Employment Trends*, 653: 11–16.

Industrial Relations Services (IRS) (1999). 'Partnership delivers the goods at Tesco'. *Employment Trends*, 686: 4–9.

Industrial Relations Services (IRS) (2001). 'We don't need no litigation'. *Employment Trends*, 719: 4–16.

Ingram, P., Wadsworth, J., and Brown, D. (1999). 'Free to Choose? Dimensions of private-sector wage determination, 1979–1994'. *British Journal of Industrial Relations*, 37/1: 33–49.

International Confederation of Free Trade Unions (ICFTU) (1996). *Behind the Wire: Anti Union Repression in the Export Processing Zones*. Brussels: ICFTU.

International Confederation of Free Trade Unions (ICFTU) (2004). *A Trade Union Guide to Globalisation* (2nd edn). Brussels: ICFTU.

International Labour Organisation (ILO) (2005). *Rules of the Game: a Brief Introduction to International Labour Standards*. Geneva: ILO.

International Trade Union Confederation (ITUC) (2008). *Annual Survey of Violations of Trade Union Rights*. Brussels: ITUC.

Ironside, M., Seifert, R., and Sinclair, J. (1997). 'Teacher union responses to education reforms: job regulation and the enforced growth of informality'. *Industrial Relations Journal*, 28/2: 120–35.

Jacobi, O., Keller, B., and Müller-Jentsch, W. (1998). 'Germany: facing new challenges', in A. Ferner and R. Hyman (eds.), *Changing Industrial Relations in Europe*. Oxford: Blackwell, 190–238.

Jefferys, S. (2000). 'A "Copernican Revolution" in French industrial relations: are the times a' changing?'. *British Journal of Industrial Relations*, 38/2: 241–60.

Jefferys, S. (2003). *Liberté, Égalité and Fraternité at Work: Changing French Employment Relations*. Basingstoke: Palgrave Macmillan.

Jenkins, S. and Delbridge, R. (2007). 'Disconnected workplaces: interests and identities in the "high performance" factory', in S. Bolton and M. Houlihan (eds.), *Searching for the Human in Human Resource Management*. Basingstoke: Palgrave Macmillan, 195–218.

Jenkins, S., Martinez Lucio, M., and Noon, M. (2002). 'Return to gender: an analysis of women's disadvantage in postal work'. *Gender, Work and Organization*, 9/1: 81–104.

Jewson, N. and Mason, D. (1986). 'The theory and practice of equal opportunities policies: liberal and radical approaches'. *Sociological Review*, 34/2: 307–34.

Jewson, N., Mason, D., Drewett, A., and Rossiter, W. (1995). *Formal Equal Opportunities Policies and Employment Best Practice*. Research Series No. 69, London: Department for Education and Employment.

Jordan, B. (1985). *The State: Authority and Autonomy*. Oxford: Blackwell.

Kahn-Freund, O. (1964). 'Legal framework'. in A. Flanders and H. Clegg (eds.), *The System of Industrial Relations in Great Britain*. Oxford: Basil Blackwell, 42–127.

Kahn-Freund, O. (1977). *Labour and the Law* (2nd edn). London: Stevens.

Kalman, D. (1999). 'Collective wisdom'. *People Management*, 25 February: 37–43.

Kandola, B. and Fullerton, J. (1994). *Managing the Mosaic: Diversity in Action*. London: IPD.

Katz, H. and Darbishire, O. (2000). *Converging Divergences: Worldwide Changes in Employment Systems*. Ithaca: ILR Cornell University Press.

Katz, L. and Krueger, A. (1992). 'The effects of the minimum wage on the fast food industry'. *Industrial and Labor Relations Review*, 46/1: 6–21.

Kay, J. (2003). *The Truth about Markets: their Genius, their Limits, their Follies*. London: Allen Lane.

Keller, B. (2003). 'The European social partners: projects and future perspectives', in D. Foster and P. Scott (eds.), *Trade Unions in Europe: Meeting the Challenge*. Brussels: Peter Lang, 115–43.

Keller, B. and Sörries, B. (1999). 'The new European social dialogue: old wine in new bottles?'. *Journal of European Social Policy*, 9/2: 111–25.

Kelly, J. (1998). *Rethinking Industrial Relations*. London: Routledge.

Kelly, J. (2004). 'Social partnership agreements in Britain: labor cooperation and compliance'. *Industrial Relations*, 43/1: 267–92.

Kelly, J. (2005). 'Social partnership agreements in Britain', in M. Stuart and M. Martinez Lucio (eds.), *Partnership and Modernisation in Employment Relations*. London: Routledge, 188–209.

Kelly, J. and Badigannavar, V. (2004). 'Union organizing', in J. Kelly and P. Willman (eds.), *Union Organization and Activity*. London: Routledge, 32–50.

Kelly, J. and Heery, E. (1994). *Working for the Union: British Trade Union Officers*. Cambridge: Cambridge University Press.

Kelsey, J. (1995). *Economic Fundamentalism*. London: Pluto.

Kerr, C. and Siegel, A. (1954). 'The inter-industry propensity to strike', in A. Kornhauser, R. Dubin, and A. Ross (eds.), *Industrial Conflict*. New York: McGraw-Hill, 189–212.

Kerr, C., Dunlop, J., Harbison, F., and Myers, C. (1962). *Industrialism and Industrial Man*. London: Heinemann.

Kersley, B., Alpin, C., Forth, J., Bryson, A., Bewley, H., Dix, G., and Oxenbridge, S. (2005). *Inside the Workplace: First Findings from the 2004 Workplace Employment Relations Survey*. London: Department for Trade and Industry.

Kersley, B., Alpin, C., Forth, J., Bryson, A., Bewley, H., Dix, G., and Oxenbridge, S. (2006). *Inside the Workplace: Findings from the 2004 Workplace Employment Relations Survey*. London: Routledge.

Kessler, I. (1994). 'Performance related pay: contrasting approaches'. *Industrial Relations Journal*, 25/2: 122–35.

Kessler, I. (2000). 'Remuneration systems', in S. Bach and K. Sisson (eds.), *Personnel Management* (3rd edn). Oxford: Blackwell, 264–86.

Kessler, I. and Purcell, J. (1995). 'Individualism and collectivism in theory and practice: management style and the design of pay systems', in P. Edwards (ed.), *Industrial Relations: Theory and Practice in Britain*. Oxford: Blackwell, 337–67.

Kessler, S. (1993). 'Procedures and third parties'. *British Journal of Industrial Relations*, 31/2: 211–25.

Kessler, S. (1994). 'Incomes policy'. *British Journal of Industrial Relations*, 32/2: 181–99.

Kessler, S. and Bayliss, F. (1998). *Contemporary British Industrial Relations* (3rd edn). Basingstoke: Macmillan.

Kingsnorth, P. (2003). *One No, Many Yeses*. London: Free Press.

Kirkpatrick, I. and Hoque, K. (2006). 'A retreat from permanent employment? Accounting for the rise of professional agency work in UK public services'. *Work, Employment, and Society*, 20/4: 649–66.

Kirkpatrick, I., Ackroyd, S., and Walker, R. (2004). *The New Managerialism and Public Service Professions*. Basingstoke: Palgrave Macmillan.

Kirton, G. (1999). 'Sustaining and developing women's trade union activism: a gendered project?'. *Gender, Work and Organization*, 6/4: 213–23.

Kirton, G. and Greene, A-M. (2002). 'The dynamics of positive action in UK trade unions: the case of women and black members'. *Industrial Relations Journal*, 33/2: 157–72.

Kirton, G. and Greene, A-M. (2005). *The Dynamics of Managing Diversity: a Critical Approach* (2nd edn). Elsevier Butterworth-Heinemann.

Kirton, G. and Healy, G. (1999). 'Transforming union women: the role of women trade union officials in union renewal'. *Industrial Relations Journal*, 30/1: 31–45.

Klein, N. (2000). *No Logo*. London: Flamingo.

Knell, J. (1999). *Partnership at Work*. London: Department of Trade and Industry.

Knight, K. and Latreille, P. (2000). 'Discipline, dismissals and complaints to employment tribunals'. *British Journal of Industrial Relations*, 38/4: 533–55.

Knowles, K. (1952). *Strikes—A Study in Industrial Conflict*. Oxford: Basil Blackwell.

Knox, B. and McKinlay, A (2003). '"Organizing the unorganised": union recruitment strategies in American transnationals, c.1945–1977', in G. Gall (ed.), *Union Organizing*. London: Routledge, 19–38.

Kochan, T., Katz, H., and McKersie, R. (1986). *The Transformation of American Industrial Relations*. New York: Basic Books.

Kochan, T. A. and Osterman, P. (1994). *The Mutual Gains Enterprise*. Boston: Harvard University Press.

Kodz, J., Harper, H., and Dench, S. (2002). *Work–Life Balance: Beyond the Rhetoric*. Institute of Employment Studies Report No.384, Brighton: IES.

Kodz, J., Davis, S., Lain, D., Strebler, M., Rick, J., Bates, P., Cummings, J., and Meager, N. (2003). *Working Long Hours: a Review of the Evidence (Volume 1—Main Report)*. Employment Relations Research Series No. 16, London: DTI.

Korczynski, M. (2002). *Human Resource Management in Service Work*. Basingstoke: Palgrave.

Kumar, K. (1986). *Prophecy and Progress: the Sociology of Industrial and Post-industrial Society*. Harmondsworth: Penguin.

Kumar, K. (1995). *From Post-industrial to Postmodern Society: New Theories of the Contemporary World*. Oxford: Blackwell.

Kuruvilla, S. and Verma, A. (2006). 'International labor standards, soft regulation, and national government roles'. *Journal of Industrial Relations*, 48/1: 41–58.

Langlois, M. and Lucas, R. (2005). 'The adaptation of hospitality and retail firms to the NMW: a focus on the impact of age-related clauses'. *Industrial Relations Journal*, 36/1: 77–92.

Lashley, C. (2000). 'Empowerment through involvement: a case study of TGI Fridays restaurants'. *Personnel Review*, 29/6: 799–815.

Latreille, P., Latreille, J., and Knight, K. (2007). 'Employment tribunals and Acas: evidence from a survey of representatives'. *Industrial Relations Journal*, 38/2: 136–54.

Leadbeater, C. (1999). *Living on Thin Air*. London: Viking.

Lecher, W., Rüb, S., and Weiner, K-P. (2001). *European Works Councils: Development, Types, and Networking*. Aldershot: Ashgate.

Ledwith, S., Colgan, F., Joyce, P., and Hayes, M. (1990). 'The making of women trade union leaders'. *Industrial Relations Journal*, 21/2: 112–25.

Legge, K. (2001). 'Silver bullet or spent round? Assessing the meaning of the "high commitment management"/ performance relationship', in J. Storey (ed.), *Human Resource Management: a Critical Text* (2nd edn). London: Thomson Learning, 21–36.

Legge, K. (2005). *Human Resource Management: Rhetoric and Realities* (2nd edn). Basingstoke: Palgrave Macmillan.

Leidner, R. (2002). 'Fast-food work in the United States', in T. Royle and B. Towers (eds.), *Labour Relations in the Global Fast-Food Industry*. London: Routledge, 8 29.

Leisink, P. (1999). 'Introduction', in P. Leisink (ed.), *Globalization and Labour Relations*. Cheltenham: Edward Elgar, 1–24.

Leisink, P. (2002). 'The European sectoral social dialogue and the graphical industry'. *European Journal of Industrial Relations*, 8/1: 101–17.

Leopold, J. (1986). 'Trade union political funds: a retrospective analysis'. *Industrial Relations Journal*, 17/4: 287–303.

Leopold, J. (1997). 'Trade unions, political fund ballots and the Labour party'. *British Journal of Industrial Relations*, 35/1: 23–38.

Leopold, J. (2006). 'Trade unions and the third round of political fund balloting'. *Industrial Relations Journal*, 37/3: 190–208.

Lewis, P. (1993). *The Successful Management of Redundancy*. Oxford: Blackwell.

Lewis, S. (1997). '"Family friendly" employment policies: a route to changing organizational culture or playing about at the margins?'. *Gender, Work and Organization*, 4/1: 13–23.

Liff, S. (1997). 'Two routes to managing diversity: individual differences or social group characteristics?'. *Employee Relations*, 19/1: 11–26.

Liff, S. (1999). 'Diversity and equal opportunities: room for a constructive compromise?'. *Human Resource Management Journal*, 9/1: 65–75.

Liff, S. (2003). 'The industrial relations of a diverse workforce', in P. Edwards (ed.), *Industrial Relations* (2nd edn). Oxford: Blackwell, 420–46.

Liff, S. and Wacjman, J. (1996). '"Sameness" and "difference" revisited: which way forward for equal opportunity initiatives?'. *Journal of Management Studies*, 33/1: 79–94.

Liff, S. and Ward, K. (2001). 'Distorted views through the glass ceiling: the construction of women's understandings of promotion and senior management positions'. *Gender, Work and Organization*, 8/1: 19–36.

Lillie, N. and Martinez Lucio, M. (2004). 'International trade union revitalization: the role of national union approaches', in C. Frege and J. Kelly (eds.), *Varieties of Unionism*. Oxford: Oxford University Press, 159–80.

Littleton, S. (1992). *The Wapping Dispute*. Aldershot: Avebury.

Lloyd, C. (2001). 'What do employee councils do? The impact of non-union forms of representation on trade union organisation'. *Industrial Relations Journal*, 32/4: 313–27.

Locke, R., Kochan, T., Romis, M., and Qin, F. (2007). 'Beyond corporate codes of conduct: work organization and labour standards at Nike's suppliers'. *International Labour Review*, 146/1–2: 21–40.

Lockwood, D. (1958). *The Black-Coated Worker*. London: Allen and Unwin.

Logan, J. (2006). 'The union avoidance industry in the United States'. *British Journal of Industrial Relations*, 44/4: 651–75.

Loveday, B., Williams, S., and Scott, P. (2008). 'Workforce modernization in the police service: prospects for reform?' *Personnel Review*, 37/4: 361–74.

Low Pay Commission (LPC) (1998). *The National Minimum Wage: First Report of the Low Pay Commission*. London: The Stationery Office.

Low Pay Commission (LPC) (2000). *The National Minimum Wage: The Story so Far*. Second Report of the Low Pay Commission, London: The Stationery Office.

Low Pay Commission (LPC) (2001a). *The National Minimum Wage: Making a Difference*. Third Report (Volume One) of the Low Pay Commission, London: The Stationery Office.

Low Pay Commission (LPC) (2001b). *The National Minimum Wage: Making a Difference, the Next Steps*. Third Report (Volume Two) of the Low Pay Commission, London: The Stationery Office.

Low Pay Commission (LPC) (2004). *The National Minimum Wage: Protecting Young Workers*. Fifth report of the Low Pay Commission, London: HMSO.

Lucas, R. and Radiven, N. (1998). 'After wages councils: minimum pay and practice'. *Human Resource Management Journal*, 8/4: 5–19.

Luce, S. (2004). *Fighting for a Living Wage*. New York: Cornell University Press.

Ludlum, S. and Taylor, A. (2003). 'The political representation of the labour interest'. *British Journal of Industrial Relations*, 41/4: 727–49.

Lunn, K. (1999). 'Complex encounters: trade unions, immigration and racism', in J. McIlroy, N. Fishman, and A. Campbell (eds.), *British Trade Unions and Industrial Politics Volume Two: the High Tide of Trade Unionism, 1964–79*. Aldershot: Ashgate, 70–90.

Lupton, T. (1963). *On the Shop Floor*. Oxford: Pergamon.

MacDonald, R. and Coffield, F. (1991). *Risky Business? Youth and the Enterprise Culture*. Basingstoke: Falmer Press.

MacDuffie, J-P. (1995). 'Human resource bundles and manufacturing performance: organizational logic and flexible production systems in the world auto industry'. *Industrial and Labor Relations Review*, 48/2: 195–221.

McArdle, L., Rowlinson, M., Proctor, S., Hammond, J., and Forrester, P. (1995) 'Total Quality Management and participation: employee empowerment, or the enhancement of exploitation?', in A. Wilkinson and H. Willmott (eds.), *Making Quality Critical*. London: Routledge, 156–72.

McBride, A. (2000). 'Promoting representation of women within UNISON', in M. Terry (ed.), *Redefining Public Sector Unionism: UNISON and the Future of Trade Unions*. London: Routledge, 100–18.

McBride, A. (2001). *Gender Democracy in Trade Unions*. Aldershot: Ashgate.

McCarthy, W. (1964). *The Closed Shop in Britain*. Oxford: Basil Blackwell.

McColgan, A. (1997). *Just Wages for Women*. Oxford: Clarendon.

McColgan, A. (2000). 'Missing the point? The Part-time Workers (Prevention of Less Favourable Treatment) Regulations 2000 (SI 2000, No. 1551)'. *Industrial Law Journal*, 29/3: 260–7.

McGovern, P., Hill, S., Mills, C., and White, M. (2007). *Market, Class, and Employment*. Oxford University Press.

McIlroy, J. (1991). *The Permanent Revolution? Conservative Law and the Trade Unions*. Nottingham: Spokesman.

McIlroy, J. (1998). 'The enduring alliance? Trade unions and the making of New Labour'. *British Journal of Industrial Relations*, 36/4: 537–64.

McIlroy, J. (1999). 'Unfinished business—the reform of strike legislation in Britain'. *Employee Relations*, 21/6: 521–39.

McIlroy, J. (2009). 'Under stress but still enduring: the contentious alliance in the age of Tony Blair and Gordon Brown', in G. Daniels and J. McIlroy (eds.), *Trade Unions in a Neo Liberal World: British Trade Unions under New Labour*. Abingdon: Routledge, 165–201.

McIlroy, J. and Daniels, G. (2009). 'An anatomy of British trade unionism since 1997: organization, structure and factionalism', in G. Daniels and J. McIlroy (eds.), *Trade Unions in a Neo Liberal World: British Trade Unions under New Labour*, Abingdon: Routledge, 127–64.

McIntosh, I. and Broderick, J. (1996). 'Neither one thing nor the other: compulsory competitive tendering and Southburg Cleansing services'. *Work, Employment, and Society*, 10/3: 413–30.

McIvor, A. (1996). *Organised Capital*. Cambridge: Cambridge University Press.

McKay, S. (2001). 'Annual review article 2000. Between flexibility and regulation: rights, equality and protection at work'. *British Journal of Industrial Relations*, 39/2: 285–303.

McKee, L., Mauthner, N., and Maclean, C. (2000). '"Family friendly" policies and practices in the oil and gas industry: employers' perspectives'. *Work, Employment and Society*, 14/3: 557–71.

McKinlay, A. and McNulty, D. (1992). 'At the cutting edge of new realism: the engineers' 35 hour week campaign'. *Industrial Relations Journal*, 23/3: 205–13.

McLoughlin, I. and Gourlay, S. (1992). 'Enterprises without unions: the management of employment relations in non-union firms'. *Journal of Management Studies*, 29/5: 669–91.

McLoughlin. I. And Gourlay, S. (1994). *Enterprise without Unions*. Buckingham: Open University Press.

Machin, S. (1999). 'Wage inequality in the 1970s, 1980s and 1990s', in P. Gregg and J. Wadsworth (eds.), *The State of Working Britain*. Manchester: Manchester University Press, 185–205.

Machin, S. (2000). 'Union decline in Britain'. *British Journal of Industrial Relations*, 38/4: 631–45.

Machin, S. (2003). 'Wage inequality since 1975', in R. Dickens, P. Gregg, and J. Wadsworth (eds.), *The Labour Market under New Labour*. Basingstoke: Palgrave Macmillan, 191–200.

Machin, S. and Wilson, J. (2004). 'Minimum wages in a low-wage labour market: care homes on the UK'. *The Economic Journal*, 114: C102–9.

MacInnes, J. (2008). 'Work–life balance: three terms in search of a definition', in C. Warhurst, D. Eikhof, and A. Haunschild (eds.), *Work Less, Live More: Critical Analysis of the Work–Life Boundary*. Basingstoke: Palgrave Macmillan, 44–61.

Macmillan, J. (1999). 'Employment tribunals: philosophies and practicalities'. *Industrial Law Journal*, 28/1: 33–56.

Mankelow, R. (2002). 'The organisational costs of job insecurity and work intensification', in B. Burchell, D. Ladipo, and F. Wilkinson (eds.), *Job Insecurity and Work Intensification*. London: Routledge, 137–53.

Marchington, M. (1989). 'Joint consultation in practice', in K. Sisson (ed.), *Personnel Management*. Oxford: Basil Blackwell, 378–402.

Marchington, M. (1994). 'The dynamics of joint consultation', in K. Sisson (ed.), *Personnel Management* (2nd edn). Oxford: Blackwell, 662–93.

Marchington, M. and Harrison, E. (1991). 'Customers, competitors and choice: employee relations in food retailing'. *Industrial Relations Journal*, 22/4: 286–99.

Marchington, M. and Parker, P. (1990). *Changing Patterns of Employee Relations*. Hemel Hempstead: Harvester Wheatsheaf.

Marchington, M. and Wilkinson, A. (2000). 'Direct participation', in S. Bach and K. Sisson (eds.), *Personnel Management* (3rd edn). Oxford: Blackwell, 340–64.

Marchington, M. and Wilkinson, A. (2005). 'Direct participation and involvement', in S. Bach (ed.), *Managing Human Resources*. Oxford: Blackwell, 398–423.

Marchington, M., Goodman, J., Wilkinson, A., and Ackers, P. (1992). *New Developments in Employee Involvement*. Research Series No. 2, Sheffield: Employment Department.

Marginson, P. and Sisson, K. (1994). 'The structure of transnational capital in Europe: the emerging Euro-company and its implications for industrial relations', in R. Hyman and A. Ferner (eds.), *New Frontiers in European Industrial Relations*. Oxford: Blackwell, 15–51.

Marginson, P., Edwards, P., Martin, R., Purcell, J., and Sisson, K. (1988). *Beyond the Workplace: Managing Industrial Relations in the Multi-establishment Enterprise*. Oxford: Basil Blackwell.

Marginson, P., Armstrong, P., Edwards, P., and Purcell, J. (1995). 'Managing labour in the global corporation: a survey-based analysis of multinationals operating in the UK'. *International Journal of Human Resource Management*, 6/3: 702–19.

Marginson, P., Gilman, M., Jacobi, O., and Krieger, H. (1998). *Negotiating European Works Councils: an Analysis of Agreements under Article 13*. Luxembourg: Office of Official Publications of the European Community.

Marks, A., Findlay, P., Hine, J., McKinlay, A., and Thompson, P. (1998). 'The politics of partnership? Innovation in employment relations in the Scottish spirits industry'. *British Journal of Industrial Relations*, 36/2: 209–26.

Marlow, S. (2002). 'Regulating labour management in small firms'. *Human Resource Management Journal*, 12/3: 25–43.

Mars, G. (1982). *Cheats at Work*. London: Allen and Unwin.

Mars, G. and Mitchell, P. (1976). *Room for Reform? A Case Study of Industrial Relations in the Hotel Industry*. Milton Keynes: Open University Press.

Marsden, D. (1999). *A Theory of Employment Systems*. Oxford: Oxford University Press.

Marsden, D. and French, S. (1998). *What a Performance: Performance Related Pay in the Public Services*. London School of Economics: Centre for Economic Performance.

Marsh, D. (1992). *The New Politics of British Trade Unionism*. Basingstoke: Macmillan.

Martin, A. and Ross, G. (1999). 'In the line of fire: the Europeanization of Labor representation', in A. Martin and G. Ross (eds.), *The Brave New World of European Labor*. Oxford: Berghahn, 312–67.

Martin, G. and Beaumont, P. (1999). 'Co-ordination and control of human resource management in multinational firms: the case of Cashco'. *International Journal of Human Resource Management*, 10/1: 21–42.

Martin, R. (1985). 'Union democracy: an exploratory framework', in W. McCarthy (ed.), *Trade Unions* (2nd edn). Harmondsworth: Penguin, 222–42.

Martin, R. (1992). *Bargaining Power*. Oxford: Clarendon.

Martin, R., Smith, P., Fosh, P., Morris, H., and Undy, R. (1995). 'The legislative reform of union government 1979-94'. *Industrial Relations Journal*, 26/2: 146–55.

Mathieson, H. and Corby, S. (1999) 'Trade unions: the challenge of individualism', in S. Corby and G. White (eds.), *Employee Relations in the Public Services: Themes and Issues*. London: Routledge, 199–223.

Mercer, S. and Notley, R. (2008). *Trade Union Membership 2007*. London: Department for Business, Enterprise, and Regulatory Reform.

Metcalf, D. (1991). 'British unions: dissolution or resurgence?'. *Oxford Review of Economic Policy*, 7/1: 18–32.

Metcalf, D. (1999). 'The British National Minimum Wage'. *British Journal of Industrial Relations*, 37/2: 171–201

Metcalf, D. (2005). 'Trade unions: resurgence or perdition? An economic analysis?', in S. Fernie and D. Metcalf (eds.), *Trade Unions: Resurgence or Demise?* London: Routledge, 83–117.

Metcalf, D. (2008). 'Why has the British National Minimum Wage had little or no impact on employment?' *Journal of Industrial Relations*, 50/3: 489–512.

Middlemas, K. (1979). *Politics in Industrial Society*. London: Andre Deutsch.

Miliband, R. (1972). *Parliamentary Socialism*. London: Merlin.

Miliband, R. (1973). *The State in Capitalist Society*. London: Quartet.

Milkman, R. (ed.) (2000). *Organizing Immigrants: the Challenge for Unions in Contemporary California*. Ithaca: Cornell University Press.

Milne, S. (2004). *The Enemy Within: Thatcher's Secret War against the Miners*, (2nd edn). London: Verso.

Milner, S. (1993). 'Overtime bans and strikes'. *Industrial Relations Journal*, 24/3: 201–10.

Millward, N. (1994). *The New Industrial Relations?*. Poole: Policy Studies Institute.

Millward, N., Bryson, A., and Forth, J. (2000). *All Change at Work*. London: Routledge.

Millward, N., Stevens, D., Smart, N., and Hawes, W. (1992). *Workplace Industrial Relations in Transition*. Aldershot: Dartmouth.

Minkin, L. (1991). *The Contentious Alliance: Trade Unions and the Labour Party*. Edinburgh: Edinburgh University Press.

Moody, K. (1997). *Workers in a Lean World*. London: Verso.

Moore, S. (2004). 'Union mobilization and employer counter-mobilization in the statutory recognition process', in J. Kelly and P. Willman (eds.), *Union Organization and Activity*. London: Routledge, 7–31.

Morgan, G. (1997). *Images of Organization* (2nd edn). London: Sage.

Morgan, P., Allinton, N., and Heery, E. (2000). 'Employment insecurity in the public services', in E. Heery and J. Salmon (eds.), *The Insecure Workforce*. London: Routledge, 78–111.

Moule, C. (1998). 'Regulation of work in small firms: a view from the inside'. *Work, Employment and Society*, 12/4: 635–53.

Mueller, F. and Purcell, J. (1992). 'The europeanization of manufacturing and the decentralization of bargaining: multinational management strategies in the European automobile industry'. *International Journal of Human Resource Management*, 3/1: 15–24.

Mukherjee, S. (1973). *Through No Fault of Their Own: Systems for Handling Redundancies in Britain, France and Germany*. London: PEP.

Mulholland, K. (2004). 'Workplace resistance in an Irish call centre: slammin', scammin' smokin' an' leavin''. *Work, Employment, and Society*, 18/4: 709–24.

Muller-Camen, M., Almond, P., Gunnigle, P., Quintanilla, J., and Tempel, A. (2001). 'Between home and host country: multinationals and employment relations in Europe'. *Industrial Relations Journal*, 32/5: 435–48.

Müller-Jentsch, W. (1995). 'Germany: from collective voice to co-management', in J. Rogers and W. Streeck (eds.), *Works Councils: Consultation, Representation and Cooperation in Industrial Relations*. Chicago: University of Chicago Press, 53–78.

Mumford, K. (1996). 'Arbitration and Acas in Britain: a historical perspective'. *British Journal of Industrial Relations*, 34/2: 287–305.

Munck, R. (1988). *The New International Labour Studies: An Introduction*. London: Zed Books.

Munro, A. (1999). *Women, Work and Trade Unions*. London: Mansell.

Munro, A. and Rainbird, H. (2000). 'The new unionism and the new bargaining agenda: UNISON-employer partnerships on workplace learning in Britain'. *British Journal of Industrial Relations*, 38/2: 223–40.

Nash, D. (2006). 'Recent industrial relations developments in the United Kingdom: continuity and change under New Labour 1997-2005'. *Journal of Industrial Relations*, 48/3: 401–14.

Neathy, F. and Arrowsmith, J. (2001). *The Implementation of the Working Time Regulations*. Employment Relations Research Series No. 11, London: DTI.

Ngai, P. (2005). 'Global production, company codes of conduct, and labor conditions in China: a case study of two factories'. *The China Journal*, 54: 101–13.

Nichols, T. (1986). *The British Worker Question*. London: Routledge and Kegan Paul.

Nichols, T. (1997). *The Sociology of Industrial Injury*. London: Mansell.

Nichols, T. and Beynon, H. (1977). *Living with Capitalism*. London: Routledge and Kegan Paul

Nolan, J. (2002). 'The intensification of everyday life', in B. Burchell, D. Ladipo, and F. Wilkinson (eds.), *Job Insecurity and Work Intensification*. London: Routledge, 112–136.

Nolan, P. and Slater, G. (2003). 'The labour market: history, structure and prospects', in P. Edwards (ed.), *Industrial Relations* (2nd edn). Oxford: Blackwell, 58–80.

Nolan, P. and Wood, S. (2003). 'Mapping the future of work'. *British Journal of Industrial Relations*, 41/2: 165–74.

Noon, M. (2007). 'The fatal flaws of diversity and the business case for ethnic minorities'. *Work, Employment, and Society*, 21/4: 773–84.

Noon, M. and Blyton, P. (2007). *The Realities of Work* (3rd edn). Basingstoke: Palgrave Macmillan.

O'Brien, R. (2002). 'The varied paths to minimum global labour standards', in J. Harrod and R. O'Brien (eds.), *Global Unions? Theory and Strategies of Organized Labour in a Global Political Economy*. London: Routledge, 221–34.

O'Connell Davidson, J. (1994). 'What do franchisors do? Control and Commercialisation in milk distribution'. *Work, Employment and Society*, 8/1: 23–44.

O'Donovan, K. and Szyszczak, E. (1988). *Equality and Sex Discrimination Law*. Oxford: Basil Blackwell.

Ogbonna, E. and Harris, L. (2002). 'Institutionalization of tipping as a source of managerial control'. *British Journal of Industrial Relations*, 40/4: 725–52.

Ogden, S. (1993). 'Decline and fall: national bargaining in British water'. *Industrial Relations Journal*, 24/1: 44–58.

Ortega, B. (1999). *In Sam We Trust*. London: Kogan Page.

Osler, D. (2002). *Labour Party PLC*. London: Mainstream Publishing.

Oxenbridge, S. (1997). 'Organizing strategies and organising reform in New Zealand service sector unions'. *Labor Studies Journal*, 22/3: 3–27.

Oxenbridge, S. and Brown, W. (2002). 'The two faces of partnership? An assessment of partnership and co-operative employer/trade union relationships'. *Employee Relations*, 24/3: 262–7.

Oxenbridge, S. and Brown, W. (2004). 'A poisoned chalice? Trade union representatives in partnership and co-operative employer-union relationships', in G. Healy, E. Heery, P. Taylor, and W. Brown (eds.), *The Future of Worker Representation*. Basingstoke: Palgrave Macmillan, 187–206.

Oxenbridge, S. and Brown, W. (2005). 'Developing partnership relationships: a case of leveraging power', in M. Stuart and M. Martinez Lucio (eds.), *Partnership and Modernisation in Employment Relations*. London: Routledge, 83–100.

Oxenbridge, S., Brown, W., Deakin, S., and Pratten, C. (2003). 'Initial responses to the Employment Relations Act 1999'. *British Journal of Industrial Relations*, 41/2: 315–34.

Oxfam (2004a). *Made at Home*. Oxfam Briefing Paper 63. Oxford: Oxfam International.

Oxfam (2004b). *Trading Away our Rights: Women Working in Global Supply Chains*. Oxford: Oxfam International.

Pai, H-H. (2008). *Chinese Whispers: the True Story Behind Britain's Hidden Army of Labour*. London: Penguin.

Pakulski, J. and Waters, M. (1996). *The Death of Class*. London: Sage.

Palley, T. (2004). 'The economic case for international labour standards'. *Cambridge Journal of Economics*, 28/1: 21–36.

Parker, J. (2002). 'Women's groups in British unions'. *British Journal of Industrial Relations*, 40/1: 23–48.

Pass, S. (2005). 'On the line'. *People Management*, 15 September: 38–40.

Phizacklea, A. and Miles, R. (1980). *Labour and Racism*. London: Routledge and Kegan Paul.

Piazza, J. (2005). 'Globalizing quiescence: globalization, union density and strikes in 15 industrialized countries'. *Economic and Industrial Democracy*, 26/2: 289–314.

Pierson, C. (1996). *The Modern State*. London: Routledge.

Piore, M. and Sabel, C. (1984). *The Second Industrial Divide*. New York: Basic Books.

Platman, K. (2004). '"Portfolio careers" and the search for flexibility in later life'. *Work, Employment, and Society*, 18/3: 573–99.

Polanyi, K. (1957). *The Great Transformation*. Boston: Beacon Press.

Pollard, S. (1992). *The Development of the British Economy 1914–1990* (4th edn). London: Edward Arnold.

Pollert, A. (1981). *Girls, Wives, Factory Lives*. Basingstoke: Macmillan.

Pollert, A. (1988a). 'The flexible firm: fixation or fact?'. *Work, Employment and Society*, 2/3: 281–316.

Pollert, A. (1988b). 'Dismantling flexibility'. *Capital and Class*, 34: 42–75.

Pollert, A. (2005). 'The unorganised worker: the decline in collectivism and new hurdles to individual employment rights'. *Industrial Law Journal*, 34/3: 217–38.

Pollert, A. (2007). 'Individual employment rights: paper tigers—fierce in appearance but missing in tooth and claw'. *Economic and Industrial Democracy*, 28/1: 110–39.

Poole, M. (1986). *Towards a New Industrial Democracy: Workers' Participation in Industry*. London: Routledge and Kegan Paul.

Poole, M. and Mansfield, R. (1993). 'Patterns of continuity and change in managerial attitudes and behaviour in industrial relations, 1980–1990'. *British Journal of Industrial Relations*, 31/1: 11–35.

Poynter, G. (2000). *Restructuring in the Service Industries: Management Reform and Workplace Relations in the UK Service Sector*. London: Mansell.

Price, L. and Price, R. (1994). 'Change and continuity in the status divide', in K. Sisson, K. (ed.), *Personnel Management* (2nd edn). Oxford: Blackwell, 527–61.

Price, R. (1983). 'White-collar unions: growth, character and attitudes in the 1970s', in R. Hyman and R. Price (eds.), *The New Working Class? White Collar Workers and their Unions*. London: Macmillan, 147–83.

Price, R. (1989). 'The decline and fall of the status divide?', in K. Sisson (ed.), *Personnel Management in Britain*. Oxford: Blackwell, 271–95.

Proctor, S., Rowlinson, M., McArdle, L., Hassard, J., and Forrester, P. (1994). 'Flexibility, politics and strategy: in defence of the model of the flexible firm'. *Work, Employment and Society*, 8/2: 221–42.

Purcell, J. (1991). 'The rediscovery of the management prerogative: the management of labour relations in the 1980s'. *Oxford Review of Economic Policy*, 7/1: 33–43.

Purcell, J. (2000). 'After collective bargaining? ACAS in the age of human resource management', in B. Towers and W. Brown (eds.), *Employment Relations in Britain: 25 Years of the Advisory, Conciliation and Arbitration Service*. Oxford: Blackwell, 163–80.

Purcell, J. and Ahlstrand, B. (1994). *Human Resource Management in the Multi-Divisional Company*. Oxford: Oxford University Press.

Purcell, J. and Hutchinson, S. (2007). 'Front-line managers as agents in the HRM-performance causal chain: theory, analysis, and evidence'. *Human Resource Management Journal*, 17/1: 3–20.

Purcell, J. and Kinnie, N. (2007). 'HRM and business performance', in P. Boxall, J. Purcell, and P. Wright (eds.), *The Oxford Handbook of Human Resource Management*. Oxford: Oxford University Press, 533–51.

Purcell, J., Kinnie, N., Hutchinson, S., Rayton, B., and Swart, J. (2003). *Understanding the People and Performance Link: Unlocking the Black Box*. London: CIPD.

Purcell, J., Kinnie, N., Swart, J., Rayton, B., and Hutchinson, S. (2009). *People Management and Performance*. Abingdon: Routledge.

Rainnie, A. (1989). *Industrial Relations in Small Firms*. London: Routledge.

Ram, M. (1994). *Managing to Survive*. Oxford: Blackwell.

Ram, M., Edwards, P., Gilman, M., and Arrowsmith, J. (2001). 'The dynamics of informality: employment relations in small firms and the effects of regulatory change'. *Work, Employment and Society*, 15/4: 845–61.

Ramsay, H. (1977). 'Cycles of control: worker participation in sociological and historical perspectives'. *Sociology*, 11/3: 481–506.

Ramsay, H., Scholarios, D., and Harley, B. (2000). 'Employees and high-performance work systems: testing inside the black box'. *British Journal of Industrial Relations*, 38/4: 501–31.

Redfern, D. (2007). 'An analysis of the role of European Works Councils in British workplaces'. *Employee Relations*, 29/3: 292–305.

Reed, H. and Latorre, M. (2009). *The Economic Impacts of Migration on the UK Labour Market*. Economics of Migration Working Paper 3. London: Institute for Public Policy Research.

Rees, G. and Fielder, S. (1992). 'The services economy, subcontracting and the new employment relations: contract catering and cleaning'. *Work, Employment and Society*, 6/3: 347–68.

Rees, T. (1992). *Women and the Labour Market*. London: Routledge.

Rees, T. (1998). *Mainstreaming Equality in the European Union*. London: Routledge.

Richards, J. (2008). 'Because I need somewhere to vent: the expression of conflict through work blogs'. *New Technology, Work, and Employment*, 23/1–2: 95–110.

Richards, W. (2001). 'Evaluating equal opportunities initiatives: the case for a "transformative" agenda', in M. Noon and E. Ogbonna (eds.), *Equality, Diversity and Disadvantage in Employment*. Basingstoke: Palgrave Macmillan, 15–31.

Rigby, M. and Marco Aledo, M. (2001). 'The worst record in Europe? A comparative analysis of industrial conflict in Spain'. *European Journal of Industrial Relations*, 7/3: 287–305.

Riisgaard, L. (2005). 'International framework agreements: a new model for securing workers rights?' *Industrial Relations*, 44/4: 707–37.

Robinson, P. (1999). 'Exploring the relationship between flexible employment and labour market regulation', in A. Felstead and N. Jewson (eds.), *Global Trends in Flexible Labour*. Basingstoke: Macmillan, 84–99.

Robson, P., Dex, S., Wilkinson, F., and Salido Cortes, O. (1999). 'Low pay, labour market institutions, gender and part-time work: cross-national comparisons'. *European Journal of Industrial Relations*, 5/2: 187–207.

Rogers, J. and Streeck, W. (eds.) (1995). *Works Councils: Consultation, Representation and Cooperation in Industrial Relations*. Chicago: University of Chicago Press.

Rollinson, D., Handley, J., Hook, C. and Foot, M. (1997). 'The disciplinary experience and its effects on behaviour'. *Work, Employment and Society*, 11/2: 281–311.

Roper, I., Cunningham, I., and James, P. (2003). 'Promoting family-friendly policies: is the basis of the government's ethical standpoint viable?'. *Personnel Review*, 32/2: 211–30.

Rosenthal, P., Hill, S., and Peccei, R. (1997). 'Checking out service: evaluating excellence, HRM and TQM in retailing'. *Work, Employment and Society*, 11/3: 481–503.

Ross, R. and Schneider, R. (1992). *From Equality to Diversity*. London: Pitman.

Roy, D. (1952). 'Quota restriction and goldbricking in a machine shop'. *American Journal of Sociology*, 5/5: 427–42.

Royal Commission (1968). *Report of the Royal Commission on Trade Unions and Employers' Associations*. London: HMSO.

Royle, T. (2000). *Working for McDonalds in Europe: the Unequal Struggle?*. London: Routledge.

Royle, T. and Towers, B. (eds.) (2002). *Labour Relations in the Global Fast-Food Industry*. London: Routledge.

Rubery, J. and Edwards, P. (2003). 'Low pay and the National Minimum Wage', in P. Edwards (ed.), *Industrial Relations* (2nd edn). Oxford: Blackwell, 447–69.

Rubery, J. and Grimshaw, D. (2003). *The Organization of Employment: an International Perspective*. Basingstoke: Palgrave Macmillan.

Russell, A. (1992). *Harmonisation of Employment Conditions in Britain: Some Causes and Consequences*. Aberystwyth Economics Research Papers, 92-08, Aberystwyth, University College of Wales: Department of Economics and Agricultural Economics.

Rutherford, S. (1999). 'Equal opportunities policies—making a difference'. *Women in Management Review*, 14/6: 212–19.

Samuel, P. (2005). 'Partnership working and the cultivated activist'. *Industrial Relations Journal*, 36/1: 59–76.

Samuel, P. (2007). 'Partnership consultation and employer domination in two British life and pensions firms'. *Work, Employment, and Society*, 21/3: 459–77.

Sawyer, T., Borkett, I., and Underhill, N. (2001). *Independent Review of Industrial Relations within Royal Mail*.

Scase, R. (1995). 'Employment relations in small firms', in P. Edwards (ed.), *Industrial Relations*. Oxford: Blackwell, 569–95.

Scase, R. (2003). 'Employment relations in small firms', in P. Edwards (ed.), *Industrial Relations: Theory and Practice* (2nd edn). Oxford: Blackwell, 489–512.

Schlosser, E. (2002). *Fast Food Nation*. London: Penguin.

Scholarios, D. and Marks, A. (2004). 'Work–life balance and the software worker', *Human Resource Management Journal*. 14/2: 54–74.

Scott, A. (1994). *Willing Slaves? British Workers under Human Resource Management*. Cambridge: Cambridge University Press.

Scott, W., Mumford, E., McGivering, I., and Kirkby, J. (1963). *Coal and Conflict*. Liverpool: Liverpool University Press.

Seifert, R. and Sibley, T. (2005). *United They Stood: the Story of the 2002–2004 Firefighters' Strike*. London: Lawrence and Wishart.

Sennett, R. (1998). *The Corrosion of Character*. London: WW Norton.

Shackleton, J. (2002). *Employment Tribunals: their Growth and the Case for Radical Reform*. Hobart Paper No. 145, London: Institute of Economic Affairs.

Shelley, T. (2007). *Exploited: Migrant Labour in the New Global Economy*. London: Zed Books.

Shen, J. (2007). *Labour Disputes and their Resolution in China*. Oxford: Chandos Publishing.

Shorter, E. and Tilly, C. (1974). *Strikes in France*. Cambridge: Cambridge University Press.

Silver, B. (2003). *Forces of Labor: Workers' Movements and Globalization since 1870*. Cambridge: Cambridge University Press.

Simms, M. (2003). 'Union organizing in a not-for-profit organization', in G. Gall (ed.), *Union Organizing: Campaigning for Union Recognition*. London: Routledge, 97–113.

Simms, M. (2007). 'Interest formation in greenfield union organising campaigns'. *Industrial Relations Journal*, 38/5: 439–54.

Singh, A. and Zammit, A. (2004). 'Labour standards and the "race to the bottom": rethinking globalization and workers' rights from developmental and solidaristic perspectives'. *Oxford Review of Economic Policy*, 20/1: 85–104.

Sisson, K. (1983). 'Employers' organisations', in G. Bain (ed.), *Industrial Relations in Britain*. Oxford: Basil Blackwell, 121–34.

Sisson, K. and Brown, W. (1983). 'Industrial relations in the private sector: Donovan re-visited', in G. Bain (ed.), *Industrial Relations in Britain*. Oxford: Basil Blackwell, 137–54.

Sisson, K. and Storey, J. (2000). *The Realities of Human Resource Management*. Buckingham: Open University Press.

Sisson, K. and Taylor, J. (2006). 'The Advisory, Conciliation, and Arbitration Service', in L. Dickens and A. Neal (eds.), *The Changing Institutional Face of British Employment Relations*. Alphen aan den Rign: Kluwer Law International, 25–36.

Smethurst, S. (2007). 'Fair traders'. *People Management*, 29 November, 28–31.

Smith, C. (1989). 'Flexible specialisation, automation and mass production'. *Work, Employment and Society*, 3/2: 203–20.

Smith, C., Child, J., and Rowlinson, M. (1990). *Reshaping Work: the Cadbury Experience*. Cambridge: Cambridge University Press.

Smith, P. (2001). *Unionization and Union Leadership: the Road Haulage Industry*. London: Continuum.

Smith, P. and Morton, G. (1994). 'Union exclusion—next steps'. *Industrial Relations Journal*, 25/1: 3–14.

Smith, P. and Morton, G. (2006) 'Nine years of New Labour: neo-liberalism and workers' rights'. *British Journal of Industrial Relations*, 44/3: 401–20.

Smith, P. and Morton, G. (2009). 'Employment legislation: New Labour's neoliberal legal project to subordinate trade unions', in G. Daniels and J. McIlroy (eds.), *Trade Unions in a Neo Liberal World: British Trade Unions under New Labour*. Abingdon: Routledge, 205–29.

Smith, R. (1999). 'The convergence/ divergence debate in comparative industrial relations', in M. Rigby, R. Smith, and T. Lawlor (eds.), *European Trade Unions: Change and Response*. London: Routledge, 1–17.

Snape, E. (1994). 'Reversing the decline? The TGWU's Link Up campaign'. *Industrial Relations Journal*, 25/3: 222–33.

Snape, E. and Redman, T. (2003). 'Too old or too young? The impact of perceived age discrimination'. *Human Resource Management Journal*, 13/1: 78–89.

Stanworth, C. and Stanworth, J. (1995). 'The self-employed without employees—autonomous or atypical?'. *Industrial Relations Journal*, 26/3: 221–9.

Stevis, D. and Boswell, T. (2007). 'International framework agreements: opportunities and challenges for global unionism', in K. Bronfenbrenner (ed.), *Global Unions: Challenging Transnational Capital through Cross-border Campaigns*. Ithaca NY: Cornell University Press, 174–94.

Stiglitz, J. (2002). *Globalization and its Discontents*. London: Allen Lane.

Storey, J. (1983). *Managerial Prerogative and the Question of Control*. London: Routledge and Kegan Paul.

Storey, J. (1985). 'The means of management control'. *Sociology*, 19/2: 193–211.

Storey, J. (1992). *Developments in the Management of Human Resources*. Oxford: Blackwell.

Strange, S. (1996). *The Retreat of the State: the Diffusion of Power in the World Economy*. Cambridge: Cambridge University Press.

Streeck, W. (1997). 'Industrial citizenship under regime competition: the case of the European Works Councils'. *Journal of European Public Policy*, 4/4: 643–64.

Strinati, D. (1982). *Capitalism, the State and Industrial Relations*. London: Croom Helm.

Stuart, M. and Martinez Lucio, M. (2005). 'Partnership and modernisation in employment relations: an introduction', in M. Stuart and M. Martinez Lucio (eds.), *Partnership and Modernisation in Employment Relations*. London: Routledge, 1–22.

Suff, R. and Williams, S. (2004). 'The myth of mutuality? Employee perceptions of partnership at Borg Warner'. *Employee Relations*, 26/1: 30–43.

Syrpis, P. (2008). 'The Treaty of Lisbon: much ado … but about what?' *Industrial Law Journal*, 37/3: 219–35.

Tailby, S. and Winchester, D. (2000). 'Management and trade unions: towards social partnership?', in S. Bach and K. Sisson (eds.), *Personnel Management* (3rd edn). Oxford: Blackwell, 365–88.

Tailby, S., Richardson, M., Danford, A., Stewart, P., and Upchurch, M. (2005). 'Workplace partnership and work–life balance: a local government case study', in D. Houston (ed.), *Work–life Balance in the 21st Century*. Basingstoke: Palgrave Macmillan, 189–210.

Taylor, B., Chang Kai, and Li Qi (2003). *Industrial Relations in China*. Cheltenham: Edward Elgar.

Taylor, L. and Walton, P. (1971). 'Industrial sabotage: motives and meanings', in S. Cohen (ed.), *Images of Deviance*. Harmondsworth: Penguin, 219–45.

Taylor, P. and Ramsay, H. (1998). 'Unions, partnership and HRM: sleeping with the enemy?' *International Journal of Employment Studies*, 6/1: 115–43.

Taylor, P. and Walker, A. (1998). 'Policies and practices towards older workers: a framework for comparative research'. *Human Resource Management Journal*, 8/3: 61–76.

Taylor, P. and Bain, P. (2005). '"India calling to the far away towns": the call centre labour process and globalization'. *Work, Employment, and Society*, 19/2: 261–82.

Taylor, P., Baldry, C., Bain, P., and Ellis, V. (2003). '"A unique working environment": health, sickness and absence in UK call centres'. *Work, Employment and Society*, 17/3: 435–58.

Taylor, R. (1993). *The Trade Union Question in British Politics*. Oxford: Blackwell.

Taylor, R. (1998). 'Annual review article 1997'. *British Journal of Industrial Relations*, 36, 2, 293–311.

Taylor, R. (no date). *The Future of Work–Life Balance*. Swindon: Economic and Social Research Council.

Taylor, S. (1998). 'Emotional labour and the new workplace', in P. Thompson and C. Warhurst (eds.), *Workplaces of the Future*. Basingstoke: Macmillan, 84–103.

Teague, P. (1989). *The European Community: the Social Dimension*. London: Kogan Page.

Teague, P. (1999). *Economic Citizenship in the European Union*. London: Routledge.

Teague, P. (2003). 'Labour-standard setting and regional trading blocs: lesson drawing from the NAFTA experience'. *Employee Relations*, 25/5: 428–52.

Terry, M. (1983). 'Shop steward development and managerial strategies', in G. Bain, (ed.), *Industrial Relations in Britain*. Oxford: Basil Blackwell, 67–91.

Terry, M. (1996). 'Negotiating the government of UNISON: union democracy in theory and practice'. *British Journal of Industrial Relations*, 34/1: 87–110.

Terry, M. (1999). 'Systems of collective representation in non-union firms in the UK'. *Industrial Relations Journal*, 30/1: 16–30.

Terry, M. (2004). '"Partnership": a serious strategy for the UK trade unions?', in A. Verma and T. Kochan (eds.), *Unions in the 21st Century: an International Perspective*. Basingstoke: Palgrave Macmillan, 205–19.

Thompson, E. (1967). 'Time, work-discipline and industrial capitalism' *Past and Present*, 38: 56–97.

Thompson, P. (2003). 'Disconnected capitalism: or why employers can't keep their side of the bargain'. *Work, Employment, and Society*, 17/2: 359–78.

Thompson, P. and Warhurst, C. (1998). 'Hands, hearts and minds: changing work and workers at the end of the century', in P. Thompson and C. Warhurst (eds.), *Workplaces of the Future*. Basingstoke: Macmillan, 1–24.

Thornley, C. (1998). 'Contesting local pay: the decentralisation of collective bargaining in the NHS'. *British Journal of Industrial Relations*, 36/3: 413–34.

Thorpe, A. (1999). 'The Labour party and the trade unions', in J. McIlroy, N. Fishman, and A. Campbell (eds.), *British Trade Unionism and Industrial Politics (Volume Two). The High Tide of Trade Unionism, 1964-79.* Aldershot: Ashgate, 133–50.

Timming, A. (2007). 'European Works Councils and the dark side of managing worker voice'. *Human Resource Management Journal*, 17/3: 248–64.

Tolliday, S. and Zeitlin, J. (eds.) (1991). *The Power to Manage? Employers and Industrial Relations in Comparative-Historical Perspective*. London: Routledge.

Torrington, D. (1991). *Management Face to Face*. Hemel Hempstead: Prentice Hall.

Towers, B. (1997). *The Representation Gap: Change and Reform in the British and American Workplace*. Oxford: Oxford University Press.

Towers, B. and Brown, W. (eds.) (2000). *Employment Relations in Britain: 25 Years of the Advisory, Conciliation and Arbitration Service*, Oxford: Blackwell.

Trades Union Congress (TUC) (1997). *General Council Report*. London: TUC.

Trades Union Congress (TUC) (2005). *TUC Equality Audit 2005*. London: TUC.

Trades Union Congress (TUC) (2008). 'Hard work, hidden lives'. Report of the Commission on Vulnerable Employment, http://www.vulnerableworkers.org.uk

Trades Union Congress (TUC) (2009). *Recession Report*, No. 3, January. London: TUC.

Tribunals Service (2008). *Employment Tribunal and EAT Statistics (GB) 2007–08*. London: Tribunals Service, http://www.employmenttribunals.gov.uk

Truss, C. (2001). 'Complexities and controversies in linking HRM with organizational outcomes'. *Journal of Management Studies*, 38/8: 1121–49.

Tsogas, G. (1999). 'Labour standards in international trade agreements: a critical assessment of the arguments'. *International Journal of Human Resource Management*, 10/2: 351–75.

Tsogas, G. (2000). 'Labour standards and the generalized system of preferences of the European Union and the United States'. *European Journal of Industrial Relations*, 6/3: 349–70.

Tsogas, G. (2001). *Labor Regulation in a Global Economy*. New York: M E Sharpe.

Turnbull, P. (1988). 'Leaner and possibly fitter: the management of redundancy in Britain'. *Industrial Relations Journal*, 19/3: 201–13.

Turnbull, P. and Sapsford, D. (1992). 'A sea of discontent: the tides of organised and "unorganised" conflict on the docks'. *Sociology*, 26/2: 291–309.

Turnbull, P. and Wass, V. (1994). 'The greatest game no more—redundant dockers and the demise of "dock work"'. *Work, Employment and Society*, 8/4: 487–506.

Turnbull, P. and Wass, V. (1997). 'Job insecurity and labour market lemons: the (mis)management of redundancy in steel making, coal mining and port transport'. *Journal of Management Studies*, 34/1: 27–51.

Turnbull, P. and Wass, V. (1998). '"Marksist" management: sophisticated human relations in a high street retail store'. *Industrial Relations Journal*, 29/2: 98–111.

Turnbull, P. and Wass, V. (2000). 'Redundancy and the paradox of job insecurity', in E. Heery and J. Salmon (eds.), *The Insecure Workforce*. London: Routledge, 57–77.

Turner, H., Clack, G., and Roberts, G. (1967). *Labour Relations in the Motor Industry*. London: George Allen and Unwin.

Tüselmann, H. and Heise, A. (2000). 'The German model of industrial relations at the crossroads: past, present and future'. *Industrial Relations Journal*, 31/3: 162–76.

Undy, R. (1999). 'Annual review article: New Labour's industrial relations settlement: the third way?'. *British Journal of Industrial Relations*, 37/2: 315–36.

Undy, R., Kessler, I., and Thompson, M. (2002). 'The impact of the national minimum wage on the apparel industry'. *Industrial Relations Journal*, 33/4: 351–64.

Undy, R., Ellis, V., McCarthy, W., and Halmos, A. (1981). *Change in Trade Unions*. London: Hutchinson.

Undy, R., Fosh, P., Morris, H., Smith, P., and Martin, R. (1996). *Managing the Unions*. Oxford: Clarendon.

United Nations Conference on Trade and Development (UNCTAD) (2006). *World Investment Report 2006. FDI from Developing and Transition Economies: Implications for Development*. New York and Geneva: United Nations.

Upchurch, M. and Donnelly, E. (1992). 'Membership patterns in USDAW 1980–1990: survival as success?'. *Industrial Relations Journal*, 23/1: 60–8.

van Roozendaal, G. (2002). *Trade Unions and Global Governance: the Debate on a Social Clause*. London: Continuum.

Virdee, S. and Grint, K. (1994). 'Black self-organization in trade unions'. *Sociological Review*, 42/2: 202-26.

Visser, F. and Williams, L. (2006). *Work–Life Balance: Rhetoric vs Reality*. London: Work Foundation.

Wacjman, J. (2000). 'Feminism facing industrial relations in Britain', *British Journal of Industrial Relations*, 38/2: 183–201.

Waddington, J. (1992). 'Trade union membership in Britain 1980–1987: unemployment and restructuring'. *British Journal of Industrial Relations*, 30/2: 287–324.

Waddington, J. (2003a). 'Annual review article 2002: heightening tension in relations between trade unions and the Labour government in 2002'. *British Journal of Industrial Relations*, 41/2: 335–58.

Waddington, J. (2003b). 'Trade union organization', in P. Edwards (ed.), *Industrial Relations* (2nd edn). Oxford: Blackwell, 214–56.

Waddington, J. (2006). 'The performance of European Works Councils in engineering: perspectives of the employee representatives'. *Industrial Relations*, 45/4: 681–708.

Waddington, J. and Hoffman, R. (2003). 'Trade unions in Europe: reform, organisation and restructuring', in D. Foster and P. Scott (eds.), *Trade Unions in Europe: Meeting the Challenge*. Brussels: Peter Lang, 33–63.

Waddington, J. and Whitston, C. (1995) 'Trade unions: growth, structure and policy', in P. Edwards (ed.), *Industrial Relations: Theory and Practice in Britain*. Oxford: Blackwell, 151–202.

Waddington, J. and Whitston, C. (1997). 'Why do people join unions in a period of membership decline?'. *British Journal of Industrial Relations*, 35/4: 515–46.

Walby, S. (1997). *Gender Transformations*. London: Routledge.

Waldinger, R., Erickson, C., Milkman, R., Mitchell, D., Valenzuela, A., Wong, K., and Zeitlin, M. (1998). 'Helots no more: a case study of the Justice for Janitors campaign in Los Angeles', in K. Bronfenbrenner, S. Friedman, R. Hurd, R. Oswald, and R. Seeber (eds.), *Organizing to Win: New Research on Union Strategies*. Ithaca: ILR Press, 102–19.

Wall, T. and Wood, S. (2005). 'The romance of human resource management and business performance, and the case for big science'. *Human Relations*, 58/4: 429–62.

Wallis, E., Stuart, M., and Greenwood, I. (2005). '"Learners of the workplace unite!": an empirical examination of the UK trade union learning representative initiative'. *Work, Employment, and Society*, 19/2: 283–304.

Walsh, J. (2005). 'Work–life balance: challenging the overwork culture', in S. Bach (ed.), *Managing Human Resources* (4th edn). Oxford: Blackwell, 148–77.

Walsh, J. (2007). 'Equality and diversity in British workplaces: the 2004 Workplace Employment Relations Survey'. *Industrial Relations Journal*, 38/4: 303–19.

Walters, S. (2002). 'Female part-time workers' attitudes to trade unions in Britain'. *British Journal of Industrial Relations*, 40/1: 49–68.

Walton, R. (1985). 'From control to commitment in the workplace'. *Harvard Business Review*, 63/2: 77–84.

Walton, R. and McKersie, R. (1965). *A Behavioral Theory of Labor Negotiations*. New York, McGraw-Hill.

Ward, K., Grimshaw, D., Rubery, J., and Beynon, H. (2001). 'Dilemmas in the management of temporary work agency staff'. *Human Resource Management Journal*, 11/4: 3–21.

Warhurst, C. (2008). 'The knowledge economy, skills and government labour market intervention'. *Policy Studies*, 29/1: 71–86.

Warhurst, C. and Thompson, P. (2006). 'Mapping knowledge in work: proxies or practices?' *Work, Employment, and Society*, 20/4: 787–800.

Warhurst, C., Eikhof, D., and Haunschild, A. (2008). 'Out of balance or just out of bounds? Analysing the relationship between work and life', in C. Warhurst, D. Eikhof, and A. Haunschild (eds.), *Work Less, Live More: Critical Analysis of the Work–Life Boundary*. Basingstoke: Palgrave Macmillan, 1–21.

Wass, V. (1996). 'Who controls selection under "voluntary" redundancy? The case of the Redundant Mineworkers Payments Scheme'. *British Journal of Industrial Relations*, 34/2: 249–65.

Waterman, P. (2001). *Globalization, Social Movements and the New Internationalisms*. London: Continuum.

Watson, D. (1988). *Managers of Discontent*. London: Routledge.

Webb, J. (1997). 'The politics of equal opportunity'. *Gender, Work and Organization*, 4/3: 159–69.

Webb, J. and Liff, S. (1988). 'Play the white man: the social construction of fairness and competition in equal opportunity policies'. *Sociological Review*, 36/3: 532–51.

Webb, S. and Webb, B. (1920a). *Industrial Democracy*. London: Longmans, Green and Co.

Webb, S. and Webb, B. (1920b) *The History of Trade Unionism* (revised edn). London: Longmans, Green and Co.

Wedderburn, D. and Craig, C. (1974). 'Relative deprivation in work', in D. Wedderburn (ed.),

Poverty, Inequality and Class Structure. Cambridge: Cambridge University Press, 141–64.

Wedderburn, Lord (1986). *The Worker and the Law* (3rd edn). Penguin: Harmondsworth.

Wedderburn, Lord (1989). 'Freedom of association and philosophies of labour law'. *Industrial Law Journal*, 18: 1–38.

Wedderburn, Lord (1991). *Employment Rights in Britain and Europe*. London: Lawrence and Wishart.

Wedderburn, Lord (1992). 'Laws about strikes', in W. McCarthy (ed.), *Legal Intervention in Industrial Relations: Gains and Losses*. Oxford: Blackwell, 147–208.

Wedderburn, Lord (1995). *Labour Law and Freedom*. London: Lawrence and Wishart.

Wedderburn, Lord (2001). 'Underground labour injunctions'. *Industrial Law Journal*, 30/2: 206–14.

Weiss, L. (1997). 'Globalization and the myth of the powerless state'. *New Left Review*, 225: 3–27.

White, G. (1999). 'The remuneration of public servants: fair pay or New Pay?', in S. Corby and G. White (eds.), *Employee Relations in the Public Services*. London: Routledge, 73–94.

White, G. (2000). 'The pay review body system: its development and impact'. *Historical Studies in Industrial Relations*, 9: 71–100.

White, M., Hill, S., Mills, C., and Smeaton, D. (2004). *Managing to Change?* Basingstoke: Palgrave Macmillan.

White, P. (1983). 'The management of redundancy'. *Industrial Relations Journal*, 14/1: 32–40.

Wichert, I. (2002). 'Job insecurity and work intensification: the effects on health and well-being', in B. Burchell, D. Ladipo and F. Wilkinson (eds.), *Job Insecurity and Work Intensification*. London: Routledge, 92–111.

Wigham, E. (1973). *The Power to Manage*. London: Macmillan.

Wilkinson, A., Godfrey, G., and Marchington, M. (1997). 'Bouquets, brickbats and blinkers: Total Quality Management and employee involvement in practice'. *Organization Studies*, 18/5: 799–819.

Wilkinson, A., Marchington, M., Goodman, J., and Ackers, P. (1992). 'Total Quality Management and employee involvement'. *Human Resource Management Journal*, 2/4: 1–20.

Wilkinson, R. and Pickett, K. (2009). *The Spirit Level: Why More Equal Societies Almost Always do Better*. London: Allen Lane.

Williams, S. (1997). 'The nature of some recent trade union modernization policies'. *British Journal of Industrial Relations*, 35/4: 495–514.

Williams, S. (2003). 'Conflict in the colleges: industrial relations in further education since incorporation'. *Journal of Further and Higher Education*, 27/3: 307–16.

Williams, S. (2004). 'Accounting for change in public sector industrial relations: the erosion of national bargaining in further education in England and Wales'. *Industrial Relations Journal*, 35/3: 233–48.

Williams, S. and Scott, P. (2008). *Shooting the Past? The Modernisation of Conservative Party Employment Relations Policy under David Cameron*. Paper presented to the Portsmouth Employment Relations Network, December.

Williams, S., Adam-Smith, D., and Norris, G. (2004). 'Remuneration practices in the UK hospitality industry in the age of the National Minimum Wage'. *Service Industries Journal*, 24/1: 171–86.

Willman, P. (1989). 'The logic of "market share" trade unionism: is membership decline inevitable?'. *Industrial Relations Journal*, 20/4: 260–70.

Willmott, H. (1993). 'Strength is ignorance; slavery is freedom: managing culture in modern organizations'. *Journal of Management Studies*, 30/4: 515–52.

Wills, J. (2000). 'Great Expectations: three years in the life of a European Works Council'. *European Journal of Industrial Relations*, 6/1: 85–107.

Wills, J. (2002). 'Bargaining for the space to organize in the global economy: a review of the Accor-IUF trade union rights agreement'. *Review of International Political Economy*, 9/4: 675–700.

Wills, J. (2004a). 'Organising the low paid: East London's Living Wage Campaign as a vehicle for change', in G. Healy, E. Heery, P. Taylor, and W. Brown (eds.), *The Future of Worker Representation*. Basingstoke: Palgrave Macmillan, 264–82.

Wills, J. (2004b). 'Trade unionism and partnership in practice: evidence from the Barclays-Unifi agreement'. *Industrial Relations Journal*, 35/4: 329–43.

Winchester, D. and Bach, S. (1995). 'The state: the public sector', in P. Edwards (ed.), *Industrial Relations: Theory and Practice in Britain*. Oxford: Blackwell, 304–34.

Winchester, D. and Bach, S. (1999). 'Britain: the transformation of public service employment relations', in S. Bach, L. Bordogna, G. Della Rocca, and D. Winchester (eds.), *Public Service Employment Relations in Europe: Transformation, Modernisation or Inertia?*. London: Routledge, 22–55.

Wolf, M. (2004). *Why Globalization Works*. New Haven: Yale University Press.

Women and Work Commission (2006). *Shaping a Fairer Future. Final Report of the Women and Work Commission*. London: Women and Equality Unit.

Wood, A. (1994). *North–South Trade, Employment and Inequality: Changing Fortunes in a Skill-driven World*. Oxford: Clarendon.

Wood, J. (1992). 'Dispute resolution—conciliation, mediation and arbitration', in W. McCarthy (ed.), *Legal Intervention in Industrial Relations: Gains and Losses*. Oxford: Blackwell, 241–73.

Wood, R. (1992). *Working in Hotels and Catering*. London: Routledge.

Wood, S. (1989). 'The transformation of work?', in S. Wood (ed.), *The Transformation of Work*. London: Unwin Hyman, 1–43.

Wood, S. and de Menezes, L. (1998). 'High commitment management in the UK: evidence from the Workplace Industrial Relations Survey, and Employers' Manpower and Skills Practices Survey'. *Human Relations*, 51/4: 485–515.

Wood, S. and Goddard, J. (1999). 'The statutory union recognition procedure in the Employment Relations Bill: a comparative analysis'. *British Journal of Industrial Relations*, 37/2: 203–45.

Wood, S., Moore, S., and Ewing, K. (2003). 'The impact of the trade union recognition procedure under the Employment Relations Act 2000-2', in H. Gospel and S. Wood (eds.), *Representing Workers*. London: Routledge, 119–43.

Woolfson, C. (2007). 'Labour standards and migration in the New Europe: post-communist legacies and perspectives'. *European Journal of Industrial Relations*, 13/2: 199–218.

Worrall, L., Cooper, C., and Campbell, F. (2000). 'The new reality for UK managers: perpetual change and employment instability'. *Work, Employment, and Society*, 14/4: 647–68.

Wray, D. (1996). 'Paternalism and its discontents'. *Work, Employment, and Society*, 10/4: 701–15.

Wrench, J. (1986). *Unequal Comrades: Trade Unions, Equal Opportunity and Racism*. Policy Papers in Ethnic Relations No. 5, Centre for Research in Ethnic Relations, University of Warwick.

Wrench, J. (1987). 'Unequal comrades: trade unions, equal opportunity and racism', in R. Jenkins and J. Solomos (eds.), *Racism and Equal Opportunities Policies in the 1980s*. Cambridge: Cambridge University Press, 160–86.

Wrench, J. and Virdee, S. (1996). 'Organising the unorganised: "race", poor work and trade unions', in P. Ackers, C. Smith, and P. Smith, P (eds.), *The New Workplace and Trade Unionism*. London: Routledge, 240–78.

Yu, X. (2008). 'Impacts of corporate code of conduct on labor standards: a case study of Reebok's athletic footwear supplier factory in China'. *Journal of Business Ethics*, 81: 513–29.

INDEX

A

AA 207
ABB 67–8
absenteeism 342, 347–9
actual practices 193
adaptability 96–7
Adidas 69
Advisory, Conciliation and
    Arbitration Service 328,
    352, 357–60
  help-line service 359
Aeroparts 225, 226
affinity groups 147–8
affirmative action programmes
    131
Age Concern 133
age discrimination 125, 133, 139,
    142, 143
Age Diversity in Employment code
    of practice 133
Agency Workers' Directive 83, 95,
    96, 98
agency workers and employment
    flexibility 42
Agenda for Change 269–70, 272,
    381
agreement negotiation 352–4
airline industry 204, 321
Alcan 306
Allied Domecq 239
Amalgamated Society of
    Locomotive Engineers
    and Firemen (ASLEF) 21
Amazon 183
Amicus trade union 241
see also Unite
annual leave entitlement 292
annualized hours 290–1, 348, **381**
anti-discrimination 95
see also public policy, anti-
    discrimination legislation
    and equality at work
anti-unionism in the United
    States 178

arbitration 354–5, **381**
see also Advisory, Conciliation
    and Arbitration Service
Argentina 334
Article 6 agreements 230–1
Article 13 agreements 230–1, 233
Association of Supervisory,
    Technical and Managerial
    Staff 214
'atypical' workers, union
    organization of (case
    study) 80–1
Aubry law (1998) 288
Australia 245, 312
  Congress of Trade Unions'
    'Organizing Works'
    programme 247
Austria 286
autocracy, benevolent 199–200

B

B & Q 133, 229
BAE Systems 311
ballots 337
Bangladesh 78
Barclays 237, 238, 239, 242
bargaining:
  distributive 352–3
  equality 156–8, **381**
  individual 9
  integrative 352
  multi-employer 258–9, 262,
    263, **382**
  power 353–4
  productivity 172
  single-employer 258
  see also collective bargaining
BECTU union 283
Belgium 286
Benefits Agency 268, 327
bilateral approach 74
blogs 350
'Blue Book' 172–3

BMW 42, 53, 64, 315–16
Body Shop 183
Boeing 67–8, 346–7
Bolton Committee of Enquiry on
    Small Firms 198
Boots 290
Borg Warner 241
'bossnapping' phenomenon 379
British Airways and industrial
    conflict (case study)
    367–8
BSkyB 183
BT 148–9, 247, 266
Bulgaria 113
bulletins 302
bureaucratic control 204
Burke Group 183
business performance 192–4
BusinessEurope 103, 234

C

Cadbury: Bourneville plant 173–5
Cadbury code of practice 275
call centres 62, 189, 204, 348
Cambodia 76
Canada *see* North American Free
    Trade Agreement
Cashco 60
Central Arbitration Committee
    (CAC) 179, 183, 228
Central Restaurant Group 205
Central Trains 289
challenging trade unions 175–95
  statutory union recognition
    179–84
  union exclusion 176–9
  see also human resource
    management 184–95
Charter of the Fundamental
    Rights of the European
    Union 110–11, 112, 117
child labour 72–3, 76
Child Support Agency 324

China 70, 334, 355

Citizens' Advice Bureaux 17, 364

Civil Service 268

civil society organizations (CSOs) 223

class actions 139

'closed shops' 88, 91, 173–4

co-determination 222

Coastguard Service 343

codes of conduct see corporate

codes of practice 275

coercive comparisons 59, **381**

coercive role of the state 24–5

collective agreements 276, 292, **381**

collective bargaining 10, 11, 12, 14, 16, 18, 26–8, **381**

   contraction 259–64

   coverage by industry sector (2004) 259

   coverage by workplace and organization size (2004) 260

   evolution and development 257–9

   free 84

   globalization 58

   nature of employment relations 31

   pay 256, 264–5

   regulation of employment relations 372

   representation and rise of representation gap 215

   state policy 85, 86

College Employers' Forum 269

Colombia 25

Commission

   communication techniques 224, 300–2

   direct 177, 186, 300–1

   downward 300–1

   upward 300

Commission for Racial Equality 130, 138

see also Equality and Human Rights

Communication Workers' Union (CWU) 6, 36–7, 245, 247

Community union 212, 250

compensation awards 363–4

compensation culture 361, 362–3

competitive pressures 321–2

compositional approach 218, 220

conciliation 354–5, **381**

see also Advisory, Conciliation and Arbitration Service

Confederation of British Industry (CBI) 83, 96, 103, 114, 293–4

conflict see industrial conflict

consent 205–7

Conservative Party/government 85, 93, 377–8

   challenging trade unions 176, 184, 187, 188

   dispute resolution 357, 362

   European Union integration 104, 105, 108

   nature of employment relations 33

   non-union forms of representation 230

   pay determination 261, 263, 268, 270

   pay inequality, low pay and National Minimum Wage 275, 276, 279, 280

   public policy: neo-liberalism 87–92

   public policy, anti-discrimination and equality 131

   self-employment 44

   strikes 335–6, 337

   union representation and rise of representation gap 217, 219–20

   working time 291

consultation, joint **381**

consultative committees 227

consultative forums 225

contesting the employment relationship 375–7

contexts 32–4

contracts 4–6, 53

control 204, 206–7

convergence 58, **381**

cooperation 7, 205–7

corporate codes of conduct 75, 76–8, **381**

corporatism 86–7, **381**

'cost minimization' approach 202–3

Costa Rica 76

Council of Europe 111

Council of Ministers 103, 104, 228, 234, 294

'country-of-origin principle' 110

Cranfield School of Management 235

custom and practice 10, **381**

CVC Capital Partners 207

Czech Republic 286

D

Danone 65

Deloitte & Touche 148

Delta Airlines 204–5

dignity at work 72, 247, 248, 249

disability discrimination 125, 129, 138, 139, 142, 161

see also Disability Rights Commission

Disability Discrimination Act (1995) 129, 131, 139

   (Amendment) Regulations (2003) 132

Disability Rights Commission 131, 138

see also Equality and Human Rights Commission

disciplinary procedures 355–7

discipline in the workplace 26

discrimination 106, 143

   direct and indirect 129, 130

   positive 130, 131, **382**

   pregnancy 122

   religion or belief 125, 139

   sex 106, 158, 361, 363, 364

   sexual orientation 139

see also disability; race/ethnicity

dispute resolution 352–65

   Advisory, Conciliation and Arbitration Service 357–60

   agreement negotiation 352–4

   collective disputes procedures 354–5

   employment tribunals 360–4

   grievance and disciplinary procedures 355–7

   procedures, collective 354–5

disputes over pay in public sector 271

distributive bargaining 352–3

divergence 58, **381**

diversity:

  management **381**

  representation in trade unions 158–62

see also equality and diversity

Donovan Royal Commission 27, 258, 360

dual function of labour 18

dual system of represenation 221–2

Dubai 334, 335

Dura Automotive Systems 309

Dynamex Friction 338

E

e-unions (case study) 253–4

East Asia 66

Eastern Europe 113–14, 115, 116

Economic and Monetary Union 120

efficiency rationale 31–2

efficiency savings 320–1

effort bargain 6

electrical contracting industry and national bargaining 262

Electrical Contractors' Association 261

electronic mail 300

Electronic Point of Sale (EPOS) 322

Emergency Powers Act (1920) 85

employee 7

  appraisals 147

  councils 226

  communicating with employees 300–2

  forums 225

  interests *see* representation

  involvement and participation 28–31, 91, 299–307, **381**

  reorganization of work 302–7

  networks 147

  surveys 300

employers 17–19

employers' associations 18–19, 269, **381**

Employers' Forum on Age 125, 143

employers and management 17–19

Employment Act:

  (1988) 88

  (1990) 90, 174

  (2002) 94, 95, 132, 135–6, 217

  (2008) 94, 97–8, 283

Employment Bill (2009) 377

Employment Equality (Age) Regulations (2006) 132, 133

Employment Equality (Religion or Belief) Regulations (2003) 132

Employment Equality (Sexual Orientation) Regulations (2003) 132

Employment Relations Act:

  (1991) 90

  (1999) 93–4, 179

  (2004) 94, 179

Employment Service 267

employment tribunals 139–40, 360–4, 373–4, **381**

empowerment 302, 303–4, 305–6, **381**

EnerSys 178

enforcement arrangements 138

Engineering Employers' Federation (EEF) 18

Equal Opportunities Commission 122, 125, 130, 138

see also Equality and Human Rights Commission

equal opportunity **381**

equal pay 157, 361

Equal Pay Act (1970) 129, 131

Equal Pay (Equal Pay for Work of Equal Value) Regulations (1983) 129

Equal Rights and Treatment of Part-Time Workers Directive (1997) 107, 132

Equal Treatment Directive

  (1976) 131

  (2000) 132

equality 95, 156

Equality Act (2006) 132

equality agenda and trade unions 154–6

equality at work *see* public policy, anti-discrimination legislation and equality at work

equality bargaining 156–8, **381**

Equality Bill (2009) 140

equality and diversity 141–53

  diversity, management of 146–9

equal opportunities policies:

  critical assessment 143–6

  understanding 142–3

Equality and Human Rights Commission 132, 138–9

equity objective 31–2

Esso: Fawley oil refinery 172–3, 206

Ethical Trading Initiative: 'Base Code' 76–8

ethnicity *see* race/ethnicity

Euro 120

Europe 67, 292–3

see also Eastern Europe

European Association of Craft, Small and Medium-Sized Enterprises (UEAPME) 103

European Central Bank 120

European Centre of Enterprises with Public Participation and of Enterprises of General Economic Interest (CEEP) 103

European Commission 103, 105, 106, 108, 134, 291, 293–4

European Convention on Human Rights 111

European Court of Justice 103, 112, 116–17, 291, 292–3

European Directives 36, 107, 374

European Economic Area 230

European Employment Strategy 108–9, **381**

European Industry Federations 103

European integration 102–18

enlargement of European Union 112–17

  'Lisbon agenda' and the erosion of the social dimension 108–10

  'social dimension' 103–8

European Metalworkers' Federation 103

European Parliament 103, 110, 117, 234, 294

European Social Charter 111

European Trade Union Confederation (ETUC) 103, 117, 231

European Union:
   accession dates 113
   agency workers 42
   anti-discrimination legislation 95–6
   equality at work 134
   flexible employment 52
   globalization 60, 61, 63, 65
   institutions 103
   Labour policies 96
   nature of employment relations 23, 33
   non-union forms of representation 225
   pay inequality, low pay and National Minimum Wage 273
   regulation of employment relations 373
   self-employment 45
   strikes 334
   work pressures data 319
   working time 286, 287

European Union Constitutional Treaty 111–12

European Works Councils 106, 230–4, **381**

European Works Councils Directive (1994) 107, 225, 230, 232, 233, 234

Eurotunnel 227

executive pay 275

experiencing employment relationship 374–5

export processing zones 67, 68–9, 70, 72, 74

F

Fair Labor Association (FLA) 75

fair representation 160

'fair tips' campaign 256

Fair Wages Resolutions 276

family-friendly policies see work-life balance

fast-food industry 178

see also in particular McDonald's

female employees 33, 51, 52

feminism 15, 156

fiddles 345–6

Fire Brigades Union (FBU) 92, 100–1, 339, 353

Fixed-Term Contract Workers Directive (1999) 107, 132

fixed-term contracts 53

Fixed-term Employees Regulations (2002) 132

flexible employment 33, 42, 51–5, 58, 150
   challenging trade unions 190
   equality and diversity 145, 149, 151
   Labour policies 95
   migrant labour 54
   patterns in 'new' economy 43
   public policy, anti–discrimination and equality 136, 137, 138
   redundancy and job insecurity 314–15
   representation and rise of representation gap 218
   working time 289–90
   workplace inequality 127
   see also homeworking; part-time; self-employment; shift-working; temporary

flexible specialization 47–8, **381**

'flying squads' 178

Ford: Halewood plant 314

Foreign and Commonwealth Office 289–90

foreign direct investment 56, 69

formal employment relations 201

Fox, Alan 12

framework agreements 105–6

Framework for Equal Treatment in Employment and Occupations Directive (2000) 107

France 112, 276, 286, 288, 294, 379

franchise 45–6, **381**

fraternalism 199

free-trade agreements 74

freedom of association 72

freelance workers 44–5, 375

Friction Dynamics 338

further education sector 268–9

future prospects for employment relations 377–80

G

gangmasters 94

Gangmasters Licensing Authority (GLA) 57, 98

garment workers' unions 64

gender issues 107, 125–7, 134, 138, 142, 143, 154
   diversity in trade unions 158, 161
   equality and diversity 144
   female employees 33, 51, 52
   pay gap 127, 128
   public policy, anti-discrimination and equality 137
   segregation 126–8
   trade unions and equality 155–6, 157
   see also Equal Opportunities Commission; 'glass ceiling'

General Motors 59

General, Municipal and Boilermakers' Union (GMB) 115, 207, 237, 247, 248

Generalized System of Preferences (GSP) 74–5

Germany 221–2, 276, 286

'glass ceiling' 128, 144, 145

Glaxo-SmithKline 275

Global Union Federations 64–5

globalization 33, **381**
   contesting employment relations 376
   international labour standards 66–78
      approaches 73–7
      'race to the bottom' 66–70
      regulation 70–3
   Labour policies 97
   multinationals and union responses 56–66
   trade union internationalism 61–5
   and strikes 334–5

go-slows 343–4

government agencies 7

Greece 112, 286

Greenbury code of practice 275

grievance procedures 355–7

Growth and Stability Pact (1996) 120

Guardian newspaper 147–8

Guatemala 74

H

hairdressing industry and National Minimum Wage (case study) 296–7

Hampel code of practice 275

harmonization 124, **382**

  positive and negative 110–11, 115

Her Majesty's Revenue and Customs 267, 282–3

Hewlett-Packard 193, 206

homeworking 47, 375

Horizontal Amending Directive (2000) 292

hotel industry and human resources management (case study) 210

human resource management 15, 19, 170, 184–95, 298

  commitment-based 190

  employee involvement and participation 302

  experiences of employees 375

  high commitment 190–4, 206

  and hotel industry (case study) 210

  interpretation 187–90

  management of employment relations 185–7

  pay 264

  and performance 190–4

  strikes 333

see also sophisticated human resource management

Hutton, John 97

I

IBM 196–7, 202, 350

Iceland 230

ideology 7

immigrant worker centres 250

incentive-based payment systems 265–6

incomes policies 85

Indian call centre industry 62

individual agreement derogation 293

individual bargaining 9

individualism 196–7, 217–18

industrial action **382**

  ``secondary **383**

industrial conflict 7, 13, 328–68, **382**

  British Airways (case study) 367–8

  contesting employment relations 376–7

  future prospects for employment relations 379–80

  organized 342–4

  see also dispute resolution; strikes; unorganized conflict

industrial democracy 29

industrial harmony thesis 198

industrial tribunals *see* employment tribunals

informal employment relations 200–1

information and communications technology-based monitoring and surveillance techniques 306, 322–3

Information and Consultation Directive 225, 227–9

Information and Consultation with Employees Regulations (2004) 227–9

Institute of Directors 275

integration 59

integrative bargaining 352

intelligent flexibility 304

intended practices 193

intensification of work 318–25, **384**

  causes 320–3

  effects 324–5

  public sector (case study) 327

interim labour injunction **382**

Internatioal Transport Workers Federation 64

International Confederation of Free Trade Unions 69

International Framework Agreements 64–5, 73

International Labour Organization 72, 73–4, 337

Declaration of Fundamental Principles and Rights at Work 70–1

international labour standards **382**

see also globalization:

International Monetary Fund 57, 87

International Trade Union Confederation (ITUC) 25

internet and virtual industrial conflict 350

intranet 300

involvement *see* employee involvement and participation

Ireland 112, 113, 114, 115, 266, 276

Irish Ferries dispute 116

Italy 286

ITCO 60

J

JCB 299

job:

  insecurity 314–17

  involvement meetings 301

  quality 325

  tenure 315–16, **382**

Johnston and Johnston 124

joint consultation 29–30, **382**

Joint Industry Board 262

Joint Industry Councils 257

joint regulation 9, 10, 16, **382**

Joseph Rowntree Foundation 319

juridification **382**

justice 247, 249

'Justice for Janitors' 246, 341

K

Kettle Chips 183

'knocking' 348

Knowco 197

'knowledge work' 42, 46–51

L

labour:

  injunctions 336

  internationalism, obstacles to 63

labour: *(Continued)*
market flexibility 96–7
power 5
problem 11
rights abuses 68–9
standards 66
Labour Party/governments 82–3,
    85, 86, 87, 88
challenging trade unions 179,
    184, 188
dispute resolution 362
European Union integration
    106, 108, 112
future prospects for employment
    relations 377, 378
knowledge economy 48
nature of employment
    relations 33
non-union forms of
    representation 230
partnership agreements 237
pay inequality, low pay and
    National Minimum Wage
    275, 276, 277
policies, interpretation of
    96–9
policies/legislative programme
    93–6
public policy, anti-discrimina-
    tion nd equality 128–9,
    133, 135, 137–8, 140
regulation of employment
    relations 373, 374
strikes 336, 337, 338, 339
and trade unions 99–101
union representation and rise
    of representation gap
    216, 217, 220
working time 291
Laissez-faire ideologies 4
'last-in, first-out' 308
Latvia 114
Laval/Vaxholm dispute (Sweden)
    116–17
leave arrangements 150
see also parental leave
Legal and General 238, 240
legalism 362
legislation 10, 373–4
lesbian, gay, bisexual and
    transexuals (LGBT) 33,
    125, 148, 159, 161

liberal approach and diversity in
    trade unions 158–9
liberal interventions and equality/
    diversity 160
liberal market economies 58
liberal-pluralist approaches 23–4
Liechtenstein 230
Liftco 227
Lindsey oil refinery walk-out 330,
    379
'Lisbon agenda' and the erosion
    of the social dimension
    108–10
Lisbon Treaty 112, 116
'living wage' campaigns in
    London 250, 279, 341
London Citizens 250, 279
London Underground 343
long-hours culture 286–8
Low Pay Commission 277–9, 283

M

Maastricht Treaty 105–6, 120
McDonald's 170
challenging trade unions 175,
    178, 185
globalization 60, 63
non-union forms of
    representation 233
unorganized industrial conflict
    347
Macpherson inquiry 134
managed activism 250
management 7, 17–19
chain 300
style **382**
managerial discretion and pay
    259–64
managerial innovation in pay-
    setting arrangements 264–5
managerial prerogative 8–9, 18,
    19, **382**
equality and diversity 144
managing with trade unions
    171, 172
non-union environments 201
regulation of employment
    relations 373
state policy 85
typologies of management
    style 204

managerial relations 6
managing employment relations
    169–210
market economy 206–7
non-union firms 202–4
trade unions 171–5
typologies of management
    style 204–6
see also challenging trade unions;
    non-union environments
see also non-union environments
manufacturing industry 42–3, 258
Manufacturing Science and
    Finance Union 158, 248
Margam Way agreement 241
maritime shipping 64
market economies 206–7
co-ordinated 58
market relations 6
Marks and Spencer 197, 202
Marxism 14, 24–5
mass-production-based economy
    47–8
maternity leave 95, 135, 137, 149
Maternity and Parental Leave
    Regulations (1999) 132
mediation 354
Merrill Lynch 148
Mexico:
maquiladora sector 67, 75
see also North American Free
    Trade Agreement
Middle East 71
migrant labourers 54, 247, 250,
    335, 375
migration 57, 113–15
Miners' Federation of Great Brit-
    ain 213
miners' strike (1984-5) 89
minimum wage 95, 97–8
see also National Minimum Wage
Minimum Wage Act (1998) 94
Ministeel 197, 203
mobilization theory 337–41, 376,
    382
motor vehicle manufacturing
    industry 64
multi-employer bargaining 258–9,
    262, 263, **382**
multinationals 66–7, 68, 69, 70,
    75, 77, **382**

American, in UK and Ireland 60

contesting employment relations 376

corporate codes of conduct 73

equality and diversity 150

non-union forms of representation 230, 232, 233

workplace inequality 124

mutual gains model 236–7, 241

N

national action plans 109

National Coal Board 89

National Economic Development Council 86

National Federation of Women Workers 154

National Health Service 144, 237, 238

pay determination 268–9, 270, 272

National Information and Consultation of Emmployees Directive (2002) 107

National Library for the Blind 237

National Minimum Wage 256, 277–9

dispute resolution 360

European Union integration 110, 115

experiences of employees 374

future prospects for employment relations 377

and hairdressing industry (case study) 296–7

homeworking 47

impact 279–83

Labour policies 93, 94, 96

nature of employment relations 33

non-union forms of representation 224

public policy, anti-discrimination and equality 133

rates (1999–2009) 278

regulation of employment relations 373

representation and rise of representation gap 216

National Union of Journalists 283

National Union of Mineworkers 89

National Union of Teachers 270

nature of employment relations 3–37

collective bargaining 26–8

contexts 32–4

custom and practice 10

discipline in the workplace 26

effort bargain 6

employers and managers 17–19

feminist critique 15

industrial democracy 29

involvement and participation 28–31

outcomes 31–2

pluralist orthodoxy, challenges to 14–16

regulation 7–11

relevance 4

Royal Mail (case study) 36–7

state 22–5

trade union repression globally 25

trade unions 19–22

unemployment in UK (1979-2009) 32

unitary and pluralist perspectives 12–14

wage-work bargain 4–7

neo-corporatism 86

neo-liberalism 24, 93, 97–8, 101, 314, 316, **382**

European Union integration 109, 114, 117

policy agenda 58

regulation of employment relations 374

strikes 334

neo-unitary **382**

Netherlands 112, 286

New Deal programmes 95

'new' economy 41–81

agency workers and employment flexibility 42

'atypical' workers, union organization of (case study) 80–1

flexible labour market 51–5

franchise arrangements— self-employment 46

homeworking 47

manufacturing and service industries (1979–2008) 43

occupational change and knowledge-workers, rise of 46–51

self-employment (1984-2008) 44

temporary and part-time employees (1984–2008) 52

see also globalization

New International Division of Labour 67

new public management 186–7, **382**

New Zealand 90, 245

News International 176–7

newsletters 300, 302

Nike 69, 75, 76

Nippon CTV 340, 356

Nissan 179, 304

non-governmental organizations 17, 63

non-union environments 195–201

small firms 198–201

sophisticated human resource management 195-8

non-union firms 202–4

non-union representation 221–34

development 222–6

European Works Councils 230–4

Information and Consultation Directive 227–9

in practice 226–7

North America 63, 68

North American Agreement on Labor Cooperation 75

North American Free Trade Agreement 74–5

Norway 230

notice boards 300

O

occupational change 46–51

in 2000s 49

during 1990s 48

open method of coordination 102, 109, **382**

Opportunity 2000 144, 145

Opportunity Now 143

opt-out provision (working time) 293–4, 377–8

Organization for Economic Cooperation and Development 276

organization of trade unions 243–51

  assessment 247–51

  characteristics 245–7

  recruitment 244–5

organizational commitment 192

organizational competitiveness 320–1

outcomes 31–2

overtime 173, 289

  bans 343–4

  systematic 288–9

  unpaid 289

P

Panasonic 232

parental leave 135, 137, 138

  maternity leave 95, 135, 137, 149

  paternity leave 95, 135–6, 137, 149, 150

Parental Leave Directive (1996) 107, 132, 135

part-time employment 33, 51, 52

  equality and diversity 151

  organizing unionism 244

  public policy, anti-discrimination, and equality 133–4, 136, 137

  redundancy and job insecurity 315

  representation and rise of representation gap 218

  working time 289, 290

  workplace inequality 126, 127

Part-time Workers (Prevention of Less Favourable Treatment) Regulations (2000) 132

participation:

  cycles 30

  'waves of interest' 30–1

see also employee involvement and

participation partnership agreements 234–43, 261, **382**

  assessment 241–2

  outcomes of partnership 238–41

  reasons for partnership 236–8

Partnership Fund 237

passive acquiescence 200, 203

paternalism 199, 202

paternity leave 95, 135–6, 137, 149, 150

pay 255–84

  collective bargaining, contraction of and rise of managerial discretion 259–64

  collective bargaining, evolution and development of 257–9

  determination 263, 268–72, 372

  disputes in public sector 271

  equal 157, 361

  incentive-based systems 265–6

  inequality 273–4

  managerial innovation in pay-setting arrangements 264–5

  payment by results schemes 265–6

  performance-related 264, 265–8, **382**

  regulation (low pay) 274–7

  review bodies 269–71, **382**

  statutory floor of wages 281

  statutory minimum wage 276

  see also National Minimum Wage

perceived practices 193

performance management systems 322

performance targets 322

performance-related pay 264, 265–8, **382**

Permira 207

Pertemps 317

PharmCo 267

Philippines 69

PhoneCo 348

physical injury at work 324

Pirelli 303

Pizza Express 183, 224, 225, 237

Pizza Hut 350

pluralism 27

pluralist 186, **382**

pluralist agenda 171–4

pluralist assumption and non-union forms of representation 224

pluralist concern 19

pluralist orthodoxy, challenges to 14–16

pluralist perspectives 12–14, 16, 202

pluralist policy and representation and rise of representation gap 214

Poland 112, 114, 286

Police Federation 271

Police Negotiating Board 271

political context 82–120

  trade unions and the Euro (case study) 120

  see also Conservative Party/ government; European integration; Labour Party/ government; State policy

political fund ballots 91

Portugal 276

positive action **382**

Post Office Counters 10

post-Fordism 47, **382**

Posting of Workers Directive (1996) 107, 117

power:

  balance 14

  imbalance 24

  relations 60

pre-hearing reviews 362

pregnancy discrimination 122

private employment agencies 53–4

private equity 207

Private Finance Initiative 100

problem-solving groups 302–4

procedural agreement **382**

procedural individualization **382**

Proctor and Gamble 67

productivity bargaining 172

proportionality 160

protected period 338

protectionism **383**

psychological damage from work 324

public policy, anti-discrimination legislation, and equality at work 128–41

legal framework development during 2000s 131–7

legal and policy framework 137–40

public policy and equality legislation 129–31

public services 42

Q

Qualified Majority Voting 104, 105, 106, 291

quality circles 302, 303

quality management 302–3

see also Total Quality Management

quitting 342, 349–50

R

RAC Motoring Services 290

Race Directive (2000) 107

Race for Equality 143

Race Relations Act (1976) 129, 130

Race Relations Act (2000) 134

Race Relations Amendment Act (2000) 132

'race to the bottom' 66–70, 110, 117, **383**

race/ethnicity 125, 128, 134, 138, 140, 142–4

disadvantage 144

discrimination 34, 125, 143, 155

diversity in trade unions 161–2

see also Commission for Racial Equality

radical approach/interventions 146, 159–60, **383**

Rail, Maritime and Transport Union (RMT) 100–1

recessions 32, 299

redundancy 307–14, **383**

compulsory 312–13

consultation 313

forced voluntary 312, 313

level and rate of 310, 312

process and experience of 310–14

voluntary 312–13, **384**

Reebok 77

Reform Treaty 112

regime competition 61, **383**

regional arrangements 74

regulation: of employment relationship 7–11, 371–4

hard **382**

soft **383**

religion or belief discrimination 139

religion or belief and equality and diversity 142

religious dress at work 125

reorganization of work 302–7

representation at work 211–54

declining unionization and 'representation gap' 216–20

e-unions (case study) 253–4

trade unions, development of in the twentieth century 212–15

trade unions and workers' interests 215–16

see also non-union representation; organization of trade unions; partnership agreements

representative democracy model 21

representative forums 225

repression of labour interest 24

'reserved seats' 159–61

responsible autonomy 204

reward mechanisms 191

reward schemes 264

'right' to manage see managerial prerogative

Road Transport Directive (2002) 292

Romania 113

Royal Commission on Trade Unions and Employers' Associations 172

Royal Mail 6, 36–7, 126, 202, 330–1, 336, 339

rule-based approach 7–10

Ryanair 188

S

sabotage 329, 342, 346–7

'scammin' 348

Scandinavia 274

Scope 248

segregation, horizontal **382**

self-employment 44–5, 46, 375, **383**

self-organization 159–62

Service Employees International Union 246

service sector 42–3, 204, 218, 347

Service Workers' Union 245

Services Directive (Bolkestein Directive) 109–10

sex discrimination 106, 158, 361, 363, 364

Sex Discrimination Act (1975) 129

sexual orientation 137, 142

discrimination 139

see also lesbian, gay, bisexual and transexuals (LGBT)

shift-working 289, 290

shop stewards 173–4, 214, 215–16, **383**

Shopco 304, 305

Siemens 290

'Silver Book' agreement 269

Single European Act (1987) 104, 105

Single European Market 104, 230

single-employer bargaining 258

single-status agreements 124

single union agreements 178–9

SIPTU 116

'slammin' 348

small firms 198–201

Social Action Programme 104, 106

Social Chapter 83, 95, 102, 105, 106

future prospects for employment relations 378

non-union forms of representation 225, 230

regulation of employment relations 373

working time 291

Social Charter (1990) 105

social class 123–5, **383**

social clauses 73–4, **383**

social context 33–4

social contract and state policy 86–7

social dialogue 105, 106, **383**

social dimension of the European
Union 74, 75, 82, 96,
107, 117
erosion of 108–10
regulation of employment
relations 373
social divisions 121–65
diversity representation in
trade unions 158–62
equality bargaining 156–8
trade unions and equality
agenda 154–6
work–life balance 149–53,
164–5
workplace inequality 122–8
see also equality and diversity;
public policy, anti-dis-
crimination legislation,
and equality at work
social dumping 383
social partners 383
sophisticated human resource
management 186, 383
employee involvement and
participation 299
'hard' approach 189
market economies 206
non-union firms 195–8, 202–3
non-union forms of
representation 224
pay 264
'soft' approach 189
South Korea 72
South West Water 227
Spain 276, 286, 294, 346
Special Negotiating Body 230–1
standardization 59
state 22–5
state policy 83–92
growing state intervention
85–7
public policy under
Conservatives:
neo-liberalism 87–92
voluntarism 84–5
status divide 123–5, 383
Stonewall 17, 223
stress-related ill-health 324
strikes 329–42, 376, 383
breadth of 331
composition of employment 333

declining level of 331–3
duration 331
economic factors 333
frequency 331
as global phenomenon 334–5
legislation and industrial
action 335–7
meanings and measurement
330–1
mobilization theory 337–41
official 330
unofficial/wildcat 330
structural adjustment programmes
334
sub-contracting 45
substantive agreement 383
substantive individualization 383
substitutionist approach 183
suggestion schemes 300
supressionist methods 183
'sweating' 200
Sweden 113, 232
'sweetheart' deals 178–9, 182
systems-based approach 7

T

take-up gap 152
team briefings 177, 300, 302, 383
teamworking 190–1, 302–5, 383
Telecomco 54
Telecorp 341
Telewest 245
Temporary Agency Work Directive
(Proposed) 107, 108
temporary employment 51, 52,
134, 315–16
term-time working arrangements
150
Tesco 202, 235–6, 238, 239, 240,
242, 261
TGI Fridays 305
The East London Communities'
Organization (TELCO)
341
three-step approach 362
tipping 205, 256
Total Quality Management 302–4,
383
'totting' 345
Trade Union Act (1984) 88

trade unions 7, 10, 12–14, 16, 18,
19–22, 100, 383
contesting employment
relations 376
decline and dispute resolution
363
density by sector and industry
220
derecognition 176–7, 181, 383
diversity representation 158–62
education 22
and equality agenda 154–6
and the Euro (case study) 120
future prospects for employment
relations 378
general 21
globalization 58
growing power 18–19
industrial 21
internationalism 61–5
and the Labour party 99–101
learning representatives 217
lesbian, gay, bisexual and
transexuals (LGBT)
representation 159
major unions 22
managing 171–5
membership and density
(1892-1979) 213
membership and density
(1980-2008) 218
occupational 21
recognition 183, 244, 372–3,
383
regulation of employment
relations 372
repression globally 25
revitalization 212
state policy 84, 87, 88–9, 91
suppression 183
see also challenging trade
unions; organization;
representation
Trades Union Congress (TUC) 22,
23, 83, 179
Commission on Vulnerable
Employment 364
equality 155
equality audit 157
globalization and multinationals
76

'New Unionism' project 245

'Organizing Academy' 247

organizing unionism 246, 248

redundancy and job insecurity 310

representation and rise of representation gap 214

state policy 85, 86

working time 293, 294

Worksmart 253–4

Transport and General Workers' Union (TGWU) 174, 183, 243, 244, 338

see also Unite

Treasury 268

Treaty of Amsterdam (1997) 106, 108

Treaty of European Union see Maastricht Treaty

Treaty of Rome 102, 103, 112

tripartism 85–6, **383**

'Typetalk' 247–8

U

unemployment 32–3, 218–19

unfair dismissal 360, 364

unfair practices 179

unilateral approach 74

Union of Construction and Allied Trades and Technicians (UCATT) 21

Union of Democratic Mineworkers 89

Union of Industrial and Employers' Confederations of Europe (UNICE) 103, 105, 106

see also BusinessEurope

Union of Shop Distributive and Allied Workers (USDAW) 91, 235–6, 244

Unison 21, 101

diversity in trade unions 160–2

equality 158

partnership agreements 237, 242

strikes 341

unitary approach 12–14, 15, 19, 202, **383**

challenging trade unions 186, 188

non-union forms of representation 224

Unite 21, 23, 379

challenging trade unions 183

diversity in trade unions 158

organizing unionism 243, 248

pay 256, 262

representation and rise of representation gap 214

United Distillers 239, 240

United States:

challenging trade unions 177, 178, 191

equality and diversity 146, 147, 148

and European Union integration 104

Federal Bureau of Investigation 346–7

globalization and multinationals 60, 61, 62, 63, 65, 67, 74, 76

and Jordan bilateral agreement 74

'Justice for Janitors' 246, 341

mutual gains model 236–7, 241

Organizing Institute 247

organizing unionism 245, 246, 249, 250

pay inequality, low pay and National Minimum Wage 277, 279

public policy, anti-discrimination, and equality 131

recessions 299

and Singpore bilateral agreement 74

unorganized industrial conflict 349

writers' strike 329

see also North American Free Trade Agreement

unorganized conflict 342–50

absenteeism 347–9

assessment 350–1

fiddles 345–6

quitting 349–50

sabotage 346–7

V

vertical segregation **383**

Visteon 379

voice objective 31–2

voluntarism 84–5, 86, 87, **383–4**

W

wage-work bargain 4–7, 10, 11, 18, 255

wage/wages:

councils abolition 276

drift 258

premium 220

see also pay

Wal-Mart 68, 178

War on Want 78

Warwick Agreement (2004) 100, 292

Washington Consensus 57–8

water industry 263

WaterCo 200

Waterstone's 350

Webb, Beatrice, and Sidney 26

Weber, Max 23

welfare to work agenda 95

Whitley Councils/principles 258–9

'winter of discontent' (1978–9) 87, 99–100

work experience, unpaid 283

Work and Families Act (2006) 94, 132, 137

work–life balance/family-friendly policies 136, 149–53

employer attitudes to (case study) 164–5

equality and diversity 141

experiences of employees 374–5

Labour policies 94–5, 98

public policy, anti-discrimination, and equality 131–2, 135–7

trade unions and equality 156–7

working time 289

work-to-rule 343–4, **384**

Worker Registration Scheme 113–14

worker unrest see labour problem

workers see employees

Workers' Union 243

workforce agreements 225, 292

workforce meetings 300, 302

working conditions 68–9
working time 284–94
    legal regulation 291–4
    number of hours usually worked
        each week by full-time
        employees in main job in
        selected EU countries 286
    trends 286–91
Working Time Directive (1993)
        96, 107, 108, 285, 291,
        292, 293

Working Time Regulations
        (1998) 225, 285, 291,
        292–3
workplace inequality 122–8
    disadvantage at work 125–8
    social class and status divide
        123–5
works councils in Germany 222
World Trade Organization 58
    Singapore Declaration (1996)
        74

Writers Guild of America 329
writers' strike (United States)
        329

X

XL 299

Z

zero-hours contracts 290
Zimbabwe 25